HBJ *Harcourt Brace Jovanovich, Inc.*

COMPREHENSIVE PROGRAM FOR SCIENCE

Classroom textbooks with correlated workbooks, laboratory materials, teacher's manuals, tests, filmstrips, and slides

SELECTED PROGRAM FOR
JUNIOR HIGH SCHOOL AND SENIOR HIGH SCHOOL

Concepts in Science
    Life: Its Forms and Changes
    Matter: Its Forms and Changes
    Energy: Its Forms and Changes

The Earth: Its Living Things
The Earth: Its Changing Form
Science 700 (a visual resource)

Biology: Patterns in the Environment
Biological Science: An Inquiry into Life
BSCS Inquiry Slides
Biology 500 (a visual resource)
Exploring Biology
Your Health and Safety in a Changing Environment
    Thomas Gordon Lawrence, Alice Schriver,
    Douglas F. Powers, M.D., Louis J. Vorhaus, M.D.

The Physical World
Concepts in Chemistry
Concepts in Physics

PROFESSIONAL SOURCEBOOKS FOR THE TEACHER

Teaching Elementary Science: A Sourcebook for Elementary Science
Teaching Elementary Science Through Investigation and Colloquium
Teaching High School Science: A Book of Methods
A Sourcebook for the Biological Sciences
Teaching High School Science: A Sourcebook for the Physical Sciences

Your Health and Safety
In a Changing Environment

Authors

Thomas Gordon Lawrence, M.A.
Formerly Chairman,
Department of Biological Sciences
Erasmus Hall High School
Brooklyn, New York

Alice Schriver, Ed.D.
Professor of Health
University of North Carolina at Greensboro
Greensboro, North Carolina

Douglas F. Powers, M.D.
Clinical Professor of Child Psychiatry
Medical College of Virginia
Richmond, Virginia

Louis J. Vorhaus, M.D.
Assistant Professor of Clinical Medicine
Cornell University Medical College
New York, New York

Educational Consultants

L. Clovis Hirning, M.D.
Chief School Psychiatrist
Northern Westchester County, New York
Associate Professor of Psychology
Western Connecticut State College
Danbury, Connecticut

Jane Joyce, M.A.
Late Teacher of Human Science
Southwest High School
Kansas City, Missouri

Herb Lewis, M.S.
Superviser, Health and Physical Education
Jefferson County Public Schools
Louisville, Kentucky

Barbara Worrel, M.E.
Supervisor of Health and Physical Education
Cincinnati Public Schools
Cincinnati, Ohio

HBJ Harcourt Brace Jovanovich, Inc.
New York   Chicago   San Francisco   Atlanta   Dallas

The chapters for which each author is responsible are the following:
Mr. Lawrence, 2, and 13 through 21; Professor Schriver, 1, 3 through 12, 35, and 36;
Dr. Powers, 22 through 28; Dr. Vorhaus, 29 through 34. Lois Balcolm was an
editorial consultant for chapters 1 and 24.

ACKNOWLEDGMENTS: For permission to reprint copyrighted material, grateful acknowledgment is made
to the following publishers:

Medical Economics Company, Oradell, N.J. 07649: Photograph on page 45, top left, Copyright © 1972.
All rights reserved.

The Condé Nast Publications, Inc.: Photographs on page 151 reprinted from *Glamour;* Copyright © 1966
by The Condé Nast Publications, Inc. Photograph on page 153 reprinted from *Mademoiselle* © The Condé
Nast Publications, Inc. 1967. Photograph by George Barkentin.

Harcourt Brace Jovanovich, Inc.: Illustrations on pp. 97, 112, 248, 312, and 314 from ''Human Body,''
research and copyright © 1963, 1960, 1957 by Harcourt Brace Jovanovich, Inc. Illustration on page 133
adapted from ''Human Body,'' research and copyright © 1963, 1960, 1957 by Harcourt Brace Jovanovich,
Inc. Illustrations on pages 209 and 249 copyright © 1972, 1968 by Harcourt Brace Jovanovich, Inc. Reproduced
from *Life: Its Forms and Changes* by Brandwein *et al.* Illustration on page 312 reproduced from *Your
Biology,* Second Edition by Smith and Lisonbee. Drawn by Caru Studios, New York, N.Y. Research and
copyright © 1957 by Harcourt Brace Jovanovich, Inc. Illustration on page 430 from *The Rorschach
Technique* by Bruno Klopfer and Helen H. Davidson, © 1962 by Harcourt Brace Jovanovich, Inc.

Page 607, newspaper headlines ''Narcotics Deaths on Increase Here,'' ''Drugs Are a Bad Scene Ex-Addicts
Tell Students,'' and ''Drug Use Rises in City's High Schools'' © 1968/69/70 by The New York Times
Company. Reprinted by Permission. ''City Asks U.S. to Curb Barbiturates'' reprinted by Permission of
New York Post. © 1972, New York Post Corporation.

Chart on page 625 reprinted from *Sportsmanlike Driving,* © 1970 by The American Automobile Association.
Published by McGraw-Hill Book Company. Reprinted by permission of The American Automobile Association
and McGraw-Hill Book Company.

Cover and Title Page photograph: Mimi Forsyth, Monkmeyer

ISBN 0-15-369525-0

CONTENTS

UNIT THREE / Achieving Fitness

UNIT FOUR / Your Body's Supply Systems

UNIT FIVE / Your Changing Self: Growth and Development

UNIT SIX / Your Changing Self: Social Development

UNIT ONE
You and Your Health

1/ *What Is Health?*

What is *health?* "Health is not being sick," you might answer. But is *physical* well-being enough? What about your *mental* well-being and *social* well-being? Do you think you could continue to remain in fine physical condition if you were constantly worried about something? Your health is determined by the interplay of many factors. In this chapter and throughout the text you will be enlarging your concept of health and discovering those attitudes and behaviors important in maintaining health.

A PROBE INTO HEALTH—Upon what does health depend? You can begin your probe into the meaning of health with questions like these:

1. What is meant by "symbols of health"? Give some examples from your own experience.

2. In what ways are large cities less healthful than rural areas?

3. Thinking about health, what physical factors come to mind? what mental-emotional factors? what social factors?

4. What is meant by psychosomatic illness? Give an example.

5. What personal health responsibilities do you now have? What health responsibilities will you have as an adult?

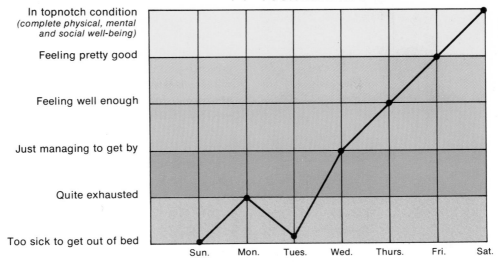

1-1 YOUR HEALTH GRAPH

In topnotch condition *(complete physical, mental and social well-being)*

Feeling pretty good

Feeling well enough

Just managing to get by

Quite exhausted

Too sick to get out of bed

Sun. Mon. Tues. Wed. Thurs. Fri. Sat.

1-1 The graph suggests how your health may vary from day to day. Have you ever reached the top level of health that is possible for you? How do you know? Can you tell your level of health just by how you feel?

YOUR GOAL OF HEALTH

How healthy are you? And what is your measure of how healthy you are? Is it the way you feel? The way you look? How well you do in your favorite sport? How others say you look?

Symbols of Health

Like many of us, you probably depend upon symbols of health. Health is talked about a great deal — or rather, symbols of health are talked about a great deal. You hear about foods and gadgets that will slim you down, build you up, improve your complexion, or increase your "zest for living." Unfortunately, many of these products concentrate on developing symbols of health, rather than health itself.

A symbol is something that stands for something else, and reminds us of it. The suntan, for example, is a symbol of health. It has come to stand for health and vigor. We see a tan and think of vigorous outdoor exercise, which we associate with health. The error is in assuming that the tan means "exercise," but many people get their tans without ever moving from a blanket on a beach.

Vitamin pills have become a symbol of health. All of us know people who take vitamin pills without doctor's orders, and then neglect to choose meals that would supply the vitamins they need. There are many other symbols of health. Can you name some?

The World Health Organization of the United Nations has defined health as "a state of complete physical, mental, and social well-being and not merely the absence of disease or infirmity." Notice that no symbols of health are included in this definition of health. Notice, too, that other conditions besides physical conditions are included.

If you were to graph your own health in the coming weeks, as in Figure 1-1, how much would it vary? How often would you reach your top score? What three conditions are required for the highest degree of health? How are they all connected? How can you achieve them?

Physical, mental emotional

social

1-2 The three sides of health: (top) physical; (center) mental-emotional; (bottom) social. How do these three factors overlap?

HEALTH IS MANY-SIDED

Though pep and energy are important, they are only part of the health picture. What advertisements call a "zest for living" and what we refer to as "health" must be looked at from three viewpoints: the *physical*, the *mental-emotional*, and the *social*.

Physical and mental-emotional health determine how you look, how you think, how you act, and how you feel. These factors, in turn, largely influence your social life. We can also turn this statement around, for social health has its *own* effect upon your physical and mental-emotional health. Social health is not merely "how you get along with others," but how healthy a neighborhood you have, and even how healthy a state and country you have—and what they do to promote the health of their citizens. In other words, social health involves everything in your *environment* (you, your family, school, friends, home town, county, state, country, and the whole world).

No wonder the subject of health is quite complicated, since *all of these factors overlap and interact*. In this course, you will sometimes be studying the physical, mental-emotional, and social factors separately. At other times you will learn how they operate in combination. Some chapters will stress "the physical you," others the "mental-emotional you"—but in these and other chapters, "the total you" will also be discussed.

The Physical Foundation

Physical health is in many ways basic to "total" health. Yet you may never have given much thought to the complicated mechanisms of your body, especially if your own health has been generally good.

What physical factors come to mind first when you think about health? Very likely the absence of disease, or having a sturdy stomach that doesn't get upset from foods you eat may represent health to you. Or perhaps you think of strong muscles with which to keep in shape with work, exercise, and play. You will learn more about all of these factors: something about diseases in Unit 7, food and digestion in Chapters 3, 4, and 14, and strength and physical fitness in Unit 3.

If you have a tendency to catch cold easily, or to be too heavy or too thin, or if you are sensitive to certain foods or troubled with a skin condition, you will think of these factors when you consider physical health. These topics may turn up in more than one place in your book—in chapters on infections and disease and food and digestion, and in the chapter on appearance.

So far we have named health factors that are clearly physical and individual. But we quickly see, as has been pointed out, that all three areas of health interact and influence each other. For instance, in Unit 6 you will find that some conditions which seem to be entirely physical (such as being overweight) may be complicated by *emotional* causes. In Units 2 and 7 you will read about influences on your physical health that stem directly from the *social* health of the community in which you live.

In many respects the large city is a less healthful place to live than is a rural environment; it has higher rates of chronic disease, alcoholism, drug addiction, and mental illness. Air pollution is also a greater problem; one which we hear a lot about at the present time. However, large cities also have public and private health agencies which may be superior to those in small communities, and this somewhat offsets the hazards. Local, state, and national health services provide many protections for their citizens, including such widely different programs as licensing doctors and hospitals, providing school lunches, building parks, playgrounds, and sports facilities, maintaining the purity of food and water, supporting mental health clinics, and countless others.

1-3 Health is many-sided. Is it possible that a break between classes, affording an opportunity to relax and talk with friends, could have a favorable effect on physical health?

Finally, Unit 8 takes up something you have probably always thought of as purely "physical" and due to chance: the injuries resulting from accidents. Yet accidents do not just happen; they are always caused, usually by carelessness. And emotional factors—worry, anger, exuberance—may lie behind the carelessness. Accidents are another case of physical and mental-emotional overlapping.

Mental-Emotional Health

With mental-emotional as with physical health, we may think first simply of the absence of disease—the serious mental disorders or emotional disturbances for which people are hospitalized. But mental-emotional health means much more than this.

Most of us have had experiences at some time when we became so emotionally upset —from anger, disappointment, hurt feelings, embarrassment, or whatever—that we simply could not function. We could not work or study efficiently and were unable to enjoy things or people that usually gave us pleasure. To have such emotions is perfectly normal, but when someone is so incapacitated by them that everything else in life is thrown out of gear, then this, too, is "ill health," just as much as is an attack of "flu." And it is just as important to treat this kind of illness as any other. Mental-emotional health problems will be discussed in Unit 6.

Social Factors

What about social health factors? If you think a minute, you will realize that most of your relationships with others, both personal and impersonal (such as what you read about your fellow citizens in the newspapers), involve your emotions. Or to put it the other way around: *most* of your emotional upsets involve people, directly or indirectly. So if handling your emotions successfully is part of health, your social life is almost inevitably part of it, too.

In fact, to speak of mental-emotional health or social health means about the same thing —in some ways—but their *components* are easily distinguishable. While the social factors refer to people and situations that concern you, the mental-emotional factors are yours—what you think and how you feel as *you*, and what your responses are to people and situations.

If your thinking and emotional reactions are lively, varied, and sensitive, yet controllable even under pressure, it is almost a sure bet that you get along well with family and friends—and strangers. But nobody ever made a perfect score on this! Every one of us has social problems to one degree or another. You will have a chance to explore personality relationships in Unit 6, especially in Chapters 23 and 27.

As important as individual social relationships may be, however, there is a broader sense in which your immediate social environment (family, friends, and neighbors) influences both your physical and your mental-emotional health. For example: ambition or a strong motivation to "get ahead"—in school for the teen-ager, in business or in a profession for the adult, in recreational sports for all ages—is an attitude toward life that

1-4 Have you ever felt like the boy in this picture? What are some of the factors that could have contributed to his feelings?

1-5 Ice skating provides an enjoyable activity for people of all ages. What recreational activities are you interested in?

1-6 A game of bridge can be a relaxing social pastime.

1-7 A group of community volunteers discusses activities that might improve social relationships within their community.

may pervade a whole social group. It may be almost entirely absent in another group, and in a third it may be present in a moderate degree, well balanced by other values. The presence or absence of this trait, especially within the family but also within a community, affects the emotional health of each individual member. Effects range all the way from a healthy win-or-lose enjoyment of competition in the more balanced social climate to opposite extremes—anxiety when there is too much "drive" and apathy when there is too little.

Then there are the social relationships that go beyond our immediate circle to include the larger community—town, city, state, and nation—and these also affect our health. We have mentioned air pollution, pure food, pure water, and drug control as examples of health problems in which society takes a hand. Through legislation and through public and private agencies, the community does much to protect the health of all its members. Now, you are on the receiving end of such protection. Soon, when you are a voter, you will help decide what protective measures are needed. Chapters 5 and 31 will inform you about these and other health problems.

UNITY OF THE MIND AND BODY

Although we have grouped some of the many health factors that you will be learning about under the headings where each *primarily* belongs, we have stressed that many of them overlap and have even pointed out some instances where the interrelationship is especially close. Perhaps the most important thing to emphasize at this point is that although we have to "take the body apart" in order to study it, the mind and body of an individual *function as a unit.*

Health Is Psychosomatic

There is a name for the physical and emotional interaction within this overall unity. It is called **psychosomatic** (sy-koh-soh-MAT-ik) from the Greek words *psyche,* mind, and *soma,* body. Even with laboratory animals there is a strong relationship between emotions and bodily health or illness. When cats are subjected to prolonged fright or anger, they develop serious stomach injury. **Psychosomatic medicine** studies and treats conditions in which mind and body interact. Nobody notices the interaction in healthy

1-8 Now that you are a teen-ager, your health is increasingly in your hands. How are you planning to handle this responsibility?

people, for when mind and body interact healthfully, neither causes the other trouble. Good health is psychosomatic, and we are not surprised to learn that some illnesses are also psychosomatic. Stomach *ulcer* (UL-ser) is a disease thought to be largely psychosomatic in origin and partly caused by frequent anger, fear, and anxiety. Ulcers are discussed in Chapter 14. That ulcers or other physical injury can result when mental and emotional strain is prolonged shows how important it is to understand and be able to handle our emotions. You will read more about this in Chapter 27.

Health Is Homeostatic

There is a process by which the body maintains an internal balance among *all* its parts, even (as you will discover in Chapter 19) between each one of its billions of cells and the fluids surrounding them.

This process is called *homeostasis* (ho-me-oh-STA-sis) from the Greek words *homoios*, meaning like or similar, and *stasis*, meaning standing.

Homeostasis is of utmost importance, not only in maintaining health but in sustaining life itself. Examples are the way your body temperature remains unchanged despite exposure to intense heat or cold, and the way you remain in good health although your body cells are producing wastes that could poison you if they were not promptly destroyed or removed. Other physiological mechanisms, such as respiration, circulation, and even growth itself, are subject to similar self-regulation.

Your Health Is in Your Hands

Of course you are not 100 percent responsible for your health! Heredity starts us off with a bundle of traits and tendencies, most of which we cannot change. And when disease and accidents strike, there is little we can do—except to get the best medical care.

But we have emphasized all along that *health* includes much more than absence of disease or injury. In this broader sense that goes *beyond* mere freedom from sickness, you do have an important choice. You can neglect the everyday health factors until your troubles pile up, or you can learn to handle your problems wisely and keep a high "total health score." This is what we mean by "your health is in your hands"!

You are the one person in the world who must learn the most about what you are like. Your parents have cared for you in the past and continue to, but the day when you take charge of your own life and health is not that far away. Fortunately, most people have many more assets than liabilities in matters of health. But everybody has his own mixture of strong and weak points. The more you know about your health, the better able you will be to make all the strong points *count* for you and to handle any weaker ones without serious damage to yourself or others.

Good health, then, combines physical, mental-emotional, and social fitness in effective balance. Are you ready to learn more about it?

What You Have Learned

What kind of health practices should you apply in maintaining your health? Check your understanding of the chapter. On a separate sheet of paper, number 1 through 12 and insert the answer from the vocabulary list below. Use each expression, but use each one only once.

count	life	promote
enjoy	mental-emotional	psychosomatic
exposed	physical	social
homeostasis	popular	you

Symbols of health are usually based on (1)_____ beliefs. Vigorous exercise is one of the basic factors that (2)_____ good health. The most effective exercise is the kind that you (3)_____ most. The way you look, act, think, and feel is determined by the state of your (4)_____, (5)_____, and (6)_____ health.

Your mind and body function as a unit, and their interaction within this unit is called (7)_____. Your body maintains an internal balance among all of its parts in a self-regulatory process called (8)_____. This process is of utmost importance not only in maintaining health but in sustaining (9)_____ itself. An example of this process is the way your body temperature remains unchanged when (10)_____ to extreme heat or cold.

The one person in the world who must learn the most about your strong and weak health points is (11)_____. The more you know about health, the better able you will be to make your strong points (12)_____ for you.

What You Can Do

1. Form a committee consisting of three groups. Have one group list the physical factors that are important to health, one the mental-emotional factors, and one the social-health factors. For example, for physical health, you might list immunization; for mental-emotional health, overcoming hurt feelings; for social health, being a cooperative member of the family.

   Have all the committee members then get together to discuss how the factors that they have listed affect their health. Do you observe any overlapping among the three lists? Can you agree to put all the factors under one heading? Why is this so? Should you compose a fourth list?

2. Keep a record of situations in which the mind influences the body, such as, "She became so angry that she burst into tears." Do the same with situations where the body influences the mind, such as, "His toothache made him feel cross and unhappy."

Things to Try

1. Make a collection from magazines of advertisements for various products that claim they will "slim you down," "restore your blood," or "improve your complexion." Discuss your collection in class. How many of the advertisements tell all the important facts?

2. Take a poll of your classmates and find out how many of them take a vitamin pill every morning. How many know why they take them? How many are taking them under a doctor's advice? Which vitamins may be harmful if taken in excess?

Probing Further

Sociology: The Study of Human Relationships, by W. LaVerne Thomas and Robert J. Anderson, Harcourt Brace Jovanovich, 1972. The social factors that may affect your health are examined, such as family structure, patterns of American education, the "youth culture," and special urban and rural problems.

Growing Up Socially, by E. Weitzman, Science Research Associates, 1969. Find out how mature you are socially. Read some of the ways in which teen-agers have solved their problems of living with others.

Understanding Yourself, by W. C. Menninger, Science Research Associates, 1966. Here you may learn the ways in which your personality takes shape.

Health Concepts in Action

Does this statement help express what you have learned? Would you change or add to it?

> **Health is the result of the interaction of social, mental, and physical factors.**

Applying this concept of health, which health practices would you

—continue?

—change?

—begin?

Will you now, as a result of your study, change any of your health objectives?

2 / You — an Overall View

You are taking a journey in a machine far more wonderful than a jet airplane. Your life is the journey, your body is the machine, and you are the pilot. Think about the many things your body does as it takes you through a day in your life. Your heart is more powerful, for its size, than any other pump. Your hand can make more kinds of movements than any device ever invented. Your brain is far superior to the finest computer. How is your body built, and how does it operate?

A PROBE INTO THE BODY — Why does the health of one part of the body depend upon the health of the entire body? To find out, you will be probing questions like these:

1. Which elements are a major part of your body make-up?

2. How can you tell that cells are alive?

3. What is a tissue? What types of tissues are in your body?

4. What are the different systems of your body? How is their work coordinated?

THE BUILDING BLOCKS IN YOUR BODY

In Chapter 1 you read that everything you do is dependent on your physical body, your emotional reactions, and your social interactions. An event such as buying a new dress or a pair of pants will include all three sides of you. The size, color, and style you choose will depend on your physical make-up. Buying the item will probably make you feel good, and you may ask approval of your choice from your parents and friends.

In order to be able to discuss these three basic parts of you, we must know more about each part. In this chapter we will begin by looking at what you are made of. We will learn about your body's substances and about its structure.

What Is Your Body Made Of?

Do you know whether your body contains many of the same materials that are found in air, water, and earth? It does. If we could take all the complex parts of the human body and break them down into the simplest materials they contain, we would end up with the materials you see in Figure 2-1. These substances, called *elements*, will not be broken down into other substances that are simpler.

More than half of your weight is oxygen. It is found in the air you breathe and in the water you drink. In your body it doesn't remain a gas such as you would find in a tank of oxygen used by a hospital for its oxygen tent. Instead, it is combined with other elements in the list in Figure 2-1 to make different substances. For instance, oxygen and hydrogen combine to make water, which is found in your body in large amounts. Oxygen, hydrogen, and carbon combine to make sugar, which is also found in your body.

None of the different elements that make up your body is found inside you in its pure state. Each of them combines with others to

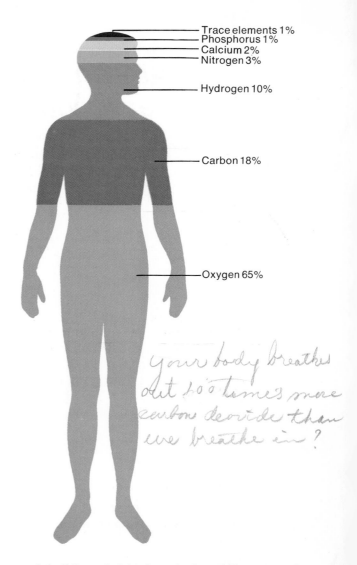

Trace elements 1%
Phosphorus 1%
Calcium 2%
Nitrogen 3%

Hydrogen 10%

Carbon 18%

Oxygen 65%

your body breathes out 100 times more carbon dioxide than we breathe in?

2-1 If the materials of your body could be separated into the elements of which they are made, your body make-up would be as shown above.

make the many different materials that your body contains. You could not eat pure carbon and digest it; pure carbon is either "black lead," such as that which makes up part of the "lead" in your pencil, or the carbon of a diamond. You can eat sugar, though; and, as you have just read, the sugar contains carbon.

2-2 How much are
you worth?

Notice how much of your body is made up of oxygen, and how small a part of it is made up of copper, iron, and iodine.

Would it insult you to learn that all the elements in your body could be bought for a few dollars? This is all they would cost— but you can feel important again because no one can buy these materials and come even close to "building" a human being. Why is this so?

Your body, and that of every plant and animal, is built up of tiny living building blocks called *cells*. The cells are made up of many different combinations of elements. It is hard to tell just what cells are like, but it is easy to see what they look like under the microscope (Figure 2-3). Most cells are so small that you would have to put hundreds of them (thousands for the white blood cell shown) side by side to measure an inch. The cells that give the blood its red color are even smaller. You could put a drop of blood containing 5,000,000 of these red blood cells in a box this size: ▱ Although some nerve cells are over three feet long, even these cells are so thin that you have to magnify them 100 times to see them clearly. You can now begin to see how complex the human body is.

How Can You Tell That Cells Are Alive?

We say that cells are alive. What do we mean when we say that something is alive? How can you tell? Suppose you found an object that looked something like a cat and something like a stuffed pillow? What tests would you apply to find out if it was alive?

1. The first thing you would probably do would be to watch it to see if it moved— of its own accord. (Living things have some power of movement.)
2. If it didn't move of its own accord, you would pet it, pinch it, or give it a shove. (Living things are sensitive.)

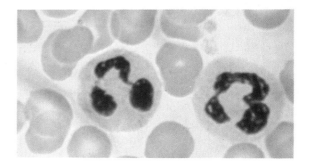

2-3 Blood cells as they appear under a microscope. The larger ones are white blood cells.

3. You would check to find out whether it breathed. (Living things breathe, or at least take in oxygen.)
4. You would put water and food in front of it. (Living things take in food and water.)
5. Eventually, you would expect it to get rid of waste matter. (Living things have to get rid of wastes.)
6. You would watch it from day to day to see if it increased in size. (Living things grow.)
7. You would feel that it had passed the test if you came in one day and found two or three little things of the same kind sitting beside it! (Living things reproduce.)

Perhaps you have been thinking, "How about plants? They are alive. Do they move? Do they do all these things?" They do. Watch a plant day by day. You will see its leaves and flowers change their positions (move) slowly. A plant has no mouth, but it takes in water and substances it uses to make food. It will pass all of the other tests, as well.

We say that the cells in your body are alive because, at one time or another, they can pass all of the seven tests listed above. Are there any other tests that you could try?

Your Living Cells

Not all of your body is alive. For example, the part of a hair extending above the skin is not alive. You feel no pain when your hair is cut, but you do when living cells at the root are disturbed by pulling the hair. Fingernails and toenails also are not alive — except at the root. The outer layers of the skin are composed of dead cells. Rub yourself hard, and some dead skin cells will fall off. They are so small that you cannot see them unless a large number come off together. All these cells were alive at one time, and they grew from cells that are still alive — at the roots of your hair, at the base of your nails, and inside your skin.

HOW CELLS GET ENERGY

You already know that the tiny cells of your body are made of many complex combinations of the elements listed in Figure 2-1. You also know that a living cell must get food. How does your body manage to get foods like carbon, hydrogen, and oxygen to your cells?

Since you can't eat and digest pure carbon, let's combine it in a certain way with hydrogen and oxygen to make sugar. The sugar is an entirely different substance; it doesn't look or taste at all like the carbon in the lead of your pencil. You can eat the sugar and digest it (some forms of sugar don't even have to be digested), after which your blood takes it to your body cells in tiny particles called *molecules* (MOL-uh-kyools). A molecule is the smallest particle of any substance that can exist by itself. Some molecules are made up of only one element; others are combinations of elements. If you break up a molecule of sugar, you will have carbon, hydrogen, and oxygen as separate elements.

How Food Gets into Your Cells

The blood brings the molecules of food to the cells. Yet a cell has no mouth. How can it take food in? What you have just read about molecules will help to explain how cells take in their food.

All molecules move. They move faster and faster as the temperature rises. When you boil water, the heat makes the water molecules move around violently and countless molecules escape into the air from the surface of the water.

The different kinds of molecules that your blood carries to your body cells are constantly sliding and bumping past one another. It is somewhat like the scene shown in Figure 2-4. Every now and then a molecule of sugar will move right out of your bloodstream and into one of your cells. The sugar molecule

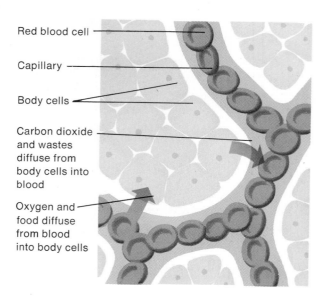

Red blood cell

Capillary

Body cells

Carbon dioxide and wastes diffuse from body cells into blood

Oxygen and food diffuse from blood into body cells

2-4 Molecules of food, oxygen, carbon dioxide, and other substances pass through the walls of tiny blood vessels and cell membranes by a process called diffusion.

does so by pushing its way between the molecules in the wall of the blood vessel and between the molecules in the covering of the cell. (After all, blood vessels and cell coverings are made up of molecules, too—thin sheets of molecules.) The covering of the blood vessel and the covering of the cell give way just enough to let the sugar molecule in, then close up again right away. In another place, a molecule of some other food might push into the cell. Water molecules might slide in at still another place. This is how your cells are nourished. The overall process is called *diffusion* (dif-YOO-zh'n). Of course, you had to swallow the water and eat the food before this could happen. The foods you ate were digested in your stomach and your intestine and then they passed through the wall of the intestine into the blood vessels. The blood carried them to the cells that needed them. Of course the substances carried in the blood no longer resembled the foods that you took in.

How Your Cells Do Their Work

You are sprawled in an easy chair, wishing you had finished your homework. Looking at television, you don't seem to be doing any work. A lot of work is going on inside you, though. What work? See if you can think what it is. Oh, yes, you are digesting your supper. Digestion is work—sometimes hard work when you eat the wrong foods! What else? You are breathing; your muscles have to work to make you breathe. Your heart is working; you know what would happen if it stopped beating. How do your cells produce the energy for this work?

Energy is the ability to do work. You must have energy to live. When you have a lot of energy, you can do a lot of work—whether you actually do it or not. You can't see energy. You can't weigh it. You find out how much energy anything has by finding out how much work it can do.

Heat is one form of energy; so is light. Would you like to store up light energy from the sun so that you could use it some months from now? This is easy. Plant some lima beans in large flowerpots or boxes full of fertile soil. Water the beans regularly. Place them in sunlight for several hours each day. They will absorb some of the sunlight and change it into stored (or chemical) energy. If you take care of the plants, they will grow and produce a crop of beans.

When you get your crop of beans, cook them, eat them, digest them. Your body cells will now take the stored energy that was in the beans and use it. Some of this energy may help keep your heart beating. Some may let you turn the television off so you can read.

Your body cells need energy to do their work, but do you know how they get the energy they need from food? At one time we would have said that food was burned in our cells, in a very slow burning without any flame or smoke. There is a better term for this process, however.

When gasoline is burned in an engine or wood is burned in a campfire, we say that the fuel is *oxidized* (OKS-ih-dyz'd). Food in your body is oxidized, too, although it is not burned.

Burning produces energy principally as heat and light. Your body cells need only a moderate amount of heat, and they cannot survive on the energy of light. They need their energy as chemical energy, which they can convert to the energy of motion or use for the production of materials they require for growth and repair.

What really happens when a food such as sugar is oxidized in the body? Ultimately, it combines with oxygen and produces carbon dioxide and water, as it would if it were burned. But in place of the one sudden reaction that we know as burning, oxidation of sugar in your cells proceeds as a series of many, small-scale reactions. Each reaction provides a bit of chemical energy that cells store (until needed) in molecules of a special substance produced just for this purpose.

Along with the chemical energy derived from foods, some heat is produced as the foods are oxidized. The heat warms your body, and much of it is given off in your breath and perspiration.

> Blow your breath against the palm of your hand. Do you feel heat? Where did the heat come from? You were blowing out some of the heat your cells produce. Feel your forehead. Does it feel warm? This heat is also produced by your body cells.

Now you know why you must breathe to live. Without oxygen, food would be useless to you. (There are some living things that do not use oxygen, but they get only about 1/20 as much energy from a molecule of sugar as you do.) The carbon dioxide and some of the water formed during oxidation are carried by the blood to the lungs and are exhaled.

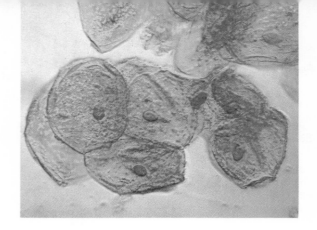

2-5 A microscopic view of the cells that line the mouth.

FROM CELLS TO ORGANS— HUMAN TISSUES

Now that you have a general idea about cells (and you will learn about them in much greater detail in Chapter 13), let's take a closer look at the different kinds of cells that make up the body.

Look at Figure 2-5. It shows living cells from the lining of the mouth. You can scrape off hundreds of them, still alive, with the flat edge of a toothpick. This won't be painful! One of these cells is much smaller than

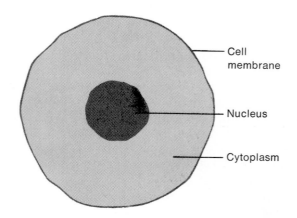

2-6 A simplified diagram of a cell. Compare this drawing with Figure 2-5. Are you able to identify the structures shown in Figure 2-5?

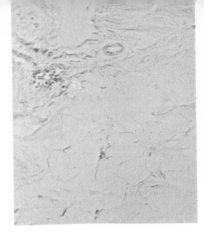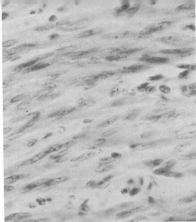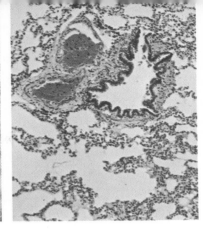

2-7 Three kinds of tissue: (*left*) fat tissue; (*center*) smooth muscle tissue; (*right*) lung tissue. How do the cells that make up these tissues differ?

the dot at the end of this sentence. The cells in Figure 2-5 are greatly enlarged. Some cells include parts which are not alive, but all the parts of the cells you can see in Figure 2-5 are living. Near the center of the cell you notice an oval body. This is the **nucleus** (NOO-klee-us). If you could push it with a tiny needle, you would find that it is tougher than the rest of the cell. The rest of the cell, surrounding the nucleus, is called the **cytoplasm** (SY-toh-plazm). Both the nucleus and the cytoplasm are living material. These cell parts are shown in Figure 2-6.

The cells lining your mouth are part of the **mucous** (MYOO-kuss) **membrane**, which lines the nose, throat, and many body cavities.

What Is a Tissue?

Cells vary in size and shape according to the kind of work they do. Cells of the same kind work as a group, though they may be found in different parts of the body. For instance, smooth muscle cells are found in different kinds of organs, but they all look alike and work the same way. Their job is to contract, and by contracting they cause motion. A group of cells of one type that carries on a special kind of work is called a *tissue*. You will learn about five different types of tissue in the next section.

Human Tissues

Figure 2-7 shows what the cells of different types of tissue look like. Study the pictures as you read about the tissues. How do the tissues shown in Figure 2-7 differ?

1. *Covering tissue.* This is usually called **epithelial** (ep-ih-THEE-lih-ul) *tissue*. Every organ of the body, inside and out, is covered or lined with this kind of tissue. The heart, the skin, the liver, the stomach, and the lungs are covered with epithelial tissue. The mouth, stomach, intestine, bladder, and lungs are all lined inside with it. Mucous membrane, some cells of which you have studied in Figure 2-5, is an epithelial tissue. Mucous membrane lines the nose, stomach, and intestines. It produces the mucus that keeps these passages moist and slightly sticky. Other epithelial membranes line the chest cavity and the cavity of the abdomen. All the glands are lined with this kind of tissue. In fact, all the juices made by the body are made by epithelial cells in the glands. Some of these juices are tears, perspiration, hormones, and digestive juices. Glands in the ears make ear wax, and certain skin glands make a waxy substance that protects the skin.

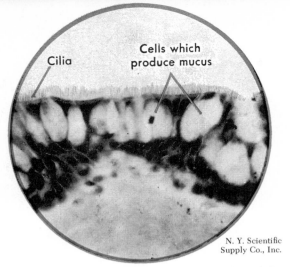

Cilia

Cells which produce mucus

N. Y. Scientific
Supply Co., Inc.

2-8 A highly magnified view of the lining of the windpipe. What is the function of the cilia?

Figure 2-8 shows the lining of the windpipe. Notice the little hairlike threads growing from the cells. They are called *cilia* (SIL-ee-uh). Cilia keep moving all the time like little whips. This whipping motion fans dust and mucus up the windpipe away from your lungs. Only certain kinds of epithelial tissue have cilia.

2. *Tissues that hold your body together.* We call these tissues *supporting*, or *connective, tissues*. Bone, *cartilage* (KAHR-tih-lij), fat, and other connective tissues furnish proper support and connect other types of tissues. Look at Figure 2-9. You will see that the cells of these tissues are often separated from each other by matter which is not alive. The living bone cells sit like little spiders in the bone they have made (Figure 2-9). If the bone should be broken, the bone cells go to work to repair it. You will read more about bones in Chapter 7.

Your ears and the tip of your nose get their shape from the cartilage inside them (Figure 2-9). Cartilage cells sit alone, or in groups of two or three, in the cartilage made by them. Cartilage, if broken, is repaired more slowly than bone. This is because all bones have blood vessels running through them, carrying the materials cells use to make and repair bone, but cartilage is very poorly supplied with blood.

2-9 Three kinds of connective tissue: (*left*) bone; (*center*) cartilage; (*right*) fibrous connective tissue. The black bodies that look like inkblots are living bone cells. Study the photographs carefully. How does the structure of cartilage and bone differ?

Courtesy CCM: General Biological, Inc.

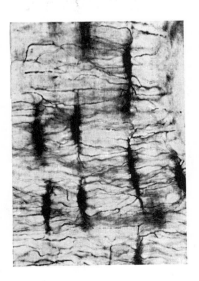
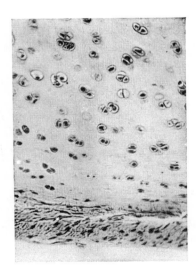
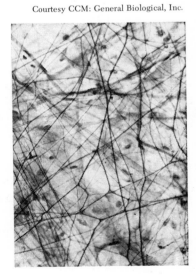

A strong connective tissue holds the bones and all the other organs of the body in their places. Some connective tissue has long, tough strings that make the tissue strong (Figure 2-9).

Fat is connective tissue made of cells which contain drops of fat. The drop of fat is much bigger than all the rest of the fat cell (Figure 2-7). Fat cells are found under your skin, around joints, and in many other places. They protect you against jars and blows. When you don't eat, your body uses the fat as food.

3. *Blood.* Does it seem strange to call blood a tissue? It is a kind of connective tissue in which the matter between the cells is liquid. The liquid is called **plasma** (PLAZ-muh). Red blood cells and white blood cells float in the plasma (Figure 2-10). Red blood cells carry oxygen from the lungs to the rest of the body. White blood cells kill germs and destroy foreign matter that enters the body. The plasma carries food, wastes, and many other materials.

4. *Muscle tissue.* Figure 2-11 includes a view of your skeletal muscle tissue and also shows heart and smooth muscle tissue. Both the skeletal muscle cells and the heart muscle have stripes. The smooth muscle cells are called smooth because they have no stripes. They each have one nucleus, while other muscle cells have more than one.

A muscle cell does only one thing when it works—it contracts. That is, it gets shorter. As soon as it stops working, it generally goes back to its original length. When a muscle contracts, it pulls whatever it is attached to, making it move. When the big muscle in the front of each upper arm contracts, it pulls your lower arm up.

5. *Nerve tissue.* **Nerve cells** do the work in your brain and nerves. They are built to carry impulses quickly.

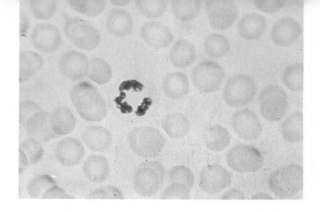

2-10 Red and white blood cells float in the plasma. Red cells carry oxygen to the cells. What is the function of white blood cells?

2-11 Three types of muscle cells: (*top*) skeletal; (*center*) heart; (*bottom*) smooth. Striated or skeletal muscle is attached to the skeleton. Heart muscle makes up the heart wall. Smooth muscle forms the walls of some internal structures.

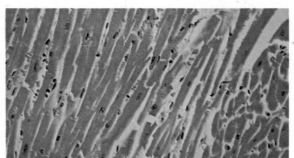

■ As soon as you read this sentence, make your hand shake as fast as you can. Did it take long for it to start to shake?

When you made your hand shake, impulses had to speed from your eye to your brain. They whizzed from one cell to another in your brain. Then not one, but several impulses rushed to muscles in your arm. These impulses caused some muscles to contract, others to relax. Many messages flashed back to your brain to let you know how you were doing. Some came from your eyes; others from many places in your hand and arm. To make your hand shake, opposing sets of muscles had to contract and relax very quickly and just at the right time. Otherwise they would have interfered with each other, and your arm would have stopped shaking.

The body of a nerve cell (which can be seen in Figure 2-12) is rounded, but each nerve cell grows out into long living threads. The threads are too long to be illustrated accurately. If you grow to be six feet tall, some of these threads will be over three feet long, but they are much too thin to be seen without the aid of a microscope. Nerve cells are placed with their long threads end to end from one cell to the next. The nerve impulses then travel along the threads from cell to cell.

HOW THE PARTS OF YOUR BODY WORK TOGETHER

You have read about some of the things that your body must do so that you can live. You know from experience that a baseball or football team is made up of players who specialize in becoming expert at playing a particular position. Each must be expert at performing his part so the entire team can play the game. All pitchers, or all quarterbacks, do not make a team. In the body, too, groups of organs are organized so as to be experts in different kinds of work and duties.

2-12 The body of a nerve cell. What is the function of nerve cells?

Large groups of one kind of cells do one type of work. Groups of other kinds of cells do other types of work. For example, the cells that make up your bones form a framework for your body, while those that make up your muscles have a different job. To help you understand the different types of work done by your body cells, we will take a look at the finished products—the nine major systems of organs in your body.

Your 206 Bones—the Skeleton

Your skeleton, or skeletal system, helps to support the rest of the body. Figure 7-2, page 112, shows what the skeleton looks like. Some of your 206 bones are separate, like the bones in the arms and legs. They are bound together at the joints by tough **ligaments** (LIG-uh-m'nts). Some bones grow together in solid joints, like the bones that form the skull. As you grow older, some of your smaller bones may unite completely, so that you have fewer bones. Your skeleton does three big jobs.

1. It gives shape and support to the body.
2. It helps you walk, eat, breathe, and move. Without bones you would have to perform all these functions in an entirely different way, as other forms of life do.
3. It protects organs like the heart, lungs, and brain.

Your Muscles

About one half of your body is muscle (Figure 6-4, page 97). The work of the muscles is movement, which makes other parts of the body, such as the bones, move. When you want to walk, run, jump, speak, or swallow, the muscular system does the work.

Your bones are moved by the skeletal muscles. These muscles are attached to the bones by tough *tendons*. Can you see why these muscles are called skeletal? They are also called *voluntary muscles* because you can make them move when you want to.

You also have *involuntary muscles*. These muscles keep on doing their work whether you think about them or not. You cannot make the involuntary muscles move or stop moving whenever you decide to do so. There are two different kinds of involuntary muscles in the body.

1. The heart, which keeps your blood flowing, is built mostly of muscle. This kind of muscle (Figure 2-11) is found nowhere else in the body.
2. Smooth muscles (Figure 2-11) are found in the stomach, intestine, and many other organs inside the body. They cause the motions for digestion and other vital processes. Whenever something moves in your body, a muscle had a part in it.

Control Unit Number One: The Nervous System

Nearly all of your muscles move only after they receive an impulse from a nerve. The heart is the only muscle with its own control system. This system makes the heart beat, but it, too, has nerves to keep it from making the heart beat too fast or too slow. Your body activities could not be maintained and regulated without nerves and nerve impulses. Your nervous system (see pages 204–08) is your top-level control unit. It consists of four main parts.

1. Sense organs, such as your eyes and your ears. They sense changes taking place in your environment.
2. Nerves, which carry impulses both ways between the brain and other organs.
3. The *central nervous system*. This includes the brain and the spinal cord. Your brain is your control center for thought, memory, and all sense impressions, such as sight, hearing, taste, and touch.
4. The *autonomic* (aw-tuh-NOM-ik) nervous system. This is a set of nerves that controls digestion, heartbeat, and other activities not under the conscious control of the central nervous system.

Your Nervous System at Work

Let's see how the parts of your nervous system work during one minute of your day.

It's 8:00 A.M. You are a high school boy walking to school. You see Anne Roberts across the street. Your eyes form her image and your two *optic nerves* (the nerves connecting your eyes and your brain, for sight) take a message to your brain. The message flashes from one brain cell to another. You think "She's very pretty. I wish I knew her better." As the message goes to other brain cells, you recall "I've thought she was nice for a long time."

Anne sees you, smiles, and says "Hi!" Your eyes and ears rush this big news to your brain. The first thing your brain does is send a message to your heart to make it pound faster. Then you decide to walk with Anne, and your brain sends an order through your spinal cord to your muscles—which start taking you across the street. As you do this, your brain does something you don't want it to do. It sends an order through your autonomic nerves to little muscles in the blood vessels of your face. They relax and let more blood flow to your cheeks. In other words, you blush.

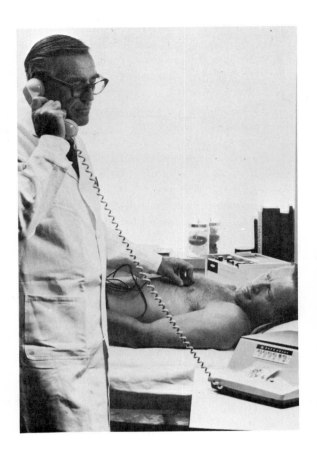

2-13 There are many advances in maintaining the health of body systems. (*Top left*) This patient lives in a very small town where few specialists in medicine are available. His electrocardiogram is being sent directly from his bedside over telephone lines to a distant computer for analysis. (*Below*) How noise pollution harms hearing is being tested by noise-abatement bureaus of large cities. (*Bottom*) This complex scanner uses radioactive materials to locate a tumor earlier and more accurately than ordinary X rays would locate it.

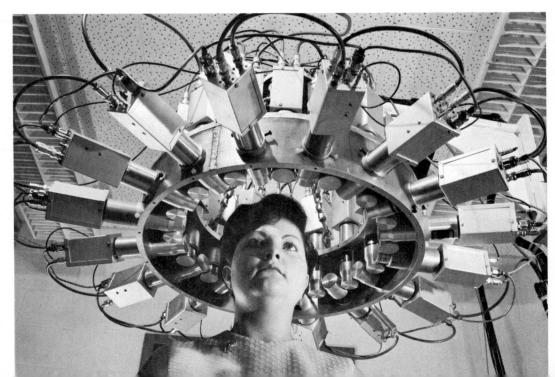

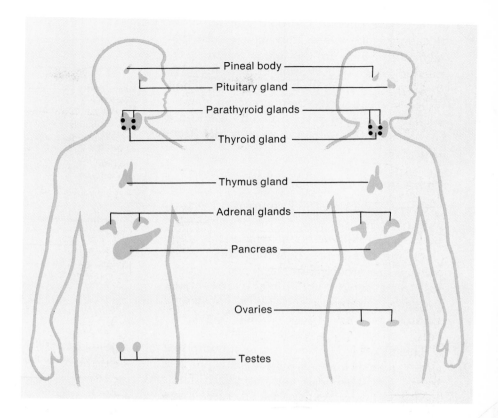

2-14 The endocrine glands are a vital control unit for your body. They produce hormones that help to regulate your body functions.

Pineal body
Pituitary gland
Parathyroid glands
Thyroid gland
Thymus gland
Adrenal glands
Pancreas
Ovaries
Testes

Once you have controlled your bashfulness, orders go to your throat to make you say "Hello!" in a firm voice, and another order cancels the one that made you blush. By 8:01 A.M. your brain sends an order to your heart that means "Take it easy; slow down to normal." All this time thousands of messages have been dashing along nerves throughout your body to keep your brain informed and to keep your heartbeat, breathing, digestion, movement, balance, and hundreds of other activities going on as they should.

Control Unit Number Two: The Endocrine Glands

How tall you grow and many other things about you are controlled by tiny amounts of chemicals in your blood. The chemicals are produced by your *endocrine* (EN-duh-kryne) glands. These glands are located in various parts of your body and range in size from tiny specks to organs larger than your hands (Figure 2-14). The chemicals they produce are called *hormones* (HOR-mohns).

The endocrine glands have no openings— that is, no tubes to let the hormones they make pass out. Therefore, they are called *ductless* (tubeless) glands. You will study them in detail later. The blood absorbs hormones from the endocrine glands through the walls of the smallest blood vessels that pass through these glands. Then the blood carries the hormones to the body cells they affect, and, depending upon the nature of the hormones, different cells are stimulated to work or are regulated in their growth.

You have many other glands besides the endocrine glands. These other kinds of glands have openings to pour out the juices that they make. Often they have a tube that takes this juice to the place where it is needed. Since duct is another word for tube, these glands are called duct glands. Their juices are called by their common names, such as tears, *saliva* (suh-LY-vuh—the liquid in your mouth), perspiration, and *bile* (from your liver).

Your Circulatory System

Every cell in the body must receive food and oxygen and get rid of wastes. This pick-up and delivery service is the job of the circulatory system. The circulatory system also carries around the hormones you have just read about. The blood carries food, oxygen, hormones, and other substances through millions of tubes called blood vessels.

The blood is kept moving by a pump that never quits as long as you live—this pump is your heart. The heart gets the rest it needs between beats. All the blood vessels are hooked up; there are no dead-end tubes in your circulatory system. The blood rushes from the heart to all parts of the body in blood vessels called *arteries*. These branch and rebranch until they form an amazingly fine network of tiny tubes called *capillaries* (KAP-'l-air-ees). The capillaries pass through every part of the body—skin, muscles, brain, and even the bones. Each capillary network covers only a short distance. After spreading out among the cells, the capillaries unite to form larger vessels called *veins*. The veins carry the blood back to the heart. The heart then pumps the blood to the lungs, where the blood loses the carbon dioxide it took from the cells and picks up a fresh supply of oxygen. See Figure 17-3, page 313.

Your Breathing or Respiratory System

To live you must breathe; otherwise your

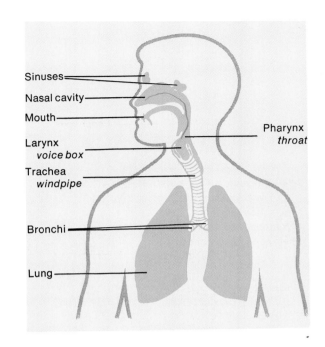

2-15 A simplified diagram of the respiratory system. Can you trace the path of air through the respiratory system?

Labels: Sinuses, Nasal cavity, Mouth, Larynx *voice box*, Trachea *windpipe*, Bronchi, Lung, Pharynx *throat*

body cells would not get oxygen and could not get rid of carbon dioxide. Figure 2-15 shows how air passes through your nose, throat, windpipe, and *bronchial* (BRONK-ee-ul) tubes to the lungs. The lungs are so light that they would float in water. This is because they are built like a sponge, with thousands of tiny air spaces resembling bubbles. The walls of these spaces are so thin that oxygen passes from the air to the blood on the other side of the wall by diffusion, just as food passes from blood vessels to body cells. Carbon dioxide passes from the blood to the *air sacs* in the lungs in the same way. You then breathe out the carbon dioxide before you inhale more fresh air.

The air you breathe out has only three fourths as much oxygen, but more than 100 times as much carbon dioxide as the air you breathe in. See if you can trace the complete path of the air you breathe into your body. Use Figure 2-15 as a guide.

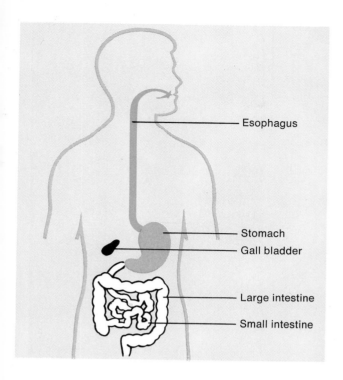

Esophagus

Stomach
Gall bladder

Large intestine

Small intestine

2-16 A simplified diagram of the digestive system. Where does digestion begin?

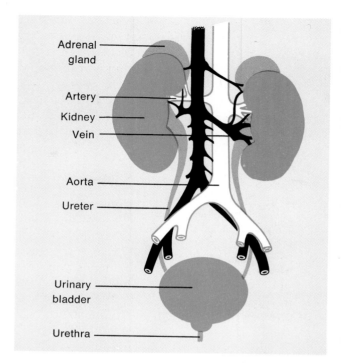

Adrenal gland

Artery

Kidney

Vein

Aorta

Ureter

Urinary bladder

Urethra

2-17 A simplified diagram of the excretory system. What does the word "excrete" mean?

Your Food Factory— the Digestive System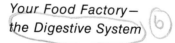

Suppose you have been playing baseball. After nine innings the cells in the muscles of your arms could use a good meal. There is only one way that you can get food to these cells. Before you can use most foods, they have to be digested in your food factory, the digestive system (Figure 2-16).

All of the food you eat has to pass through a long tube called the *alimentary* (al-ih-MEN-tuh-ree) canal. This consists of the mouth, *esophagus* (uh-SOF-uh-gus), stomach, small intestine, and large intestine. (The large intestine doesn't digest the food. It gets rid of the food parts that cannot be digested and put into the blood.) Besides the alimentary canal, the digestive system includes glands that pour digestive juices into the canal.

Digestion starts while you cut and grind the food with your teeth. After you swallow the food, it is churned by muscles located in the walls of the stomach and small intestine. The digestive juices are chemicals that act upon the food to change large, complex molecules into smaller, simpler molecules, which the cells of your body can use.

The Excretory System

Every cell continually pours wastes into the blood. The blood has to get rid of these wastes. The lungs, the liver, and the kidneys remove wastes from the blood and send them out of the body. Sweat glands get rid of small amounts of wastes. All these organs help regulate body activities when they *excrete* (eks-KREET) wastes. Excrete means "to get rid of." (The large intestine, a part of your diges-

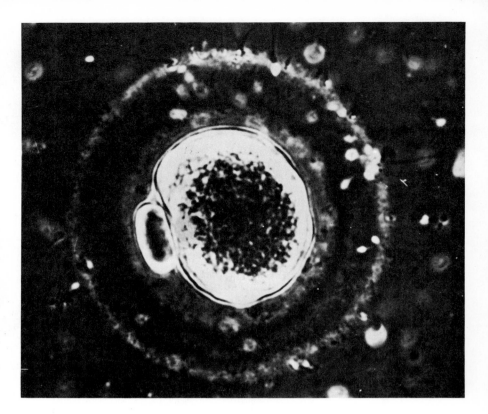

2-18 The fertilization of a human egg cell. Although many sperm cells can be identified in this photograph, only one will penetrate the egg cell.

Courtesy L. B. Shettles, Ovum Humanum, Hafner Publishing Co., N.Y.

tive system, removes the part of food that cannot be digested and has therefore never actually become a part of your body cells or blood. In this sense, the large intestine is not an excretory organ.)

Look at Figure 2-17 on the previous page. Which of the organs of the excretory system are shown in this diagram?

The lungs and sweat glands help regulate body heat by giving off excess heat during the processes of breathing and perspiring. The liver helps regulate the amount of food in the blood, and the kidneys (along with the sweat glands) help regulate the amount of water in the blood. All this is in addition to the regulatory work these organs do in excreting wastes.

You have read briefly about how the endocrine glands regulate growth. Later you will learn more about their role in growth and about how they regulate the development of your reproductive system.

How Life is Continued— the Reproductive System

In human beings, as in most animals, there is a system of organs that continues the life of the species. This is the *reproductive* system. The organs which produce the cells for the new life are the two *ovaries* (OH-vuh-reez) in the female and the two *testes* (TESS-teez) in the male.

The ovaries and testes are also ductless glands, giving hormones to the blood. (See page 412.) These hormones cause many of the physical differences between men and women.

The female sex cells are called *eggs* and the male sex cells are called *sperms*. The union of an egg cell and a sperm cell is called *fertilization.* A *fertilized egg* results. Under the right conditions a human fertilized egg develops into a new human being. In the female, the *uterus* (YOO-ter-us) is the organ in which the unborn child develops.

What You Have Learned

What kind of health practices should you apply in maintaining your health? Check your understanding of the chapter. On a separate sheet of paper, number 1 through 20 and insert the answer from the vocabulary list below. Use each expression, but use each word only once.

air
blood
cells
connective tissue
endocrine
energy
epithelial tissue

fertilization
food
hormones
hydrogen
iodine
iron
molecules

oxidation
oxygen
reproductive
sugar
tissue
water

Your body is composed of a number of elements. By weight, more than half of you is the element (1)_____. This element is found in the (2)_____ and (3)_____ you take into your body. The element (4)_____ combines with oxygen and carbon in (5)_____ molecules. Then there are such elements as (6)_____ and (7)_____ that are essential to body function.

Your body, like that of all plants and animals, is built of tiny living building blocks called (8)_____ that are made of many complex combinations of elements. In order to survive, the building blocks must have (9)_____ that is carried to them by the (10)_____ in tiny particles called (11)_____ (12)_____ is the ability to do work. It is produced in the form of chemical energy largely from the (13)_____ of the food you eat.

A group of cells that carry on a special kind of work is called a (14)_____ of which there are several types. All the body organs are covered with (15)_____. The tissues that hold your body together are called (16)_____ The (17)_____ glands produce (18)_____ that regulate your body functions. A new life is formed by the (19)_____ system. The union of a sperm and egg is called (20)_____

What You Can Do

1. Raise one arm high overhead and keep the other arm lowered by your side for a few minutes. Now place both hands, palms down, on your desk. Does one hand look different from the other? What does this tell you about the circulation of the blood?

2. Sit with your legs crossed at the knee. Hang a pocketbook or book bag over the instep of your raised foot and lift the bag as high as you can. Locate the muscles that are raising the bag.

Things to Try

1. Place one hand on the biceps of the opposite arm (see Figure 2-13). Bend and straighten your arm several times. Can you feel a change in the shape of the biceps? Can you feel the tendon that attaches the biceps to your lower arm? Now clench your fist and slowly bend your arm as though you were lifting a heavy weight. Does the biceps feel the same as before? If not, why is this so?

2. Hold a piece of glass in your hand and blow your breath onto its surface. Why does the glass cloud over? Where do the droplets of moisture come from? What body system is involved? What waste products are being eliminated through your breath?

3. Look at the back of your hand and think of the various tissues of the body. How many tissues can you see in your hand? Feel your knuckles. Beside the bones, what tissues are in your knuckles?

Probing Further

Man and His Body: The Story of Physiology, by Gordon McCull, Natural History Press, 1967. This book explains, in easy language, how the body functions. The book begins at the level of the cell and proceeds to clearly develop each body system.

Biological Science: An Inquiry into Life, by J. A. Moore and others, Harcourt Brace Jovanovich, 1968. A modern approach to the biological sciences, including interesting discussions of body systems and related scientific history and findings.

Health Concepts in Action

Does what you have learned support this statement?

The body is organized into specialized parts that interact in maintaining healthy functioning.

Applying this concept of the body, which health practices would you

— continue?

— change?

— begin?

Will you now, as a result of your study, change any of your health objectives?

A Visit
to the
Doctor

An annual visit to a doctor should be on your "must" list. In the following photographic essay you will accompany Tom on his visit to the doctor. It is the first time Tom has seen this doctor. The doctor first discusses Tom's medical history with him, taking notes on previous illnesses, operations, immunizations, changes in weight, and other matters. He is also interested in illnesses in Tom's immediate family. The more he knows about Tom and his family, the better able he will be to interpret his medical findings.

After completing Tom's medical history the doctor shows Tom into the examining room. After Tom has undressed, the doctor joins him and begins the physical examination. Tom tells the doctor of any problems so that the doctor can pay special attention to them during the examination. A seemingly unimportant complaint could give the doctor a clue to some illness.

The doctor prepares to make use of a wide variety of equipment . . .

 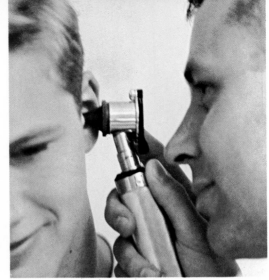

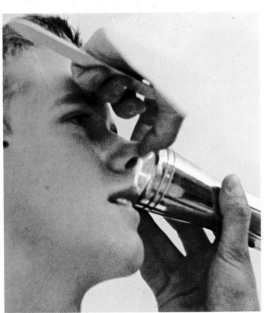 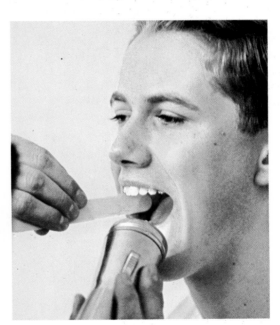

Tom's eyes, ears, nose, and throat are carefully examined. The doctor checks his pupils by shining a flashlight into his eyes. He uses an otoscope to look at Tom's eardrums. Next the doctor checks Tom's nostrils, and then his mouth and throat. He may suggest that Tom visit an ophthalmologist, a hearing specialist, or a dentist for further examination.

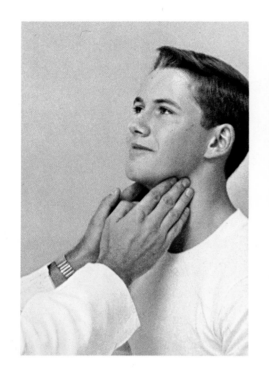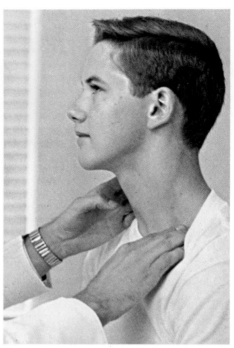

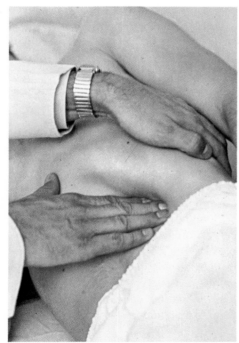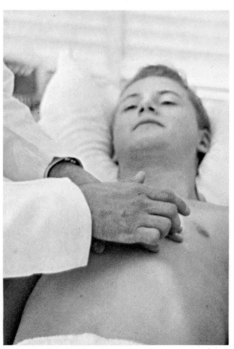

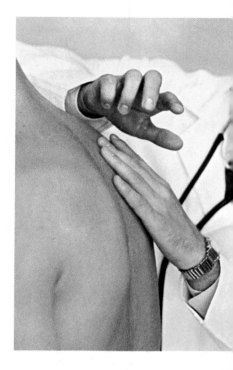

Next the doctor palpates, or feels, for enlargement of glands. He checks the lymph nodes of the throat and neck, and the thyroid gland below and to the sides of the Adam's apple. He may also check the lymph nodes in the armpits and in the groin. Enlarged lymph nodes can indicate trouble, chiefly the possibility of infection. The doctor also palpates the spleen (*opposite, lower left*). If there is enlargement of the spleen, it could indicate the need for special blood tests to check for a possible blood disorder.

Now the doctor percusses, or "thumps," Tom's chest and back (*opposite, lower right, and this page, top*). From the sounds he hears he may be able to tell whether there is enlargement of the heart, fluid in the lungs, or other abnormalities inside the chest cavity. This can be an important indication of physical trouble. The doctor then adjusts his stethoscope and prepares to take Tom's blood pressure and to listen to Tom's heart and breathing sounds. This too is a vital part of a physical examination.

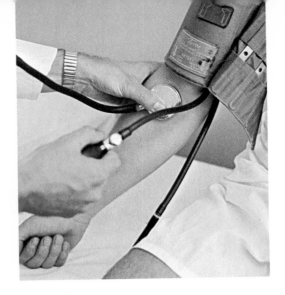

Here the doctor is taking Tom's blood pressure with the aid of an air-inflated rubber cuff, a manometer, or gauge, and a stethoscope. With the stethoscope he can hear the sound made by the blood rushing through the blood vessels.

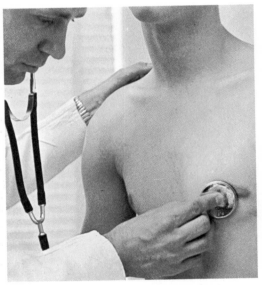

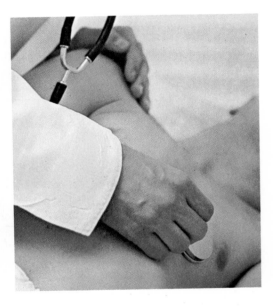

Next the doctor listens to Tom's breathing movements through the front and back walls of the chest. He also listens to the heartbeat and to the sounds made by the blood passing through the valves of the heart.

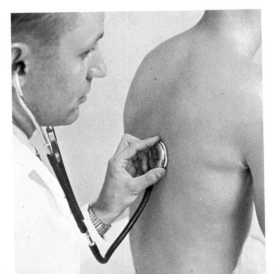

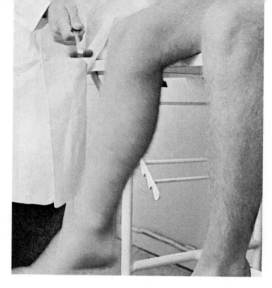

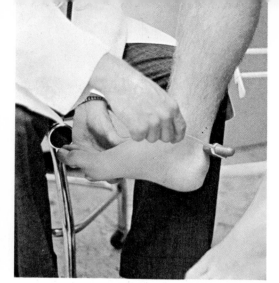

Since some diseases affect the nervous system, the doctor checks to see whether a detailed neurological examination is necessary. To test Tom's nerve reflex reactions, the doctor taps the tendon below the kneecap and the tendon at the back of the ankle; then he lightly scratches the sole of Tom's foot. After this, the doctor concludes Tom's physical examination by measuring and weighing him. Since teenagers are still growing rapidly and gaining weight, this is an important part of the physical examination. Now Tom will get dressed and, while the doctor enters the data in Tom's medical record, Tom will go to the laboratory for some additional tests.

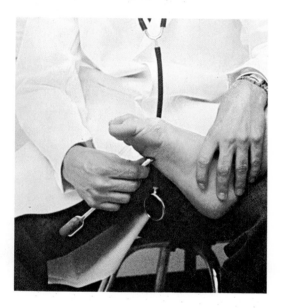

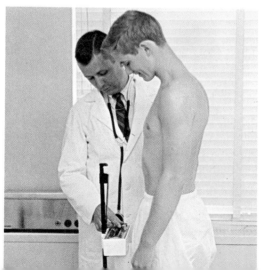

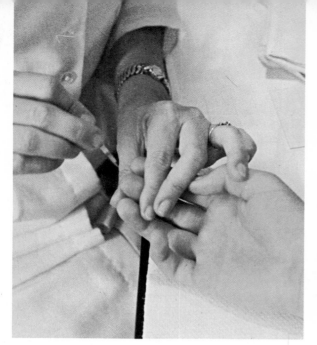

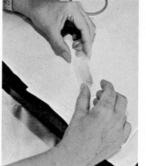
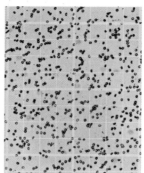

A specimen of blood is taken from Tom's fingertip. A count of the red and white blood cells will be made, and the hemoglobin content will be determined. Tom will also leave a sample of urine, which will be tested in many ways. One test will be for sugar, a sign that further tests for diabetes should be made. Tom then returns to the doctor to hear the results of his physical examination and to find out if the doctor recommends additional studies, such as an X-ray examination. When the results of the laboratory tests are complete, Tom's medical record will be up to date. The visit over, the nurse sees Tom to the door, telling him that he need return only if the laboratory tests prove unsatisfactory.

UNIT TWO
Daily Needs
Supplied by
Your
Environment

3 / The Foods You Eat

"How do I look?" This is a question most teen-agers ask. The answer will depend partly on how you reply to the question, "How do I feel?" Whether you look and feel well or ill will depend a great deal on how you nourish your body. The foods you eat are essential to physical health, and a well-nourished body gives you a sense of emotional and social well-being. You must eat to live, but maintaining an adequate diet is not always easy unless you know how to go about it.

A PROBE INTO NUTRITION—What is an adequate diet? To find out, you will be probing questions like these:

1. Why must you eat? What five types of nutrients are needed?

2. What are some valuable sources of complete and incomplete proteins?

3. How is the energy value of food determined? How many calories do you need daily?

4. Why does the body require minerals?

5. Why do we need a number of different vitamins? Should you supplement your daily diet with vitamins? Why?

6. How can you overcome a dislike for certain foods? How do your emotions influence your diet?

3-1 You need a lot of energy to keep up the pace of this dance. How do you get that energy?

WHAT KINDS OF FOOD DO YOU NEED?

Why do you have to eat? Why do you need food? Here are three main reasons.

1. Foods provide substances that your tissues need for growth and repair. The process of tissue growth continues until you become an adult. The process of tissue repair continues as long as you live.
2. Foods furnish you with energy. Energy provides body heat, makes it possible for you to move about, and helps you think.
3. Foods help regulate the work done by your body.

All foods contain chemical compounds called *nutrients* (NU-tree-ents) that are used for one or more of the functions listed above.

Your Environment and the Foods You Eat

The area of the country where you live as well as your family background may influence your eating habits. Families of various na-tional backgrounds have settled in certain areas of America, where they continue their national customs. Certain foods and types of cooking have become associated with partic-ular areas. Typical of these areas are the New England states with their many fish dishes, the Southern states with their ham and chickens, the Pennsylvania Dutch country with its many unusual foods, the Mexican border states influenced by the highly spiced Spanish foods, and the New Orleans area with its Creole preparations.

Another environmental influence is seen especially among people of low economic levels who live in rural regions. In areas where low-income groups predominate, the people must depend on foods available from local sources. Foods that are grown locally are usually less expensive than those that are shipped into an area. Other valuable local foods are fish from streams in the area or from the ocean, wild birds and animals from woods and mountains, and greens that grow wild in backyards and fields.

Whatever may be the environment where you live, it is important that you know the essentials of nutrition. This will help you make right choices from available foods.

Five Essential Nutrients Plus Water

Five essential classes of nutrients and water are necessary for the healthy functioning of the human body. They are *carbohydrates, fats, proteins, minerals,* and *vitamins.* Sources and deficiency effects of these nutrients are shown in Figure 3-2. A similar chart for vitamins is shown in Figure 3-10. To eliminate any one of these nutrients from your diet is to court trouble. Now let us see what each nutrient does for the body. Does your daily diet include all of the essential nutrients?

3-2 ESSENTIAL NUTRIENTS

Nutrients	Common Sources	Deficiency Effects
Carbohydrates	Sugar, honey, preserves, cakes, cereals, bread, dried fruits, potatoes, rice, spaghetti, wheat, corn, barley	Loss of weight Lack of energy
Fats	Bacon, lard, vegetable oils, butter, nuts, margarine, mayonnaise, peanut butter, olives, avocados, egg yolk, chocolate	Loss of weight Lack of energy Skin disorders Sensitivity to cold
Proteins	*Complete:* animal products—milk, cheese, eggs, meat, fish, poultry *Incomplete:* plant products—dried peas, beans, lentils, bread, cereals, nuts, peanut butter	Lack of energy Retarded growth Poor muscle tone Low resistance Poor body function
Calcium	Milk, milk products, leafy and green vegetables, oranges, eggs, dried fruit	Slow blood clotting Poor tooth and bone formation Retarded growth and repair; tetany
Phosphorus	Meat, fish, poultry, milk, cheese, nuts, whole-wheat products	Poor tooth and bone formation Retarded growth and repair
Iron	Eggs, lean meat, soybeans, nuts, dried fruits, whole-grain or enriched cereals, leafy and green vegetables, liver, oysters	Anemia Iron-deficiency diseases
Iodine	Seafoods, iodized salt	Thyroid gland defects Goiter

Carbohydrates

Carbohydrates (starches and sugar) are the prime source of energy. They contain the chemical elements carbon, hydrogen, and oxygen. *Carbo* comes from carbon; *hydrate* from the Greek word for water. Carbohydrates are so named because the hydrogen and oxygen in them are usually in the same proportion as in water. In most countries more than one half of the calories needed in the diet are supplied by carbohydrates.

Starches are found in all grain products, such as flour, bread, cereals, cakes, macaroni, and noodles. Starches are also found in such vegetables as potatoes, beans, and peas. Sugar is found in all fruits, honey, molasses, and in many vegetables. All of these foods contain other nutrients in addition to sugar. See Figure 3-2 for other sources of carbohydrates.

3-3 What essential nutrients are included in this meal? Is this a well-balanced meal?

Fats

Fats contain the same chemical elements as carbohydrates, although not in the same proportions. Fatty compounds are key substances in the structure of the cell membrane and other membranes. They are also important as energy sources. An ounce of fat supplies more than twice as much energy as an ounce of carbohydrate or protein.

Fats that have become part of your body serve important functions. They insulate you and help control body temperature, they form substances that insulate nerve fibers, and they help absorb shocks and injuries. The body is supplied with fats from animal sources, dairy products, and plant oils. See Figure 3-2 for common sources of fats.

Reducing Your Intake of Fats

Some teen-agers have strong feelings about fats and believe that every possible ounce should be eliminated. As you see here, fats have important body functions that are performed by no other nutrient. A certain amount of fat tissue is vital to good health. If you are fat-conscious, it is well to consider the *calorie* (KAL-eree) values of the foods that you eat, but it is unwise to eliminate totally all fats from your daily diet.

Saturated and Unsaturated Fats

Fats are divided into two general types based on their principal characteristics. ***Saturated fats*** tend to increase blood ***cholesterol*** (co-LES-ter-rol)—a fatlike substance found in the brain and the nerves and in the blood. Saturated fats are found in animal foods such as beef, pork, or lamb, and in solid cooking fats. ***Unsaturated*** fats tend to lower blood cholesterol. They are mainly of vegetable origin and are included in vegetable cooking oils, such as corn oil.

3-4 What kinds of nutrients are these girls getting in their foods? Which kind of food is better for them? Why?

However, none of the fats is completely of either type. A convenient general guide to determining the type of fat is that the unsaturated fats, such as those in corn oil and other vegetable oils, melt at room temperature. The saturated fats, such as bacon, beef, and lamb grease, harden at room temperature.

A fat-controlled diet is sometimes recommended by physicians for people suffering from *atherosclerosis* (ATH-er-oh-skler-oh-sis), in which there is a high level of cholesterol and various fats in the blood. The fat deposits

3-5 Which one to buy? With so many different kinds of fats for sale, the housewife is left with a difficult decision.

cling to the inner wall of the artery, causing it to narrow and making it more difficult for the blood to flow through. Eventually, these deposits may completely block an artery—usually an artery to the heart, brain, or kidneys. A fat-restricted diet should be undertaken only when prescribed by your physician.

Proteins

Proteins furnish the body with energy and much more. During the growing years they help form new tissues, and throughout life they provide material for tissue repair. Protein comes from the Greek word meaning "to take first place," and this is just what proteins do in your diet. Proteins, like the fats and carbohydrates, contain carbon, hydrogen, and oxygen. In addition, they contain nitrogen. During digestion your body splits proteins into *amino* (a-MEE-noh) *acids.* These amino acids form the building blocks of protein molecules. See Figure 3-2 for some common sources of proteins.

The human body uses some 20 amino acids in building proteins. Some of these amino acids can be synthesized in the body. However, eight or more amino acids are *essential* because the body can only get them through the foods you eat. **Complete proteins** contain all of these **essential amino acids.** Complete proteins come mainly from animal sources, such as liver, milk, eggs, cheese, fish, and meats. Among foods on the market today, you will find cottage cheese the least expensive of the complete proteins. **Incomplete proteins** contain fewer of the essential amino acids, and these proteins come mainly from vegetable sources. You will find them in such foods as beans, peas, peanuts, cereals, and lentils. It is possible to get all the amino acids you need from plant proteins, provided that you eat the proper variety of plant foods so that all of the essential amino acids will be supplied.

■ List all of the foods you eat at dinner for one week. Beside each food that contains protein place a *C* for complete protein or an *I* for incomplete protein.

Minerals

Minerals are present in a wide variety of foods in the form of water-soluble salts. They appear in particles small enough to pass through the walls of the small intestine into the bloodstream. They require no digestion. Several purposes are served by the minerals. They are used

1. *As building materials.* Calcium and phosphorus build bones and teeth; iron is an essential ingredient of **hemoglobin** (HEE-moh-glo-bin) in the red blood cells. Hemoglobin is the red coloring matter of the blood that carries oxygen from the lungs to the tissues and carries carbon dioxide away from the tissues.
2. *As essential ingredients of several body secretions.* An example of this function is the need for iodine in the thyroid secretion of the hormone thyroxin.
3. *As aids to favorable climate for cells.* Sodium chloride keeps the blood and tissue fluid slightly salty. Other minerals in the body protect the blood and tissue fluid from becoming acid.
4. *As regulators of body processes.* Minerals affect the clotting of the blood, beating of the heart, and functioning of muscles, nerves, and glands.

The minerals to be concerned about are calcium, phosphorus, iron, and iodine. When these four are adequate in the diet, the other minerals needed only in "trace amounts" will be supplied. Among the minerals needed only in trace amounts are copper, magnesium, zinc, sodium, chlorine, fluorine, sulfur, cobalt, and potassium. These minerals are found in the same foods as those that contain the four most important minerals.

Calcium and phosphorus usually work in combination and are found in much the same foods. Milk is one of the best sources. Such vegetables as broccoli, beans, and turnip greens, and such fruits as oranges and grapefruit are rich sources of calcium and phosphorus. Meat contains ample amounts of phosphorus, but little calcium. These minerals are important for building bones and teeth, for normal coagulation of the blood, and for the body's ability to maintain muscle and nerve sensitivity. They also help promote the rhythmic functioning of the heart and aid the passage of fluids through cell walls.

Iron is usually present in adequate amounts in the normal diet. Foods rich in iron are eggs, meat, green vegetables, and iron-enriched bread. Iron is needed in the manufacture of *hemoglobin.*

Iodine is found in seafoods, in vegetables grown in iodine-rich soil, and in iodized table salt. It is needed for the proper functioning of the thyroid gland. Some areas, such as the Great Lakes Region and parts of the northwest section of the United States, tend to be deficient in sources of iodine. People in these regions add iodine to their diet by using iodized table salt and eating

3-6 A patient with goiter, an enlargement of the thyroid gland. This condition may develop from insufficient iodine in the diet.

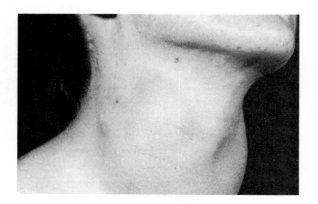

seafoods shipped in from other sections of the country. A *goiter* (enlarged thyroid gland) occurs when the diet is deficient in iodine. See Figure 3-6. You will read more about this condition in Chapter 22.

Minerals are present in almost all foods. By eating a variety of foods, you are assured of getting the minerals needed for body function. However, in hot weather, when you perspire freely, it is good to add a few extra shakes of table salt (sodium chloride) to your food. This helps restore the salt lost with perspiration. Salt is essential to maintaining proper water balance in the body.

Using Figure 3-2 as a guide, list the essential nutrients in each of the foods you eat for one entire day. Include all of your snacks.

Vitamins

Vitamins are organic compounds built by plants and animals. All of the vitamins play essential roles in nutrition and body welfare. They contain carbon, hydrogen, oxygen, and other elements. Vitamins are widely distributed among foods in the American diet.

Vast advertising compaigns have successfully produced a large market for vitamin pills and capsules. It is not necessary for a healthy person to take vitamin pills, so long as he has a varied diet. Buying vitamin pills is more expensive than obtaining them from foods. Also, in foods there are other essential nutrients along with the vitamins. However, if you become ill and are put on a restricted diet, your physician may want to fortify your diet temporarily with certain vitamins. By following the plan of eating well-balanced meals daily and using vitamin pills only when prescribed, you will get all of the vitamins that your body needs. Let us find out about these essential vitamins.

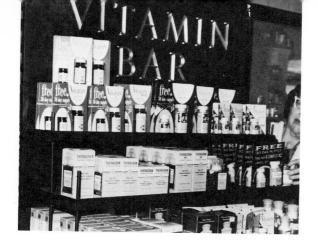

3-7 Many different kinds of vitamins can be purchased in your drug store. Will a balanced diet supply you with all the vitamins you need?

Kinds of Vitamins You Need

Scientists have identified a large number of vitamins, but only nine of them need serious consideration in your diet. They are vitamins A, C, D, *thiamine* (THY-a-min) *riboflavin* (ry-boh-FLAY-vin), *niacin* (NY-uh-sin), and vitamins B_{12}, E, and K.

Why You Need Vitamins

Vitamin A is needed for the prevention of night blindness, an impairment of vision in dim light. It is also essential for building bones, forming cells of teeth, and keeping the skin, mucous membranes, and eyes healthy. Vitamin A is found in animal food sources dissolved in fat. It is found in plant sources in the form of *carotene* (KAIR-uh-teen), which must be converted by body action into active vitamin A. Carotene is the yellow, orange, or red pigment found in such foods as sweet potatoes, carrots, egg yolk, and corn.

The *vitamin B complex* includes a whole family of vitamins, some known by chemical names, some by a letter, some by both. They are all intimately related in function and are of highest importance to growth and energy.

Thiamine (B_1) is needed for healthy nerves, good muscle tone in the digestive tract, and proper digestion of carbohydrates. Thiamine taken in excess of body needs is not stored to any extent in the body. It is found in pork, whole-grain cereals, liver, lean meat, and nuts. An insufficient amount of thiamine in the diet may lead to various nerve disorders and muscular difficulties. Severe deficiencies may produce the disease **beriberi**, in which the heart as well as nervous system is affected.

Riboflavin (B_2) is needed for healthy functioning of the nervous and digestive systems and of the skin and for general body resistance. A deficiency of riboflavin may cause inflammation of the tongue and cracking of the lips and corners of the mouth. Like thiamine, it is not stored to any extent in the body but must be eaten in the daily diet. Riboflavin is found in such foods as liver, cheese, leafy vegetables, beans, peas, lean meat, milk, and fish.

Niacin is needed to protect the health of the skin and nerves and as an aid to digestion. Like thiamine and riboflavin, it is not

3-8 Do you take vitamins without doctor's orders? Vitamins A and D in excess are stored by the body and may build up to harmful levels.

stored in the body. Niacin is found in such foods as whole-wheat products, peanuts, almonds, dried beans and peas, tuna fish, and lean meat. A lack of niacin in the diet may cause *pellagra* (puh-LAY-gruh). Pellagra causes the skin to become dry and red with scaly patches. It causes nervous and digestive disorders.

Vitamin B₁₂ helps to increase the red blood cells and to keep the spinal cord healthy. It is produced by bacteria in the large intestine and is stored in the liver. Vitamin B_{12} is used in the treatment of *pernicious anemia* (per-NISH-us uh-NEE-me-uh), a form of *anemia* in which the blood does not have enough normal red blood cells. Pernicious anemia will be discussed in greater detail in Chapter 16, where you will learn about other kinds of anemia, also. B_{12} is also found in such foods as liver, kidneys, leafy vegetables, milk, eggs, and cheese.

Folic acid is another B vitamin that is also used in the treatment of pernicious anemia. It is needed for metabolic function, growth, and development. The food sources for folic acid are the same as those for vitamin B_{12}.

Ascorbic acid, vitamin C, is needed to maintain firm, healthy gums. It aids in the formation of intercellular cement that binds together the cells of the capillary walls. When ascorbic acid is lacking in the diet, capillary walls weaken and blood leaks through the gums and other tissues. This disease, called *scurvy*, is readily prevented by eating citrus fruit, cabbage, tomatoes, and strawberries. Surplus amounts of ascorbic acid are not retained by the body, so regular daily amounts are needed in your diet.

Vitamin D helps the body to absorb calcium and is sometimes called the sunshine vitamin because it is formed by action of the *ultraviolet rays* of the sun upon fatty substances present in the skin. Milk and some other foods can be enriched with vitamin D by exposing them to ultraviolet radiation.

Food treated in this way can be identified by the phrase on the label, "enriched with vitamin D."

Vitamin D is vital for strong bones and teeth. When it is lacking in your diet, a disease called *rickets* may occur. Rickets affects the bones and causes various types of bone deformities (Figure 3-9) such as bowed legs and enlarged joints. It was discovered that sunshine, cod liver oil, and the oil of other bony fish are excellent preventatives of rickets.

There is evidence that a person can get too much vitamin D with harmful results. Persons who take too much vitamin D daily may develop calcium deposits in muscles or in kidneys (kidney stones), or elsewhere.

Vitamin E is shown by experiments to be beneficial to normal reproduction in some animals. Its use within the human body is still not well understood. Vitamin E is found in such foods as wheat germ, egg yolk, leafy vegetables, nuts, and cereal.

3-9 An Indonesian girl suffering from rickets. How can this disease be prevented?

3-10 THE ESSENTIAL VITAMINS

Vitamins	Common Sources	Effects of Deficiency
Vitamin A	Liver, butter, egg yolk, milk, cream, carrots, ice cream, apricots, green and leafy vegetables, tomatoes	Night blindness Rough skin Susceptibility to infection
Thiamine (vitamin B_1)	Pork muscle, beans and peas, liver, whole grains, nuts, oysters, kidneys, and peanuts	General poor health Susceptibility to poor appetite, indigestion, and impaired nerve function Beriberi
Riboflavin (vitamin B_2)	Liver, cheese, eggs, leafy vegetables, beans, lean meat, peas, milk, fish, and egg yolk	Unhealthy skin, mouth, and eyes General poor health
Niacin (vitamin B group)	Liver, peanuts, peanut butter, almonds, tuna fish, salmon, lean meat, whole-wheat products, beans, and peas	Unhealthy skin and nerves Low energy Pellagra
Vitamin B_{12}	Liver, kidneys, meat, leafy vegetables, milk, eggs, and cheese	Anemia
Folic acid	Green vegetables, liver, and kidneys	Anemia
Ascorbic acid (vitamin C)	All citrus fruit (limes, oranges, lemons, grapefruit), tomatoes, raw cabbage, peppers, strawberries, cantaloupe, and potatoes	Unhealthy gums and capillaries Susceptibility to infection Scurvy
Vitamin D	Egg yolk, butter fat, liver, oils from livers of fish	Deficient use of calcium and phosphorus in bones and teeth Rickets
Vitamin E	Lettuce, watercress, wheat germ, peas, milk, and butter	Effects have not yet been clearly defined in man
Vitamin K	Leafy green vegetables	Hemorrhage

Vitamin K is needed for normal clotting of the blood. It, like vitamin B₁₂, is produced by bacteria in the large intestine. Leafy green vegetables are good food sources of vitamin K.

List the foods you have eaten today. Using Figure 3-10 as a guide, identify the vitamins contained in those foods. Have you had all of the essential vitamins? If not, what foods should you eat for dinner?

Water

Water is needed for all body functions. About two thirds of the body is composed of water. Water holds other nutrients in solution both inside and outside of the cells. Blood and *lymph* (LIMF), for example, are principally water. Lymph is derived from blood plasma which has passed out from the capillaries. It surrounds the body cells. A loss of 10 percent of water from the body is serious. A loss of 20 percent, as in severe bleeding or extreme perspiration, may cause serious damage to the tissues and is a threat to life.

There is, however, normal body water loss of about two quarts per day. This takes place when water and waste products are excreted through the skin as perspiration, through the lungs in exhalation, through the intestines as feces, and through the kidneys as urine. Many factors affect the rate of water loss. Among these are: climate, working in hot areas, vigorous activities, and fever.

The body constantly strives to maintain its vital water balance. You become aware of this by the powerful sensation of thirst. If you respond to normal thirst, your water intake will probably be adequate. Normal fluid need is roughly estimated at six to eight glasses (8-ounce glasses) per day. This amount is in addition to the water in your foods.

Roughage

Some *roughage* (RUF-uj) is needed in the daily diet to promote the elimination of feces. Roughage is the indigestible fibrous part of foods. It passes along through the digestive system to the colon (large intestine), from which it is expelled in normal bowel action. Roughage is present in the husks and outer coats of grains and seeds, the skin of fruit, and in fibers of stems and leaves. See Figure 3-13 for a check of roughage content in foods.

3-11 Here Arnold Palmer is playing a vigorous game of golf in a warm climate. This will result in a considerable loss of water through perspiration.

3-12 Do you eat enough foods that contain roughage? Make a list of all the roughage foods you have eaten today.

3-13 ROUGHAGE VALUE OF FOODS

Harsh-fibered foods	Soft-fibered foods	Foods lacking fiber
1. Raw fruit with skins and seeds	1. Raw-fruit pulp without skins or seeds	1. Fats
2. Raw vegetables, such as carrots, celery, etc.	2. Cooked fruits	2. Milk products
3. Coarsely ground whole-grain cereals	3. Most cooked vegetables	3. Eggs
4. Certain cooked vegetables, such as leafy greens, peas, and corn	4. Finely ground whole-grain cereals, softened by long cooking	4. White-flour bread
		5. Cakes and pastries
		6. Meats
		7. Highly milled cereals, such as cream of wheat
		8. Corn flakes
		9. White or puffed rice

3-14 Your calorie needs vary according to your age, sex, build, and occupation. How would the calorie needs of these three people differ?

HOW MUCH FOOD DO YOU NEED?

The amount of food needed in the daily diet is estimated by its *calorie* content. The calorie is a measure of the energy you get from the food you eat. Expressed in familiar terms, a calorie is the amount of heat that will raise the temperature of 1 quart of water nearly 2° F, or the temperature of 1 kilogram of water 1° Celsius. (Scientists call this the *great calorie*, but we will simply say *calorie*.) Of all the food elements, proteins, carbohydrates, and fats provide almost all of the calories. Foods vary in their calorie content as they vary in their nutritional value. For example, a serving of fish and a serving of meat may provide you with the same protein value, but the calorie content of the meat may be much greater than that of the fish. In our weight-conscious society there are millions of people who count calories but are totally unaware that the calorie is not a nutrient.

All foods contain energy. When food is utilized in the body, it provides energy for body processes, movement, and responses. It is this energy available in foods that is measured in terms of calories. One speaks of the calorie content of food. In Figure 3-17 you will find the calorie values and the percentage of nutrients found in common foods.

To find out how much energy there is in a quantity of food, we put the food in a box called a *calorimeter* (kal-er-IM-uh-ter). You can see a diagram of one in Figure 3-15. Notice that the food is in a small metal box. This box is in another metal box full of water. The box with the food contains no air—just pure oxygen. When we make an electric spark jump across the wires, the food flames up and is burned. All we have to do now is to find out how much heat passed out into the water. Since we know how much water was in the box, we can note its change in temperature and find the number of calories that the food produced.

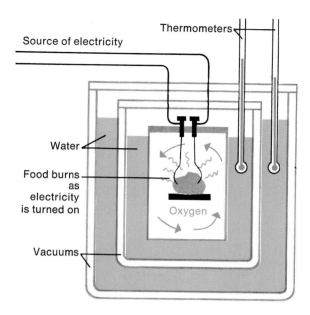

Source of electricity

Thermometers

Water

Food burns as electricity is turned on

Oxygen

Vacuums

3-15 Diagram of a calorimeter. Pure oxygen is used to make the foods burn completely.

How Much Energy Do You Use?

Work is going on inside your body constantly, even while you are resting or sleeping. Your heart beats, your breathing continues, your temperature is maintained, and all the cells of your body carry on their life processes. The energy needed for this internal work, while you are at rest and have no food in your digestive tract, is known as your **basal metabolism.**

In addition to the energy you require for your basal metabolism, you need energy for growth, for movement, and for all your daily activities.

All this energy must come from calories — from the food you eat. Figure 3-16 gives examples of the energy needs of young people — expressed in calories of food to be taken in. You can see from the table that the amount of energy needed is tied to many factors: age, sex, height, and weight. Thus, if you are shorter or taller than the example for your

3-16 CALORY NEEDS OF BOYS AND GIRLS

Boys

Age in years	Weight	Height	Calories
10–12	77 lb	55″	2500
12–14	95 lb	59″	2700
14–18	130 lb	67″	3000
18–22	147 lb	69″	2800

Girls

Age in years	Weight	Height	Calories
10–12	77 lb	56″	2250
12–14	97 lb	61″	2300
14–16	114 lb	62″	2400
16–18	119 lb	63″	2300
18–22	128 lb	64″	2000

These calory allowances are suggested by the Food and Nutrition Board, National Academy of Sciences-National Research Council for normal persons living in the United States under ordinary environmental stresses.

age, or weigh less or more, this will affect the calories you need.

Does the table take everything into account? Are there any factors that may affect your calorie needs that have not been included? How might recovery from an illness affect your calorie needs?

■ Keep a record of the food you eat for several days. Then look ahead at Figure 3-17, and calculate how many calories your diet provides on an average day. Does this figure fall within about 10 percent of the range of calorie allowances in Figure 3-16?

3-17 COMPOSITION OF FOODS, 100 GRAMS, EDIBLE PORTION

Key: Zero indicates that the amount is probably none or too small to measure. Dashes indicate a lack of reliable data for a nutrient believed to be present in a measurable amount.

Food	Approx. measure	Food energy (Calories)	Protein (gm)	Fat (gm)	Carbohydrate (gm)	Calcium (mg)	Phosphorus (mg)	Iron (mg)	Vitamin A value (IU)	Thiamine (mg)	Riboflavin (mg)	Niacin (mg)	Ascorbic acid (mg)
Asparagus, cooked, boiled	2/3 cup, cut pieces	20	2.2	0.2	3.6	21	50	0.6	900	0.16	0.18	1.4	26
Bacon, broiled or fried, drained	12 strips, drained 6"	611	30.4	52	3.2	14	224	3.3	0	0.51	0.34	5.2	—
Beans, lima, cooked, boiled	2/3 cup	111	7.6	0.5	19.8	47	121	2.5	280	0.18	0.10	1.3	17
Beef, hamburger, cooked	2 small patties	219	27.4	11.3	0	12	230	3.5	20	0.09	0.23	6	—
Bread, white, enriched	4 slices	269	8.7	3.2	50.4	70	87	2.4	Trace	0.25	0.17	2.3	Trace
Broccoli, boiled	1 large stalk, or 2/3 cup	26	3.1	0.3	4.5	88	62	0.8	2,500	0.09	0.20	0.8	90
Butter	7 tablespoons, or 14 pats	716	0.6	81	0.4	20	16	0	3,300	—	—	—	0
Cabbage, shredded, cooked	2/3 cup, cooked short time	20	1.1	0.2	4.3	44	20	0.3	130	0.04	0.04	0.3	33
Candy, chocolate	2 small bars	528	4.4	35.1	57.9	94	142	1.4	10	0.02	0.14	0.3	Trace
Carrots, raw	1 large carrot, 1 cup shredded	42	1.1	0.2	9.7	37	36	0.7	11,000	0.06	0.05	0.6	8
Cheese, Cheddar (American)	approx. 4 oz, average serving	398	25	32.2	2.1	750	478	1	1,310	0.03	0.46	0.1	0
Cheese, cottage, uncreamed	5 to 6 tablespoons	86	17	0.3	2.7	90	175	0.4	10	0.03	0.28	0.1	0

Food	Measure												
Doughnuts, cake type	3 average	391	4.6	18.6	51.4	40	190	1.4	80	0.16	0.16	1.2	Trace
Egg, fried	2 medium	216	13.8	17.2	0.3	60	222	2.4	1,420	0.10	0.30	0.1	0
Grapefruit, raw	1/4 medium, 4 1/4" diam	41	0.5	0.1	10.6	16	16	0.4	80	0.04	0.02	0.2	38
Ham, roasted	3 1/3 slices, 4" x 2 1/2" x 1/8"	394	21.9	33.3	0	10	225	2.9	0	0.49	0.22	4.4	--
Jams and preserves	5 tablespoons, average, assorted types	272	0.6	0.1	70	20	9	1	10	0.01	0.03	0.2	2
Lamb, roasted	2 1/2 slices, 3" x 3 1/4" x 1/8"	266	25.8	17.3	0	11	212	1.8	--	0.15	0.27	5.6	--
Lettuce, raw	9 small leaves	18	1.3	0.3	3.5	68	25	1.4	1,900	0.05	0.08	0.4	18
Liver, beef, fried	2 1/2 slices, 3" x 2 1/4" x 3/8"	229	26.4	10.6	5.3	11	476	8.8	53,400	0.26	4.19	16.5	27
Milk, cow, fluid (pasteurized and raw), whole	3 1/4 oz	65	3.5	3.5	4.9	118	93	Trace	140	0.03	0.17	0.1	1
Orange juice, raw, all commercial varieties	3 1/4 oz	45	0.7	0.2	10.4	11	17	0.2	200	0.09	0.03	0.4	50
Pork, fresh, roasted	1 1/2 medium chops	410	20.9	35.6	0	9	213	2.7	0	0.47	0.21	4.2	--
Potatoes, cooked, baked in skin	1 medium, 2 1/2" diam	93	2.6	0.1	21.1	9	65	0.7	Trace	0.10	0.04	1.7	20
Potato chips	50 pieces, 2" diam	568	5.3	39.8	50	40	139	1.8	Trace	0.21	0.07	4.8	16
Rice, polished, white, enriched	3 cups	109	2	0.1	24.2	10	28	0.9	0	0.11	1.2	1	0
Salad dressings, commercial, mayonnaise	8 tablespoons	718	1.1	79.9	2.2	18	28	0.5	280	0.02	0.04	Trace	--
Spinach, boiled, drained	1/2 cup	23	3	0.3	3.6	93	38	2.2	8,100	0.07	0.14	0.5	28
Tomato juice, canned or bottled	1/2 cup	19	0.9	0.1	4.3	7	18	0.9	800	0.05	0.03	0.8	16
Tuna, canned, in oil, solids and liquid	3/4 cup with juices	288	24.2	20.5	0	6	294	1.1	90	0.04	0.09	10.1	--

Adapted from *Composition of Foods*, Agriculture Handbook No. 8, Consumer and Food Economics Research Division, Agriculture Research Service, USDA, Washington, D.C., Revised 1963.

What You Have Learned

What kind of health practices should you apply in choosing the food you eat? Check your understanding of the chapter. On a separate sheet of paper, number 1 through 24 and insert the answer from the vocabulary list below. Use each expression, but use each one only once.

amino acids
area of country
calories
carbohydrates
cholesterol
economic status
family background
insulate

iodine
iron
milk
new
nitrogen
repair
roughage
saturated

shocks
temperature
thirst
3,000 – 3,400
2,300 – 2,500
unsaturated
unwise
vitamins

Your eating habits are influenced by many things in your environment, including your (1)____, (2)____, and (3)____. Most of your energy comes from (4)____ that also provide more than one half of the (5)____ you need.

To maintain good health you need fats to help control body (6)____, absorb (7)____ from blows and falls, and to (8)____ nerve fibers. It is (9)____ to totally eliminate all fats from your diet. Fats are divided into two general types: (10)____, found mainly in animal foods, which tend to increase blood (11)____, and (12)____ fats, found mainly in vegetable foods.

While you are still growing, proteins help form (13)____ tissue and throughout life they provide material for tissue (14)____. Proteins are an important source of (15)____. The human body uses some twenty (16)____ to form the building blocks of protein molecules.

Minerals are present in a wide variety of foods. One of the best sources of calcium and phosphorus is (17)____. A mineral needed for the proper functioning of the thyroid gland is (18)____. A mineral needed for the manufacture of hemoglobin is (19)____.

(20)____ composed of organic compounds built by plants and animals are vital to your daily diet. Water is essential to life, and your body makes known its need for water through the sensation of (21)____. Body wastes must be eliminated regularly. A certain amount of (22)____ is needed in the diet to promote normal elimination of solid waste matter. The amount of energy you obtain from food is measured in calories. The average high school boy needs at least (23)____ calories per day. The average high school girl needs at least (24)____ calories per day.

What You Can Do

Read about the diet of the people in a foreign country in which you are interested—China, Mexico, India, or France, for example. What foods supply these people with the needed carbohydrates, fats, proteins, minerals, and vitamins?

Things to Try

1. Keep a careful list of all the foods you eat for two days. Include all snacks. Using the table in Figure 3-2 on page 40, check your list to see if you have had each of the essential nutrients on both days.
2. At the grocery store, or in your family kitchen, check the foods that have been enriched or fortified with nutrients. List the nutrients that have been added: for example, vitamin D in milk.

Probing Further

Food Is Your Best Medicine, by H. G. Bieler, Random House, 1966. This is a factual account of the vital role played by food in the maintenance of good health, as confirmed by similar material in your text.

Composition of Foods: Raw and Processed, Bureau of Home Economics, Department of Agriculture, Washington, D.C., 1967. This publication gives a complete list of foods. It will supplement the partial list of foods given in Figure 3-17.

Foods Without Fads: A Common-Sense Guide to Nutrition, by Earl W. McHenry, Lippincott, 1960. The essentials of nutrition explained simply.

Nutrition and Physical Fitness, by Jean Bogert, Saunders, 1966. This volume stresses the importance of good eating habits.

Health Concepts in Action

Does this statement reflect what you have learned?

The individual is interdependent with his environment, from which he obtains the nutrients needed to maintain health.

Applying this concept of nutrition, which health practices would you

— continue?

— change?

— begin?

Will you now, as a result of your study, change any of your health objectives?

4 / A Balanced Diet

"How soon will dinner be ready?" asks the hungry teen-ager. He can satisfy his hunger by a wise choice of foods or by a foolish one. But the other functions of food in the body are not carried out as readily. There is a difference between food and nutrition. For this reason, biologists and nutritionists have worked out special meal patterns which they call a balanced diet.

A PROBE INTO EATING PATTERNS—How can you improve your own diet? To find out, you will be probing questions like these:

1. How can hunger be wisely satisfied? unwisely satisfied?

2. How can your choice of foods affect your school work? your participation in sports? your appearance?

3. How can foods help protect you from illness?

4. How do your feelings about your weight influence your food choices?

5. What are some common foods to which people are allergic?

6. Can highly advertised "health foods" be checked for their nutritive value? How?

4-1 The chef of this hospital kitchen is demonstrating the three R's of conserving food values and tastes: reduce the amount of water used; reduce the surface area exposed to air; reduce the cooking time. How might these three R's affect your choice of cooking ware?

PLANNING MEALS

We all must eat to live in health, and this should be one of our daily pleasures. A wise selection of tasty, well-balanced foods and drink is a genuine aid to healthy living, good personal appearance, and a positive outlook on life. Selecting too many low-calorie foods leads to underweight. The opposite can happen, and frequently does, when you eat more high-calorie foods than your body requires. This leads to overweight. Even when a diet has the right calorie content but fails to include some of the essential nutrients, malnutrition or "hidden hunger" will result. Only a diet composed of the recommended amounts of all the essential nutrients is a *balanced diet*.

Balancing Your Diet

There have been many different systems worked out to guide us in the selection of a balanced diet. It remains an unresolved question among scientists as to whether the diet should be balanced every day, once a week, or in some other period of time. You learned in the preceding chapter that some —but not all—nutrients are stored in the body. Calcium, for example, is generously stored in the bones and need not be replenished daily. But certain vitamins, such as ascorbic acid (vitamin C), are not stored in the body. They must be included in each day's diet. So, to be on the safe side, it seems best to balance your diet daily.

Recommended Daily Dietary Allowances

For practical purposes, modern scientific information on human nutrition is summed up in a table called "Recommended Daily Dietary Allowances." Allowances for protein and the major minerals and vitamins are shown in Figure 4-2. Look for your age and sex group, and you will see the allowances recommended for you. This table is the result of extended, continuous research by the Food and Nutrition Board, National Academy of Sciences—National Research Council.

"The allowance levels are intended to cover individual variations among most normal people as they live in the United States under usual environmental stresses.

	Age (years)	Weight (lbs)	Height (in.)	Calories	Protein (gm)	Fat-soluble vitamins		
						Vitamin A activity (IU)	Vitamin D (IU)	Vitamin E activity (IU)
Infants	0–1/6	9 (4kg)	22	kg × 120	kg × 2.2	1,500	400	5
	1/6–1/2	15 (7kg)	25	kg × 100	kg × 2.0	1,500	400	5
	1/2–1	20 (9kg)	28	kg × 100	kg × 1.8	1,500	400	5
Children	1–2	26	32	1100	25	2,000	400	10
	2–3	31	36	1250	25	2,000	400	10
	3–4	35	39	1400	30	2,500	400	10
	4–6	42	43	1600	30	2,500	400	10
	6–8	51	48	2000	35	3,500	400	15
	8–10	62	52	2200	40	3,500	400	15
Males	10–12	77	55	2500	45	4,500	400	20
	12–14	95	59	2700	50	5,000	400	20
	14–18	130	67	3000	60	5,000	400	25
	18–22	147	69	2800	60	5,000	400	30
	22–35	154	69	2800	65	5,000	—	30
	35–55	154	68	2600	65	5,000	—	30
	55–75	154	67	2400	65	5,000	—	30
Females	10–12	77	56	2250	50	4,500	400	20
	12–14	97	61	2300	50	5,000	400	20
	14–16	114	62	2400	55	5,000	400	25
	16–18	119	63	2300	55	5,000	400	25
	18–22	128	64	2000	55	5,000	400	25
	22–35	128	64	2000	55	5,000	—	25
	35–55	128	63	1850	55	5,000	—	25
	55–75	128	62	1700	55	5,000	—	25
Pregnant				+200	65	6,000	400	30
Nursing				+1000	75	8,000	400	30

The allowance levels are intended to cover individual variations among most normal persons as they live in the United States under usual environmental stresses. The recommended allowances can be attained with a variety of common foods, providing other nutrients for which human requirements have been less well defined.

The symbol g represents grams; kg, kilograms; mg, milligrams; mcg, micrograms; IU, International Units.

Water-soluble vitamins							Minerals				
Ascorbic acid (mg)	Folacin (mg)	Niacin (mg equiv)	Riboflavin (mg)	Thiamin (mg)	Vitamin B_6 (mg)	Vitamin B_{12} (mcg)	Calcium (g)	Phosphorus (g)	Iodine (mcg)	Iron (mg)	Mag-nesium (mg)
35	0.05	5	0.4	0.2	0.2	1.0	0.4	0.2	25	6	40
35	0.05	7	0.5	0.4	0.3	1.5	0.5	0.4	40	10	60
35	0.1	8	0.6	0.5	0.4	2.0	0.6	0.5	45	15	70
40	0.1	8	0.6	0.6	0.5	2.0	0.7	0.7	55	15	100
40	0.2	8	0.7	0.6	0.6	2.5	0.8	0.8	60	15	150
40	0.2	9	0.8	0.7	0.7	3	0.8	0.8	70	10	200
40	0.2	11	0.9	0.8	0.9	4	0.8	0.8	80	10	200
40	0.2	13	1.1	1.0	1.0	4	0.9	0.9	100	10	250
40	0.3	15	1.2	1.1	1.2	5	1.0	1.0	110	10	250
40	0.4	17	1.3	1.3	1.4	5	1.2	1.2	125	10	300
45	0.4	18	1.4	1.4	1.6	5	1.4	1.4	135	18	350
55	0.4	20	1.5	1.5	1.8	5	1.4	1.4	150	18	400
60	0.4	18	1.6	1.4	2.0	5	0.8	0.8	140	10	400
60	0.4	18	1.7	1.4	2.0	5	0.8	0.8	140	10	350
60	0.4	17	1.7	1.3	2.0	5	0.8	0.8	125	10	350
60	0.4	14	1.7	1.2	2.0	6	0.8	0.8	110	10	350
40	0.4	15	1.3	1.1	1.4	5	1.2	1.2	110	18	300
45	0.4	15	1.4	1.2	1.6	5	1.3	1.3	115	18	350
50	0.4	16	1.4	1.2	1.8	5	1.3	1.3	120	18	350
50	0.4	15	1.5	1.2	2.0	5	1.3	1.3	115	18	350
55	0.4	13	1.5	1.0	2.0	5	0.8	0.8	100	18	350
55	0.4	13	1.5	1.0	2.0	5	0.8	0.8	100	18	300
55	0.4	13	1.5	1.0	2.0	5	0.8	0.8	90	18	300
55	0.4	13	1.5	1.0	2.0	6	0.8	0.8	80	10	300
60	0.8	15	1.8	+0.1	2.5	8	+0.4	+0.4	125	18	450
60	0.5	20	2.0	+0.5	2.5	6	+0.5	+0.5	150	18	450

Revised 1968, by the Food and Nutrition Board, National Academy of Sciences—National Research Council. Designed for the maintenance of good nutrition of practically all healthy persons in the U.S.A.

4-3 "The Four Essential Food Groups." Have you had the proper number of servings from each group today?

The recommended allowances can be attained with a variety of common foods, providing other nutrients for which human requirements have been less well defined." ("Recommended Daily Dietary Allowances.")

■ In Figure 4-2, find the correct line for your age and sex. Keep an accurate record of all the foods you eat for three days. Check each food for its approximate calorie value, minerals, and vitamins. Estimate how close your three-day diet comes to the recommended daily allowances.

The Four Essential Food Groups

The "Recommended Daily Dietary Allowances" is the official American guide for the maintenance of good nutrition, but its use of technical terms makes it somewhat difficult to use in daily meal planning. An easier, simpler system for selecting your daily well-balanced diet was introduced in 1958. The U.S. Department of Agriculture, Division of Human Nutrition, published and distributed throughout the United States a guide called "The Four Essential Food Groups" (Figure 4-3). This guide is based on the recommendations found in the Daily Allowances, and when you use it in planning, your daily meals will contain enough of each of the five essential nutrients to equal a well-balanced diet.

How to Vary Your Calorie Count

The number of servings recommended for each of the four food groups may be varied, to provide more or fewer calories as needed by various members of the family. You will notice on the chart (Figure 4-2) that your age group requires somewhat more calories than your father if you are a boy, or than your mother if you are a girl. For younger children or older members of the family, servings can be adjusted to suit their calorie requirements.

To figure out the calorie allowance of a particular person, the standards in the table (Figure 4-2) have to be modified according to differences in body size. Larger calorie allowances must be provided for someone whose body size is greater than the so-called "reference man or woman" used for each age range, and smaller allowances should be provided for someone smaller in size. Weight can be used as the basis for judging size if the person is neither overweight nor underweight.

In the age range of 22 to 35, the reference man is 22 years old and weighs 154 pounds, and the reference woman is 22 years old and weighs 128 pounds. They are both considered to live in a temperate environment of about 68° F, and to be moderately active physically. In the other age ranges, such as 14–18, the reference person is in the middle of that range.

(From "Recommended Daily Dietary Allowances." See Figure 4-2.)

Selecting Your Food from Each Group

When you go shopping for food or are eating out at a public place, there are some choices you can make within each of the four food groups. Let us consider recommended amounts for each group.

1. *Milk Group.* Four 8-ounce glasses daily. This group includes milk, cheese of all kinds, and ice cream. In place of whole milk, you may substitute buttermilk; skim, dry, evaporated, or condensed milk; natural or processed cheese; or ice cream. Milk is the leading source of calcium in your diet. It contains complete proteins, vitamin A, riboflavin, and other essential nutrients. When sub-

stituting cheese or ice cream for milk, the following amounts would apply: American cheese (1 slice − 1 oz) = 3/4 glass of milk. Cottage cheese (1/2 cup) = 1/3 glass of milk. Ice cream (1 cup − 1/2 pint) = 1/2 glass of milk.

2. *Meat Group.* Two or more daily servings. Included in this group are meats, poultry, fish, eggs, and cheese. You may use as substitutes dried beans, peas, and nuts. It is from this group that the main course of your meal is selected, and that establishes the price of the meal. A serving equals 2 or 3 ounces of lean meat, poultry, or fish—without counting the bone; 2 eggs; 1 cup of cooked dried beans or peas; 4 tablespoons of peanut butter. This group is rich in proteins, iron, thiamine, riboflavin, and niacin.

3. *Vegetable and Fruit Group.* Four or more daily servings. You may count as a serving about 1/2 cup of vegetables or fruit. The vegetables and fruit are interchangeable; you may select all fruit, for example, or all vegetables. However, you do require at least one serving daily of ascorbic acid (vitamin C), and every other day you need one serving of vitamin A (Figure 3-10, page 47). This group usually provides the side dishes, salads, appetizers, and sometimes the dessert course of the meal. The fruit and vegetables may be fresh, canned, frozen, or dried.

4. *Bread and Cereal Group.* Four or more daily servings. These are the energy foods. When they are enriched and of whole grain, they also furnish good amounts of proteins, thiamine, iron, and niacin. A serving is about 1 slice of bread or 1/2 to 3/4 cup of cereal. Included in the group are: crackers, rice, macaroni, noodles, dumplings, muffins, cakes, and cookies.

Your Snacks Also Count

There is nothing wrong with eating between-meal snacks. The "snack break" often provides a needed energy lift at midmorning, afternoon, or evening. When you have worked or played vigorously, the sugar in your blood may need replenishing. The amount of sugar in your blood rises when you eat. But this does not mean that your snacks should consist of large amounts of sweets, for, as you will learn, your digestive system changes starch into sugar. Have you noticed that, when you chew a cracker, it soon begins to taste sweet? The sugar that you may need, or the starches to make the sugar, can be found in fruits and vegetables.

But there is one thing to keep in mind about eating snacks. They can easily lead to your consuming more calories than you need or want.

In the preceding chapter, you learned how energy is measured in calories and how the caloric content is figured. Often, when you are counting calories, you forget to count the caloric values of the snacks that you eat. It is well to remember that your daily diet includes all of the foods and liquids you consume within the day. This includes the food you eat as snacks as well as at regular meals. Of course all of the calories count.

What About Breakfast?

The word breakfast means "to break your fast." The fast refers to that longest period of time between meals—nighttime, or the period between dinner (or supper) and breakfast. Suppose you eat breakfast at seven and lunch at noon; that would be just five hours between meals. Then from lunch to dinner or supper at, say, six o'clock would be six hours. Now look at the long fast of thirteen hours between dinner or supper at six in the evening and breakfast at seven the next morning. It makes you wonder how your body sustains itself for such a long time.

4-4 Snacks are very important, especially to the "calorie counter." Are the snacks you eat chosen wisely in terms of nutrients and calories?

It is mainly because you sleep during most of these thirteen hours that you can endure them without feeling "hunger pangs." Hunger pangs are the body's way of letting you know that it needs food. While you are asleep, all of your body processes slow down; there is much less demand for energy. But the processes of the body—digestion, circulation, respiration, building and repair of tissues—go on, and the time comes for replenishment of fuel. Breakfast becomes an important meal to furnish you with foods to restore the energy you need to start the new day.

What You Need for Breakfast

You need about one quarter, or 25 percent, of your protein and calorie allowances at breakfast. In Figure 4-2 you saw that in the 15–18 age group, girls require 58 grams of protein and 2,300 calories, while boys require 85 grams of protein and 3,400 calories, each day. Put this in terms of your breakfast needs, and you find that your age group requires 14 to 22 grams of protein and from 575 to 850 calories. Here is a sample breakfast that comes close to providing these requirements.

4-6 SAMPLE BREAKFAST

Foods	Portions	Calories	Proteins
orange juice	6 oz	80	1.5 gm
boiled egg	1	75	6
toast	2 slices	130	4
milk	8 oz	160	8.5
butter	2 tsp	65	
jam or marmalade	2 tbs	110	
Total		620	20 gm

4-5 What kind of breakfast do you eat? Is it a "quickie" breakfast like the above two? The breakfast below provides 25 percent of your daily calorie and protein needs. Why is it important to eat an adequate breakfast?

MANY FACTORS
INFLUENCE YOUR DAILY DIET

Your daily diet is subject to many influences, and normal physical hunger is one of these. But there are psychological influences, too, that appeal to your appetite, such as smelling bread fresh from the oven as you pass the bakery, looking at a basket of rosy-colored peaches, or just talking about a tall chocolate float. And there are other factors.

Your Feelings and Your Diet

How you feel about foods may affect your choices of foods. You probably like some foods better than others; you may even dislike some foods. Within the "Four Essential Food Groups" (Figure 4-3) you should find most of your "likes." Sometimes you can

overcome your "dislikes" by eating one or more of them in combination with foods that you like very much.

There are many possible reasons for disliking certain foods. It may be that some food is new or strange to you and you hesitate to try it. It could be the result of some emotional experience. In fact, the evening you were scolded during dinner for some mistake you had just confessed may be associated with your present dislike for the foods served at the meal. Of course, you may have a true *allergy* (AL-er-gee) or sensitivity to some particular food or class of foods, such as wheat or dairy products, and this could cause you to want to avoid them. We will discuss allergies and food fads and fallacies a little later on in this chapter.

Your Emotions May Affect Your Appetite

Your emotions can lead your normal appetite astray. Have you noticed that when you get good news, you feel hungry? Or, if you failed to get the part in the class play that you tried for, did your appetite "just leave you"?

No two people seem to respond to emotional stimulation in the same way. For example, one of your friends may have been just too excited during a weekend trip to eat. A classmate may have become hungry because of disappointment over not making a team.

To deny the normal appetite for food is often associated with feelings of defeat, insecurity, failure, or some compelling desire to reduce. Since you must eat to live, it is unwise to get into the habit of not eating when emotionally disturbed. On the other hand, it is equally unwise to overindulge a large appetite. Overeating is often associated with feelings of loneliness, not being wanted, or being bored. Such overindulgence is almost certain to lead to overweight and a problem of reducing.

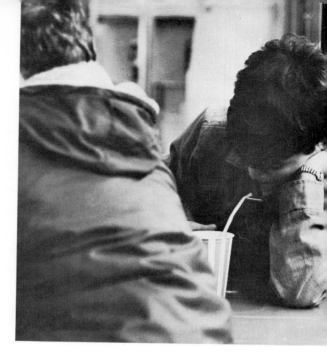

4-7 Your emotions may affect your appetite. Have you ever reacted like the boy in this picture? How does good news affect your appetite?

The Cost of Foods Influences Diet

If you are on a limited budget, your diet will be influenced by the foods you can afford. However with careful planning, your diet can contain the essential nutrients needed for health.

When you go shopping for food, you need to remember what you learned about the essential food nutrients. In Figure 3-17 on pages 52 and 53, you find a large variety of foods listed for each required nutrient. From these lists you can select the foods you need at various prices, depending on how much you can spend. You can obtain complete protein from expensive beefsteak or from inexpensive cottage cheese. You can obtain fats from bacon or from peanut butter.

As a general rule, the dried foods are the least expensive, and they contain many important nutrients. Next come canned foods, which also supply a great variety of nutrients. Somewhat more in cost are the frozen and fresh foods. Perhaps the most expensive foods are certain cuts of meat and the pre-packaged, prepared meals, ready to be cooked or merely heated.

It is possible to prepare delicious and tasty low-cost meals, and the more you learn about nutrition, the better you will be able to do this.

Social Forces Influence Your Diet

Among the many social forces that play a part in what, how, and when you eat are your friends. Also, you are likely to be influenced by the foods grown or available in the area where you live. If you live inland, you probably eat fewer fish foods than do people who live along the coast. Then there are the well-known regional patterns of eating. In one region, for example, you find that

4-8 These children are learning how to shop for food. They will learn about the cost of food as well as the nutrient value of different foods.

a common dish is grits; in another region it may be potatoes; in still other regions it may be rice. Perhaps the strongest influence is your family pattern of eating. Long before you were old enough to give much thought to your diet, you had become accustomed to eating what the family ate, and this has now become your pattern.

Your selection of diet also is influenced by the demands of fashion for a slim figure, perhaps including certain food fads advertised to produce an almost "weightless" figure. Such social forces as these are not easy to resist, and you may, at times, find yourself their victim.

You can see how complicated the selection of a daily well-balanced diet may become for some people. For many other people it is an uncomplicated, natural process. But for everyone, it seems clear that you need to know and use the nutritional facts about foods, to recognize the possible effect of emotional reactions on your eating habits, and to be aware that there are many social forces that play a big part in your pattern of eating.

YOUR WEIGHT

There are at least two factors that have caused most of us to become weight-conscious—one, the social pressures created by fashion designers; and two, the findings of medical research scientists—a more worthy reason. The compelling desire for weight control seems to be mostly for the improvement of appearance, especially if you enjoy good health. But weight control is also important to the improvement or control of certain existing body conditions.

What You Should Weigh

Your weight depends, to a large extent, on your body framework (skeleton). You will see in Chapter 8 a description of three types

4-9 Social forces influence our diet. The "weight-less" figure is currently very popular. Do you find yourself influenced by such fads?

of Actuaries, which represents many large insurance companies. The findings have been adopted as our standard weight tables.

The tables in Figure 4-10 show what your weight should be at age 25, based on your height and body build. By age 25, it is thought that you should have come close to the weight noted on the chart and that after age 25 you should maintain this weight, except during pregnancy or illness.

Growth patterns of children and adolescents are highly variable, and so is the age at which people reach maturity. For these reasons it is not possible to construct accurate height and weight charts for these years.

■ Use your thumb and forefinger to pinch the skin on your upper arm. Is the fold of skin and fat over 1-inch thick? You may be overweight. Is it under ½-inch thick? You may be underweight. The "pinch test" is helpful, but only your doctor can tell you for certain whether you are overweight or underweight.

of body build—small, medium, and large builds. You inherit your particular body build whether it is tall and slim with small bones, short and heavy-set with large bones, or in between with medium bones. Your diet cannot change your body framework very much, although lack of certain minerals in your diet, such as iron, calcium, and phosphorus, may lead to bone disorders or deformity.

But, within limits, you can control your weight and avoid building up too much body fat. Such control sometimes calls for medical supervision, although in uncomplicated cases you can, by proper diet, achieve weight control by personal effort.

What you should weigh is determined by age, height, and body build. Some years ago a vast research project was conducted throughout the United States by the Society

Normal Weight Gain

There is a natural, normal, and gradual increase in body weight from childhood to adulthood. This is to be expected and is not to be confused with an unusual weight gain. If normal weight gain fails to occur over a period of several months, it is wise to consult your physician. Any sudden weight change, whether you gain or lose, calls for medical attention.

When You Have a Weight Problem

There comes a time, for almost everyone, when he is eager to add or take off a few pounds. Girls usually want to lose weight to improve their figures. Boys often want to gain weight to improve their physiques or to qualify for sports. Older people strive to keep their weight within recommended limits for reasons of health and appearance.

4-10 DESIRABLE WEIGHTS FOR MEN
of ages 25 and over

Height (with shoes on) 1-inch heels Feet Inches	Small frame	Medium frame	Large frame
5 2	112–120	118–129	126–141
5 3	115–123	121–133	129–144
5 4	118–126	124–136	132–148
5 5	121–129	127–139	135–152
5 6	124–133	130–143	138–156
5 7	128–137	134–147	142–161
5 8	132–141	138–152	147–166
5 9	136–145	142–156	151–170
5 10	140–150	146–160	155–174
5 11	144–154	150–165	159–179
6 0	148–158	154–170	164–184
6 1	152–162	158–175	168–189
6 2	156–167	162–180	173–194
6 3	160–171	167–185	178–199
6 4	164–175	172–190	182–204

Weight in pounds according to frame (in indoor clothing).

DESIRABLE WEIGHTS FOR WOMEN
of ages 25 and over

Height (with shoes on) 2-inch heels Feet Inches	Small frame	Medium frame	Large frame
4 10	92– 98	96–107	104–119
4 11	94–101	98–110	106–122
5 0	96–104	101–113	109–125
5 1	99–107	104–116	112–128
5 2	102–110	107–119	115–131
5 3	105–113	110–122	118–134
5 4	108–116	113–126	121–138
5 5	111–119	116–130	125–142
5 6	114–123	120–135	129–146
5 7	118–127	124–139	133–150
5 8	122–131	128–143	137–154
5 9	126–135	132–147	141–158
5 10	130–140	136–151	145–163
5 11	134–144	140–155	149–168
6 0	138–148	144–159	153–173

For girls between 18 and 25, subtract 1 pound for each year under 25.

Courtesy of the Metropolitan Life Insurance Company.

If You Are Overweight

The records of insurance companies show that you have the best chance for healthy, long life when you keep your weight fairly close to the average for your age, sex, height, and body build.

People who are overweight tire easily and are more likely to develop certain disorders than are people of normal weight. They seem more prone to high blood pressure, hardening of the arteries (*arteriosclerosis*—ar-ter-ee-oh-skler-OH-sis), and kidney ailments. In addition, excess weight puts a strain on the heart, and it probably lowers general efficiency.

Being overweight affects personal appearance and often creates a problem and extra expense when buying clothing. In most cases, the remedy for overweight conditions among teen-agers is a simple prescription: *If you want to lose weight, eat less—but keep your diet balanced.*

In addition to overeating, there are sometimes other reasons for becoming overweight. Among them are physical inactivity,

4-11 Boy, can those kids eat!

family patterns of eating, malfunctioning glands, and heredity. You can correct the physical inactivity yourself by adopting a schedule of activity. Family eating patterns can be discussed with family members and changes in diet can be made. However, all of the other reasons for overweight call for medical appraisal and supervision. Whatever the cause of your weight problem may be, you will need medical advice before you start any major reducing program.

Your Emotions and Your Weight

Habits of eating are, for most people, formed early in life by parental training. If the training has been wise, you probably now adjust readily to emotionally uncomplicated eating patterns. If parental training has been unwise, indifferent, or lacking, you may have developed patterns of behavior that now unfavorably affect your eating practices.

4-12 Do you want to gain weight? These foods can help. Which is the richest in protein? in fat? in starch? in sugar? Whether overweight or underweight, you should eat a balanced diet.

The habit of overeating can be established early in life and may result in obesity in later life. For example, if parents give undue importance to a child's eating habits, he may learn to use food as a tool for gaining attention and satisfaction. For him, food becomes a substitute gratification instead of a means of satisfying hunger. By such practices, the child fails to learn how to make satisfactory emotional adjustments in everyday situations.

Another example is seen in a person who fails to make a normal adjustment to the opposite sex. Such a person may find emotional release in excessive eating. This, in turn, creates an overweight problem and another hurdle to desirable social relations.

A similar course of events may lead to undereating. The parent struggling with a personal weight problem may reject foods in such a manner that the child feels included in the rejection. In his self-rejection, the child attempts to punish himself and his parent by refusing to eat, and he may threaten starvation. Such extreme behavior has been observed.

These examples, and similar unsatisfactory food practices, are a reminder of the importance of adopting healthy patterns and attitudes toward eating.

Some Practical
Weight-reducing Hints

When you are concerned about taking off a few pounds or you just want to hold your present weight, you may find the following hints helpful:

1. Work hard at changing your eating habits. Be sure you include servings recommended for each group in the "Four Essential Food Groups" (Figure 4-3). This will provide you with about 50 to 80 percent of the calories you need to maintain your present weight.

2. Eat when you are hungry, but select low-calorie foods.
3. Drink water before, during, and after meals. This gives you a feeling of fullness.
4. Eat slowly and take small bites. This helps you feel that you are eating more.
5. Avoid "crash" diets. Be content to reduce slowly, and you will find it easier to keep your weight down after you have lost as much weight as you wish.
6. Practice daily general good health habits—vigorous exercise, plenty of sleep, regular meals—and find interesting things to do.

To Gain Weight,
Eat More

It is often as difficult to gain as to lose weight. To gain weight, eat both more food and more high-calorie foods. Do this slowly to give your body a chance to adjust to the larger amounts of food. For your between-meal snacks, feel free to enjoy such weight producers as chocolate milk shakes, sundaes, nuts, and pastries. Breakfast should be given special attention. Allow plenty of time to eat a nourishing meal. Your daily health habits should include plenty of sleep, daily exercise, and frequent meals. If you are seriously underweight, you should have a medical check-up.

Other Reasons
for Underweight

In addition to not eating enough or not eating the right kinds of foods, there are other reasons for underweight. It may be due to some irregularity in the digestive system, or to the presence of some infection. Problems of this type call for medical advice and supervision; diet alone will not prove effective.

FOOD ALLERGIES

He was six feet tall, broad-shouldered, and carried himself like an athlete. He was an athlete. Still his eyes were watery, his nose inflamed, and he had pink, swollen patches on his face. "What's the trouble?" asked his friend. "Strawberries again," said the big athlete. "I couldn't resist the shortcake."

Tracing the Allergy

Some people are allergic to certain foods that are entirely acceptable to other people. Among the common food offenders to which some of you may be allergic are strawberries, chocolate, shellfish, tomatoes, wheat products, and even milk. Allergies show up in a variety of ways, such as skin rashes, hives, digestive disturbances, and swollen areas around the face. These conditions are all uncomfortable, and some are painful. If you experience such reactions, you should see your physician. He can suggest appropriate substitutes for foods that are essential to your diet; he can also test you for possible allergies in case you are uncertain about what is causing your discomfort.

FOOD QUACKERY

Recently, an official of the U.S. Food and Drug Administration said that nutritional quackery is costing ten million Americans over 500 billion dollars a year.

Many present-day exaggerated beliefs about diet come from an emotional approach to foods or from ignorance. The food quack takes advantage of both factors. The modern version of the old "medicine man" is the food-supplement salesman. He calls himself a "nutrition adviser" and gladly gives free "doorstep diagnoses." He warns against the use of foods grown in depleted soil and the use of chemical additives. No attempt is made to justify these terms and their implied dangers.

This approach creates fear and false hope in the minds of people, and the food quack sells his food supplements. One of the greatest dangers is the false sense of value placed in food supplements by people who may be in need of medical attention.

The present emphasis on weight reduction and health has brought forth an avalanche of "health foods." Honey and vinegar,

4-13 Help! Get those strawberries out of here!

4-14 Health foods have become a popular food fad. Have you ever visited a store like the one shown here?

exotic herbs, grasses, seaweed, and seawater selling at $3.50 per pint are only a few. From all of these, the food faddist selects according to his beliefs and pays the high price demanded by the food quack.

For those who suffer from nutritional deficiency, or who think they do, the safe and inexpensive way to solve such a problem is to consult a reliable physician.

Food Fallacies

References to food fallacies can be found through much of man's recorded history. For example, "Pliny, naturalist of ancient Rome, wrote that Nero ate leeks [similar to onions] several days each month to clear his voice." Other beliefs held that certain foods gave tranquillity and happiness to the departed spirits. "At one time, the Romans believed that the souls of those who had passed on resided in beans, consequently, they [beans] were eaten at funerals." (*Food Facts Talk Back*, The American Dietetic Association.)

In more modern times, bogus "health groups" appear from time to time, advertising their fallacies. Sometimes these groups have a commercial sponsor. In addition, certain food fallacies based on superstition have persisted over the years. Some examples, none of which have any scientific basis are: fish is a "brain food"; you will be ill if you eat lobster and ice cream at the same meal; seasonings injure foods. (In times past, highly seasoned foods might have produced illness, but the reason was that the seasoning was used to hide the fact that the food was spoiled.)

Falling for fads and fallacies results in the waste of money, and threatens health.

■ Fact or Fancy Test

Listed below are some popular ideas on nutrition—some are sound fact, some are pure fancy. Is your nutrition knowledge fact or fancy? On a paper, write the numbers 1 through 24. Place a T (true) or an F (false) after each number. Answers follow the test.

1. Brown sugar has fewer calories than white sugar.
2. Honey may be eaten by diabetics.
3. White and whole-wheat bread have about the same caloric value.
4. Aluminum cooking utensils are harmful.
5. Tomatoes cause an acid stomach.
6. Fish and milk are safe to eat together.

F 7. Yogurt makes you live longer.

F 8. Raw milk is better than pasteurized milk.

F 9. Artificial coloring changes the nutritional value of food.

T 10. Enriched breads and cereals are better for you than plain ones.

F 11. Everyone needs to take vitamin pills.

F 12. Processing of food destroys all food value.

T 13. Mineral oil should never be used in foods.

T 14. Many reducing diets are harmful.

F 15. Foods high in phosphorus are good for the brain and nerves.

F 16. Raw eggs are more wholesome than cooked ones.

T 17. Neither onions nor garlic cures a cold or purifies the blood.

T 18. The body can handle both alkaline and acid foods.

T 19. Yogurt is a tasty, more expensive form of milk. It has no more vitamins, calcium, or calories than regular whole milk.

T 20. Milk and cheese do not cause constipation. They have little residue because they are so completely digested.

F 21. All diseases are caused by faulty diet.

T 22. Iodine must be included in the diet.

F 23. Adding spices to foods destroys their nutritive value.

F 24. Every ache, pain, discomfort, and other symptom of fatigue or illness is caused by vitamin or mineral deficiency.

Answers:

24 F.
17 T, 18 T, 19 T, 20 T, 21 F, 22 T, 23 F,
10 T, 11 F, 12 F, 13 T, 14 T, 15 F, 16 F,
1 F, 2 F, 3 T, 4 F, 5 F, 6 T, 7 F, 8 F, 9 F.

What You Have Learned

What kind of health practices should you apply in balancing your diet? On a separate sheet of paper, number 1 through 20 and insert the answer from the vocabulary list below. Use each expression, but use each one only once.

19 allergy
15 bored
5 bread and cereals
8 breakfast
9 cottage cheese
13 failure
11 family

12 friends
20 health
19 high calorie
2 hunger
1 live
14 lonesome
16 low calorie

3 meat
4 milk
7 one quarter
10 peanut butter
18 snacks
6 vegetables and fruit

Everyone must eat to (1)_____. You eat in response to a built-in mechanism called (2)_____. A well-balanced daily diet is based on proper selections from the "Four Essential Food Groups." These groups include (3)_____, (4)_____, (5)_____ and (6)_____. You need (7)_____ of your protein and calorie allowances at (8)_____. You can plan balanced low-cost meals. For example, you can obtain complete protein from inexpensive (9)_____ as well as from expensive beefsteak. You can also obtain fat from inexpensive (10)_____

Social forces and emotions influence what you eat. The earliest and perhaps strongest social influence on your diet is your (11)_____. Another important influence is your (12)_____ Your emotions can lead your normal appetite astray. When you are hungry and still do not want to eat, it is often due to a feeling of (13)_____. On the other hand, you may overeat when you are (14)_____ or (15)_____

There comes a time for almost everyone when he wants to gain or lose weight. When you want to gain, you eat more frequently and more (16)_____ foods. When you want to lose weight, you eat less food, but more (17)_____ foods. (18)_____ can lead to consuming too many calories.

When people are sensitive to certain foods that are harmless to other people, they have a food (19)_____. The practice of "falling" for food fads can endanger your (20)_____

What You Can Do

1. When you are in a hurry at meal time, do you bolt your food and wash it down with liquids? Or, do you chew your food thoroughly? At your next meal keep these questions in mind. How did you do?

2. Make out a menu for a balanced daily diet that would not be considered expensive.

3. Make a list of your favorite foods. How many of these foods originated in a different country? From your classmates' lists choose a few foods that you have never tasted. Find out how to prepare these foods and try some of them.

4. Your doctor tells you that you are a few pounds too heavy, and you would like to lose weight. How would you go about planning a sensible reducing diet?

5. Your doctor suggests that you are a few pounds underweight, and you would like to gain a few pounds. How would you go about planning a sensible weight-gaining diet?

6. Keep a daily list of all the snacks you eat from the time you wake up until you go to sleep. Using a calorie guide, record the total calories eaten in snacks. How do these snacks affect your daily calorie intake? Remember, a snack is anything not eaten at a meal.

Things to Try

1. In certain areas of the United States, as you have learned, there are deficiencies in some of the essential nutrients. Locate some of these

areas, list the deficiencies, and explain what the people in these areas can do to overcome the deficiencies.

2. Describe two reducing diets that you have heard or read about. For each one, list the nutrients they contain in one column. In a second column, list the essential nutrients that are lacking. Compare the two lists.

3. Collect the labels from canned foods. Compare the prices of these foods with comparable amounts of frozen foods and with comparable amounts of fresh foods. Which are more expensive?

Probing Further

Your Weight and How to Control It, by Morris Fishbein, M.D., Doubleday, 1969. If you have a weight problem, you will find this volume a useful, reliable supplement to your text material.

Introductory Nutrition, by Helen Andrews Guthrie, Mosby, 1967. This beginning college textbook makes a useful reference book on the science of nutrition.

The Prudent Diet, by Norman Jolliffe, M.D., Simon and Schuster, 1965. Much useful information on sound nutrition is included in this book prepared for those concerned with the effect of diet on heart disease.

Health Concepts in Action

Do you agree with this statement? Would you change or add to it?

> **To maintain health, food patterns must provide a chemical balance of nutrients.** yes

Applying this concept of nutrition, which health practices would you

—continue?

—change?

—begin?

Will you now, as a result of your study, change any of your health objectives?

5 / Controlling Environmental Pollution

In the summer of 1972, a grayish-brown haze of heavy smog blanketed the picturesque town of Riverside, California. The smog was "imported" by winds from surrounding counties. Other towns and cities had already suffered many smog episodes. Los Angeles, New Orleans, New York City, and many other parts of the country had been engulfed at some time in the choking atmosphere known as smog.

In addition to air pollution, food and water pollution may seriously affect your health. The pollution of these three vital elements—food, water, and air—causes life-threatening injury to people and to our food plants and animals.

A PROBE INTO THE ENVIRONMENT—Is your environment healthful? To find out, you will be probing these questions:

1. How may foods be contaminated in growing and processing?

2. From what sources does radiation in foods come?

3. About how much water do you use each day?

4. In times of water shortage, what home appliances would be restricted in use?

5. What new sources of water supply are now being considered?

6. What are the environmental conditions that contribute to smog? What is meant by temperature inversion?

7. What are the irritants in air pollution that may affect your health? your property?

8. How has population growth affected the environment?

PROTECTING THE ENVIRONMENT

For your daily quota of food, water, and oxygen, you are vitally dependent on the environment in which you live. As you learned in Chapter 1, the environment includes all the external conditions and influences—biological, physical, and social—that affect your life and growth.

To obtain the best value from food, you must eat safe food. The water you take into your body must be clean water. The air that you breathe must be clean air.

Natural and Man-made Hazards

The hazards in the environment may be those produced by nature or by man's activities. Hazards in the air, for example, may be natural hazards such as fog or pollen. Or they may be the by-products of our agricultural and industrial progress in the form of smoke, fumes, and other wastes. Scientists now believe that it is possible to remove many of the hazards and to control others for the benefit of all of us.

Pollution (puh-LOO-shun) of the air is readily seen in this familiar example. On a clear, cold morning observe the column of smoke arising from the chimney of a factory or home. Hot fumes and airborne particles are being carried aloft. As they cool, waste particles fall out and drop, polluting the area close to the ground. Unfortunately, other forms of pollution of the environment are not as obvious as this kind. Only in recent years have we come to recognize their importance.

Environmental Protection Agency

The control of the environment is both a public health problem and an individual one. Average citizens, agricultural management, and industrial management share the responsibility with government of creating

5-1 Air pollution can be seen all around you. Make a note of how many different air pollution sites you see on your way to school.

a more healthful environment in which to live, raise a family, work, and enjoy leisure time.

Some of the major responsibilities for maintaining a safe environment have now been centralized within one federal agency, the Environmental Protection Agency. The EPA began operating in late 1970, with about 15 organizations, over 5,000 employees, and a budget of over 1½ billion dollars.

The Environmental Protection Agency is concerned primarily with controlling water pollution, air pollution, and solid wastes. It also sets the standards for safe radiation levels in the environment, and enforces these standards. The EPA has thus taken over some of the responsibilities for environmental

5-2 Chemical pesticides are commonly used by farmers. What objections have been raised against the use of such pesticides?

water run off

health that were formerly scattered among such agencies as the Department of the Interior, the Federal Radiation Council, the Atomic Energy Commission, and the Department of Health, Education, and Welfare.

SAFE FOOD

To be safe, food must be kept free from harmful substances during the growing and marketing processes. It must also be kept free of contamination from dirty cups, spoons, or other utensils during cooking and serving.

Today's farmer uses many new pest controls to improve his crops. Some of these controls are chemicals called *pesticides.* Pesticides check or destroy pests of all sorts — fungi, weeds, insects, and rodents. Some of these chemicals are still in the experimental stage of use, and scientists are not yet in agreement as to their safety.

Value of Pesticides

A familiar example of a pesticide is the chemical known by the abbreviated name *DDT.* DDT was first used on a large scale during World War II to control pest-borne diseases among military and civilian populations. It is credited with saving five million lives during the war years.

Since then, DDT and a score of other chemical agents have been successful in checking the spread of such age-old diseases as yellow fever, malaria, typhus, bubonic (black) plague, and *encephalitis* (en-sef-eh-LY-tis), or sleeping sickness.

The use of pesticides has also greatly increased the size and quality of our food supply by reducing pest damage to food and

5-3 This man is a research worker in a pest-control laboratory. He is testing the effects of various pesticides on insects.

livestock. Without pesticides, many of the inexpensive foods now in common use would be luxury items available only to a few. Without pesticides, the great expansion of the beef, dairy, fruit, and vegetable industries in this country would probably not have been possible.

Safe Use of Pesticides Still in Doubt

When Rachel Carson's book *Silent Spring* was published in the sixties, it provoked wide interest in the harmful effects of pesticides on wildlife, as well as on farm products and fish used for food. Government investigations were launched to determine the effects on people of DDT and other chemicals.

Since then, the dangers of pesticides have continued to receive attention. Reports in the daily papers tell of "fish kills" in rivers. There is evidence that pesticides can run off the land or drift in the air to pollute the environment many miles away from where they were used.

DDT has now been banned in this country in favor of other pesticides. The new pesticides are also toxic but are less long-lasting in the environment. However, the National Research Council points out that about 5 million tons of DDT have already entered the ocean, with about 20,000 tons now in the bodies of sea plants and animals.

Questions of safe use of pesticides continue to be raised by scientists and others. As one answer to the doubt and debate, scientists are experimenting with a number of nonchemical methods of pest control.

Other Methods of Pest Control

Biological control is one of the oldest methods of pest control, first used prior to 1920. Harmless insects of one species that are known to devour harmful insects of another species are placed in an infested area. Here the insects fight it out, and hopefully the harmless ones win.

Releasing sterilized insects so that they will mate with normal insects is another control method. Since no offspring can be produced by the mating, the insect population eventually dies out. This method has worked against the screwworm, a serious pest of livestock.

Raising insect-resistant plants is an ideal method because they are harmless, effective,

5-4 How safe are the fruits and vegetables at this market? What alternative methods of pest control can you think of?

and cheap. However, it takes **entomologists** (en-toh-MOL-oh-jists—scientists who study insects) and plant breeders ten or more years to develop suitable varieties of plants. Already, many such plants have been developed. Some varieties of winter wheat are now resistant to the Hessian fly; certain varieties of corn are resistant to the European corn borer and corn worm; several varieties of pest-resistant cotton are in the process of development.

These are just some examples of the non-chemical methods of pest control. Many others are in experimental stages. Among them are chemical attractants, which lure insects to traps.

Microbes, Additives, and Radiation

There are three primary sources of contamination of foods—microbes, additives, and radiation.

Microbes gain entrance into food through improper handling and processing. Among the more prevalent germs are **salmonella** and **staphylococci** (staf-ih-loh-KOK-seye), bacteria that multiply quickly and are the chief causes of infections transmitted by food. They produce food poisoning and gastroenteritis.

Milk is especially favorable as a carrier of such diseases as typhoid fever and tuberculosis. The causative germs are destroyed, however, when the milk is pasteurized. For the process of pasteurization see Chapter 29.

Additives are substances put into foods to serve a variety of purposes. The use of additives has been under federal control since 1958. You are familiar with such additives as iodine in salt and vitamin D in milk. These are nutritive additives. You also know of non-nutritive sweeteners that are sugar substitutes. Additives are also used as preservatives, thickeners, neutralizers, bleaching agents, and as flavoring. All food additives must meet

5-5 This scientist is trying to reduce a mosquito population by biological control rather than pesticides. He develops sterile male mosquitoes which then mate with other mosquitoes without producing young. Here he is separating mosquitoes at different stages of development.

Ingredients: Enriched bleached flour, water, shortening with freshness preserver, sugar, leavening, dried cultured buttermilk, salt, rice flour.

5-6 Do you ever read food labels? This one is from a pancake mix. Look at some labels from other foods and make a list of the additives.

established standards provided by federal law, and, when a harmful one is discovered, that food is withdrawn from the market. Not long ago an unsafe ingredient was identified in an imitation vanilla extract and the product was withdrawn from the market.

■ See how many products you can find in the grocery store that list food additives on their labels: for example, vitamin D added to milk. Why do you think the use of additives is under such strict control by the federal government?

Radioactive (ray-di-oh-ACK-tiv) fallout has greatly increased in the last few years. This increase of fallout is not entirely due to nuclear weapon testing, as you might well think. It also results from more extensive use of X rays and other types of radiation in hospitals, industrial plants, and research laboratories. From the earliest use of atomic weapons, there has been concern over the possible contamination of food and milk by radiation. Extensive testing through the nation shows the presence, to some degree or other, of radioactive fallout in these products. But it is generally accepted that the level of contamination is not high enough to be detrimental to health. However, this is a matter that is still open to debate, investigation, and further research.

Consumer Protection

The consumer in the United States is protected by federal, state, and local laws governing the preparation of milk and other foods for sale. Many city and county health departments check the pasteurization of milk. They also license and inspect restaurants, meat-packing plants, and other businesses connected with food preparation or sale. In Chapter 31, you will learn more about federal controls protecting our food supply.

CLEAN WATER

Clean water, like safe food, means water that is free from physically harmful substances. It means water free from pollution. The U.S. Public Health Service defines pollution in water as "the presence of any foreign substance—organic, inorganic, radiological, or biological—in water, with such pollution tending to degrade the water's quality to the extent that it constitutes a hazard or impairs the usefulness of water."

When you speak of clean water, that is, water fit to drink, you may call it *potable water*. This is a good word to remember if you travel abroad. Clean water may not be as plentiful in some countries as it is in our own, so it must be conserved. When traveling, look at the faucets. Sometimes one is labeled potable, the other *nonpotable*. Nonpotable water is not safe for drinking or brushing your teeth, although it is fine for rinsing out your clothes.

5-7 Detergent pollution in a stream. How can such pollution be avoided? What can you do?

Lots of People Living Close Together

The population of the United States has increased two and one-half times since 1900. People have moved from rural areas into towns and cities until, by now, the census shows that half of the total population is squeezed into one and one-half percent of our land. This is the basic cause of water pollution—lots of people living very close together.

Back in the early 1900's, when you wanted to build a house, stake out a farm, or set up a factory, you just made sure that a stream was nearby. If there was no stream, you dug a well and got your water from it. The factories piped water in for tanning leather for shoes and making other products and then discharged the waste-laden water back into the stream. At that time, the streams were capable of cleansing themselves by natural processes. Before long, more people moved in, towns grew up, and many more factories were started. The water from the towns and factories became more and more polluted with both human and factory wastes. The streams were no longer capable of cleansing themselves.

5-8 What will I come up with next?

The Need for Water Sanitation

Water sanitation includes controlling pollution by human wastes, which can carry disease. Among the important water-borne diseases are typhoid fever and dysentery. The community must also control contamination by industrial and agricultural wastes. Among these are many types of chemicals—pesticides, insecticides, and weed killers. These, you recall, may also contaminate food. Then there are greases, oils, salts, sludge, detergents, and animal and vegetable waste matter. The list may seem long, but it could be much longer. There are many new synthetic waste materials that have not as yet been identified.

Types of Water Pollutants

The Department of Health, Education, and Welfare lists eight categories of pollutants, each with its own hampering, or dangerous effect on water and health.

1. *Sewage* includes both domestic and food-processing wastes. Some sewage pollution of lakes and rivers is due to pleasure boats. Frequently, galley and toilet wastes are dumped directly into the water. This practice becomes a serious menace where boats are anchored in large numbers. Even more serious is the practice of some towns and cities of dumping such wastes, untreated, directly into rivers.

5-9 These men are helping to save ducks threatened by an oil slick that spread across Cape Cod beaches.

2. *Infectious agents* are found in the waste that comes from slaughter houses, chicken farms, mortuaries, and hospitals.

3. *Plant nutrients* are the fertilizers that are used on farms to stimulate crop growth. When it rains they wash off into the nearby streams and lakes. In the water, they continue to stimulate growth of plant life, which soon chokes the streams and kills off many of the fish.

4. *Organic chemical foreign wastes.* These are the newer and, perhaps, the more dangerous forms of pollution. Among them are detergents, pesticides, and other chemicals. They have not been in use long enough to determine their long-range effect on health, but they are under suspicion. Pesticides are washed into the streams from fields when it rains. Both these and the fertilizers are not always totally removed in normal water treatment.

5. *Mineral and chemical* pollutants from natural sources have to be recognized.

There are salts from natural rock deposits, and sulfates and acids from coal mining, along with wastes from quarries and other natural sites.

6. *Sediment* as a form of pollution became a problem when the forests around our watersheds were cut down. This exposed the land to the full force of the spring rains, floating soil into the streams to be carried along and gradually deposited as sediment.

7. *Radioactive wastes* are another of our newer forms of water pollution. They get into water from uranium mining, atomic reactors, medical laboratories, hospitals, and certain types of industry. At the present time, the level of discharge of radioactive wastes into our streams is considered by scientists to be small, but we are warned that if the present rate should increase, the consequences to health could be serious.

8. *Heat* is seldom thought of as a pollutant. But large amounts of water are drawn from streams into factories and returned to the streams hot or warm from the manufacturing process. This occurs in such factories as steel mills, coke ovens, petroleum refineries, and nuclear power plants. The heated water kills fish and other aquatic life.

Interstate Pacts Help Control Water Pollution

With water as with foods, scientists and engineers are seeking better methods of controlling contamination. The present emphasis is on interstate area control within a given watershed. A watershed is a ridge that divides one drainage area from another, the entire area draining into the same streams and lakes. An example of interstate area control is the Ohio Valley Water Sanitation Pact, a project of eight states.

This cooperative pact furnishes sewage-treatment facilities for about ninety-five percent of the watershed's population; it also provides control facilities that curb industrial waste discharge in about ninety percent of the area's industries. Similar cooperative projects are in operation or being planned for many parts of the country.

Industry Faces the Problem of Waste Disposal

Industry is the greatest contributor to stream pollution, and it uses the greatest amount of water. Many of the larger industries have installed waste-control equipment that is usually effective in clearing our streams. But there are factory owners who seem indifferent to the problem or are reluctant to spend money for the equipment. In one mountain area, for example, where a factory provides the only available jobs for hundreds of workers, the management expressed this view to the press: "We came here because there was water available to run this factory and because there was a stream to carry the wastes away. If we can't have this, we'll move elsewhere." Fortunately, such attitudes are slowly giving way to the more vigorous enforcement of state antipollution laws.

5-10 In this new method of garbage disposal, compressed and coated blocks of garbage are used in land fills or other construction.

Government Assists in Fighting Pollution

Most state and local governments have antipollution laws to protect their water supplies. However, the enforcement of these laws is sometimes hampered by lack of funds, not enough trained personnel, public indifference, and political considerations.

In an effort to strengthen state and local governments, federal laws such as the Water Quality Act have been passed. The federal laws not only set standards for water quality, but also provide grants to help the states meet these standards. Grants totalling over 1 billion dollars have already been made available to improve sewage-treatment facilities in cities. Nevertheless, much remains to be done.

Tapping New Sources of Water Supply

Another national concern is water shortages. Some scientists believe our supply is adequate, although they admit that in some areas, due to lack of processing, storage, and distribution facilities, danger of water shortage does exist.

New sources of water are sought. One of these is sea water, which can be converted to

5-11 This plant is able to produce one million gallons of fresh water from sea water daily.

fresh water by a process called **desalting**. Scientists have done this successfully, but as yet it is too expensive a process for practical use. The reuse of water is another effort toward conservation. Industry and government have made great strides in perfecting ways of purifying water for its reuse.

The Uses of Water

Water is used in great quantities for the manufacture of all sorts of products. For example, it is estimated that it takes one thousand gallons of water to produce one pound of high-grade paper. The second greatest user of water is agriculture with its vast irrigation systems and large number of stock. Towns and cities use great quantities of water to fight fires, wash streets, and for other health protection and sanitation activities.

Now consider the use of water in the home. It is estimated that in a home with running water, each person uses about twenty gallons per day. Broken down, this may mean the use of five gallons to wash, shave, and brush your teeth; five to seven gallons each time you flush the toilet; five more gallons each minute you stand in the shower with the

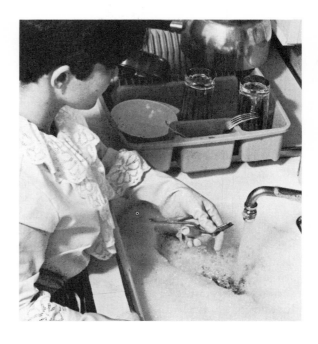

5-12 Do you ever stop to think how much water you use each day? It is estimated that each person uses twenty gallons a day. How much of this water is wasted? Three cases of water being wasted are shown on this page. Is your family guilty of water-wasting practices?

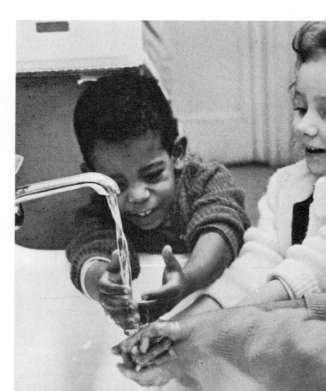

water turned on, and even more than this for a tub bath. In addition, there is the water you drink and that which is used in preparation of foods.

■ Try to estimate the amount of water you use for one day, excluding the water used in the preparation of food. Use the hints given above to help you with your estimate.

Twenty gallons of water per person per day only begins to tell the story. When the amount of water used for air conditioners, automatic dishwashers, garbage disposers, and washing machines is added to the amount consumed by personal use, an estimated 150 gallons of water are used each day in the average American home.

CLEAN AIR

Clean air, like safe food and clean water, means air free from physically harmful substances. It refers to air free from an overburden of atmospheric moisture. It means air free of pollutants from industry, family life, and nature. You have often heard people speak of pure air. There probably is no such thing as pure air, since air purity is a matter of degree that can change with the weather.

Why Is Air Pollution Increasing?

Air pollution increases in proportion to the increase in population and to the number and kinds of industries. The use of new chemicals and fertilizers by industry and agriculture has added to pollution. Perhaps the greatest increase comes from the estimated 88 million motor vehicles in the United States. These motor vehicles throw off into the atmosphere a daily dose of about 240,000 tons of carbon monoxide, hydrocarbons, and nitrogen dioxide gases.

5-13 How do motor vehicles contribute to the air pollution problem? What can be done about it?

Sources of Air Pollution

Nature contributes to pollution in the form of great sand and dust storms, forest fires, and ash dust from erupting volcanoes. Fog and mist that result from changes in the temperature help to trap pollutants.

Living things throw off literally tons of harmful pollens into the wind, which carries them great distances. The pollens come from trees, flowers, weeds, and grasses. Decaying matter in woods and swamps pours out gases and odors into the air. Then there are the molds that grow in damp areas of grass, leaves, and soil. Their microscopic spores are shaken into the air by the wind and still another pollutant is added.

People, too, make a contribution. They do this when they burn trash in the backyard; when they let their car idle for a long period of time on a cold morning; when they use a power mower. The burning of soft coal and wood in fireplaces, stoves, and furnaces adds still more pollution. Can you think of any other ways that people contribute to air pollution?

■ Check to see what laws there are in your community that regulate burning of trash outdoors and using outdoor fireplaces and incinerators. Have you and your family been obeying these laws?

Agriculture, in its use of pesticides, weed killers, and fertilizers, plays a heavy role in air contamination. These products have far-reaching effects since they are readily caught up into the air and carried great distances.

Transportation and industry put the greatest amount of pollution into the air. Some forms, such as smoke, can easily be seen, while others, such as the gases, are invisible. Ordinary smoke is composed of particles of carbon and ash. In more dense smoke, such other substances are present as microscopic particles of steel filings, lead, oil, and grease.

The invisible gaseous pollutants are waste products from burning coal and gasoline; they rise from chemical and heating plants and from oil refineries. Among the dangerous gases are oxides of sulfur and nitrogen. Another dangerous pollutant is **carbon monoxide,** the only odorless gas among them. All of the others you can detect by your sense of smell. You will read more about carbon monoxide in Chapter 15. Some of the gases tend to deplete the oxygen content of the air and produce a hazard that often occurs in the mining industry.

Testing Oxygen Content

Before the development of our present instruments for testing the oxygen content of air, miners carried a caged canary into the mine with them. When the canary showed signs of breathing difficulty and lost its coordination—fell from its perch—the miners knew it was time to clear out. They knew that either the oxygen supply in the mine was near the danger point or that other gases, such as methane, had accumulated to dangerous levels.

Smog

The name *smog* was originally given to a mixture of *smoke* and *fog*. This type of pollution has long been common in urban areas such as London, England. A typical London smog contains small droplets of water suspended in air (fog) intermingled with smoke from many fireplaces, stoves, and furnaces. The smoke contains sulfur compounds released in burning coal and low-grade heating oils. Another form of smog, which is associated with Los Angeles, is almost entirely gaseous, including gasoline vapors. It contains only one percent of microscopic carbon and ash particles. (See the table of major air pollutants on page 87.)

Today, however, the name smog is used for any polluted atmosphere in which visibility is poor, even if little smoke or fog is present. Los Angeles smog is typical of this modern form of air pollution. One of the more obvious effects of smog is shown in Figure 5-15.

Air-Pollution Disasters

The first recorded air-pollution disaster in the United States occurred in Donora, Pennsylvania in 1948 when a heavy fog settled over the town and did not lift. The atmosphere became so polluted with industrial waste that daytime turned into night. Some

5-14 NATIONAL SOURCES OF MAJOR AIR POLLUTANTS
(millions of tons per year)

Source	Carbon Monoxide	Sulfur Oxides	Hydrocarbons	Nitrogen Oxides	Particulate Matter	Other, Miscellaneous	Total
Transportation	66	1	12	6	1	*	86
Industry	2	9	4	2	6	2	25
Power plants	1	12	*	3	3	*	20
Space heating	2	3	1	1	1	*	8
Refuse disposal	1	*	1	*	1	*	4
Total	72	25	18	12	12	4	143

* Less than 1

From *Air Pollution Primer*, National Tuberculosis and Respiratory Disease Association, 1969.

5,000 people became ill, and seventeen died.

The London fogs have been more disastrous than that of Donora. London has been blanketed by industrial wastes and fog at least four times. In one smog that lasted only a few days, 750 deaths resulted from its effects.

New Orleans has been the scene of an "asthma epidemic" which was caused by air pollution. Within a twenty-four hour period, hundreds of the population were treated for labored breathing, coughing, and other symptoms of acute respiratory distress.

Los Angeles is the city most frequently affected by smog. Its residents have come to expect many days when smog will irritate their eyes and respiratory passages.

New York City and much of the northeast coast suffered their first major smog in November 1966. Hundreds of people were treated for coughs, labored breathing, and other symptoms of acute respiratory distress. Many longtime sufferers of respiratory ailments were hospitalized.

Other cities in the United States have experienced smog episodes that were brief and caused little damage. Smog is a threat that hangs over the head of all industrial areas. Do you live in an area that has had a major smog problem?

5-15 Smog in Los Angeles is usually not visible, but it causes burning irritation of the eyes.

5-16 If this smog keeps up, we will soon need gas masks!

5-17 New York City blanketed by heavy smog.

Temperature Inversion

Air close to the surface of the earth, containing pollutants, is usually warmer than the layer of air above it. The warm air, being lighter, rises and carries fumes and other pollutants away with it. However, frequently, there is a *temperature inversion.* That is, air close to the ground is cooler and heavier than the layer of warm air above it. When this happens, the warm air acts as a lid that prevents the polluted air from rising.

Temperature inversion was present and there was lack of wind-flow during the smog disasters in Donora, Los Angeles, and New York City.

Damage Caused by Air Pollution

The damage caused by pollutants in our air touches every individual and costs him money. The homeowner finds his recently painted house darkened and the metal work on his porch rusted. The electric company sees corrosion on its electric contact points. Car owners are distressed to find the paint deteriorating, pock marks on the chrome trim, and cracks appearing in the tires. Farmers find dark spots on peaches, corn, and grapes. Have you noticed any other effects of air pollution? Is there anything you can do to improve the situation?

Then there are the accident hazards caused by poor visibility. The airplane pilot does not always have instrument landing equipment to bring him through smog. Bus and truck drivers, burdened by loads of people or produce, fight their way through atmosphere thickened by pollutants. The same problem is faced by any automobile driver. It is a true danger and one that accounts for many accidents.

The Link Between Pollution and Health

Your entire respiratory system is involved in obtaining the necessary amount of oxygen from the air you breathe. When this air is contaminated with gases and tiny solid particles, the soft, velvety membranes lining your nose, mouth, and throat may become irritated and inflamed. If the exposure is severe or continues over a long period of time, the respiratory tract becomes susceptible to infectious diseases such as colds, chronic bronchitis, pneumonia, and influenza.

Air pollutants do have an ill effect on all of us, but they more seriously harm those who are already suffering from respiratory ailments, or those who are very susceptible to such infections.

The Clean Air Act

In 1963, Congress passed the Clean Air Act providing grants to the states to help them clean up the air. In 1970, amendments to the Act gave the federal government power to set national standards of air quality. The bill also set tough fines for industries violating these standards.

Automobile manufacturers have been given until 1975–76 to develop an automobile in which the exhaust of toxic gases has been reduced by 90 percent. This is intended to help remove the vast sea of fumes that floats around areas of heavy traffic. Before federal legislation was enacted, the state of California, alarmed by the spread of smog into many urban areas, had led the way with a law requiring all new cars sold within the state to be equipped with approved exhaust controls.

The Impact of Environmental Health

The relatively new science of environmental health seeks solutions to the mounting threat to health due to contamination of our food, water, and air. The attention of society is attracted to this new science as individuals become aware of the present and future dangers of pollutants. Federal laws have been enacted to strengthen state and local action and to stimulate an all-out war against these dangers. Environmental health requires the cooperation of all of us.

5-18 Any day in a large city, one can see pollutants in the air. This aerial view of New York City shows pollutants being added and helps to pinpoint the sources. What are large cities doing about the problem? Can one city's effort alone solve the problem?

What You Have Learned

What kind of health practices should you apply in maintaining your health? Check your understanding of the chapter. On a separate sheet of paper, number 1 through 18 and insert the answer from the vocabulary list below. Use each expression, but use each one only once.

air pollution   fumes   smog
crowded   oxygen   smoke
diarrhea   people   temperature inversion
dysentery   pesticides   typhoid fever
fog   pollen   unknown
food   respiratory   water

In order to survive, you are vitally dependent on your environment for (1)_____, (2)_____, and (3)_____. Within your environment, there are hazards produced by nature, such as (4)_____ and (5)_____ along with those produced by man, such as (6)_____ and (7)_____. (8)_____ occurs when these waste particles fall toward earth. The name (9)_____ was originally given to air polluted by a mixture of smoke and fog. A higher layer of air that acts as a lid preventing the pollutants from rising is called a (10)_____. Air pollution affects our (11)_____ system.

Our food supply has been remarkably increased through the use of (12)_____ in the control of insects and rodents. But scientists are not yet agreed as to their safe use on foods for (13)_____

Water is a necessity of life, and water pollution may become critical in some areas where there are (14)_____ conditions. Among the common waterborne diseases are (15)_____, (16)_____ and (17)_____ This explains the precaution you learn when camping outdoors: never drink water from (18)_____ sources.

What You Can Do

1. Find out about your community water supply. Does it come from underground or from surface sources? Learn, by a visit to the filtration plant, how the water is treated to make it potable.

2. Invite a garageman to show your class how a smog control device for an automobile operates. Have these devices been successful? Are they required in the state where you live?

3. Have your class take sides and debate the pesticide theory: "Pesticides destroy wildlife and may be harmful to personal health," versus "Pes-

ticides destroy pests that ruin crops and they help the farmer grow more food." Do some research reading in order to have good reasons to back up your side in the debate. Some good references are given under "More You Can Learn" below.

Things to Try /

1. Locate the watershed in the area where you live. Find out what is being done to prevent pollution of the water along your watershed.

2. Some day when you are exposed to smog, wear a gauze mask over your nose and mouth. After a few hours of exposure, remove the mask and observe the discoloration on the mask. How would such pollution of the air be likely to affect your health?

3. Make a list of the problems discussed in this chapter which you can personally help solve: for example, burning trash in your backyard.

4. Find out what is being done about air pollution in your community. Are there any community groups involved in programs to help cut down air pollution? Go to their meetings and find out what is being done and what you can do to help.

Probing Further /

Man and His Environment, by Frederick Rasmussen, Houghton Mifflin, 1971. Investigates living things, how the environment affects living things, and how man affects the environment.

"Air Pollution Primer," by Rena Corman, *National Tuberculosis and Respiratory Disease Association,* 1971. A thorough explanation of the processes of air pollution, the properties of contaminants, and the health effects of the different types of air pollution including radioactivity.

Clean Air—Clean Water for Tomorrow's World, by Reed Millard and the Editors of Science Book Associates, Messner, 1971. An up-to-date discussion of specific pollutants, their effects, and what agencies and governments can do about them.

Our Polluted World: Can Man Survive?, by John Perry, Watts, 1967. Tells of air and water pollution and the effect of man on his environment.

That We May Live, by Jamie L. Whitten, Van Nostrand, 1966. A good account of the place of pesticides in today's world.

Silent Spring, by Rachel Carson, Fawcett World, 1970. This fascinating best seller provoked heated debate among scientists, especially as to the ill effects of pesticides on humans.

"The Fouling of the American Environment," *Saturday Review,* May 22, 1965. A collection of articles on pollution in this issue, prepared by distinguished scientists, adds to the material in the text.

"Pollution: Everybody's Adversary," *Today's Health,* March 1966. This issue contains a special report by a group of distinguished scientists concerning all forms of pollution.

Health Concepts in Action

Does this statement agree with your own ideas?

> **To maintain healthy structure and functioning, the individual is dependent on a healthful environment.**

Applying this concept, which health practices would you

—continue?

—change?

—begin?

Will you now, as a result of your study, change any of your health objectives?

UNIT THREE
Achieving Fitness

6 / Your Physical Fitness

94 – 227

Who is the most physically fit person you know? If asked a question like this, most of us tend to choose someone who is very muscular and "looks athletic." But muscle development is only one part of physical fitness. If you have the bubbling energy and endurance needed to enjoy your daily work and play—and to cope successfully with stress—*you* may be the most physically fit person you know! Physical fitness provides the foundation for general fitness for living.

A PROBE INTO FITNESS—How can you improve your physical fitness? To develop a plan, you will be probing questions like these:

1. How do the activities of your daily life compare with those of teen-agers before the turn of the century?

2. Why did only the physically strong among our primitive ancestors survive? Is this true today?

3. Where does your energy come from? How does exercise help improve your energy level?

4. What events triggered the physical fitness movement in America?

5. What is the purpose of taking the physical fitness test?

6. What other qualities, in addition to physical ones, are needed for total fitness?

6-1 These women from Thailand *must* be physically fit to do their work. Could you survive in their way of life?

THE IMPORTANCE OF KEEPING PHYSICALLY FIT

Not so long ago, young men and women of fifteen or sixteen led a very different kind of life from yours. There was a time when most humans *had* to be physically fit to survive and live in the world. Each morning you awake and eat before going to school, but they were self-starters who rose and, of necessity, hunted for their breakfast. You leave home and drive to school, unless you live within a few blocks of it. They left their crude shelters, walked or ran for many miles, and hunted for food as they went.

During your school day you take flat little plugs, or discs, of metal from your purse or pocket and trade these for your lunch; your ancestral teen-agers labored with stones to make the tools to help them hunt. You may now, if you wish, drop a coin in a slot to get what once required the risk of a girl's or boy's life.

With little exertion you can push buttons, turn knobs, flip switches, and make telephone calls for the needs that once kept youths in constant exercise, moving through forests, up hills and down, climbing trees, scaling cliffs, quarrying stones, and, if they were fortunate, carrying wearisome burdens of food back with them.

As man became more advanced and built up complex civilizations, the way of life changed a great deal—but young men and women of your age still walked wherever they went, unless they were fortunate enough to own a horse. Some things could be bought; others continued to require personal skill and effort.

Today your effort is largely mental, not physical. The coin, pushbutton, knob, and switch have solved problems you are not aware you otherwise might have faced.

But your life of physical ease has created problems your ancestors did not face. You are larger and potentially stronger than your ancestors, but you are less well developed and probably weaker by comparison. You may not get enough physical exercise—not even enough to be physically alert and feeling at your best.

Your Structural Endowment

Your body is engineered for physical activity; think for a moment of its general

6-2 We live in a world of buttons, knobs, and switches. Our meals can easily be obtained by inserting a coin.

structure. Bones, joints, and muscles with their tendons and ligaments make up the *musculoskeletal* (muscle-bone) *system.* Bones are of many sizes and shapes and provide the framework upon which the rest of the body is suspended. The bones are articulated into several types of joints that permit different degrees of motion.

Your muscles make up about 40 to 50 percent of your body weight. Muscles help to determine your body's shape, and contraction of your muscles is the process that makes motion possible in any part of the body. You can move your head, arms, and legs. You can do more than this; you can run, jump, crawl, and climb. See page 97 for views of the muscular system.

You will learn later about how energy for muscular activity is supplied. For now, think only about the fact that your primitive ancestors had the same potential for activity and energy production that you have. They, however, strengthened their bodies through vigorous activity. Today you no longer need

to make your tools, or hunt and kill game, or, in fact, even walk very much. As a result, although people grow taller and their feet are larger, due perhaps to improved nutrition and medical care, many have underdeveloped muscles. As long ago as the fourth century B.C., Hippocrates observed "That which is used develops, and that which is not used wastes away." Here in our century, we find that from lack of vigorous use in daily living, our muscles fail to reach their optimum potential of development and strength.

How Your Body Does Its Work

Your body accomplishes the tasks of daily living by the use of energy. Everything that you do, every body function, whether you are awake or asleep, requires energy. You have observed that some of your acquaintances seem to have more energy to expend than do others. Let us suppose that the necessary provisions for energy—nutrition, freedom from injury and emotional stress, and other factors—are equal among you. Perhaps the abundant energy observed in certain persons may be attributed to constitutional inheritance. In order to understand

6-3 This "city of tomorrow," exhibited at the last New York World's Fair, features moving sidewalks and a new concept in building design. How will this modern city affect your physical fitness?

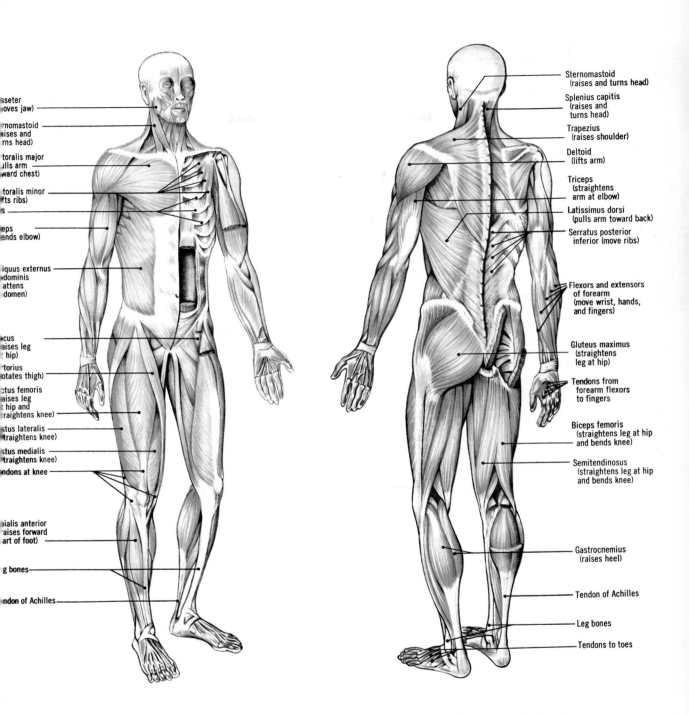

Masseter
(moves jaw)

Sternomastoid
(raises and
turns head)

Pectoralis major
(pulls arm
toward chest)

Pectoralis minor
(lifts ribs)

Biceps
(bends elbow)

Obliquus externus
abdominis
(flattens
abdomen)

Psoas
(raises leg
at hip)

Sartorius
(rotates thigh)

Rectus femoris
(raises leg
at hip and
straightens knee)

Vastus lateralis
(straightens knee)

Vastus medialis
(straightens knee)

Tendons at knee

Tibialis anterior
(raises forward
part of foot)

Leg bones

Tendon of Achilles

Sternomastoid
(raises and turns head)

Splenius capitis
(raises and
turns head)

Trapezius
(raises shoulder)

Deltoid
(lifts arm)

Triceps
(straightens
arm at elbow)

Latissimus dorsi
(pulls arm toward back)

Serratus posterior
inferior (move ribs)

Flexors and extensors
of forearm
(move wrist, hands,
and fingers)

Gluteus maximus
(straightens
leg at hip)

Tendons from
forearm flexors
to fingers

Biceps femoris
(straightens leg at hip
and bends knee)

Semitendinosus
(straightens leg at hip
and bends knee)

Gastrocnemius
(raises heel)

Tendon of Achilles

Leg bones

Tendons to toes

6-4 Two views of your muscular system. The muscles shown here are skeletal muscles—that is, they are muscles that are attached to bones. Your muscles work by contracting. When they contract, they become thicker and shorter; thus, they exert a pull on the bones to which they are attached and movement is the result.

how hereditary characteristics are transmitted, it is necessary to know certain facts about the living cell. You will learn these facts in Chapter 13 and in Chapter 20.

It is interesting to note here, however, that among your primitive ancestors only the strong survived the perils and rigors of life common in those days. The weak perished for lack of capacity to defend themselves. The constitutional capacity of the strong was passed along from generation to generation. In today's modern society, due in part to advances in medical science, improved shelter, improved sanitation, and the absence of primitive perils, both the weak and the strong survive and pass along their constitutional capacities.

The abundance of energy evident in some persons and absent in others may, perhaps, indicate an inheritance of capacity to perform the tasks of daily living without undue strain or fatigue. Such persons may also possess reserve energy with which to meet emergencies. Such capacity exists, although, as already noted, it is not always utilized in today's way of life. The automobile has made walking almost obsolete; our pushbutton existence tends to produce atrophy at an increasingly early age.

Your Source of Energy

Where does your energy come from? All your energy comes from nutrients supplied to your cells through the blood. As you know, these nutrients, which come from your food, are used to build and repair tissues and keep the rest of your life processes going.

The same source of energy is needed for the action of the muscles. Therefore when you exercise, the heart and lungs must work more efficiently. They have to bring more blood to and from the muscle cells to increase their supply of food and oxygen and to remove wastes. This increased blood flow benefits not only the muscle cells but all the cells and organs of the body. Here, perhaps, is the crux of the **Physical Fitness Movement**: regular exercise has been found to benefit *all* the systems of the body.

IMPROVING PHYSICAL FITNESS

An early advocate of the importance of physical activity was President Theodore Roosevelt. At the turn of the century he encouraged youth to follow his own example of developing a healthy body from a sickly one by leading the "strenuous life."

6-5 Wait for me—I need a ride to school!

The Physical Fitness Movement

The need for a Physical Fitness movement was brought into sharp focus in the United States by a number of events that caused national concern. During the two world wars, many young men were rejected for military service because of low levels of physical and/or emotional or mental fitness. This revealed that an alarming number of American youths were not as healthy as we had supposed them to be. Moreover, tests given to boys and girls in the United States and in several European and Far Eastern countries showed that youths of the same age in other countries were often superior in physical performance to American youths.

In the fifties, during President Eisenhower's term of office, he appointed a federal commission to study and to recommend corrective measures for the improvement of youth fitness. Then, in 1961, President Kennedy established the President's Council on Youth Fitness. President Kennedy urged each school to adopt three recommendations of the Council:

1. Identify the physically underdeveloped pupil and work with him to improve his physical capacity.
2. Provide a minimum of fifteen minutes of vigorous activity every day for all pupils.
3. Use valid fitness tests to determine pupils' physical abilities and evaluate their progress.

Succeeding presidents have continued to support the work of the President's Council. President Lyndon B. Johnson extended the work of the Council, developing physical fitness programs for people of all ages, not merely young people. The Council was renamed "The President's Council on Physical Fitness" to clarify the Council's larger role.

The Council provides guidelines for school physical fitness programs. Although the guidelines apply chiefly to physical activities, the Council also emphasizes that spiritual, emotional, mental, and social fitness are an important part of total fitness.

Tests for Physical Fitness

According to the Council, you can judge the state of your physical fitness by your ability to pass three standard screening tests which measure your physical strength, flexibility, and agility. The tests consist of:

1. *pullups* (with modified pullups for girls) to test the strength of your arms and shoulders;
2. *situps* to test your flexibility and abdominal strength;
3. *squat thrusts* to test your agility.

These three screening tests are pictured and described on pages 100–102. If you fail to pass any one or all of the tests, the Council suggests certain remedial exercises to bring you up to par. Examples of these remedial exercises are given on page 103. You may take the screening tests again and again until you can successfully pass all three tests.

A passing score represents a minimum level of achievement of muscular development. You will probably wish to bring your score as far above the minimum level as the general state of your health, discussed with your doctor, permits. Keep in mind that passing or failing these tests is *not* an indication of the general state of your health since your muscular development is, of course, only one factor in your overall physical-condition.

Progress in Youth Fitness

The national emphasis on youth fitness has proved beneficial. American girls and boys aged 10–17 are generally, as shown by recent scores, more fit today than they were when tested about a decade ago.

Three Screening Tests for Physical Fitness

Three tests that measure strength, flexibility, and agility are: *pullups* (arm and shoulder strength); *situps* (flexibility and abdominal strength); *squat thrusts* (agility).

If you fail any test, retest yourself every six weeks, until you pass.

A convenient way to carry out the program is to work with a partner. Your partner can act as scorer for you while you take the test, and vice versa. After each test, record the results.

The only equipment needed is a chinning bar, a stopwatch (or a watch with a sweep-second hand), and record forms.

Pullups / Boys (See Figure 1)

Equipment:

A bar, of sufficient height, comfortable to grip.

Starting Position:

Grasp the bar with palms facing forward; hang with arms and legs fully extended. Feet must be free of floor. The partner stands slightly to one side of the pupil being tested and counts each successful pullup.

Action:

1. Pull body up with the arms until the chin is placed over the bar.
2. Lower body until the elbows are fully extended.
3. Repeat the exercise the required number of times.

Rules:

1. The pull must not be a snap movement.
2. Knees must not be raised.
3. Kicking the legs is not permitted.
4. The body must not swing. If pupil starts to swing, his partner stops the motion by holding an extended arm across the front of the pupil's thighs.
5. One complete pullup is counted each time the pupil places his chin over the bar.

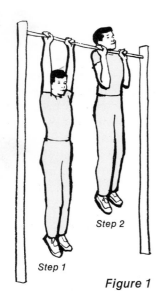

Step 2

Step 1

Figure 1

To Pass:

Boys, ages 10–13:1 pullup. Boys, ages 14–15:2 pullups.
Boys, ages 16–17:3 pullups.

Modified Pullups / Girls (See Figure 2)

Equipment:

Any bar adjustable in height and comfortable to grip. A piece of pipe, placed between two stepladders and held securely, may be used.

Starting Position:

Adjust height of bar to chest level. Grasp bar with palms facing out. Extend the legs under the bar, keeping the body and knees straight. The heels are on the floor. Fully extend the arms so they form an angle of 90 degrees with the body line. The partner braces the pupil's heels to prevent slipping.

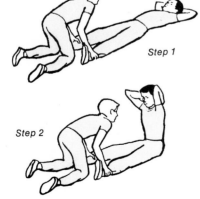

Step 1

Step 2

Figure 2

Action:

1. Pull body up with the arms until the *chest* touches the bar.
2. Lower body until elbows are fully extended.
3. Repeat the exercise the required number of times.

Rules:

1. The body must be kept straight.
2. The chest *must* touch the bar, and the arms must then be *fully extended.*
3. No resting is permitted.
4. One pullup is counted each time the chest touches the bar.

To Pass:

Ages 10–17: eight modified pullups.

Situps / Boys and Girls (See Figure 3)

Starting Position:

Pupil lies on his back with legs extended, feet about 1 foot apart. The hands, with fingers interlaced, are grasped behind the neck. Another pupil holds his partner's ankles and keeps his heels in contact with the floor while counting each successful situp.

Step 1

Step 2

Figure 3

Action:

1. Sit up and turn the trunk to the left. Touch the right elbow to the left knee.
2. Return to starting position.
3. Sit up and turn the trunk to the right. Touch the left elbow to the right knee.
4. Return to the starting position.
5. Repeat the required number of times.
6. One complete situp is counted each time the pupil returns to the starting position.

To Pass:

Boys, ages 10–17: 14 situps. Girls, ages 10–17: 10 situps.

Squat Thrust / Boys and Girls (See Figure 4)

Equipment:

A stopwatch, or a watch with a sweep-second hand.

Starting Position:

Pupil stands at attention.

Action:

1. Bend knees and place hands on the floor in front of the feet. Arms may be between, outside, or in front of the bent knees.
2. Thrust the legs back far enough so that the body is perfectly straight from shoulders to feet (the pushup position).
3. Return to squat position.
4. Return to erect position.

Scoring:

The teacher carefully instructs the pupils how to do *correct* squat thrusts. The teacher tells the pupils to do as many correct squat thrusts as possible within a 10-second time limit. The teacher gives the starting signal, "Ready!—Go!" On "Go" the pupil begins. The partner counts each squat thrust. At the end of 10 seconds, the teacher says, "Stop."

Rule:

The pupil must return to the erect position of attention at the completion of each squat thrust.

To Pass:

Girls, ages 10–17:3 squat thrusts in 10 seconds.
Boys, ages 10–17:4 squat thrusts in 10 seconds.

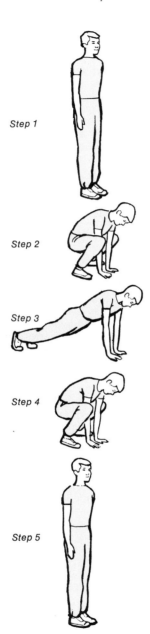

Step 1

Step 2

Step 3

Step 4

Step 5

Figure 4

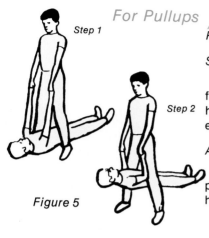

Step 1

Step 2

Figure 5

For Pullups / Arm and shoulder strength developer.

Reclining Pullups (See Figure 5)

Starting Position:

One pupil lies on back. His partner stands astride him, looking face to face, feet beside reclining pupil's chest. Partners grasp hands, with fingers interlocked. Reclining pupil's arms are fully extended.

Action:

*Count 1.—*Pupil on floor pulls up with arms until chest touches partner's thighs. His body remains straight, with weight resting on heels. The standing partner supports but does not aid action.
*Count 2.—*Return to starting position.

For Situps / Abdominal strength and flexibility developer.

Pull Stretcher (See Figure 6)

Starting Position:

Two pupils sit facing each other, legs apart and extended, so that the soles of their feet are in contact. Pupils grasp hands with fingers interlocked.

Action:

One pupil attempts to bring his own trunk as close to the floor as possible. The other pupil aids by pulling his partner forward. The exercise is continued as partners reverse actions. The legs must be kept spread and straight throughout the exercise.

Figure 6

For Squat Thrusts / Agility developer.

Kangaroo Hop (See Figure 7)

Starting Position:

Pupil assumes a semi-squatting position. Knees are flexed with the weight on the balls of the feet and the trunk erect. Place the hands on the hips.

Action:

Jump as high and as far forward as possible, keeping hands on hips, landing in the starting position.

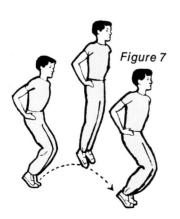

Figure 7

6-6 The President's All America Team. Each of these boys and girls has won a Presidential Physical Fitness Award. Do you think you could make the team?

As an added incentive to youths to continue in the program, the ***President's Fitness Award Program*** has been established. Winners of the award are boys and girls aged 10–17 who score at, or above, the 85th percentile on the Youth Fitness Test of the American Association for Health, Physical Education, and Recreation. The award consists of a certificate, suitable for mounting, bearing the presidential seal and the President's signature. In addition, there is an embroidered award emblem in gold, red, white, and blue, that may be worn on clothing. (See Figure 6-6.) Further information regarding this program may be obtained from the President's Fitness Awards, 1201 Sixteenth St., N.W., Washington, D.C. 20036. See also the pamphlets listed on page 109.

Endurance Fitness and Aerobics

The screening tests on pages 100–103 are designed to test your muscular development. However, fitness depends also upon the condition of your heart and lungs and their endurance under stress. Most of us can produce enough energy for our daily tasks. But when we have to put out a bit more effort, we become easily fatigued and winded. We have little reserve capacity to meet emergency work and play requirements. The heart and lungs of the physically fit person, on the other hand, are able to deliver the extra blood and oxygen needed.

With this concept of fitness in mind, Major Kenneth H. Cooper of the United States Air Force developed another way of testing fit-

6-7 Chris Evert's endurance and agility made her a leading contender in tennis championship matches by the time she was sixteen.

include walking, jogging, bicycling, running in place, swimming, skipping rope. To qualify as aerobic exercises—that is, exercises which build heart and lung endurance—they must be carried on at least four times a week, for a certain length of time, and at a certain pace.

The point system worked out by Major Cooper shows at what pace and for what length of time to carry out the exercises to get the "training effect" that helps build endurance. The point system is geared to your age, sex, and general level of fitness at the start of the program.

The Value of Jogging and Other Sports

Today, as a result of studies like those carried out by Dr. Cooper, we know much more about exercise and its effects on the body than we did at the turn of the century when people thought they could keep fit just by doing their "daily dozen of calisthenics." We know that those sports activities that require rhythmic, sustained action are more likely to develop endurance than activities that require just spurts of action.

6-8 Bicycle riding is a good sport to carry over into your adult life. What other sports fit into this category? Roller Skating

ness. In this test, you try to cover as much distance as possible in 12 minutes flat, alternating walking with running when you get out of breath. Then you compare your results with standards on a chart to find out how much endurance you have.

This test is an indirect measure of maximum oxygen intake—that is, the amount of oxygen that your heart and lungs are able to supply to your muscles when you are doing very heavy work.

Aerobics (meaning: *with oxygen*) is the name of the exercise program that Major Cooper has developed to improve the capacity of the heart and lungs to deliver oxygen to the body under stress. Aerobic exercises

Therefore, activities like swimming and bicycling are even more beneficial to the body than sports like tennis or football.

In the broad realm of sports, you can probably find some that are appealing enough to make you want to learn the skills needed to take part in them. Here are some other possibilities in addition to those mentioned under aerobic activities: dancing, roller skating, ice skating, volleyball, ping pong, bowling, gardening, and skiing. The list is almost endless. In making your choice of sports, try to select sports that will be useful in your leisure time as well as at school. You may also want to select a land sport and a water sport, an indoor sport and an outdoor sport, a winter sport and a summer sport.

You are wise to enter into as many sports as possible. Properly selected sports activities are an enjoyable and effective way of striving toward the goal of physical fitness.

Your Muscles Need Daily Action

Fitness cannot be stored up, any more than sleep or rest can. To remain in condition, your heart, lung, and skeletal muscles require a certain minimum of daily work — that is, exercise. Therefore, maintaining fitness is a lifetime goal. To remain physically fit, you will need to establish an activity program that will continue, with some modifications, for the rest of your life.

The amount of exercise you get in your daily tasks will no doubt vary from season to season. This is a factor to keep in mind when planning your fitness program. If you work as a caddie on a golf course or a lifeguard at the pool, or engage in a great deal of dancing or sports, you will find that each of these activities is adding to your physical fitness. On days that you have gained a great deal of exercise from your routine chores or from sports, you may not need to carry out any special exercise workouts.

THE GOAL: TOTAL FITNESS

In a pamphlet called *Seven Paths to Fitness*, The American Medical Association has suggested the following as vital steps toward the achievement of total fitness:

1. Proper medical care
2. Adequate nutrition
3. Proper dental care
4. The right kind and amount of exercise
5. Satisfying work
6. Healthful play and recreation
7. Adequate rest and sleep

You can see that physical fitness is but one element of total fitness, even though it is an exceedingly important one. Mental, emotional, and social fitness affect your physical fitness for better or worse. In turn, all of these factors are improved when you are as physically fit as is possible for you.

Throughout this book, you can discover how to improve your general, or total, fitness — to achieve vitality, endurance, and efficiency in daily living.

What You Have Learned

What kind of health practices should you apply in maintaining your health? Check your understanding of the chapter. On a separate sheet of paper, number 1 through 15 and insert the answer from the vocabulary list below. Use each expression, but use each one only once.

5 ability to move	3 40 to 50 percent	physical fitness movement
1 bones	6 Hippocrates	4 shape
12 energy	14 increases	9 sports
11 exercise	2 joints	7 survive
13 food	8 physical	10 work

Your body is designed for physical activity. The (1) _bones_ are articulated into several types of (2) _joints_ that permit various degrees of movement. Your muscles make up about (3) _40 to 50_ percent of your body weight and give the body (4) _shape_ and (5) _ability to move_. As early as the fourth century B.C., (6) _Hippocrates_ observed: "That which is used develops, and that which is not used wastes away."

Your primitive teen-age ancestors had to use their muscles in order to (7) _survive_. Today, your muscles may grow soft because there is no need to use them. To promote muscular development you should add vigorous (8) _physical_ activities to your daily routine. You can do this by participating in such activities as (9) _sports_, (10) _work_, and (11) _exercise_.

You accomplish your daily tasks through the use of (12) _energy_ which you obtain from the (13) _food_ that you eat. When you are active, your body's need for energy (14) _increases_. The (15) _physical fitness movement_ is designed to help you reach your optimum physical potential.

What You Can Do

1. Suppose you have made a poor score on the pullup test (Figure 1) and you want to improve. Which of the following activities would most likely be of greatest benefit to you? On a separate sheet of paper, number 1 through 14. Next to appropriate numbers, insert A—Good, B—Fair, and C—Poor.

A 1. playing golf	B 8. sawing wood
A 2. jumping rope	C 9. playing in the band
A 3. throwing a ball	A 10. playing volleyball
B 4. rowing a boat	C 11. delivering newspapers
A 5. running the 50-yard dash	A 12. mowing the lawn
B 6. paddling a canoe	A 13. washing the family car
B 7. practicing the broad jump	B 14. playing tennis

2. While sitting quietly, take your pulse and record the count on a piece of paper. Now walk briskly up and down a flight of stairs. Stop and record your pulse rate again. Sit quietly for five minutes. Now run as fast as you safely can up and down the same flight of stairs. Stop and note your pulse rate again. Compare the three pulse rates: are they approximately the same or do they vary? If they differ, what causes the variation? Does your body benefit from a vigorous run? Explain.

3. What type of physical fitness program does your school have? Is there an adult physical fitness program in your community? How could one be organized?

Things to Try

1. The scores made on the physical fitness tests by 10- to 17-year-old girls in 1964—65 were better than those made in 1957—58 in all tests except the softball throw. Why do you think the muscles used for this throw are weak? With regular exercise, both boys and girls can strengthen these muscles:

   a. Stand within a six-foot area at the front of which is a restraining line. Do not cross the line until after the ball has left your hand.

   b. Use a 12-inch softball and throw overhand.

   c. Have a partner put a marker down at the spot where your ball first touches ground.

   d. Measure the distance of your throw on a straight line from the marker where your ball first touched ground to the restraining line. An excellent throw would be:

   Girls 13 years old— 94 feet
   14 100 feet
   Boys 13 years old—175 feet
   14 187 feet

2. The scores made on the physical fitness test by 10- to 17-year-old boys in 1964–65 were better than those made in 1957–58 in all tests. However, the score increase that showed the least improvement was in the fifty-yard dash. What muscles and organs do you think need strengthening for better records in the dash? With practice, both boys and girls can build power for the dash:

   a. Stand behind a starting line, preferably with another runner. It is more challenging to race with another runner.

   b. Have someone start you off by saying: "Are you ready? Go!" As the starter says "Go," he should lower his arm as a signal to the timekeeper.

   c. Exactly fifty yards from the starting line, mark off a finish line.

d. Have someone with a stopwatch stand at the finish line and record the time of your dash in seconds and tenths of seconds.
An excellent time would be:

$$\begin{array}{ll}\text{Boys 13 years old} - & 6.9 \text{ seconds} \\ \qquad\quad 14 & 6.6 \text{ seconds} \\ \text{Girls 13 years old} - & 7.5 \text{ seconds} \\ \qquad\quad 14 & 7.4 \text{ seconds} \end{array}$$

Probing Further

Vim, President's Council on Physical Fitness, Washington, D.C. This booklet, available from the U.S. Government Printing Office, Washington, D.C., 20402, for 25¢, presents a complete exercise plan for girls 12 to 18.

Vigor, President's Council on Physical Fitness, Washington, D.C. This companion booklet to Vim, above, presents a complete exercise plan for boys 12 to 18.

The New Aerobics, by Kenneth H. Cooper, M.D., Bantam Books (paperback); M. Evans and Company (hardcover); New York, 1970. A follow-up of Dr. Cooper's first book, Aerobics, which presents a new concept of physical fitness and showed how systematic exercises such as jogging and walking can be used to achieve fitness.

The Magic of Walking, by Aaron Sussman and Ruth Goode, Simon & Schuster, New York, 1967. An entertaining and useful book which encourages walking as relaxation and healthful sport.

Youth Fitness Test Manual, American Association for Health, Physical Education, and Recreation, Washington, D.C., 1965. This booklet contains the tests and national norms for physical fitness in schools and for the President's Physical Fitness Award Program.

Health Concepts in Action

Would you agree with this statement? Would you change or add to it?

> **Physical fitness—which contributes to total fitness—is maintained by regular physical activity.**

Applying this concept of fitness, which health practices would you

—continue?

—change?

—begin?

Will you now, as a result of your study, change any of your health objectives?

7 / *Your Body Framework*

"But doctor," Bill remarked, "you said I only broke one bone in my ankle. Why does this cast go all the way up to my knee?"

As you will see, the bones of your ankle must mesh properly with the bones of your lower leg where they meet, and therefore the leg bones must also be supported. When almost any bone in your body is broken, you are likely to suffer inconvenience and discomfort until it mends, since even the smallest bone is an important part of your body framework.

A PROBE INTO THE SKELETAL SYSTEM—How can you maintain a healthy body framework? To find out, you will be probing these questions:

1. What are the main functions of bones?

2. How are bones connected? What protects them from grating against each other? Which joints allow the most movement?

3. How do bones grow and repair themselves? Why is a compound fracture more serious than a simple one?

4. How is the spine held erect? What is the function of the cartilage discs in the spine?

5. Why is good posture important? How can you maintain good posture while standing? while sitting?

6. What should you consider when selecting shoes?

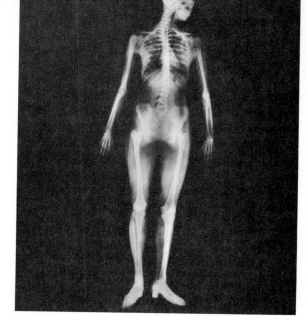

7-1 An X-ray photograph of the human skeleton. The skeleton gives shape and support to your body and protects your vital organs.

THE SKELETAL SYSTEM

You often become aware of your skeletal system when you or someone you know has an accident in which a bone is damaged. There are different kinds of *orthopedic* (or-thuh-PE-dik), or bone, disorders. Some orthopedic disorders may be the result of injury; others of disease or undue stress. Whatever their cause, orthopedic disorders affect the body framework and perhaps the body's shape, and may interfere with the functioning of organs.

Parts of Your Skeleton

Your bones, joined together by ligaments (bands of tough connective tissue), form the inside framework or architecture of your body. Bones are of many shapes and sizes, each adapted to specialized work. When the main job is protection, bones are curved to form a cage or basket, like the *pelvis* and *ribs*. When support is the main function, the bones are heavy like the *femur* (upper leg bone). When dexterity and skill are required, the bones are short and small as in the fingers, or *phalanges* (fa-LAN-jeez). When the bone

is to act as a lever when moved, it is long like the *humerus* (upper arm). When flexibility is needed in a group of bones, the separate bones in the group are short like those of the *wrist* and *ankle*.

The place where two bones come together is called an articulation, or *joint*. The joints are of various types, each adapted to its work. You will learn more about types of joints later on. Without joints, your body framework would be fixed or immobile, much like the framework of a house. Through the action of your muscles and the movement of your joints, your body is constantly shifting its position. This calls for constant adjustment and is one of the problems to be mastered in your effort to maintain good posture.

Functions of the Skeletal System

Your bones perform many functions without which you could not live. The main mechanical functions are

1. To provide rigid support for the body weight against the pull of gravity and to make possible an upright posture.
2. To protect soft tissues and vital organs.

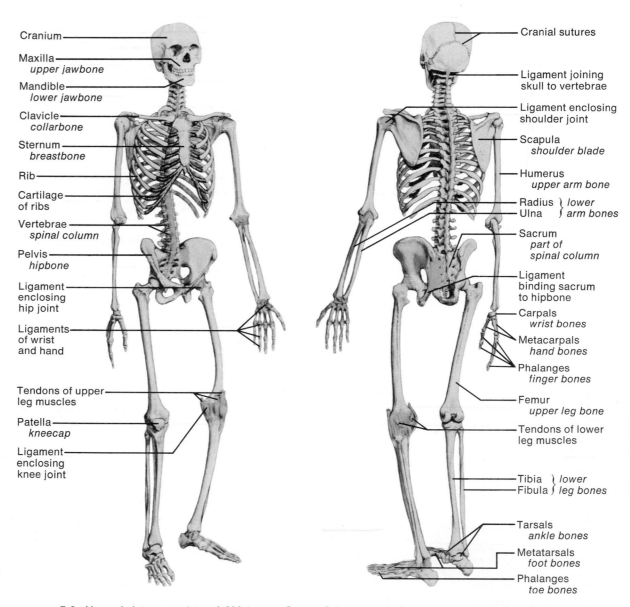

Cranium

Maxilla
upper jawbone

Mandible
lower jawbone

Clavicle
collarbone

Sternum
breastbone

Rib

Cartilage
of ribs

Vertebrae
spinal column

Pelvis
hipbone

Ligament
enclosing
hip joint

Ligaments
of wrist
and hand

Tendons of upper
leg muscles

Patella
kneecap

Ligament
enclosing
knee joint

Cranial sutures

Ligament joining
skull to vertebrae

Ligament enclosing
shoulder joint

Scapula
shoulder blade

Humerus
upper arm bone

Radius } *lower*
Ulna } *arm bones*

Sacrum
*part of
spinal column*

Ligament
binding sacrum
to hipbone

Carpals
wrist bones

Metacarpals
hand bones

Phalanges
finger bones

Femur
upper leg bone

Tendons of lower
leg muscles

Tibia } *lower*
Fibula } *leg bones*

Tarsals
ankle bones

Metatarsals
foot bones

Phalanges
toe bones

7-2 Your skeleton consists of 206 bones. Some of these bones have grown together, as in your cranium and in the lower part of your spinal column. Most of your bones, however, remain separate, yet are connected by some means. Your ribs and most of your vertebrae are connected by tough, stiff cartilage, which greatly restricts movement. Other bones are jointed and held together by tough but flexible ligaments, which do not restrict freedom of movement.

The skull protects your brain; the spinal column (backbone) encloses the delicate spinal cord. Ribs, sternum (breast bone), and spinal column shield your heart and lungs. The spinal column and pelvis protect the abdominal organs.

3. To serve as points of support and leverage for lifting and bending. Tendons (tough, cordlike tissue) supply the attachment between most of the muscles and the bones.

■ Lift your arm from the elbow as shown in Figure 7-3. Notice how far your hand goes through the air. Do this again while you clasp the muscle at the front of the upper arm with your other hand. Note how small the movement of the muscle itself is. Your muscles pull your bones, which then make the bigger movements.

7-3 Which muscle contracts as this boy bends his arm? Try this yourself. How much does the muscle move?

Other Functions of the Bones

In addition to these mechanical functions, your bones are storehouses for minerals, especially calcium and phosphorus, and they are the manufacturing system for red blood cells and some white blood cells. All bones do not serve all of these purposes, but all do store minerals and serve as attachments for muscles.

Your 206 Bones

Your skeleton is made up of 206 bones and it is divided into the *head,* the *trunk,* two *arms,* and two *legs.* Your skull is made up of the *cranium* (KRAY-nee-um) and the skeleton of the face. The eight bones of the cranium enclose the brain, and fourteen other bones form the skeleton of your face. If you examine a skull, you can see wavy lines, or

7-4 Football can be a rugged sport. Can you see why thorough conditioning is essential to minimize the chances of being hurt?

sutures (SOO-chers), where the bones are joined. The skull bones of an infant have spaces between them filled with a fairly soft material. These spaces gradually fill up with bone, until at 18 months all the bones have joined to make the entire skull firm.

The *spinal column*, or *backbone*, is the central support for the whole body. The backbone of a grown person has thirty-three bones (Figure 7-5), each of which is called a *vertebra* (VER-tuh-bruh). The first seven *vertebrae* (VER-tuh-bree) form the neck. To each of the next twelve, a pair of ribs is attached. The following five vertebrae, which form the "small of the back," have no attached bones; they are called the *lumbar* (LUM-ber) vertebrae. *Lumbago* (lum-BAY-goh), an old name for lower-back pain, comes from *lumbar*. Just below the five lumbar vertebrae are five bones fused into one and

flattened out. They form the *sacrum* (SAY-krum), to which the hipbones are attached. Last comes the *coccyx* (KOK-siks), four bones fused into one.

Each vertebra is a bone with a hole in its center. The holes fit over each other to form a long hollow, the *spinal canal,* which runs lengthwise in the backbone. The *spinal cord,* composed of millions of nerve cells that are continuous with the brain, rests inside the spinal canal (Figures 7-2 and 7-5).

Your backbone has to take shocks and be flexible, as well as have great strength. Your shock absorbers are pads, or discs, of cartilage between the vertebrae (Figures 7-5 and 7-7).

A column of bones would topple over unless there was something to bind it together. Your backbone is held in place by strong

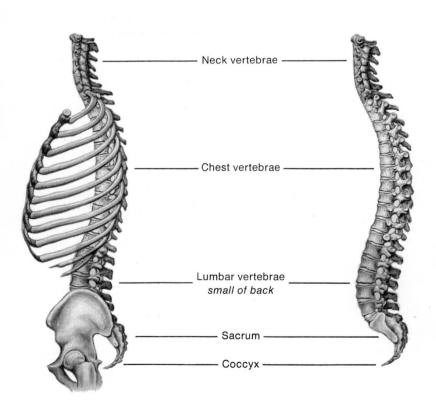

Neck vertebrae

Chest vertebrae

Lumbar vertebrae
small of back

Sacrum

Coccyx

7-6 One vertebra. Where would the spinal cord be in relation to this vertebra?

7-5 Your spinal column, or backbone, consists of thirty-three vertebrae. Have you ever seen an X-ray photograph of your spinal column?

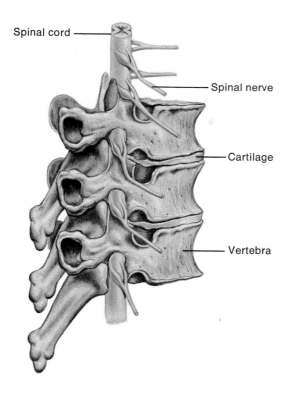

Spinal cord

Spinal nerve

Cartilage

Vertebra

7-7 Three vertebrae from the backbone. How do the vertebrae protect the spinal cord? Why is the cartilage between the vertebrae important?

ligaments and muscles. When your muscles on both sides pull with the same force, the bones are held in line so that you don't bend to either side. When you do bend to one side, you contract, or shorten, the muscles on that side and relax them on the other. The motion of your backbone is limited by the cartilage discs and by the tough bands of ligament. It is limited further by your ribs and by bony outgrowths from the back of each vertebra.

■ Run your hand along the back of your spine. Do you feel the bumps? These are the ends of the bony outgrowths from the back of the vertebrae. If you lean back too

far, these outgrowths meet and stop your movement.

If you view it from the side, the spinal column shows four curves (Figure 7-5). These balance with each other without strain on the muscles, since they curve alternately. Try to locate these curves in your own spine.

Your chest is formed by your twelve pairs of ribs, the spinal column, and the breastbone (Figure 7-5). The front end of each rib is made of cartilage. The first seven pairs of ribs, called *true ribs,* are attached in front to the breastbone. The other five pairs are called *false ribs,* because three of them are connected only to the cartilage of the rib above, while the lowest two pairs, the *floating ribs,* are not attached in front at all. Your ribs are moved by means of muscles attached to the vertebrae. There are also muscles and ligaments stretched directly between ribs.

Your arms are suspended from the *shoulder girdle.* This is made up of the two collarbones and the two shoulder blades (Figure 7-2). The word girdle is used because these bones form a sort of ring around the body. Since the upper arm has but one bone and the forearm two, you can twist your forearm and wrist while you hold your upper arm steady. Try it.

Your wrist and hand have twenty-seven bones. In the wrist, there are eight small bones (*carpals*) that articulate with each other and with the bones of the forearm and hand. The five bones of the hand (*metacarpals*) articulate with the wristbones and the finger bones (phalanges). There are fourteen finger bones, three in each finger and two in each thumb.

The legs are fastened to the trunk by the *pelvis* (PEL-viss), or hip girdle, composed of the two hipbones and the sacrum (Figure 7-5). The leg bones correspond to those of the arms, except that the ankle has one bone less than the wrist, and the knee is protected by the *patella* (puh-TEL-luh), or kneecap.

The ankle and foot have twenty-six bones. The seven anklebones (*tarsals*) articulate with each other and with the foreleg and foot bones. The heel bone (*calcaneus*) is the largest of the tarsals, and the next in size is the *talus.* The talus transfers weight to the heel bone and other tarsals. The five foot bones (*metatarsals*) articulate with the anklebone and the toe bones (phalanges). Each toe has three bones except the big toe, which has two bones.

How Your Bones Are Joined Together

The joints are the places where bones are joined. You have many types of joints—too many to mention in this book. According to the amount of motion they permit, we call them (1) *immovable*, (2) *slightly movable*, and (3) *freely movable.*

In the immovable joints, the bones are locked tightly. The sutures of the skull are immovable joints that were formed in infancy when the skull bones grew together.

You have many slightly movable joints. Examples are those between the vertebrae (Figure 7-8) and those between the sacrum and the hipbones. In these joints, the bones are separated by means of broad, flat discs of tough cartilage that can be squeezed and stretched a little. Slightly movable joints permit limited bending and twisting.

Most of your joints are freely movable *joints,* which allow considerable movement, as in the elbow, knee, shoulder, and wrist.

Where the ends of the bones come together, they are enlarged into heads, which give them a larger surface to strengthen the joints. Each head is covered with smooth, tough cartilage; this covering helps the bones to glide on each other. It also takes up some of the shock when the bones of the joint are pressed together.

In addition to being padded by cartilage, the bones of a joint are held together by strong ligaments attached to the outside of

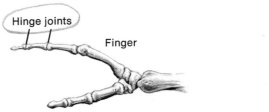

Gliding joints

Wrist

Immovable joint

Skull

1st vertebra

2nd vertebra

Pivot joint

Hinge joints

Finger

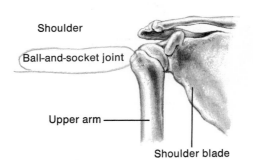

Shoulder

Ball-and-socket joint

Upper arm

Shoulder blade

7-8 What is the function of each of these joints? Are you able to swing your arm all the way around at the shoulder in a true circle?

the bones above and below the joint. One of these ligaments (the *capsule*) surrounds the whole joint in a closed, airtight sac. This sac is lined with a thin membrane and filled with fluid that looks like the white of an egg. The fluid "oils" the joint.

Think of the great variety of motions the different parts of your body can make. This variety is made possible by your many freely movable joints, not all of which are alike. Four of the most important kinds of freely movable joints, shown in Figure 7-8, are

1. *Gliding joints*, as in your wrist. These have nearly flat surfaces that glide over each other.
2. *Pivot joints*, as in your neck. These allow rotating movements, such as turning your head (made possible by the joint between the first and second vertebrae).
3. *Hinge joints*, as in your fingers, elbows, and knees. These work only one way, like most doors.
4. *Ball-and-socket joints*, as in the shoulder and hip joints. These have a ball that rotates in a socket. Watch a baseball pitcher "winding up" to see the great freedom of movement this kind of joint gives. See Figure 7-9.

BONES GROW
AND MEND THEMSELVES

Your bones are alive, as you will discover if you fracture one. It must be alive because it will mend. (If you ever do suffer a broken bone, get a doctor to set it for you immediately. Otherwise it may mend improperly and cause many problems.) You have additional proof that your bones are alive—they grow! Have you ever noticed how pink a fresh meat bone is? It is pink because of its blood supply, which feeds the living cells in it. How bones can be so hard and still be alive is surprising, but the process by which bones develop is even more surprising.

7-9 What joints does pitcher Vida Blue make the most use of?

The Composition of Bones

Hard as a bone is, one third of it is made of living *organic* (or-GAN-ik) *matter*. The other two thirds is nonliving, or *mineral matter*. The organic matter includes many cells—bone cells, cartilage cells, nerve cells, fat cells, and others. Inside many bones, in the *marrow*, are the cells which make your red blood cells and many of your white blood cells. A bone is a busy place; blood vessels and nerves run everywhere in it, except in the very hardest part of the mineral matter.

7-10 A cross section of bone as seen under a microscope. What is the function of the many canals formed in bone? *Carry blood vessels and nerves through bone*

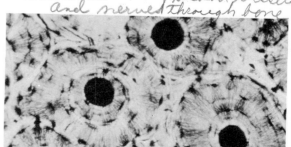

■ You can separate the organic matter from the mineral matter in a bone. Soak a bone in strong vinegar for several days. The mineral matter will dissolve. What you have left will bend like rubber. It will have the shape of the original bone, but it will be tough and flexible instead of hard. You can tie it in a knot. The organic matter in the bone makes it tough and hard to break. See Figure 7-11.

■ Take another bone and heat it for some time in an oven. This will remove the organic matter. What you have left is the mineral matter, which will also have the shape of the original bone but will be very light in color. Notice how little it weighs. Crush it with your fingers—it will fall to pieces. The mineral part of the bone makes it hard and brittle.

If older people romped about and took the falls that children do, they would have a great many broken bones. Children have more living matter in their bones than older people do. Thus, their bones have a certain amount of "bounce," which makes the bones less likely to break. Even a broken bone is a less serious thing in a young person, be-cause it still has strong powers of growth and repair.

A bone always has a covering. The tough *periosteum* (pehr-EE-os-tee-um) covers all of the bone except for the ends. It is richly sup-plied with blood vessels which branch into the bone at various openings. The peri-osteum is vital in producing bone cells and in nourishing the bone. At joints where one bone moves on another, the covering is carti-lage.

Two Kinds of Cartilage

The amount of cartilage in a bone depends on the age of the bone. Infants have a great amount of *temporary cartilage* in their bones. This makes their bones elastic and pliable. As the bones grow older, cartilage cells are replaced by bone cells and minerals that make bones capable of bearing greater weight, but they become less elastic and pli-able. Figure 7-12 compares an infant's wrist before the cartilage has been replaced with the wrist of an adult.

But in some parts of the body, the cartilage becomes permanent and is retained through-

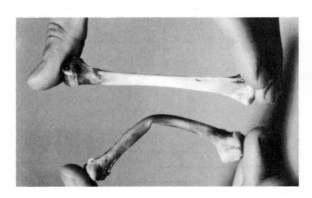

7-11 Why is this bone so flexible after being soaked in strong vinegar?

7-12 (*Top*) An X-ray photograph of a child's wrist. (*Bottom*) The wrist of an adult. Why is it advanta-geous for infants and young children to have so much cartilage in place of bone?

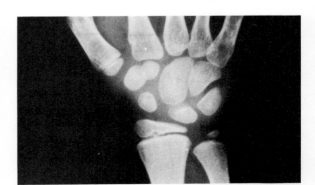

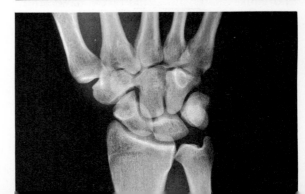

out life. Such permanent cartilage is found in the lobe of the external ear, the tip of the nose, the rings of the trachea, and the discs between the vertabrae of the spinal column.

How Do Bones Live and Grow?

A marvelous arrangement of cells, blood vessels, and nerves is located in the bone framework. If you have a large, dried bone available, look at it closely. You may be able to see some of the largest of the tiny holes through which blood vessels once entered it. Now look at Figure 7-10. The large, dark spots you see are some of the many canals that carry blood vessels and nerves through the bone. The other dark spots arranged in circles around the canals are the hollows where the bone cells live, each by itself. These cells are fed by lymph, which carries food supplies from the bloodstream. The lymph seeps out of the bone canals and finds its way to the cells through tiny holes in the bone.

Your bones may grow until you reach the age of 20 to 25 years. Your tiny bone cells take phosphorus, calcium, and other materials from your blood to make bone.

As mentioned previously, a large part of the bone-to-be in babies is cartilage or membrane. At certain points, the periosteum sends two types of cells into the cartilage: (1) cells that destroy the cartilage and (2) bone-building cells to make hard bone.

Growth begins at both ends of each bone and works toward the center; it also works from the center toward the ends. While the bone is growing longer, it is also increasing in diameter, but when the two kinds of cells meet, the bone is completely *ossified* (OSS-ih-fyde) and unable to grow more in length. (The word *ossify* means to change into hardened bone.) Many living bone cells are caught in the construction work and left scattered throughout the bone. These remain where they are for upkeep and repair work.

Fracture—a Break in the Bone

A fracture is a break in the bone; it may be partial or complete. Partial fractures are more common in children whose bones are still pliable. In children, the bone can bend enough to break some of the fibers without breaking the whole bone. This is called a **greenstick** fracture. This exercise will show you how such a fracture happens:

■ Take two twigs, one green and juicy, the other hard and dry. Bend them both sharply. You will see how the greenstick fracture got its name.

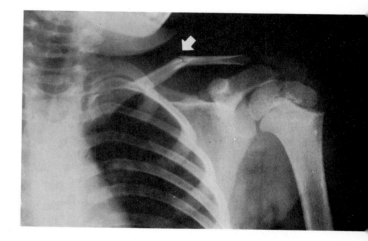

7-13 Three types of fractures: (*top*) greenstick; (*left*) simple; (*right*) compound. How do they differ?

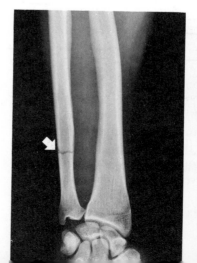
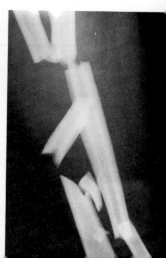

There are two kinds of **complete** fractures, **simple** and **compound.** A *simple* fracture is one that has no open wound (Figure 7-13). In a *compound* fracture, there is an open wound extending through the skin to the fracture area (Figure 7-13). In a compound fracture, the broken end of the bone may have penetrated through the skin, or if the fracture was caused by a bullet or sharp instrument, there would also be an open wound. A compound fracture is more serious than a simple fracture since the area has become contaminated, and infection is likely to set in. All fractures call for immediate medical attention.

How Fractures Heal

When a bone is broken, blood plasma and white cells pour into the gaps between the broken parts. A sticky deposit called **callus** (KAL-us) forms from the blood. It helps to hold the broken bone together. Living bone cells and the cells of the periosteum start to grow and divide to form other cells like themselves. These cells make bone that takes the place of the callus. What happens in repair is much like the growth of bone when it is first formed in the infant. The new bone slowly becomes as hard as the rest of the bone.

Conditions Bones Need to Grow and Repair

The special needs of growing bones include:

1. *Plenty of calcium, phosphorus, and vitamin D*—for bone cells to use in building bone.
2. *Exercise*—to keep blood and lymph circulating through all the canals and tiny openings in the bone, and to put enough stress on the bones to stimulate their healthy growth.
3. *Plenty of rest*—to allow cartilage to expand and to relax muscles, thus releasing their pull on the bones.

Some Causes of Orthopedic Problems

Improperly formed bones may result from such diseases as **osteomyelitis** and **tuberculosis** of the bone. Osteomyelitis includes various bone infections. Malformed bones may also result from nutritional deficiencies that cause *rickets*. Some bone disorders arise from hereditary factors.

In recent years, the incidence of malformed bones has declined, largely because of advances in nutrition research and medical treatment. But the incidence of disabling orthopedic conditions caused by cerebral palsy, muscular dystrophy, and childhood accidents has not declined.

Damage to bones can result from purely mechanical factors, as when constant muscle strain pulls a bone out of normal position. If this strain continues over a long period, the bone tends to grow out of proper alignment. The cartilage discs between the bones then grow thicker on one side than on the other, causing the bone to slant. Certain occupations, such as mining, contribute to this kind of problem.

Although poor posture can also be a factor in causing poorly aligned bones, its real disadvantage is that it is a social handicap. A person who hunches or has a pronounced swayback is not likely to make a good first impression. Someone with an upright, well-balanced posture, on the other hand, looks as though he is brimming with life and would be fun to know. Next time you are at a party or other gathering, see how much you judge strangers by their posture. You might be surprised at how important posture is in first impressions.

It is easy to fall into habits of poor posture. A very tall boy or girl, for example, whose best friend is short is likely to assume a rather stooped posture. Also, youths who feel they are too tall will purposely walk stooped

A   B   C   D

7-14 A guide to posture. (A) *Good.* Straight line from ear through shoulder, hip, and instep; chest high, abdomen flat; back curves normal; weight over arches of feet. (B) *Fair.* Head slightly forward; chest flat; shoulders slightly drooping; abdomen prominent; hollow back. (C) *Poor.* Head forward; chest flat; shoulders drooping; abdomen sagging; extreme hollow back. (D) *Very poor.* Head drooping; chest flat; shoulders rounded; abdomen sagging; extreme hollow back; weight on heels.

A   B   C   D

7-15 How would you rate on this posture test? (A) *Good.* Head, trunk, and thigh in straight line; chest high and forward; abdomen flat; back curves normal. (B) *Fair.* Head forward; abdomen prominent; exaggerated curve in upper back; slight hollow in back. (C) *Poor.* Head forward, abdomen sagging; shoulder blades prominent; hollow back. (D) *Very poor.* Head forward; very exaggerated curve in upper back and neck; abdomen sagging and protruding; chest flat and sloping; extreme hollow back.

to give the impression of being shorter. Later on, youths usually discover that being tall can be an attractive trait. Other common habits that contribute to poor posture are sitting on one foot, standing continually with your weight on one leg, or always carrying books or heavy loads under the same arm. Any of these habits, and similar ones, should be avoided, especially during the years that the bones are still growing and taking shape.

YOU CAN DEVELOP GOOD POSTURE

Practically every one has been told at some time or other to "straighten up" or to "hold his shoulders up." Actually, correct posture means something other than the ramrod stiffness implied in such commands. Today we think of posture as the easy, graceful use of your body in maintaining balance. Your posture changes from moment to moment as you bend, lift objects, walk, play, or work. These changes are reactions of your muscles to a physical force from outside the body, the force of gravity. Like all other objects on earth, your body is subject to a pull toward the center of the earth, the pull of gravity. You learn to adjust to this pull and force by contracting your muscles.

What Good Posture Does for You

1. *Gives you a feeling of physical well-being.* When posture is correct, there is less strain on the muscles and you can play or work longer and harder. Exercise strengthens muscles and gives them practice in moving the bones with speed and ease. With strong muscles to hold bones and internal organs in proper relationship, there comes a sense of physical well-being.

   A variety of exercise is needed to make certain that your muscles are developing evenly. When one part of your body is exercised much more than other parts, muscles develop unevenly. The baseball pitcher's pitching arm is likely to be somewhat larger than his other arm. But the basketball player is likely to have more evenly developed arms.

2. *Enhances your general appearance.* Posture expresses personality, attitude, poise, and alertness. This is important at any time, but especially when you are applying for a job or when you want to make a good impression. Often you are judged by your appearance long before you have a chance to speak or take part in a group, hence your posture may become a social asset. Good body balance and control lends grace and rhythm to movement, and well-co-ordinated movements give you a sense of confidence. Moreover, the shape of the neck, shoulders, and the rest of the body is at its best when good posture is maintained.

Your Posture and Your Feelings

You may not realize it, but your body responds to your emotions. You have seen actors use certain postures to express some strong emotion such as courage, love, fear, sorrow, or joy. As you watch the actors, you sense what they feel, even before they speak. Your posture can give away your own feelings. It is not easy to stand or move gracefully when suffering from worries, hurt feelings, shyness, or boredom.

Things to Consider

1. One of the chief signs of fatigue may be a slouched posture, due to loss of muscle tone. You have experienced loss of muscle tone after playing a vigorous game or after a long run or swim. This is temporary posture fatigue. A good meal and a night's rest are all that you need to remedy it.

7-16 Look at the way you are sitting. Which picture do you resemble? What can you do to improve your posture?

Another type of fatigue, more difficult to remedy, comes from muscle strain. Whenever the weight-bearing bony framework (skeleton) is out of alignment, the muscles are put under strain to maintain body balance. This causes muscular fatigue that may lead to ungainly, slumped posture. Have you ever suffered from muscle strain?

2. *Nutrition.* Eating the right foods that nourish your bones and muscles is important to good posture. When your diet is lacking in any one of the essential nutrients (Chapter 4), the body suffers and becomes weak. A deficient diet may eventually lead to malnutrition and structural defects of the bones.

3. *Skeletal growth.* Your bones may have grown quite long suddenly, and you may be faced with a posture problem that calls for adjustment to your new size. You may feel self-conscious about your height, particularly if your friends have not caught up with you, and find yourself stooping, without realizing it, to hide your new size. Have you ever done this?

How to Stand Erect—Easily

1. Hold your head so that your chin is at right angles with the column of your neck and the crown of your head is directly above your spine.

2. Raise your chest so that the tip of the breastbone (sternum) is the bone farthest out in front of you. This helps the shoulder blades (scapulae) lie flat. Your arms hang relaxed in their sockets.

3. The position of your hip girdle (pelvis) is very important in good posture. When you raise your chest, the abdominal muscles flatten which helps keep them firm. As you purposely tighten the abdominal muscles, the pelvis rotates and straightens the spine at the small of the back.

Your Body Framework / **123**

7-17 This is one way to "improve" your posture. What are some better and safer ways?

4. Stand with your feet parallel, about two inches apart, neither toeing in nor toeing out. Your body weight should fall mostly on the balls of your feet and toward the outside border. Your knees should be "easy," not stiff but slightly flexed. When you are in good balance, you should be able to raise your heels from the floor without changing the alignment of your posture.

■ Stand beside a pole or the edge of an open door, as shown in Figure 7-18. Place your body in proper alignment as described above and as shown in Figure 7-14 and Figure 7-15. Now raise your heels slightly from the floor. Your body should not sway either forward or backward from the straight line of the door or pole. Practice this until it becomes an easy straight up and down movement.

How to Practice Good Posture While Sitting

Your body position from your hips to the crown of your head remains the same when sitting as when standing. Sit well back touching the back of the chair, your body weight supported by your hips and thighs. Rest your feet comfortably on the floor.

Sitting tall and relaxed, with your weight supported by hips and thighs, makes possible long periods of sitting without fatigue. It may be hard for you to believe that this position is more comfortable and less tiring, if you have formed the habit of resting your weight on your shoulders and the end of your spine. Such a position forms a little bridge of your back, puts strain on muscles, and compresses your chest and abdomen.

When you sit at a desk or table, the chair you use is important. The seat should slope slightly backward to prevent any forward-sliding tendency, and your feet should rest comfortably on the floor. The lower part of your back should be supported by the chair back. The height of the desk or table can also add to your comfort. It should be high enough to rest your forearms on the top surface, at right angles to your upper arm.

Try This for Fun

When you ride on a bus or subway or sit in a waiting room, look at the different ways people are sitting. You will find this amusing

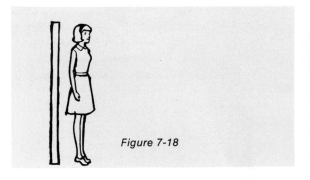

Figure 7-18

and perhaps a bit of a shock. Which of these postures do you admire? Which would you like to imitate?

YOUR FEET

Nature has fortunately provided you with pairs of things such as eyes, ears, arms, and feet. When a foreign object gets into your eye, you can close it and still see out of the other eye. So it is with your arms. An injury to one arm that results in its being put into a sling still leaves your other arm free; but it is not so with your feet. You need both feet to support and carry your body weight properly. You already know this if you have had an injured foot that required a cast. Your body balance was difficult to hold; you had to use a cane or crutch to take the place of the injured foot.

Your Foot Arches

Your foot is designed for weight-bearing and for absorbing the shocks that come with walking, running, and jumping. There are muscles that control the movements of your foot; short ones within the foot, long ones in the leg. The leg muscles are attached to your foot by tendons. Ligaments and tendons hold the bones in position to form two main arches — *longitudinal* and *transverse.*

The *longitudinal* (long) arch extends from the heel to your great toe, along the inside of the foot. The *transverse* (short) arch crosses the ball of the foot from the great toe to the little toe. Although the arches are very strong and good shock absorbers, they can be injured. For this reason, when you jump down from a height it is safer to land with your knees bent, so that the powerful leg muscles can help absorb part of the shock.

Your Feet Can Become Troublesome

There are many reasons why feet become weak and painful. Some reasons are poor general health, incorrect body posture, or improper use of the feet. However, the most common cause seems to be found in poorly fitted shoes and hose. *Corns, calluses,* and *bunions* are a few problems that result from wearing the wrong size and shape of shoes.

7-19 A normal footprint. What do footprints tell you about your feet? Be sure to try the exercise on page 126.

7-20 Your foot bones form two arches. Would an X-ray photograph of your foot look like this? How might it differ?

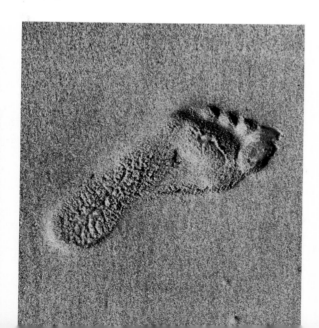

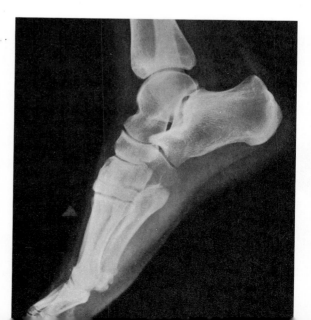

You seldom think of hose as being an offender, but hose that are too short or narrow can hold the foot in an unnatural, often painful, position. This is particularly true with the use of nylon hose, since nylon does not stretch very much.

Various foot problems are also caused by wearing high heels. High heels are fine for dress occasions when you will not be standing long hours or walking long distances. When high heels are worn all of the time or for long periods of time when you are active, the fatigued muscles give way and posture defects appear. The head juts forward; the abdomen protrudes causing the lower back to hollow, and the hips project unnaturally and prominently to the rear (Figures 7-14 and 7-15). This is the body's natural reaction in its effort to hold you upright and maintain body balance.

You have heard of *flat feet* and *fallen arches.* These occur when the ligaments and muscles that hold the arch in place become stretched. Flat feet (without visible arches) are not necessarily either weak or painful. Some people are born without arches and have naturally flat feet. But fallen arches may

7-21 What kinds of shoes do you wear? Fit and comfort as well as style should always be considered when buying shoes.

be painful and sometimes result in flat feet. Toeing out when you walk is a common cause of fallen arches. This position stretches the ligaments and muscles and allows the bones to slide out of their correct place in the arch. Your ankles tend to turn inward. This causes the line of weight-bearing to be off center, producing weak, awkward feet.

If your feet are normal, you do not need any arch support. However, if you have let your arches fall or weaken, you may need to wear shoes with arch support whenever you are on your feet for long periods of time.

■ Try this exercise as a test of your arches. Remove your shoes and hose, wet the soles of your feet, then stand on a sheet of paper. Step off the paper and you will see the imprint of your feet. While your footprint is still wet, trace the outline of each foot with a pencil. Now compare your footprint with the one shown in Figure 7-19.

Corns are hard, thickened areas of the outer layers of the skin. They usually develop on the toes due to pressure from shoes that are too tight. Pain is caused when the core of the corn presses the tender tissue beneath. A *callus* is similar to a corn, but it usually spreads over a larger surface. Calluses develop due to rubbing or irritation of the outer layers of skin. This is nature's way of protecting an irritated area, by building up layers of dead tissue.

A *bunion* is more serious since it involves bone at a joint. Bunions may be caused by wearing shoes that are too short or of a shape that hampers the normal line of your toes. Very pointed shoes that are too short are the great offenders, as they press the toes together into an unnatural position. The big toe is pressed inward at the tip and outward where it joins the foot bones. This pressure causes inflammation of the joint, and a bony enlargement called a bunion is formed. In its early stages of growth, a bunion can be stopped by wearing correct shoes. In later stages, after the bunion has formed, surgery for its removal and straightening of the toes may be needed.

How to Select Your Shoes

In choosing shoes, first consider your own particular shape of foot. Then find the last that best suits your foot. A last is a wooden form, carved as a replica of a normal foot, upon which the shoe is built. Lasts are built to suit several types of feet. You can determine your foot type by drawing a straight line from the center of your heel to the middle toe. If this line divides your foot fairly evenly, you have a "straight" foot. If more of your foot is toward the outside of the line it is called an "outflare"; if more is toward the inside of the line it is called an "inflare." (These terms are used in the shoe trade.)

Your shoes should fit snugly under the arch and at the heel. The ball of your foot should fall directly over the widest part of the shoe sole. Your shoes should be long and wide enough to allow plenty of room for your toes to spread normally. It is well to allow at least one-half inch of space between your longest toe and the tip of the shoe. Wiggle your toes to test the length and width. Do this while sitting, standing, and walking around. Try on both shoes; your feet are seldom exactly the same size. What is the best time of day to try on shoes? Why?

How to Walk Gracefully

The way you use your feet as you walk, stand, sit, run, and go up and down stairs controls your carriage and gait. You will agree that graceful carriage lends distinction to anyone and is a valuable social asset as well as a physical one. Walking is a natural movement that you have been doing since you were a year or so old. As you grew taller you had to adjust to longer legs, arms, feet,

and bodies. As a result, you may have developed an awkward carriage, round shoulders, and a drooping head. If this happened to you, it is now important for you to practice walking to regain graceful, easy movement. While you practice, remember the functional posture points mentioned.

As you walk, each step you take originates from the hips, not from the knees or ankles. Your feet are pointed straight ahead. It is as though you were walking along a straight line, the right foot falling to the right of the line, the left foot falling to the left of the line. Your arms should swing freely from the shoulders in easy rhythm with your stride. In stepping forward, the heel and the ball of the foot strike the ground at nearly the same time, the heel touching first. Now push off from the ball and toes of your other foot, not from the heel. This strengthens your arches and gives a buoyant spring to your step.

It's Up to You

Who can have good posture? Everyone can strive to find the posture that puts his body into best alignment and reduces daily fatigue. You have learned the guidelines for the correct alignment of your body framework. In applying these guidelines, it is well to remember that good posture can be mastered with just a little effort.

Posture is a habit. When you assume good skeletal alignment and practice it week in and week out, you get the feel of that position. Your muscles and the nerves that stimulate them get used to that position, and it becomes a habit. It becomes you. And as you go about your daily tasks and find that there are some habits that you will want to correct, it may comfort you to know this wise old saying: "Habit is habit, and not to be flung out of the window by any man, but coaxed downstairs a step at a time." (Mark Twain [Samuel Langhorne Clemens], *Pudd'nhead Wilson's Calendar*, Ch. 6.)

What You Have Learned

What kind of health practices should you apply in maintaining your health? Check your understanding of the chapter. On a separate sheet of paper, number 1 through 20 and insert the answer from the vocabulary list below. Use each expression, but use each one only once.

7 abdominal organs	6 heart and lungs	8 periosteum
12 badly aligned	1 ligaments	3 red blood cells
14 balance	17 longitudinal	15 rhythm
20 bunion	9 marrow	19 shoes
4 brain	2 minerals	5 spinal cord
16 confidence	13 muscle	18 transverse
11 fracture	10 ossified	

   Your bones, held together by (1)_____, form the framework of the body. In addition, the bones are storehouses for (2)_____, and they are the manufacturing system for (3)_____. Your bones protect the soft tissues and vital organs. The skull protects the (4)_____, the spinal column encloses the (5)_____, the ribs, sternum, and spinal column shield the (6)_____, and the pelvis and spinal column protect the (7)_____.

   The tough (8)_____ covers all of the bones except for the ends. Inside the bone, in the (9)_____ are cells which make your red blood cells and many of your white blood cells. When a bone is completely (10)_____, it is unable to grow any longer. A (11)_____ is a break in a bone.

   Poor habits of posture, especially during your growing years, can cause (12)_____ bones. Such a condition is caused by constant irregular (13)_____ strain that pulls a bone out of position. We think of posture as the easy, graceful use of the body in maintaining (14)_____. Body control gives grace and (15)_____ to movement and provides a sense of (16)_____.

   When in an upright position, your body weight rests on your feet, which are supported by the (17)_____ and (18)_____ arches. The most common cause of foot trouble is poorly fitted (19)_____. Shoes that are too short may cause a joint defect called a (20)_____.

What You Can Do

1. On a skeleton or a large picture of a skeleton, locate the bones you use when you write, step on a bus, sit down, and kick a ball.

2. Get a fresh joint that is not too closely trimmed from the meat market. Locate the ligaments that cover the joint. Find the tendons that bind the muscles to the bones. Compare the texture of the muscles with those of the tendons and ligaments. Cut away the ligaments and look at the ends of the bones. Can you find the layer of cartilage?

3. Locate and name the types of joints you would use in the following activities: making a fist, swinging your leg from the hip, bending your trunk sideward, and rotating your ankle.

Things to Try

1. Mark a six-foot line, two inches wide, on the floor or ground. Stand on the line with one foot in front of the other, both feet on the line. As a test of your balance, see if you can walk the line without raising your arms. Now close your eyes and walk again. Repeat the walk, eyes open and eyes closed, until you can walk the line without raising your arms to help your balance.

2. Keep a check for an entire day of the number of times you catch yourself standing with your weight on one foot, and sitting with your weight resting on your shoulders and on the end of your spine.

Probing Further

Essentials of Healthier Living, by J. J. Schifferes, Wiley, 1972. Chapter 9 of this text emphasizes the modern functional approach to good posture.

The Armor Within Us: The Story of Bone, by Joseph Samachson, Rand Mc-Nally, 1966. The often overlooked properties of bone as a living, growing tissue are given greatest emphasis in this entertaining, introductory book.

Health, by Oliver E. Byrd, Saunders, 1966. The vital physiological need for exercise in modern living is stressed in Chapter 6 of this text.

Health Concepts in Action

Does what you have learned support this statement?

> ***Fitness depends upon maintaining the health of the skeletal system.***

Applying this concept, which health practices would you

- —continue?
- —change?
- —begin?

Will you now, as a result of your study, change any of your health objectives?

8 / Your Body in Action

Sally telephoned her friend Jane to tell her the skiing party had been called off because of a heavy snowstorm. "But what can we do all day?" Jane moaned. "I get so restless just sitting around." "Well, why doesn't everyone come over here and we'll dance to records?" Sally suggested.

Vigorous, healthy teen-agers who are accustomed to daily exercise find it difficult to face an inactive day. Your muscles respond to habit, and once vigorous activity is established as a routine, it becomes a daily need.

A PROBE INTO YOUR MUSCLES—How does your overall fitness depend on healthy muscle action? To find out, you will be probing questions like these:

1. What is muscle tone? Why is it of value? Are muscles ever completely relaxed?

2. How are muscles attached to bones? How do muscles move bones?

3. What is the "oxygen debt"?

4. What are some ways of overcoming fatigue?

5. How does tension build up in the body? What dangers arise from prolonged tension? Name some causes of present-day tension.

8-1 What type of physique do you have? Is it similar to any of the ones shown here?

MUSCLES GIVE THE BODY FORM AND MOVEMENT

Your muscles are important because they are essential to all movement. They also give your body form. It is estimated that by your age your muscles comprise about one half of your body weight. But muscles serve other vital functions of your body as well. Muscular action is essential for circulation, respiration, digestion, and elimination. In addition, the vital organs—heart and lungs—are developed and strengthened through the use of the large muscles.

How Muscles Are Kept in Good Working Order

Interesting, too, is the fact that the various systems of the body are indirectly involved in keeping your muscles in good working order. For example, the digestive system changes food into products the blood can absorb and carry to the muscles as nourishment. The respiratory system takes air to the lungs and passes the oxygen from it into the blood, so that the oxygen can be carried to muscle (and all other) cells. The circulatory system carries food and oxygen to the muscles, and it carries the waste products away.

The nervous system also performs an important function. The fibers that make up muscles are connected with the central nervous system and receive impulses from it. For example, if you touch a hot stove with your finger, an impulse travels to the central nervous system. There the appropriate centers respond to this incoming impulse and relay the message to your muscles to take your finger off the stove. If you have had this experience, you know that it all happens in a split second.

Nerve impulses flow steadily to your muscles from the central nervous system; the more vigorous your activities become, the more impulses are needed to sustain the activity. At all times, even when you are resting, nerve impulses keep your muscles in a constant state of readiness for action. This means that your muscles are partially contracted, a state known as *muscle tone*. Good muscle tone is essential to the maintenance of correct posture as well as for effective movement.

Your Body Build

The size and shape of your bones and muscles at any one time make up your body build, or *physique* (fi-SEK). In Chapter 7 you learned about the requirements for bone growth and the contribution made by heredity. Your muscles depend on the kind of food you eat for their growth. Muscle growth is also dependent on how much you use them. These factors will largely determine both the heaviness or lightness of your muscles and their relative strength or weakness. But no matter what type of body build or how much physical stamina you may have inherited, your actual size and shape at any given time will show the effect of other important factors. Among these factors are congenital (present at birth) defects in structure, such as a heart or blood vessel defect, and any serious illnesses or accidents you may have recently suffered.

Hereditary influence is chiefly responsible for the so-called body types—the tall, slender type at one extreme, the short, stocky type at the other, with an "average" type in between. These variations in body type, or build, are largely determined by the size, shape, and density of your skeleton and by your hormones. But the width and girth (measurement around) of various body parts show the bulk of the muscles and the amount of fatty tissue beneath the skin. Your body build then, like the color of your eyes, cannot be changed from one type to another.

Accepting Your Body Build

Your particular body build indicates a given type of outward appearance that you learn to accept just as you must accept having brown or blue eyes. In case you are not pleased with your body build, you modify its appearance as best you can. One way to do this is by selecting clothing that compliments your figure. This is an easier task for girls than it is for boys, who have fewer choices of what they wear. If you are extra tall, for instance, vertical stripes will tend to make you look even taller. If your neck is short, broad collars for girls and high ones for boys will be equally

uncomplimentary. But no matter what your body build may be, you will be able to compliment it by careful grooming.

How Your Muscles Are Arranged

Your muscles are, for the most part, arranged in paired sets, with one muscle on each side of the body segment it is to move. When one muscle of a set contracts, or shortens, the other muscle relaxes. You may see this action when "making a muscle" in your arm. Clasp your upper arm with your hand, bend your elbow, and you can feel your *biceps* (two-headed muscle) harden. At the same time, the muscles on the back of your arm called the *triceps* (three-headed muscle) will become soft and relaxed. The biceps and triceps, then, are paired muscles. See Figure 8-2. The muscles that bend a body part such as the elbow or knee are called *flexors* while those that straighten it out are called *extensors.* When a muscle is in good health,

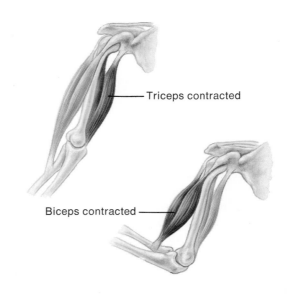

8-2 Movements of muscles in the upper arm: (*left*) the arm is straightened by contraction of the triceps muscle; (*right*) the arm is bent as the biceps contracts.

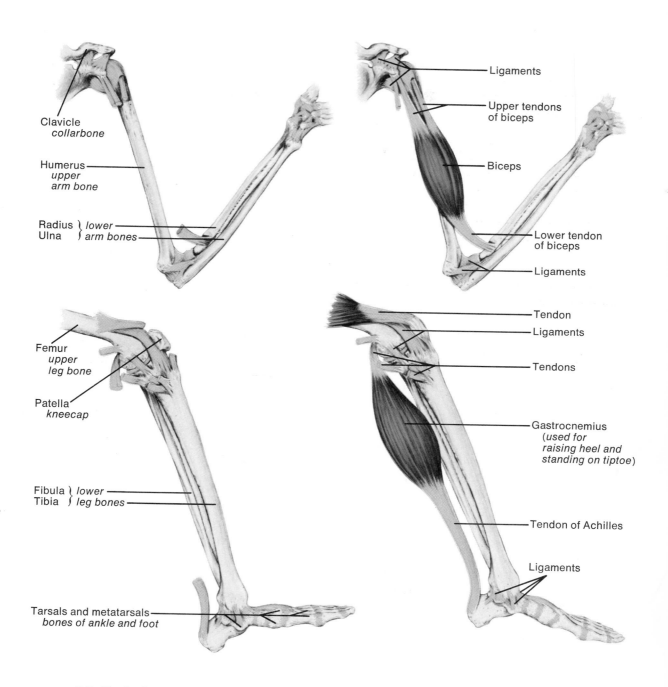

Clavicle
collarbone

Humerus
*upper
arm bone*

Radius } *lower*
Ulna } *arm bones*

Ligaments

**Upper tendons
of biceps**

Biceps

**Lower tendon
of biceps**

Ligaments

Femur
*upper
leg bone*

Patella
kneecap

Fibula } *lower*
Tibia } *leg bones*

Tarsals and metatarsals
bones of ankle and foot

Tendon

Ligaments

Tendons

Gastrocnemius
(*used for
raising heel and
standing on tiptoe*)

Tendon of Achilles

Ligaments

8-3 The basic structure of an arm and leg (the left arm and leg, viewed from the inner side) helps clarify how your bones and muscles work together. The ends of the arm and leg bones are enlarged to form heads. Where the heads of two bones come together (as in the knee joint), they are padded by cartilage and bound together by flexible ligaments.

the extensor will relax when the flexor is working. As an exercise, find the flexors and extensors of your foreleg.

Another important muscle of the arm is the *deltoid* which lifts your arm. See Figure 8-3. The term *deltoid* comes from the Greek letter delta, which is shaped like a triangle. You can feel the deltoid contracting (working) when you put your hand over the top of your arm and then raise your whole arm to shoulder height.

The muscles that cover the skeleton are called *skeletal muscles.* They are of many shapes—long, thin, flat, round, even diamond shaped—each designed for the work it is to do. The skeletal muscles are also called *voluntary muscles*, that is, they are muscles that you can consciously direct.

Beneath the outer layers of muscles, there are others called the *deep muscles.* As an example, there are three layers in your forearm. Some of these move one finger, or clench your fist, or move your wrist. Notice the muscles in your forearm as you try these exercises:

■ Pull one finger down hard and very slowly, then straighten it out stiff again. Can you tell which muscle pulls it down and which extends it? These muscles, like your biceps and triceps, are typical of many in the body. When one works, its mate relaxes.

Move your fingers up and down as if you were playing the piano. Do you see the long tendons that raise your fingers? The muscles that pull them are in your forearm. While you move the fingers of one hand up and down, use the fingers of the other hand to trace the long tendons through your wrist to the muscles of your forearm.

How Muscles Are Attached to Bones

Your muscles are attached to bones, as you learned earlier, by *tendons.* Of the many

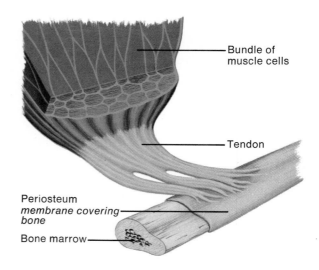

Bundle of muscle cells

Tendon

Periosteum *membrane covering bone*

Bone marrow

8-4 What is the relationship between the tendon, bone, and muscle?

tendons in your body, the strongest and toughest one is of special interest. It is called the *tendon of Achilles,* named for the Greek hero who supposedly could not be injured in any other part of his body. You can trace it with your fingers by starting at the heel and moving up to the calf muscle to which it attaches.

How Muscles Move Bones

Muscle fibers are able to contract, or shorten. When a muscle contracts, it pulls a bone toward it. Draw up your lower arm and feel the *biceps* on the front of your upper arm. A pair of tendons attach the biceps muscle to your shoulder. The shoulder does not move when the muscle contracts. This point of attachment is called the **origin**. The other end of the biceps is attached to the *radius* bone of the lower arm. This bone is movable and the point of attachment is called the **insertion**. When the biceps contracts, the muscle shortens and your lower arm is drawn up.

Other muscles, like those in your neck,

are attached in such a way as to produce slower motion than that of your forearm, but with less pull. As a result, your neck muscles do not tire so quickly from their job of holding your head up. Still other muscles, like those of your hip, are arranged so that they exert great force with little effort.

Looking at Muscle Cells
Under the Microscope

Skeletal muscle cells (the cells in your big muscles) are quite different from any other cells in the body. Although they are from 1/25 of an inch to 1 1/2 inches long, you cannot see them without a microscope because they are only about 1/2,500 to 1/250 of an inch wide. You see parts of several muscle cells, or *fibers*, as they are called, in Figure 8-5. Notice that they are shown cut across at the right. The artist had to draw them this way. Having enlarged the width of each fiber as he did in this drawing, he would have had to show each from 8 to 15 feet long to keep length and width in proportion.

Each cell is wrapped in a thin membrane, so clear that you could see through it. From each cell fine threads of connective tissue weave their way along the length of the muscle between other cells, until they grow onto the bones at either end of the muscle. The tendons are made of the threads from all the cells of the muscle (Figure 8-4). Thus, through its own connective threads, each cell exerts its pull on the bones. The part of the muscle nearest the tendon has more connective tissue. This tissue makes it tougher than the central portion.

Under the microscope you can see that each skeletal muscle cell has fine marks across it. Because of these stripes, skeletal muscles are also called *striped*, or **striated**, (STRY-ayt-'d) muscles (Figure 8-6).

Groups of parallel fibers, or cells, are bound together in small bundles the size of the lead in a pencil. They are wrapped in connective tissue that extends from the tendon at one end to the tendon at the other end.

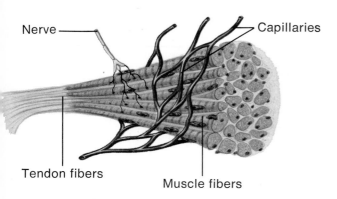

Nerve —

Capillaries

Tendon fibers

Muscle fibers

8-5 An enlarged view of skeletal muscle, showing several muscle fibers cut in two. Why are nerves and capillaries necessary to muscles?

8-6 A photomicrograph of skeletal muscle. Why is skeletal muscle also called striated or striped muscle?

Small bundles are grouped to make larger ones; these are bound together to make up the whole muscle.

What Makes Your Muscles Contract?

The living muscle is characterized by its ability to contract, or shorten. Contraction of a muscle takes place in response to a variety of stimuli, usually thought of as stimuli from the nervous system. But other forces can also stimulate muscular contraction, such as mechanical, thermal, and chemical stimuli. For example, muscular contraction can be caused by applying a brief electric current.

Our understanding of the chemistry of muscular contraction is still incomplete. Your muscles act somewhat like an engine for the conversion of fuel (chemical energy) into power or motion. The skeletal muscles contain glycogen (GLY-kuh-jen), a carbohydrate formed from the sugar in our food. When glycogen is converted back into the sugar and the sugar is oxidized in the mus-

8-7 This photomicrograph shows nerve endings distributed over skeletal muscle. What is the function of these nerve endings?

Courtesy CCM: General Biological, Inc.

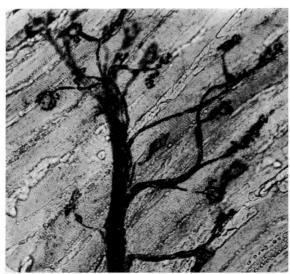

cles, the energy needed for muscle activity is released. In this energy-releasing process such waste products as carbon dioxide and lactic acid are formed. The blood carries away carbon dioxide. The lactic acid is broken down into carbon dioxide and water, which can be disposed of, and some is re-formed into glycogen.

When you engage in vigorous activity, and the number of contractions your muscles must make exceeds a certain limit, the lactic acid cannot be disposed of as fast as it is formed. Some of it flows into the bloodstream. When lactic acid builds up in muscle tissue and in the bloodstream, the accumulation interferes with the chemical reactions required for muscle contraction. Such a situation causes true muscular fatigue.

Even when your body is at complete rest, it requires oxygen and produces the waste products of carbon dioxide and lactic acid. But when you are at rest, sufficient time elapses between the muscular contractions for the waste products to be carried away. Hence fatigue does not occur. Fatigue will be discussed later in this chapter.

What Is the "Oxygen Debt"?

You have all experienced the body reaction that follows a race up a flight of steps. You puff and pant for several minutes. During this short, vigorous run the oxygen demands of your muscles were not satisfied; you could not take in oxygen fast enough. There developed, so to speak, an "oxygen debt." An oxygen debt is somewhat like a money debt. Suppose you earned $20 and with it you bought a jacket that cost $30. You are in debt for $10 and will have to work a little while longer to repay the $10 debt. This, in a sense, is what you are doing when you puff and pant following your run up the stairs. You are repaying the oxygen debt to your muscles by breathing in quantities of oxygen to replenish the amount that you have used.

8-8 Kipchoge Keino of Kenya is an internationally known runner who has set many records. How does he repay his "oxygen debt"?

During sudden, vigorous activities, there is not enough time for the respiratory and circulatory systems to adjust in order to supply sufficient oxygen. As a result, lactic acid builds up and, for a variable period of time following exertion, the lactic acid demands oxygen for oxidation. It is during this over-time period that the oxygen debt is paid back.

Muscle Tone Provides for Instant Action

Muscle tone keeps your muscles ready for instant action. Muscle tone also has a steadying effect in much the same way as a firm grip on the steering wheel of your bicycle helps to steady the wheel.

The partial contracture, or tonicity, of your muscles is maintained without significant fatigue because it uses such an extremely small amount of energy. At any one moment, parts of the muscles are in a state of contraction while others are resting and relaxed. This division of labor makes it possible for you to maintain various postures when you sit or stand, while other body parts are in action.

There are conditions, however, in which the muscles can lose their tonicity. Some cases of **poliomyelitis** (poh-lee-oh-my-eh-LY-tis) are an example of this condition. A muscle that has lost its tonicity is described as being **atonic**. At the other extreme, there is the condition called **hypertonic** in which the muscle becomes tightly contracted. An example is a muscle cramp.

How Your Smooth Muscles Work

Smooth muscle cells look "smooth." They are not striated like those in skeletal muscle. They are also much shorter. You would have to place 50 of the longest ones end to end to measure an inch. The longest striated muscle cell is 150 times as long as the longest smooth muscle cell. A smooth muscle cell has one nucleus, while a skeletal muscle cell is a strange cell in this respect, having many nuclei. Figures 8-6 and 8-9 show these two kinds of muscle cells.

Smooth muscle forms thin sheets of tissue in such hollow organs as the stomach, intestines, blood vessels, and the bladder. Smooth muscles make the pupil of your eye contract when you look at a bright light. When a freezing wind strikes you, tiny, smooth muscles make your hairs "stand on end."

Smooth muscles, like those lining the alimentary canal, contract to reduce the diameter of the canal and squeeze and push along its contents. They cause the movements of your stomach and intestines. Compared to the instant action of skeletal muscles, smooth muscles take their time. However, smooth muscle tires slowly and can continue to contract for a long time.

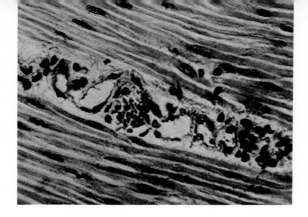

Courtesy CCM: General Biological, Inc.

8-9 A photomicrograph of smooth muscle. Where would you find smooth muscle? Why is smooth muscle also called involuntary muscle?

8-10 A photomicrograph of cardiac muscle. How is cardiac muscle similar to smooth muscle and to skeletal muscle? *striated*

Smooth muscle is also called *involuntary muscle*. This is because it works under the control of a part of your nervous system without your knowing or thinking about it. You cannot start or stop the motion of your stomach when you wish, although your thoughts and emotions speed up or slow down the action of the stomach and the other organs having smooth muscle.

How Your Heart Muscle Works

Cardiac (KAHR-dee-ak), or heart, muscle cells are different from all other muscle cells. They are *striated* somewhat like skeletal muscle cells, but they are *involuntary,* like smooth muscle cells. You have no conscious control of them, although your emotions often speed up or slow down their action. They contract more quickly than smooth muscle and more slowly than skeletal muscle. As you see in Figure 8-10, the fibers of heart muscle fuse with each other in places. You will read more about heart muscle in Chapter 17.

Your Muscles Can Be Injured

One of the ways to avoid injury to your muscles is to keep them in good, healthy working order by using them. The well-coordinated muscle moves smoothly and

rhythmically and responds to normal stress and strain without injury. There are, however, unusual situations where injury seems unavoidable. Being in too big a hurry and not being alert is often a contributing factor in muscle injury.

Muscle strain is a common injury that is the result of overextension. The fibers of the muscles are stretched beyond normal limits and are partially torn. The more serious muscle strains are those involving the back muscles. These strains are often caused by lifting heavy objects. Rest and warm applications will give muscles relief and an opportunity to heal.

Sprains are injuries to the ligaments that hold the joints together, to tendons that connect muscles to bones, to muscles, and to blood vessels that are stretched and sometimes ruptured. Sprains can occur at any joint, and they are often serious, since there is a possibility that there may also be a bone chip or fracture. To be on the safe side, it is well to get an X-ray picture in order to determine the extent of damage to the bone. You cannot judge this from the amount of swelling that is present.

Cold, wet applications, or an ice pack that is applied immediately and continued for an hour or so, will relieve pain and help control swelling. Once the discoloration appears, warm applications to improve circulation are indicated.

A *dislocation* is the displacement of a bone end from the joint. Here, too, the ligaments, tendons, muscles, and blood vessels are involved. Dislocations are always serious and call for medical attention.

One type of *hernia*, or rupture, occurs when a loop of intestine (bowel) pushes through a weak point in the muscular wall of the abdomen. Hernia may result from unusual muscular effort in pushing or lifting heavy objects or from severe coughing. Medical attention is indicated for the repair of hernia. There is real danger in the use of artificial

8-11 Skiing is fun but requires practice and skill to enjoy it safely.

devices to hold a hernia in place, unless they are prescribed by a doctor.

Bursitis (bur-SY-tis) also involves the muscles. The bursae are small sacs of fluid found in most joints that can become inflamed for a great variety of reasons. The inflammation causes pain, and the surrounding muscles become stiffened. Cold applications and rest are sometimes effective, but in severe cases medical aid is needed.

Paralysis is another muscle abnormality. It is a nerve affliction that causes loss of voluntary muscle movement. Paralysis occurs in cases of poliomyelitis and stroke and in other neuromuscular disorders.

Muscle cramp is familiar to almost everyone. Often it occurs when you fail to "warm up" your muscles properly before engaging in vigorous activity. The muscle contracts and fails to relax, causing pain, and sometimes it disables the body part entirely. Massaging the muscle usually helps to relax it. Lack of oxygen to a muscle may also cause cramping.

In addition to the above abnormalities of muscles, the muscles are subject to a number of *neuromuscular diseases*. Examples of these are the following:

Muscular dystrophy is characterized by the progressive wasting away of the muscle.

Parkinson's disease (shaking palsy) is a group of symptoms caused by various disorders. Symptoms may include tremor, muscle rigidity, decreased range of movement.

Multiple sclerosis is characterized in general by loss of muscular coordination, difficulty in maintaining balance, paralysis, and numbness.

FATIGUE—NATURE'S WARNING THAT YOU NEED REST

The feeling of fatigue is a common experience and represents, in most instances, an announcement by your body that you need rest. Just as hunger, thirst, and sleepiness

8-12 Exercise is often a good way to release tension. Which form of exercise shown is more relaxing?

indicate the body's need for food, water, and sleep, so it is with fatigue. Normal fatigue calls for rest, relaxation, recreation, change of pace, or sleep. Usually a night of good sleep will relieve normal fatigue.

When you feel normal fatigue, your body responds in several ways to restore and refresh itself. One of these is the chemical process in which lactic acid and other fatigue products are eliminated. Another way is by the biological process in which cells are rested and restored. Both of these restorative processes function at a maximum during rest, especially during sleep.

Your Need for Sleep

We spend about one third of our lives in sleep, but up to now science has given us no universally accepted explanation of the fundamental mechanism of sleep. At the end of this chapter, there are some interesting references on sleep that you will want to read.

The fact that all higher animals need sleep is known and well accepted. During your growth period throughout childhood and youth, you need more sleep than is needed by the fully grown adult. Then again at an older age, when the repair processes are slowed down, sleep is needed in greater amounts. People seem to vary as to the amount of sleep they need, but to be on the safe side most teen-agers can use eight or nine hours of sleep with profit. You will read more about sleep in Chapter 12.

The Fatiguing Effect of Undue Tension

Sometimes, it seems, we fail to respond to normal feelings of fatigue. Some situation may occur that prevents us from being aware of our fatigue. You have read earlier about the cause of true muscular fatigue and how it can be corrected by variable amounts of rest, sleep, and nourishment. But there is also fatigue that is less healthy and that requires other measures to be taken. This is called undue tension. Tension means tightening, and, therefore, in muscles it indicates contraction.

Your muscles, and at times the whole body, can reach a state of undue tension. This occurs when unnecessary and excessive muscular contractions mount up that are beyond the needs of your body for maintenance of muscle tone or the performance of motor movements. You can recognize tension in the stiff, awkward performance of a beginner in any skill or sport. You say he is "trying too hard." This is because he is using too many muscles and is contracting them too frequently. You may also have seen evidence of undue tension in facial expressions such as unnatural blinking of the eye, a twitching lip, tapping of fingers or a foot, and other unnecessary movements.

When excessive muscular contraction or undue tension is present, your nerves are also involved since a muscular contraction, for the most part, is the result of a nerve impulse. Here again, as with the muscles, when the nerve impulses exceed the need for muscle contraction a state of nervous tension builds up. The two seem, then, to be inseparable, for where there is tension both muscles and nerves are involved. During excessive tension, there is also an increased demand made upon the heart and circulatory system.

Your heart must pump a little harder and blood vessels must contract a little more. As a result, tension becomes a factor in **high blood pressure**, or **hypertension**.

Some Causes of Undue Tension

Sometimes muscle and nerve tensions build up as a result of illness or repeated accidents, but more often they result from daily living. We are faced in this twentieth century with many difficult situations, all of which to some degree or other touch the lives of teen-agers as well as of other age groups.

There is the growing population with its consequent crowding wherever you go—in schools, stores, theaters, housing, and recreation areas. As the population grows, competition becomes keener. You must strive harder to excel, or just to keep up with your peers, while you compete for school marks, to make the sports team or band, to be elected to some club or office, or to get into the college

8-13 Crowding is a common cause of tension. How do you react to crowded conditions?

8-14 Sailing is a great way "to get away from it all." What do you do to relieve tension?

or university of your choice. Then there is the rising standard of living that at times causes people to strive for success beyond the limits of their capacity. Youth is caught up in this pressure, too, when they strive sometimes beyond their endurance to earn enough money to buy a car of their own or to satisfy some other desire.

In today's world, too, most boys must face the dual role of military service and preparation for a career, while many girls face the dual role of preparation for a career and marriage. There are many circumstances to be considered in making these choices and, in fact, deciding which should come first. For some people this is a frustrating experience that can mount into undue tension.

How to Avoid Undue Tension

Much more is known about how to avoid the fatiguing effects of undue tension than is known about how it may be relieved. Perhaps the first preventive measure to be considered by busy teen-agers is to adopt the habit of planning your time. Making out a daily schedule does not have to be a big production. In fact, it can simply be a mental plan—a plan that smoothly coordinates the things that you must do with those that you want to do, and allows for periodic rest breaks when you do not do anything at all. Relaxing, unwinding even for a brief ten minutes, three or four times a day gives

your muscles and nerves refreshing recovery breaks.

As you learn more about yourself, your strengths and limitations, you begin to appreciate the need to consider your strong points. When you select a career, you should strive to set reasonable, attainable goals for yourself.

Your body is a coordinated whole; each system benefits from the healthy condition of the other systems. It is important, therefore, that as you strive for healthy muscles you also continue all of the other health practices you are learning about in this text. Your daily, routine health behavior becomes still another means of defeating tension and fatigue.

Another good approach to the relief of undue tension is through physical activity. It will not matter whether the exercise you take is for fun or work, whether it is waxing the floor, dancing, swimming, painting the garage, building a bookcase, playing a hard game of tennis, or boxing.

Sometimes all that is needed for the relief of undue tension is a change of pace. Here the choice of some absorbing recreational activity in which you can lose yourself proves beneficial. Such activities as playing bridge, collecting stamps or coins, playing the piano or banjo, reading about some hobby you enjoy, going to a good movie, or any other activity that completely absorbs your attention will help you change pace.

What You Have Learned

What kind of health practices should you apply in maintaining your health? Check your understanding of the chapter. On a separate sheet of paper, number 1 through 18 and insert the answer from the vocabulary list below. Use each expression, but use each one only once.

asleep	flexors	relaxes
central	food	rest
contraction	heredity	tendons
contracts	lactic	tension
exercise	ligaments	time
extensors	movement	tone

Your muscles are essential to all body (1)_____. Nerve impulses flow steadily to the muscles from the (2)_____ nervous system and keep the muscles in a state of partial (3)_____ that is known as muscle (4)_____. Your body build is determined by such factors as (5)_____, (6)_____, and (7)_____.

Most muscles are arranged in paired sets. When one muscle of a pair (8)_____, the other muscle (9)_____. The muscles that bend a body part such as the forearm are called (10)_____, and those that straighten it are called (11)_____. Muscles are attached to bones by (12)_____, and joints are held together by (13)_____.

A feeling of fatigue is nature's warning that you need (14)_____. In normal fatigue, the body refreshes itself by eliminating (15)_____ acid and other products of muscle fatigue. This chemical process functions best when you are (16)_____. But, when your muscles contract in excess of their normal need to maintain tone, another type of fatigue called undue (17)_____ occurs. It is important to your well-being to avoid tension, and one good way to do this is by planning your (18)_____.

What You Can Do

1. Place your relaxed forearm and hand on your desk. One at a time, tap each finger on the desk. How are you able to move your fingers? Where are muscles that are moving them? Can you see the muscle action?

·2. Notice how you feel when fatigued from a day of vigorous physical activity. Then notice how you feel when fatigued from a day of tests. Are these feelings approximately the same or are they quite different? What should you do in each case to refresh yourself?

3. You are a forward on your class basketball team, and have missed two weeks of practice due to illness. You return to practice feeling fine; however, your coach says you may warm up with the team but not compete for a while. Why are you being limited to just the warmups?

Things to Try

1. Try this fatigue test. Start tapping with your fingers on your desk as rapidly as you can. You will see that at high speed the degree of fatigue mounts quickly. In fact, it rises out of proportion to the work your muscles are doing. Soon your muscles will tire; fatigue sets in, and you will have to stop to rest.

2. Select a skill that you have learned, such as ice-skating, knitting, fly-casting, surfing, water-skiing, or tennis. What were the principal muscles you used in learning the skill?

Probing Further

Sleep: The Mysterious Third of Your Life, by J. and M. Kastner, Harcourt Brace Jovanovich, 1968. An entertaining and interesting summary of what science has learned of the importance and functions of sleep.

Efficiency of Human Movement, by Marion R. Broer, Saunders, 1966. This volume emphasizes the importance of healthy muscles.

"Maybe You Need More Sleep," by Robert O'Brien, *Reader's Digest,* February 1960. This article challenges the idea that everyone needs the same amount of sleep and further explains our need for sleep.

Science and Medicine of Exercise and Sports, by Warren R. Johnson, Harper, 1960. Selected parts of this volume describe the approach of medicine and science to the body's need for exercise.

Health Concepts in Action

Does this statement bring together ideas you have gained from this chapter?

Vital body functions depend upon the action of muscles.

Applying this concept, which health practices would you

    —continue?

    —change?

    —begin?

Will you now, as a result of your study, change any of your health objectives?

9 / *Your Appearance*

How you look to other people often inspires such comments as, "She's the image of her mother," or "He's a chip off the old block." Your appearance does, of course, depend partly on inherited features. But many aspects of your appearance depend also upon you. There are many ways in which you can complement your appearance. How many such ways can you think of right now?

A PROBE INTO YOUR APPEARANCE—What habits of personal care will help you look—and feel—your best? To decide, you will be probing questions like these:

1. What are the six main functions of the skin?

2. What structures in the skin give you personal identification? Are they permanent?

3. What happens to the skin when you are embarrassed? frightened? excited? cold? Can you control these reactions?

4. How often should you shampoo your hair?

5. What are the benefits of brushing your hair and massaging your scalp daily?

6. What are the functions of the four types of teeth?

7. What is fluoridation? Is the water fluoridated in your community?

8. How can you prevent dental caries?

HOW IMPORTANT IS APPEARANCE?

Making the most of your appearance requires not only effort but understanding. You need to know the structure and function of the skin, hair, and teeth. You also need to understand how to care for them.

The use you make of these physical qualities is an important factor in your appearance and poise. It will be equally important in your acceptance by others and in the way you feel about yourself.

You as a person, or personality, are of course more than the way you look. But cleanliness, neat and appropriate clothes, and well-cared-for skin, hair, and teeth are natural expressions of a pleasing personality. A well-groomed and healthy-looking person is attractive.

How Your Skin Protects You

Your skin is the largest organ of the body. It is tough, strong, and elastic. It varies a great deal in thickness on different parts of the body. Think of the skin on your eyelids, for example, compared with the thicker skin on the soles of your feet. The skin covers about seventeen square feet of surface in adults and weighs about five pounds. Destruction of more than one third of its surface, by scalding or burning, is usually fatal. Your hair and nails are modifications of skin that have developed to serve special needs.

Your skin is highly adapted to its many functions. It has to accommodate itself to changes in your body size and weight. You may see how elastic it is, how it stretches and shrinks. Pull a small part of the skin of your forearm as far as it will go, release it, and watch the skin snap back into shape. Sometimes when the skin is stretched, it falls into folds that may become permanent with continued use. You see this in wrinkles of the face formed by smiling or frowning.

Your Skin Serves Many Functions

1. Your skin forms a barrier against foreign substances and germs.
2. Your skin forms a waterproof sac that encloses and insulates the body.
3. The blood vessels in your skin cool the body when it is too warm and retard loss of heat when it is cold.
4. In addition to its multiple-functioning network of blood vessels, your skin has an equally remarkable network of nerves.
5. Your skin helps to regulate the water balance in your body.
6. Perhaps the skin's most remarkable property is its power to regenerate, that is, to heal itself.

9-1 Greatly enlarged cross section of skin. How do the epidermis and dermis differ? What part of each hair is alive?

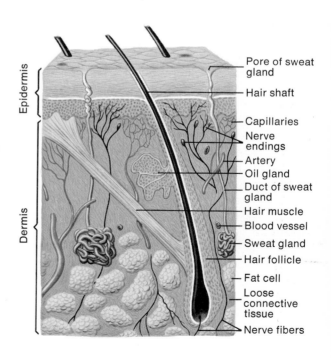

Epidermis

Dermis

Pore of sweat gland

Hair shaft

Capillaries

Nerve endings

Artery

Oil gland

Duct of sweat gland

Hair muscle

Blood vessel

Sweat gland

Hair follicle

Fat cell

Loose connective tissue

Nerve fibers

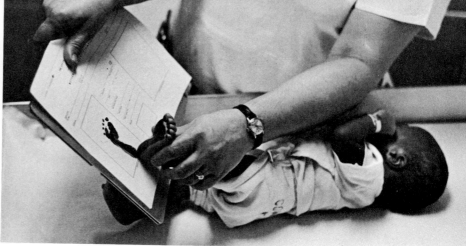

9-2 Skin is frequently used for identification purposes: (*left*) a thumbprint showing individual markings; (*right*) a newborn baby being footprinted in the hospital.

Your Fingerprints Are Unique

Your skin shapes your facial and body contours like those of no other person. It forms such distinctive markings that your fingerprints are different from those of any other person. Not even identical twins have exactly the some fingerprints. The skin of your fingertips is heavily grooved with ridges, whorls, furrows, loops, and arches.

Look at your palm and finger tips and you can see these identifying structures (Figure 9-2). Use a magnifying glass for a closer look. Now place the glass over the fingers of a friend's hand and see how different his markings are from yours. These markings are made from rows of tiny *papillae* (puh-PIL-ee) that grow up from the *dermis*. The dermis is an under layer of skin that gives the skin strength and elasticity. The papillae look like tiny fingers. In some there are minute blood vessels, in others there are nerve endings. Each *papilla* (puh-PIL-uh)—singular for papillae—stays in the same place all of your life. Your fingerprints will not change unless you suffer a severe cut or burn. Fingerprints are used for identification by the police, armed forces, and some government agencies. In hospitals, a footprint is made of newborn babies to make certain that each mother gets her own child.

Your Skin Records Emotional Reactions

Your skin carries many messages. The blush that comes from embarrassment or shame, sweat on your forehead and palms as you wait for an appointment with the principal or as your parents read your report card, or gooseflesh when the score is tied in basketball with thirty seconds left to play are just a few examples; you are probably aware of many more.

These are physical signs of emotional reactions that you cannot keep from showing whether you want to or not. You cannot start or stop them because they are triggered by the part of the nervous system that does not respond to your will. They are all normal reactions that your skin records, and they tend to disappear when the cause of the emotion ceases.

Your Renewable Overcoat

Look at your hand. What you actually see won't be there when you look at your hand next week. The skin cells that form the sur-

9-3 Your skin records your emotional reactions. Can the boy control his physical emotions?

pliable, and waterproof. During adolescence, the sebaceous glands become more active. They may overproduce and cause oily skin or oily hair. This condition is often accompanied by acne. Frequent shampoos are needed to control oily hair. As an aid in controlling oily skin, you need a daily warm bath and warm face washes two or three times each day.

Sometimes the opposite occurs and there is insufficient secretion of sebum. In such a condition, the skin and hair become dry and lackluster. It is thought that this condition may be due to a deficiency of vitamin A in your diet or the result of an illness. Eating well-balanced daily meals is important for the healthy functioning of the skin.

TAKING CARE OF YOUR SKIN

The structure of your skin, as you have seen, is not like that of any other person. So the care of your skin becomes a personal matter. The methods of care used by your family or friends may not prove beneficial for you. This seems true also when you need treatment for plant poisoning or infections of the skin. You need your own prescription. It is well to first learn the principles of skin care and then vary these according to your own needs.

Attention to Health Comes First

Good general health is basic to healthy skin. Your skin gets all of its nourishment from within, no matter how convincing the advertisements may be for "skin food." You cannot "feed" your skin by rubbing creams on it. What you can do with creams is relieve dry skin. If your diet is faulty or your digestion, circulation, or other body processes are not functioning properly, your skin will show the effects.

Lack of sleep, overstimulation, or general fatigue, for example, can change the skin's

face of your skin will fall off or be rubbed off before then because they are no longer alive. If they rub off in large enough pieces, you can see them. Usually, however, the groups of skin cells rub off in such small pieces that you cannot see them (except for dandruff, which is made of large groups of skin cells that rub off the scalp).

These outer skin cells are called the *cuticle* (KYOO-tih-k'l). They are part of the larger *epidermis* (ep-ih-DER-mis), or main outer portion of skin (Figure 9-1). The *dermis* is a second layer under the epidermis.

Underneath the cuticle are the "mother cells" of the epidermis. They grow all the time. As they grow, they divide to make new cells to replace the cells of the cuticle that are always dying, drying up, and falling off.

How Your Skin Oils Itself

The *sebaceous glands* (se-BA-shus) that are found in the dermis secrete an oily substance called *sebum* (Figure 9-1). The functions of sebum are to help keep the skin and hair soft, normal color. Unusual pallor, blueness, or yellowness of the skin may be a sign of serious illness, and is a sign that you should consult a doctor. Fever usually makes the skin look flushed.

How to Cleanse Your Skin

Most people are aware of the importance of cleanliness to personal appearance and to being accepted socially. But cleanliness is also essential for proper functioning and protection of the skin.

Bathing

The skin can be kept clean by bathing. A daily warm bath may be necessary to remove the secretions of oil, sweat, and the accumulation of dirt, dust, and scales from the skin. It also keeps the pores of the skin open and free to function. But for some people who have dry skin or certain other skin conditions, a warm bath twice a week may be more desirable.

A warm bath—about body temperature—is relaxing, and when taken before bedtime is conducive to sound sleep. Very hot baths—above 98° F—should be taken only on medical advice. If you are going outdoors following a warm bath, it is well to follow it with cool water. This helps your skin contract and prevents too rapid loss of body heat.

A cool shower or tub dip is an excellent tonic for your skin, providing you react well to it and feel warm afterwards. It should be taken in a warm room, followed by a brisk rubdown.

Cleansing Materials

The best way to clean your skin is with soap and water. Except in rare skin conditions, this beauty treatment is the best on the market. It removes all the accumulation of dirt and bacteria on the skin, makes your skin soft and pliable, and stimulates.

Among the many other cleansing agents are cold cream, vanishing cream, cleansing lotions, and chemical preparations that combine various oils with alcohol. Such preparations are helpful for the few people who are allergic to soap or who have extra sensitive skins. Even if you have a normal skin, you may want to use a cream cleanser to remove make-up or to soften your skin if it is dry.

Deodorants and Antiperspirants

It is easy to look and smell clean and fresh after a bath, but it is not always easy to stay that way. If you perspire freely, you may find it helpful to use one of the many preparations on the market for limiting and deodorizing perspiration. A *deodorant* is a preparation that masks or diminishes body odor, while an *antiperspirant* retards or checks the flow of perspiration.

9-4 Cleansing cream may be helpful in particular cases, but soap and water are usually best for washing your face. What do you use?

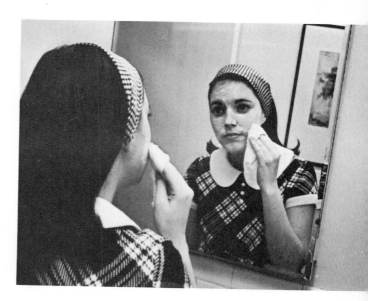

Some preparations that contain aluminum salts inhibit both odor and flow. These types are safe to use in limited areas, except on sensitive skins. Trial and error is probably your best method of deciding what to use since the effectiveness of products varies with individuals. A safe trial can usually be made by following the directions printed on the package.

If perspiration is a problem for you, checking your clothing is important. Stale perspiration quickly becomes offensive, and it can rot, stain, or take color out of some fabrics.

How Should a Girl Care for Her Face?

You should give your face special care for three reasons: (1) To insure proper functioning and protection of the skin. (2) Because you have more oil and sweat glands in the face than elsewhere. (3) Because your face is constantly exposed to dust, wind, and fumes that may be in the air. Because girls usually wear makeup, they may have to follow special cleansing procedures.

Your night routine. Use a mild soap or cleansing cream or both. If your skin is oily, you should use soap; if it is dry, use cleansing cream.

When you use soap, first wet a clean washcloth or facial sponge in moderately hot water. Hold it against your face. Repeat until your skin pores are relaxed and the circulation is increased. Then make a good lather on the washcloth or sponge and rub your face gently but firmly. This cleans the pores and exercises the muscles of the skin without irritating the surface of the skin. Rinse your face with fresh warm water. Remove all the soap; if you leave any, it may irritate your skin and make it dry and rough. To finish, rinse your face in cold water and dry it thoroughly. If you wish, apply a mild astringent to help make the pores contract again.

When you use cleansing cream, let it remain on your skin long enough to enter the pores. Then apply a hot washcloth to stimulate the circulation before you wipe off the cream. Go on with the thorough washing and rinsing described above. Even if your skin is oily but tender, you may get the best results by cleansing it first with cream and then with soap and water.

Your morning routine. If your skin is oily, use soap and water and a washcloth in the morning. Repeat this routine at noontime or after school and then again before bedtime. Use hot water, followed by a cold rinse. A normal skin can simply be bathed in cold water and patted dry with a soft towel.

Experiment to find the treatment that keeps your face in best condition. In any case, do three things: (1) Keep the sweat and oil glands clean to help prevent blackheads and pimples. (2) Stimulate the circulation to bring about adequate nourishment and removal of wastes. (3) Exercise the skin and underlying muscles by careful rubbing to help keep them firm and healthy.

What About Cosmetics?

Cosmetics, when wisely and sparingly applied, may enhance a girl's appearance and boost her morale as well. There are hundreds of cosmetic products on the market: face powders and bases, lotions and creams, rouges, lipsticks, fingernail polishes, mascaras, eyebrow pencils, and eye shadows. Most cosmetics are harmless when properly applied. Some may be harmful to a few girls with delicate skins or allergies. And, there are "non-allergenic" products for such skins. But just to be safe, try all eye makeup and other cosmetics in small quantities before you use them.

There is an art to applying makeup, and too much makeup can be very unattractive. Study Figure 9-5 for examples of how makeup can be used and misused. No matter how appealing the advertisements for cosmetics may be, it is well to remember that no cos-

9-5 The proper use of cosmetics can enhance your appearance. These two photographs are of the same girl. Do you agree that she is more attractive in the photograph on the right? How does her use of cosmetics change her appearance? Which hair style is more becoming? Why?

metic can produce any marked changes in your skin. Washing with soap and water encourages healthy skin, which remains the basis of youthful good appearance.

How Should a Boy Care for His Face?

Read the instructions for girls about washing the face. You will find them useful. If your beard has begun to grow, you have the extra problem of shaving. When you shave, draw the razor across the hairs in the direction in which they lie. Avoid cutting your beard "against the grain." The pattern of hair growth varies from man to man. The hairs under the chin and on the neck usually lie at a different angle from the other hairs. If you shave against this angle, you may irritate the skin.

If you use an electric razor, follow the manufacturer's instructions.

After shaving, rinse off all of the soap with water. A face lotion may then be used. Most lotions have an alcohol content that has some value as an antiseptic. But if your skin is sensitive, a cream lotion will be more soothing. Many men find that a dash of cold water on the face after shaving is all they need to keep their skin in fine condition.

THE WEATHER AND YOUR SKIN

The weather—hot, cold, windy—causes most people some concern for their skin. For those with delicate skin, precautions against weather irritations become important. Sunburn, chapping, and cracking all need special attention.

How Your Skin Tans

Tanning of the skin is a little like taking a picture with a camera. When you take a picture, the light makes parts of the film turn dark. When you tan, the light makes cells in your skin turn dark. It has nothing to do with the heat of the sun. The work is done by the ultraviolet rays, the same rays your skin uses in order to make vitamin D (you read about Vitamin D in Chapter 3). Some people tan readily, others slowly. There are some people with very pale skin who seem never to tan at all.

Here is what happens when you tan in sunlight. Part of the "mother cells" beneath the cuticle are *pigment-producing* cells. Pigment is coloring matter. The ultraviolet rays of the sun cause the "mother cells" to make the pigment that tans your skin. The more

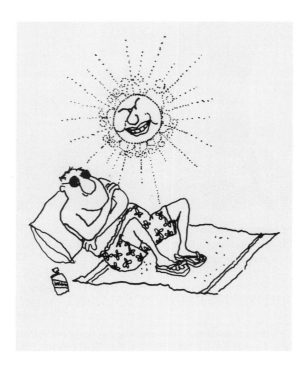

9-6 The sun is not always friendly! Painful burns can be avoided if you start with a short exposure time and gradually increase it.

pigment producing cells you have, and the more active they are, the darker will be your tan.

This pigment, or tanning, will then protect the dermis, or inner skin, from the sun's rays (Figure 9-1). This is why the sun does more harm to a light skin. With little protection against the sun, a light skin burns easily.

Sun-bathing and Sunburn

Getting a good suntan is a popular activity, almost a ritual with some people. Basking in the sunshine produces a fine sense of relaxation and well being, if it is not overdone.

If you want a good tan, get it gradually. Start out with fifteen minutes of exposure the first day, and add a few minutes each day for about two weeks. This process allows your skin time to produce its pigment to give you

a tan, and it avoids painful skin burns. Suntan lotions can also be helpful in preventing sunburn. Try several kinds, until you find the best one for you.

Overexposure to the sun can cause burns. Sunburn is like burns from any other source, and should be treated in the same way (see Appendix, page 652). Overexposure may also cause heat cramps or *heat prostration* (see Chapter 19 and Appendix, page 652). Continued overexposure, over

9-7 Sun-bathing is a popular pastime for people of all ages. Do you enjoy basking in the sun? Can this activity ever become dangerous?

9-8 Freckles are often a very attractive feature. Do you have freckles? Do more freckles appear when you are exposed to sunlight?

a period of years, can cause wrinkles and leathery, coarse skin.

Another result from exposure of the skin to the sun is a crop of freckles. They are caused by the same mechanism as skin tanning. But in freckles, the pigmentation appears in spots and clusters instead of spread out as in a tan.

Chapping

Your skin, particularly on your face and hands, is exposed to all sorts of weather. Chapping is caused by cold, hot sun, and wind that dries out, and sometimes cracks, the epidermal layer of the skin. A good oil-base cream used before and during exposure will help prevent chapping. When cracking and bleeding occur, you probably need medical advice.

SPECIAL SKIN PROBLEMS

Not too much is known about how to treat skin blemishes. The reason is that our skins differ so greatly. You have previously read about food allergies in Chapter 4. Many skin problems are also due to allergies. A soap that helps one boy's skin may set another boy's hands and face "on fire." A cream that soothes one girl's face may make her sister break out in a rash. Nonetheless, you will find that most of the advice in this section will work well for everyone.

Blackheads and Pimples

Blackheads are clogged, enlarged pores tipped with dirt or chemically changed oil from the sebaceous glands (Figure 9-9). It requires persistent treatment to get rid of them. One way is to steam your face with a moist, hot towel to open the pores. Cleanse the face thoroughly with a washcloth and mild soap, then rinse with cold water. Follow this with a mild antiseptic, such as rubbing alcohol, then apply a soothing cold cream. Repeat this procedure every few days. This should help the pores to discharge their oil and wastes, and will help to wash the blackheads away.

Pimples are caused when bacteria enter the pores. Pimples should never be squeezed or pinched. This is because the hard circle usually found at the base of a pimple walls it off from the underlying skin; squeezing may break the wall and release infection to other parts of your body.

Acne

Sometimes teen-agers suffer from a condition that causes blackheads, pimples, swellings, and other blemishes. In severe cases, these conditions leave scars that may last for years. This condition is called *acne* (AK-nee). Acne may be caused by overactive glands that usually produce too much oil,

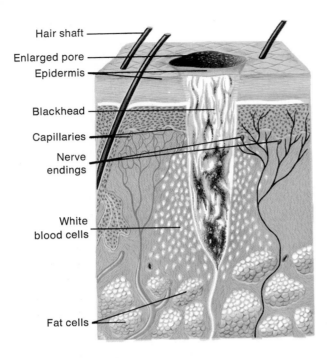

Hair shaft

Enlarged pore

Epidermis

Blackhead

Capillaries

Nerve
endings

White
blood cells

Fat cells

9-9 A diagram of a cross section of skin showing a blackhead. What are blackheads? How are they formed? How should they be treated?

but it may not be merely a skin disorder. At your age, the body is going through many rapid changes, some of which make your skin (although not the rest of your body) less able to resist bacteria. The person, rather than merely the acne, may have to be treated. You need to apply all health measures to effect a cure. The most important measures for overall health are: (1) 8 or 9 hours of sleep a night; (2) regular elimination; (3) two or more hours of daily exercise; (4) proper diet; and (5) careful skin care.

The best diet for those with acne includes fruits, vegetables, lean meats, and high-protein, low-fat foods.

How to Care for Skin with Acne

1. Using a washcloth, wash the affected areas gently with ordinary soap and hot

water two or three times a day. Dry the skin with a rough towel. This treatment removes some of the oil and blackheads from the skin. It helps free the pores of dead cells.
2. To prevent spreading infection, avoid picking at the face or other affected areas. By all means, use only your own towel and washcloth.
3. Regular brushing and shampooing of the hair are needed to remove excess

9-10 Planing surgery is often used to remove scars caused by acne: (top) scars resulting from acne; (bottom) skin after removal of scars by surgery.

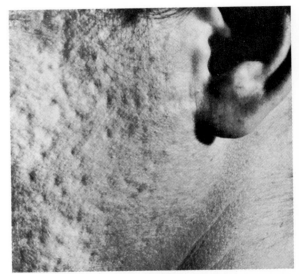

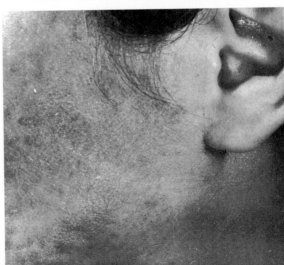

oil. Oiliness of the scalp may cause dandruff and make acne worse.

4. Avoid greasy creams, salves, and oily preparations, since there is already an excess of oil on the skin.

5. Remove blackheads to prevent swollen or pus-containing sores. To do this, use a blackhead remover that can be purchased at the drugstore. First, soften the skin by holding a bath towel soaked in hot water against the skin for a few minutes. Then, place the hole of the blackhead remover over each blackhead, and press gently to remove it.

6. Try sunbathing. Start with a few minutes exposure daily and gradually increase the amount.

Boils and Carbuncles

Boils often begin in the hair follicles and are primarily caused by bacterial infections. A **simple boil** has a single core and may be no more than a pimple. A mass of boils, close together and with several cores, is called a **carbuncle.**

Boils generally occur where the skin and hair roots are irritated or chafed. These areas are commonly found on the back of the neck and in the armpits. They should not be squeezed or pinched, as the walled-off infection may then spread to other parts of the body.

Small, simple boils can be protected by covering them with a bandage until the boil comes to a head in about a week, breaks, and releases its small core and pus. The area should continue to be bandaged until healing is complete. For large or painful boils, you should promptly see your physician.

Warts and Moles

Warts are small growths on the skin. They often appear on the hands. Most of them are rough, although there is a smooth kind that hangs on a little stalk. These stalked warts are more likely to grow in the armpit. Warts are probably caused by a virus, but they often go away without treatment. If one starts to grow, see a doctor. It may not be a wart! Incidentally, the old superstition is not true; you don't get warts from toads.

Moles are skin growths of a darker color than the rest of your skin. Most moles are harmless unless irritated. Large, hairy, raised moles are no more dangerous than small, flat, smooth ones. The first rule in dealing with moles or other growths is: don't irritate them. Don't scratch or cut them, and don't squeeze or pick at them. Don't subject moles on any part of the body to friction from belts, straps, collars, or seams of clothing. If you have moles that cannot be protected from rubbing or scratching, you should have them removed. Any mole that becomes sore should be removed by a physician. Another rule for moles: if they begin to grow or *turn darker* in color, see your doctor. A mole that grows, darkens in color, gets sore, or bleeds may be the beginning of a skin cancer.

Don't treat your own moles or warts. Dark brown or blue-black moles, in particular, should be checked periodically by the doctor for any signs of change.

Athlete's Foot

Ringworm of the face or scalp and **athlete's foot** are much the same thing, except for location. The cause is a **fungus,** a form of plant life that thrives in animal tissue and which is hard to kill. Fungi live best in warm, moist spots and thrive in shower rooms and on swimming pool decks. Athlete's foot attacks toes and feet, making the skin itch, crack, and peel. The condition is extremely difficult to cure.

Rarely, athlete's foot causes **abscesses** (AB-sesses) and may cripple the feet for days or weeks. An abscess is a pus collection that forms in an infected area. To prevent athlete's foot, wash your feet with extra care. Dry them thoroughly, especially between the toes. Change your hose daily, and use a drying powder between your toes. The fungus causing athlete's foot may be present almost anywhere you are, and it attacks when the skin of the feet is in weakened condition. The term "athlete's foot" is really not accurate, since this condition is not peculiar to athletes.

Many boys and girls fear that they have athlete's foot when the trouble really is that their feet have become so warm and moist that the skin breaks down between their toes. If not treated properly, this condition leaves you more vulnerable to athlete's foot. The girls who slip their shoes off from time to time help their feet in two ways. They not only relieve pain caused by tight shoes; they also allow their toes to dry if they have been perspiring. This lessens the danger of any kind of foot infection. If you think you have athlete's foot you should see a doctor.

Ringworm has nothing to do with worms. Like athlete's foot, it is caused by a fungus. It grows in rings of various sizes, and it is very hard to treat when it occurs in the scalp.

Other Common Skin Troubles

Impetigo (im-peh-TY-goh) is an infection that spreads rapidly through the skin. This infection is caused by bacteria and may be caught from infected towels, clothing, or by contact. It is most common on face, hands, and neck, and it is extremely contagious. See a doctor immediately if you think you may have impetigo.

Scabies (SKAY-beez) is a Latin word which means *the itch*. This disorder is caused by a *mite*, a tiny, eight-legged creature. The mite digs into the skin and burrows under the surface. As it crawls, it causes intense itching. Since mites multiply rapidly, scabies requires a doctor's care. Scratching often results in infection. An individual who scratches because of scabies often gives himself impetigo.

Cold sores are the same thing as **fever blisters.** They are due to a virus that many people have all the time. The sores, which form only when the body is upset, are little blisters full of liquid, most often occurring on the lips or the skin around the mouth. Some people get the sores whenever they have a cold, a fever, sunburn, or indigestion. One treatment is to apply camphor or alcohol. Another—to let them alone. Don't squeeze them. The danger is that they may become infected when they break.

Eczema (EK-suh-muh) is most often due to an allergy. Certain foods, drugs, dyes, perfumes, plants, petroleum products, poisons, and many other things can cause it.

If you have eczema, your skin is spotted by red, swollen patches, which ooze a clear fluid. Such skin becomes scaly later. Don't try to treat eczema. See your doctor at the first sign of eczema.

Head lice are soft, gray insects which sometimes creep from one child's head to that of another in school or at play. More often they are picked up from a borrowed comb, brush, or hat. Lice suck blood from their victims. Their bites are so irritating that the victim scratches and may cause an infection. The best preventive for lice is cleanliness. If you should contract lice, see your doctor.

Warning—Avoid Risky Home Remedies

Except for simple measures of cleanliness as described in this chapter, let your skin alone. Avoid home remedies and popular skin treatments. These may help one person, have no effect on another, and be harmful to a third. If an unusual skin condition appears, see your physician. Some skin conditions are serious, and sometimes they mask other serious diseases.

WHAT ABOUT YOUR HAIR?

There is some growth of hair over the entire skin excepting the palms of your hands and soles of your feet. Each hair grows from a *hair follicle* (FOL-ih-k'l), a part of the epidermis that has pushed down like the root of a plant into the dermis (Figure 9-1). Cells within the follicle push upward, grow together, and harden into hair. As long as the cells in the follicle remain active, a hair can grow; but when they die, lost hair will not be replaced.

The *shaft* of a hair, above the scalp surface, has three layers of horny dead cells. These three layers of cells have heavy walls of the same protein found in the walls of cuticle cells. Your nails and the horns of some animals are made of the same substance. In a hair, only the middle layer of cells has color. The color of your hair depends on the kind and amount of pigment you have. As you grow older there is less pigment, and the hair turns gray and then white.

Curly or Straight Hair?

You may have wondered why some people have straight hair and others curly hair. Straightness or curliness depends on two things: whether the hair is round or flat when cut across, and whether the hair follicle is straight or curved. A straight follicle and a round cross section go with straight hair; a curved follicle and a flat cross section go with curly hair.

Have you ever been reading a "thriller" alone in a room at night, when a door banged behind you? Did a chill run down your spine and "gooseflesh" rise all over you? This condition in your skin is caused by little muscles attached to the roots of small hairs, so tiny that you need a lens to see many of them (Figure 9-1). As a rule, each hair slants to one side, but when you are cold or fright-

ened, a muscle contracts around the base of the hair and causes it to stand up. You then experience "gooseflesh."

The part of the hair that you see is not alive. You can give it a permanent wave, or cut it, and you feel nothing. Only the root of a hair is alive and the hair growth takes place at the root.

Why Brush Your Hair?

Brushing your hair every day stimulates blood circulation in the scalp, and in the neck and shoulders. Good circulation is necessary for the growth of hair. When brushing, avoid

9-11 Brushing your hair every day will stimulate scalp circulation and leave your hair looking clean and lustrous. How often do you brush your hair?

digging into the scalp as this may irritate the skin and lead to infection. Massaging your scalp also aids circulation. Both brushing and massage will result in cleaner, healthier, more lustrous-looking hair.

■ If you are at home, you might try this. Brush your hair and massage your scalp before reading further. Repeat this once a day for the next two weeks. Then see if your scalp feels cleaner and your hair looks more lustrous.

How to Shampoo Your Hair

Most people should shampoo the hair at least once a week, but more often if the scalp is oily and exposed to fumes and dust in the air. Liquid or cream shampoos are better than using a cake of soap, since they are easier to rinse from the hair.

Wet your hair thoroughly with warm water, apply the shampoo, and work the lather into your scalp with your finger tips. Rinse off the first suds and apply shampoo again. Again work the lather into the scalp and hair, then rinse the hair several times until all lather is removed. If you are using hard water, a few drops of lemon juice or vinegar will help remove the lather.

Dandruff

Two different conditions go under the name of *dandruff.* Ordinary dandruff is dead cuticle cells that are shed from the scalp in the same way they are shed from the rest of your skin. Dried oil on the scalp causes the shedding cells to stick together, forming the flakes that make dandruff so noticeable. This dandruff can be cleared up by improving general body care, frequent shampoos, and by keeping comb and brush clean.

Another, more severe, type of dandruff results from low resistance, nervous tension, or sometimes an infecting germ. Dandruff

from such sources is harder to deal with than ordinary dandruff and generally requires medical care.

Baldness

Most boys and girls your age have strong, healthy hair, and few girls or women are ever bothered with baldness. However, as they get older, many boys and men begin losing their hair.

Hair loss can be treated if it is caused by a scalp condition or illness. Notice whether or not your scalp looks healthy. Have you kept it clean and free of excessive dandruff? Have you brushed your hair and massaged your scalp regularly? If so, it may well be that you cannot avoid baldness permanently. Baldness is nearly always inherited, and, if so, cannot be avoided.

Excess Hair

The best way to temporarily remove unwanted hair is by shaving, using either a manual or an electric razor. You may have heard that shaving causes the hair to grow in thicker and coarser than it was. This is false. Your hair will look so at first, but when it has grown to normal length, its texture will be the same as before shaving.

There are other temporary hair removers called *depilatories.* Pumice stone is used to rub off the hair; wax or chemical preparations are used to peel off the hair. These may cause skin irritation in some people. Before using any chemical preparation first test it on a small area of skin. Bleaching unwanted hair with hydrogen peroxide will make it less conspicuous.

The permanent way to remove hair is by *electrolysis* (the electric needle). When done by a technician working under direction of a *dermatologist* (a skin specialist), this is a safe, although somewhat expensive, procedure.

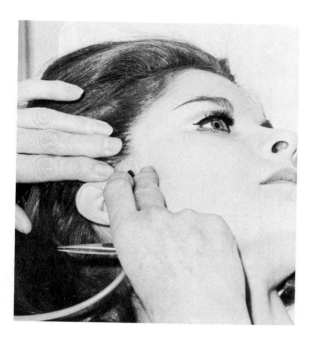

9-12 Electrolysis is the permanent way to remove unwanted hair.

CARING FOR YOUR NAILS

Your nails, like your hair, are modified skin structures. They develop from the outer layer of the skin. Good-looking nails depend partly on your health and partly on grooming.

How Your Nails Grow

Nails are made of the same protein that makes hair. You might think of a nail as many hairs fused together to make a horny plate. The part under the nail, called the **nail bed,** is made up of rows of papillae. The pink color of the nail bed comes from its many tiny blood vessels. Your nail grows in length as new cells are formed at its root. The new cells push the nail forward, and the rate of growth varies with age. If a nail is torn off, a new one will slowly grow in to replace it, providing the root cells and nail bed are not destroyed.

Trimming Your Nails

Your fingernails should be filed or clipped to conform to the shape of the finger tips. When they are a little longer than the finger tips, they act as protection for the tips and are helpful in picking things up. With toenails, there is sometimes a problem of ingrown nails, especially of the big toes. To prevent this, trim all toenails straight across. Infections are common with ingrown nails; if you have one, you should see your physician.

Cleaning Your Nails

Good grooming calls for scrupulously clean nails. A nail brush, used vigorously, will usually clean the nails, or an orange stick may be used to remove dirt from under the nails. There is danger of cutting the delicate flesh under the nail when a knife blade or the pointed end of a nail file is used.

Cuticle and Hangnails

The **cuticle** is the hardened skin around your nails. It may be gently pushed back with an orange stick. This is readily done just after washing your hands in warm water,

9-13 If desired, the softened cuticle of the nails may be pushed back gently with a padded orange stick.

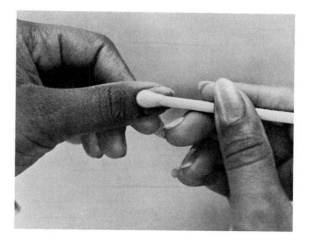

while the cuticle is softened. The cuticle should not be trimmed, as it will grow in heavy and coarse.

A *hangnail* is a sliver of cuticle that is hanging loose along the edge of a nail. It should be carefully clipped with small scissors sterilized in alcohol. Hangnails should not be pulled for danger of possible infection.

HOW TO CARE FOR YOUR TEETH

Sound teeth are a fine asset. They are important to your appearance, and they are indispensable to healthful living. The teeth that show when you talk and smile make an immediate impression. When they are clean, white, and regularly formed, the impression is favorable.

What Teeth Are Like

There are four types of teeth, each designed to perform a special function in eating. The *incisors* (in-SIZ-zors), located in the front of the mouth, cut food. The *cuspids,* located at the corners of the mouth, have a long, heavy root and a sharp, pointed crown. They tear food. The *bicuspids,* located back of the cuspids, have two projections on the crown (cusps) and one or two roots. They tear and crush food. The *molars,* located in the back of the mouth, have several projections on the crown and two or three roots. They grind food. See Figure 9-14.

In Figure 9-15, you can see the various parts of a tooth and their relation to each other. Each tooth has three parts. The *crown* is the part that projects above the gum and is covered by *enamel,* the hardest substance in the body, harder even than any of your bones. The *neck* is the narrow section at the gum line. The *root* lies below the gum line and is covered by a bonelike substance called *cementum.*

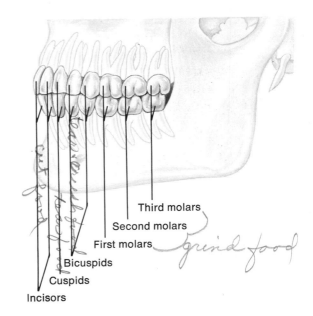

Third molars
Second molars
First molars
Bicuspids
Cuspids
Incisors

9-14 You have four different kinds of teeth: incisors, cuspids, bicuspids, and molars. Are you able to find these teeth in your own mouth? Where would you find your wisdom teeth in your mouth? What kind of teeth are they? Do you have any of your wisdom teeth?

Directly inside the enamel and cementum is a softer, bonelike substance called *dentine.* Inside the dentine is a space known as the *pulp cavity* that contains blood and lymph vessels, nerves, and a spongy material called *pulp.* The blood vessels and nerves enter the pulp cavity through *root canals* located in the tip of each root. The health of the tooth depends on the flow of blood through capillaries of the pulp and its nerve supply. In this way, the tooth is nourished by nutrients from your diet.

Below the gum line the root is surrounded by a thin, soft tissue called the *peridontal membrane.* This membrane absorbs the shock from chewing, provides for slight movement of the teeth in the jaw, and forms a surface between the teeth and jawbone that lies directly outside.

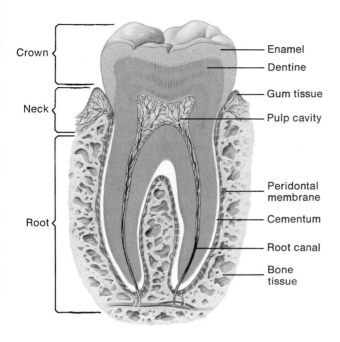

Crown
Neck
Root

Enamel
Dentine
Gum tissue
Pulp cavity
Peridontal membrane
Cementum
Root canal
Bone tissue

9-15 An enlarged diagram of a tooth. How are your teeth nourished? What nutrients are necessary for healthy teeth and gums?

How Teeth Develop

All of us usually develop two sets of teeth that started growing from embryonic tooth buds some months before birth. The first set of twenty, ten each in the upper and the lower jaw, are known as *deciduous* (de-SID-yoo-us), *primary*, or "baby" teeth. They begin to erupt through the gums during the sixth or seventh month after birth and are usually completed by the third year. The primary teeth are shed and replaced by permanent teeth that they guide into place.

Primary teeth have definite functions to perform and some, especially the primary molars, are needed until the tenth to twelfth years. They are important for chewing and good speech, and they provide symmetry to the face and preserve space for the permanent teeth. Their importance to health is not generally recognized, and many serious dental problems later in life result from poor care and the premature loss of these primary teeth.

The second, or *permanent set* of teeth, consists of thirty-two teeth, sixteen each in the upper and lower jaw. The first of these to erupt through the gums are the *six-year molars.* There are four of these, two each in the upper and lower jaw, and they appear at about six years of age, or about the same time the child is losing his front primary teeth. Since they do not replace any primary teeth, they are often mistaken for primary molars.

The last of the permanent teeth to appear are the third molars, or *wisdom teeth.* They erupt during the late teens or early twenties. Sometimes they come in at a wrong angle, or are *impacted* against the second molar, and have to be extracted.

This is not a serious loss to the process of chewing since there are enough other molars to do the job.

9-16 An X ray of a child's skull showing the primary, or "baby," teeth and the permanent teeth waiting to come in. Can you identify both sets of teeth? The heavy, white areas show dental caries.

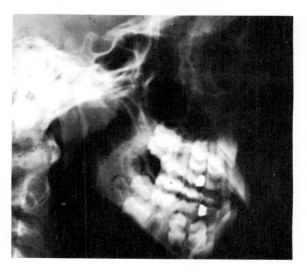

Dental Caries

Dental caries is a localized disease process that destroys tooth structure and produces cavities in teeth. It is more commonly known as *dental*, or *tooth*, *decay*. Decay begins with a small opening in the enamel. Such an opening or crack may be caused by bacterial action, by an accident, by cracking hard nuts between the teeth, by some flaw in the enamel, or within some area that is hard to clean. Once the enamel has been penetrated, bacteria and acids enter the pores of the much softer dentine. The decay spreads faster through the dentine until it reaches the pulp cavity. This allows food, heat, and cold to reach the nerves, often causing toothache.

When the blood and lymph vessels and nerves within the pulp cavity are exposed, they may become infected, and an *abscess* may form either within the tooth or at the tip of the root. Soreness and pain usually result. As the infection spreads, the face may swell and there may be pain. Your dentist can tell by X-ray examination the extent of the damage and type of treatment necessary.

Causes of Dental Caries

Early studies suggested that there might be a single causative factor for dental caries. This gave rise to the misleading saying that "a clean tooth cannot decay." Further dental research, however, shows the problem of dental caries to be more complex, and we now regard other factors important in addition to cleanliness.

One of these causes is the action of bacteria on fermentable carbohydrates, principally sugar, in the mouth. This process produces an acid that is capable of dissolving the hard tooth enamel.

Another cause of dental caries may be found in the diet. Calcium and phosphorus, and vitamin D, which regulates the utilization of these minerals in the body, are essential while the teeth are forming and throughout their growth. Milk, vegetables, and fish foods are rich sources of calcium and phosphorus. Vitamin D is likely to be deficient in natural foods during the winter months, but it can be obtained from vitamin D milk and cod-liver oil.

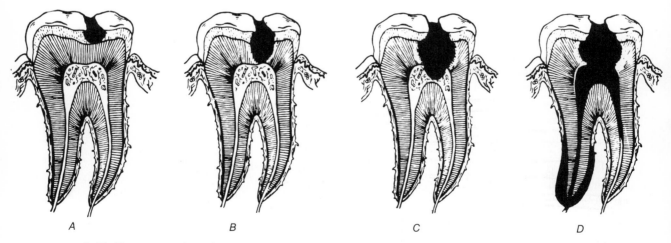

A	B	C	D

9-17 The stages of tooth decay. From left to right: (A) decayed enamel; (B) decayed enamel and dentine; (C) decayed pulp; (D) abscessed root. Pain usually starts in the second stage as a reaction to very hot or very cold foods or liquids. Why may pain become severe in the third and fourth stages? Do you recall when you last visited your dentist? If more than six months have elapsed since then, make an appointment now to have your teeth examined as soon as possible.

Controlling Dental Caries

At the present time there is no positive way to prevent all tooth decay. But you can make wise use of the control measures that are available. Important daily measures are (1) eating well-balanced meals; (2) reducing your daily intake of sweets; (3) brushing your teeth after eating and before going to bed. If you are away from home where you cannot brush, then rinse your mouth thoroughly with water.

At least once a year, have your teeth and gums examined by a dentist. You might also consult him about the possibility of applying sodium fluoride directly to the surface of your teeth. This is fairly expensive treatment, but may cut dental caries about 40 percent. This measure is recommended in areas where the drinking water is deficient in fluorides.

Fluoridation of Water Supplies

Perhaps the best and least expensive measure against dental caries is the addition of one part fluorine per million parts of water to drinking water in municipal and private water supplies. This is called *fluoridation* (FLOO-rid-a-shun). Experiments across the nation have proved the effectiveness of this measure in the prevention of dental caries, especially among growing youngsters. However, despite the proven worth of fluoridation, there remain some localities that are reluctant to add fluorine to the water supply.

Cleaning Your Teeth

The purpose of brushing your teeth is to remove food particles from between the teeth and crevices in the chewing surfaces. Brushing also helps prevent tartar deposits from forming, and it stimulates the circulation of blood in the gums.

The acids that cause tooth decay begin their work while you are still eating and can do much damage if you wait until bedtime to brush. The teeth should be brushed as soon as possible after eating, even after eating snacks. If you cannot brush, rinse your mouth thoroughly with water. Many people, including students, do not know how to brush their teeth properly. The proper method is illustrated in Figure 9-19. If you practice this method, it will soon become a good habit.

Selecting Your Toothbrush and Dentifrice

Many toothbrushes are too large to be of practical use. An effective brush should have a head that is small enough to reach all surfaces of your teeth. It should have firm bristles and a flat brushing surface. The relatively new *electric toothbrush* has certain advantages, especially for handicapped persons. It is easy to manipulate and mechanically efficient. It can do nothing, however, that hand brushing cannot do, and it cannot in any way replace professional dental care.

9-18 One way of fluoridating water is shown here. A fluoride is poured into the small pipe. From there it flows into the community water supply.

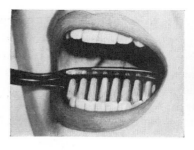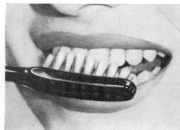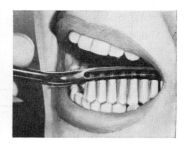

9-19 Do you brush your teeth correctly? (*Left*) Brush away from the gums to clean back surfaces. Brush up on lower teeth, down on upper teeth. (*Center*) Clean the front surfaces by brushing away from the gums in the same manner used for the back surfaces. (*Right*) Brush in little circular movements to clean the chewing and grinding surfaces. When you have finished, rinse your mouth thoroughly with warm water containing a pinch of salt or baking soda.

Using a *dentifrice*—toothpaste or powder—makes brushing more pleasant, but it is to be regarded as an aid rather than a treatment. A good dentifrice contains a harmless, abrasive substance that aids in cleansing. An inexpensive cleanser can be made by combining bicarbonate of soda with table salt. The highly advertised dentifrices that guarantee to "whiten" or "brighten" the teeth have not, as yet, been proved by controlled experiments to be effective.

Bad Breath and Mouthwashes

Halitosis—offensive or bad breath—can be a social handicap, as the advertisements all say. But there are things that can be done about bad breath; the first is to find the cause. Constant bad breath is usually a symptom of some condition that needs correction. For example, neglected decay in teeth and pockets of food particles may cause bad breath. Medical diagnosis and treatment is needed to determine the cause.

Mouthwashes have only a temporary effect and cannot be relied on to reach the fundamental causes of bad breath. Their useful function is for rinsing the mouth after eating when it is not possible to brush your teeth. A safe, inexpensive mouthwash can be made from a solution of salt or soda and water.

Other Dental Disorders

Broken teeth should be repaired or replaced for the sake of your health and your appearance. Teeth are frequently chipped, cracked, or broken by biting on metal objects, cracking nuts, or trying to loosen bottle caps. All of these can be avoided by reminding yourself not to do them. Broken teeth are highly subject to dental caries.

Stained teeth can be made more attractive by your dentist, who uses special cleansing instruments and abrasives.

Lost teeth can and usually should be replaced. When not replaced, the adjacent and opposing teeth gradually shift their position in the jaw. This shift affects the proper alignment of the upper and lower teeth. It interferes with proper chewing of food.

Diseased teeth are not always painful, but they can affect your health and lower your resistance to other diseases. Having your teeth checked regularly by your dentist is a good way to avoid such conditions.

What You Have Learned

What kind of health practices should you apply in maintaining your appearance? Check your understanding of the chapter. On a separate sheet of paper, number 1 through 20 and insert the answer from the vocabulary list below. Use each expression, but use each one only once.

adolescent   follicle   regenerate
caries   foreign objects root
cementum   germs   sebaceous
crown   hair   shaving
dermis   nails   soap
electrolysis   papillae   water
enamel   peridontal

Your skin shields you against (1)_____ and (2)_____. Your (3)_____ and (4)_____ are modifications of skin, developed to serve special needs. The remarkable property of skin is its power to (5)_____ itself. Your skin forms such distinctive markings that your fingerprints are not like those of any other person. These markings are made by rows of (6)_____ that grow up from the (7)_____. The skin is kept soft by the secretion of oil from the (8)_____ glands. These glands are more active during your (9)_____ years. The best way to clean your skin is with (10)_____ and (11)_____.

There is some hair growth over most of the body, except on the palms of your hands and soles of your feet. Each hair grows from a hair (12)_____ of the skin. The safe way to temporarily remove unwanted hair is by (13)_____, and the permanent way is by (14)_____.

The part of your tooth that projects above the gum line is the (15)_____; it is covered with (16)_____. Below the gum line is the (17)_____, covered by (18)_____. Below the gum line the tooth is covered by the (19)_____ membrane that forms a surface between the tooth and jaw bone. Decay that causes tooth cavities is called dental (20)_____.

What You Can Do

1. Make a careful, honest list of the things about your physical appearance that you would like to improve. You may find that some of these you can correct yourself; others you will need help with, such as crooked teeth. Start working on those that you can correct, one at a time, until you change all of them. If possible, make plans to have those corrected that you cannot take care of alone.

2. Make a collection of cosmetic advertisements and look at the cosmetic displays in the drugstore. Study the claims that are made for these products. How true do you think these claims are?

3. Find out from your classmates what they have heard of as a "cure" for warts. Do warts ever go away without treatment? What should you do if a wart begins to grow in size?

Things to Try

1. Find out how many of your classmates are opposed to public fluoridation of water supplies. What is the basis for their opposition?
2. Try making a fingerprint file. Press the right side of your forefinger tip against an inked stamp pad, roll your finger from right to left to pick up the ink. Now roll your finger tip from right to left on a piece of white paper and you will see your fingerprint. Make prints of your other fingers in this same way and you will have a set of prints. Compare your friends' prints with your own: you will notice how different they are. You can also make footprints of your dog or cat.

Probing Further

Effective Oral Hygiene, The American Academy of Periodontology, 211 East Chicago Ave., Chicago, Illinois, 60611. This booklet and other literature on the teeth and gums is available free from the Academy.

Know Your Skin, by John H. Woodburn, Putnam, 1967. Explains many things about the skin and hair, including how the skin responds to emotions, insect bites, poisons, skin infections.

Understanding Dentistry, by Minna Lantner and Gerald Bender, Beacon Press, 1969. A very readable, thorough, and well-written book which covers all aspects of tooth care and dentistry, including tooth growth and decay, dental practices, and how to choose a dentist.

Health Concepts in Action

Does this statement agree with your own ideas?

> **Maintaining one's appearance contributes to physical, mental, and social fitness.** Yes

Applying this concept of a healthful appearance, which health practices would you

—continue?

—change?

—begin?

Will you now, as a result of your study, change any of your health objectives?

10 / *Sports and Sportsmanship*

"But Dad," exclaimed Henry, "I've never been sick a day in my life! Why do I have to take a physical examination?" "Now Henry," replied his father, "if you are going out for competitive sports, your school says you must have a physical examination, and I agree with them."

Taking a thorough preseason history of a player and giving him a physical examination are the most important precautions in the prevention of sports injuries. Another feature of the preseason examination is the proper matching of players, since teen-agers grow at different rates and show great variations in size.

A PROBE INTO SPORTS—How can you improve your health through sports? To find out, you will be probing these questions:

1. How do sports contribute to your physical growth? to your social growth?

2. What does sportsmanship mean to you? What values are found in teams and individual sports that will be useful to you in adult life?

3. Why is protective gear required in some sports?

4. What protections for the player and the school are listed in the "Bill of the Athlete"?

5. Which sport has the greatest number of fatal accidents? Why is this so?

6. Why does the American Red Cross stress the precaution "throw, row, go"? Who should "go"?

SPORTS FURNISH A BASIC NEED

In Chapters 6 and 8 you learned the value of regular physical activity in maintaining fitness. Sports are an enjoyable way to meet this basic need. You nourish your body daily with food and drink and refresh it with rest and sleep. As far as possible, you should also give your body the exercise it needs. Requirements vary from person to person. However, at least a half hour to an hour of daily vigorous physical activity should usually be aimed for. Even the ill need some exercise each day; exercise has become common practice as post-operative therapy.

Sports for Fun and Friendship

You have learned earlier of the biological and chemical effects of exercise on muscular growth and efficiency. These, in themselves, produce a sense of well-being. Part of the fun in sports is making use of well-coordinated muscles in leisure-time sports activities.

Participating in sports does not always mean formal, competitive events. The "pick-up" games, pairing friends against friends, are the fun and friendship way of sports, and the physical exercise will be just as beneficial. Often, too, in the "pick-up" games, it is possible to drain off some of your troublesome feelings and be refreshed and relaxed emotionally as well as physically.

Play and sports are great social common denominators that can provide fun and build friendships among people wherever you happen to live. If you are a newcomer in a community, you will find companionship by participating in the sports that are available.

Value of Sportsmanship

One of the great benefits of participating in sports is that you learn to cooperate with teammates and you try, by fair means, to outwit your opponent. You play to win, but

10-1 Volleyball is an enjoyable group activity. It is a social game as well as a competitive sport. Is volleyball played at your school?

you learn how to be a good loser. When you win, you learn how to accept victory without boasting. Rules, you find out, have a purpose. They help guarantee fair competition, and they protect you from injury. You learn the value of team play where the team is more important than the individual.

There are many ways of demonstrating your sportsmanship as a player. You do this when you learn and obey the rules; when you master the skills needed for winning and safe play; when you observe the customs and etiquette of each sport. As a spectator, you applaud the good plays of the visiting team as well as those of your own team, and you respect the decisions of the officials. The "fans" of the visiting team are guests of your school, and you show them every courtesy.

When you think about these qualities of sportsmanship, you see how they apply to other activities in your school: such activities as your clubs, committees, group work—everywhere that students are engaged together in activities. They become socially

10-2 Tennis is a fast-moving sport and fun to watch. This picture was taken at a National Singles match at Forest Hills, New York.

10-3 Interest in baseball begins at an early age. This photograph was taken at a Little League game between the United States and Japanese champions.

useful to you in your community activities. And you find there is a great feeling of satisfaction in being counted on as a cooperative member of a team, whether in a sport or on the program committee for your school dance.

Batter Up! Play Ball!

"Batter up" sounds the call for spring and for our national sport. It may be heard from vacant lots, farm yards, sand lots, back yards, and on the diamonds of playgrounds, open fields, and big-league ball parks. It is baseball no matter where it is played. People of all ages and both sexes come to watch or to play, for baseball is a sport of great fascination for both players and spectators.

Baseball evolved in America from various bat-and-ball games that our early settlers brought with them from England. "Rounders" and "town-ball," as the earlier games were called, gave way to the organized sport of baseball with the adoption of a code of rules that was printed in 1845. A year later, the first match on record was played.

The Civil War interrupted the development of what was then club baseball, but it produced even larger numbers of followers. The game was played in base camps and behind the lines. At war's end, the troops took baseball home to their communities. In 1872, the magazine *Sports and Games* pronounced baseball the "national game of the United States."

Football—a Rugged Sport

Football was developed mainly in colleges from the English game rugby, which the early colonists brought to America. As early as 1840, Yale conducted scrimmages on the college lawn, but the first intercollegiate match, between Princeton and Rutgers, was not played until 1869.

By the 1900's, football had become so rough and dangerous that many colleges considered dropping it as a sport. But President Theodore Roosevelt, an enthusiast of all sports, intervened and called representatives from Yale, Harvard, and Princeton to

10-4 Skilled skating is needed in ice hockey, long a favorite sport in Europe and Canada.

10-5 Which sports do you enjoy more? Those sports in which you compete with your classmates, or those in which you compete with yourself?

10-6 Both professional and amateur basketball are popular sports. Which do you enjoy more? Why?

the White House to discuss this matter. The outcome of the session was the introduction of the forward pass and other changes that made the game more open, less hazardous, and faster.

From these beginnings, football has grown to the tremendous popularity that it enjoys today. The enthusiasm for football soon penetrated high schools, and today it has great popularity as an interscholastic and a professional sport.

Basketball—"Made in America"

Unlike many other sports, the exact origin of basketball seems to be clearly established. History records that in the winter of 1891–92, Dr. James Naismith, an instructor at the YMCA Training College (now Springfield College) at Springfield, Massachusetts, invented the game. His object was to provide exercise and competition between the football and the baseball seasons. He fastened peach baskets overhead on the walls at opposite ends of the gymnasium and, using what is now a soccer ball, organized teams for play. The purpose of his new game was to toss the ball into one basket and prevent, as far as possible, the opponent from tossing the ball into the other basket. Fundamentally, the game is the same today, although there have been improvements in equipment and many changes in rules. During World War I, American soldiers introduced the game in Europe and it soon became a world sport.

Swimming — an Ancient Sport

As far back as there are written records, you can find reference to swimming the world over. Its actual origin is not revealed, however, in writing or in sculpture. But we do know that man, unlike most animals, is not a natural swimmer.

Among early records you may see, in the British Museum, art work dated 880 B.C. showing a fugitive swimming a river to escape his captors. Also, history relates that elaborate baths, used for swimming, were located in ancient Rome. One of these, called Caracalla, covered twenty-nine acres and was completed about A.D. 217.

The first mention of competitive swimming is found in Greek history, and in Rome swimming was considered an essential skill, as is seen in the Roman adage "He has neither learned to read nor to swim."

In America, *The Art of Swimming* by J. Frost was published in 1818 and contained letters from Benjamin Franklin about the art of swimming. On his trip to Europe, Franklin was requested to teach swimming to the nobility. He was, at that time, America's best swimmer and a dedicated teacher.

Long-distance swimming was the early form of competition, and the English Channel — Dover to Calais — became the great challenge. Matthew Webb, in August 1875, was the first to conquer these choppy waters. His time was 21 hours 45 minutes. Later other swimmers were also successful, but in August 1926, Gertrude Ederle of New York City lowered the Channel record with her triumphant swim in 14 hours 34 minutes. Since that time, the record has been lowered by a number of swimmers.

Today, competition at short as well as long distances, indoors and outdoors, attracts thousands of swimmers the world over. It has been an important event in Olympic competition since the start of modern Olympic games in 1896.

Interest in swimming has grown rapidly in America with the increase of public and private pools, beaches, and artificial lakes. Schools, clubs, and community centers offer instruction in swimming and conduct contests that attract thousands of people of all ages. Swimming provides great pleasure in addition to wholesome exercise and what some believe to be the therapeutic effects of water and sun.

10-7 Swimming can be an enjoyable social activity as well as a highly competitive sport.

Other Sports

Many other sports were introduced in America and enjoyed periods of enthusiastic popularity. Lawn tennis and croquet started out as the fashionable lawn games of polite society. Archery was revived from its ancient form and joined the lawn games. These were played by both men and women. Tennis gradually developed into the active sport we know today. By 1900, with the establishment of the international Davis Cup matches, tennis became a serious sport, no longer merely a lawn pastime.

Such sports as polo, sailing, riding, rowing, and fox-hunting were the pleasure of the wealthy, leisure class. Since these were expensive sports to maintain, their popularity was not so widespread. But they did play a part in maintaining a lively interest in sports.

Bicycling and roller-skating had great appeal to large numbers of people. Here were sports that almost everyone could afford, and they soon swept the country.

By the early 1900's, a number of events had taken place that greatly influenced the development of organized sports. Our puritan inheritance, so opposed to play and sports, had been largely overcome. Roads were improved and modes of transportation had increased. Trains, automobiles, and aircraft opened vast areas for sports, not earlier within reach. Sports had withstood the test of wars, time, and depression. Now, in the second half of the 1900's, the list of sports has reached great proportions and new sports continue to be added. The general public has a long list of sports from which to choose. Young and old alike find pleasure in everything from shuffleboard to skiing. There is today a sport available to suit the age, disposition, and skills of practically everyone. Do you have a favorite sport? Is it an individual or team sport? Do you get more satisfaction from playing an individual or team sport?

Selecting Sports

Many things enter into your choice of sports. Among these are the variety of sports offered in your school sports program, at your home, in your community, and in summer camp. Then, too, the climate where you live will determine which outdoor sports can be engaged in. You may, for instance, have snow-skiing, ice-skating, and tobogganing; or it may be water-skiing, scuba-diving, or sailing.

Your own natural disposition will play a part in your choice. Some teen-agers prefer the team sports and the excitement of co-ordinated effort of teammates. Others enjoy playing against one or two opponents, while still others like competing against their own scores, as in golf.

Sometimes your choice may be guided by your size and build. Also, you may wear glasses or suffer from some orthopedic problem. Being very tall and slender may rule out football, just as being short and stocky may rule out basketball. They are ruled out, that is, for interscholastic competition, but often you can play on your class team where your opponents will be more nearly your own size. Also, you can learn the skills and rules and be an appreciative supporter of your team.

A wise choice of sports can add real enjoyment to your life, and when school days are over, you will find much pleasure in using many of the skills you have learned. School days are, perhaps, the best time for team sports that require a large number of players. Such sports include football, basketball, baseball, softball, field hockey, soccer, and speedball. Later on, you may enjoy the individual and dual sports that you can play with a friend or two. Among these are swimming, golf, riding, climbing, sailing, skiing, skeet shooting, hunting, tennis, badminton, and bowling, to mention just a few. How many others can you think of?

Activities for the Handicapped

There are many games, and even some sports, the student can take part in even if he has defective sight or hearing loss or if he has been crippled. Swimming is perhaps the favorite of these sports. Many determined and courageous students develop skills in such sports as rope climbing despite the loss of a leg. Others, handicapped by a loss of hearing or sight, develop into good skaters, and one-armed players compete successfully in tennis. The physically handicapped student has only to keep in mind that he should choose an activity that does not risk injury to himself or to others.

SAFETY IN SPORTS

Participating in sports can be a healthful and exhilarating experience, and time spent in play can soothe away tension. But sports, like most other activities, have some potential hazards. Part of learning to play any sport involves recognizing the potential hazards of the game, in order to find out how best to avoid being injured. Safety rules and protective gear, along with the rules of play, are designed to safeguard you against hazards and possible injury. You are asked to walk, and not run, on the wet deck at the pool. If you play football, you wear a mouth-guard to protect your teeth. In field hockey, your shins are protected by shinguards. You wait on the golf course, before you drive, until the players ahead of you have taken their second drive. Each sport has its own equipment, its own protective gear, its own safety precautions, and its own rules of play that are meant to safeguard you against accidents.

There may be times when you feel that your coach or instructor is heartless when he or she refuses to permit you to play without wearing your protective gear; when a game is called off because of darkness or a wet

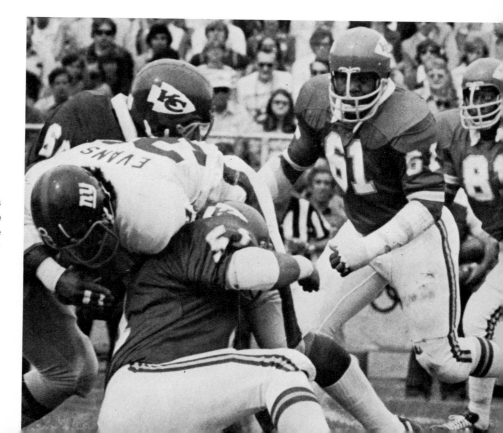

10-8 Safety in sports is very important. What is the value of protective gear in football? What other sports require protective gear?

field or court; when a "winded" player is removed from the game. These are the precautions a coach or instructor is expected to take for your protection.

"Bill of Rights of the Athlete"

As a participant in school sports, you are entitled to equipment and safety devices suitable to the sport and to medical care, if needed. These provisions, like the rules of play, are a kind of guarantee for you. They assure you of a good chance to enjoy your sports with maximum safety, and they assure you of proper care in case of an accident. Under such conditions, you may expect to experience healthy growth and development without the handicap of injury.

The American Medical Association's Committee on the Medical Aspects of Sports has set forth its recommendations for safety in sports in the "Bill of Rights of the Athlete." These are the practices that you, the player, have the right to expect. In brief, these "Rights" are as follows:

"1. *Good Coaching.* The coach who teaches unsportsmanlike tactics to win at any price is today almost extinct. Almost all coaches today are competent instructors in the technical aspects of the game, ignorance of which, of course, greatly increases the incidence and severity of injury.

"2. *Good Equipment.* The manufacturers of equipment take their responsibility seriously and are continually modifying and improving the various types of protective devices worn in contact sports. The problem lies in the false economy of using worn-out, outmoded, or ill-fitted gear.

"3. *Good Medical Care,* which has three major aspects:

    (*a*) A thorough preseason history and a physical examination of each player. These constitute the most important factors in the prevention of injuries. Many of the sports tragedies that occur every year are due to medical conditions—such as heart disease, hypertension, and diabetes—which went unrecognized.

"Another important part of the preseason examination, particularly in high schools and preparatory schools, is the proper matching of players. Boys grow at different rates. Some at 15 have mature and well-coordinated musculo-skeletal systems. Others are small and soft, having barely entered adolescence; and still others are large-boned, skinny, and uncoordinated, being in a period of rapid bone growth, with barely compensated nerves and muscles. To mix these types on a team is to court trouble. Well-matched teams are safer and provide much more fun for all concerned.

    (*b*) A doctor (ideally the same one) should be available throughout the season and should be present at every game. To let a trainer or coach decide whether an injured player should continue to play or be removed from the game, and, if removed, whether he should be carried or walk off the field, is to gamble with a player's future.

    (*c*) The doctor's authority in medical matters should be absolute and unquestioned. It is quite true that the great majority of sports injuries are not serious, will heal despite even bizarre treatment, and will leave no permanent disability, but the day of regarding this problem as 'minor' and beneath the dignity of a proper doctor is gone." (*Today's Health*

Guide, American Medical Association, W. W. Bauer, M. D., editor [*Chicago, 1970*], pp. 236-237.)

Swimming Safety

Of all the sports, swimming has the most hazards and accounts for the greatest number of fatal sports accidents. Among teen-agers and young adults, only automobile accidents cause more fatalities. Every year about 6,500 persons drown while swimming or boating or by breaking through ice, or falling into the water from docks, piers, bridges, or river banks. This is sufficient reason for everyone to learn how to swim safely and how to help a swimmer in trouble.

Perhaps the first precaution is to learn to swim. Swim well enough to take care of yourself, except under the most unusual circumstances. No matter how well you swim, it is important to have someone with you who could help, in case of an emergency. When the temperature of the water is around 70 to 78 degrees, the body is relaxed and comfortable. Sixty degree water may be exhilarating to some, but the output of energy, to counter the loss of body heat, may lead to rapid exhaustion.

When big thunderclouds appear in the sky, it is time to get out of the water. Water attracts lightning and presents a hazard to swimmers.

Swim only in a familiar outdoor area,

10-9 Two rescue holds in swimming: (*top*) the head carry; (*bottom*) the cross-chest carry. Always follow the advice of the Red Cross water safety course: "throw, row, go," in that order. The only person who should "go" is a strong swimmer thoroughly trained in lifesaving procedures.

where you know how deep the water is and whether there are dangerous currents or tides. If possible, swim only where a lifeguard is on duty. Never swim in polluted water, since you are bound to get some water in your mouth. Nonswimmers should remain in shallow water, even though they may be using water wings, floats, inner tubes, or planks. On such equipment, it is easy to be floated into deep water. Floating is a skill that everyone can and should acquire. It is helpful when you tire, and it may save your life when in trouble and awaiting rescue.

When you feel tired or chilled, it is time to stop swimming. These feelings are your body's warning signals that you have had enough.

Some Causes of Water Accidents

Panic is a sudden, unreasoning, overwhelming fear that may attack nearly anyone in the face of real or imagined danger. Nonswimmers and novices are particularly susceptible to panic, but it can strike seasoned swimmers as well.

Exhaustion is another frequent cause of swimming accidents. There are innumerable possible causes. Some of these may be going into the water when overheated or overtired, when still recovering from an illness, when the water is too cold, or when you disregard the limits of your own strength.

Cramp causes pain and discomfort, and sometimes panic. Cramp most often occurs in the muscles of the feet, legs, and hands due to poor blood circulation resulting from fatigue or cold. The muscle contracts into a hard knot that prevents movement of the affected part. You can relieve cramp by assuming a back-floating position, drawing the knees toward the abdomen, and exerting pressure and kneading on the muscle. An expert swimmer may take a deep breath, roll to a face-down position, and grasp the cramped muscle firmly. If the muscle does not relax, then rubbing and kneading may help to restore circulation.

Currents, caused by the movement of water, add an element of danger to swimming in oceans and rivers. Two kinds of currents menace bathers in the ocean. These are

10-10 Look before you leap! Never dive into strange waters—unseen objects may be dangerous.

tides and undertow. Tides move large masses of water and may run for great distances. An undertow is the receding movement of water that runs back under oncoming waves; it can be quite violent, but it runs for short distances. In rivers, currents are deceptive as to their direction of flow, which is often strong. When caught in a current of any type, you should swim diagonally across it. If you should be caught in a very strong current, it may be best to float or tread water until you reach still water, or until help arrives. In any case, try to avoid wearing yourself out by swimming against the current. Even the best of swimmers find it difficult, if not impossible, to "buck" a current.

Additional Precautions

Night swimming on a hot evening can be refreshing and fun but should be limited to the experienced swimmer. Floodlights should be placed so as to light the entire swimming area adequately. If possible, swimmers should be in pairs, and a lifeguard is essential.

When swimming a long distance, you should arrange to have someone accompany you in a boat.

Often there are notices posted along the beach or near a lake or river to warn swimmers of possible hazards. The good swimmer looks for these notices and observes them.

Diving is a fine skill to learn and to use in familiar waters. To dive into strange waters is to run the risk of striking unseen objects.

The water is no place for rough play, ducking nonswimmers, and similar acts. Such behavior creates hazards that often lead to accidents.

The nonswimmer should have a life preserver as a part of his "must" gear whenever he is afloat in any kind of small craft. Life preservers are now readily available almost everywhere. Often, in indoor pools the nonswimmers are required to wear red bathing caps to help lifeguards look after them.

To the Rescue

The instinct to assist a person in danger of drowning prompts many persons to heroic rescue attempts for which they are poorly, or not at all, fitted. The desire to help too often ends tragically for both victim and would-be rescuer. Swimmers trained by the American National Red Cross in lifesaving can safely go to the rescue of a swimmer in trouble. But others, without this training, use good judgment when they resort to other types of aids for rescue.

Many potential drownings occur near shore. In such cases, a rescuer may be able to throw the victim a rope, or reach him with a sweater, pole, or anything else close at hand. If the swimmer is farther out and a boat is nearby, the rescuer can row out, extend an oar to the victim, and tow him in. In lifesaving, the Red Cross stresses the precaution of "throw, row, go," in that order. The "go" is reserved for the strong swimmer who has had training in lifesaving procedures and knows how to protect himself while making a drowning rescue. Courses of this type are available in many communities. If you are a strong swimmer, you may want to take such a course.

Artificial Respiration

Saving a person's life in a near-drowning accident does not end when the victim is brought to shore. Artificial respiration is immediately indicated. Mouth-to-mouth resuscitation is now considered the best method. The techniques of this procedure are simple and easy to apply, even by small children. It is a good procedure for the whole family to know. Refer to Figure 10-11 as you read this section.

"If there is foreign matter visible in the mouth, wipe it out quickly with your fingers or a cloth wrapped around your fingers.

1. Tilt the head back so the chin is pointing upward (A). Pull or push the jaw into a jutting-out position (B and C). These maneuvers should relieve obstruction of the airway by moving the base of the tongue away from the back of the throat.

2. Open your mouth wide and place it tightly over the victim's mouth. At the same time pinch the victim's nostrils shut (D) or close the nostrils with your cheek (E). Or close the victim's mouth and place your mouth over the nose (F). Blow into the victim's mouth or nose. (Air may be blown through the victim's teeth, even though they may be clenched.) The first blowing efforts should determine whether or not obstruction exists.

3. Remove your mouth, turn your head to the side, and listen for the return rush of air that indicates air exchange. Repeat the blowing effort. For an adult, blow vigorously at the rate of about 12 breaths per minute. For a child, take relatively shallow breaths appropriate for the child's size, at the rate of about 20 per minute.

4. If you are not getting air exchange, recheck the head and jaw position (A, B, or C). If you still do not get air exchange, quickly turn the victim on his side and administer several sharp blows between the shoulder blades in the hope of dislodging foreign matter (G). Again sweep your fingers through the victim's mouth to remove foreign matter.

Those who do not wish to come in contact with the person may hold a thin cloth over the victim's mouth or nose and breathe through it. The cloth does not greatly affect the exchange of air." (Supplement on Artificial Respiration, American National Red Cross, pages 4–6.)

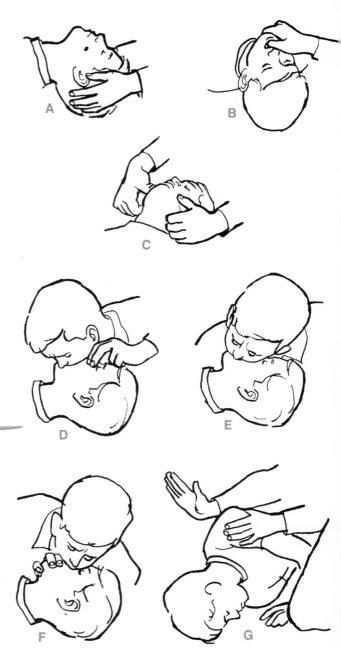

10-11 The mouth-to-mouth method of artificial respiration. Refer to the instructions at the left of this figure for a step-by-step description of what is taking place. Have you performed this type of artificial respiration? Have you ever watched someone else do it?

Check List for Safety in Water Sports

1. Learn to swim and relax in the water. Until you have accomplished this, you should wear a life belt whenever you are in the water or on the water in small craft.
2. Never swim alone.
3. Swim at places known to be safe, preferably places supervised by lifeguards.
4. Beware of unfamiliar areas; they may have treacherous currents, deep holes, hidden objects, and other hazards.
5. Don't swim when overheated, over-tired, right after eating, or when the water is unusually cold.
6. Before diving, make sure there are no hidden objects and that the water is deep enough.
7. If you are going on a distant swim in open water, have someone accompany you in a boat.
8. Don't overestimate your own ability; it is difficult to judge distance over water accurately.
9. Be sure to learn new skills with an instructor before you try them out on your own.
10. Don't stand or try to change seats in small craft while underway.
11. If a boat overturns, stay with it and don't try to swim a long distance to shore.
12. If you get a leg cramp, don't panic. Draw your knees up to your chest, or catch hold of your toes and pull, or kick vigorously with both feet. Try to relax and assume a floating position.
13. There is no place in, or on, the water for horseplay. Horseplay should be forbidden.
14. A swimming rescue should be attempted *only* by persons trained in lifesaving.

What You Have Learned

What kind of health practices should you apply in maintaining your health? Check your understanding of the chapter. On a separate sheet of paper, number 1 through 19 and insert the answer from the vocabulary list below. Use each expression, but use each one only once.

9 basketball	17 exhaustion	7 officials
2 competitive	4 fair competition	16 panic
6 cooperating	15 fatal	14 shin guards
18 cramps	10 football	11 swimming
19 currents	12 hazards	1 two
8 1872	5 injury	
3 exercise	13 mouth guards	

Teen-agers need a minimum of (1) *two* hours of daily vigorous activity to help them grow strong. Participation in sports does not always mean formal (2) *competitive* events. "Pick-up" games also provide good physical (3) *exercise*. Rules for sports help guarantee (4) *fair competition* and they protect the player against (5) _injury_. You demonstrate sportsmanship by (6) _cooperating_ with teammates as a player and by respecting the decisions of (7) _officials_ as a spectator.

Although baseball evolved from various English bat-and-ball games, it was pronounced our national sport in (8) _1871_. Nineteen years later, America introduced its own original game of (9) _basketball_. Before either of these dates, colleges were playing (10) _football_, a game developed largely from the English game rugby. Another popular intercollegiate and interscholastic sport is (11) _rowing_, the oldest sport on record.

Part of learning any sport involves recognizing the potential (12) _hazards_ of the game. To avoid unnecessary injury you are required to wear such protective gear as (13) _arm guards_ for football and (14) _shin guards_ for field hockey. Records show that in swimming there are more (15) _fatal_ accidents than in other sports. Among the frequent causes of water accidents are (16) _panic_, (17) _fatigue_, (18) _cramps_, and (19) _currents_.

What You Can Do

1. Make a list of the potential hazards you should guard against in each of these sports: football, field hockey, basketball, baseball, swimming, scuba diving, skiing, and ice-skating.

2. When engaging in sports, why is it good practice to remove wrist watches, bracelets, and rings?

3. What is the purpose of the general rule that only gym shoes are to be worn in the gymnasium? Is it to avoid scratching the floor? Is it so everyone will look alike? Or is it to avoid accidents?

4. When participating in competition, what should you do when you know you have committed a foul? Raise your hand? Play on as though nothing had happened? Decide that it is up to the official to call the fouls?

Things to Try

1. While swimming at a nearby lake, one of your friends calls urgently for help just as you approach the shore. How would you respond to his cry?

2. Suppose you decide to draft a "Code of Sportsmanship." What items will you include in such a code?

3. Try practicing some skill you are interested in and keep a record of your improvement. For example:

   a. The number of goals you can make out of each five tries from the basketball foul line.

   b. The distance you can throw a baseball, softball, or basketball.

c. The time it takes you to swim the length of your pool or to run a fifty-yard dash.

d. The distance you can jump in a running broad jump or in a standing broad jump.

e. The time it takes you to climb up the climbing rope in the gymnasium.

Probing Further

New York Times Guide to Spectator Sports, by Leonard Koppett, Quadrangle Books, 1971. Includes chapters on swimming, fencing, baseball, football, hockey, track and field, gymnastics, and other popular sports.

Bill Talbert's Weekend Tennis, by Bill Talbert, Doubleday, 1970. The beginner will find here much useful and entertaining information about tennis strategy and equipment.

How to Play Baseball, by Bud Harrelson, Atheneum, 1972. In a conversational style, the author advises you how to improve fielding, hitting, base running, and other techniques. There are hints for all builds and abilities.

First Aid Textbook, American National Red Cross, Doubleday, 1957. This text contains procedures for artificial respiration, rules for watercraft use, and precautions for water sports, some of which are explained in your textbook.

Safety Education, by Florio and Stafford, McGraw-Hill, 1969. Safety procedures in all walks of life are explained in this textbook.

Today's Health Guide, American Medical Association, 1970. This important volume includes material on play, sports, and recreation.

Health Concepts in Action

Does this statement agree with your own ideas?

Participation in sports contributes to physical, mental, and social fitness.

Applying this concept of sports, which health practices would you

— continue?

— change?

— begin?

Will you now, as a result of your study, change any of your health objectives?

11 / Keeping in Touch Through Your Senses

A great roar of applause resounded in the gymnasium when your team sank the winning basket just as the final whistle blew. Many of your senses were stimulated during the game. You saw the ball go into the basket for the winning points. You heard the final whistle and applause. You felt your hands clapping together, and you also felt the pressure of the crowd as you left the gymnasium. You smelled and tasted the hot dogs you ate on the way home. How many different senses were stimulated?   *All*

A PROBE INTO YOUR SENSES—How can you protect your sight and your other senses? To find out, you will be probing these questions:

1. How does an ophthalmologist differ from an optometrist?

2. What are some common symptoms of eye trouble? Do you suffer from any of them?

3. In what way is clear hearing of value to you?

4. How are the ears tested?

5. What are the odors to which your sense of smell normally responds?

6. Your taste buds recognize four different tastes. What are they?

7. To what sensations does the skin respond, in addition to touch?

8. Can pain ever be of value to you? What is meant by referred pain?

11-1 How often do you have your eyes examined? There are many eye clinics, such as the one shown, that will give you expert eye care.

YOUR HEALTH AND YOUR SENSES

Your senses play many roles. They enable you to see, hear, smell, taste, and touch. Stimulation of your senses brings about emotional response and has some effect on social behavior. For example, think of the basketball game discussed in the introduction to this chapter.

It is through the special organs of sense that you keep in touch with other people and with your environment. The use you make of your senses is a key factor in your physical, mental, and social well-being.

The Wonders of Vision

Your eyes tell you more about the wonders of the world and the people around you than any other sense organ. They acquaint you with the knowledge in this book as well as with the distant stars.

The eye has been called "the mirror of the soul" because the eyes are popularly believed to reflect emotions and feelings toward other people. In fact, eyes probably do not "twinkle" or "soften." More likely, the whole facial expression is the reflector of emotions and feelings. But the eyes do reflect our state of physical health.

Where Do You Go for an Eye Examination?

Before consulting anyone about your eyes, you should know about the three specialists in this field. The *ophthalmologist* (op-thuh-MOL-uh-jist), or *oculist*, is a physician who specializes in eye care and eye surgery. He has a doctor of medicine degree. He can use medication in examination and treatment, prescribe glasses, and determine whether the eye trouble is mechanical or the result of infection or disease.

The *optometrist* (op-TOM-e-trist) is a specialist trained to measure your vision and to prescribe glasses. He may not use medication or perform surgery on the eyes. The *optician* (op-TISH-an) is a highly skilled technician who measures, grinds, and mounts lenses that are prescribed by the ophthalmologist and the optometrist.

How Eyes Are Examined

Many of you are familiar with the Snellen Eye Chart used in some schools as a *screening test*. Snellen introduced his chart in 1863 and with it established 20/20 as *normal vision*. While standing twenty feet away from the chart, you are asked to read letters or distinguish the symbol *E* pointing in different directions. If you can read the line marked 20 with each eye, you can see what you should see at a distance of twenty feet. Most people can read from the line marked 30 through the line marked 15, and that is considered within the normal range. This test, along with the observations of the teacher, is meant to screen those who should be referred for a professional eye examination.

Modern Devices for Eye Examination

With the use of the *ophthalmoscope* (of-THAL-mo-skohp), the eye specialists can look into the interior of the eyeball. With

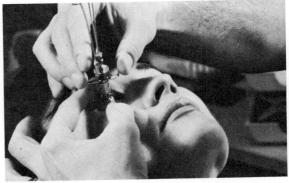

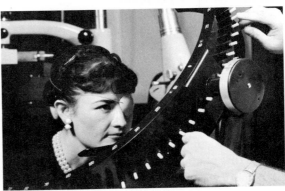

11-2 The Snellen Eye Chart is frequently used for initial eye testing. If this girl can read line 8, she has 20/20 vision.

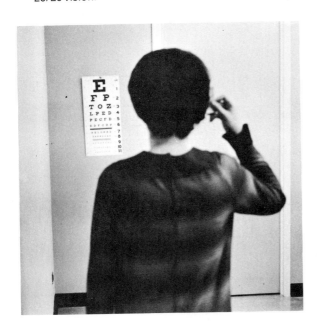

11-3 Three instruments used in eye examination. *(Top)* The ophthalmoscope enables the doctor to view the interior of the eye. *(Center)* The tonometer is used to test for glaucoma. *(Bottom)* The perimeter tests the extent and limitations of the patient's field of vision.

the *tonometer* (to-NOM-e-ter) they can test for *glaucoma,* a serious eye disease that is discussed on page 190. Notice the chart in Figure 11-7; this is used to test for *astigmatism* (a-STIG-ma-tis-um). Astigmatism will be discussed on page 188. For testing side vision, they use the **perimeter** (per-RIM-e-ter). These and many other devices are used for detection and diagnosis.

Some Common Signs of Eye Problems

You may detect many of the following symptoms before they are observed by your teachers or any other person. When you notice them, it is time for you to have an eye examination.

Troubled by: frequent headaches, dizziness, blurring, seeing double, watering, redness, encrusted eyelids, and frequent styes.

Behavior signs: rubbing eyes, holding body tense when looking at distant objects, thrusting head forward, not paying attention to chalkboard, map, or wall chart lessons, and being irritable.

When reading: blinking continually, holding book too close or far away, closing one eye, frequently losing the place on the page, and confusing letters.

On the playground: poor ability in eye-hand coordination, as in catching balls or shooting baskets, and frequent stumbling.

How You See

The eye is a sphere that fits neatly into its bony socket in the skull. Refer to Figure 11-4 as you read on. The outside of the eye has three layers:

1. The outer protective layer, the **sclera** (SKLEE-ra), is transparent where it crosses the front of the eye to form the **cornea**. The cornea permits light to enter the eye and serves to protect the eye from injury. The rest of the sclera is

11-4 Two views of the eye: (*left*) external structures; (*right*) internal structures. In what ways is the eye protected from injury? What are the functions of the eye muscles? What conditions can result if the eye muscles are not able to work together?

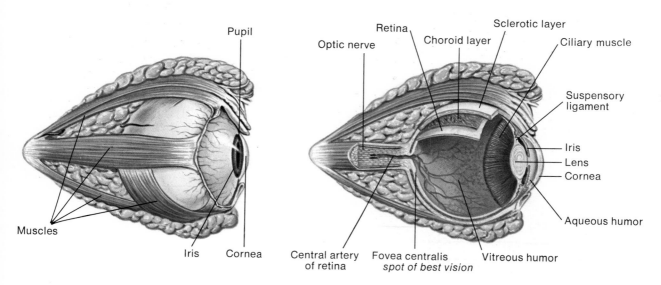

Pupil

Retina

Optic nerve

Choroid layer

Sclerotic layer

Ciliary muscle

Suspensory ligament

Iris

Lens

Cornea

Aqueous humor

Muscles

Iris   Cornea

Central artery of retina

Fovea centralis *spot of best vision*

Vitreous humor

A

B

smooth and white, and the part that you can see is called the "white of the eye."

2. A dark middle layer, the *choroid* (KOH-roid), protects the inside of the eyeball from glare. It carries the largest number of blood vessels that nourish the eye.
3. The inner layer, the *retina* (RET-in-a), is the light-sensitive portion of the eye.

How Your Eyes Focus

A pattern of light enters the front of the eyeball through the *cornea* (transparent portion of the sclera). It then travels through the *pupil*, the opening in the *iris*. The clear, *crystalline lens* lies behind the pupil. The iris, the colored portion of the eye, lies behind the cornea. The iris adjusts the size of the pupil to regulate the amount of light entering the eye. This adjustment influences the brightness and clarity of the image. Between the cornea and the crystalline lens, there is a substance called the *aqueous* (AK-wee-us) *humor*. Aqueous means watery. Humor means fluid. This fluid and the

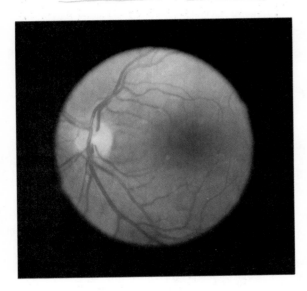

11-5 The surface of the retina as seen through an ophthalmoscope. Notice the lighter area. This is the beginning of the optic nerve.

curved cornea seem to magnify the image seen in much the way an object is magnified when seen through a tumbler of water.

■ Place two tumblers on the table. Fill one tumbler with water. Behind each tumbler place a small object, such as a thimble. Look through each tumbler. Observe how much larger the thimble appears through the tumbler filled with water.

After penetrating the aqueous humor, the light rays penetrate the clear, *crystalline lens*. The lens adjusts to focus the light rays on the *retina*. The process by which the lens adjusts is called *accommodation*. It bulges to accommodate for near objects and flattens for far-away objects. The large space between the crystalline lens and the retina is filled with a clear, jellylike substance called *vitreous* (VIT-ree-us) *humor*. Vitreous means glasslike.

The *retina* contains two kinds of light-sensitive cells, called *rods* and *cones* because of their shape. The cone cells are closest together in the center of the retina and are sensitive to bright light and color. In other parts of the retina, the cones are intermingled with the rods. In regions close to the center of the retina, there are more cones than rods. In regions farther away, there are more rods than cones. Much less light is needed to stimulate the rods than is needed to stimulate the cones.

The center of the retina, *fovea centralis,* is the *spot of best vision.* The rod cells distributed throughout the retina are sensitive to larger forms and to dim light. At one point at the back of the eyeball, the sclera, the choroid, and the retina (the three outer layers of the eye) are pierced to allow for the passage of *optic nerve* and blood vessels. Since there are no rods or cones at this point, it is called a *blind spot*.

■ To locate your blind spot in each eye, close your left eye and focus on the *X* below with your right eye.

X   **O**

Keep looking at the *X* while you move the book first closer and then farther away. Stop when you cannot see the *O*. Its image is now on your blind spot. Repeat with the other eye. Close your right eye and focus the left eye on the *O*. Now try with *both* eyes open. Look at the *X*. Does the *O* vanish? It should not. Can you figure out why you cannot find your blind spot when both eyes are open?

It is the rods that make it possible to see objects in dim light. Since the rods give no sensation of color, objects appear gray in twilight. Animals that sleep in the daytime and hunt for food at night have only rods in the retina.

The outer part of the rods contains a pigment called *visual purple* that is bleached by light but is re-formed in darkness. Visual purple can be rapidly re-formed only when there is a constant supply of vitamin A present in the body. A deficiency of vitamin A in your diet causes a condition called *night blindness,* decreased ability to see in dim light. See Figure 3-10, Chapter 3, for food sources of vitamin A. Individuals who suffer from night blindness are particularly prone to twilight accidents.

■ Using Figure 3-10 as a guide, list all of the foods containing vitamin A that you have eaten today.

How Your Eyes Move

Your eyes move by the action of three *matched pairs of muscles* that turn the eyeballs. One pair moves the eye to left and right. A second pair moves the eye upward and downward. The third pair moves the eye downward and inward, and upward and inward.

When the muscles of your eyes are well-coordinated, or balanced, the corresponding muscles in each eye are working together. That is, both eyes turn right or left, up or down, in harmony. But when one eye turns right, for example, while the other eye continues to look straight ahead, this is called *muscular imbalance.*

In addition to these three pairs of muscles, there is a ring of muscle inside each eyeball. This is the *ciliary muscle*, which regulates the shape of the lens as images of far and near objects are focused.

■ How quickly do your ciliary muscles adjust from distant vision to reading? Look out of the window, then suddenly try to read. For a brief instant the words will be blurred before you can read them clearly. If you read in a moving car or bus, the distance from your eyes to the book changes all the time; thus your ciliary muscles have to change constantly, too. This causes strain that may give you a headache or an upset stomach.

Kinds of Vision

As light rays enter the lens, they are refracted (bent) and brought to focus on the retina. Unfortunately, few eyes refract light rays perfectly. Notice the three types of refraction shown in Figure 11-6.

In normal vision, the light rays entering the eye are focused by the lens to fall precisely on the "screen" of the retina.

In *myopia* (my-OH-pee-a), or nearsightedness, the light rays entering the eye are bent but come to focus before they reach the retina. In this condition the lens is thicker and more convex than normal, or the eyeball is too long. Myopia is corrected with concave lenses that shift the point of focus farther back onto the retina.

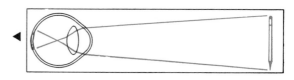

11-6 (A) If your eyesight is normal, this is how you would see the statue and girl.

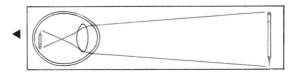

(B) If you are nearsighted, this is how the girl and statue look.

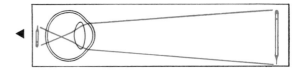

(C) If you are farsighted, this is how the girl and statue look.

11-6 Using one eye at a time, look out the window at both a distant object and an object within 20 feet of you. Focus first on one, then on the other. Do you see each clearly? If not, plan to visit an eye specialist and have your eyes examined.

In *hyperopia* (hy-per-OH-pee-a), or far-sightedness, the light rays entering the eye focus behind the retina. The eyeball in hyperopia is too short. Hyperopia is corrected by convex lenses that reduce the divergence of light rays and bring them to focus on the retina.

Presbyopia (prez-by-OH-pee-a) is farsightedness of old age. Corrective glasses are needed for reading, and often bifocal lenses are required. Bifocals contain a lens for distant sight in the upper part and one for close sight at the bottom.

Astigmatism means "without a point." The incoming light rays focus at different points instead of at a single point. It is caused by an uneven curvature of the crystalline lens. It can be corrected by specially ground glasses.

Strabismus (crossed eyes) is common in

11-7 Test for astigmatism. Hold the book directly in front of you at a comfortable reading distance, close one eye, and look at the center of the figure. Do the same for the other eye. Do some lines appear darker than others? If so, you may have a common eye defect—astigmatism.

very young children and frequently corrects itself. It is caused by muscle irregularities that cause the eyes to turn toward the nose. Crossed eyes can be corrected by special glasses and exercises.

The use of the eye varies from **monocular** (one-eyed) vision to **binocular** (two-eyed) vision. One eye may be farsighted and the other nearsighted. In such a case the person may close one eye alternating with the other to achieve a clear image and thus create one-eyed vision. In monocular vision, height and width can be seen but not depth. Objects look flat. This condition can be corrected by visual reeducation and eye exercises.

Peripheral vision is the ability to see a given area that surrounds the point of focus.

■ Near the top center of the chalkboard, put a good-sized chalk mark. Stand in the back center of the room and focus on the chalk

mark. Notice the distance you can see around the chalk mark. This is your peripheral vision.

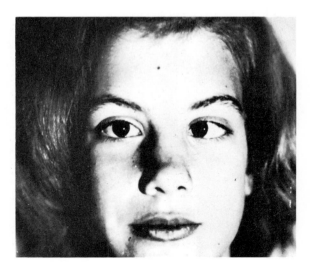

11-8 This child is cross-eyed because the muscles of her two eyes do not work together.

Peripheral vision is important to your safety. In driving a car, for example, a person who knows he has a narrow field of vision must learn to turn his head frequently to see cars that might be approaching from side or cross streets.

Persons who cannot distinguish one or more of the basic colors—red, green, yellow, blue—are said to be *color blind.* About ten out of a hundred males and less than one out of a hundred females have some degree of color blindness. It is probably due to a lack of color receptors in the retina. It is usually an hereditary condition passed from a colorblind grandfather through a normal mother to a colorblind grandson. It is a **sex-linked** characteristic that you will read more about in Chapter 20.

Diseases of the Eye

Cataracts are the leading cause of blindness in America. A cataract is a cloudiness of the lens that interferes with the normal passage of light rays through the lens. The cloudiness cannot be removed, but the lens can be removed. Vision can be restored to 20/30 or better.

11-9 Have you noticed that the red light is always above the green light? This is a protection for people with red-green colorblindness.

Glaucoma is a disease in which the pressure within the eyeball is increased. It is the second leading cause of blindness in America. Although glaucoma cannot be prevented or cured, visual loss can be avoided by early detection and treatment.

Retinal detachment may be due to disease or to injury. It means the separation of the innermost layer of the eye, the retina, from the choroid layer just behind it. These two layers are normally in close contact, but when the retina is pushed up or peeled away from the choroid, all or part of the vision is blocked out.

A person may have early indications that his retina is becoming detached. If he seeks prompt treatment, eye surgeons can often use a laser beam effectively to make the repair.

Corneal Scarring

Scarring, or opacity, of the cornea sometimes follows inflammation, ulceration, or injuries of various kinds. If the scarring is extensive enough it can cause blindness. The corneal transplant operation has proved successful in many cases. The transplant is made by replacing the scarred cornea with a healthy one. Healthy corneas are obtained from eye banks. The corneas are taken after death from persons who have previously signed a statement donating their eyes to the eye bank.

In 1944, eye banks were established in various parts of the country to make available to surgeons a supply of fresh or preserved corneal tissue for use in corneal transplants.

Eye Infections

Acute conjunctivitis (kon-JUNGK-ti-vy-tis), or pinkeye, is an infection of the **conjunctiva** (kon-JUNGK-ty-va), the lining of your eyelids. The same membrane also covers the *cornea.* The eyes become red; the lids swell, and may be stuck together in the morning by a thick secretion. It is highly contagious and may occur in epidemic form in schools. Conjunctivitis is contracted by touching your eyes with objects—handkerchiefs, washcloths, towels, eyeglasses, or eye cosmetics—that have been used by a person with the infection.

A *sty* is an infection of the glands connected with the roots of the eyelashes. The sign of a beginning sty is a red swelling at the margin of the eyelid, pain, and tenderness. Later, a yellow spot filled with pus forms in the red swelling as the sty comes to a head. Applications of hot compresses will hasten this development. Any attempt to prick or squeeze a sty may result in a dangerous infection.

Gonorrheal (gon-oh-REE-ul) *infection* of the eye is caused by the gonococcus germ. *Gonorrhea* (gon-oh-REE-uh) is the most prevalent of the *venereal* (ven-EAR-e-ul) diseases. Venereal diseases are contagious and are usually acquired through sexual relations. You will read more about these diseases in Chapter 29. Gonorrhea can be transmitted from a mother to her child at birth. The use of silver nitrate drops in all infants' eyes at birth has greatly reduced blindness from this infection.

Your Built-in Eye Protection

Your eyes are equipped with their own protective apparatus. The eyeball is protected in its bony socket. The *cheekbone* and *forehead* guard it against blows. Through reflex action the eyelids snap shut when anything comes toward the eye. The *eyelashes* filter foreign particles from the air, and the *eyebrows* prevent perspiration from running into the eye.

The *eyelids* cover the eyes in sleep and in daytime protect them from external injury, foreign bodies, undue exposure, and bright light. They serve to keep the eyeballs moist and clean by spreading tears over their surface. The windshield wiper and washer on an automobile function in this way, too, except that you have to turn a switch when you want them to function, but your eyes do all of this automatically.

Tears are secreted by the *lacrimal glands.* These glands are located in the outer angle of each eye. After the tears are brushed across the eyeballs by the eyelids, they drain off through the *tear ducts*, located at the inner corner of the eye, into the nose. Without this continuing washing of the conjunctiva by tears, this delicate membrane would soon become dry and inflamed.

Conserving Your Eyesight

The lenses of glasses can now be made of shatter-resistant glass or of plastic, and these are recommended. There is only a small additional cost.

Lighting should provide for comfort and efficiency. Good lighting calls for light that is steady, uniform, adequate, and free from glare or shadow. The amount of light in a room can be measured by a *lightmeter.* The unit of light measurement is a *foot-candle*. One foot-candle is the light cast by a standard one-inch candle at a distance of one foot. The type of light and the fixtures that you use are important in obtaining adequate light.

The most favorable type of room lighting is *indirect light,* where the light shines on the ceiling and is reflected into the room. Another type of good light is *diffused light* from fluorescent tubes. Fluorescent light gives even, general illumination with little glare or shadow. For reading or close work, additional light is furnished by table or floor lamps. When selecting lamps, look for the approval seal of the Illumination Engineering Society (IES) to be assured of proper light-giving design. When writing, light should come from the left side for right-handed persons, and from the right side for left-handed persons. This prevents shadows from forming over your work.

Glare is bright light that strikes the eye directly or is reflected from objects. Both are harmful and may induce nervousness, irritability, and fatigue. *Direct* glare refers to light shining into the eye, as from the sun or an unshaded light bulb. *Indirect* glare is light reflected from such surfaces as snow, water, glass-covered pictures, polished floors and furniture, and glossy paper.

To reduce indoor glare, window shades can be adjusted, and dull-finish wax can be used on furniture and floors. For outdoor glare, glasses that are dark enough to cut out about 70 to 80 percent of the light should be worn. They should neither enlarge nor reduce the size of objects seen through them. Neutral colors in this order are recommended – gray, green, and tan.

Eyewashes of any type should be used only when prescribed for you. Your eyes have their own natural lubricant (tears).

What About Contact Lenses?

Some teen-agers dislike wearing glasses for a number of reasons. They may not feel attractive wearing them or they may regard them as a hindrance. Of course, in recent years new styles in frames have made many teen-agers want to wear glasses, and almost everyone can find a style that is attractive.

More and more teen-agers and adults are turning to *contact lenses.* Besides their cosmetic value, contact lenses help certain people to see better, and they are very helpful to those who participate actively in sports.

Two things seem to stand in the way of wider use of contact lenses. One is the high cost as compared with conventional glasses. The other is the fear some people have of placing anything in contact with the eyes. Contact lenses are now made of paper-thin plastic. Many people find them very comfortable after wearing them for a while.

Bifocal contact lenses are available and useful to those who have had a cataract operation. They are also used to match different iris colors, such as one blue eye and one brown eye. They can be tinted for *photophobia* (abnormal sensitivity to light), and they do not steam up as eyeglass lenses do.

Is Television Viewing Harmful?

Television viewing is no more harmful than watching anything else. Here are some hints. *For comfort in viewing television you should:*

1. Have the entire room well lighted.
2. View from a straight-ahead position, with your head on a level with the screen.
3. Sit at a distance from the set that is about eight times the width of the screen. For a seventeen-inch screen,

11-10 This girl is placing a contact lens in her eye. Do you or any of your friends wear contact lenses?

you would sit about eleven and one-third feet away.

4. If you wear glasses for distant seeing, wear them for television viewing.
5. Avoid long periods of viewing; move about frequently.
6. Occasionally rest your eyes by shifting them away from the screen.

Your Emotions and Your Eyes

Recently it has been demonstrated experimentally that there is a correlation between how you feel—your emotional response—and your eyes. The pupil of the eye contracts in bright light and dilates in dim light (Figure 11-11). This is its physiological function. It is now shown that the pupil responds in a similar way to other stimuli. This is an emotional reaction.

The pupil of the eye has now been observed to dilate when stimulated by interesting and pleasing sights, such as meeting your best friend. But the pupil contracts when unpleasant, frightening, or distasteful sights are seen, such as a dead animal on the road. When what you see is uninteresting or boring, there seems to be no pupil response. See Figure 11-12.

The eye plays a dual role of responding in a similar way to both physical and emotional stimulation. For example: your eyebrows pucker over a puzzling problem and in bright light; your eyelids flicker to clear away dust and harmful materials; your tear glands overflow with a cinder in the eye and from grief. As to crying, in our culture crying seems to be regarded as a weakness acceptable in girls and women but considered unmanly in boys and men. Crying, like laughter, is a natural, normal, emotional response of both sexes that provides comfort and relief.

How You Can Protect Your Eyes

1. The first precaution is to have your eyes examined at least once every two

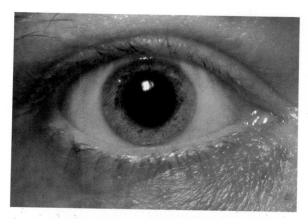

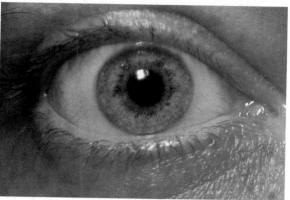

11-11 (Top) In dim light your pupil enlarges to allow in all possible light. *(Bottom)* In bright light the pupil contracts to shut out light. Are your pupils enlarged or contracted at this moment?

years. If you need glasses, by all means wear them and keep them clean.
2. When symptoms of eyestrain appear, seek professional advice.
3. Do not rub your eyes. Use only your own washcloths and towels.
4. Protect your eyes with a face shield when doing things that involve hazards to the eyes.
5. Use care in handling sharp objects, firearms, and power tools.
6. When you have an eye infection or injury, get immediate medical assistance.
7. Protect your eyes against strong light

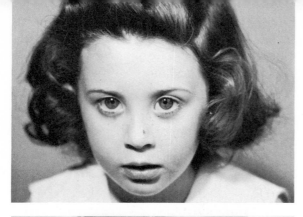

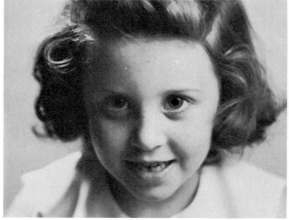

11-12 Your emotions also affect the size of your pupils. The child at the top has been frightened and her pupils are smaller than at the bottom. The picture at the bottom was taken when she was pleased.

during infectious diseases, such as measles.

8. Do not look directly at or near the sun; avoid reading where strong sunlight shines on your reading matter.

9. Provide plenty of light, but avoid glare, when reading, writing, or doing any close work.

10. Avoid reading and close work when ill.

11. When you must study for a long period of time, rest your eyes by looking at a distant object every few minutes.

12. Avoid reading on moving trains, buses, and automobiles where your eye muscles must make constant adjustments.

13. If you read in bed, hold your book at least fourteen inches straight in front of your eyes.

14. When reading or working at your desk, hold the printed matter at least fourteen inches from your eyes, with good light coming over your shoulder.

YOUR HEARING

In today's fast-moving world, the ability to hear clearly is vital to your well-being. It helps you in communicating with other people and in this way contributes to your social acceptance. Being able to hear clearly is necessary for success in your school work. It is an important means of keeping in contact with the environment, and it helps protect you from danger.

It is estimated that twenty million Americans have subnormal hearing. Two things seem to keep people from seeking help for hearing loss: (1) They cling to the hope that the loss is temporary and will right itself. (2) Many people fail to realize that in the great majority of cases, hearing loss can be restored.

Where You Go for an Ear Examination

In some schools, screening tests are given to determine if your hearing is within a normal range. An *audiometer* (aud-ee-OM-et-er) is an instrument used to measure the power of hearing, the audibility, and the intensity of sound. If your hearing is not within a normal range, you are referred for further testing to an ear specialist, an *otologist* (oh-TOL-oh-jist). An otologist is a medical doctor who specializes in the care and treatment of the ears.

The otologist may use the *audiogram*, which shows the degree of hearing loss, and the *binaural* (both ears) *selectometer*, which

11-13 This child is having her hearing tested with an audiometer. Has your hearing ever been tested with this instrument?

helps him determine the exact correction needed for fitting hearing aids.

Parts of the Ear

Each ear has three parts: the *outer ear*, the *middle ear*, and the *inner ear*. The parts that you see, the *lobe* and *ear canal*, make up the outer ear. The ear canal leads to the *eardrum* (tympanic membrane) and the middle ear. In the middle ear there are three tiny bones (the smallest bones in the body) called the *hammer* (malleus), *anvil* (incus), and *stirrup* (stapes) because of their resemblance to these objects (Figure 11-14).

The middle ear is connected with the throat by the *Eustachian* (you-STAY-kee-un) *tube*. The Eustachian tube functions to equalize the air pressure within the middle ear with the air pressure outside of the body. The inner ear contains the *semicircular canals* that are essential to balance and the awareness of your position in space. It also contains the *cochlea* (KOK-lee-uh), which is shaped like a snail and contains the sensory cells (hair cells) of hearing. The movements

of the stirrup are transmitted through a membrane called a "window" to the fluid in the cochlea.

What Is Sound?

Sound is the result of vibrations in the air, in liquids, and in solids. It has pitch, intensity, and timbre. *Pitch* depends on the number of vibrations per second. *Intensity* refers to loudness or softness of sound. It is measured by units called *decibels. Timbre* (TIM-ber) means the quality of the sound.

How you Hear

The outer ear is shaped to catch sound waves and direct them into the ear canal. You have noticed a dog cock its ears. Many animals have the ability to turn the outer ear toward the source of sound, but people have lost this ability in the process of evolution.

There are usually hairs on the skin lining the ear canal. The hairs, along with wax secreted into the ear, catch particles of dust and in this way protect your eardrum.

Your ear canal directs sound toward the eardrum, a thin, tough, slightly rounded membrane. It is the eardrum that separates the outer ear from the middle ear. The eardrum vibrates with the sound waves and transmits the vibrations to the three middle ear bones. When these tiny bones—hammer, anvil, and stirrup—are set in motion, they transfer the vibrations to the inner ear. This is done by the stirrup that is attached to the "window" of the cochlea.

As the stirrup vibrates, it transmits vibrations across the "window" membrane between the middle and inner ears. Each vibration continues through the fluid of the cochlea until it reaches special nerve endings (hair cells). Nerve impulses are then conducted to the *auditory nerve* that carries them to the brain where they are identified as sounds.

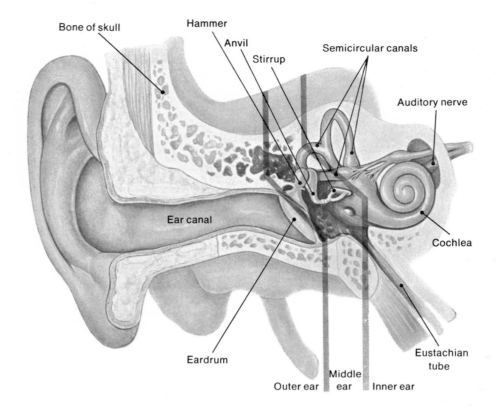

Bone of skull
Hammer
Anvil
Stirrup
Semicircular canals
Auditory nerve
Ear canal
Cochlea
Eardrum
Eustachian tube
Outer ear
Middle ear
Inner ear

11-14 A diagram of a human ear. When sound waves strike the eardrum, a chain of reactions starts, quickly reaching your brain as sound messages. Can you trace the path of sound waves and impulses through the ear?

How Pressure Is Equalized in Your Ears

The major function of the Eustachian tube, which enters the middle ear from the throat is to equalize external and internal pressure on the eardrum. Air is interchanged between the throat and the middle ear.

Usually you are not aware of this passage of air, but when you make a quick change in elevation by plane, automobile, or elevator, you may feel a popping sensation in your ear as the pressure is suddenly equalized. The tightly stretched eardrum, which has bulged inward or outward because of the pressure, has merely snapped back into place. You can relieve the feeling of pressure by frequently swallowing or yawning.

Hearing Defects

There are two general types of defective hearing, *transmission* and *sensory.* In *transmission deafness* there is failure of the mechanism to transmit sound through the ear canal, eardrum, and middle ear. In *sensory deafness* there is loss of function of sensory cells in the cochlea or the auditory nerve.

Heredity is sometimes a factor in hearing loss. Injuries, such as blows and skull fractures, may also impair hearing. Another cause of deafness is infections. Bacteria and viruses from diseased tonsils, head colds, and many of the children's diseases may infect the ears and cause damage.

Deafness may also be caused by illness of the mother during pregnancy. German measles is the worst offender. It has been reported that as a result of the 1963-64 epidemic of German measles about 4,500 infants may have been born with impaired hearing.

Impacted wax is common and can cause temporary hearing loss. In some persons, wax hardens and forms a plug in the ear canal. It can be painlessly removed by an otologist, but home remedies are not recommended.

Mastoiditis is inflammation of the mastoid cells in the bone surrounding the ear. It is serious because of the thin wall between the cells and the brain. Early treatment with one of the antibiotic drugs is usually successful.

Inflammation of the ear (*otitis*) or of the middle ear (*otitis media*) causes pain, fever, and deafness. The attention of an otologist is always needed.

Things to Avoid

Avoid violent blowing of the nose, especially when you have a cold or other respiratory infection. Germs can go through the Eustachian tube to the middle ear.

Avoid swimming in stagnant water or pools that are not regularly inspected. Water-borne germs from unclean water can cling to the ear canal and cause infection.

Avoid putting anything in your ear "smaller than your elbow."

Avoid diving feet first, without holding your nose tightly shut.

Avoid striking anyone on the ears, even in fun. Some people have extra-sensitive ears.

Avoid exposing your ears to loud blasts or shrill sounds. Sound waves of great intensity can rupture the eardrum.

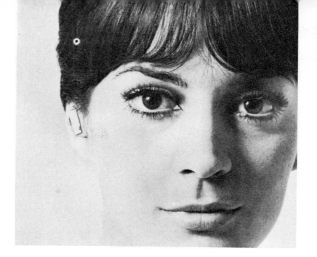

11-15 This hearing aid weighs just over one tenth of an ounce. It was designed for the full range of mild hearing losses.

Aids to Hearing

Modern hearing aids are the accepted remedy when hearing loss reaches the level where you are deprived of the pleasure of sound, where your work depends on clear hearing, and when your safety is threatened. *Hearing clearly is a necessity in modern living, not a luxury.*

Through the benefits of electronic research, hearing aids are now efficient, compact, and relatively inexpensive. Some hearing aids have combined functions, such as *hearing glasses* where the hearing aid is placed inside the shaft of the glasses frames, or hearing aids that are part of a tie clasp or pin. There are the in-the-ear type that are so tiny they cannot be seen, and the behind-the-ear type, which are transistorized.

A hearing aid that fits behind the ear is successful because the bones of the skull can carry some vibrations to the cochlea.

■ You can find out how the bones carry sound. Have a classmate hold his hands tightly over your ears. Click your teeth. Tap on a tooth with your fingernail. Hold a toothpick between your teeth and make it vibrate. You will hear all of these sounds.

11-16 This construction worker must have a highly developed sense of balance. How is your sense of balance maintained?

It should be pointed out that hearing aids do not always furnish the immediate benefit that glasses provide for vision. A certain amount of training is needed for their comfortable use. But the benefits you get from their use make the training period infinitely worthwhile.

Your Feelings and Your Sense of Hearing

There seems no ready explanation as to why people in general are reluctant to admit that they do not hear clearly. It has been observed that school children, and high school and college students, bluff their way through their lessons by depending on others nearby to repeat what was said, by learning to read lips, and by many other tricks in an effort to hide hearing loss.

In this noisy world you struggle to hear against the rumble of traffic, the shrill ring of bells, and others talking in the same room. To many people, these are the everyday sounds of the environment that they get used to. In fact, city dwellers often find the silence of the country so uncomfortable that they cannot sleep at night. Country people, on the other hand, find the rushing rumble of traffic in the city equally disturbing.

Each person has his own toleration level for sound, but for everyone there is a high-intensity threshold of sound that produces pain. Being constantly exposed to sound at the threshold of pain may cause deafness in certain individuals.

YOUR MANY OTHER SENSES

We no longer consider the senses as referring only to sight, hearing, smell, taste, and touch. Today, the physiologist adds to this list such sensations as pressure, pain, position, heat, cold, vibrations, and balance.

Balance

One of the forces you are normally not aware of is the pull of the earth, called gravity. You become aware of it, however, when something goes wrong with the sensory organs that control balance.

In addition to the cochlea and the semicircular canals, the inner ear contains two small sacs, the *saccule* (SAK-yool) and the *utricle* (YOO-trih-k'l). All of these together form the *labyrinth of the ear,* so called because of its twisted shape. The utricle and the saccule help you to know whether you are upright or swaying to one side. They also help to keep you in balance when you are moving.

The saccule and utricle let you know which way is up or down. Of course, if you can see you know this. But when swimming under water or walking in complete darkness, you must rely for direction on these sensory organs of balance.

The semicircular canals contain fluid and are arranged at right angles to one another. Whenever your head is tilted or rotated, the fluid moves and stimulates a nerve. This makes you aware of the movement, and reflex action prompts you to compensate by moving your head in the opposite direction.

Under normal conditions, the fluid in the canals moves fast enough to maintain balance. But when there are rapid and continuous waves of motion, the canals may not be able to readjust quickly enough. The result is *motion sickness.* Motion sickness is produced by unaccustomed motion. You can develop auto, air, elevator, sea, and train sickness. Once you become used to these motions you can usually outgrow motion sickness. However, for those who are very sensitive, there are antimotion-sickness medicines that can be taken. But they must be taken well in advance.

Your Sense of Smell

The sensory end-organs for smell, called the *olfactory* cells, are located at the top of the inner surface of the nose. The olfactory cells are imbedded in the mucous membrane, and from them other nerve fibers pass to the brain, where the odor is identified.

The olfactory cells pick up odors from molecules released into the air from various substances. There are seven odors to which you normally respond individually and when they are combined: burnt, acid, putrid, spicy, fragrant, fruity, and resinous.

Your Sense of Taste

Taste is the sense by which you recognize flavors. The end-organ receptors are called *taste buds.* Impulses from the taste buds are carried to the brain where they register as taste sensations. Your taste buds are located primarily on the tongue. They can recognize four different tastes: sour, sweet, bitter, and salt. They react only to substances in solution. When stimulated, they cause secretion of saliva in the mouth, and gastric juice in the stomach.

Your Sense of Touch

Your skin, because of its many nerve endings, acts as an important sensory organ of touch. Through it you receive a great deal of information about your environment. Touch—*tactile sensation*—is but one of five types of sensations to which the end organs of the skin respond. They are also stimulated by pain, pressure, heat, cold, and combinations of these.

The layers of your skin contain nerve endings that respond to these stimuli. The nerves involved eventually come together and communicate with the spinal cord. Some areas of the body have more end organs of touch than do others. For example, your lips and finger tips are far more sensitive than are your arms, legs, and back.

Internal Pain and Pressure

Sensations of pain and pressure from the interior of the body—stomach, colon, bile ducts—are very common. You are aware of sensations from muscles and joints, of hunger, thirst, sleepiness, and fatigue, of fullness of the bladder and rectum. But these pain and pressure sensations are different from those you receive from the skin. There may be a dull ache that is not so definitely localized as the sharp, clearly localized pain and pressure from the skin. There are probably fewer pain fibers in the internal organs than on the skin, and they respond to stimuli in a different way. It is possible to cut almost any internal organ without producing pain.

Referred Pain

Referred pain is pain that originates in one part of the body but is felt in a different part. Heart pain, for example, can radiate into the arm or shoulder, or it can imitate an intestinal upset. Patients with sinus infection sometimes experience severe aching in their teeth. The precise reason for referred pain is not clear.

What You Have Learned

What kind of health practices should you apply in maintaining your health? Check your understanding of the chapter. On a separate sheet of paper, number 1 through 21 and insert the answer from the vocabulary list given below.

anvil	hyperopia	retina
astigmatism	myopia	sclera
auditory	ophthalmologist	smell
choroid	ophthalmoscope	stirrup
cochlea	optician	styes
eardrum	optometrist	taste
hammer	pinkeye	touch

There are three specialists in the field of vision. The (1)_____ is a physician who specializes in eye care; he performs surgery, and prescribes medication. The (2)_____ is a specialist trained in measuring visual acuity and prescribing glasses. He does not perform surgery or use medication. The (3)_____ is a highly skilled technician who measures, grinds, and mounts lenses that are prescribed by the other specialists. The instrument used to look into the interior of the eyeball is the (4)_____

The eye has three covering layers. The outer layer, the (5)_____ is smooth and white; the part you can see is called the "white of the eye." A dark middle layer, the (6)_____ protects the inside of the eye from glare. The inner layer, the (7)_____ is the light-sensitive portion of the eye.

As light rays enter the lens of the eye, they are refracted (bent) and brought to focus on the retina. There are several refractive errors in which the light rays fail to focus properly on the retina. One of these is (8)_____, or nearsightedness, where light rays come to focus before they reach the retina. One is (9)_____ or farsightedness, where the light rays focus behind the retina. Another is called (10)_____ where the light rays focus at different points instead of on a single point.

Among the common eye problems are infections of the conjunctiva, commonly called (11)_____ and infections of the glands connected with the roots of the eyelashes, called (12)_____

Loss of ability to hear clearly can be a serious handicap. Sound enters the ear through the outer ear canal and strikes the (13)_eardrum_, which is the outside protective membrane of the middle ear. Three small bones in the middle ear, the (14)_ear_, (15)_anvil_, and (16)_stirrup_ receive the sound and carry it to the inner ear. As the third small bone vibrates, it sends the sound to the (17)_cochlea_ of the inner ear. From the inner ear, the sound reaches the (18)_auditory_ nerve that carries it to the brain, where it is identified.

In addition to the senses of sight and hearing, there are other senses valuable to your health and safety, such as (19)_taste_, (20)_touch_, and (21)_smell_

What You Can Do

1. Examine a camera in class. Find the opening through which light enters the camera—the lens—and the place where the film is inserted. Which parts of the eye do each of these camera parts resemble? Take a picture with the camera out of focus and have it developed. Take the same picture with the camera in focus and have it developed. Compare the two pictures. What can you learn from these snapshots about the importance of having refractive errors of the eye corrected?

2. Find an alphabet chart of the sign language used by the deaf. See how long it takes you to learn this alphabet. Can you use it in a simple sentence?

3. Try lip reading. You might make this a game similar to charades. Have one team make up a short sentence and say it with their lips without speaking. Then have the opposing team try to read their lips and guess the words used in the sentence.

Things to Try

1. Here is a blindfold test: On a tray, place food samples that represent the various taste sensations of sour, sweet, bitter, and salt. With your eyes tightly blindfolded, see how many of the foods you can identify by tasting them.

2. Try the same blindfold experiment for the sensation of smell. On a tray, place samples of such things as fragrant flowers, fruit, burned toast, vinegar, and decayed potato. See how many sensations of smell you can identify.

3. Stand behind a classmate who has covered his left ear tightly with his left hand. Hold a watch close to his right ear so he can hear its ticking clearly. Now, slowly move the watch away from his ear. Ask your classmate to raise his hand when he can no longer hear the ticking. Notice the distance you were able to move the watch away from his ear. Repeat with the other ear. Compare the two distances. Are they the same or different? What does this mean?

4. Fill a small clear glass bowl with water. Hold the bowl about an inch above this page and observe the size of the print through the bowl. Empty the water from the bowl and again observe the size of the print. Do you notice any difference?

5. Using a small box of colored crayons, give a classmate a test for color blindness.

Probing Further

Your Sight:Folklore, Fact and Common Sense, by Bernard Seeman, Little, Brown, 1968. An excellent general source book on the eye and vision, including safety, eye hygiene, and medical problems.

"How Color Affects Your Life," by John E. Gibson, *Today's Health,* September 1962. This article presents a useful guide on how color can excite the emotions and affect your sense of time and distance. It supplements your text material.

"Let's Take the Din Out of Living," by William R. Voth, *Today's Health,* Feburary 1965. This article shows the effects of high pitch and low pitch sounds on people and the difference in reactions to sounds between city and rural dwellers.

The First Book of The Human Senses, by Gene Liberty, Franklin Watts, 1961. This volume presents a full range of discussion on all of the organs of sense and supplements similar text materials.

Health Concepts in Action

Does what you have learned support this statement?

> *Ability to interact with the environment depends upon efficient functioning of the sense organs.*

Applying this concept of sensory fitness, which health practices would you

— continue?

— change?

— begin?

Will you now, as a result of your study, change any of your health objectives?

12 / *Your Brain and Nerve Network*

When John returned to the classroom after taking an aptitude test given by the school psychologist, everyone wanted to know what the test was like. "One thing I had to do," said John, "was to move twenty-four pegs that were in one board to another board with twenty-four holes in it, while the psychologist timed me with a stopwatch." The psychologist explained that the score achieved in this kind of test depends upon the coordination of eye and hand by the nervous system. Would a sleepless night before the test have affected John's test score? Why do you think so?

A PROBE INTO THE NERVOUS SYSTEM—How can you keep your nervous system working at top efficiency? To find out, you will be probing these questions:

1. Why is it important to understand how the nervous system functions?

2. What composes the communication unit of the nervous system?

3. How are habits formed? How do they differ from reflexes?

4. You can develop habits of feeling as well as habits of action. Give two examples.

5. What is the difference between normal and chronic fatigue?

6. What is the right way to fight fatigue? the wrong way?

7. What are the physiological benefits of sleep? the psychological benefits? Why do you dream?

YOUR NERVOUS SYSTEM
AND NERVE CELLS

The nervous system is the body's communications system. Along with a system of very important glands, which you will study in Chapter 22, it regulates the activities of all of the other organ systems. The nervous system enables you to communicate with other people and with your environment. In order to better understand its function, you can divide it into three related systems. The *central nervous system* consists of the brain and spinal cord (Figure 12-1). The **peripheral** (peh-RIF-er-al) **nervous system** is made up of all the nerves that connect the spinal cord and brain with other parts of your body. The *autonomic nervous system* is made up of nerves associated with many of your organs and part of your brain. But, unlike the central and peripheral systems, the autonomic system does its work without your

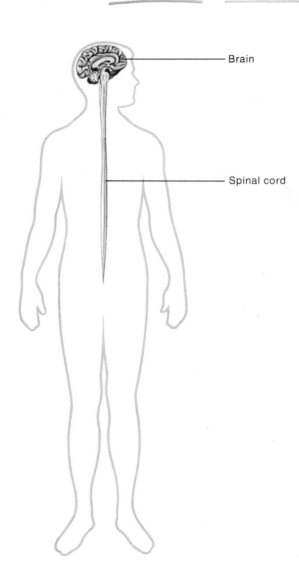

Brain

Spinal cord

12-1 The brain and spinal cord make up the central nervous system. Why are they given this name?

intervention—to keep your heart beating, to keep you alive.

The three systems that together make up your nervous system work in unison to keep you alive, alert, and in good health.

Neurons—Units of Communication

The individual cells of the nervous system are the **neurons** (NYOO-rons). Each neuron has a **cell body** and two or more threadlike extensions. The extensions that carry impulses *toward* the cell body are called **dendrites** (DEN-drytes). Those that carry impulses *away* from the cell body are called **axons** (AK-sons).

How a Message Is Transmitted

A **nerve impulse** is an electrochemical change that travels away from the cell body down the *axon*, where it is picked up by the *dendrites* of another neuron. The dendrites transmit the change (and the small electric charge that it includes) to the next cell body, where an axon takes over and transmits the impulse away from the cell body. (See Figure 12-2.)

There are three kinds of neurons. **Sensory neurons** carry stimuli from various sense organs to the brain or spinal cord. **Motor neurons** carry impulses from the brain or other nerve centers to the muscles or glands. **Associative**, or **connecting, neurons** serve as connections between one another and between sensory and motor neurons. Associative neurons make up the **gray matter** of the brain and spinal cord.

The axons and dendrites of neurons constitute the nerve fibers. The fibers of sensory and motor neurons are grouped in bundles—the *nerves*. There are **sensory nerves, motor nerves**, and **mixed nerves**, depending on the kind of fibers they contain. Sensory and motor nerve fibers together make up mixed nerves.

The fibers in a nerve vary in size. The

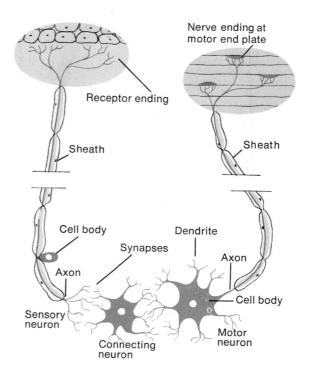

12-2 A neuron is a unit of communication. This picture shows the three types of neurons and how they are related. How is a nerve impulse transmitted?

thinnest fibers can transmit an impulse at about the rate of from three to four feet per second. The thicker, high-speed nerve fibers that serve the farthermost parts of the body can carry impulses at a speed of about 450 feet per second, or 300 miles an hour. By this you may see that communication to even widely separated limbs and organs is almost instantaneous.

The places where the axons of motor neurons pass impulses to muscles are called **motor end plates** (Figure 12-3). Each axon branches into from 10 to 100 end plates.

Not all impulses end in muscles, although many do—as when you jerk away a burned finger, or blink, or decide to change position to relieve the discomfort of being in one position too long. Many impulses end in glands (as when you think of sour lemon and begin to secrete saliva).

The Peripheral Nervous System

The peripheral nerves that extend outward from the brain are called *cranial nerves*. Those that extend from the spinal cord are called *spinal nerves*. These nerves (Figure 12-4) are primarily related to conscious activities and sensations of the body. This means that in most cases you know what is going on when they are at work.

Sensory nerves, or sensory fibers in mixed nerves, carry information from your sense receptors to the brain and spinal cord. The receptors include skin receptors of many kinds as well as those for sight, taste, smell, hearing, and balance. You can see that you have many messages for your sensory nerves to carry.

Motor nerves, or motor fibers in mixed nerves, carry orders from the central nervous system to effectors—chiefly muscles and glands.

Here is a familiar example of the work of both kinds of nerves: When you see an object

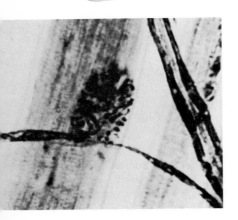

12-3 A photomicrograph of a motor end plate. What is the function of a motor end plate?

Clay Adams, Inc.

12-4 The peripheral nervous system is made up of 31 pairs of spinal nerves. Is the peripheral nervous system under your conscious control?

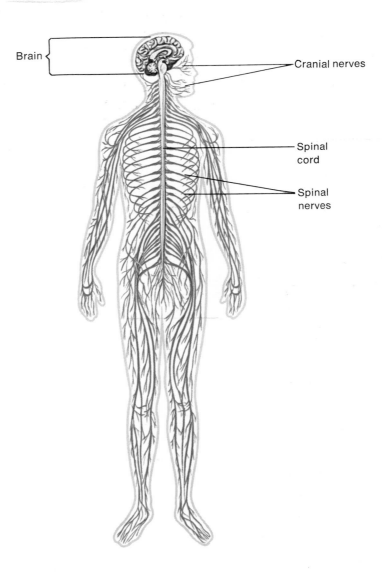

Brain

Cranial nerves

Spinal cord

Spinal nerves

flying toward you, you duck to avoid being hit. The sensory message of danger originated in the eyes. The sensory nerve that carried the message was the *optic nerve*. In your brain, the message was interpreted and routed to many motor nerves leading to muscles of your neck, shoulders, arms, and body. When you ducked, it was a coordinated movement of many muscles attached to different bones, not one or a few muscles in your neck alone.

Many of the impulses carried to the central nervous system by the peripheral sensory nerves are a signal to the body to make a physical adjustment. Others are more complex in terms of your mental attitude and interests. For example, your motor responses to some sensory impulses may be to paint a picture or to burst into song.

The Autonomic Nervous System

The autonomic system, like the peripheral system, consists of nerves. Both systems of nerves have **ganglia** (GANG-glee-a), concentrations of neuron cell bodies. These occur in the roots of the spinal cord for the spinal nerves, and usually near the spinal cord for the autonomic nerves. In a few instances in the autonomic system, the ganglia themselves are further concentrated into a nerve **plexus** (PLEX-us). The *solar plexus* is one, the *cardiac plexus* another. A plexus is a very complicated relay station. When it is working properly, you are not even aware of it, but you are aware of it when it is not working! A hard blow to the pit of the stomach interrupts the work of the solar plexus, and a blow over the heart may stun the cardiac plexus. The two sensations that are strongest in such injury are pain and internal paralysis—interrupted heartbeat, loss of the ability to breathe, and so on. "The breath is knocked out of you," as the saying goes.

Such occurrences are part of the evidence that the autonomic system (Figure 12-5) con-

trols functions that are involuntary, such as digestion, heartbeat, blushing, and perspiration. All these vital activities occur without your conscious involvement. Can you affect them when you wish?

■ Try *thinking* a change in your rate of breathing. You can, as you know. Try it with your rate of heartbeat, using a watch with a second hand to check your efforts. Lastly, try perspiring by force of will. What are your results?

The work of your autonomic system is carried on and balanced by two of its subdivisions. The **parasympathetic** (pair-a-sim-puh-THET-ik) **division** and the **sympathetic division** produce opposite effects, as can be seen in the list that follows.

Parasympathetic	Sympathetic
Promotes secretion of digestive juices	Inhibits secretion of digestive juices
Promotes digestive tone and movements of intestine	Inhibits tone and contractions of intestines
Relaxes heart rate	Speeds heart rate
Dilates blood capillaries in skin	Constricts blood capillaries in skin
Constricts air passages to lungs	Dilates air passages to lungs
Increases bladder wall contraction	Inhibits bladder contraction
Promotes peristalsis	Inhibits peristalsis
Constricts pupil of eye	Dilates pupil of eye

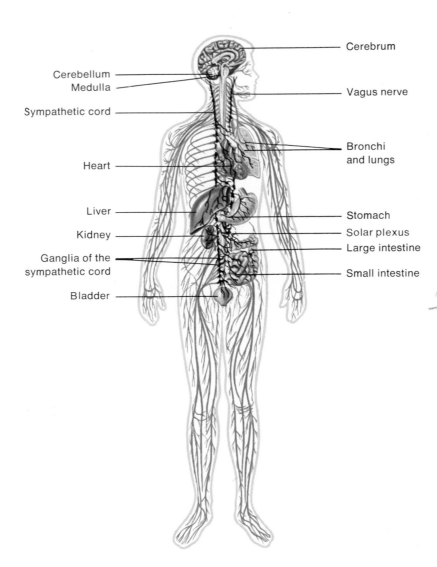

Cerebrum

Cerebellum
Medulla

Sympathetic cord

Heart

Liver

Kidney

Ganglia of the
sympathetic cord

Bladder

Vagus nerve

Bronchi
and lungs

Stomach
Solar plexus
Large intestine

Small intestine

12-5 The autonomic nervous system controls your internal organs. It has two divisions: the parasympathetic and the sympathetic. How do they differ? Do you have any control over your autonomic nervous system?

You can see that when the parasympathetic nerves are stimulated, you relax, breathe quietly, are ready to eat, carry on digestion at a normal rate, and can lose heat gradually through the enlarged blood capillaries of the skin. However, when the sympathetic nerves are stimulated, all these quiet activities so vital to living are interrupted—you get ready for an emergency! Digestion stops; heart rate increases; air passages to the lungs enlarge, and you breathe more deeply and rapidly; blood capillaries in the skin constrict, and your body temperature and blood pressure go up; increased blood pressure "pushes" water out of the skin capillaries as perspiration.

Normally, parasympathetic and sympathetic nerves work smoothly in balance, controlled by a part of your midbrain and a lower brain part (which you will also read about in this chapter). What are some other examples of parasympathetic-sympathetic action?

The Reflex Arc

The central nervous system analyzes sensory information and directs the motor and glandular response. This is true for peripheral nerve action and for autonomic nerve action, although different parts of the brain are involved, depending upon whether or not you are aware of what is going on. Sometimes the pathways from sensory neurons to associative neurons to motor neurons are very complicated, involving several parts of the brain. But sometimes they are not. The simplest level of nerve action is a *reflex*. The nerve impulse follows a path, called a *reflex arc*, which often bypasses the brain. A classic example of a reflex is the action that follows touching a hot stove with your hand. Your arm reacts at once, without waiting for a conscious decision to be made by your brain. This kind of short, simple nerve pathway is of great advantage to your health and safety. Reflex arcs also take care of regaining your balance after stumbling and many other necessary, quick actions.

A reflex arc involves at least three neurons —a sensory neuron, an associative neuron in the spinal cord or brain, and a motor neuron that stimulates action. There are a number of reflex arcs that pass through the spinal cord but not the brain. However, a connecting neuron carries an impulse to the brain so you become aware of what has happened.

In your body's nerve pathways, the axon of one neuron lies close to, but not attached to, the dendrites of another nerve cell. The microscopic gap between them is called the *synapse* (SIH-naps). Nerve impulses bridge the synapse by secretion of a chemical substance across the gap. Most nerve axons are

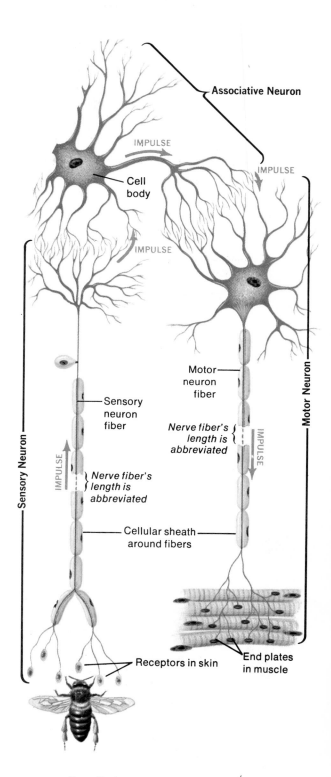

12-6 A simple reflex arc. What is a synapse? How does it function in the reflex arc? Follow the path of the reflex arc in this diagram.

branched at the end, and they can synapse with many other neurons. Even in the simple reflex-arc example, sensory impulses must cross two synapses in order to reach the motor nerve (Figure 12-6). At both synapses, branching of impulses to other neurons occurs. Thus, the message can go to the brain even as action is taken, and the action itself is not by one muscle cell but many, since numerous motor neurons are stimulated.

Protective Function of Reflexes

Reflexes, for the most part, have a protective function, especially against injury and foreign objects. However, despite the body's normal reaction to these situations, it can with time be conditioned to tolerate some of them.

One foreign object the body deals with is the *contact lens*, discussed in Chapter 11. The contact lens is a foreign object when placed in the eye, and the eye responds by reflex action, blinking and tearing, in an effort to wash the foreign object out. Time, motivation, and determination are needed to overcome this inborn response.

The body can even condition reflexes that have to do with heat and cold, or with pain. Every housewife knows that burns from hot pans in the kitchen hurt most when one is learning to cook. Later, many small burns are ignored. As for cold, the man who works in a refrigeration plant "learns" not to shiver continuously as he works.

How Habits Are Formed

The synapses appear to be important in controlling action and thinking, especially in learning new skills. You may recall when you learned to add columns of numbers or to play a musical instrument that each new effort was intense and awkward. Gradually the impulses move through the appropriate synapses more accurately and quickly (15 +

4 *always* added to 19, and you began to find the notes of the scale more easily). Eventually the impulse pathways became "automatic" (you could add 15 + 4 in your head, and your hand automatically played middle C when you saw that note written next in the score). When this happens, we say that we have developed a series of *conditioned responses*, automatic responses to a particular stimuli.

All sorts of skills that you now take for granted — walking, talking, riding your bike — were acquired in much the same way as any conditioned response. In fact, most skills are really sets of conditioned responses.

A habit is a more complex type of conditioning. A habit is not triggered by only one stimulus, and we have conscious control of whether or not we have a particular habit.

It is easier to form a new habit than to change an old one. In forming a habit, you learn to respond to certain particular stimuli. For example, if you want to form the habit of brushing your teeth before going to bed, put your toothbrush near the bed or sink so you will see it just before going to bed. Soon you

12-7 Swimming is a learned skill. How does a skill differ from a conditioned response?

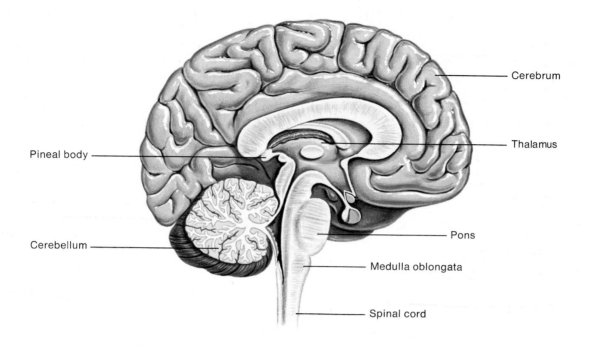

Cerebrum

Thalamus

Pineal body

Pons

Cerebellum

Medulla oblongata

Spinal cord

12-8 The brain is composed of several different parts. Each part works closely with the other parts but also has important individual functions. Can you give some examples of how parts of the brain work together? How is the brain protected against injury?

find that you no longer need to put it out. You are responding to the pattern (stimulus) of a routine before getting into bed—brush your teeth.

But suppose you have a habit you want to break. Unlearning it isn't easy. Let's say that you respond with "huh" when someone speaks to you, and you want to change the habit. It will be easier to change if you will substitute some other response, such as "Yes?" or "Yes, Mr. Taylor," or "Yes, Susan," rather than try to break the connection between the old stimulus and response of "huh" by suppressing *any* reaction. In this way you substitute a new response for an old, undesirable one, without ignoring the stimulus.

The Central Nervous System

The central nervous system is the communications center of the body. It includes, as you know, the *brain* and the *spinal cord*. The brain interprets the meaning of the sensations picked up by the receptors of the peripheral nervous system. You are aware of what is going on. Parts of the brain also control what responses are made to stimuli of the autonomic system, but you are *not* aware of what is going on.

The brain and spinal cord are protected against damage by a bony framework and protective membranes (Figures 12-1 and 12-8). The brain is encased in the *skull*, and the spinal cord is enclosed within the *backbone*.

Within their bony covers, both the brain and the spinal cord are further protected by three membranes, the *meninges* (meh-NIN-jeez). Between the inner two membranes, there is a space that is filled with *cerebrospinal* (ser-eh-bro-SPY-nal) *fluid*. The fluid acts as a cushion against shock, and nutrients pass through it from the blood to the nerve cells. The fluid also carries waste products from the nerve cells. The wastes are then carried away by the circulatory system.

The brain is composed of a number of different parts, each working with the others, but each performing specialized functions (Figure 12-9). The large, upper part of the brain, the *cerebrum* (SEHR-uh-brum), is divided into two hemispheres, or parts, and is covered by a wrinkled layer of *gray matter* called the *cerebral cortex*. The folds of gray matter are called *convolutions* (kon-vuh-LOO-shunz). The convolutions increase the surface area of the gray matter, making it possible to accommodate more neurons. It is here in the gray matter that thinking, planning, learning, conscious perception, and other complex functions occur. Its organization is at the highest level of the brain, and its vastly greater development accounts for the dominance of man in the animal kingdom.

Specialized areas of the cerebrum have been identified that control sight, hearing, speech, motor activities, and other functions (Figure 12-10). It is known that the functions of the cerebrum depend on electrical impulses that it receives and records. But the way the cerebrum actually functions in thought and action is not yet fully understood.

There is much crossing-over of neuron pathways from the cerebrum's two hemispheres. The motor area on the right side controls movement on the left side of the body. The motor fibers from the cerebrum actually do cross over to the opposite side as they enter the spinal cord. Hence, if there is

12-9 YOUR BRAIN AND SPINAL CORD

Part of Central Nervous System	What You Need It For
Cerebrum	Consciousness and conscious activities. (Exercise of will power, memory, learning, speech, writing, reason, planned movements, etc.)
Cerebellum; and brain stem up to cerebrum	Balance and coordinated movement. (Walking—provided a stimulus is given, avoiding obstacles in path, balancing the body, sitting erect)
Medulla	Vital physical activities. (Breathing, reflexes of blood vessels, control of heartbeat, and other reflex actions necessary for life)
Spinal cord	Simple reflexes. (Pulling leg away when pinched, etc.)

damage to the right side of the cerebrum, the left side of the body will be affected.

The *cerebellum* (sehr-uh-BEL-um) lies under the back part of the cerebrum. It functions in coordinating your body's muscle movements, as in maintaining posture and balance, or as in walking, swimming, and other activities.

Two smaller parts of the brain—the *hypothalamus* and the *pons* (PONZ)—contain control centers for regulation of body temper-

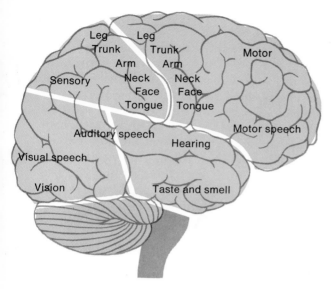

12-10 Specialized areas of the cerebrum control many activities. How do you think these specialized control areas were identified?

ature and other functions. They are also connecting stations between the spinal cord and other parts of the brain.

The *medulla oblongata* (meh-DUHL-a ob-lon-GA-ta) lies under the cerebellum. It contains the vital centers that regulate breathing, heart action, digestion, and blood circulation. The medulla provides connections for nerve fibers that pass from upper parts of the brain into the spinal cord. It and the hypothalamus also regulate autonomic nerve action. Injury to the medulla can cause instant death.

The *spinal cord* is suspended in a cylinder formed by the bones of the spine. These bones, along with the meninges and the cerebrospinal fluid mentioned earlier, protect the cord from shock just as the brain is protected. The spinal cord is composed of millions of nerve cells, many of them continuous with the brain. It is the pathway for sensory nerves that carry impulses up the cord to the brain and for motor nerves that carry impulses from the brain.

Diseases of the Central Nervous System

There are many diseases that affect the central nervous system. Some of the more common diseases include stroke, tumors of the brain and spinal cord, and infections, such as polio. Stroke is caused by a blood clot or by a blood vessel breaking in the brain. You will learn more about stroke in Chapter 32. Tumors are abnormal growths that may or may not be cancerous. Certain tumors may develop in the cerebrum, cerebellum, or spinal cord. The location will determine the symptoms. Most tumors place pressure on nerves and may result in paralysis. In many cases, tumors can be successfully removed by surgery.

Infections of the nervous system are caused by bacteria, *viruses* (VY-rus-ez), and other organisms. Viruses are exceedingly small and puzzling. Outside of a living cell, they are as inactive as any nonliving substance, but inside a cell they reproduce and cause infections. Polio, or *poliomyelitis*, some forms of *meningitis* (men-in-JY-tis) and *encephalitis*, and *rabies* (RAY-beez) are virus infections of the central nervous system. You will read more about viruses in Chapter 29.

Polio is also called *infantile paralysis* because it most often attacks children. It may strike persons of any age, but it rarely attacks anyone over forty. It is caused by any of three (or possibly more) related strains of viruses that may damage the motor cells of the spinal cord and thus paralyze the muscles in certain parts of the body. Sometimes the viruses settle in the medulla of the brain and cause paralysis of the breathing muscles. When this happens, the patient may have to be placed in an iron lung, which mechanically produces artificial respiration.

Fortunately, there are many more nonparalytic cases than paralytic ones. That is, polio frequently occurs in a mild form. Many adults had, as children, mild attacks by

12-11 A photomicrograph of the virus that causes poliomyelitis.

different virus strains that produced no paralysis but left them immune to the disease. The symptoms are common to many other diseases: fever, headache, sore throat, upset stomach with vomiting, sore muscles, and dizziness. During a polio epidemic, any suspicious symptoms, particularly if muscle pain or spasms develop, should have immediate medical attention.

As yet, we have no drug that will destroy the viruses once a person develops polio. In the early days of the illness, rest is very important. Later, massage and properly directed exercise are helpful if paralysis develops. Exercise may prevent muscles from shrinking and save those muscle fibers whose connecting nerve cells have not been killed by the virus. Even with the best treatment, many patients have to wear steel braces permanently. Fortunately, more than 50 percent of the people who have polio in a severe enough form to be recognized recover completely without having reached the paralytic stage.

Scientists had to solve many problems before they could find a vaccine to prevent polio. They had to find living tissues, other than human, in which the viruses would thrive and reproduce. Then they had to weaken or kill the viruses in such a way that they would not cause the disease in man but would protect man against all three known strains of the virus. Only then would a vaccine be both safe and effective.

Dr. Jonas Salk grew all three strains of polio viruses in cultures of monkey kidney cells. He then treated the viruses with formaldehyde to destroy their ability to cause polio. The Salk dead-virus vaccine was shown to be safe when it was given to more than 1,800,000 school children in the largest medical field trial in history.

American scientists have also developed several different _live_-virus vaccines. In these vaccines, the living viruses have been so weakened that they can no longer cause polio, although they can still protect a person from getting the disease. One advantage of the live-virus vaccine is that it can be taken by mouth. The live-virus vaccine developed by Dr. Albert Sabin is now the vaccine most widely used to prevent polio.

Rabies is a virus disease that kills both men and animals if the virus reaches the brain. It takes, on the average, from two to six weeks after the initial infection for rabies to develop. Infection occurs when the victim is bitten by a rabid dog, squirrel, bat, or other animal in which the disease occurs.

Dogs suspected of rabies should be kept caged by public health authorities for ten days. If they are still alive and in good health then, rabies is improbable. If the dog dies, its brain should be examined to find out if rabies was the cause of death. There is no known cure for rabies if it actually develops, hence, preventive treatment is very important. (A preventive treatment was developed by Pasteur.) You should always consult your doctor if bitten by an animal.

See Figure 12-13 for a chart showing the major causes and effects of numerous disorders that affect the central nervous system.

12-12 (*Left*) Dr. Jonas E. Salk, developer of the dead-virus polio vaccine, shown in his laboratory. (*Right*) Dr. Albert B. Sabin developed the live-virus polio vaccine, which is presently the most widely used polio vaccine. How do these vaccines differ?

YOUR FEELINGS AND YOUR NERVOUS SYSTEM

The nerves form a communications network throughout the body. Through this network the body acts on the mind, and the mind acts on the body. Mind and body work together; they are not separate units.

Sometimes a physical reaction may arise from an emotional situation, *or* an emotional reaction may occur as the result of physical distress. For example, a person may experience an upset stomach either because of eating spoiled food or because he does not want to take a test in school. In the first case, the autonomic nervous system responds to a normal impulse of the stomach, to rid itself of an irritating substance. In the second case, the autonomic nervous system responds to impulses from the brain itself. The effect in this case is to help the person escape from the emotional stress situation.

One way or another, whatever stimuli occur, a response will follow, whether it is withdrawal of a finger from a source of pain, laughter at a funny story, restlessness as a result of boredom, breathing more deeply after exercise, or singing because of happiness or loneliness.

Effects of Prolonged Stimulation of the Nervous System

Sometimes the nervous system is stimulated over a long time during stress. It may be because you are ill and missing many days of school, or you are preparing for a big test, or it may be because you do not feel really accepted by a group of boys and girls you like. The effects of prolonged stress may show up as restlessness, lack of desire to participate in normal activities, or inability to concentrate, relax, or sleep.

You have learned how the sympathetic

12-13 DISORDERS OF THE CENTRAL NERVOUS SYSTEM

Disorder	Cause	Effect
Aphasia	Injury to speech center of brain	Defect or loss of power of expression
Stroke (apoplexy)	Clot, hemorrhage of blood vessel in brain	Depends on area of brain involved
Cerebral palsy	Injury to motor areas of the brain or lack of oxygen to the brain at birth	Paralysis or difficulty with motor function and/or coordination
Concussion of brain	Violent blow to the head	Loss of consciousness
Encephalitis (sleeping sickness)	Virus infection of brain areas	Headache — pain — deep sleep — coma
Epilepsy	Possibly injury, inflammation, or poor blood supply to the brain; often unknown	Mild to violent convulsions or seizures
Meningitis, cerebrospinal	Infection of meninges (membranes) of brain and spinal cord	Fever — chills — stiff neck — skin rash
Multiple sclerosis	Destruction of the myelin sheath that surrounds nerves	Weakness — numbness — lack of coordination
Neuritis	Inflammation of nerve fiber sheath	Tenderness — pain — limited movements

Disorder	Cause	Effect
Parkinson's disease	Degeneration of nerves at base of brain	Tremor—rigidity of muscles—speech impairment
Poliomyelitis	Virus infection of the brain and spinal cord	Muscle weakness—partial or extensive paralysis
Rabies	Virus from rabid animal entering open wound, affecting central nervous system	Pain at site—insomnia—acute muscle spasm—depression—death if untreated before symptoms appear
Shingles (Herpes zoster)	Virus infection of sensory nerves	Pain—blisters on area supplied by affected nerves
Tumor (brain and spinal cord)	Abnormal cell growth	Pressure on nerves—inhibits activity of normal cells—destruction of normal cells

division of the autonomic nervous system acts as mediator in helping you meet emergencies. In addition to this help, there are things that you can do to help overcome such stress situations. The first thing, of course, is to check up on your everyday health habits —food, elimination, sleep, rest, and exercise. Undue excitability, called *restlessness* or *nervousness,* often can be remedied by physical exertion—a good swim, a long hike, boxing, or wrestling. Working on a hobby or helping a friend with his hobby often helps you recapture the ability to concentrate and relax.

Habits of Feeling

You can develop habits of feeling as well as habits of action. In both cases they can be desirable habits or undesirable ones. Suppose, when you were quite small, you were badly frightened when a cat scratched you. The next time you saw a cat, it was easy for your impulses to travel the same pathway, and you were frightened again. The result may be that you are still afraid of cats.

You can change habits of feeling in somewhat the same way that you change habits of action, but it is not easy. Habits of feeling too often are associated with the way you want to feel. If your fear of cats is just that, and not really a dislike, take the direct approach and play with a kitten when you next have the opportunity. If you actually dislike cats but want to be more tolerant of them, spend some time with a friend who has a cat and observe how your friend and the pet adjust to each other.

All of this goes for your habits of feeling about different kinds of people, too. If one of your friends has another friend whom you feel is a kind of person you do not really like, spend some time with both of them if you can. With understanding, better habits of feeling can develop.

Habits of Relaxing

Making relaxation a regular part of your busy day is as important to your feelings as it is to your muscles and organs. Here is a suggestion. Stretch out on your back for from five to fifteen minutes and deliberately stop thinking, just as you would turn off the television set. All the body functions tend to slow down and assume a calm, smooth rhythm. You can make relaxing a habit simply by repeating it at intervals when you can, during the day and evening.

People sometimes associate the need to relax with being an older person. Older people do need to relax, but high school students who are still growing need regular relaxation even more. Even during a brief five minutes, the body has the opportunity to get ahead with its building and repair functions.

Engaging in recreation is another way to relax. Literally, recreation means to recreate, that is, to give fresh life. Recreation takes many forms. A good guide to choosing a relaxing form of recreation is to look for the opposite type of activity from what you have been doing. If you have been working wholly mentally, choose an outdoor activity, prefer-

12-14 Painting is one way of relaxing. What is your favorite method of finding relaxation?

ably one that is vigorous. If you have been working out with the team every afternoon preparing for the coming sports season, choose a good book and sit quietly, watch television, or listen to some music you like. Visiting friends is a good way to relax any time. Do you leave enough time for relaxation?

The Environment Affects
Your Nervous System

The external environment where you live, like the internal environment of your body organs, affects your nervous system. You react and adjust to everything from your home and family, to your school and school friends, to the world and its problems.

People react differently to their environment. Many are happy with it; some accept it as part of daily living; others believe it is a threat to their well-being.

There are special problems of living in the world today. Even the small ones seem strange, as when you dial a wrong number and get a recorded announcement instead of a friendly voice offering help. Recorded messages are being used more and more today, not only by the telephone company, but in large cities by movie theaters, railroads, and airlines to give information in answer to your call. These robot voices work against the nerve tone of your conditioned responses, for you are accustomed to answering when spoken to, yet you know it is useless.

Negotiating a purchase with a coin-operated machine can also be frustrating. It cannot discuss the product with you, or

12-15 Your environment can affect your nerves. Do noisy class changes affect you?

apologize and correct its mistake when it has given you the incorrect change.

Recorded voices and machines are factors you will have to face more and more in your life, along with larger crowds, because our human population is growing at an alarming rate. You will face more environmental noise, too—today's jet planes crashing through a sonic barrier overhead are only a beginning. Life is less stable than it once was and, in a sense, is "subject to change without notice." People move about more today than they ever have before, as the advances of technology close some types of industries and open others, often in far-away, strange places. In Chapter 5 you read about the population shifts from rural to urban, suburban, and industrial areas. Crowded urban and industrial areas create the need for a whole new approach to community living, and they create a conflict between the impulse to follow old habits and customs and the demands of the new environment for change in your way of life.

All your adjustments to modern life will not be problems, however. Along with the problems, ranging from the ones just discussed to worldwide matters of war or peace, you have many benefits of modern knowledge to anticipate—such as a longer life, better physical health, and a better education. The effects of your environment upon your nerves will probably balance out well.

THE EFFECTS OF FATIGUE AND SLEEP

Fatigue is the sensation of being tired and is the body's message to you that you need rest. When fatigue is kept within your physiological limits, it is useful. It can help insure restful sleep, and it gives a general feeling of well-being. The problem is not to prevent fatigue, but rather to keep it within useful bounds.

Causes and Conditions of Fatigue

Fatigue is caused by the accumulation of waste products in the tissues at a faster rate than the body can throw them off. It is a condition of the cells and organs that have undergone excessive activity, resulting in loss of power to respond to stimulation.

Symptoms of fatigue are complicated and show up in a variety of ways. For example, the swimmer is obviously fatigued at the end of a hundred-yard race, but the student who has studied all weekend for a final may be equally fatigued, but in a different way. Both of these types are *normal fatigue,* and the body needs only time to restore itself. There is a more complex kind of fatigue, called *chronic fatigue,* in which the cause is not so readily seen or understood. It may be the result of physical or psychological activity. Chronic fatigue is not useful, and it can be a threat to health and happiness.

Normal or Physiological Fatigue

Here is a simple exercise to try that may help you understand muscle fatigue:

Flex and relax the index finger of your hand as rapidly and as many times as you can. Before long, there will be discomfort in your wrist and forearm. The discomfort will increase to a feeling of pain that will grow so intense you will have to stop the exercise.

Several things are demonstrated in this exercise. *First,* the more vigorously you exercise, the faster the muscle fatigues. *Second,* fatigue in one set of muscles soon affects others nearby. In a similar way, eye fatigue from excessive use of eye muscles, tired feet from an evening of dancing, or tired arms from bowling can cause the whole body to

12-16 What kind of fatigue is this girl showing? Can emotions influence fatigue?

feel fatigued. *Third,* the sensation of pain is a warning that you have reached your physiological limits. In this case, fatigue is a *protective* mechanism.

Physiological fatigue occurs when muscle action demands more oxygen than is available. The waste products of muscle fatigue, such as lactic acid and carbon dioxide, build up in the muscles at a rate faster than they can be accommodated. Slowing down and rest are needed to provide time for the body to restore a proper balance.

Nerve cells also show fatigue, although they are more resistant to fatigue than muscles are. Continued stimulation of nerve cells depletes their energies and causes fatigue products to mount up. Changes may occur in nerve endings making it difficult, sometimes impossible, for impulses to pass. Nerve fatigue requires longer and more frequent rest periods before nerve cells can be restored to normal efficiency.

Environmental factors may contribute to fatigue, such as poor illumination, the reading of fine print over a long period of time, uncomfortable chairs, and insufficient ventilation. Other common contributors to fatigue are ill-fitting clothing, eyestrain, and weak feet.

Chronic or Pathological Fatigue

Chronic fatigue is a symptom that something is wrong. When a person comes home in the evening tired and cross instead of tired and hungry, or if he cannot eat, sleep, or find pleasure in his normal activities, he needs to investigate his condition. His excessive fatigue may be a symptom of disease or body disorder—anemia, tuberculosis, or poor nutrition or circulation. He needs a medical check-up.

If no disease or body disorder is found, the fatigue may be due to other causes, such as a conditioned inability to relax, work requiring more strength or aptitude than he has, or boredom with the routine of school, social life, or home activities. All of these conditions, and many others, may cause chronic fatigue. Most of them, with proper guidance, can be remedied by revising the routine of daily work, play, study, rest, and sleep.

The first thing, however, in treating chronic fatigue is to find the cause and to eliminate it, if possible. If it is due to illness, the illness can be treated. If it is due to emotional strain, a way must be sought to eliminate or adjust the situation causing the strain. Unfortunately, there are times when the cause cannot be readily removed, but the feeling of strain can be lessened if everyone concerned frankly admits the problem and tries sincerely to work out a solution. Rest may not prove too helpful in emotional strain; the better therapy would be to find and, if possible, to eliminate or minimize the cause.

Wrong Ways of Fighting Fatigue

The use of **chemical stimulants** to postpone or counteract fatigue is the wrong way to fight fatigue. Chemical stimulants excite the nervous system, sending out more and more impulses over already-fatigued nerve pathways. In rather a short time, the body "kicks back" at the overstimulation by producing nervousness, confusion, and severe "let-down" feelings. Some students who take "pep pills" to help them stay awake while cramming for tests find out too late that the nervousness, confusion, and "let-down" reactions may come during the test in class. Such sensations often render a student incapable of finishing his examination.

Right Ways of Fighting Fatigue

Correct ways of fighting fatigue call for some planning on your part. Here are some suggestions:

1. Organize your time each day so that your required duties get full attention.
2. In between these duties, set aside time for a few minutes of rest, as mentioned earlier.
3. Plan to relax—and this is not the same as rest. You can relax by doing something different. If you have been studying, for instance, you can relax by doing something physical.
4. Plan time for enough refreshing sleep.

The Importance of Sleep

It is estimated that people spend about one third of their lives in sleep. If you average eight hours of sleep each night, you will spend 2,920 hours in sleep this year.

The mechanism of sleep has puzzled scientists for centuries. Many theories have been advanced, but thus far none has been universally accepted. But it is agreed that when you feel sleepy it is nature's message that your body needs recuperation and rest. And everyone agrees that sleep is necessary to life.

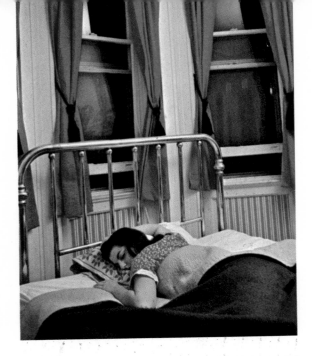

12-17 Good ventilation is essential for a restful night's sleep. Do you keep your window open when you go to sleep?

Some Benefits of Sleep

During sleep, most of the measurable physical functions slow down. Body temperature falls, muscles relax, heartbeat slows, blood pressure and pulse rate fall, breathing slows, and secretion from nearly all glands lessens. It is during this period of minimized body activity that the body recuperates and repairs itself. During the normal activities of the day, body cells of some types wear out and must be replaced. During sleep, growth and regrowth take place more rapidly, since cells are being restored faster than they are being worn out. For example, it has been shown that the cells of the skin divide and make new cells about twice as fast when you are asleep as when you are awake.

The benefits of sleep on the brain and nervous system are not so readily measured, but some reactions seem clear. During sleep you become seemingly unconscious, unaware, and more or less unresponsive to your environment. In approaching sleep, one by one the senses become inactive—first vision, then taste, smell, hearing, and finally touch. You rest and relax even though the nervous system and brain become temporarily very active during parts of your sleep—you even have many visual images as you sleep, and eye movement becomes extremely active as you dream. Your dreams themselves often sort out the problems of the day, and you handle them in your sleep in refreshingly novel ways! All this activity is part of the explanation of dreams, and even of talking in your sleep and sleepwalking (somnambulism). Exactly why dream activity varies from one night to another in any particular person cannot be explained.

Dreams

In recent years many laboratory experiments have been performed in an effort to understand dreams and the purposes they might serve. For one such experiment, the subjects were divided into two groups. One group was allowed to dream; the other subjects were awakened when they began dreaming. Those who were not allowed to dream showed extremely undesirable behavior during their waking hours, such as irritability and lapse of memory. They also developed enormous appetites. The conclusion drawn was that dreaming is necessary to physical and mental health. The dreams apparently serve as a safety valve for relieving the tensions and burdens of waking life.

How Much Sleep Do You Need?

Some scientists believe that the amount of sleep a person needs is influenced by his rate of growth. By this guide, rapidly growing infants need more sleep than do teenagers, and teen-agers need more than adults. Then in old age, when the repair processes of the body are slower, more sleep is again required. Another suggestion advanced by many scientists is that the amount of sleep you need depends on the kind of work you do. If it is heavy work—mental or physical—you need more sleep.

In some ways sleep requirements are a highly individual matter, but eight hours per night is commonly accepted for most people. Edison is reported to have slept only five or six hours a night, but he had a cot in his laboratory and was fond of taking catnaps during the day. Many creative people consistently sleep less than eight hours a night, others more. To look and feel your best, you probably need from eight to ten hours of sleep each night. This is not a prescription, however, for the amount of sleep you feel you need may be the result of habit. Some families have rigid rules regarding sleep requirements; some are more flexible. Also, there are those who resort to sleep not merely for rest but to escape unpleasant duties or situations. They get more sleep than they actually need.

How can you tell if you are getting enough sleep? You have had enough sleep when you awake feeling refreshed, alert, and ready to meet the new day. With either too little or too much sleep, you will not feel as well.

What Happens When You Lose Sleep?

There are few or no harmful physical effects from occasional loss of sleep. But there is research evidence to show that psychological reactions may appear in the form of restlessness, irritability, and inability to concentrate. Recent research findings point out that missing an hour of sleep each night over a long period of time may do more harm than losing several hours on one particular night. If your sleeping habits are generally good, you can afford an occasional late night. You are wise, of course, to take the late night when the demands of the next day will be light.

"Sleeping Like a Log"

There is no such thing as "sleeping like a log." Studies made with recording devices have definitely shown that the sound sleeper changes his position every 10 to 15 minutes. He does this to give relaxation to different sets of muscles. It follows, then, that there is no best position for sleep. Any position that is comfortable will serve.

It is recognized that some hours of sleep are deeper, or more sound, than others. *Deep sleep* may come before or after midnight and lasts from two to four hours. It is of great importance to the restorative mechanisms of the body. Evidence that there are different levels of sleep is shown by the *electroencephalograph* (ee-LEK-tro-en-SEF-a-lo-graf), or EEG, a device that traces "brain wave" patterns. See Figure 12-18.

12-18 An electroencephalograph traces brain wave patterns and may be used to detect different levels of sleep.

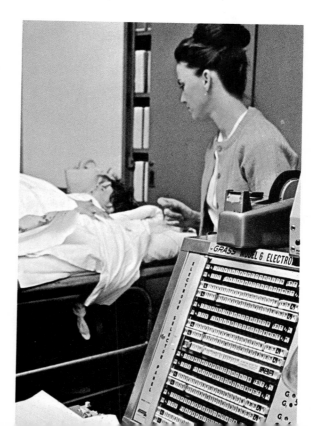

There are many factors that contribute to deep sleep. Among them are the environmental conditions. A comfortable bed in a darkened, quiet, agreeably cool room is an example.

Insomnia—Inability to Sleep

Even the best-adjusted person may occasionally have difficulty falling asleep. This is *temporary insomnia* and can be brought on by looking forward to some exciting event, worrying over some school problem, or even thinking about a mystery story. None of these is serious; the situation usually corrects itself, and soon you are sleeping normally.

Sometimes, however, insomnia is severe, persistent, and eventually chronic. The cause may be due to some disease or body disorder, or may be associated with excessive fatigue, hunger, an uncomfortable bed, cold or worry, noise, lights, fear, stimulating beverages, or some long-range problem.

Your Feelings and Insomnia

Some people accept insomnia as their lot in life; others seek the cause and work hard to remedy the condition. Here are some of the homemade techniques for getting to sleep: taking a warm bath, drinking warm milk, reading a dull book, walking around the block. Then there are gadgets for sale. The slumber salesman offers earplugs, eyeshades, special mattresses, bed boards, and phonograph records of hypnotic sound, to mention only a few. When insomnia becomes chronic, medical supervision is usually needed.

New Day—New Experiences

With or without the best conditions of sleep and work, the amazing durability of your neurons and nerves through all that you do each day, and each year, is one of the mysteries of your health. Since almost everything you do requires nerve coordination, you surely would plan to make nerve cells replaceable if you were designing a human body in which limited kinds of cells could be replenished. But this is not the case. Your neurons and nerves are with you for life, while skin cells, blood cells, liver cells, and certain others can be regenerated.

All this points to the importance of your being concerned with your health—your diet, your balance of activities, your rest and sleep, and your outlook. Your nervous system—and therefore you—will be better and last longer for the care you give it.

What You Have Learned

What kind of health practices should you apply in maintaining your health? Check your understanding of the chapter. On a separate sheet of paper, number 1 through 18 and insert the answer from the vocabulary list below. Use each expression, but use each one only once.

autonomic
central
cerebellum
cerebrum
conscious
fatigue

insomnia
learned
medulla
motor nerves
parasympathetic
peripheral

reflex arc
sensory nerves
spinal cord
sympathetic
synapse
waste

The nervous system includes three closely related systems. The (1) *Central* nervous system, which includes the brain and spinal cord, is the communication center of the body. It is largely concerned with (2) *learned* activities of the body. The (3) *peripheral* nervous system is made up of all the nerves that connect the spinal cord and brain with parts of your body. (4) *Sensory* nerves carry information from your sense organs to the brain and spinal cord. (5) *Motor neurons* carry information from the central nervous system to the muscles and glands. The (6) *autonomic* nervous system controls involuntary body functions, such as heartbeat. It has two subdivisions. The (7) *sympathetic* subdivision helps the body get ready for an emergency, and the (8) *parasympathetic* subdivision governs such functions as constricting the pupil of the eye to protect it from bright light.

The central nervous system analyzes information and directs the desired motor response. The simplest pathway that a nerve impulse can take is called a (9) *reflex arc*. In your body's nerve pathways, the axon of one neuron lies close to, but not attached to, the dendrites of another nerve cell. The microscopic gap between them is called the (10) *synapse*. Conditional responses, like reflexes, do not require constant attention, but they are different from reflexes in that they must be (11) *conscious*.

The brain is composed of several parts that work together, but each has a specialized function. The large, upper part of the brain, the (12) *cerebrum* provides the highest level of learning, deciding, and remembering. The (13) *cerebellum* lies under the back of the large upper part and functions in muscle coordination. Connecting the rest of the brain with the spinal cord is the (14) *medulla*, which contains vital centers that regulate breathing, heart action, and circulation. It also serves as the connection for nerve fibers that pass from the upper part of the brain into the spinal cord.

Suspended within a cylinder formed by bones of the spine is the (15) *spinal cord*, which forms the junction of many sensory and motor nerves. The sensation of being tired is called (16) *fatigue*. It is caused by an accumulation of (17) *waste* products. The inability to sleep is called (18) *insomnia*.

What You Can Do

1. Keep a list for a week of the number of times during the day that you relax. How do you relax? Do you lie on your back or just sit in a comfortable place for a few minutes? Do you take a slow bike ride, a leisurely swim, or a walk with a friend? Do you watch television or listen to records?

2. Check your habits and find one that you would like to improve. Practice faithfully. How long was it before you noticed some results? How long was it before you were able to break a bad habit?

3. Have you ever tried not to blush or perspire? Do you think that you can succeed? Make a list of body actions that you cannot control.

Things to Try /

1. Obtain a sheep or calf brain from the meat market. Open it up and locate the gray matter and the white matter. Can you find where the nerves are attached?

2. Try the knee-jerk reflex test. Sit on a table and let your legs hang free from the knee down. Have someone strike you just below the knee with the side of his hand. Does your leg jerk up? Can you explain what has happened?

Probing Further /

The Nervous System: The Inner Networks, by Alvin Silverstein and Virginia B. Silverstein, Prentice-Hall, 1971. An easy-to-read, informative book about the nervous system.

Sleep, by Gay Gaer Luce and Julius Segal, Lancer, 1970. An interesting account of the effects of sleep deprivation, of learning during sleep, and of the nature of dreams.

The Human Brain: Its Capacities and Functions, by Isaac Asimov, Houghton Mifflin, 1964. A clear, up-to-date presentation of the way the brain is constructed and how it controls the body.

Health Concepts in Action /

Does this statement help express what you have learned?

> *The individual senses, interprets, and responds to his environment through the coordinating activity of the nervous system.*

Applying this concept of the nervous system, which health practices would you

    —continue?

    —change?

    —begin?

Will you now, as a result of your study, change any of your health objectives?

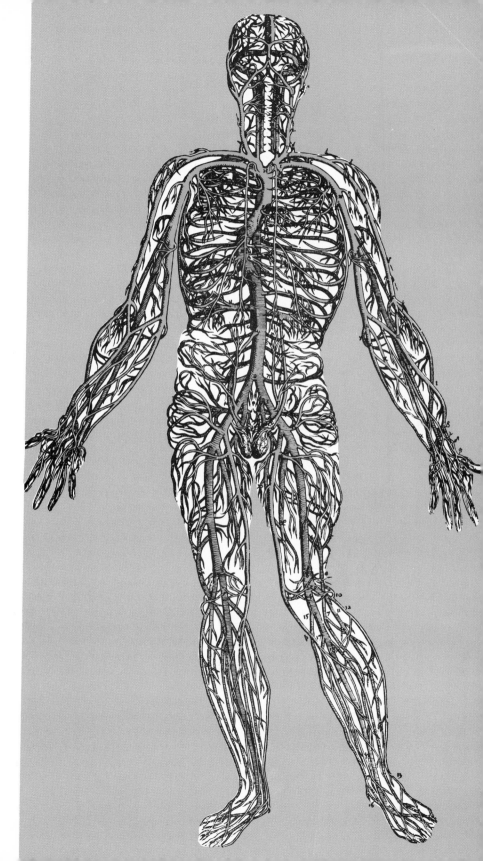

UNIT FOUR
Your Body's Supply Systems

16th century schematic drawing of
circulatory system. By permission of
The Bettman Archive

13 / Your Cells

228 - 365

Years ago a French-American doctor named Alexis Carrel snipped a tiny bit of heart tissue from the small, unconscious beginning of a chicken that was still inside the egg. Thirty-six years later, that bit of tissue was still feeding, growing, and producing more of itself. The cells, the living part of the tissue, grew so fast that after a while Carrel frequently had to remove part of the tissue and throw it away. If he had not done this, the living mass would soon have outgrown its container.

A PROBE INTO YOUR CELLS—Why do all your activities depend upon the activities of your cells? To find out, you will be probing questions like these:

1. What is a cell? What typical structures are found in cells? What are their functions?

2. Why is the nucleus called the control center of the cell? Why are chromosomes and genes so important?

3. What is metabolism? How do cells get their food?

4. How long do different kinds of cells live? How do cells produce new cells?

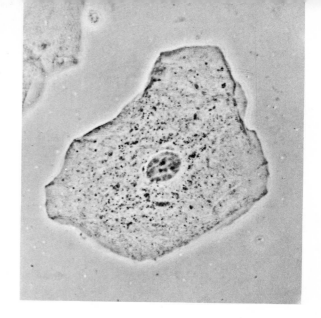

13-1 Photomicrograph of a cheek cell. What parts of this cell can you identify?

WHAT IS A CELL?

Cells are tiny living structures that make up all of the living parts of the body of every man, woman, and child—and of every plant and animal. Our bodies are built entirely of cells and substances made by them. You have read about many kinds of human cells in Chapter 2.

How Cells Are Built

Imagine yourself reduced to the size of a sugar molecule—small enough to dissolve in a droplet of water that wouldn't moisten the period at the end of this sentence. At this size you can set off on an exciting trip into the interior of a living human cell. At first your way seems blocked by a great, curved wall. In reality it is a very thin *cell membrane* surrounding the cell. It admits some molecules and keeps out others. For this reason it is called a *semipermeable* (sem-ee-PER-me-a-b'l) *membrane.* You will get through it without difficulty—a lucky thing for you. If you were larger on this imaginary trip—the size of a protein molecule—you would have to be digested first!

Once inside the cell, you would be in the *cytoplasm*. The cytoplasm includes all the structures and substances enclosed by the cell membrane except the *nucleus* and its contents. It also contains a complex system of membranes that appear to connect with the cell membrane. These membranes are the *endoplasmic reticulum* (EN-doh-plas-mick re-TIH-kyoo-lum), shown in Figure 13-2. Possibly—we don't know for sure—the endoplasmic reticulum is a transport system for materials passing from the cell membrane to the nucleus and from the nucleus to the cytoplasm.

There are many "small organs," or *organelles* (or-gan-ELLS), in the cytoplasm. While exploring the cell, you would come across the *ribosomes* (RY-boh-sohms). Studies indicate that ribosomes are the protein factories of the cell. You will read more about them in a later chapter. You would also see the *mitochondria* (my-toh-KON-dree-a). These are centers of *cell respiration*—"power plants" where energy is made available to support cell activities. You will read more about cell respiration later, too—on page 236.

As you traveled through the cell, you

13-2 A diagram of a cell. What are organelles? Which organelles can be identified in the photomicrograph of a cell shown below?

Cell membrane
Vacuole
Endoplasmic reticulum
Chromosomes
Cytoplasm
Nucleus
Nuclear membrane
Centrosome
Centrioles
Ribosomes
Mitochondria

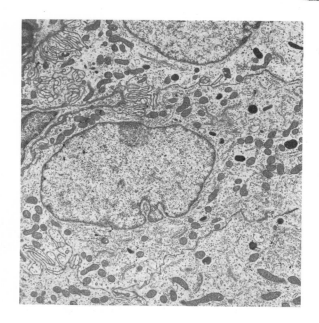

would come to fluid-filled cavities in the cytoplasm. These are the *vacuoles* (VA-kyoo-oles). Vacuoles may contain water, dissolved sugar, salt, and many other substances. Some vacuoles may contain waste products.

Eventually, you would come to the nucleus, the control center of the cell. The nucleus is surrounded by a *nuclear membrane*, which separates the nuclear materials from the rest of the cell. Once inside the nucleus, you would have some difficulty in making your way through the 46 extremely long, coiled, slender *chromosomes* (KROH-moh-sohms). See Figure 13-3. The *genes* (JEENZ), which control development and heredity, are transmitted from parent to child by the chromosomes. Heredity will be discussed in some detail in Chapter 20.

If you were to stay a while in the nucleus, you would note that the chromosomes seem to attract a host of smaller molecules. You would see the smaller molecules become attached to each other to make new, longer molecules that would then pass out into the cytoplasm to help manufacture proteins. Here is evidence that the nucleus is in charge of the cell and most of the things the cell does.

You may have read that the nucleus is the most important part of the cell. If this is stretching the truth it is only because almost *every* part of the cell is most important. The rest of a human cell cannot live on indefinitely without the nucleus. This is true of

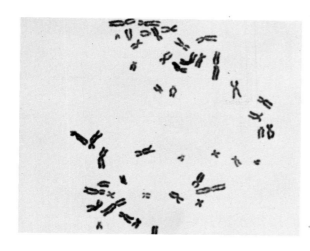

13-3 Chromosomes as they appear in a cell that is about to divide. In dividing cells the chromosomes become much shorter and thicker.

our red blood cells, the only cells in our bodies that normally lack nuclei. They can live for a few months without nuclei, however, so we tend to think of them in this way—having no nuclei. Other cells would not do nearly as well if they lost their nuclei. Most of them would die within a few days. The cell nuclei cannot live separately, either. They die almost immediately upon being removed from the cells.

As you pass back through the cytoplasm, ready to make your way out through the cell membrane, you might come close in your route to a *centrosome* (SEN-tro-sohm) and the two rodlike *centrioles* (SEN-trih-ohlz) inside it. These structures play an important role in cell division.

Cells That Move and Cells That Travel

When scientists take human cells and grow them in tissue cultures, as Alexis Carrell did, the cells often change their shape and move about in the glass culture dish. The cytoplasm of the cells has a constant, flowing motion. The cell membrane may pro-

duce numerous projections (see Figure 13-4), and the cytoplasm enters these projections and moves the cell along, as the part left behind is pulled forward. This suggests a kind of contraction, as in the muscle tissue of your body. The cytoplasm of these moving cells in tissue cultures is not muscular, but it does have some ability to contract. These cells can even do something you cannot do—*a single cell* can *surround* its "prey," or food, by moving into two projections, one on each side of the food! This kind of movement is called *amoeboid* (a-MEE-boid) *motion* because it is like the movement of a very common microscopic organism, *Amoeba* (uh-MEE-buh). In Chapter 16 you will learn how our white blood cells pursue bacteria in this way, then surround and destroy them, protecting the body from infection. Some other cells in the body also defend us by literally engulfing bacteria. All of these cells move by amoeboid motion.

13-4 Amoeboid motion is very important in the control of infection. What types of cells have this type of movement?

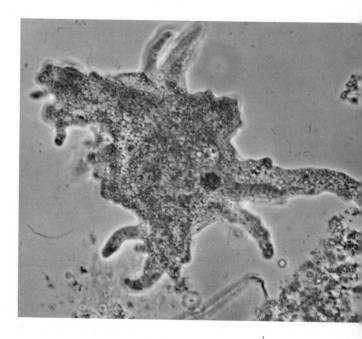

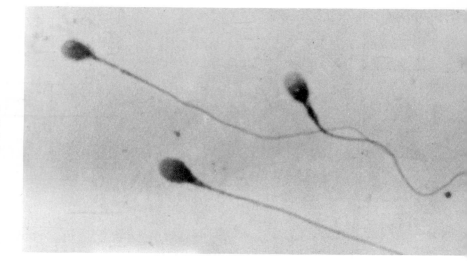

13-5 How do these sperm cells move? Why is this type of motion necessary to their functioning?

The delicate passages of the **_trachea_** (TRAY-kee-uh), or windpipe, and its branches are protected from dust and bacteria by millions of surface cells with microscopic, hair-like threads called *cilia*. The cilia carry dust and bacteria that were taken in with the air back toward the throat and mouth. This dust mixed with mucus is removed when you cough, sneeze, or clear your throat. You will read more about these cells, too.

Sperms (male sex cells) must swim to an *egg cell* to fertilize it. What happens then is a part of your study of heredity (Chapter 20). Each sperm is able to swim by means of a long, very thin **_flagellum_** (fla-JEL-lum— from a word meaning *whip*). The plural of flagellum is **_flagella_** (fla-JEL-la). See Figure 13-5. Many one-celled organisms move with the aid of cilia and flagella. These types of motion and amoeboid motion are found in animals, all the way from one-celled animals to you.

How Are Cells Fed?

A cell requires energy to carry on activities such as digestion, growth, and movement. To obtain its energy, the cell must have food and oxygen. Yet, some of the most important cell activities take place at least partly without the cell doing any work. Molecules of water, carbon dioxide, and oxygen pass in or out through the cell membrane. Some other kinds of molecules do the same thing. How can a cell secure life-giving oxygen without doing any work to get it? See Figure 13-6.

All molecules are in ceaseless motion except at the lowest possible temperature, absolute zero. Molecules vibrate in solids, constantly slide and bump against one another in liquids, and dash wildly in gases. When you boil water, the heat makes the water molecules move about violently and countless numbers escape from the water's surface. All of these collisions cause the molecules to spread apart from one another and distribute themselves equally in a given space. This distribution of molecules is known as *diffusion*. You read about diffusion in Chapter 2.

Suppose you open a new bottle of household cleaner at home. Does the label say it contains ammonia? As you open the bottle, the ammonia molecules begin to diffuse into the air, and air molecules begin to diffuse into the bottle. If you leave the bottle open indefinitely, the household cleaner will begin to smell less strong. Why? *In diffusion, the molecules move from a region of greater molecular concentration to a region of lesser molecular concentration.* (See Figure 13-7.) You can see how this occurred with the bottle of household cleaner. The same ammonia used in the household cleaner is sometimes used on little pads to help revive persons who have fainted. When someone feels faint, you unwrap the pad and squeeze it. One whiff of the diffusing ammonia and the patient coughs himself awake.

In your body there is more oxygen in the air sacs in the lungs than there is in the blood. Many more oxygen molecules *diffuse* through the thin membrane of the air sac and through the thin wall of the tiniest blood vessels into the blood than diffuse the other way. With carbon dioxide the story is different. Since there is more carbon dioxide in the blood than in the air sacs, it diffuses in the opposite direction. A substance must either be dissolved in water or be soluble in the cell membrane itself to diffuse through the membrane.

Fatty materials and some fat solvents, such as ether and alcohol, dissolve readily in the substances of the cell membrane and pass into the cell.

You can easily observe many examples of diffusion:

■ Have someone open a bottle of perfume in a still, closed room while you stand several feet away. How long is it before you smell the perfume?

■ Place some crystals of copper sulfate in a glass of clear water. How soon does the water turn blue? Keep the glass with the water and copper sulfate as long as you can. Compare the length of time that it took for perfume to travel three feet through the air with the time

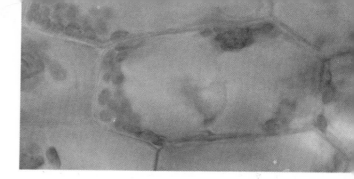

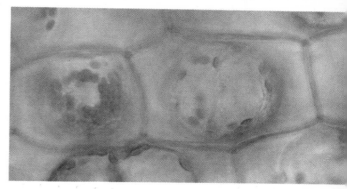

13-6 (*Top*) Cells of a green leaf as they normally appear under a microscope. (*Bottom*) Cells after water has diffused through the cell membrane. Did water go into or out of the cells?

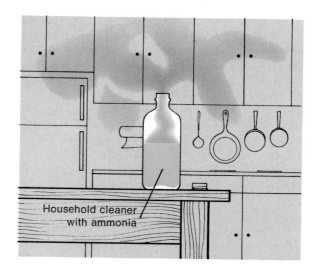

Household cleaner with ammonia

13-7 The ammonia in this household cleaner is diffusing out of the bottle. What are some other common examples of diffusion?

it takes for copper sulfate molecules to diffuse one inch through water. Why the difference? Hint: the molecules of a liquid are very much closer together than the molecules of a mixture of gases, such as air.

■ Place dry lima bean seeds or dried prunes in saucers of water. What happens after a few hours? The swelling of the seeds and the prunes is due to diffusion of water through the cell walls and cell membranes.

A Mostly One-Way Diffusion

After you have caused dried fruit to swell with water, can you make the fruit shrivel again?

■ Take a glass of water and add as much salt as will dissolve in it. Now drop your plump, water-filled fruit into the salty water. Examine the glass every hour. Can you account for what happens? Why did the fruit swell in plain water and shrink in salty water? If you would like to prepare a mixture that tastes better than the salty one, drop the swollen fruits into a thick solution of sugar in water. Will the same thing happen—will the fruit shrink?

The swelling or shrinking of seeds and fruits is due to the movement of water through a semipermeable membrane. *This movement is from an area of greater concentration of water molecules to an area of lesser concentration of water molecules.* Water moves faster through living membranes than do the substances dissolved in it. We refer to the movement of water molecules by a special name, *osmosis* (oz-MOH-sus). See Figure 13-8.

Cell membranes allow water molecules to pass through more easily than sugar molecules. This is why the fruit swells or shrinks, with gain or loss of water, instead of equalizing the concentration of sugar between the fruit and the water around it.

Active Transport in and out of the Cell

We could not live without the transport by diffusion of oxygen, carbon dioxide, water, many digested foods, and other substances. But diffusion of many things in liquids is very slow, as you saw with the copper-sulfate crystals in water. Diffusion is *too* slow to supply the needs of a cell that is using energy every moment. Then, too, diffusion can only carry molecules from where they are more concentrated to where they are less

13-8 What type of diffusion is being illustrated here? Explain what is happening in each picture.

A   B   C

concentrated. Yet cells have the power to take in certain substances when there is a small concentration of them in the outside solution and a large concentration in the cells. Obviously, this takes work (and energy). This passage of substances through a cell membrane by means of energy-requiring processes of the cell is known as **active transport.** The tiny amounts of iodine that we eat with our food travel in the blood to the thyroid gland. Thyroid-gland cells already contain a much greater concentration of iodine than the blood does—and yet they readily absorb most of the blood's iodine through active transport.

We used to think that all digested foods were absorbed by means of diffusion, but now it appears that cells lining the intestine take in much of the glucose and other simple sugars, digested fats, and some minerals by active transport. These cells have to work and use energy. Active transport is of vital importance because it allows cells to take in needed materials at a faster rate—even when they are in scarce supply. Just as important, it allows cells to get rid of unneeded or injurious substances at a faster rate—even when these are piling up and are already more abundant outside than inside the cell. Unfortunately, this doesn't seem to work with some poisons, such as alcohol and ether, which dissolve readily in the materials of the cell membrane.

YOUR CELLS AND YOUR ORGAN SYSTEMS

Secretion (seh-KREE-shun) is the manufacture of useful substances by cells. It also includes their being concentrated together, ready for use. Cells of glands secrete enzymes, hormones, tears, saliva, and many other substances. Skin cells secrete perspiration, which helps keep us from being overheated. They also secrete oils, which prevent the skin from drying excessively and being destroyed. We might say that bone cells secrete bone, cartilage cells secrete cartilage, and fat cells secrete fat. Nerve cells secrete substances that act on other nerve cells and cause them to go into action.

You will study many examples of secretion that are essential to your health. You can begin by secreting something right now!

■ Think of words like *sour lemon* or *salt,* or very pleasant things like *thick, juicy roasts.* Does your mouth begin to fill up with saliva?

Little Cells and Big Cells

Cells come in many sizes and shapes. Red blood cells are among our smallest, although they are enormous compared to bacteria. Nerve cells may be more than a yard long yet, throughout most of their length, only one thousandth of an inch in diameter! Red blood cells are discs, thinner in the middle than around the edge; white blood cells change their shape and crawl like an amoeba. Sometimes they pinch in the middle until they look as if they were going to be torn in half. Our oval cartilage cells sit by one's or two's in cartilage, while bone cells sit in the bone that they secreted, looking something like inkspots, or spiders that have been stepped on. Most cells have one nucleus; voluntary muscle cells have many; red blood cells have lost their nuclei and have none.

Different Kinds of Cells for Different Jobs

You have studied the work of muscle, bone, and nerve cells. In this unit, you learn of the work of cells of the body's *supply* systems. It may seem strange that cells as different from each other as fat cells, nerve cells, and muscle cells should all have the same fundamental structure. All

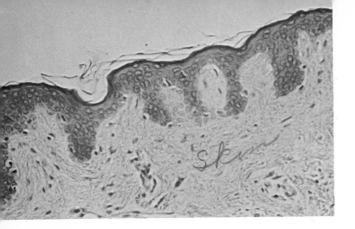

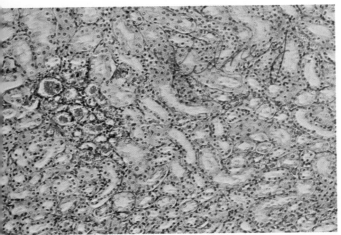

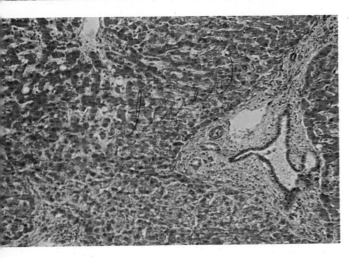

13-9 Three types of cells: (*Top*) skin cells; (*Center*) kidney cells; (*Bottom*) liver cells. How are these cells alike? How do they differ? Which of these cells has the shortest life span? Why?

cells except the red blood cells, which lack nuclei, are similar in structure. And even the red blood cells are not unlike other cells when they are very young, before they have lost their nuclei.

Some cells are more useful after they die. This is true of the cells of the fingernails and toenails and of the hair. Dead cells on the outer surface of the skin help to protect the living cells underneath them.

LIFE INSIDE THE CELL

Respiration, digestion, excretion, and the other chemical changes that take place in cells are together called **metabolism** (meh-TAB-oh-lizm). **Cell respiration**, the series of chemical changes by which oxygen and food substances are used and energy released, is an extremely complicated and marvelously efficient process. As you remember, the mitochondria are the centers of cell respiration. It is in the mitochondria that energy from the oxidation of glucose is made available to the cell. Oxidation involves the addition of oxygen or the removal of hydrogen from a molecule, with the release or transfer of energy. Most of the oxidation in a cell is brought about by the removal of hydrogen—from glucose, fats, and other substances. Every time the energy-rich association of a hydrogen atom with a carbon atom in glucose—or a fat, or small remnants of protein—is broken, energy is made available. The oxidation in a cell occurs in small steps, each of which releases or transfers small quantities of energy. Cell respiration provides the energy required for the countless activities of each cell. The cell would die instantly if deprived of energy.

How Long Do Cells Live?

If you live to be 100 years old, most of your nerve and muscle cells will also reach the age of 100 years. On the other hand, the outer cells of the skin and the cells that line the intestine will be "youngsters." Throughout your life these types of cells are constantly pushed toward the surface by the growth of cells beneath them. Once at the surface, they live only a short time and then fall off. They are replaced by some of the newer cells that have formed beneath them.

In your blood, one type of white blood cell lives only about five days, while another type lives from 100 to 200 days. Red blood cells live about 120 days.

If you do survive to the age of 100 years, your hundred-year-old nerve cells will still let you know whenever something hurts, and the hundred-year-old muscle cells in your heart will still pump your blood as before.

How Cells Make Cells

You cut yourself. If it is a small, clean cut, you needn't worry. You know that your tissues will soon repair the wound. It will heal, and you hope it won't leave a scar. All the work of repair is done by cells. Millions of white blood cells and many connective-tissue cells travel to the wound. Cells around the edge and at the base of the wound are stimulated to grow and divide, and they gradually fill the wound with new tissue.

The only way that new cells can be made is by growth and division of old cells. You can imagine the amount of cell division needed for a seven-pound baby to develop into a 170-pound man.

We humans have just two kinds of cell division; you will read more about this in Chapter 20. You will also read about the chromosomes and genes that control the development of cells and thus of the entire body. We have 23 *pairs* of chromosomes in our cells. In the most common type of cell division, or rather in the nuclear division that takes place *before* cell division, the chromosomes duplicate all of their genes and assemble them until there are two

13-10 How long do cells live? In a crowd of people, who would have the oldest cells? Are some cells very young no matter how old a person is? *yes*

chromosomes of each kind in place of one. This nuclear process is called *mitosis* (my-TOH-sis). Cell division then occurs. Each new cell gets the same number and kinds of chromosomes the parent cell had before mitosis. In the other kind of cell division, a process called *meiosis* (my-OH-sis) occurs. Here the nuclear production of new chromosomes does not keep pace with cell division. Each new cell gets only *one* chromosome of each pair, or a total of only 23. This kind of cell division occurs only when sex cells—the sperms and the eggs—are produced.

As you read this book, millions of cells in your skin, bone marrow, and the lining of your mouth, throat, stomach, and intestine are dividing to make millions of new cells. All of the new cells now forming in your body, and those of all the people on earth, are the result of an unbroken line of human cell divisions from the time of the first man on earth.

What You Have Learned

What kind of health practices should you apply in maintaining your health? Check your understanding of the chapter. On a separate sheet of paper, number 1 through 24 and insert the answer from the vocabulary list below. Use each expression, but use each one only once.

22 active transport	21 diffusion	14 mitosis
18 amoeboid movement	5 endoplasmic reticulum	24 nerve cells
17 Carrel	19 flagella	3 nucleus
1 cell membrane	13 genes	6 organelles
16 centrioles	23 iodine	4 red blood cells
12 chromosomes	15 meiosis	9 ribosomes
20 cilia	8 metabolism	11 secretion
2 cytoplasm	7 mitochondria	10 vacuoles

All of our cells are surrounded by a thin (1)_____. Just inside this we find the (2)_____, which includes all of the living part of the cell except the (3)_____. The only cells of the body that lack this last structure are the (4)_____. A complex system of membranes, the (5)_____, appears to connect with the cell membrane. The many "small organs" in the cytoplasm are known as (6)_____. Among the most important of these are the (7)_____, which serve as our cell "power plants." Their work and all of the various chemical changes that take place in the cell are included under the term (8)_____. Another important activity centers in the (9)_____, where protein is made for the cell. (10)_____ are fluid-filled cavities in a cell. Many kinds of useful substances are made by cells. This process is called (11)_____.

Inside the nucleus of a typical human cell are 46 long, coiled (12)_____. The (13)_____ are transmitted by these structures from parent to child; they control heredity and development. New cells are produced by the division of an already existing cell. Usually (14)_____ occurs when a cell divides, causing each new cell to get the same number and kinds of chromosomes as the old cell had. In the other kind of cell division, (15)_____ takes place. This results in each new cell getting only half as many chromosomes as the original cell had. Two rodlike structures, the (16)_____, play an important role in cell division. While studying the growth of tissues, the French-American doctor, (17)_____, kept some chicken-heart tissue alive and growing for 36 years.

Living cells grown in tissue culture sometimes move about the dish they are kept in. This process is called (18)_____. In reproduction, sperms move in quite a different way. They swim toward the egg by means of their long, thin (19)_____. Mucous membrane cells do not move about in the body, but in the air passages the beating of their (20)_____ protects us by helping to get rid of dust and bacteria.

Cells are supplied with oxygen, water, and a number of other useful substances by (21)_____ without the cell having to do any work or use up any of its own energy. When there is a larger concentration of a substance inside a cell than there is on the other side of its cell membrane, the cell must use (22)_active transport_ to bring the substance across its cell membrane. This is the method the thyroid gland cells use to accumulate large amounts of (23)_Iodine_

Cells come in many shapes and sizes. Some human (24)_nerve cells_ may be more than a yard long.

What You Can Do

1. In your notebook, fully explain each of the following statements. Then, in class, compare your answers with those of your classmates. Later you can correct or improve the explanations you previously wrote.

    a. Although millions of cell divisions occur throughout a person's life-time, the number and kinds of chromosomes in most of a man's cells are the same.

    b. The cytoplasm of a cell is just as important as the nucleus.

    c. Our lungs are protected by millions of little, hairlike living threads.

    d. Certain of our cells can move about actively.

    e. If you open a bottle of perfume at one end of a closed room and stand at the other end of the room, you will eventually be able to smell the odor of the perfume.

    f. Dry seeds and dried fruits placed in water swell in size.

    g. Some of the cells of our bodies live much longer than other cells.

    h. Under the best conditions, chickens rarely live longer than fifteen years. Most chickens will be on the dinner table long before they reach that age. Yet chicken tissue has been kept alive for more than twice as long as the life span of even the oldest chickens.

2. Read the following statements. Write down the letter that appears before each statement. If a statement is true, write _true_ after the number. If a statement is _false_, replace the italicized word with a correct one. Write the correct word next to the appropriate letter.

    a. Carrel made his famous experiment, using tissue from a _white rat_. _False_

    b. A sugar molecule has less difficulty in passing through a cell mem-brane than does a _protein_ molecule. _True_

    c. _Ribosomes_ are believed to be the "protein factories" of the cell. _true_

    d. A human body cell has _48_ chromosomes.

    e. _Nerve_ cells are the only cells in the human body that normally lack nuclei. _False_

    f. _Centrioles_ play an important role in cell division. _true_

g. *White blood cells* surround and destroy bacteria. *True*

h. The air tubes in the lungs are protected from dust by millions of *flagella.* *True*

i. To obtain energy, a cell must have food and *carbon dioxide.* *True*

j. The mitochondria are the centers of cell *respiration.* *True*

Things to Try

1. Charts to illustrate the different kinds of human cells. You will learn much about human cells if you organize a committee to prepare a number of charts and display them on a bulletin board with the title, "Cells of the Human Body." You will easily find drawings to copy and photographs from which you can make outline drawings. Consult this book and several of the books recommended at the end of this chapter. Consult your teacher about the size you should make your drawings. If you do this, you may be able to present to your class a valuable teaching aid when you remove your charts from the bulletin board.

    When you make your charts, first draw lightly, but very accurately, with a soft, No. 1 pencil. Then go over your pencil outlines with a magic marker or with India ink. Colored charts are attractive, but if you color your charts, use *light* colors and do not apply color too heavily. Neat, clear lettering is very important.

2. Try making models of cells, using various materials. For example, a plastic container could represent the cell membrane. The container could then be filled with materials of different consistency to represent the cytoplasm, nucleus, and so on.

3. If you can secure the use of a microscope, you can learn a great deal by examining prepared slides of human cells and tissues. The easiest slides to examine are those that show a number of individual cells of the same kind—blood cells or teased-out muscle cells, are examples. Slides with sections cut through the thyroid gland or the brain are much more difficult to understand unless you have some knowledge of anatomy. Slides of the following will make the descriptions in this chapter and in Chapter 2 seem more real to you: ciliated epithelial cells; section through ciliated epithelium (this comes from the mucous membrane of the air tubes); flat epithelial cells from mucous membrane of mouth (these cells form what is called *squamous* epithelium); slides of the three types of muscle cells—smooth, skeletal, heart; and human blood (showing red cells, white cells, and platelets). It would also be interesting to observe a slide of frog or salamander blood to note the contrast with human blood. How does their blood differ from human blood?

Probing Further

The Cell, by Carl P. Swanson, Prentice-Hall, 1969. A small book with a great deal of up-to-the-minute information and very interesting illustrations. You should enjoy reading this book, although you may have some difficulty with the account of mitosis and meiosis.

The Life of The Cell, by J. A. V. Butler, Basic Books, 1964. A more advanced but very interesting account of the nature, origin, and development of cells.

The Microstructure of Cells, by Stephen W. Hurry, Houghton Mifflin, 1964. This is an excellent paperback book; the book is well illustrated with enlarged electron microscope photographs. When you examine the illustrations, some of which show structures enlarged up to 360,000 times, you will realize how the structure of cells is studied.

Health Concepts in Action

Does this statement bring together ideas you have gained from this chapter?

Health is based on the activities of cells—the structural and functional units of the body.

Applying this concept of cells, which health practices would you

—continue?

—change?

—begin?

Will you now, as a result of your study, change any of your health objectives?

14 / *Digestion*

Two patients occupy the same room in a hospital. Both, of course, must have food. One, an older man whose broken leg bone is mending, has enjoyed his breakfast of fruit juice, cereal, poached eggs, toast, and coffee. The other patient, a boy of sixteen, is very ill after an emergency operation for a ruptured appendix. He has no appetite and is nauseated even by a glass of water. A nurse enters the room carrying a bottle of liquid which she hoists on a metal stand. The liquid contains three substances that all the cells of the body must have to live—water, salt, and glucose sugar. The liquid is to be injected directly into a vein in the boy's arm because his digestive system cannot function properly.

A PROBE INTO THE DIGESTIVE SYSTEM—What are some of the many factors that influence how your digestive system functions? To find out, you will be probing these questions:

1. What are the parts of the alimentary canal? Where does digestion take place? What are enzymes?

2. How does digested food travel to all of your body cells?

3. Can your state of mind interfere with your digestion? How? Why do some people eat too much?

4. How is it possible for people of different countries to all be healthy while living on very different diets?

5. What are some diseases of the alimentary canal?

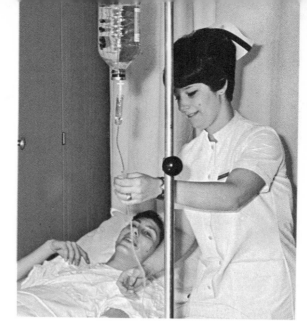

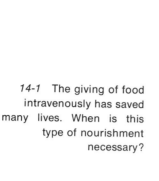
14-1 The giving of food intravenously has saved many lives. When is this type of nourishment necessary?

THE PROCESS OF DIGESTION

The process, described on the preceding page, of introducing dissolved foods directly into a vein is called **intravenous** (IN-tra-VEE-nuss) **feeding.** Amino acids, vitamins, and other minerals besides salt can also safely be injected into a patient's veins. Yet if the nurse had attempted to inject milk, eggs, or toast, she might have killed him. Why is it safe, and often life-saving, to introduce some nutrients directly into the bloodstream, while to inject most foods would be deadly?

Injecting the proper amounts of water, salt, amino acids, glucose, and vitamins can benefit the patient because the particles of these nutrients are so small that they can pass through a cell membrane. Thus, they can enter the living cells that need them.

The bits of food that we swallow would cause clots if we injected them into the bloodstream. Such clots could cause death as they passed through the heart, lungs, or brain. Even if the starches and proteins eaten at breakfast were broken into their molecules, they still could not be used by our cells because the molecules are too large to pass through cell membranes. Most foods have to be *digested,* or broken down, before the body can use them.

The Alimentary Canal

Food is digested in the *alimentary canal,* which consists of the mouth and throat, gullet or *esophagus* (uh-SOF-uh-gus), stomach, small intestine, and large intestine (Figure 14-3). The canal is very long in comparison to the size of the body. A man 6 feet tall may have a canal 30 feet long. For most people the canal is about five times as long as the body. Long as it is, most of it is so folded and looped that it is packed into a very small space.

Digestion goes on in three parts of the alimentary canal—mouth, stomach, and small intestine. Your food is broken down in two ways—by *mechanical action* and by *chemical action.*

Mechanical Digestion

In mechanical digestion, food is broken up into small bits and thoroughly mixed with digestive juices. The process begins with

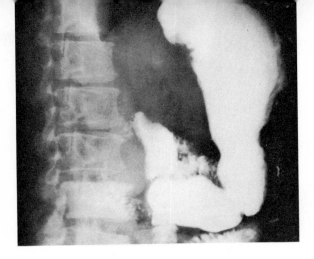

the chewing of food in the mouth. Then the stomach and the small intestine churn and break it up into still smaller pieces.

If you see a film that shows digestion, you may be surprised at the way the stomach and small intestine twist and contract. By giving a person a meal of *barium sulfate* (BAHR-ee-um SUL-fayt), which shows up in X-ray photographs, a doctor can actually watch the stomach in action. Sometimes it pinches itself so violently that it looks as if it would break in two.

14-2 Compare the shape of the stomach in this X-ray picture with that in Figure 14-3. Do they differ? If so, how?

14-3 What are the main functions of your digestive system? Where does digestion start? Imagine that you have just eaten a cracker; follow the digestion of the cracker through your digestive system.

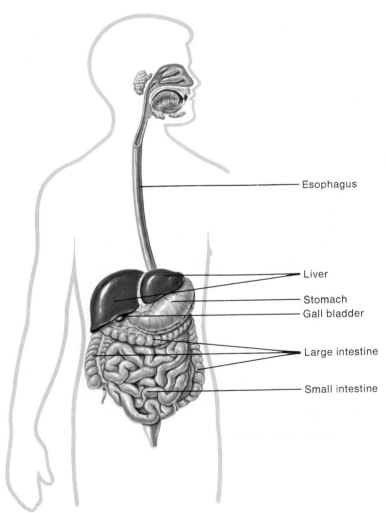

Esophagus

Liver

Stomach

Gall bladder

Large intestine

Small intestine

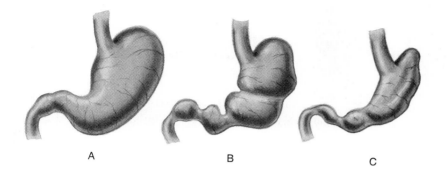

14-4 Peristalsis in the stomach. (*Left*) Immediately after a heavy lunch. (*Center*) Two hours later. (*Right*) Four hours after lunch. Why is the stomach smaller in the picture on the right?

A   B   C

Chemical Digestion

Although mechanical digestion treats the food particles roughly, fat remains fat, and protein remains protein. Most of the molecules are still too large to pass through a cell membrane. It is chemical action that breaks large food molecules down into small ones that can pass through cell membranes. This action is caused by *enzymes* (EN-zymz) made by glands in the digestive system. An enzyme is a juice that can make other substances change without changing itself. Therefore, a very small amount of an enzyme can cause a large amount of digestion. Many enzymes are present in your digestive juices. Each enzyme can affect only one certain kind of foodstuff. An enzyme that works on protein has no effect on starch.

When enzymes digest a food, they split up the molecules of the substances that make up the food.

For example, when you chew certain starchy foods, an enzyme in your saliva starts the digestive process by breaking starch into *malt sugar*, so called because it is found in the malt that flavors your malted milk. Malt sugar is also called *maltose* (MAWL-tohs).

■ Would you like to demonstrate that starchy food changes to sugar as you chew it? Get a cracker and put a piece of it in your mouth. What immediate taste do you get? Now chew the piece of cracker thoroughly. It will begin to taste sweet as the starch molecules are broken into malt sugar.

The cells of your body cannot use malt sugar, since its molecules, although smaller than those of the starch, are still too large. However, in the small intestine, the malt sugar is digested to glucose, a sugar that has molecules small enough for your cells to use.

Digestion in the Mouth

In the days when our ancestors had no knives and forks, teeth were even more important than they are now. While you are chewing, the food mixes with saliva, which flows into the mouth through ducts of the three pairs of *salivary* (SAL-ih-vehr-ee) *glands*. The *parotid glands* are the largest salivary glands. They lie in front of and slightly below the ears. The *submaxillary glands* lie in the lower jaws, and the *sublingual glands* lie under the tongue. Refer to Figure 14-5. The salivary glands make from 1 to 2 quarts of saliva every day. It is colorless and slightly sticky, and it has one important enzyme, *ptyalin* (TY-uh-lin), also

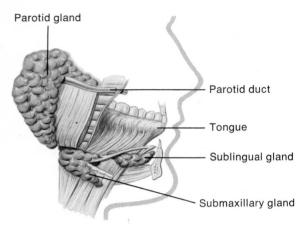

Parotid gland

Parotid duct

Tongue

Sublingual gland

Submaxillary gland

14-5 The salivary glands of the mouth. Does all digestion begin in the mouth?

called **salivary amylase** (AH-mil-ase), which aids in the digestive breakdown of starch molecules. Saliva moistens and softens all food, but it acts chemically only on starch. You should chew starchy foods well to give this enzyme time to work.

Saliva helps you to swallow. If your mouth were perfectly dry, you couldn't swallow solid food. The tongue, teeth, and saliva work together to form the food into round, moist masses.

Chew Your Food!

Train yourself to chew your food. Chewing not only grinds the food into small bits; it mixes it thoroughly with saliva. Saliva can work on starch only if it comes in contact with each little particle. Plenty of saliva helps to stimulate the flow of gastric juice. Drinking plenty of healthful liquids is a good practice, but don't wash your food down with water or other fluids. This practice may result in swallowing food before it is thoroughly chewed and even in choking on pieces of food too large to be swallowed. However, there is no reason to forbid water with your meals. If you are thirsty, drinking water may help both appetite and digestion.

How Does Food Get to Your Stomach?

What makes food travel from the mouth to the stomach? Is it gravity? You can make an observation to find out. You will need a cat and a bowl of milk. If the cat is thirsty, a bowl of water will do. Note that the cat drinks with his head down—lower than his stomach. The milk is swallowed *against* gravity. A horse would show this better. A giraffe drinking water would show it best of all.

As soon as you swallow, a ring of muscle contracts just behind a morsel of food and starts a wavelike motion along the gullet. Successive rings of muscle contract to push the food along. This action is known as **peristalsis** (pehr-ih-STAL-sis), and it continues to push the food—although more slowly—through the stomach (Figure 14-6) and the small and large intestines.

Digestion in the Stomach

The stomach (Figure 14-3) is a muscular pouch which can hold about 2 quarts. When full, it is about 1 foot long and 5 inches across. It lies mostly to the left of the center of the body, with the large end well up under the ribs. This upper portion of the stomach acts as a storehouse. It holds foods until they can be churned and mixed with digestive juices. The round masses of food that you swallow don't break up right away in the stomach. Until they do, the enzyme of saliva keeps on digesting starch to sugar. When the masses break up, this digestion of starch stops, because the stomach juices are strongly acid (the enzyme of saliva cannot work in a strong acid).

The digestive juice of the stomach is called **gastric** (GASS-trik) **juice.** This is made by cells within the millions of tiny gastric glands in the wall of the stomach (Figure 14-7). Besides water, the gastric juice contains an enzyme and other substances.

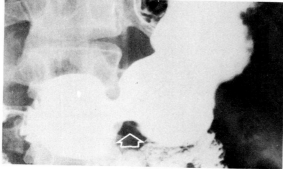

14-6 X-ray photograph of the stomach before and during peristalsis. Is digestion ever completed in the stomach?

14-7 Millions of tiny gastric glands line the stomach wall. What is their function?

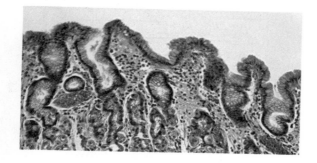

1. **Pepsin.** This enzyme begins the digestion of proteins. It breaks them down into **peptones** and **proteoses**. These products must still undergo further breakdown in the small intestine before protein digestion is completed.
2. **Hydrochloric** (hy-druh-KLOR-ik) **acid.** Have you ever vomited when your stomach was upset? Did it burn your mouth and throat? If so, you were feeling the hydrochloric acid from the gastric juice. Hydrochloric acid makes pepsin work much faster. In fact, pepsin can work only in the presence of an acid. The acid also helps to dissolve mineral matter. It is believed that it helps protect us by killing many bacteria we swallow with food. Hydrochloric acid curdles milk, changing one of the milk proteins into solid curds. (Cottage cheese is the curds of cow's milk.)
3. **Mucus.** Gastric juice dissolves tough meat. Why, then, doesn't the stomach digest itself? One reason is that the gastric juice contains mucus, which forms a protective coating over the stomach lining.

In the lower end of the stomach, the food changes to a semi-fluid mass about as thick as pea soup. This is called **chyme** (KYME). To go from the stomach to the small intestine, the chyme has to pass—by means of peristalsis—through a ring of muscle called the **pylorus** (py-LOH-rus). The pylorus acts like a valve, to keep food in the intestine from "backing up" into the stomach. A meal takes from 2 1/2 to 5 hours to pass through the stomach, while water, which needs no digestion, passes through the stomach in a few minutes.

Digestion in the Small Intestine

The small intestine (Figure 14-3) is longer than all the rest of the alimentary canal put together. It is a hollow tube about 1 inch in diameter and 20 feet long, looped and folded in the middle of the abdomen. Since the muscles in the intestinal wall, like those of the esophagus and stomach, are constantly contracting to force the food along, there has to be something to keep the intestine in place. Otherwise, it might throw itself into tight loops and knots that could cut off both circulation of blood and movement of food. This could be fatal. The intestine is held in place by a thin membrane called the **mesentery** (MESS'n-tehr-ee), which is attached at the back of the abdomen near the backbone. (The blood vessels and nerves that supply the intestine are in the mesentery.) Since this membrane is not strong enough by itself to support the weight of the intestine, it needs the help of the muscles in the wall of the abdomen. There are three things you can do to strengthen these muscles and keep them strong:

1. Get enough exercise.
2. Stand and walk erect, with your abdomen "tucked in."
3. Don't let youself get fat. (Layers of fat cause a sagging "stomach," really a sagging abdomen.)

The small intestine is not only longer, but also more important than all the rest of the alimentary canal. The greatest part of digestion goes on in here—the mouth and the stomach merely start the work. As you have learned, the food (chyme) is a liquid about as thick as pea soup when it leaves the stomach. Some of the starch has been changed to malt sugar, and proteins have been changed to peptones. However, your cells cannot use malt sugar or peptones.

Three digestive juices work on the food in the small intestine:

1. *Pancreatic* (pan-kree-AT-ik) *juice.* This is made in the pancreas and poured into the small intestine through a little duct, or tube (Figure 14-8). It has three types of enzymes. *Pancreatic amylase* digests any remaining starch to malt sugar, as does the enzyme in saliva. *Trypsin* (TRYP-sin) digests protein. *Pancreatic lipase* (LY-pays) digests fats, but it cannot work unless it has the help of bile.
2. The churning of the stomach and small

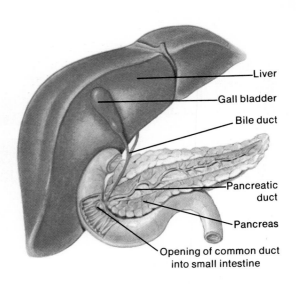

14-8 How do these structures aid digestion? What substances do they secrete? How are fats digested?

intestine breaks up fats and oils into tiny droplets that can be attacked by pancreatic lipase. *Bile*, which has no enzymes of its own, contains salts that act like soap or detergent to prevent the droplets from coming together again. The liver secretes bile, which is stored in the **gall bladder**, a pear-shaped bag that lies close against the liver (Figure 14-8). Bile is necessary for the digestion of fats. If the liver passages are clogged, the supply of bile is cut off. When this happens, fats pass through the intestine without being digested. You will read more about bile in Chapter 18.

3. *Intestinal juice.* This is made by millions of tiny glands in the lining of the small intestine. It has several enzymes. A team of enzymes finishes the digestion of proteins, breaking down *peptones* and *proteoses* into *peptides.* Further breakdown changes peptides to *amino acids.* Other enzymes work on different kinds of sugar, changing them to glucose and other simple sugars. One works on

malt sugar, one on table sugar, another on milk sugar.

How Are Nutrients Changed in Digestion?

You will remember that some nutrients are *not* digested. They are ready for use when you swallow them. Among these are water, salt, glucose, fruit sugar, and vitamins. All of these have molecules small enough to pass through a cell membrane. At the end of digestion, all of your food is ready to enter your cells, because:

1. All carbohydrates (starch and sugars) have been changed to glucose and other simple sugars.
2. Proteins have been broken down into amino acids.
3. Each molecule of fat has been broken into two very different kinds of molecules. These are fatty acids and **glycerol** (GLISS-er-ohl). Most fatty acids are not sour like the acids you know. Brushless shaving cream contains a mixture of fatty acids. Glycerol is another name for **glycerin** (GLISS-er-in), a thick, clear, syrupy liquid.

How Digested Foods Get into the Blood

Food in the stomach or the intestine is still "outside the body," in a sense. To be of any use, food has to get into the cells. As you know, the blood takes digested food to all parts of the body. Hence, the food must get into the blood once it has been digested. The stomach wall absorbs water, certain minerals, and sugar very slowly. However, the largest part of these substances goes right on through the stomach to the small intestine. Almost all of the digested food is absorbed by the blood through the wall of the small intestine.

Which will dry you faster after a bath—a

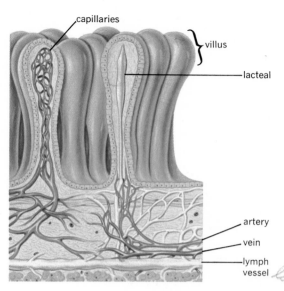

14-9 Villi in the small intestine. How does food get into the villi? What is a lacteal? What is its specialized function?

large towel or a small one? You know the large one will, because it has the most *surface* to take up the water. The small intestine has a very large surface for absorbing food, because it has thousands of ridges or folds in its inner lining and about 5,000,000 tiny projections called **villi** (VIL-eye). In the first part of the intestine, the villi are flat; farther on, they look like little fingers (Figure 14-9). They absorb the completely digested food.

There is a network of blood capillaries inside each **villus**. Everything a villus takes in goes into these capillaries, except the digested fats. The blood then carries the substances it absorbed—glucose, water, salt, vitamins, amino acids, etc.—to the liver. The liver stores some, changes others, and lets some go on in the bloodstream.

What happens to the digested fats? They are absorbed by the villi also. In the center of each villus is a small lymph vessel, called a **lacteal** (LAK-tee-ul), Figure 14-9. This takes in the digested fats, which are then carried along with the lymph and enter the bloodstream only when the lymph does.

The Large Intestine

The large intestine (Figure 14-3) is about 2 inches in diameter and 5 to 6 feet long. It starts just in front of the right hipbone, goes up the right side, crosses over below the stomach, and goes down the left side. Finally it curves toward the center of the abdomen and descends in a section called the *rectum* (REK-tum) to the outside opening, the *anus* (AY-nus). The anus is controlled by a ring of muscle which keeps the tract closed except during *defecation* (def-uh-KAY-shun), which is the act of eliminating wastes, called *feces* (FEE-sees), from the intestine.

The first part of the large intestine, as far as the rectum, is the *colon* (KOH-l'n). No food is digested in the large intestine. The solid parts of the watery material that enters it are mostly fragments of food that could not be digested, including fibers from roughage. Mixed with this material are mucus, dead cells thrown off by the lining of the intestine, and billions of bacteria, living and dead. Billions of bacteria live in the large intestine. As long as they stay there, they seem to do no harm; in fact, many of them make vitamin K and some of the B-complex vitamins. The harm is done when these bacteria get into the wrong place—for instance, the kidneys or the gall bladder. When the bacteria that cause intestinal diseases are swallowed, it is a serious matter.

The chief work of the large intestine is to absorb water (and probably vitamins made by the bacteria) and to eliminate waste material in comparatively solid form.

The Appendix— a Frequent Troublemaker

Figure 14-10 shows how the small intestine empties into the large one. Notice the pouch at one side. This is the *caecum* (SEE-k'm). It was given this name, from a Latin word meaning "blind," because it is a sort of

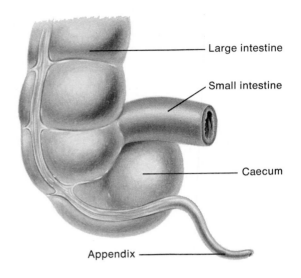

14-10 The appendix shown in relation to the large and small intestines. What might happen if an infected appendix is not removed?

blind alley. The caecum itself gives no trouble, but the little wormlike projection, the *appendix*, gives enough trouble for something many times its size. It is a blind, or dead-end, tube from 2 to 6 inches long. The appendix serves no known function, and we do not know what function it may have had for our ancestors.

If the opening to the appendix gets plugged, it becomes infected, germs multiply in it, and it becomes inflamed and full of pus. This is what happens in *appendicitis* (uh-pen-dih-SY-tis). See Figure 14-11. This disease is so common and so dangerous that you should know its symptoms. The three most typical symptoms are

1. *Lasting pain in the abdomen.* Pain is not always over the appendix. The pain most often starts near the center of the abdomen and a few hours later shifts to the lower right side of the abdomen, over the appendix. Pain may also start

on either the left or right side of the abdomen. Later, the right abdomen becomes extremely painful to the touch.

2. *Nausea.* The patient is almost sure to be more or less sick at his stomach and to lose his appetite. Frequent vomiting and diarrhea are possible.

3. *Fever.* The trouble here is that the fever doesn't always appear in the early stage, and it is usually low. Don't wait to see if fever develops before having other symptoms checked by your doctor.

Important: If there is any suspicion of appendicitis, never take a laxative or enema. Never use massage or a hot-water bottle. Any of these may cause an infected appendix to burst, or rupture. If this happened, millions of bacteria would be liberated in the cavity of the abdomen, where the tissues have very little resistance against germs. The condition that develops when the appendix bursts is called *peritonitis* (pehr-ih-toh-NY-tis). This can prove fatal; it is far more dangerous than appendicitis. You will read more about peritonitis on page 259.

14-11 An X-ray photograph of an appendix. What steps should you follow if you suspect appendicitis?

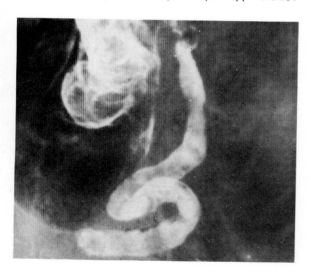

You are safe in doing only one thing when you suspect appendicitis: *Call a doctor.* In the meantime, remain quiet, eat nothing. Any activity in the intestine may make the condition worse.

Prepare Foods Correctly

Starch should be thoroughly cooked, since your digestive system is not built to take care of raw starch. Heat actually can start the process of digestion in starchy foods. When we digest starch in the mouth or intestine, the starch molecules first split to form a substance called *dextrin* (DEK-strin). The dextrin then breaks up into molecules of sugar. Heat can also change starch into dextrin. Thus, the taste of a crust of bread and of toast is partly due to dextrin. One of the few natural starchy foods that we don't need to cook is the banana.

Most *protein foods* can be digested when raw just as well as when cooked. Cooking them too quickly at high temperature makes them tough. A good cook often softens tough meat by slow cooking. Egg white, beans, peas, and tough meat are easier to digest when cooked. Cooking does another good thing for egg white, as well as for fish. Raw egg white and some raw fish have a substance that destroys *biotin* (BY-oh-tin), one of the B complex vitamins. (We haven't mentioned biotin before because almost any kind of diet gives you enough of it.) Cooking eggs or fish destroys the substance that destroys the biotin.

Fats are needed in small amounts. You may be eating more fat than you think, because eggs, pastry, cakes, cheese, cream, nuts, and most meats contain large amounts of fat. How much fat you should eat depends on what you do and where you live. You could use a great deal of fat if you lived in an extremely cold climate or spent your days chopping down trees. Most of us are better off if we eat only small amounts of fat in summer and moderate amounts in winter.

Be careful with fats (and sugar) if you have complexion trouble. Fats mixed with other foods, as in pastries and rich stews, slow up the digestion of the other foods. Fats coat their particles so that enzymes cannot reach them until the coating of fat is dissolved in the small intestine or melted off by the heat of the stomach. On the other hand, fats, more than any other nutrient, give you that satisfied feeling after a meal.

Vitamins are often lost in cooking. Vitamins A and D are *not* hurt by cooking. These two do *not* dissolve in water. Your problem in cooking is with the B complex group and with vitamin C. All of these dissolve in water. If you throw away the water in which you cook vegetables, you throw away a valuable part of these vitamins. Drink the liquid or use it in soups. Cook your vegetables and fruits in tightly covered dishes with very little water. Cook them only long enough to soften them.

What about canned and frozen fruits and vegetables? Those prepared commercially keep most of their vitamins. Heat alone does not do much to destroy vitamin value. It is heat in the presence of oxygen that does the damage. The commercial canners are able to work so rapidly, that canned and frozen products often have more vitamins than "fresh" vegetables cooked at home. Fresh market vegetables may lose half their vitamin C in one to two days after they are gathered. If kept cool and moist, they lose less.

Prevent Constipation by Correct Habits

Infrequent or difficult bowel movements are termed **constipation**. Many people are afraid of constipation when they don't need to be. Laxatives may sometimes be needed, but making a habit of rushing food through the stomach and intestine prevents proper digestion and deprives a person of much of the value of his meals.

Occasionally, constipation is a real problem. One should consult a doctor if the condition is serious. What can you do to prevent (or help to remedy) it? Follow these rules:

1. Eat a good normal diet.
2. Eat some bulky foods, or roughage. Roughage, as you know, is food that has fibers in it that you cannot digest. Fruits, raw vegetables, and bran are good sources of roughage. (Too much roughage, however, sometimes makes constipation worse instead of better.)
3. Have regular habits. This is important. One should have a set time and *enough* time for the colon to act naturally.
4. Exercise the muscles of the abdomen. This helps stimulate normal peristalsis in the colon.
5. Take plenty of drinking water and other liquids. This will insure that you mix enough water with the solid parts of your foods, and should also stimulate peristalsis.
6. Get enough rest and relaxation. If constipation persists, see a doctor.
7. *Interesting fact:* So many people make their condition worse by worrying and taking too many laxatives, that a standard medical reference book has a section called "Imaginary Constipation."

Diarrhea

Of the two disorders—constipation and *diarrhea* (DY-a-ree-uh)—diarrhea is more likely to mean real trouble. Diarrhea is a loose bowel movement. In diarrhea, food is not retained long enough to be properly digested. It is not only a health problem in itself, but also a symptom of many serious diseases. It may also be due to food poisoning. Sometimes it follows eating foods that have a laxative effect, as many fruits often do. If diarrhea continues for more than a day or two, or if there is also fever or vomiting, you should consult a doctor promptly. After all, you are losing valuable food and causing yourself physical discomfort—often pain— even if no other danger is present.

MENTAL AND EMOTIONAL INFLUENCES AFFECTING DIGESTION

Your state of mind can help or harm your digestion. When your appetite is keen, when you look forward to the meal, your digestive glands go to work before you taste the food. They start making saliva and gastric juice. Fear, anger, worry, and depressed spirits "put the brakes on." They may slow down the digestive glands, and they can slow or stop peristalsis.

A good-natured cat was fed a "meal" of barium sulfate, which shows up clearly in X-ray photographs. The photographs showed that the cat's stomach was making its normal movements. When an unfriendly dog came into the room, the cat's stomach ceased activity. The X-ray photograph showed this plainly. An hour after the dog was removed, the cat's stomach was still "on strike."

We have much evidence to show that it is better for people not to eat when emotionally upset. The setting for a meal should be pleasant. Everyone at the table should try to make each meal a pleasure for himself— and for everyone else.

Do Worry and Anger Cause Ulcers?

What is the connection between mental and emotional states and physical health? Doctors find that worry, fear, and anger seem to help cause *ulcers* in the stomach and the intestine. An ulcer is a sore somewhat like an open wound.

If you could see an ulcer, it would look as if layers of flesh had been eaten away, leaving the raw tissue. In people with ulcers, the stomach makes more hydrochloric acid than

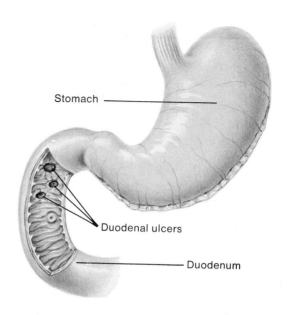

14-12 Possible locations of ulcers in the duodenum. Are ulcers related to emotional strain?

is needed for digestion. This acid irritates the lining of the stomach and the *duodenum* (doo-oh-DEE-num), or first part of the intestine, and may help to destroy part of this lining. If the process continues long enough, an ulcer develops. The emotional strain of anger and worry increases the flow of acid, and alcohol, tobacco, and bad eating habits are likely to make an ulcer worse. See Figure 14-12.

There is a curious thing about the pain of a stomach or a *duodenal* (doo-oh-DEE-n'l) ulcer—it is relieved by eating, especially if the food is something soothing and easy to digest, such as milk. Certain drugs also may relieve the pain, and the patient must be well nourished with easily digested food, especially proteins. Yet a most important part of treatment for ulcers is believed to be relief from the emotional tension that seems to help cause ulcers in the first place.

When someone finds out that he has an ulcer, a doctor will put him on a strict diet of soft, bland, easily digestible food. An ulcer patient eats several small meals frequently, rather than the regular three meals a day. This keeps the stomach full and helps absorb the hydrochloric acid to prevent it from attacking the stomach lining.

If the ulcer persists, it may be wise to seek psychiatric help to relieve any underlying tension or anxiety that may be aggravating the ulcer.

Is There an Ulcer Type?

Stomach and duodenal ulcers are more likely to attack men than women. In fact, ulcers are almost three times more common among men than among women. When more than two thousand doctors were questioned, half of them thought that the patient's type of personality was the most important cause of ulcer. The next most important cause mentioned by the doctors was the pressure of the environment.

Ulcer victims are most likely to be anxious and insecure. Many people think that men with ulcers are most often big business leaders and executives. Actually, many men with jobs carrying less responsibility suffer from ulcers. Farm life seems to be no protection; one survey showed ulcers more common in rural areas than in cities.

Exercise

Exercise speeds up your rate of breathing and your circulation. It helps to give you an appetite. Exercise that you enjoy helps to take your mind off your work. Many people who are inactive and have indigestion would find that games, walks, and other physical activity would help them.

Your food may not digest properly if you are very tired, or if you engage in heavy exercise too soon after eating. Try to relax for 20 to 30 minutes before and after eating, especially if you are very tired or if you plan heavy physical activity afterward.

Digestive System— the Victim of Our Emotions?

Bad news sometimes results in indigestion. A distressing sight, a strange-looking food, or an unpleasant odor can temporarily kill the appetite. Fright can stop the flow of saliva and make the mouth turn dry. Our digestive systems may react differently to similar happenings. Suppose that two motorists are harshly "bawled out" by a traffic policeman. The first becomes angry, and his stomach feels as if it were on fire. His stomach contracts violently and pours out acid. Some of the acid may spray up into the gullet and cause the burning sensation we call **heartburn**, although it has nothing to do with the heart. The other man is frightened. His stomach acts in just the opposite way and goes limp. He may say later that he had butterflies fluttering in his stomach, or that he felt as if he had just finished a ride on a roller coaster. His stomach is still and pale. The angry man's stomach would be seen to be a furious red in color, if you could look into it. As we are all different in some ways, reactions to anger and fear may sometimes be reversed; the stomach of the angry man may turn pale and stop working, and the frightened man may feel a volcano inside as his stomach churns violently. The impulses that cause these reactions start out in the brain and are carried to the glands and smooth muscles of the digestive system by our autonomic nerves. (The autonomic nervous system was discussed in Chapter 12.) Autonomic impulses are sent out without our being conscious of them. Sometimes a person will become nauseated and may vomit when nervously upset by an incident that would not disturb someone else.

How do we know that emotional upsets cause changes in the color of the stomach lining? How do we know that emotional upsets also cause increased or decreased activity in the digestive tract? Facts about such changes in the stomach were discovered by doctors who observed patients with openings from the body wall into the stomach.

Long before the rise of modern surgery, back in 1822, a young French-Canadian hunter, named St. Martin, was accidentally shot in the stomach from a distance of only three feet. This happened at an American army post in Michigan. The young American army surgeon, William Beaumont, who took charge of St. Martin's case, became the first doctor to look directly inside a living human stomach and to watch it as it contracted and relaxed. He was able to take out and replace pieces of food as they were digested and to see the living lining of the stomach change from bright red to a pale yellowish color — and then change back to red. Beaumont received this great opportunity because St. Martin's wound healed in such a way that it left an opening in his stomach. Beaumont learned much about digestion, but he did not account for the color changes.

About 120 years later, in 1943, Dr. Stewart Wolf and Dr. Harold G. Wolff studied a man called Tom who had scalded his gullet drinking boiling hot chowder when a boy. As the gullet healed, a scar formed preventing food from reaching the stomach. As a result, an opening had to be cut from the skin into the stomach. Hence Tom, like St. Martin long before, had a "window" into his stomach through which he fed himself with a funnel. The two doctors learned that Tom's stomach was sensitive to the effects of emotions. When Tom was angered his face turned red — and so did his stomach lining. At the same time, his stomach churned violently and produced an unusual amount of hydrochloric acid. The doctors noted that when they touched the bright red lining with a glass rod, it bled, indicating that it was now easily injured.

When fear made Tom's face turn pale, his stomach lining again followed the example of his face and also turned pale. The stomach stopped its normal contractions. But now the doctors found that touching the lining with the glass rod caused no injury, and neither did pinching or applying acid. The experiments with Tom when he was angry are evidence for the suspicion that a man's emotional state has a good deal to do with his chance of developing a stomach ulcer.

A patient with cancer of the gullet gave the same doctors the chance to learn about the nervous control of the stomach's behavior. This patient also had to be fed through a hole into his stomach. As with Tom, anger made this patient's face and stomach lining both turn red. To remove the cancer, the surgeon had to cut the branch of the vagus nerve that runs to the stomach. The vagus is the large autonomic nerve that speeds up stomach action and slows down the heart. From the time that the branch of the vagus was cut, fits of anger that reddened the patient's face had no apparent effect on his stomach.

Recently a part of another person's stomach was left uncovered by the skin. When this man was furious, the contractions in his stomach increased. But when he was calm, or even sad, the contractions decreased. When he experienced extreme excitement and showed either elation or horror, the contractions almost ceased.

Indigestion or "Indigestion"

One of the complaints you hear sometimes is "I had an attack of indigestion." The indigestion that our friends talk about may be anything from a slight, vague distress to severe pain. It may be due to eating too much, gulping one's food, being allergic to foods, being constipated, smoking excessively, or eating poorly cooked or greasy foods, very sour foods, or unripe fruits. As a rule, people of your age don't suffer from much indigestion.

Indigestion may also be due to gas in the stomach or intestine. Gas in the stomach,

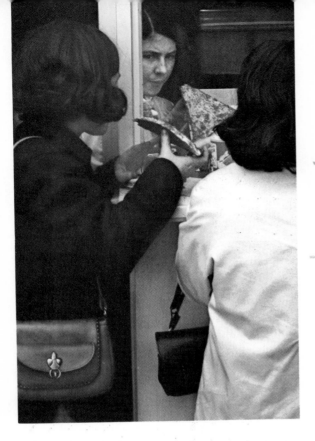

14-13 Do you give yourself enough time for each meal? How can gulping your food affect your digestion?

which can be painful, is often nothing but air. Many people swallow air when they eat. It can be most annoying when one is weakened following an operation and cannot eat normal meals. A large bubble of air can really hurt by the pressure it causes as it goes down the gullet.

The symptoms that people describe as indigestion may indicate anything from conditions of no importance to serious and even potentially deadly diseases. In older persons, indigestion may be due to an ulcer, a disease in the liver, gall bladder, or pancreas, or cancer. If your only symptoms are vague uneasiness, fullness in your stomach, slight nausea with no other difficulty, or less appetite than usual, it may be best to ignore these feelings. However, severe pain or continued milder pain, acute discomfort, or prolonged vomiting should be checked by a physician.

Three symptoms often noticed in indigestion are:

Heartburn is a burning sensation coming from the gullet when the contents of the stomach back up into it. Very strong acid from the stomach can irritate the gullet, but the mere pressure of food retained in the gullet can also be painful.

Flatulence (FLA-tyoo-lence) is an excessive accumulation of gas in the stomach or intestine. Carbon dioxide from soft drinks can join with swallowed air to cause painful distention of the stomach. Gas in the intestines comes mostly from the action of intestinal bacteria upon food. Patients compelled to remain in bed after serious operations sometimes suffer from the painful pressure of gas in the intestine. As soon as these patients are able to eat solid food and can move around a bit, the gas pains usually disappear.

Nausea (NAU-ze-uh), an urge to vomit, may be caused by tension on the walls of the gullet, stomach, or the duodenum. Sudden sweating may accompany nausea, along with faintness, weakness, dizziness, and headache. Alarming thoughts and unpleasant emotions help to cause nausea. Unpleasant odors and sights and severe fright may precipitate nausea. Sometimes a person will feel that he has slight indigestion, and even a touch of nausea, and then find that he feels quite comfortable after a good meal.

A common-sense rule about your digestion is not to eat foods that you know have often upset your stomach. Give yourself enough time for each meal. Eat a balanced diet (see Chapter 4), chew your food thoroughly, and do not gulp liquids with your meals. A pleasant, relaxing atmosphere is best for meal time, with company and conversation, but without excitement and arguments.

Why Do People Eat Too Much?

As you know, our thoughts and our emotions may strongly influence our digestive systems, sometimes for the better, as when we get pleasure and satisfaction from eating the right amounts and kinds of food. Only too often, though, people devour meals which they know from experience will upset them or give them actual pain. Sometimes the mind acts the other way and prevents some persons from eating as much or as nourishing food as they should.

You have heard of drug addiction. You know that many persons are victims of alcohol and cigarettes and cannot give these things up, even though they know that they are probably injuring themselves. Can food also be a sort of addiction? Unfortunately, eating too much is one of Americans' most common bad habits, even though the medical journals point out that being overweight tends to shorten life and to increase the dangers of heart disease, stroke, liver disease, and general discomfort. You can hardly pick up a newspaper or magazine without reading of the perils of *obesity* (oh-BEES-i-tee)—the condition of being very fat. Yet, according to a recent publication of the Department of Health, Education, and Welfare, obesity is increasing. The booklet also states that adolescence is often the critical time that may decide whether a person is to grow up to be a compulsive eater, who overeats in much the same way that some persons smoke and drink too much. Many children look to food for satisfactions that they should get from exercise, play, friendly competition, adventure, study, or work. Loneliness, and feelings of inadequacy or of being neglected may inspire people to eat too much and too often. Sometimes consuming food may result from feelings of fear or impulses toward aggression which one dare not carry out. Many people overcome the overeating habit, just as many overcome the smoking habit.

Many parents and a great many teachers have known plump adolescent girls who finally decided that enough was enough and then showed determination in successfully slimming themselves to normal weight. The problem then is to maintain normal weight, which requires constant attention.

SOCIAL AND ENVIRONMENTAL INFLUENCES AFFECTING DIGESTION

Our relationships with other people have a profound effect upon our mental and emotional life, and through these upon all of the functions of our bodies and especially upon digestion and the digestive system. Social activity often leads to overeating. When we entertain others, or when they entertain us, both we and they often eat things that we might not have eaten otherwise. In many persons it leads to drinking—and overdrinking.

What we eat is largely dictated by the customs of the people that we live among. Few Americans wish to eat octopus, a favorite in Italy and China. Some people cannot imagine eating snails, highly esteemed in many European and Oriental countries. Rabbit is a favorite dish in many European countries. You can visit American restaurants for years and never find rabbit on the menu, although we have plenty of rabbits. Various religions forbid the eating of certain foods.

It may seem strange to Americans raised on a diet rich in animal proteins to see husky Chinese workers living on a mainly vegetable diet, or, at least, on a diet composed mainly of plant products with no milk, little meat, and not much fish. By eating large amounts of soybeans along with wheat products, the northern Chinese manage to get sufficient amounts of all the amino acids they need. A very different diet is found among many Eskimos. They live almost entirely on animal food, as their climate is too cold and

14-14 Different countries have very different types of diets. This is an outdoor market high in the Andes of South America.

the growing season too short for the crops which supply us with grains and vegetables. It has been found that Eskimos living mainly on fish and seal and whale meat and fat seem quite healthy and do not seem to have any excessive deposits of cholesterol in their arteries. (You will find a discussion of cholesterol and hardening of the arteries in Chapter 32.) However, when a diet similar to that of the Eskimos was tried out at Bellevue Hospital in New York, the results were not so good. This brings up the thought that perhaps through the ages, different human populations have become adapted to some extent to the types of food available to them, as they have become adapted to some extent to the climatic conditions of their home lands.

Social and environmental conditions may directly affect health. In those countries where it is the custom to eat raw fish or raw meat, people are much more likely to suffer from parasitic worms found in the meat than they are in countries like our own where meat and fish are cooked. In a somewhat similar way, in countries where politeness requires one to dip his hand into the same dish that everyone else eats out of, there would seem to be more danger of infection.

Very important for the tremendous drop in the death rate and the great increase in length of life is the great improvement in water and food supply. Pure food and pure water have not only meant much greater length of life; they can make a great difference in the way one plans one's life. It was one thing to plan one's future when the average life span was thirty years. It is a bit different now that the average life span is about seventy years.

Trouble in the Alimentary Canal

Colitis (koh-LY-tiss) is inflammation of the colon. Some cases are mild, others very serious. In **ulcerative colitis,** the inner wall of the large intestine may bleed easily and have many small abscesses. Severe diarrhea is one of the most annoying symptoms. Large ulcers form in the colon wall in severe cases. There may be different causes: infection by bacteria, allergic reaction to food, spasms due to nervous upsets. Some authorities believe that psychological upset, during which nervous impulses damage the colon and thus permit bacteria to invade the wall, may be a chief cause. Treatment includes rest, plenty of water, and a diet with no roughage. Sulfa drugs, antibiotics, adrenal hormones, and even surgery may be used.

Spastic colon, or **irritable colon**, is very different from, and far less serious than, ulcerative colitis, although it is sometimes referred to as **mucous colitis**. The principal symptom may be chronic constipation. Persons with this condition are usually anxious, tense, and hurried. They often eat too fast and at irregular hours. Sometimes allergy to foods plays a part. Many patients make their condition worse by overuse of enemas and laxatives. The best remedies for the condition are the rules for avoiding constipation on page 252.

Gastritis (gas-TRY-tiss) is inflammation of the mucous membrane that lines the stomach. It may be caused by alcohol, certain drugs, poisons, infections of the stomach wall, measles, scarlet fever, certain other diseases, and foods to which the patient is allergic.

Hemorrhoids (HEM-oh-roidz) are enlarged veins in the rectum. In some persons they may result from obstinate constipation. A bleeding hemorrhoid is not dangerous, but it is advisable to consult a doctor—to make sure that the bleeding is not the result of a more serious condition.

Peritonitis was once a leading cause of death. It is an inflammation of the lining of the abdominal cavity and is most often due to a burst appendix, gall bladder, or other organ in the abdomen. Until less than a hundred years ago, surgeons feared to open the abdomen to remove an infected appendix because of the peritonitis that almost always followed. With the improvement of surgical techniques and the introduction of antibiotics and sulfa drugs, such operations have become safe and common.

Don't Let Poisons Be Swallowed!

The home medicine cabinet has saved many lives; it has also caused many deaths. Most home cabinets contain some poisons, and too often these can be reached by small children. Other persons sometimes swallow dangerous liquids because they fail to read the label correctly, or absentmindedly pick up the wrong bottle without looking at the label. Drugs which are perfectly harmless when used properly may be deadly when taken in large quantity or by small children. Accidental poisoning is three times as common among children under five years as it is among older boys and girls.

Aspirin kills more small children than any other drug; hence, it is very important to keep candy-flavored aspirin where toddlers cannot reach it. Many small children are killed by barbiturates (sleeping pills). Aside from drugs, common causes of poisoning include kerosene, lead, lye, ammonia, rat poisons, and fly sprays. You might be surprised to learn that among the products which are eaten and prove deadly are shampoo, rubbing solution, bleaches, moth balls, and furniture polish.

What to Do for Swallowed Poisons

If you suspect that a person has swallowed a poisonous substance, the first step is to *call a doctor, hospital, or your local Poison Control Center.* Since the treatment depends upon the kind of poison, try to find out what poison was swallowed. This will be most helpful to the doctor in guiding treatment. If you cannot find out what the poison was, try to describe the person's symptoms as accurately as possible. From the symptoms, it may be possible for the doctor to identify the type of poison.

The next step, even while waiting for medical help, is to *dilute the poison with milk or water.* This step is so important that it is best to have another person call for medical help while you administer this first aid treatment immediately. Regardless of the type of poison, you can give about 1 to 2 cups of fluid to a person aged one to five years old, and up to 1 quart of fluid to a person over five years old.

CAUTION: *If a corrosive substance has been swallowed, do not give so much fluid that you cause vomiting.* It is important to avoid inducing vomiting if the person has swallowed a corrosive substance such as an acid or alkali, or kerosene, gasoline, or other petroleum distillates (unless the latter contains dangerous insecticide, which must be removed). It is also important to avoid inducing vomiting if the person is unconscious. Corrosive substances can burn and destroy tissues during the vomiting process, and petroleum distillates can become deadly if drawn into the lungs.

In diluting corrosive substances, you can follow the principle that acids and alkalis neutralize each other. For acidic substances such as sulfuric, nitric, or hydrochloric acid, iodine, or silver nitrate, give the person a glass of milk, water, or 1 tablespoon of milk of magnesia mixed with 1 cup of water. For alkaline substances, such as washing soda, ammonia water, household bleach, or drain cleaners containing lye, you can give milk, water, vinegar, or any fruit juice (particularly lemon or orange juice).

If the swallowed poison is a noncorrosive substance, give an *emetic* (eh-MET-ik), something to make the patient vomit. Milk, water, or 2 tablespoons of salt in a glass of warm water can act as an emetic. After giving the fluid, you can also help induce vomiting by placing the blunt end of a spoon or your finger at the back of the patient's throat. When vomiting begins, place the person face down with his head lower than his hips, to prevent the escaping material from entering the lungs.

Keep the person warm in all cases of poisoning, and be prepared to treat him for shock (see Chapter 17).

For some years, it has been common practice to include the so-called "universal antidote" in first-aid kits or medicine chests. However, many doctors now consider this mixture quite ineffective. Instead, powdered activated charcoal is being recommended as a useful antidote for a number of poisons, including overdoses of certain common drugs. However, activated charcoal does not work against all poisons, such as lye and other caustic alkalis. Research is continuing to determine for which poisons activated charcoal is the best first-aid treatment.

What You Have Learned

What kind of health practices should you apply in maintaining your health? Check your understanding of the chapter. On a separate sheet of paper, number 1 through 24 and insert the answer from the vocabulary list below. Use each expression, but use each one only once.

amino acids	fats	small intestine
bacteria	heartburn	soybeans
banana	irritable colon	stomach
barium sulfate	lacteal	sugar molecules
capillaries	large intestine	tenseness, and anxiety
cells	large molecules	that satisfied feeling
digested	peristalsis	ulcers
enzymes	protein	villi

Most of the food we eat consists of (1) _amino acid_, which cannot pass from the intestine into the blood or from the blood into our (2) _cell_. Therefore, it must be (3) _digested_, or split into particles that can pass through cell membranes. All food containing fat, starch, and (4) _protein_ must be digested.

Most digestion occurs in the (5) _____. Only a small amount of digestion takes place in the mouth and (6) _stomach_. (7) _enzymes_ produced in the mouth, stomach, pancreas, and small intestine do the chemical work of digestion. In other words, they split starch molecules to make (8) _sugar_, protein to make (9) _fats_, and (10) _large molecules_ to make fatty acids and glycerol. Using a special kind of X-ray machine, you could see the stomach and intestine vigorously contracting and squeezing the food along by (11) _peristalsis_

The small intestine has a very large surface for absorbing digested foods because it has thousands of tiny projections called (12) _villi_. There is a network of (13) _capillaries_ inside each of these projections. Digested fats are absorbed by the (14) _lacteal_ in the center of each projection. It is mostly water and undigested particles of food that pass from the small intestine into the (15) _large intestine_. Here billions of (16) _bacteria_ live on the remnants of a person's food and manufacture vitamin K and some of the B-complex vitamins.

Fats and many protein foods can be digested just as well raw as cooked. The (17) _banana_ is one of the few natural starchy foods that we don't need to cook. Fatty foods, more than any others, give us (18) _satisfied feeling_ after a meal.

If your doctor should wish to X-ray your stomach, he will probably ask you to swallow some (19) _barium_. Anger, fear, and worry seem to help cause stomach (20) _ulcers_. A far less serious but often painful condition, which occurs when stomach acid sprays up into the gullet, is called (21) _heartburn_. Frequent anger, fear, (22) _tension, anxiety_ help to bring on and aggravate many troubles of the digestive system, including (23) _irritable colon_.

If you travel around the earth, you find that different people may get all the nutrients they need, even though their diets seem to be not at all similar. By eating a mainly vegetable diet, along with wheat, northern Chinese workers manage to get all of the amino acids they need. They usually eat only small amounts of fish and meat but consume large amounts of (24) _soybeans_

What You Can Do

1. How much have you learned by personal experience about appetite and digestion? How much can you learn from the experiences of your friends and acquaintances?

   a. Have worry, anger, fear, joy, excitement, or other emotions ever affected your appetite or digestion or those of other persons that you know? Mention: (a) person or persons involved; (b) temperament of person (calm, excitable, good humored, serious, always joking, etc.); (c) what happened to cause the emotion; (d) how appetite or digestion was affected.

b. When are you most likely to feel hungry? Is it when you are alone? when studying? when excited? when worried? when having a good time with your friends? under other circumstances? Or do you usually get hungry at about the same time each day regardless of what you are doing?

c. Make a list of the foods you like best. Try to start with your favorite (if you have a favorite) and list the others in the order of your preference. Try to get the other members of your class to do the same thing. Now compare lists and find out how many "votes" each of your favorite dishes get. Check the dishes that got the most votes and your own favorites for their nutrient value. Consult Chapter 14 and Chapters 3 and 4.

2. Discuss each of the following good health practices in class. Then list each practice in your notebook. Do you follow each of these practices? Explain why these are good health practices.

a. Relax for 20 to 30 minutes before and after eating a heavy meal, especially if you are tired or if you plan heavy physical activity afterward.

b. Try to make each meal a pleasant, relaxed occasion for yourself and others.

c. Carefully wash all fruits or other foods that are eaten raw.

d. Avoid eating too many fatty or fried foods.

e. Try to make sure that all starchy foods except bananas are cooked thoroughly.

f. Chew your food thoroughly.

g. Drink as much water as you wish at meals, but do not gulp mouthfuls of water to wash down your food.

h. If you develop persistent pains in the abdomen, call a doctor.

Things to Try

1. Have each student in your class find a recent article in a magazine or newspaper, or a chapter in a book that contains information on psychosomatic illnesses affecting the digestive system. Try to keep the discussion to one theme at a time, so that it does not leap from stomach ulcer to colitis or food allergy while questions on the first topic are still being debated.

2. Find out how many of your friends drink water with their meals and how much water each one usually drinks. Does the water help or hurt their appetites?

3. Have a class discussion on the topic "How Different Peoples Get the Same Nutrients from Different Foods." If there are students from different parts of the country, they may make valuable contributions. So may boys or girls who were born in other countries or whose parents were foreign-born. You can find many interesting articles containing such information in magazines. Travel books and cookbooks can also be of help.

Probing Further /

Today's Health, a monthly magazine published by the American Medical Association. You can find current issues and back numbers of this magazine in your school library, the public library, or both. It contains easy-to-read articles on everything connected with health, including emotional, social, and environmental factors as they affect the workings of the body.

The Human Body: What It Is and How It Works, by Mitchell Wilson, Golden Press, 1959. Although written over a decade ago, this book is well worth reading. With large, full-color illustrations on each page, this book tells you about foods and digestion and all the organ systems of the body in simple language.

Health Concepts in Action /

Does what you have learned support this statement? Would you change or add to it?

> **The digestive system converts food into substances the body's cells can use for energy and growth.**

Applying this concept of digestion, which health practices would you

— continue?

— change?

— begin?

Will you now, as a result of your study, change any of your health objectives?

15 / *Respiration*

Imagine that you are one of the first astronauts hurtling through space on an expedition to Mars. Before anyone can make this trip and return alive, many problems must be solved. Scientists must find out how to supply men with enough oxygen during the months that they must travel in an airtight vehicle.

A PROBE INTO THE RESPIRATORY SYSTEM—What are the many factors that influence your respiratory processes? To find out, you will be probing these questions:

1. What processes are included under the term *respiration?*

2. How is your breathing controlled without your having to think about it?

3. What disturbances of breathing may sometimes be due to emotions? What is hyperventilation?

4. How can we help avoid colds? What complications may sometimes follow colds?

5. Why is the humidity of the air in heated buildings important?

6. How are pneumonia and tuberculosis treated today? What are some of the factors that contribute to emphysema?

15-1 Years ago three French scientists ascended five miles into the air in a balloon like this. What was learned from their work?

WHY WE BREATHE

How to breathe at great heights above the earth's surface had already become a problem almost a hundred years before the first spacecraft and long before the first airplane. More than thirty years before the Wright brothers built the first successful airplane, the city of Paris was waiting eagerly for a great balloon ascension. At last Gaston Tissandier (tih-sahn-DYAY) and his two companions boarded their huge balloon and cast off the ropes that held it (Figure 5-1). Soon they were up a thousand feet, then five thousand, a mile, and more. It was not very long before they saw northern France like a map below them.

Tissandier and his friends were good scientists. They had prepared themselves for high altitudes by taking a supply of oxygen so that they would not be suffocated when they rose to heights where the air is very thin. They were the first airmen to do this. When the balloon had risen to 8,000 feet (above 1½ miles), they noted that their hearts were beating faster. At 2 miles up (above 10,000 feet) Tissandier had begun to think that perhaps he could not see and hear as well as usual. At 3 miles up there was no doubt about it.

Tissandier kept a record of how he felt on the way up. At 24,600 feet (over 4½ miles up) he found that he could hardly move—and didn't want to. "Body and mind become feebler little by little," he wrote. "There is no suffering. On the contrary, one feels an inner joy. . . . I soon felt myself so weak that I could not even turn my head to look at my companions. I wished to take hold of the oxygen tube, but found I could not move my arms." His mind was still clear when the balloon was about 5 miles up. "I wished to call out that now we were at 8,000 meters (26,200 feet), but my tongue was paralyzed. I shut my eyes, fell down powerless, and lost all further memory." Why had the three men failed to use the oxygen they took with them?

They had carried the oxygen in small balloons, but since the balloons would not hold very much, they were determined not to use the precious gas until it became absolutely necessary. By the time they had tried to open the little balloons for a life-giving breath, they were too weak to make their muscles obey their wills. When the balloon landed, only Tissandier was still alive and he was

15-2 An artist's concept of a lunar city of the next century. A lunar city will present some unusual respiratory problems as there is no atmosphere on the moon. Men will have to wear special suits that will provide oxygen, and oxygen will have to be supplied to all buildings. Some of the features of this lunar city include a nuclear power station at the extreme top left. At top center there is a large industrial complex. Hovering overhead is the moon orbiting station, which serves as a transfer point for passengers shuttling between earth and moon. Notice the moving sidewalk at the lower left.

unconscious. His two friends had both died from lack of enough oxygen.

What Is Respiration?

Tissandier and his two friends helped us to understand what happens when breathing becomes labored or stops. The body cells fail to get oxygen; the muscles weaken and become paralyzed; the brain falters; the mind loses consciousness. Finally, the skin turns blue; the body grows cold; soon the heart stops. Unless natural breathing or artificial respiration can be started without much delay, the cells of the body begin to die. First to go are the delicate cells of the brain. In order to explain why our life depends on breathing we have to understand what is meant by *respiration.*

Every living cell in every living thing has to expend energy all the time to live. In order to grow, move about, play, and work, you need still more energy. The process by which the body releases energy to go on living and to carry on its activities is respiration. Respiration includes (1) breathing; (2) the transfer of oxygen from the air through lungs and blood to body cells; (3) the complicated process called *cell respiration* that takes place inside all of our cells. Cell respiration was explained in Chapter 13 as a series of small-scale chemical reactions. Each of these reactions yields a little energy for the use of the cell.

Oxygen comes into action only after the cell has taken most of the energy from glycogen, sugar, or another substance that the cell is using. Then each oxygen atom unites with two hydrogen atoms from a food molecule to form water. This water and carbon dioxide (which has also been split off from the food) leave the cell and are carried by the blood to the lungs. All of us must take in oxygen and get rid of carbon dioxide as long as we live. How do astronauts breathe on the moon? Will men ever be able to live on the moon? See Figure 15-2.

Your Breathing Apparatus

You have two entrances for breathing—the regular entrance and the emergency entrance. The emergency entrance is the mouth. Breathing through the mouth is a lifesaver when the nose is clogged by a cold. You also breathe through the mouth when you must take in a great deal of air in a short time.

■ Would you like to find out why you should use your mouth only as an emergency breathing entrance? Then start breathing deeply through your mouth right now. Unless the air around you is very moist you will soon find your throat uncomfortably dry. Breathe through your nose again. Isn't nose breathing much better?

On its way from the nose to the lungs, the breath you just took was drawn through your throat cavity. It then went on through the voice box, the windpipe, or *trachea* (TRAY-key-a), two large tubes called the *bronchi* (BRONK-eye), and a series of smaller passages called the *bronchial tubes.* Locate the voice box, windpipe, bronchi, and bronchial tubes in Figures 15-3.

Many things can obstruct the air passages. Children sometimes put beans, coins, and other strange objects in their nostrils. Sometimes the bony structure is such that the doctor has to operate to allow free air passage. He may also have to remove soft growths called *polyps* (POL-ips) that sometimes partly close the nostrils.

Many people have died as a result of objects lodging in the windpipe. This usually results in violent choking. If the victim is a very small child, hold him upside down by his feet and slap him sharply between the shoulder blades.

Here are some further instructions for first aid from the American Red Cross:

1. Let the patient try to cough up the object. Do *not* probe with your fingers into

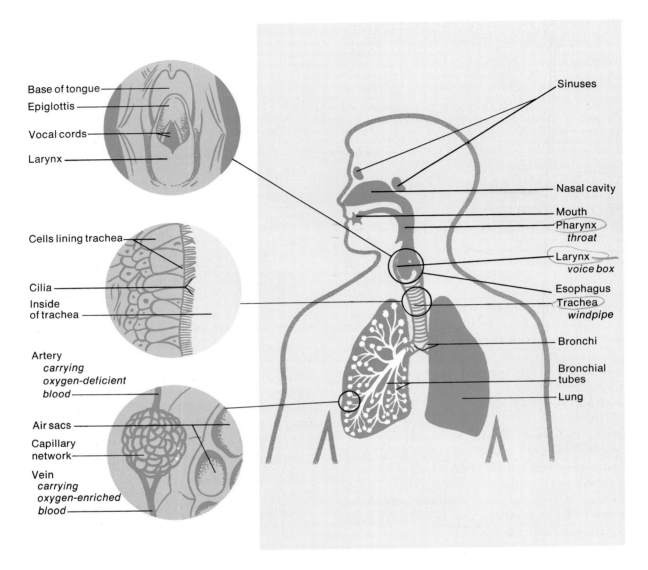

Base of tongue
Epiglottis
Vocal cords
Larynx

Sinuses
Nasal cavity
Mouth
Pharynx *throat*
Larynx *voice box*
Esophagus
Trachea *windpipe*

Cells lining trachea
Cilia
Inside of trachea

Bronchi
Bronchial tubes
Lung

Artery *carrying oxygen-deficient blood*
Air sacs
Capillary network
Vein *carrying oxygen-enriched blood*

15-3 The respiratory system. In the circle at the lower left you see a capillary network such as the one that surrounds each air sac in the lungs. Why does the blood change color as it flows through these capillaries? In the drawing at the right, what is the relationship between the windpipe and gullet in the throat? How is food kept from entering the lungs?

the throat; if you do, you may push the object farther down toward the lungs.

2. Do not distract the patient from his attempt to cough and breathe by showing alarm or asking questions.

3. Do *not* slap a person on the back. This may make him gasp a mouthful of air which may pull the object down into his lungs.

4. Always take him to a physician or the nearest hospital emergency room unless he has expelled the object.

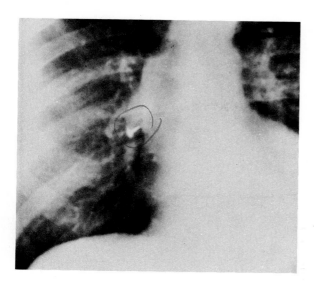

15-4 An X-ray photograph showing a tack that has lodged in a lung. How do you think a situation like this could have come about?

5. If breathing stops, give artificial respiration and try to clear the airway with fingers or forceps.

Don't give small children such foods as peanuts, popcorn, or cake containing nuts until they have their first teeth and have learned to chew their food. Give them only finely chopped meat, and *don't* leave needles, pins, nails, or other such small items around where toddlers can find them.

Your Air-Conditioning System

Every one of us is born with an air-conditioning system that filters, warms, and moistens the air that enters our lungs. If we did not have this system we would soon die, because the lungs would be clogged with dirt and bacteria. They would be injured by cold, and they would dry out and stop functioning.

The hairs at the entrance of each nostril strain out large particles of dust. These hairs grow only in the lower part of the nose.

Smaller bits of dust and bacteria by-pass the hairs. Fortunately, these are usually caught like flies in flypaper by the slightly sticky mucus that coats the moist mucous membrane that lines the upper part of the nose and all the other air passages. Yet if all this foreign material remained where it landed, the mucous membrane would be injured and the nose and the smaller air passages would be stopped up. You have a living sweeping squad to take care of this problem.

From the time you take your first breath, *cilia* sweep bacteria, dust, and excess mucus to the throat cavity to be coughed up or swallowed.

Cilia are at work in all of the air passages— beginning a short distance above the outer openings of the nostrils and continuing all the way down to tiny tubes $1/50$ of an inch in diameter within the lungs (see Figure 2-8). There are hundreds of thousands of cilia to every square inch of mucous membrane in the nose, windpipe, bronchi, and bronchial tubes. They are even inside the voice box. Cilia work all the time, day and night. They beat strongly on the upstroke and then swing back gently. As a result, they carry mucus, bacteria, and dust away from the lungs.

The mucous membranes, to which the cilia belong, do other work of great importance. Because they are damp, they moisten the incoming air. Because they are warmed by many blood vessels, they cause the air delivered to the lungs to be at the right temperature.

Inflammation of the mucous membranes of the nose, leading to excess "running of the nose," is known as **rhinitis** (ry-NY-tis—from a Greek word meaning "nose"). It may be caused by a virus, chilling drafts, exposure to colds, allergies, irritating dust or chemical fumes, or defects in the structure of the air passages. Some persons suffer from rhinitis after an emotional upset. The expression **nasal catarrh** (kuh-TAHR) was formerly used for some types of rhinitis.

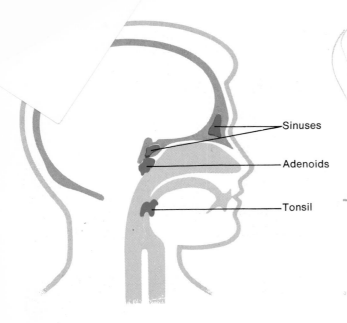

15-5 In this cross section of the head, you see some of the sinuses, the adenoids, and one of the two tonsils. The two tonsils and the adenoids help destroy germs that enter your nose or mouth.

The Nasal Sinuses

You have a number of air spaces in the bones of your head. Some of these air spaces are shown in Figure 15-5. They all open into the nose. They are the nasal *sinuses* (SY-nus-ez), which supply mucus for the nasal cavity. They also help by reducing the weight of the head. When the sinuses become infected and fill up with pus, they may cause severe headaches. Sometimes an allergy is the cause of the trouble. The sinuses are hard to treat because their small openings readily close when the mucous membrane is swollen. Infected sinuses should be treated by a doctor. Usually nose and throat specialists treat infected sinuses.

The Throat—Where Two Lifelines Cross

At the back of the nose and the mouth is your throat cavity, or *pharynx* (FAIR-inks).

Here two important streams of traffic have to cross—air from the nose on its way to the lungs, and food and water from the mouth on their way to the stomach.

At the bottom of the throat cavity, there are two openings, as you see in Figure 15-3. Air goes down the one in front to pass through the voice box and then down the windpipe. Food and water enter the gullet, which lies behind the windpipe. A living trap door called the *epiglottis* (ep-ih-GLOT-is) protects us from wrong-way traffic. The door closes automatically when you swallow and opens to let you breathe. Sometimes, when you are laughing or talking while you eat, the door fails to work. Then a bit of food may drop through the voice box into the windpipe. This is dangerous because fragments of food carrying millions of bacteria might enter the air passages of the lungs. Serious illness might occur if you were not able to cough up the food.

The opposite accident occurs when you swallow air. This may cause pain in the stomach.

Sore Throat

Sore throat is a painful inflammation of the throat, or pharynx, or of a part of it. An infection in the mucous membrane of the throat is called *pharyngitis* (fair-in-JYE-tis). This is most often due to viruses, but more serious cases are usually caused by bacteria. *Strep throat* is a sore throat caused by the streptococcus bacterium. It can make one quite ill with chills, fever, and difficulty in swallowing.

The Voice Box—
a Useful Musical Instrument

The voice box, or *larynx* (LAIR-inks), is a hollow box made of cartilage and lined with mucous membrane. The sharp-edged V in

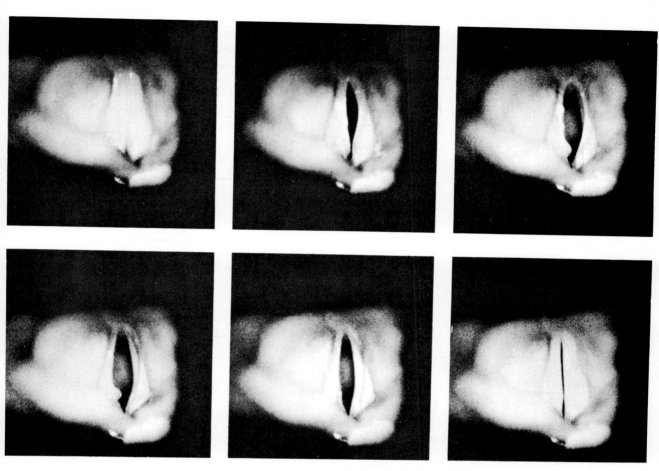

15-6 These photographs show how the vocal cords move when you produce sounds of low pitch. These pictures were taken with high-speed photography.

front is called the "Adam's apple." According to fable, when Adam ate the apple a piece of it stuck here in his throat. Touch the front of your throat and find the voice box. Now swallow. Can you feel it bob up and down? When the voice box rises, it presses against the epiglottis. This closes the trap door.

You make sounds by vibrating your two vocal cords (Figure 15-6). These cords stretch across the inside of the voice box. They are elastic bands of tissue covered with mucous membrane. To speak or sing, you contract little muscles that stretch the cords and make them tense. Then, as you breathe

out, the air makes the cords vibrate. The more you contract the muscles, the thinner the cords are stretched and the higher the sound becomes.

Men have larger Adam's apples than women, and grown men have larger ones than boys. Most men have deeper voices than women or children because the larger voice box has longer, thicker cords. Early in adolescence our voice boxes grow larger. This is why your voice is deeper now than when you were a small child.

■ You can make an imitation vocal cord with a blade of grass. Put your thumbs together and stretch the grass between them. Then put your mouth close to the grass and blow. The more you stretch the grass, the higher the note. Experiment with grass of different widths. Do this exercise out in the open, not at home—and not in school! Your parents and teachers may not enjoy the "music."

Laryngitis is inflammation of the larynx, or voice box. Like pharyngitis, it often follows the common cold. It may also follow pharyngitis, tonsillitis, and infected sinuses. Bad weather, excessive use of the voice, and the breathing in of irritating dust or gases make one more likely to develop laryngitis. A person becomes hoarse, his voice changes considerably, and he may become unable to speak for the time being. Treatment includes complete rest for the voice and preferably bed rest. Cough syrups and tablets may be helpful, and steam inhalations may speed recovery.

The Bronchial Tree—Windpipe, Bronchi, and Bronchial Tubes

After passing through the voice box, the air you breathe in goes down the windpipe, or trachea, a strong tube about 1 inch in diameter and 4 1/2 inches long (Figure 15-3). Feel your windpipe below the voice box. Notice how hard it is. Does it seem to be made of rings, one on top of another? The "rings" are horseshoe-shaped pieces of cartilage, open at the back, which strengthen the tough walls of the windpipe. Across the open ends of the cartilage strips are bands of muscle. You cannot feel this side because it is at the back, away from the surface of the neck.

The fact that there is no cartilage on the back side of the windpipe helps when you swallow. This is because the gullet lies in the neck just behind the windpipe and touches the windpipe where the muscle re-

places cartilage. When food is swallowed, the gullet bulges and the muscle "gives" (muscle has much more "give" than cartilage).

In the chest the windpipe divides into two smaller tubes called the bronchi. Each bronchus enters the lung on its side of the body and then divides into many smaller branches. These are called the bronchial tubes. They keep dividing until they become tiny tubes reaching into all parts of the lungs.

In the X-ray photograph (Figure 15-7), the windpipe, the bronchi, and the bronchial tubes look like the trunk and branches of a tree turned upside down. Doctors sometimes call them the bronchial "tree." Inflammation of the bronchi is called **bronchitis** (bron-KY-tis). This may be caused by the spread of germs following a cold or some other disease of the respiratory system. A person with bronchitis usually coughs a great deal. He is often short of breath and may find it difficult to breathe.

The Lungs—Where the Blood Picks Up Oxygen

Each of the smallest air tubes ends in a group of little *air sacs* as shown in Figure 15-3. The word *sac* means *bag*, and the clusters of air sacs look like tiny balloons. The important work of the lungs is done in the air sacs. In order to give enough oxygen to the blood and to take enough carbon dioxide from it, air must be exposed to as many capillaries as possible. The capillaries form a network around each air sac. The wall of a capillary is only one cell thick, and the wall of an air sac is also only one cell thick. Both together are thinner than the finest tissue paper. Hence, the molecules of oxygen have only a very short distance to go from the air to the blood. Similarly, carbon dioxide has only a short distance to go from the blood to the air.

The lungs have hundreds of millions of air

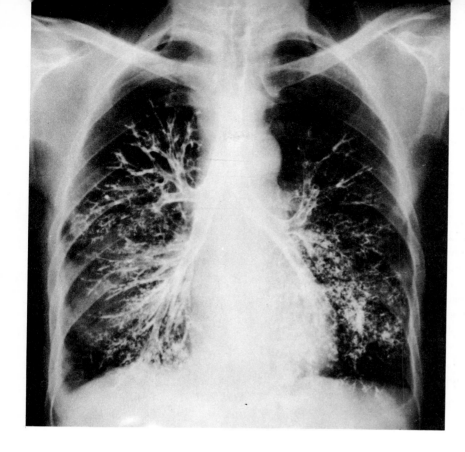

15-7 An X-ray photograph of your respiratory system, showing the bronchial "tree." What structures form this "tree"?

sacs; if all the air sacs in the two lungs were flattened out, they would cover an area of more than 1,000 square feet!

Why Breathing Doesn't Hurt

Why aren't your lungs injured by rubbing against the inner wall of your chest when you take a deep breath? They are not injured because each lung is protected against friction by a double membrane moistened with liquid. This membrane is called the *pleura* (PLOOR-uh). One layer surrounds the lung; the other lines the chest cavity. When the pleura becomes inflamed, the rubbing of the two layers causes intense pain. This condition is called *pleurisy* (PLOOR-ih-see).

Empyema (em-pye-EE-muh) is a severe form of pleurisy in which pus forms between the pleural membrane and the lung. It almost always follows another infection. The first choice for treatment is usually *penicillin* (pen-uh-SILL-in), an *antibiotic* (an-tee-by-OT-ik). Antibiotics will be discussed in Chapter 30.

MAINTAINING RESPIRATION

The air you breathe out is saturated with moisture from your lungs. It has about one-fourth less oxygen and more than 100 times as much carbon dioxide as it did when it was breathed in. To put it another way, the air you breathe in contains 21 percent oxygen and much less than 1 percent carbon dioxide, while the air you breathe out contains only 16 percent oxygen and more than 4 per-

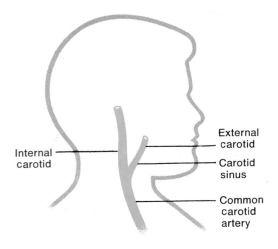

15-8 The region of the carotid sinus. The nerve cells in this area serve as monitors of changes in the amount of gases in the blood.

cent carbon dioxide. This explains why you could not live very long without a change of air.

How Breathing Is Regulated

Why do you continue to breathe when asleep? Why will a man breathe under water if he remains there long enough, even though he knows that breathing water into the lungs may kill him? Why do you breathe at regular intervals without needing to think about it? The reason is that a part of the brain called the *medulla* sends nerve impulses to your breathing muscles to make them contract. What makes the medulla do this? The medulla reacts in this way to changes in the amount of carbon dioxide and oxygen in its blood vessels.

You breathe faster and deeper during exercise because carbon dioxide accumulates in your blood. This causes the medulla to send out the breathing impulses more frequently. Blood flowing through the two arteries in the neck affects groups of nerve cells near these vessels, which act as moni-toring stations of changes in blood pressure and amounts of carbon dioxide, oxygen, and acids in the blood. These nerve cells send impulses to the medulla to stimulate it to "order" the breathing muscles to work harder. See Figure 15-8. The principal control is in the medulla itself, however, as it responds to the concentration of carbon dioxide in the blood flowing through it. Once the amount of carbon dioxide and oxygen has returned to normal, the medulla stops sending "work harder" messages to the breathing muscles.

How You Breathe

You live at the bottom of an ocean of air. This great mass of air extends at least 500 miles above the surface of the earth. The weight of the gases above makes the atmosphere at sea level push against everything with a pressure of almost 15 pounds per square inch. When you inhale (breathe in), you expand the chest cavity and air rushes in. To exhale (breathe out), you allow the chest cavity to spring back to a smaller size. This forces the air out. The lungs themselves move passively in the chest.

When you breathe in, two sets of muscles go to work. The chest muscles contract. This raises the chest upward and outward. The *diaphragm* (DY-uh-fram) also contracts. This makes the lungs expand downward. The diaphragm is a dome-shaped sheet of muscle; it divides the chest cavity from the abdomen.

When you breathe out, the reverse action takes place. The chest muscles and the diaphragm relax. The chest becomes smaller, presses on the lungs, and forces the air out of them. See Figure 15-9.

Types of Breathing

Some people do chiefly "rib breathing" (by making the chest rise and fall); others depend mostly on the diaphragm. Most of us use a combination of the two in which the diaphragm does about 60 percent of the work.

■ What type of breathing do you use? Put your hand over your stomach just beneath the rib cage and feel what happens as you breathe normally. Does your chest rise and fall very much? If so, you tend to use rib breathing, rather than diaphragm breathing or a combination of both.

Full breathing is a result of strong diaphragm and chest muscles. Stooped shoulders crowd the lungs so that they cannot expand fully. You do not need to think about the actual breathing movements if your health is good and if you get enough wholesome exercise. Exercises you enjoy, such as hiking, swimming, rowing, and active games, are better than formal breathing exercises.

How Much Can the Lungs Hold?

You take in about a pint of air in an ordinary breath. Figure 15-10 shows instruments used to measure breathing capacity. The amount of air you can force out after taking the deepest possible breath is called your *vital capacity.* This depends on your size, build, muscular development, and breathing habits. For the average adult man, the vital capacity is from six to eight pints. From the time you take your first breath, your lungs always retain some air, however. No matter how forcibly you breathe out, about two pints of air remain in the lungs.

How Mental and Emotional Influences Affect Respiration

Have you ever been awakened by the sudden loud ring of a telephone and surprised by the weakness and high pitch of your voice as you answered it? Have you noticed that often people's voices become shrill with fear or anger or even with pleasant excite-

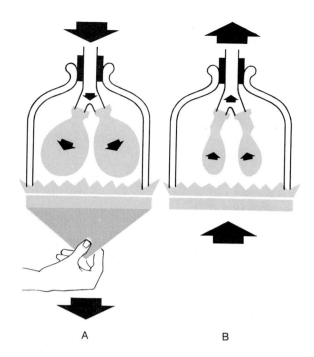

15-9 With this apparatus you can investigate the mechanics of breathing. Can you identify the breathing structures represented by the glass tubing, the balloons, and the rubber sheeting? Describe what is happening in each part of this drawing.

ment? These are examples of some of the ways that we control the air we breathe in. Have you ever found that unexpected news, good or bad, made you "catch your breath," or that boredom or being forced to pay close attention made you yawn? They are other cases in which emotional responses affect the way that we control our breathing.

Grief or pain may make one sob, that is, weep, sigh, or cry along with a convulsive catching of the breath. Excited talking or laughing may cause food, liquids, or saliva to go down the "wrong way," that is, into the windpipe instead of into the gullet. This may result in severe choking. Excitement and nervousness tend to make us breathe faster. Sometimes unpleasant excitement may stop breathing. You may observe this when an angry or frustrated small child holds his

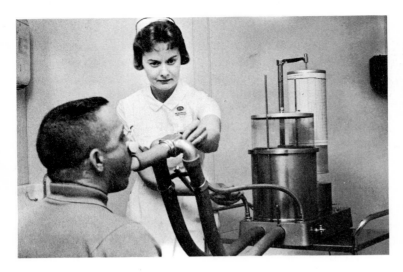
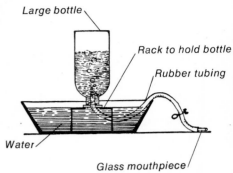

Large bottle

Rack to hold bottle

Rubber tubing

Water

Glass mouthpiece

15-10 A spirometer is used to test the capacity of the lungs. Why is this an important test of lung function? What diseases may reduce lung capacity?

breath. Enraged infants sometimes become blue in the face from lack of oxygen as a result of prolonged breath holding.

Mental and emotional upsets sometimes even cause prolonged and distressing hiccups. Most of us have at some time had mild attacks of hiccups, those repeated involuntary contractions of the diaphragm accompanied by brief stoppage of breathing and gasping sounds. Usually hiccups are due to any of a number of physical conditions.

Have you ever *hyperventilated?* Many people do. Hyperventilation is breathing more frequently or more deeply than one needs to, long enough for the blood to absorb more oxygen and lose more carbon dioxide than it should. In extreme cases of hyperventilation, a person may become agitated and light-headed. He may have muscle spasms and may faint. The effects of hyperventilation show that even though our lungs must continually get rid of carbon dioxide, we still need a certain amount of carbon dioxide in the blood to keep us in good condition. Prolonged anxiety sometimes results in hyperventilation that is handicapping.

Smoking Affects Respiration

When the English settlers first saw American Indians smoking tobacco, they were astonished. What a strange sight it seemed! Men breathing in hot smoke from dead leaves—and enjoying it. It was not long, of course, before many of the English had themselves formed the habit of smoking. Many people form the habit of smoking today in somewhat the same way that early explorers and settlers did. They see others smoking; they are curious and perhaps envious—and soon they are smoking themselves.

Smoking is harmful to the respiratory system in several ways. As you have learned, the cilia that line the air passages from the nose to the air sacs in the lungs play an important role in defending the body against disease. The cilia beat constantly, sweeping layers of mucus and dust, bacteria, and other invading particles up from the lungs to the throat. Cigarette smoke first weakens, then paralyzes the cilia. In time, the smoke may kill them, and this important defense for the lungs is lost.

Death rates in various age groups have been found to be higher among smokers than among nonsmokers. In addition, certain diseases occur much more frequently among cigarette smokers than among nonsmokers. Of these diseases, those that affect the air passages are cancer of the lung, mouth, and larynx; bronchitis; and emphysema. You will learn more about smoking and the other diseases that are believed to be linked to smoking in Chapter 33.

How Changes in the Atmosphere Affect Respiration

You read what happened to Tissandier and his friends when they made the first balloon ascension carrying oxygen—and failed to use the oxygen. As one goes up in a balloon or open airplane or when one climbs a mountain, air pressure grows less and less, and less and less oxygen enters the lungs. As a result, the blood can carry less oxygen to the tissues. Every cell begins to suffer from lack of oxygen, especially those of the brain. Today, of course, space vehicles and pas-senger airplanes are pressurized, that is, the air inside the sealed cabin is kept at near-normal atmospheric pressure. Hence, the persons inside the cabin breathe in some-thing like a normal amount of oxygen. Actually, when a plane is flying at a height of 32,000 feet, the air pressure inside the cabin is kept about equal to that of the outside air at an elevation of 8,000 feet—about 3,000 feet above the altitude of Denver, Colorado. Some persons, especially those with serious lung disorders, find themselves in distress even at this level of air pressure.

In the Andes mountains region of South America and in Tibet, people live, do the hardest kind of work, and play sports in the thin air at altitudes of 12,000 feet and more. Yet a person traveling in these regions usually finds himself breathless after very moderate exertion. Travelers are impressed by the tremendous chest development of the native Indians. The number of red blood cells also is greatly increased in those people who spend much time at high altitudes. Can you explain why? Usually, most people can become adapted to the high altitude in a week or two.

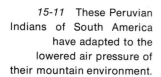

15-11 These Peruvian Indians of South America have adapted to the lowered air pressure of their mountain environment.

The Importance of Humidity
in the Air We Breathe

Except when we climb or fly to high altitudes the air, pure or contaminated, outdoors or indoors, almost always has all the oxygen we need or can use. The important substance that is most likely to be in short supply is water vapor. There is always some water vapor in the atmosphere, but the amount may be from as little as 1/10 of 1 percent to as much as 2.5 percent. In very dry air, the sun's light may come through so completely that one can soon receive a dangerous sunburn if he leaves his skin exposed. In very **humid** (HYOO-mid—meaning *moist*) air, tropical heat may be unbearable. Our respiratory systems, however, can adapt well to dry desert air, provided we drink plenty of water.

Worse than dry desert air is the air of many modern homes and apartments where artificial heat may make the air drier than it is on the Sahara desert. The resulting drying-out of the mucous membranes of the nose can be very uncomfortable and can increase the danger of colds and other respiratory infections. To keep our air passages in good condition, the **relative humidity** (degree of moisture that is present in the air as compared with the largest amount that the air could hold) should range from 40 to 50 percent. Electric humidifiers can be helpful in adding sufficient moisture to indoor air.

IMPORTANT RESPIRATORY DISEASES

The **cold** is the commonest of all diseases and it occurs about 25 times as often as any other disease. The average American has about three colds a year. The cold is primarily a virus disease—doctors know a *number* of viruses that can cause colds by attacking the mucous membrane that lines the breathing passages. Some of the attacking viruses may be present at all times. Rhinitis, the inflammation of the mucous membrane of the nose, is always present when you have a cold.

Avoiding Colds

How can we prevent colds? Scientists are still investigating this problem. Enough sleep, personal cleanliness, healthful exercise—all of these may help. But it is most important to avoid contact with those who have colds.

It is commonly believed that an even body temperature is important in resisting and curing colds. Sitting with cold or damp feet, sudden chilling from a draft, or rapid cooling when damp with perspiration may make us liable to attack by a cold virus. However, the importance of such factors is still not clear.

No truly successful preventive measure or medicine for colds is yet known. Research seems to indicate that none of the usual remedies has significant preventive or curative value. The best procedure known is to go to bed at the beginning of the cold, keep warm, eat easily digested foods, and drink plenty of liquids. Fruit juices rich in vitamin C may help. There is no proof, though, that large quantities of vitamins can prevent colds. If, like most adults and teen-agers, you refuse to go to bed, at least try to stay home for a few days and don't expose yourself to drafts or chilling. Steam inhalations will often give much relief.

Some years ago, new drugs called **antihistamines** (an-tee-HISS-tuh-meens) were hailed as almost certain cold preventives if taken within the first 24 hours of the onset of the cold. At present it is generally believed that they have no effect in preventing or curing colds, but that they may give certain patients relief from some of the symptoms of colds. Aspirin often helps relieve headache and the generally miserable feeling that accompanies colds.

15-12 What other remedies can you suggest for the common cold?

Colds not properly cared for may develop into more serious conditions, such as mastoid, sinus, or ear infections, bronchitis, influenza, or pneumonia. Advanced symptoms to watch for include fever, earache, sore throat that lasts more than a few hours, severe tightness in the chest, difficulty in breathing, and pains in the back and legs. You should call a doctor if you have any of these symptoms.

Scarlet Fever

Like strep throat, scarlet fever is caused by streptococcus bacteria. If there is a pink-red rash, we call it scarlet fever; if not, it is usually called streptococcus sore throat. Scarlet fever is usually more serious than strep throat. Both may have severe complications leading to deafness and heart and kidney disease.

Penicillin, other antibiotics, and sulfa drugs have enormously reduced the number of deaths from scarlet fever. In most cases, penicillin is the only drug needed. When there is a case of scarlet fever in the family, a single injection of long-acting penicillin will usually protect other members of the family.

Influenza

Influenza is an infection of the respiratory tract by any of three different viruses. Symptoms of influenza are fever, backache, aching limbs, and marked tiredness. There may be symptoms of a cold, sore throat, and bronchitis. If you have fever and aches, go to bed and call a doctor. Although the acute stage usually lasts only one to five days, the patient may be left partially exhausted for some time longer. Good care is important to prevent complications such as pneumonia. We now have highly effective vaccines that can immunize one against some types of influenza. However, no one vaccine can protect against all the influenza viruses. At long intervals, there are world-wide epidemics. The epidemic of 1918–19 is thought to have killed more than 20 million people.

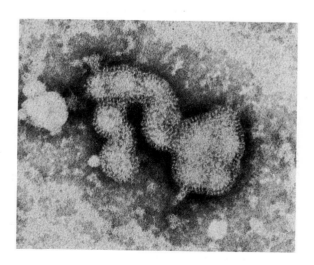

15-13 One of the viruses that causes influenza. Have you ever had the "flu?"

Pneumonia

For many years *pneumonia* (nyoo-MOHN-yuh), along with influenza, which so often led to pneumonia, was the greatest of all killers. Pneumonia is the name given to several different kinds of inflammations of the lungs. The death rate from these diseases fifty years ago was more than six times what it is now. The great drop in the death rate has been largely due to the use of sulfa drugs and antibiotics, especially penicillin.

Pneumonia usually comes on suddenly, with a feeling of being chilly or an actual chill, fever, cough, rapid breathing, pain in the chest, and blood-tinged cough or mucus from the nose. If you have these symptoms, call a doctor at once, and go to bed.

The most common type of bacterial pneumonia is *lobar pneumonia,* and it is usually caused by the *pneumococcus* (NYOO-moh-COK-kus) bacterium. Other bacteria may also cause pneumonia. *Virus pneumonia* develops more slowly than lobar pneumonia and is usually a milder disease.

Tuberculosis

The bacteria that cause *tuberculosis* may invade any part of the body. They most commonly attack the lungs. The germs weaken and often destroy lung tissue.

In the past, tuberculosis of the lungs was one of the leading causes of death. Although this is no longer true, tuberculosis is still a serious disease.

When infection occurs, the body attempts to defend itself against the germs of tuberculosis by forming a wall around them, which prevents them from causing active illness. Many in the older generation have been infected with the germs but have never become ill. In the United States today, children rarely become infected, unless they have been in direct contact with someone with active disease. In infected individuals whose resistance is low, the protective wall around

the germs may give way, and the germs may renew their activity.

A simple test, a *tuberculin* (too-BER-kyoo-lin) skin test, will usually show whether tuberculosis germs have entered the body. Since they often invade the body without causing active disease, a positive test (marked by a temporary lump where the test was made) is not necessarily cause for alarm. However, if you show a positive reaction, you should have a chest X-ray examination to find out if the germs have done any damage.

If the tuberculin test is positive, preventive drug treatment can be given. Such treatment can prevent active disease from ever taking place. If active disease has already started, the drugs can cure it.

Through its Christmas seals, the National Tuberculosis and Respiratory Disease Association has for years carried on a campaign to eliminate tuberculosis. Your teacher can obtain valuable pamphlets and other information from your local tuberculosis association or health department.

15-14 An X-ray examination of the chest will reveal early lesions of tuberculosis before symptoms such as fatigue or coughing appear.

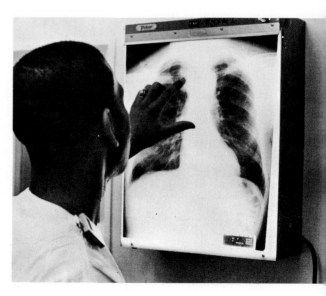

Tuberculosis can be prevented. It has been recommended that every person with a positive tuberculin test receive a year-long course of treatment with the preventive drug **INH** (short for isoniazid). If an active case of tuberculosis is found, all persons in close contact with the patient should be carefully checked for possible infection. One active case in a home or school can spread infection to many others.

In countries that have a high rate of tuberculosis infection, doctors recommend that people be immunized against tuberculosis with the vaccine **BCG,** developed by French scientists. (You will learn more about immunization in Chapter 30.) In this country, BCG is not ordinarily used because the danger of infection is so small.

Tuberculosis can be cured. Before 1947, when the use of certain new drugs began, treatment of tuberculosis was mainly a matter of complete rest in bed and proper nutrition, with an operation to remove or collapse the more seriously affected lung when necessary.

Surgery for tuberculosis is no longer common. The great cure rates in recent years have been the result of treatment by several drugs that have been developed. The three major drugs that have so dramatically cured many tuberculosis patients are isoniazid, **PAS** (short for para-aminosalicylic acid), and *streptomycin,* an antibiotic made from tiny molds living in the soil. As a result of drug therapy, hospital stays have been shortened and some patients get treatment entirely as outpatients.

Diphtheria

Diphtheria is most dangerous to young children, although it is a serious disease at any age. It is caused by certain bacteria which grow mainly in the throat and nose and cause the growth of a gray membrane on the lining of the respiratory tract. Diphtheria usually starts with sore throat, chills, aching pains, and sometimes vomiting and headache. Even when the symptoms are mild, the patient may be in great danger. Diphtheria antitoxin and antibiotics must be given promptly. If treatment is not begun until the third day, the chance of cure is greatly lessened.

The **Schick test** is given to determine whether or not a child is naturally immune to diphtheria. If not, he should be immunized with toxoid. Through immunization, diphtheria deaths have been almost eliminated today.

Whooping Cough

This highly contagious disease causes many more deaths than diphtheria and scarlet fever combined. It may leave a child so weak that he is easily susceptible to pneumonia or tuberculosis. The coughing spells often end with a sound like the word *whoop*. Whooping cough can usually be prevented by vaccination. The accepted immunization timetable for young children starts out at the age of three months or earlier with a combined dose of diphtheria toxoid, tetanus toxoid, and whooping cough vaccine. These injections are repeated at four and at five months of age. Booster shots are given later on, usually before children enter school.

Emphysema

Emphysema (em-fih-SEE-ma) is a lung disease which seems to be increasing. In one state, the known cases increased 300 percent in eight years. In this disease, the air sacs lose their elasticity, trapping air inside, and the lungs themselves may enlarge, lose their elasticity, and cease to function normally. The disease is rare in boys and girls of high school age; most of those who suffer from it are men between 50 and 70 years of age. You may already know that heavy cigarette smoking has been blamed for much of the great increase in lung cancer. *Over 90 percent* of those who have emphysema smoke and have been heavy smokers for most of their lives. Also—most of them live where air pollution is a problem.

We think that emphysema is caused by long-standing infection of the bronchial tubes. Smoking and air pollution, by irritating the mucous membrane, help to bring on infection.

Emphysema begins with slight shortness of breath. Eventually, every breath may become a struggle. Doctors have not yet found treatments that will bring about a definite cure. However, by relieving any infectious conditions, such as bronchitis, colds, and sinus disorders, the patient may be made comfortable.

Fungus Infections

Most molds and moldlike fungi grow on vegetable matter. Among the few fungi that regularly attack man are those that cause athlete's foot and ringworm. There are, however, a few fungus diseases caused by molds that usually grow in soil or on wood or other vegetable matter.

Coccidioidomycosis is a lung disease that usually clears up of its own accord. However, there may be fever with a temperature up to 104° F, with aches all over, chest pains, and, perhaps, a rash like that of measles.

Histoplasmosis produces lung cavities something like those of tuberculosis. The disease is most common in the central part of the United States (as coccidioidomycosis is in the Southwest). Sometimes it is called "summer influenza" in the Midwest.

Other fungus diseases which may attack the lungs include *blastomycosis, cryptococcosis,* and *actinomycosis.* Actinomycosis is caused by a mold related to those from which we get some of our most valuable antibiotics, such as streptomycin and chloramphenicol.

Social and Environmental Influences That Contribute to Respiratory Diseases

You know how pleasant it is to breathe in clean, fresh air when you have been a "prisoner" in a crowded, humid building. As one professor used to say, "Help yourselves to this wonderful air. And all free!" The air is still free. But how wonderful is it?

The quality of the air depends upon where you are. If you are in one of our great cities, you may well be breathing a rather poor grade of air. Automobile and truck fumes, black smoke, ashes from incinerators, dust, and cinders all contaminate the air.

For the past two hundred years, progress in industrial development has meant growing contamination of the atmosphere because of the greater burning of fuels and the production of more irritating or poisonous by-products. Increasing *urbanization* (err-ban-i-ZAY-shun—the movement of people from the country to cities and their suburbs) has made the problem more serious in two ways. More people in a given area means more burning of fuels, more automobiles and trucks, and more and larger power plants. People tend to move to areas where there are more jobs and, of course, many jobs depend on the presence of factories and processing plants. At the same time, businessmen, and even the government, tend to set up industrial plants and offices where there is a concentrated population. All of this leads to more air pollution. Refer to Chapter 5 for more information on the growing problem of air pollution.

While the illness and death rates from tuberculosis have been dropping, those from chronic bronchitis, emphysema, and asthma have been increasing. In 27 years, the number of deaths reported from emphysema increased more than 100 times. Both the increase in air pollution and the increase in

15-15 How does air pollution affect you? What respiratory diseases does it contribute to?

cigarette smoking have probably played a part in causing this increase. The lung-cancer death rate in men is ten times as great as it was thirty years ago.

Poison Gases in the Home

Two gases that may sometimes be breathed in deadly amounts in our own homes are *carbon tetrachloride* (TET-ra-KLOH-ryde) and *carbon monoxide*. Carbon tetrachloride is a clear liquid, but the vapor it forms is rapidly absorbed by the lungs. It is no longer considered a safe cleaning agent for clothes. Dangerous amounts of carbon tetrachloride may be absorbed through breathing before one is even aware of its odor. Carbon tetrachloride can cause convulsions and damage to the skin, kidneys, lungs, and eyes.

Carbon monoxide is a gas that you cannot see or smell at all. It causes more deaths than all other types of gas poisoning put together. It is a colorless, odorless gas found in automobile exhaust gas (an engine running five minutes in a small closed garage makes the air deadly), in illuminating gas, in smoke and fumes from oil heaters, coal stoves, furnaces, coke ovens, and even in

tobacco to some extent. The red blood cells readily take up carbon monoxide in the lungs. They are then unable to carry oxygen. One percent of carbon monoxide in the air would kill you in a few minutes, while much less will make you unconscious in 30 minutes.

The victim of carbon monoxide poisoning usually feels tired and has a headache. He is often dizzy and nauseated, and he may hear a ringing in his ears. Later, his heart flutters or throbs. He may, however, feel nothing and suddenly collapse.

A victim of gas poisoning should be treated at once, even though he is breathing normally. He must rid his blood of the carbon monoxide quickly to prevent later severe sickness or even death. He should be taken into fresh air (not necessarily outdoors), kept warm, and given artificial respiration immediately. Call a physician and an *inhalator* (IN-huh-lay-ter) squad from the fire department. The inhalator allows the victim to inhale oxygen. He should rest quietly. (See Chapter 10 for artificial respiration.)

Artificial respiration is necessary because the medulla has ceased to send out its rhythmical "orders" to the diaphragm and the rib

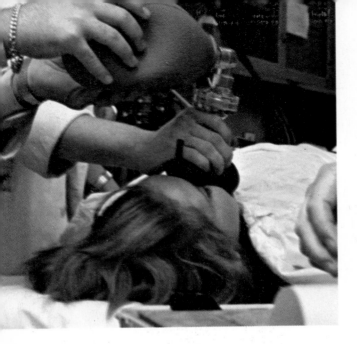

15-16 This girl has been overcome by carbon monoxide poisoning and is receiving artificial respiration. How can accidents like this be prevented?

muscles to make them contract regularly and thus make the victim breathe.

How can you avoid carbon monoxide and gas poisoning?

1. Never run an automobile in a closed garage.
2. Never sit in a closed parked car with the engine running.
3. Never ignore the odor of gas. Open the windows immediately and call the gas company if you cannot locate the source of escaping gas. (Never look for a gas leak with a match!)
4. Always have good ventilation in a room where there is a fire or smoke.
5. Never leave a gas flame burning in a room where someone is sleeping.
6. Try to avoid rubber-tubing connections for gas heaters. If you *must* use one, be sure it is the best. Inspect it often to make sure that it has not become cracked or brittle.
7. Take care that liquids do not boil over on a gas stove. They may put out the flame, and the gas will begin to fill the room.

What You Have Learned

What kind of health practices should you apply in maintaining your health? Check your understanding of the chapter. On a separate sheet of paper, number 1 through 24 and insert the answer from the vocabulary list below. Use each expression, but use each one only once.

6 air sacs	2 epiglottis	1 respiration
5 bronchi	9 filtered	11 rhinitis
21 bronchitis	3 larynx	10 sinuses
24 carbon monoxide	15 medulla	23 streptococcus
9 cilia	8 mucous membranes	19 tuberculosis
18 cold	16 pleura	22 whooping cough
13 diaphragm	12 polyps	4 windpipe
20 emphysema	17 relative humidity	14 vital capacity

Breathing and the chemical reactions inside the cells that yield energy are both included under the term (1) respiration Air is breathed in through the nostrils and then passes through the throat cavity and past a living trap door called the (2) _epiglottis_ . It then goes through the voice box, or (3) _larynx_, and continues down through a strong tube about one inch in diameter called the (4) _windpipe_. In the chest, this tube divides into two smaller tubes called the (5) _bronchi_. Each of these tubes enters the lung on its side of the body and divides to form smaller tubes, which branch and branch again to form tiny tubes that carry air to the (6) _air sacs_. Here oxygen and carbon dioxide are exchanged between blood in the capillaries and the air in the lungs.

Air must be warmed, moistened, and (7) _filtered_ before it reaches the lungs. The (8) _mucous membrane_ moisten the air, and (9) _cilia_ carry mucus, bacteria, and dust away from the lungs. The functions of the air spaces, called (10) _sinuses_, in the bones of your head seem to be to reduce the weight of the head and to supply mucus. The condition that used to be called nasal catarrh is now called (11) _rhinitis_. Sometimes soft growths called (12) _polyps_ may partly close the nostrils.

In breathing, we use both our chest muscles and the sheet of muscle called the (13) _diaphragm_. The amount of air you can force out after taking the deepest possible breath is called your (14) _vital capacity_. Day and night, awake or asleep, we usually breathe as often and as deeply as we need to. The body has an automatic system for regulating breathing, with the principal control in the (15) _medulla_ of the brain. The double, liquid-filled membrane that covers and protects the lung is called the (16) _pleura_.

If the (17) _relative humidity_ of the air in your room is too low, it can increase the danger of respiratory infections. When the mucous membrane of the nose dries out, you are more likely to suffer from a (18) _cold_. Pneumonia, tuberculosis, and diphtheria, the three greatest killers of the past among the respiratory diseases, are now much less common than they used to be. The antibiotic streptomycin and two new drugs have been successful in treating (19) _tuberculosis_. Unlike pneumonia, the lung disease (20) _emphysema_ seems to be increasing. Other important respiratory diseases include influenza; (21) _bronchitis_, or inflammation of the bronchi; and (22) _lung cancer_, which causes more deaths than scarlet fever and diphtheria combined. Both scarlet fever and a very similar serious sore throat are caused by the (23) _streptococcus_ bacterium. You should be careful to avoid breathing poisonous gases, especially odorless (24) _carbon monoxide_.

What You Can Do

An important health practice is given in each of the sentences in this section. Write the reasons for each practice in your notebook and discuss the practices in class.

1. Unless otherwise instructed by your doctor, you should engage in active exercise, such as games, rather than in formal breathing exercises.

2. You should pay attention to the frightening evidence against cigarette smoking and not start this habit.

3. For comfort, the air you breathe indoors should have a relative humidity of about 40 to 50 percent.

4. You should never sit in a closed car with the motor running.

5. You should breathe through your nose except when you need a large amount of air in a short time.

6. If the air you breathe is too dry, you are more likely to catch cold.

7. You should try to resist catching colds by protecting yourself from chilling by drafts and avoiding contact with those who have colds.

8. If you feel very tired and have fever and aches along with symptoms of a cold, you should call a doctor.

Things to Try

You might like to choose one of the following interesting topics to read about and report on. As you read the article in the magazine mentioned below, make accurate notes of the parts you plan to include in your own report. If you have personal knowledge or experience concerning the topics, you can use judgment as to how much of your experience to include. If you find other references in books, magazines, or newspapers, that will be so much the better.

1. Will researchers ever develop a protection against the common cold? To learn about some of their efforts toward this end, read, "On the Way: Vaccines to Snuff Out Sniffles," in *Today's Health,* December 1969. Consult other articles about research into cold prevention. Does a cold vaccine seem a likely possibility? Why do you think so?

2. Who has not had an attack of hiccups? Often amusing to onlookers, usually annoying to the victim, hiccups can be dangerous after operations. Read "Don't Laugh at Hiccups" in *Today's Health,* August 1966, and find out how many ways hiccups can be started and how many remedies have been used to stop them.

Probing Further

Breathing . . . What You Need to Know, by Ruth and Edward Brecher, National Tuberculosis and Respiratory Disease Association, 1968. This pamphlet gives you a brief, clear account of respiratory diseases. It will help you to form good health practices that will help protect your respiratory system.

Elements of Healthful Living, by H. S. Diehl, McGraw-Hill, 1969. This comparatively advanced book explains the structure and functioning of the respiratory and other body systems. It also gives advice on practices to keep us healthy.

The Body, by Alan E. Nourse and editors of *Life,* Time, 1964. With many beautiful colored pictures and unusual diagrams, this book briefly explains the workings of the lungs, air tubes, and other parts of the body.

Health Concepts in Action

Does this statement help express what you have learned?

Through the respiratory system, vital gases are exchanged with the environment.

Applying this concept of respiration, which health practices would you

—continue?

—change?

—begin?

Will you now, as a result of your study, change any of your health objectives?

16 / *Your Blood*

There is an automobile accident in your neighborhood. Several persons are badly injured: some are unconscious, some are bleeding badly, and some have broken arms or legs. You are a member of a first-aid rescue team whose job is to save lives and prevent further injury. The doctor in charge of the team asks you to help him first with those who are bleeding heavily. Why?

A PROBE INTO THE WORK OF THE BLOOD—What is the work of your blood, and which part of the blood carries out each kind of work? You can begin your probe with questions like these:

1. What important substances does the blood carry to every part of your body? What substances does it remove?

2. What are some of the different types of anemia and their causes?

3. What happens when blood clots? How much blood can you safely lose? How can hemophiliacs be helped?

4. What precautions are taken in giving transfusions? What is the Rh factor? What is the importance of blood banks?

5. When does a doctor order a white cell count?

6. What first-aid measures must be taken if large blood vessels are cut during an accident?

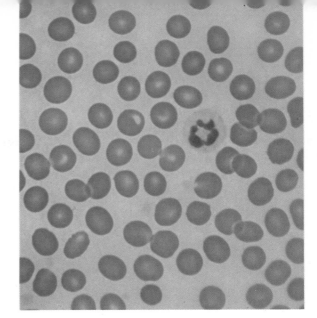

16-1 Photomicrograph of blood cells that have been stained to aid in identification of types. One kind of white blood cell is shown among the red blood cells.

THE IMPORTANCE OF BLOOD

Your muscles, bones, brain, and other organs must have a constant supply of blood, and it must be moving blood. If you wind a rubber band tightly around your finger (*danger*), the finger becomes cold, because the tight band stops the flow of blood to and from the finger. If the flow of blood is cut off for very long, the cells of the finger will die. Then the tissues will begin to shrivel. We would say that *gangrene* (GANG-green) had set in. Cutting off the flow of blood to any part of the body will soon kill that part.

The Work Done by the Blood

Every living cell in your body needs a constant supply of oxygen. Each cell also needs water, salt, sugar, amino acids, vitamins, and many other substances. Every cell produces carbon dioxide and other wastes that it has to get rid of. The blood is essential to life and health because it delivers the substances our cells need and takes away those that are dangerous or are not needed.

The following are some of the substances that the blood carries to every cell in the body: oxygen, water, salt and other minerals, glucose, amino acids, digested fats, vitamins, and hormones.

Actually, the cells of the body are not washed by the blood itself. Oxygen and other needed substances pass through the walls of the smallest capillaries into the watery fluid that surrounds all the tissues. They pass into the cells from this fluid. The cells give off carbon dioxide and other wastes into this tissue fluid. Some of the waste material given off by the cells promptly leaves the tissue fluid to enter the blood vessels. Carbon dioxide does this. Other waste materials have to make a longer trip through tubes called lymph vessels (explained in Chapter 17). The trip is a rapid one, and these wastes also soon enter the bloodstream.

Materials removed from the body cells include carbon dioxide and other waste products, and salt and other minerals. The cells take and give up substances such as water and salt according to their needs.

What Is Blood Made Up Of?

Three types of cells (red blood cells, white blood cells, and platelets) make up a little less than half of the blood, about 45 percent.

The other 55 percent of the blood is a liquid called *plasma*. Although plasma shows no color under the microscope, it is pale yellow when collected in any quantity.

All of these parts of the blood are necessary for health — and life.

RED BLOOD CELLS

If you could focus a microscope on one of the smallest capillaries in your body (as you can do on the tip of a goldfish tail), you would see the red blood cells being carried along in single file. They would be packed so closely that you might wonder how the plasma could move them along. Each red blood cell is shaped somewhat like a doughnut, except that it is slightly hollowed in the middle instead of having a hole completely through it (Figure 16-2). When blood is drawn from the body, the red cells stick together in rows, like stacks of pennies.

Red blood cells are so small that you could put a drop of blood containing about 5,000,-000 in a box this size: ▫ A box this size would be a cubic *millimeter* (MIL-ih-mee-ter). Doctors speak of the number of red blood cells in this space as the "red-cell count." The red-cell count is about 5,000,000 per cubic millimeter for a grown man. For an adult woman the count is about 4,500,000. Newborn babies have about 500,000 more red cells in a drop this size than do grown people, although they have much less blood than adults. See Figure 16-3. Have you had a blood count taken recently?

You have about 20 to 30 trillion (20,000,-000,000,000 to 30,000,000,000,000) red blood cells in your body. That is, you have about 7,000 times as many red blood cells as there are people on the earth! Red blood cells are often called red *corpuscles* (KOR-pus-'lz). *Corpuscle* comes from a Latin word meaning "small body."

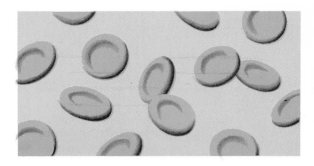

16-2 A drawing of red blood cells. How would you describe their shape? What is the main function of the red blood cells?

16-3 A sample of blood is placed in a laboratory counting chamber. Using a microscope, a technician makes a count of red blood cells by finding the average number of these cells in each small square. Why is this information important?

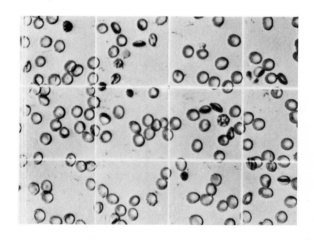

The main work done by red blood cells is to take oxygen from the lungs to all the cells of the body. They also help to carry carbon dioxide from the tissues to the lungs.

The red cells in the blood have no nucleus. You cannot see any structures in them under a school microscope. The most important part of a red blood cell is the coloring matter, called *hemoglobin*; it picks up and carries the oxygen.

The blood in your veins is dark red. Expose a drop of this blood to the air and it instantly turns bright red. This is because the combination of oxygen with hemoglobin turns the hemoglobin a bright red. Hemoglobin combines with oxygen whenever exposed to air in the lungs.

The Short and Busy Life of Red Blood Cells

Red blood cells are made in the red *marrow* of the bones. (Marrow is the soft tissue inside the bones.) Red cells are made all the time, about 2,000,000 every second!

How are blood cells made? All cells are made in the same way; each new cell results when a cell which is already in existence splits in two. Certain cells in red bone marrow split in half to form red blood cells. Figure 16-4 shows what happens. At first a red blood cell has a nucleus, but its nucleus is lost as the cell matures. Follow the red blood cell's development in Figure 16-4.

Red blood cells get many knocks and jolts as they are pumped through the blood vessels. Finally, they wear out and break into pieces, which are often so small that they look like dust under the microscope. Red blood cells live from about 100 to 120 days. About 2,000,000 of them break up every second. Note that the red blood cells are made and destroyed at the same rate.

Broken pieces of red cells are removed from the blood in the *liver* and in the **spleen**, by cells that resemble white blood cells, but are larger. (The spleen is a spongy, bean-shaped organ which lies at the left of and behind the stomach.) The large scavenger cells seize and engulf the tiny fragments of old red cells. Spleen and liver cells also destroy old red cells which have ceased to be useful but have not yet broken up; however, they do not attack healthy red cells.

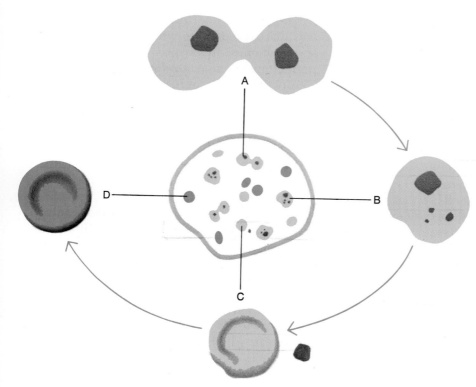

16-4 From an enlarged view of various cells in bone marrow, four stages in the development of a red blood cell are further enlarged. (*A*) Division of mother cell in bone marrow. (*B*) Young cell with nucleus and traces of hemoglobin. (*C*) The nucleus is expelled by the cell, which is now red with hemoglobin. (*D*) Mature, *disklike* cell, soon to be discharged into the blood.

After the spleen and liver cells have digested the broken-up red cells, they save most of the iron that was in them and return it to the blood. The blood takes the iron back to the bones where it is used over and over again in making new red blood cells.

Anemia and Other Blood Diseases

If you become pale or tire too easily, your doctor will make a blood count to find out if you are *anemic* (uh-NEE-mik), which means suffering from *anemia*. An anemic person either does not have enough red cells, or else there is not enough hemoglobin in his red cells. All the cells of his body suffer from lack of oxygen, since it is the hemoglobin in the red cells that carries the oxygen.

In making a blood count, a drop of blood is taken from your finger and spread out on a microscope slide. By counting the number of red cells in the little squares (Figure 16-3), a doctor finds whether you have enough red cells in the blood. To estimate the amount of hemoglobin your red blood cells have, the doctor compares the color of a drop of your blood with the colors on a printed standard scale. The pictures on page 36 show you some of the steps in taking blood for a blood count.

An anemic person may look pale, because his blood is not as red as that of a person with normal blood. He tires easily, because his muscle cells do not get enough oxygen. He may become thin, because oxygen is needed to oxidize the food in the cells so that energy can be released and used to put the materials together that repair or form tissue.

Temporary anemia may be due to loss of blood. *Iron-deficiency anemia* is due to lack of enough iron, a necessary part of hemoglobin. This type of anemia may be cured and prevented by eating foods rich in iron. These include liver, heart, red meat, egg yolk, oysters, green vegetables, and prunes. In severe cases the doctor may prescribe medicines rich in iron. (Anemia may also be caused by certain other deficiencies in diet.)

WARNING: Keep iron pills out of the reach of young children. Serious poisoning has resulted when children have swallowed a number of iron pills.

Folic acid deficiency anemia results from lack of enough folic acid, a vitamin plentiful in liver, green leafy vegetables, yeast, and mushrooms. As vitamin C is needed for the body to make proper use of folic acid, lack of enough vitamin C can cause the same type of anemia as lack of folic acid itself.

In *pernicious anemia* the bone marrow fails to make enough normal red blood cells. Before 1926 it meant certain death. In that year two American doctors (George Minot and W. P. Murphy) discovered that liver contained "something" that caused diseased bone marrow to produce enough healthy red blood cells. This relieved the symptoms of anemia. Deaths from anemia soon became rare when the patients were fed enough liver or liver extract.

Later the wonderful "something" in liver was discovered to be vitamin B_{12}. (You read about vitamins in Chapter 3.) It will not *cure* pernicious anemia; it *relieves* the condition. The patient has a permanent defect and has to take the vitamin as long as he lives. Pernicious anemia is not actually caused by a poor diet, because some people develop the disease while eating the very same foods as do others who remain in the best of health. The trouble is due to the failure of the stomach to make a substance called the *intrinsic* (in-TRIN-sick—from a Latin word meaning "on the inside") *factor.* The intrinsic factor passes from the stomach to the intestine. Without the intrinsic factor, the intestine can absorb very little vitamin B_{12}. If enough vitamin B_{12} is given, some will pass through the intestinal wall and arrest the disease.

Polycythemia (po-li-sy-THEE-mi-ah) is a disease in which the red blood cells greatly increase in number. Too much of any good

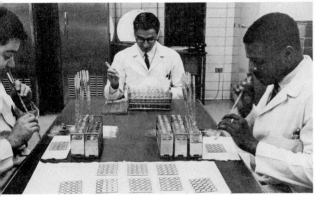

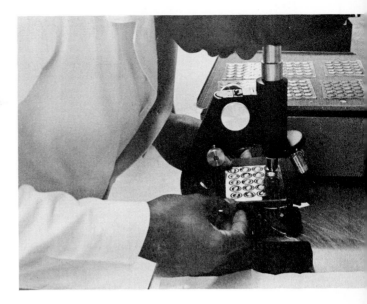

16-5 When you need to have your blood tested, the nurse will first take a blood sample. Then laboratory technicians will prepare the blood for microscopic study. The blood is then studied under the microscope and various chemical tests may be done. Can you think of some reasons why blood must be tested?

thing can be bad, and that is the case with blood cells. The condition is treated in different ways, depending on its cause. Bloodletting, *radioactive* phosphorus, and a variety of chemical agents have been used in treatment. In the disease known as *leukemia* (lyoo-KEE-mee-uh), there are too many white cells rather than red cells. You will learn more about leukemia in Chapter 32.

WHITE BLOOD CELLS— YOUR MICROSCOPIC ARMY

Whenever bacteria or other enemies invade your tissues, your microscopic army of white blood cells moves forward to fight them. White blood cells are colorless, not white (Figure 16-6). There are about 8,000

in each cubic millimeter of blood, or one white blood cell to every 600 or 700 red cells. Several different kinds of white cells live in the blood. Most of them are somewhat larger than the red blood cells, but a few are smaller. The largest white blood cells are more than twice as large in diameter as the red cells.

Every white blood cell has a nucleus. In most of them the nucleus is "pinched in" so that it is almost split into from two to five parts. Under the microscope you can see some kinds of white blood cells move to attack bacteria and other foreign objects, such as bits of dead cells. They surround and engulf the bacteria and then digest them.

Sometimes as many as 20 bacteria can be seen in one white blood cell (Figure 16-7). Often the bacteria remain alive inside the

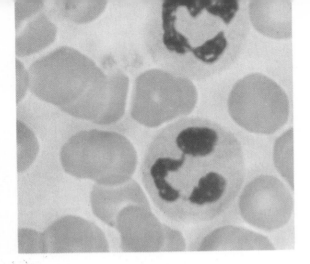

16-6 A photomicrograph showing two white blood cells. How do white blood cells differ from red blood cells in structure and function?

white blood cell, and the battle goes on. The white blood cell begins to digest the bacteria, and the bacteria pour out poisons that may kill the white blood cell.

When the skin is cut or punctured and germs enter the body, your reserve army of white blood cells goes into action. Millions of them hasten to the infected spot. Since the cells have no rigid framework to hold them in one shape, they make themselves very flat and *squeeze* their way out of the smallest capillaries to attack the germs. The battlefield is strewn with dead germs and cells. While most of the white blood cells are fighting the invaders, others work with connective tissue cells to build a wall to keep the infection from spreading. Dead and living white blood cells and bacteria form yellow matter called *pus*, and a walled-off accumulation of pus is called an *abscess*.

"Blood Poisoning"

On rare occasions the battle between white blood cells and bacteria goes against the cells, and they are not able to destroy or isolate the bacteria. This is particularly likely to happen when there is infection in the

walls of blood vessels or the lining of the heart. This condition, once called blood poisoning, is now referred to as *bacteremia* (back-ter-EE-mi-ah), meaning bacteria in the circulating blood.

When the bacteria multiply in the bloodstream, the condition is often called *septicemia* (sep-ti-SEE-mi-ah). The most serious condition results when the bacteria in the blood invade many spots throughout the body and form numerous abscesses. This is more likely to occur with staphylococcus bacteria. The patient must rest in bed and receive ample food and water. If he is too weak to eat, he must be given blood, plasma, or amino acid solutions intravenously. Antibiotics are given to control the bacteria. Sometimes the doctor must give the largest amounts of antibiotics that the patient's body can tolerate.

Destroying bacteria is only one of the important jobs done by white blood cells. White blood cells make substances that work against snake venom and the poisons produced by some bacteria. They also work to wall off splinters and other foreign matter, and dead tissue, so that the body can get rid of these unwanted things.

16-7 Photomicrograph of a white blood cell engulfing bacteria. When would a white blood cell count be important?

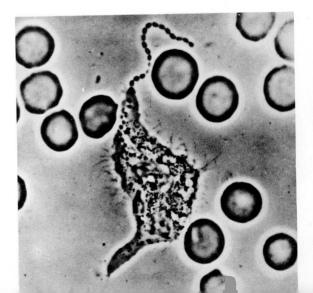

■ Have you been troubled by pimples or by an infected cut or wound? Did the presence of the pus irritate you? Did you realize that pimples and wounds are battlegrounds for your white blood cells? Discuss with your teacher and classmates some ways in which you can eliminate many common causes of accidental infection.

White-Cell Count

When the doctor suspects appendicitis, he makes a "white-cell count." He does this in the same way that he would make a count of red blood cells (Figure 16-3). If he finds too many white cells, it may mean an infected appendix, since bone marrow makes white cells faster when there are more bacteria to fight. Abscessed teeth, diseased tonsils, and other infections may also cause a jump in the number of white blood cells. Do you see why a white-cell count is an important tool for a doctor to use?

Where Are the White Blood Cells Made?

Like all other cells, white blood cells are made when certain cells split in two. Most white blood cells are made "next door" to the red cells in the bone marrow. The white cells are made in much the same way as the red cells are made (Figure 16-4). Other white blood cells are made in the spleen and some in the *lymph nodes.* (You will read about the lymph nodes in Chapter 18.)

Too Few White Blood Cells

Agranulocytosis (a-gran-yoo-loh-sy-TOH-sis) is a rare disease, but a dangerous one. The name refers to the disappearance of the *granulocytes* (GRAN-yoo-loh-sytes) which are the most numerous of the different kinds of white blood cells and the ones that act as our first line of defense against bacteria. The pa-

tient suffers from high fever, chills, ulcers in the mouth and extreme weakness.

The reduction of white blood cells can be the result of various kinds of damage to the tissues that make the white cells. The damage might be caused by radiation beyond certain levels. In rare instances, certain drugs used to treat other conditions might cause such damage in unusually sensitive persons.

PLATELETS AND PLASMA

Billions of tiny, flat bodies called platelets are carried throughout the body by the plasma. There are about one tenth as many platelets as red blood cells. They are from one third to half as large as the red cells. Like the red cells, platelets have no nucleus. However, they have no hemoglobin either. Most of the time they seem to do nothing. Yet they are important in the clotting of blood. When a blood vessel is cut and bleeding occurs, the platelets break up and give off a substance needed for the blood to clot.

Plasma—the Liquid Part of the Blood

Plasma forms more than half of the blood. Plasma is about 90 percent water, with more than 200 other substances dissolved in it. As the blood travels through the body, living body cells take various materials from the plasma and give up other things to it.

Some of the substances (other than red and white blood cells and platelets) which the plasma carries are

1. *Food materials*, which include amino acids, sugar, tiny drops of fat, vitamins, and dissolved minerals (such as common salt, iodine, and calcium).
2. *Dissolved gases*, mostly carbon dioxide being taken to the lungs.
3. *Wastes* other than carbon dioxide that cells of the body must get rid of.

4. *The blood proteins.* These are needed for blood clotting and fighting disease germs. They prevent **dropsy**, a condition in which water leaks out of the blood vessels into the tissues. There are three principal types of plasma proteins: (*1*) **Albumin** (al-BYOO-min) is most important in preventing the blood from losing too much water to the tissues. (*2*) **Globulin** (GLOB-yoo-lin). One kind of globulin (*gamma* globulin) is important in making antibodies. (*3*) **Fibrinogen** (fy-BRIN-oh-jen) is essential for blood clotting.
5. *Hormones.* These are substances from the endocrine glands that regulate the body in many ways, from preventing severe mental retardation to causing a boy's voice to change.
6. **Antibodies.** These are substances whose primary purpose is to fight disease. Most antibodies are made by the blood itself or by the lymph tissue or connective tissue.

16-8 A centrifuge is used in the laboratory to separate the blood cells from the plasma.

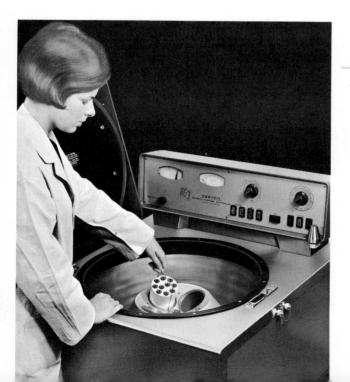

Why Bleeding Stops

A cut, or even a scratch, might have caused your death when you were a baby except for one thing. Your blood was able to form a clot that stopped bleeding. Clots form when body cells are injured and when blood is exposed to the air (Figure 16-9). Here are some of the steps that occur when a clot forms:

1. Some platelets break up. Platelets and injured body cells give off chemicals which start a series of changes.
2. As a result, the dissolved protein fibrinogen changes into threads of a solid called **fibrin** (FY-brin).
3. The fibrin threads stick together to form a network of threads. Blood cells get caught in this network to form a clot.

■ What are the dried scabs that form over cuts or scratches?

Clotting Time

The length of time it takes a person's blood to clot is very important. Usually the time is five minutes or less. A surgeon needs to know his patient's clotting time before he operates, so that he can guard against **hemorrhage** (HEM-er-ij), which is excessive bleeding. If you observe clotted blood which has been standing for a few hours, you will find that the clot has shrunk in size because the plasma has separated from the clot. The plasma that is left after the clot has been removed is called **serum** (SEE-rum). Serum is important in the prevention and treatment of many diseases.

Protection Against Internal Blood Clots

Blood must be able to clot normally to keep us from losing too much of it. Sometimes, however, blood clots in the wrong

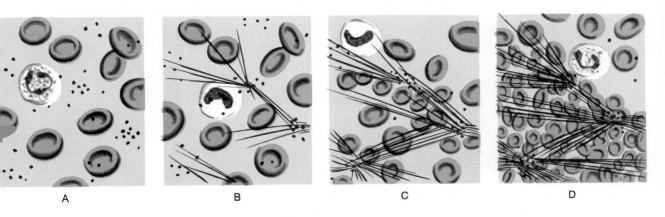

A   B   C   D

16-9   Stages in the formation of a blood clot.

place—with dangerous results. After an operation the doctor and nurse often tell the patient to move his legs and to wiggle his toes. This is to keep the blood moving and to prevent formation of clots in the veins. After injuries and in some diseased conditions such as hardening of the arteries, the injured cells may pour out substances that start the formation of a clot. The process in which clots are formed in the blood vessels is called *thrombosis* (throm-BOH-siss). A blood clot in a blood vessel can block the flow of blood to the heart or brain. You will read more about this in Chapter 32.

How to Stop Visible Bleeding

Visible bleeding may range from nose bleeding to loss of blood from a major wound. A nosebleed can usually be treated successfully, even if it does not stop in a few moments of its own accord. If a nosebleed persists:

1. Have the patient sit erect, with his head thrown back slightly. He should breathe through his mouth and loosen his collar.
2. Apply a cold, wet compress to the nose.
3. If necessary, press the nostrils together firmly for 4 or 5 minutes.
4. In severe cases, a strip of sterile gauze

or cotton can be packed gently back (not up) into the nostril, with the end protruding for removal.

If these measures are not effective in a few minutes, consult a doctor. Accidental injury of known or unknown cause may lie behind the bleeding. Tell the patient not to blow his nose for several hours.

In slight, superficial wounds, a small amount of bleeding actually does more good than harm, because it cleanses the wound and tends to wash out germs. Usually, you can easily check *capillary bleeding*, the kind occurring in most minor wounds, by placing a bandage directly over the wound. You can often slow the flow of blood from a cut finger by holding your arm above your head and letting gravity help.

If injury results in severe bleeding, you must plan to stop the flow of blood before you attend to anything else. To stop severe bleeding, you must immediately apply *pressure*, whether the blood comes from an artery or a vein. The pressure, according to the circumstances, should be (1) direct pressure on, in, or over the wound (Figure 16-10), (2) a bandage compress (sterile if possible), placed directly on the wound and held tightly in place by a snug bandage (Figure 16-11); or (3) finger pressure on pressure

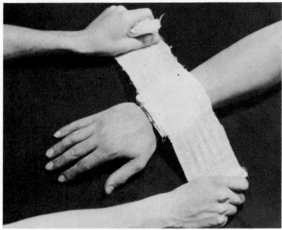

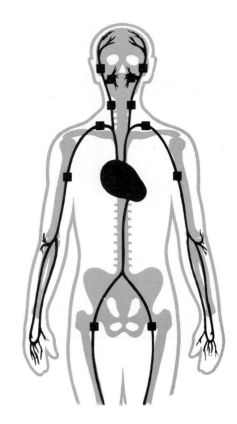

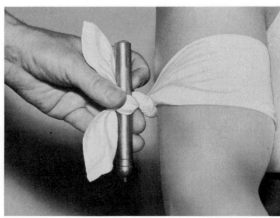

16-10 (*Top left*) Applying direct pressure over a wound to stop bleeding. Use only a sterile gauze bandage, if one is available. Otherwise, use a clean handkerchief.

16-11 (*Bottom left*) A bandage compress being applied to a wound. Several thicknesses of sterile gauze attached to a long strip of gauze make up the bandage compress. It can be tied or taped in place.

16-12 (*Top right*) The black spots on this diagram show the main points at which an important artery may be pressed against a bone. Pressure applied at any of these points will stop bleeding from a cut farther from the heart. Why must the pressure point lie between the wound and the heart?

16-13 The tourniquet. Never apply it unless bleeding cannot be stopped by any other means. Then use a belt or folded strip of cloth for the tourniquet, never a wire or cord which might cut more blood vessels. What might happen if a tourniquet is left in place too long?

points, which stops the flow of blood before it reaches the exposed wound (Figure 16-12).

The last resort for severe bleeding is a *tourniquet* (TOOR-nih-ket), a bandage placed around a limb so tightly that it stops circulation. *It should be used only when hemorrhage threatens a person's life.* Never apply a tourniquet if bleeding can be controlled in any other way. The chances are that you will go through your life without ever seeing a wound that requires the use of a tourniquet. According to the American National Red Cross, crushing wounds or large lacerations, where large arteries are severed, or cases of partial or complete severance of a body part are the only instances where application of a tourniquet may be justified. Left on too long, a tourniquet may cause the loss of a limb through gangrene. If a tourniquet does have to be used, the following procedure should be followed:

1. Place the tourniquet close to the wound and between the heart and the wound. There should be unbroken skin between the tourniquet and the wound. (Figure 16-13 shows a tourniquet applied to the upper arm.)

2. Make sure it is applied tightly enough to stop bleeding. If not properly applied, it may increase bleeding.

3. Place a big *T* with pencil or lipstick on the victim's forehead to warn that a tourniquet has been applied.

4. Once you apply a tourniquet, leave it on until a doctor arrives. Get a doctor as quickly as possible. Attach a note to the victim telling where the tourniquet is and *when* (to the hour and minute) you applied it.

5. Make a tourniquet only from flat material about two inches wide, such as a bandage, stockings, or a wide belt. *Never* use wire, rope, or sash cord; they may destroy tissues and blood vessels.

Internal Bleeding

Internal bleeding may come from the lungs, stomach, or bowels. Blood from the lungs is bright red and frothy, and is coughed up. It is usually due to tuberculosis or to a puncture wound, such as a broken rib driven into the lung. Blood from the stomach is usually dark brown and has the appearance of coffee grounds. It is commonly due to stomach ulcers or to wounds of the stomach. Blood from the bowels will be bright red if from the lower portion of the intestines, or a dark tarry mass if from the upper area.

A person with internal bleeding is usually restless, anxious, and thirsty. He may be pale and weak, and have a weak, rapid pulse. Keep him lying flat on his back, and as quiet as possible, but turn his head to one side for coughing or vomiting. Keep him warm. Avoid any kind of stimulant. If the patient has a chest injury and cannot breathe while lying flat, prop him up, but only enough to let him breathe. Call a doctor at once.

Hemophilia

This disease is due to an inherited defect that causes the blood to clot very slowly. As a result, the parents of children with this condition live in constant fear, since a slight wound can be fatal.

The curious thing about **hemophilia** (hee-moh-FIL-ee-uh), or bleeders' disease, is the fact that while usually only the males in a family have it, it is transmitted by women. That is, a man with the disease always has inherited the condition from his mother. The blood of the mother of a man with hemophilia clots more slowly than does the average person's blood, but not slowly enough to cause a dangerous condition. Until a few years ago no cases of hemophilia in women were known, but since 1951 doctors have reported a few women "bleeders." Instead of clotting in five minutes, the blood may keep flowing from a small wound for an hour or more. When bleeding is from a surface wound, pressure and cold can help. **_Thrombin_** (THROM-bin), one of the substances necessary for natural clotting, when applied as a powder or in solution, may stop bleeding. Powdered fibrinogen may also be applied. However, when the bleeding is very severe, transfusions of plasma or whole blood must be given.

How Much Blood Can You Safely Lose?

The total amount of blood in an average-sized man is about 12 to 13 pints, and in an average-sized woman about 9 to 10 pints. Healthy adults *may* recover after losing almost 40 percent of their blood, even without being given a blood transfusion. However,

16-14 Blood, already typed, is stored for future use in a hospital blood bank. Have any members of your family ever donated blood? Have any members of your family ever had a transfusion? yes

loss of about 3 pints can be fatal, especially if the loss has been rapid.

When a person gives a pint of blood to a **_blood bank,_** his plasma will go back to its normal volume in a day or two, but it will take 4 to 8 weeks before he has as many red blood cells and as much hemoglobin as he had before. A blood bank is a supply of whole blood kept in sterile bottles that are classified and labeled according to ABO blood types and Rh factor. The blood is kept in a refrigerator at a temperature about ten degrees above freezing. See Figure 16-14.

The water and the salt in your blood are important. You can lose water and salt by losing blood, by profuse sweating, and in other ways. Sick people sometimes cannot drink enough water or other liquid. They may lose too much liquid by vomiting. Doctors often inject **_normal salt solution_** when any of these things happen. It has the same salt concentration as normal plasma, which is the equivalent of one level teaspoon of salt to one pint of boiled water. This solution does not irritate the tissues or destroy blood cells, because it has the same proportion of salt as blood, saliva, tears, and the other body fluids. Injecting pure distilled water into the veins would be dangerous. Normal salt solution is not satisfactory in the case of hemorrhage. In this condition the best treatment is blood transfusion, and the next best is transfusion of plasma.

SAVING LIVES WITH BLOOD

Blood transfusions—causing the blood of one person to flow into the veins of another—were first tried out centuries ago. Even the blood of animals was used. Unfortunately, several of these experiments promptly caused the death of the patients. It was not until the discovery of the four common blood types that it became safe to give blood transfusions.

Types of Human Blood

The four best-known blood types are based on the type of red blood cells they contain. These four types of cells look the same under the microscope, but some types will cause others to clot. These four groups or types of human blood are called A, B, AB, and O. Most populations show all four blood types but in different numbers. For example, 3 percent of the North American population have type AB blood, 10 percent have type B blood, and the rest are about equally divided between types O and A blood. This is not true for *all* populations. For example, of native Australian Aborigines who have been tested, none have had type B blood. When the wrong bloods are mixed, clumping of blood cells may result. For example, type A red cells that are dropped into type B blood clump together. These clumps could cause fatal injury as they pass through the heart or brain. Doctors used to believe that it was safe to give Group O blood to persons with any of the other types, and that persons with Group AB could accept any of the other types. Group O was classed as the **universal donor** and Group AB as the **universal recipient.** Enough trouble followed, however, that doctors always try to give a patient a transfusion from his own blood group.

Blood types are inherited, like eye color and certain other traits. These traits often "skip" one or more generations. This is why your eye color and blood group may differ from those of your father or mother.

Rh Factor

A substance called the Rh factor was first found in the blood of the **Rhesus** (REE-sus) monkey and hence was named after it. About 85 percent of the human race have this factor in their blood; they are **Rh-positive**. About 15 percent lack it; they are **Rh-negative.**

The Rh factor acts like a foreign substance to anyone who is Rh-negative. If an Rh-negative person receives Rh-positive blood, his own blood will make a substance called an antibody, which will act against the Rh-positive blood. An Rh-negative person may receive *one* Rh-positive transfusion safely. If a second transfusion is given to him, the antibody will make the Rh-positive cells clump. The Rh-negative person may be killed by the second transfusion because of the clumping of the transfused blood cells.

Let us suppose that an Rh-negative woman marries an Rh-positive man. In the past many babies born of such marriages have died. The *first* child in such a marriage is usually not harmed. A second or later child may be seriously injured. If the baby inherits the Rh factor from his father, his mother's blood may produce so many antibodies against it that the baby becomes severely anemic or, worse, dies before or shortly after birth.

Doctors usually test the blood of a woman before childbirth to find out if she is Rh-negative. If she is negative and the father Rh-positive, the doctor is prepared to take the best steps to protect both the baby and the mother.

How Transfusions Are Given

To give a blood transfusion before World War I, an artery of the person giving the blood had to be connected by a tube to a vein of the person receiving it. During that war, methods were discovered to prevent blood from clotting, so that it could be taken from the donor, set aside for a few minutes, and then transfused into the patient's vein (Figure 16-15). We are now able to keep blood under refrigeration in a blood bank for 21 days or more.

During World War II scientists discovered how to remove the blood cells from blood and send the plasma to remote battlefields. They found that plasma was almost as effective as whole blood in many cases.

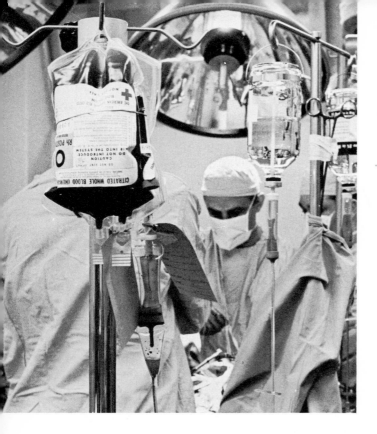

16-15 Essential to the success of this heart operation is the transfusion of blood. What must be done to a donor's blood before it can be transfused?

Plasma can be dried into a powder or sealed as a liquid and kept as long as wanted; it also has the advantage of not having to be typed.

Many Uses for Blood

Red blood cells are used in the treatment of many conditions, including anemia, stomach ulcers, burns, and infected wounds. As we can now separate the different plasma proteins, these substances can be preserved and used as they are needed. Dry gamma globulin can be kept for several years. Another type of globulin helps check loss of blood in hemophilia.

Fibrin is made into *fibrin film* (very thin sheets, foams, plastics, and glues for use in delicate surgery). These blood products are especially valuable because they are absorbed by the tissues of the body. Foreign substances are not absorbed and hence often become irritating to the tissues. Spongy *fibrin foam* is used in closing surgical and accidental wounds. Fibrin film looks like a very delicate cellophane. Surgeons use it to cover nerves and the brain after operations.

Social and Environmental Influences Affecting the Blood

What we eat may help very much to determine how healthy we are, and failing to get enough of certain nutrients can cause our blood to lack essential substances. The environment we live in may cause poor nutrition, resulting in anemia and many other serious disorders. In overcrowded countries, where food production falls short of the population increase, there tends to be a growing lack of all nutrients. Several different nutrients are necessary in the making of blood cells, hemoglobin, and plasma.

As more and more surgery is performed, more blood is needed for transfusions, and the cost of a pint of blood for transfusion has greatly increased. Some unions and some large corporations maintain their own blood banks; a person who donates blood receives credit that will allow him free transfusions later when he or his family may need them.

During World War II and the Korean War, a great many people donated blood to the Red Cross. Many still do this. However, there are a number of professional blood donors who are paid for each pint that they contribute. Many of these professional donors are in excellent health and are doing a valuable public service. There is always a slight danger, though, that professional and, for that matter, other donors may give blood contaminated with disease germs. *Serum hepatitis* (HEP-uh-ti-tis) (a disease of the

16-16 A commercial blood bank where donors are paid. What are some of the dangers in using blood from a professional donor?

liver) and malaria are the principal diseases that may be transmitted by blood transfusions. The germs of these diseases may be in a person's blood without his showing any symptoms. When these same germs are injected through a blood transfusion into another person, the latter may come down with the disease.

However, various procedures are being perfected to prevent the transmission of diseases through blood transfusions, and the advantages of blood transfusions far outweigh the risks. Many people now in perfect health would not be alive if they had not received transfusions. Many patients have received dozens of pints of blood with no ill effects.

POISONS IN THE BLOOD

Many poisons may invade the blood or be produced there. If carbon monoxide enters the lungs when one breathes, it is absorbed by the blood, where it does its damage. It combines with hemoglobin in the red blood cells and thus prevents the hemoglobin from taking up oxygen. Many substances that the body needs become poisonous when they enter the blood in excessive amounts. Among these are iron, carbon dioxide, and even oxygen.

Toxins are poisons made by living things. As you read in the section on white blood cells, disease bacteria release their toxins inside the cells, blood, or tissue fluid of the victim. Poisonous snakes, insects, ticks, and some other small animals inject their toxins into our blood or tissues when they bite us.

Snakebite

As far as poisonous snakebites are concerned, the United States gets off rather well. Recently, about 3,000 deaths from snakebite were reported around the world in one year. Only 15 of these were in this country. Our poisonous snakes belong to two families. One family includes the gaily-colored coral snakes which are found from North Carolina south and from Colorado south and west. Their poison affects the nervous system and can stop breathing. The other family, the pit vipers, include the copperhead, the cottonmouth or water mocassin, and several kinds of rattlesnakes. A pit viper has a pit on each side of its face. The pit or depression is very sensitive to temperature changes; it alerts the snake to the presence of the small, warmblooded animals it feeds upon, such as rats and field mice. The poison of rattlesnakes and the other pit vipers attacks the blood vessels, dissolving some of the smallest ones and destroying the lining of some veins and arteries.

If someone is bitten by a poisonous snake, apply a tight bandage just above the bite to cut off the flow of blood back to the heart and prevent the poison from being carried throughout

16-17 (*Top left*) Copperhead. (*Top right*) Black widow spider. (*Bottom left*) Jellyfish. (*Bottom right*)
Stingray. Each of these organisms is poisonous. What are the effects of the poisons each produces?
How would you treat a bite or sting inflicted by each of the above?

the body. The bandage is intended to prevent the nerve poison of the coral snake from reaching the brain and the poison of the pit vipers from reaching more blood vessels. The bandage should be tight enough to slow drainage through the veins, but not tight enough to prevent completely any blood from reaching the limb. You should loosen the bandage for one minute every thirty minutes. Keep the patient at rest. Do not let him walk, but arrange to get him to a doctor immediately. Don't give him alcoholic drinks. If you can get ice, you may "freeze" the area of the bite with ice packs. This should slow circulation and possibly check the flow of poison to other parts of the body.

There are now *antivenins* (AN-ti-VEH-nins, "against poisons") for the poisons of both our native families of snakes. The doctor will probably inject the appropriate antivenin as soon as possible.

The Gila monster is our only poisonous lizard. Its venom (poison) acts like rattlesnake venom. Treatment is the same as for rattlesnake poisoning.

Bee and Wasp Stings

Most of the time, a bee or wasp sting is regarded as a painful nuisance. Every year a certain number of people are killed by them, however. Some people are profoundly sensitive to the toxins of these insects. Some people succumb to the effect of great numbers of stings, as when they disturb a beehive or a hornets' nest. Worker bees leave the stinger in the wound. This should be carefully removed because it continues to pour in poison. Applying a fairly strong household ammonia solution (poison) can reduce discomfort. If there are signs of collapse, a doctor should be seen at once.

Spiders and Other Pests

Don't touch them, but the big, bright red, yellow, and black spiders and the large hairy ones are almost never dangerous. The only two United States spiders known occasionally to cause death are the small black widow and the even smaller brown house spider, sometimes called the brown widow. There have been exaggerated reports about the frequency of poisoning by these spiders, but if you do get bitten by one, it may be a serious matter. If you should be bitten, you will know it, because there is soon sharp, sometimes excruciating, pain. There is not much an untrained person can do if bitten except see a doctor as soon as possible. Our big, hairy Southwestern spiders, usually called tarantulas, are harmless to people and rarely bite. Bites by similar big spiders that come as stowaways on fruit from the tropics may be more poisonous and cause redness and swelling. An extremely small number of these tropical-spider bites have caused death.

American *centipedes* (SENT-uh-peeds) have never been known to cause death in the United States. Two of the *scorpions* (SKOR-pee-uns) in the Southwest are dangerous, especially to children under the age of three. Scorpions do not bite; they use the large stinger at the end of their tail. With all of these poisonous creatures, the danger is much greater to small children. Generally speaking, the larger and heavier the victim, the less danger there is.

Ticks are a more important nuisance — and they are common in most parts of the country. Ticks carry the germs of some serious diseases, such as Rocky Mountain spotted fever and tularemia. They may also cause a temporary "tick paralysis." A few persons have died from tick paralysis. It is important promptly to find any ticks with their heads buried in the patient's skin and promptly remove them. Never jerk a tick out of the skin of a person or a pet animal. The head may be left in the wound where it may decay and set up a serious infection. To remove ticks, cover them with oil, butter, or grease. This will clog their breathing tubes and force them to move. Holding a hot object against them will also make them release their grip.

Mites are related to ticks, but are much smaller. The disease called *itch*, or *scabies*, is caused by mites that tunnel through the skin and lay their eggs in their burrows. You read about scabies in Chapter 9. Another mite that causes intense itching is the redbug, or chigger, whose tiny red larva (young stage) injects an irritating saliva. Bathing immediately after walking through tall grass may get rid of them. A mixture of a small amount of camphor and carbolic acid (*poison*) applied to the skin will kill the mites and reduce itching. Scratching the skin greatly increases the irritation.

Biting insects of many kinds abound in many regions. Through the ages, millions of people have died of such diseases as malaria, yellow fever, and plague carried by these pests.

Mosquitoes have perhaps done more harm than any other insects. In the brief Arctic summer, mosquitoes often darken the sky and force explorers to cover their hands with gloves and their faces with netting. Mosquitoes may inject the germs of malaria, yellow fever, various kinds of *encephalitis* (often called sleeping sickness), and the tiny worms that cause **elephantiasis** (el-eh-fan-TYE-uh-sis), a condition in which the legs or arms or other parts may swell to many times their proper size. Other kinds of mosquitoes may only cause skin irritations. This can be extremely annoying to a person allergic to mosquito saliva.

Fleas and lice have also often caused widespread, deadly epidemics. Plague, the Black Death of the Middle Ages that killed one third of the population in many countries, is most often carried by flea bites, but also by direct contact with sick rats or people.

Lice carry typhus fever and other diseases caused by **rickettsias** (rih-KET-si-ahs), tiny germs intermediate in size between bacteria and viruses. Some forms of typhus and other rickettsial diseases are also carried by bites of fleas, mites, and ticks, and are also spread by contact with rats, mice, and people ill with the disease. Many other diseases in tropical countries are carried by bites of insects. You will read more about rickettsial diseases in Chapter 29.

What to Do About Bites and Stings

The following substances may be applied to relieve itching and pain and to help to prevent inflammation:

1. A paste made of baking soda and cold cream.
2. A compress moistened with ammonia water.
3. Calamine lotion.
4. Immediate application of ice.

Remove ticks, fleas, lice, or mites at once. A warm bath with plenty of soap should suffice with all except embedded ticks. Cover a clinging tick with petroleum jelly or oil to clog its breathing pores. Sooner or later, perhaps in half an hour, it will remove its head.

Stingrays and Jellyfish

Stingrays are flattened fish that lie on the sea bottom along many of our southern coasts. If you step or fall on one, it will pierce your flesh with its sting and inject its poison. Sometimes nothing worse results than the pain and tearing of the flesh. However, fever, shortness of breath, low blood pressure, unconsciousness, or even death may follow.

Soft and beautiful jellyfish, which often float about in vast numbers, can shoot thousands of tiny weapons, each with a load of poison, into the skin of anyone who touches them. Except that they do not make wounding tears in the skin, the results can be much the same as after a stingray attack. The Portuguese man-of-war is a rather large jellyfish and one of the most common offenders in warmer waters.

For first aid after stingray attacks, the wound must be immediately and thoroughly washed with fresh water. The sheath of the stinger should be removed if visible because the longer the sheath stays in the wound the more poison will be absorbed. This is one case where a tourniquet needs to be applied if the wound is in the arm or leg. Tourniquets are explained on page 299. A doctor should be secured at once if the victim appears ill. If the wound is in the chest or abdomen, the victim must be taken to a hospital.

The skin area that has touched a jellyfish must be flushed thoroughly with fresh water. Measures similar to those for relief of irritation due to insect bites can then be applied. Artificial respiration and sedatives may be needed after encounters with either stingrays or jellyfish.

What You Have Learned

What kind of health practices should you apply in maintaining your health? Check your understanding of the chapter. On a separate sheet of paper, number 1 through 24 and insert the answer from the vocabulary list below. Use each expression, but use each one only once.

15 abscess	*12* gangrene	*14* pus
5 anemia	*13* hemoglobin	*1* red blood cells
10 bacteremia	*8* hemophilia	*22* Rh factor —
4 bone marrow	*16* hemorrhage	*54* serum
20 dropsy	*11* intrinsic factor	*17* thrombosis
7 fibrin	*9* leukemia	*21* transfusion
6 fibrinogen —	*3* platelets	*23* universal donors
18 gamma globulin	*19* proteins	*2* white blood cells

Each part of the blood has its own work to do. (1)_____ carry oxygen to all parts of the body. (2)_____ destroy bacteria. Blood-clotting is aided by the breaking up of the (3)_____. Although some white blood cells are made in the lymph nodes and some in the spleen, most of them, along with the red blood cells, are made in the (4)_____. A person suffering from (5)_____ either does not have enough red blood cells or does not have enough hemoglobin in these cells.

When blood clots, soluble (6)_____ changes into threads of solid (7)_____. An inherited defect in which the blood clots too slowly is (8)_____. Other serious blood conditions include (9)_____, in which there are too many white blood cells, and (10)_____, in which there are bacteria in the circulating blood. Pernicious anemia can be caused by lack of either vitamin B$_{12}$ or a substance made by the stomach called (11)_____. When the supply of fresh blood is cut off to a finger or toe, tissues die, and we say that (12)_____ sets in.

The bright red color of blood is due to the combination of oxygen with (13)_____. The yellow material that forms after a battle between white blood cells and bacteria is called (14)_____. When there is an accumulation of this material surrounded by a wall of tissue, we call the local condition an (15)_____. A profuse escape of blood from the blood vessels is called a (16)_____. Blood-clotting is necessary to save life, yet sometimes blood clots in the wrong place — with serious results. The process in which blood clots are formed in the blood vessels is called (17)_thrombosis_

A substance dissolved in the plasma that helps to make antibodies is (18)_____. This substance, as well as fibrinogen and plasma albumin, belongs to the group of substances called plasma (19)_____. Albumin and the other members of this group of substances are needed to prevent (20)_____, a condition in which too much water leaks out of the blood vessels into the tissues.

Allowing blood from another person to flow into a person's vein is called a (21)_____. Before giving the patient such blood, the blood of the patient must be matched with that which is to flow into his veins. Not only must blood be matched for the four well-known types; it must also be checked for the (22)_R. H. factor_. Formerly persons with Group O blood were classed as (23)_universal donors_

Plasma that is left after blood has clotted and the clot has been removed is called (24)_____. This substance is important in the prevention and treatment of many diseases.

What You Can Do

Consider each of the problems listed below. After you have read your text and other references on the subject, write answers to the questions in your notebook. Also write an explanation for each topic. In class, compare your answers and explanations with those of your classmates. Does your study of these topics lead you to form good health practices?

1. Suppose that a blood test shows that you have too few red blood cells. What name is given to this condition? What might be the cause? What are some of the things the doctor might recommend to relieve or correct this condition?

2. After receiving a small cut on his hand, a person continues to wash away the blood to keep the wound from showing. Is this the wisest thing for him to do? Why, or why not?

3. Sometimes plasma, rather than whole blood, is given to patients. What might be the reasons?

4. How might social and environmental influences affect a person's blood?

5. Testing your blood, the doctor finds that you have far more white blood cells than normal. What could be the cause?

6. Taking a shower after a long hike, you find that a number of large ticks have buried their heads in your skin. What should you do? What is the danger in improperly removing ticks?

7. Sitting on the porch one night in the country, you are badly bitten by mosquitoes. What are some of the possible ill effects of mosquito bites?

8. Assume that you are to receive a blood transfusion. Ordinarily the blood that you are to receive will be carefully "cross-matched" with yours to make sure that it is of the same blood group and is the same as to Rh. Now think a bit. Under what circumstances would it be important for you to know both your blood group and whether you are Rh-positive or Rh-negative? Do you know your blood group?

Things to Try /

The study of health (and also of disease) is progressing so fast that you are likely to learn of entirely new scientific developments from newspapers, magazines, radio, and television.

You can feel the thrill of discovery by doing some research on any of the following topics and reporting your results to your class. Be sure to give your references for any new facts that you find. Besides the references given below, refer to your text and to other books listed at the end of this and other chapters.

1. *New hope for victims of hemophilia.* You will find out about interesting developments dealing with this formerly hopeless affliction in "Breakthrough for Bleeders if They Can Afford It," by A. J. Snider in *Science Digest,* August, 1971. You might also like to read "Man with 586 Blood Brothers" in *Ebony,* February 1967.

2. *What is being done about the problem of Rh?* Progress is being made in dealing with Rh incompatibility, which has often meant disaster in the past. Read "Unborn Baby's Fight to Live," by J. Blank in *Redbook,* March 1967; and "GG versus Rh Disease" in *Newsweek,* January 30, 1967.

3. *Blood banks, blood types, and blood substitutes.* These are some related subjects that you might wish to investigate. You might like to learn more about all of them or about any one. Here are two interesting articles: "Rare Blood to the Rescue," by P. Brady in *Today's Health,* May 1967; and "Blood Substitute" in *Science Digest,* February 1967.

Probing Further

Blood, by Leo Vroman, Natural History Press, 1967. This entertaining book will introduce you to many other aspects of the blood besides those discussed in your textbook.

American Red Cross. Ask your local chapter for the latest pamphlets dealing with blood.

The Machinery of the Body, by A. J. Carlson, V. E. Johnson, and H. M. Cavert, University of Chicago Press, 1961. An advanced book, which gives a detailed and accurate account of the blood and circulation.

Your Blood and You, by S. R. Riedman, Abelard, 1963. You will enjoy this account of the blood—how it carries oxygen and food, and how it is used in medical practice. The book tells about the hormones and proteins that blood contains and relates stories of men who pioneered in blood research.

Health Concepts in Action

Does this statement help bring together the ideas in this chapter?

The blood—composed of specialized cells and fluids—has transporting and protective functions in maintaining health.

Applying this concept of the blood, which health practices would you

— continue?

— change?

— begin?

Will you now, as a result of your study, change any of your health objectives?

17 / *Your Heart and Blood Vessels*

From the earliest times, people have thought of the heart as the center of our emotions. This is shown by the following expressions: "brave heart," "loving heart," "kind heart," "hardhearted," "goodhearted," "lionhearted," and "softhearted." How many more expressions can you think of that include the word "heart"? Can your emotions affect your heart?

Your life depends upon the beating of your heart, and many doctors believe that constant tension, anxiety, anger, and worry may increase the likelihood of certain kinds of heart disease. Why?

A PROBE INTO THE CIRCULATION OF THE BLOOD—How is your blood moved through your body? To find out, you will be probing these questions:

1. How is your heart constructed? What are the functions of the chambers? the valves?

3. How can an emotional upset cause a person to faint? to blush? to become pale?

2. How do clothing, exercise, and posture affect your circulation?

4. In what ways may the condition of the heart and blood vessels be affected by the food you choose? by constant tension? by too little exercise?

THE HARD-WORKING HEART

Your heart is not only a living pump, but a double pump made mostly of muscle and divided by a thick wall between the two sides (Figure 17-1). The *right* side of the heart receives *dark red* blood containing carbon dioxide from all over the body and pumps this blood to the lungs. Here the carbon dioxide is exchanged for oxygen, which turns the color of the blood to a *bright red*. From the lungs, the blood goes back to the heart—this time to the *left* side. The left side of the heart then pumps this red blood at high speed and under great pressure into a strong artery called the *aorta* (ay-OR-tuh) that leads to all parts of the body except the air sacs of the lungs. (The lungs receive blood from the left side of the heart through the aorta, and also from the right side of the heart. This will be explained later in this chapter.)

17-1 The interior of the heart. Why does the heart have four chambers?

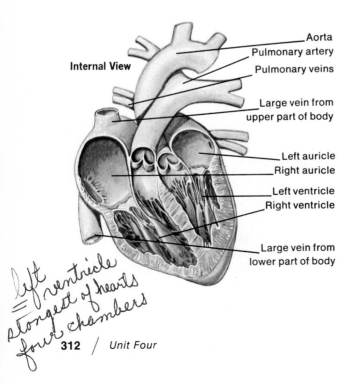

Internal View

Aorta
Pulmonary artery
Pulmonary veins
Large vein from upper part of body
Left auricle
Right auricle
Left ventricle
Right ventricle
Large vein from lower part of body

left ventricle = strongest of hearts four chambers

The Four Chambers of the Heart

Each side of the heart has two rooms, or chambers. The upper one is called the *auricle* (AW-rih-k'l) and the lower one the *ventricle* (VEN-trih-k'l), as shown in Figure 17-1. Scientists and doctors frequently use the word *atrium* (AY-tri-um—from a Latin word meaning room or court) instead of auricle. Blood from the brain, the liver, the arms, the legs—from everywhere except the lungs— enters the *right auricle* through two large veins. When the auricles contract, this blood is forced down into the *right ventricle*. The right ventricle pumps the blood through the *pulmonary* (PUL-muh-nair-ee) artery to the lungs, where it picks up a fresh supply of oxygen and gives up carbon dioxide and some water. The pulmonary veins carry the blood, bright red now because it is loaded with oxygen, to the *left auricle*, which forces it down into the *left ventricle*. The left ventricle has the thickest walls and is the strongest of the heart's four chambers. It needs to be strong because it has to pump blood with enough force to send it all over the body. With each heartbeat, the left ventricle forces some blood into the aorta in a powerful spurt. This gives all the blood in the circulation a little push forward. See Figure 17-2.

The Heart's Own Circulatory System

To pump tons of blood every day, the heart itself needs a rich supply of food and oxygen. To supply these there are arteries, veins, and capillaries in the thick heart muscle (Figure 17-3). Two arteries, called the *coronary* (KOR-uh-nair-ee) arteries, branch off from the aorta where it leaves the left ventricle (Figure 17-3). These arteries circle the heart and send many branches into the heart tissue. The circulation within the wall of the heart is called the *coronary* circulation.

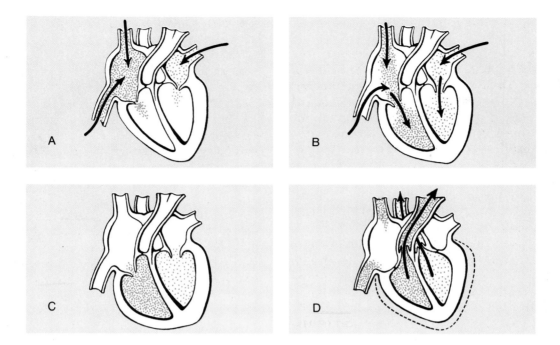

17-2 How blood enters and leaves the heart. (A) The beginning of the pumping cycle. The auricles relax; blood from the body enters the right auricle while blood from the lungs enters the left auricle. (B) The ventricles relax, allowing blood from the auricles to enter. (C) The auricles contract, forcing all blood into the ventricles. (D) The ventricles contract, forcing the blood from the left ventricle into the aorta and blood from the right ventricle into the pulmonary artery. This stage completes the pumping cycle, which will begin again with stage (A).

About 10 percent of all the blood pumped out by the left ventricle goes into the coronary circulation.

The coronary circulation is so short that the blood travels through it in two or three seconds; but the heart uses oxygen at such a fast rate that a complete stoppage in this circulation means sudden death. Such a stoppage in one of the heart's own blood vessels is the cause of almost all deaths from so-called *heart failure.* Yet one of the branches of these vessels may be blocked without causing heart failure. Most people survive a first attack. Many live for 10, 20, or 30 years thereafter.

Trouble with coronary circulation comes after years of gradual hardening of the coronary arteries. Finally, a clot starts to form on the rough inside surface of the artery (Figure 17-4). Doctors call a clot of this kind a thrombus. If it blocks a coronary artery, the patient is said to have a *coronary thrombosis.* Both heart failure and coronary thrombosis will be discussed in greater detail in Chapter 32.

Circulation of Blood Through the Body

The aorta is the largest artery in the body. It receives the blood containing oxygen from the heart, and it delivers the blood to branch arteries. As these divide again and again, the blood travels more slowly. The smallest arteries branch into millions of tiny capillaries, in which the blood moves slowly past the cells of your

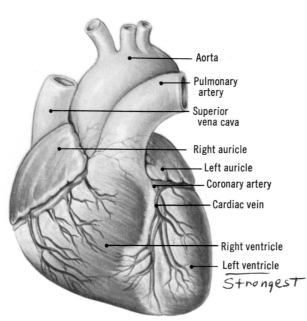

Aorta

Pulmonary artery

Superior vena cava

Right auricle

Left auricle

Coronary artery

Cardiac vein

Right ventricle

Left ventricle

Strongest

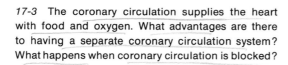

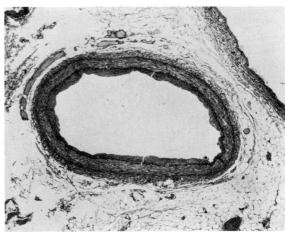

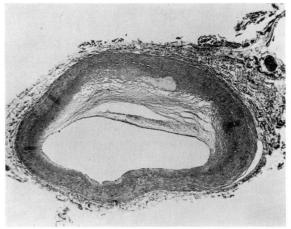

American Heart Association

17-3 The coronary circulation supplies the heart with food and oxygen. What advantages are there to having a separate coronary circulation system? What happens when coronary circulation is blocked?

body tissues. (Blood actually travels 600 times as fast in the aorta as it does in the capillaries.)

As blood flows through the capillaries, it gives up oxygen to the tissues and takes on carbon dioxide. It also loses its bright color. The blood returns to the heart so that it can be pumped to the lungs again where it picks up more oxygen and gets rid of carbon dioxide.

As the return trip to the heart begins, the capillaries join to form the smallest veins. Here the blood flows faster again. Later on, when the small veins have joined to form the largest veins, the blood flows almost as fast as it did in the aorta.

Figure 17-5 shows the plan of circulation for your body's blood supply.

17-4 Here you see photographs of successive stages in the formation of a thrombus (blood clot) in a coronary artery. Notice the deposits building up on the inside of the artery, hardening and thickening its walls. Finally, a clot completes the blockage.

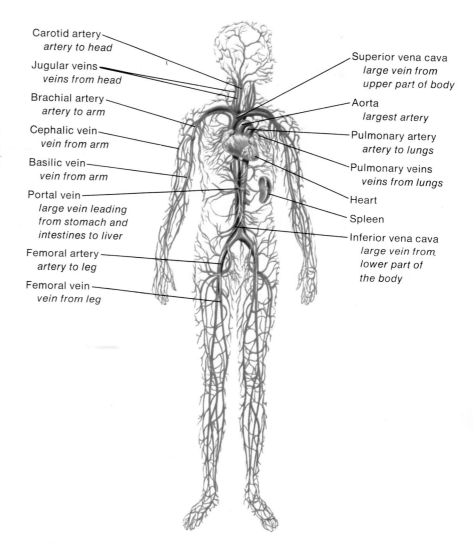

17-5 Your heart and approximately 100,000 miles of blood vessels make up your circulatory system — your body's inside transportation system. Blood carries the supplies that your muscles, bones, brain, nerves, skin, and all other parts of your body need to stay alive and work efficiently. Only the arteries and veins, your larger vessels, can be illustrated, since the capillaries that connect them are too small and too numerous to be shown

Carotid artery —
artery to head

Jugular veins —
veins from head

Brachial artery —
artery to arm

Cephalic vein —
vein from arm

Basilic vein —
vein from arm

Portal vein —
large vein leading from stomach and intestines to liver

Femoral artery —
artery to leg

Femoral vein —
vein from leg

Superior vena cava
large vein from upper part of body

Aorta
largest artery

Pulmonary artery
artery to lungs

Pulmonary veins
veins from lungs

Heart

Spleen

Inferior vena cava
large vein from lower part of the body

HOW YOUR CELLS ARE FED, WATERED, AND CLEANSED

No human cell could live if the blood ceased to flow. Yet most of the cells of your body are never touched by a drop of blood! The blood stays in the blood vessels. Red blood cells cannot escape from a capillary unless the capillary wall is torn. Water, dissolved foods, and white blood cells that have passed out of the capillaries are called tissue fluid. In other words, tissue fluid is plasma minus some of the plasma proteins and some other substances, plus a few white blood cells that can change shape and squeeze through a capillary wall. The red blood cells give up their load of oxygen as

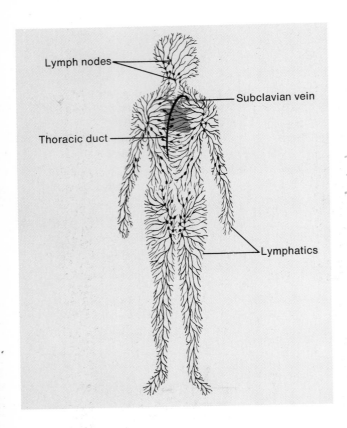

Lymph — What Keeps It Moving?

You can see that tissue fluid must be carried away from the tissues to keep them from becoming swollen and watery. It has to get back into the bloodstream, but it does not go back directly into the capillaries. Instead, it flows from the tissue spaces into small **lymph capillaries.** After the tissue fluid enters these tiny tubes, it is called *lymph*. Lymph capillaries differ in several ways from capillaries that carry blood (Figure 17-6). Lymph capillaries are larger, with many swellings and constrictions. The fluid passes into them through their thin walls. The smallest lymph vessels join to form larger tubes called **lymphatics** (lim-FAT-iks). The lymphatics join to form still larger vessels. The lymph gets back into the bloodstream by flowing into two large veins at a point near your collarbone.

The lymphatics have so many valves that they look as if they are jointed or knotted. What keeps the lymph moving? It is pushed slowly forward by the pressure of the liquid that constantly seeps out of the blood capillaries. Can you see how important exercise is to lymph movement? Every time you move, your muscles squeeze the lymph vessels, thus helping to push the lymph forward; the valves prevent it from moving backward.

Why Doesn't the Blood Flow Backward?

To keep the blood from flowing in the wrong direction, the heart has valves. The valves are flaps of tissue that hang down into each ventricle and allow the blood to flow past them from above (Figure 17-2). However, when the ventricle contracts, it forces blood upward against the valves, and the flaps are raised to close the entrance. Another set of valves guards the opening from each ventricle into its artery.

17-6 The lymphatic system. Lymph collects in the lymphatics, which join with larger vessels, eventually joining into two large veins just before they enter the heart.

the blood circulates through the capillaries. The oxygen then dissolves in the fluid that bathes the cells of your body tissues.

As the fluid washes over them, your cells take as much oxygen as they need, as well as sugar and other foods. At the same time they give off carbon dioxide and the wastes they have produced as a result of being alive. Capillaries and tissue cells are arranged in the body, with fluid filling the tiny spaces between cells. The cells in the skin, in the muscles, and even in the thick walls of a large blood vessel are all bathed by tissue fluid.

A Leaky Heart

A leaky heart isn't losing blood. However, one or more valves fail to close tightly and thus allow some of the blood to flow backward. When a valve leaks, the sharp thuds of the heartbeat become a **murmur.** By listening through the **stethoscope** (STETH-oh-skop), a doctor hears murmuring sounds and learns a great deal about how the heart is working. Have you heard the sound of your heartbeat? He can usually tell whether the sounds mean any serious damage to the valves. Many heart murmurs are not dangerous. When they occur in a child, they are often outgrown. See page 34, *A Visit to the Doctor*, for an account of how a doctor uses the stethoscope.

Valve trouble may be caused by abnormal development—that is, the valves may not be just the right size or shape. The defects often result from attacks by bacteria that cause the delicate valves to become inflamed. Bacterial attack may leave hard scars that prevent the valves from closing tightly. You will read more about this in Chapter 33.

100,000 MILES OF BLOOD VESSELS

If you could take all of the blood vessels, large and small, from the average-sized man and stretch them end to end, they would form a tube about 100,000 miles long. This is four times the distance around the earth at the equator. At its widest (the aorta and the largest veins), the tube would be a little more than one inch in diameter. At the narrowest portion (formed by the smallest capillaries), the tube would be about $\frac{1}{3,000}$ of an inch in diameter.

We have three kinds of blood vessels. *Arteries* carry the blood away from the heart. *Veins* carry blood toward the heart. Your millions of *capillaries* carry blood from the smallest arteries to the smallest veins.

The Arteries

Each time your heart beats it forces blood into your arteries in a powerful spurt. Your arteries have to withstand great pressure—and pressure that varies all the time. For this reason they have to be strong and elastic.

Arteries have thick walls with a layer of muscle, a smooth inner lining, and an outer coat of strong connective tissue (Figure 17-7). This coat is so heavy in large arteries that it keeps them from collapsing when cut. This fact, in addition to the blood pressure from within, makes it hard to stop bleeding in a torn artery. In most parts of the body the larger arteries are buried deep in the tissues, far away from the surface of the skin. Thus they are protected by all the layers of muscle and other tissue above them.

The walls of the arteries tend to become thicker and less elastic as a person grows older. This may result in the chronic condition *arteriosclerosis*, commonly called "hardening of the arteries."

Capillaries—Where the Real Work of the Blood Is Done

The aorta sends off large branch arteries to the head and to other parts of the body. These arteries branch again and again, forming tubes of smaller and smaller size with thinner and thinner walls. Finally, the smallest arteries branch into microscopic *capillaries*. The word *capillary* means *like a hair*, but capillaries are much smaller than hairs. The capillaries are so small that it is hard to picture them. The *largest* are $\frac{1}{25}$ of an inch long and less than $\frac{1}{1,000}$ of an inch in diameter. The smallest are less than $\frac{1}{3,000}$ of an inch in diameter. They are so small that the tiny red blood cells have to pass through them in single file (Figure 17-7). If you cut yourself enough to make a small drop of blood appear, the cut has probably sliced hundreds, or thousands, of capillaries!

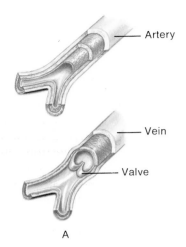
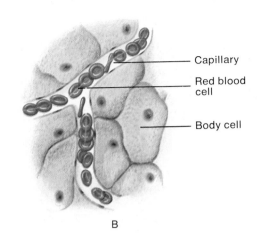

17-7 (*A*) Diagram of an artery and a vein. (*B*) Blood cells in a capillary. What is the function of each of these blood vessels? How do they differ structurally?

Artery

Vein

Valve

Capillary

Red blood cell

Body cell

A

B

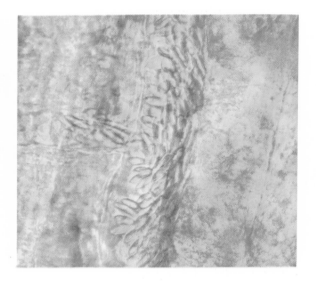

17-8 Circulation of blood in a goldfish tail. Notice how tiny the capillaries are. How many capillaries are probably injured when you cut your finger?

Why do we say that the real work of the blood is done in the capillaries? The reason is that fresh supplies of oxygen and food, and waste materials, are exchanged by the blood and body cells through the capillary walls. This is easy, because the walls are only one cell thick.

The Veins

To allow the blood to flow back to the heart, the capillaries join together to form the smallest veins. These veins join to form other larger veins, until finally the blood from all over the body (except the lungs) pours into the right auricle of the heart through two large veins. One of these brings *venous* (VEE-nus) blood from the head and arms. The other vein brings venous blood to the heart from the trunk of the body and the legs.

The walls of veins are not as thick as those of arteries (Figure 17-7). The walls of veins have some muscle and some connective tissue, but they cannot stretch or contract nearly as much as arteries do. When cut, the walls of a vein collapse. This makes it easier to stop bleeding by pressing on the vein. Most veins are closer to the surface of the body than the arteries are.

■ Look at the back of your hand. You can see the outlines of some veins, but you cannot see any trace of the arteries. Why do the veins appear bluish? Is your blood really blue? What will happen to the color of the blood when it reaches the lungs?

Many veins have valves. These valves are most numerous in the legs and the lower part of the body. The valves permit the blood to flow toward the heart, but not away from it (Figure 17-7). This is important, because the blood pressure in the veins is so low that there would be danger of the blood standing still or flowing backward in the legs. Every time you exercise, even when you move your toes, your muscles contract and squeeze the veins. This gives the blood a push. Since the valves keep the blood from going the wrong way, exercise aids your circulation.

■ To show that gravity can affect circulation in the veins, let your arm hang down until the veins become slightly swollen. Now raise your arm above your head and hold it there for 20 seconds. Account for the difference in appearance of the larger veins.

YOUR HEARTBEAT

Most muscles move only when they receive a nerve impulse—or when they are given an electric shock. Yet a heart removed from a dog or a frog, or even a man, may continue to beat for a while, even though its nerve connections have been cut. How can heart muscle do what other muscle cannot do?

The Pacemaker

The reason is that the heart starts its own heartbeats from its own *pacemaker,* a small mass of tissue located on one side of the heart near the top. The pacemaker is also called the *sinoatrial node* (SI-no-ATE-tree-ul). An impulse from the pacemaker makes the auricles contract, forcing blood into the ventricles. As the wave of contraction passes from the muscle of the auricles, it arouses an impulse in another node (a sort of assistant pacemaker) that spreads through the ventricles and makes them contract. The whole process usually takes less than one second. During most of this time, the heart is actually resting.

When the Heart Stops

Is there ever hope for a person once his heart has stopped beating? It was on New Year's Eve that one family found an answer to this question. Four-year-old Neal was playing with the electric train he got for Christmas. As he watched the train "come 'round the bend," the tall Christmas tree, with all its lights sparkling, toppled and fell across the track. There was a flash, and the boy lay still. Apparently, a "short circuit" had electrocuted Neal.

The family doctor was summoned within minutes. Exhaustive efforts failed to revive the little boy. Still the doctor did not give up. There was a happy ending to the story, which the United Press flashed to all parts of the United States on New Year's Day. The doctor had administered a shot of *adrenaline* (a-DREN-al-in), a powerful hormone, directly into the boy's heart. You will read more about adrenaline in Chapter 22. Then, after obtaining the permission of the parents, he had opened the child's chest, exposed the heart, and begun to massage it. Within a few moments the heart had started to beat. Neal breathed again.

Neal's accident with the Christmas-tree wire occurred some years ago. Today, doctors often make a stopped heart go back to work by massaging the heart without opening the chest. This is done by pressing strongly on the chest 60 times a minute while some one else does mouth-to-mouth breathing for the victim. In many cases, doctors still think it better to open the chest.

Your life, like that of little Neal, depends upon the beating of your heart. Your blood must carry necessary supplies to your body cells, and take away the wastes that the cells give off.

What Is Heart Block?

Heart block is an interruption or slowing down of the impulses that the pacemaker sends to make the heart muscle contract. A common type of heart block is one in which the "assistant pacemaker" is damaged and the ventricles beat more slowly than the auricles. As it is the contraction of the ventricles that causes the pulse, the damage may result in the pulse dropping to 30 to 40 a minute. Electricity is often useful in treating some kinds of heart block and in starting a stopped heart. Small battery-powered **electrical pacemakers** may be implanted in patients whose own pacemakers fail to work properly. Sometimes an *external* pacemaker is used. See Figures 17-9 and 32-4.

How Fast Does the Heart Beat?

You find out how fast your heart beats by taking your pulse. When you do this, you count the number of pulsations per minute in the walls of an artery.

■ Using the tips of your second and third fingers, feel your pulse at the artery on the thumb side of the inside of your wrist. Count the number of beats you feel in one minute. Time yourself with a watch.

In some people the heart beats much faster than in others. For some the rate is as low as 50 beats a minute or even less, and for others as high as 90. The average is about 72, although the rate varies with age and sex. In newborn babies the heart beats about 140 times a minute. It slows down to 85 in youth and to around 72 in the average adult. In old age the rate varies between 70 and 80. The rate for girls and women runs about 5 beats faster than for men.

Just as a small clock ticks faster than a large one, so a small heart beats faster than a large one. In some animals the heart beats at an

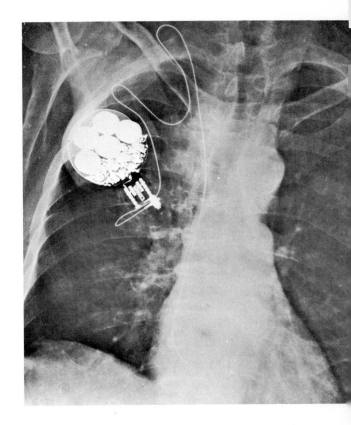

17-9 This X-ray photograph shows an electrical pacemaker placed just under the skin of the chest. What is the function of such a pacemaker?

astonishing rate. An elephant's heart beats at a rate of only 20 beats a minute, while the heart of a mouse beats 700 times a minute.

The Strength and Endurance of the Heart

As you sit in class, your heart may be pumping some 20 pints (weighing about 20 pounds) of blood each minute. In 10 minutes your heart pumps about 200 pounds of blood—quite a bit more than your own weight. The heart pumps this blood with so much force that if a vertical glass tube were connected to your largest blood vessel, the blood would rise five feet or more in the tube. In 24 hours your heart pumps many tons of blood this forcefully. Of course, it is the same blood—your 9 to 13 pints—that is being pumped over and over again.

Rest, Exercise, and Rate of Heartbeat

Your heart beats most slowly when you are lying down, because it does not have to pump blood uphill from your feet and legs. When you sit up, it goes about 4 beats a minute faster. When you stand up, it speeds up another 10 to 14 beats.

Exercise makes the heart beat faster. If the exercise is very strenuous, the heart may beat 180 times a minute. After a long swim or run, it may take an hour or more for the heart to slow down to normal. The more efficient the heart is, the more quickly it returns to normal after exercise. Proper athletic training should speed up the rate of recovery.

Trained athletes often have the slowest resting heart rates. Some famous runners have a pulse rate of 40 to 60 per minute, which may speed up very little during exercise.

■ Try this simple investigation. Take your pulse while you're seated reading. Now get up and do a few pushups as a mild exercise. Stop and take your pulse again. When you've completed your reading, take your pulse again. Is the rate back to what it was before you exercised?

Out for the Team!

Are interscholastic sports too strenuous? Some authorities think so. Most, however, believe that they are safe provided proper precautions are taken. Doctors say that a normal heart will not be hurt by strenuous athletic competition—but the doctor must make a careful examination to find out whether the heart is normal. Before you go out for any team, have your doctor give you a thorough checkup.

Suppose that you have been ill. Should you take part in a strenuous sport such as tennis or track? Not for at least a week!

High school athletics should be carefully supervised. Students should be limited in the kind and number of events in which they may compete. They should train gradually up to the peak of activity before they are permitted to compete at all. All boys and girls should be given a thorough physical checkup before being admitted to competition. Do you participate in any team or individual sport in your high school? If so, are you required to take a complete physical examination before being allowed to participate? Why is this so important?

Under the stimulus of winning for the school or of trying "to be a man," some students push themselves too far. Don't wear yourself out just to be a "regular fellow." Try to learn what your capabilities are, and stay within them.

Reserves of Blood

You need to have more blood in circulation at some times than at others. When you run a long way, play football, or do heavy physical work, more blood must go to your muscles. Some of this "extra" blood is stored in the spleen, a spongy, bean-shaped organ situated at the left of and behind the stomach (Figure 17-11). A larger amount is held in the liver and in the veins that drain into the liver. When you are at rest, about one fifth of your blood may be held in the spleen, the liver and its supplying veins, and the skin. When you need more blood in circulation, the liver and its veins release blood to the general circulation, and the muscles of the spleen squeeze stored blood into the veins. More blood goes to the muscles during exercise and to the skin at high temperatures.

17-10 Can participation in strenuous sports be dangerous? Be sure you have a physical examination before entering athletic competition.

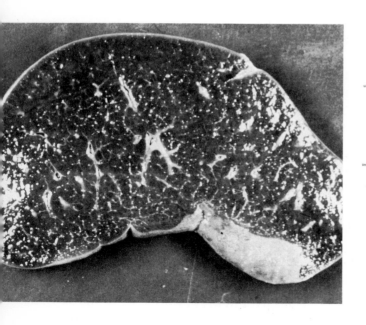

17-11 A cross-section of the spleen. What is one function of the spleen? What other organ also functions this way?

No Heart Cramps

You can get a cramp in your leg muscles, but not in your heart. Cramp is caused by the failure of a muscle to relax after it has contracted, or by a muscle contracting again before it has relaxed fully from the previous contraction. Heart muscle, fortunately, will not start a second contraction until it has relaxed from the last one. When you are excited or under great strain, it may flutter, but not cramp. We think that this is because heart muscle uses all the fuel (food) available each time it contracts. Thus it *has* to rest, at least a little, while it is refueling.

We think of the heart as working all the time. Does it? No! It *actually rests at least half the time*. This is one reason why it lasts so long and can do so much work without tiring. Some authorities think that when you are lying down and are completely relaxed, your heart rests twice as much as it works.

BLOOD PRESSURE

You must have **blood pressure** to live. Blood pressure is the force with which the blood presses against the walls of the blood vessels. It is this pressure that keeps the blood moving through the blood vessels.

How Blood Pressure Is Measured

Usually, the doctor "takes" the pressure in an artery in the upper arm. See Figure 17-12. Two pressures are registered when you are examined. One is the highest pressure when the heart contracts, called the **systolic** (sis-TOL-ick) pressure. The other is the lowest pressure when the heart muscle is resting, called the **diastolic** (dy-as-TOL-ick) pressure. 120/80, or 120 over 80, is about the average pressure for adults under age forty. This means that a person's systolic pressure could raise a column of mercury 120 millimeters (nearly five inches) and that his diastolic pressure could raise it 80 millimeters (over three inches). If, instead, a tube filled with water (which weighs much less than mercury) could be attached, the same pressures would make the water rise to about 5½ feet and then fall back to about 3½ feet, all in one second.

People vary in their blood pressures, and a fairly wide range exists of normal blood pressures for different ages.

Except during serious illness or following hemorrhage, low blood pressure is rarely a serious matter. Very high blood pressure may be dangerous. High blood pressure increases the danger of heart failure or stroke. Hardening of the arteries may tend to increase blood pressure, because it narrows the arteries and makes them less elastic. In any case, don't worry about your blood pressure unless your doctor does. It is only one of a number of symptoms that the doctor must consider.

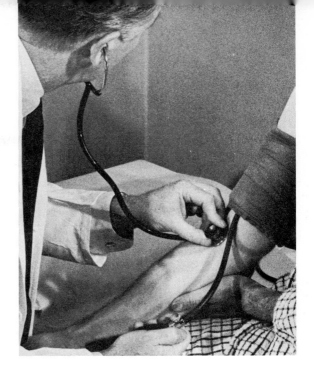

17-12 When a doctor takes your blood pressure, he also listens to the sound of the blood going through the artery. Does blood pressure normally vary much?

Shock

The word **shock** is used for several different conditions. Usually we mean the serious condition accompanied by a sharp drop in blood pressure. This often follows severe loss of blood, sudden emotional strain, or extremely harsh pain. The capillary walls relax, with the result that the capillaries can hold more blood. At the same time, plasma leaks out through the capillary walls to the tissues. Both of these things help lower the blood pressure. The heart tries to make up for this by beating faster, but since the heart now does not receive enough blood, the heartbeat weakens. The patient's skin becomes cold and clammy, and he perspires a great deal. His breathing becomes shallow, and neither his lungs nor his kidneys can get rid of wastes properly. He begins to be poisoned by the wastes. This and lack of oxygen may cause death if untreated.

What Can You Do for Shock?

Shock may be slight, severe, or quickly fatal; it may last only a few seconds, or for hours; it may occur immediately after injury, or not for several hours following the injury. If severe, it must have prompt treatment by a doctor.

Shock may produce a dazed condition or complete unconsciousness. The face is usually pale; pulse weak and rapid; breathing feeble and irregular, perhaps gasping. Severe chilling may occur, and the patient may vomit. Shock should be one of the first things treated in all accident cases, because of its possible serious results. Prompt preventive procedures may keep it from becoming serious. These procedures should be followed:

1. *Conserve body heat.* The patient may chill rapidly because of poor circulation during shock. Keep him comfortably warm by putting a blanket under him, as well as over him (Figure 17-13), but do not make his skin too warm. This would lower his already too low blood pressure.

2. *Keep him lying down.* Keep the patient lying on his back with his head low, and keep him as quiet as possible. If he lies with his head turned to one side,

there is less danger of choking if he should vomit. It is best to raise the foot of his bed or stretcher about 12 inches above the level of his head, or to raise his feet gently if he is lying at the scene of an accident and can be safely moved. Do not raise his head or chest unless he has a head or chest injury, difficulty in breathing, or a nose bleed. In these cases, do not elevate his feet.

3. *Be cautious with liquids.* Although a person in shock needs more liquid in his system, you should be very cautious in giving him anything to drink. *Never* give anything solid. Even water or salt solution may cause him to vomit and perhaps suffocate. If he is in mild shock, you may give him small amounts of water or, better, a little "shock solution," a mixture of a teaspoonful of salt and half a teaspoonful of baking soda in a quart of water. The patient should receive only a few sips at a time.

Call a Doctor

In severe shock, a doctor must be obtained as soon as possible. The treatment he gives the patient will be determined partly by the cause of shock. The most effective treatment when much blood has been lost is transfusion of *cross-matched* blood. After

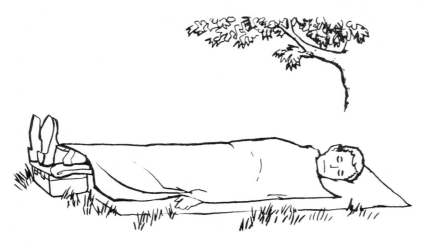

17-13 Treatment for shock. Prompt preventive procedures may keep shock from becoming serious.

blood types are matched, cross-matching is done. This is accomplished by mixing small samples of the red blood cells and sera from the donor and the recipient. These samples are then observed under the microscope to see if clumping of cells occurs. The bloods are thought to be compatible if no clumping occurs. As typing and matching blood takes a certain amount of time, the doctor frequently injects **dextran** or salt solution until the correct blood for transfusing can be obtained. Dextran is a syrupy substance made from sugar by bacteria. The bacteria, of course, are destroyed before the dextran is introduced into a person's veins.

What Can You Do for a Person Who Has Fainted?

A person faints when his brain fails to receive enough blood to maintain consciousness. Fainting may be due to weakness, excessive fatigue, lack of food, shock, or fear. The face of a person who has fainted is pale, his breathing shallow, and the pupils of his eyes normal. Keep the patient lying down, with head low and clothing loosened. Smelling salts or aromatic spirits of ammonia held to the nose for a moment or cold water dashed on the face may serve as stimulants, but these methods are not of much value. If a person feels faint and for some reason it is impossible to have him lie down, he may be helped to recover by sitting with his head bent over between his knees.

TRAFFIC JAMS IN THE BLOODSTREAM

Sometimes the blood supply to parts of the body is cut off or slowed down. When this happens, the cells in the affected part are weakened by lack of enough oxygen and food. At the same time they are poisoned by their own waste products. These cells may dry out and wither away, or become soft and mushy. A toe or foot whose circulation has been cut off turns black. When the tissues die because of poor blood supply, the condition is called gangrene, as you have already learned.

Maintain Good Posture and Wear Loose Clothing

Blood cannot force its way through pinched blood vessels. Blood flow is slowed by cramped positions and by tight clothing. Tight collars, garters, and arm bands can be harmful, because the veins in the neck and the limbs are so close to the surface that the flow of blood is easily obstructed by pressure. Elastic in clothes should be adjustable and no tighter than necessary.

Tight shoes reduce circulation, make the feet swell, and often cause much pain. If, for any reason, the audience suddenly had to run out from a theater, dozens of people's shoes would be left behind because they had been slipped off aching feet. Would *you* be among the barefooted people running from the theater? Do your shoes fit comfortably?

Varicose Veins

Varicose (VAIR-ih-kohss) veins are enlarged, sometimes painful veins. They occur most often in the legs, when the valves within the veins break down. In some cases, they look like blue or purple cords bulging under the skin. Varicose veins seem to be more common among people who have to stand a great deal in their work, particularly without moving around.

A person may be born with weak valves or weak veins. Sometimes this condition seems to run in families. In some cases, a different disease may result in varicose veins. Overweight and pregnancy tend to make varicose veins worse.

How can you help prevent varicose veins? Here are some ways:

1. Get enough exercise regularly to help veins in their job of returning blood to the heart. Muscular movement helps give the blood a push forward in your circulatory system.
2. Don't strain or lift heavy weights that are beyond your strength. When you strain, it forces blood backward against the valves in your veins.
3. Do you have to stand on your feet for a long time? Then move about now and then to relieve the back pressure in the leg veins. During rest periods, elevate your feet and legs to relieve this back pressure in the veins.

Frostbite

Frostbite is the freezing of any surface part of the body. Nose, ears, and feet are the parts most likely to suffer. There is, of course, no circulation of blood through the frozen part. Frostbitten toes, ears, or other parts of the body should be warmed quickly by immersing the frostbitten area in warm (*never* hot) water of close to, or very slightly above, normal body temperature. When tissue has been frozen for more than one-half hour, warm water should not be used at first. The air around the area should be kept cool, and heat applied only after the circulation has improved.

INFLUENCES AFFECTING THE HEART OR BLOOD VESSELS

Both emotions and environment can be important influences that affect the heart and blood vessels. In the following sections you will learn how emotions and fainting are related and how too *much* rest can be as bad as too little.

Mental and Emotional Influences

A student was displaying a tame, harmless snake to a class. As he passed down the aisle, he dropped the snake on the desk of a girl. She gasped and fainted. What went wrong?

It happened that the girl had had a medical checkup the week before. The doctor had reported her in perfect condition. Heart, nervous system, everything was in proper order. Fainting usually in no way indicates disease or weakness of the heart. In the girl's case, fainting was due to an emotion—fright. When she saw the snake, impulses went from her brain to nerves in her muscles and the wall of the abdomen. These impulses caused the blood vessels to dilate so that large amounts of blood were held in them. As a result, not enough blood reached the brain, causing her to lose consciousness and faint. Few physical disorders show so clearly the effect that the mind often has on the working of the body as fainting. As one medical authority says, fainting is "usually associated with emotional crisis." A person who has fainted on account of pain, fear, surprise, or some other emotion usually speedily regains consciousness if treated as recommended on page 325. The greatest danger in emotional fainting lies in falling or in losing control of an automobile or of something else that is potentially dangerous.

If you read novels of the eighteenth or nineteenth centuries, you may find many references to ladies fainting or at least talking about fainting. If women really did faint so much more often in those days, it may have been partly on account of the tight corsets they generally wore. Such corsets could easily slow the circulation of blood and also cause some pooling of blood in the veins and capillaries of the abdomen. It may also be that physical events caused by thoughts and emotions are much more likely to occur when we *think* that they are going to occur. As most of the reports of emotional

17-14 Is a fainting spell like this physical or emotional in origin? Have you ever fainted under similar circumstances?

fainting of former days come from the upper classes where women did not do hard physical work, and as girls and women went in far less for sports in those times, lack of exercise might have had something to do with it. You are not likely to meet a girl today who carries a vial of "smelling salts" with her, but at one time it was fashionable for a young lady to sniff daintily at the ammonia gas that rose from the crystals in the smelling salts bottle—whenever a young man seemed too bold or some shocking or alarming event occurred. A whiff of ammonia may still be used to give a slight jolt to a fainting person, though it is not necessary. A deep lungful of ammonia, on the other hand, could easily *cause* a person to faint and would be poisonous.

You must have noticed that embarrassment can make you blush. When this happens, nervous impulses rush from the brain along autonomic nerves to the smallest arteries and "tell" the muscles in the walls of these small blood vessels to relax. This allows more blood to flow into the capillaries, and as a result the skin becomes hot and red. Fear,

anger, and pain usually have the reverse effect, causing the tiny artery walls to contract so that the capillaries receive less blood and the skin becomes pale. Sometimes anger causes more blood to flow to the capillaries so that the face becomes red and hot. One man, listening to unexpected good news on the telephone, was observed to turn pale. If you tell a person that he is blushing, he very often will blush. The reason is the slight embarrassment resulting from being made conspicuous.

Psychiatrists (sye-KYE-ah-trists—doctors who treat mental ailments) consider that the following disorders may all be partly due to fears and worries, including some fears that may be buried deep in our unconscious minds: sudden increase in the heart rate to 100 or more beats per minute; shortness of breath; high blood pressure; possibly, damage to the heart itself. A person's nervous condition may make a perfectly healthy heart pound or beat faster. However, it has not been proved that such reactions actually do the healthy heart any harm.

Social and Environmental Influences

Today diseases of the heart and blood vessels are by far the most important causes of death in the United States. Advances in treatment of these diseases are described in Chapter 32.

Because diseases of the heart and blood vessels are most common among older people, one naturally wonders if part of the increase in heart disease may not be due largely to the fact that so many more persons live long enough to become "eligible" for heart and artery trouble.

While this may be true, many studies and experiments have led doctors to conclude that the conditions of social life in the United States and similar countries tend to cause people to do things that help to bring on heart and artery trouble.

Too much food. Overeating usually means overweight, and overweight means that the heart continually has too much work to do. It has been estimated that an extra pound of excess fat requires an extra mile of capillaries to feed this fat. This means that your heart has much more work to do, day after day, whether you are working or sleeping. Many of the foods that taste best to most of us are among those richest in fat: butter, cream, gravies, eggs, cheese, beef, mutton, and pork. Furthermore, these foods are all rich in the saturated fatty acids that seem to be connected with arteriosclerosis.

Tension. Many people think that we are more likely to suffer from tension and repressed emotions than people in underdeveloped countries or even in Europe. American society seems to be more competitive than many others, but we really have no way of making comparative measurements of the average amount of tension suffered by the average American and the average citizen of an underdeveloped country.

There is, however, a clear relationship between the number of cases of heart disease and arteriosclerosis and the differences in diet between countries. The United States has one of the highest death rates from coronary thrombosis. This condition is rather rare in Japan and China and in other parts of the world where rice is a principal food and the people eat little animal fat. Yet, people of Japanese and Chinese ancestry born and raised in this country have a greater rate of coronary disease than do people in Japan and China. It therefore seems that adoption of American eating habits tends to bring about an increase in hardening of the arteries.

Too little exercise. Experts who have tested American boys and girls against English and other European students claim that, in general, the Europeans were stronger and more agile than the Americans, even though our young people were taller and heavier on the average than the others. They attribute the difference to lack of exercise. The Americans are more likely to have automobiles, more likely to drive or be driven wherever they go, and less likely to take long walks or to engage regularly in strenuous exercise. Exercise is important in keeping the heart healthy. How much exercise do you get every day? Do you think that you are getting enough exercise?

Prolonged inactivity weakens the ability of the heart to adjust itself to the demands normally made on it. Six healthy young men who were required to rest in bed day and night for six weeks showed a progressive decline in the amount of blood pumped by their hearts at each beat. Their pulse rates climbed as their hearts had to beat faster. After the men were allowed to get up and take normal exercise, it took from 36 to 72 days before their hearts returned to their old efficiency.

You may know someone whose doctor made him remain in bed for some time after a heart attack. Very often prolonged bed rest is required to save the patient's life after the heart has been damaged. In such cases, as in all others, the doctor must use his knowledge and his judgment. Too much rest (that is, too little exercise) does decrease the efficiency of a healthy heart. However, a damaged heart, like a broken leg, must have rest, even though for full strength and efficiency, exercise is needed by both heart muscle and leg muscle.

What You Have Learned

What kind of health practices should you apply in maintaining your health? Check your understanding of the chapter. On a separate sheet of paper, number 1 through 24 and insert the answer from the vocabulary list below. Use each expression, but use each one only once.

3 aorta	15 diastolic pressure	21 spleen
4 arteries	22 frostbite	14 systolic pressure
1 auricle	11 heart block	17 thrombus
13 blood pressure	12 heart murmur	7 tissue fluid
5 capillaries	9 lymph	23 valves
16 coronary circulation	8 lymph capillaries	24 varicose veins
18 coronary thrombosis	10 pacemaker	6 veins
19 cramp	20 shock	2 ventricle

The right (1) _auricle_ receives blood from the body and passes it down to the right (2) _ventricle_, which pumps the blood to the lungs. The left side of the heart receives blood returning from the lungs and pumps it to the rest of the body. The left ventricle pumps the blood into the largest blood vessel, the (3) _aorta_, from which it flows through branching (4) _arteries_ to millions of microscopic (5) _capillaries_. These tiny tubes join together to form the (6) _veins_, which carry the blood back to the heart. A certain amount of plasma leaks through capillary walls to form the (7) _tissue fluid_, which bathes and feeds the cells in our tissues. Most of this liquid passes into tubes with many swellings and constrictions called (8) _lymph capillaries_. This liquid is now called (9) _lymph_.

The small mass of tissue that starts each heartbeat is called the (10) _pacemaker_. When there is an interruption or slowing down of the impulses that this structure sends to the heart muscle, we say that a person suffers from (11) _heart block_. When a valve leaks, the sharp thuds of the heartbeat become a (12) _murmur_. (13) _blood pressure_ is the force with which the blood presses against the walls of the blood vessels. The highest pressure, when the heart contracts, is the (14) _systolic pressure_, while the lowest pressure, when the heart muscle is resting, is the (15) _diastolic pressure_.

The circulation of blood within the wall of the heart is called the (16) _coronary circulation_. Sometimes a clot called a (17) _thrombus_ starts to form in an artery. If such a clot blocks an artery in the heart wall, the patient is said to have a (18) _coronary thrombosis_. Heart muscle, fortunately, does not suffer from (19) _cramp_, the failure of a muscle to relax after it has contracted.

The serious condition accompanied by a sharp drop in blood pressure is called (20) _shock_. Fortunately, normal circulation may be aided by reserves of blood stored in the skin, the liver and its supplying veins, and a spongy, bean-shaped organ called the (21) _spleen_. Circulation ceases in any surface part of the body that is frozen. This condition is (22) _frostbite_.

Sometimes the (23)_valves_, which prevent the blood from flowing the wrong way in the heart and veins, break down in certain veins, causing the condition known as (24)_varicose veins_

What You Can Do /

Discuss the following health practices in class. Are these good health practices? Explain why or why not.

1. Take active exercise every day except when you are ill.
2. Avoid unnecessary stress and worry, as well as anger and alarm.
3. Do not eat too many fatty foods, especially those with saturated fats.
4. Avoid tight clothing that restricts circulation.
5. Get enough rest, including eight hours of sleep each night.
6. Maintain a good posture, both for the sake of appearance and for your circulatory system.
7. If you feel that you are in danger of fainting, lie down or at least sit with your head bent down between your knees.
8. Have a physical examination before going out for any athletic team.
9. If a person is in shock, try to keep him quietly lying down (with his head low unless he has a head or chest injury).
10. Do not strain yourself or try to lift heavy weights that are beyond your strength.
11. If you suffer a frostbitten toe or ear and no doctor is present, immerse the frostbitten part in warm (not hot) water.
12. When tempted to overeat, remember that too much weight is both unattractive and hard on your heart.

Things to Try /

1. Here are two problems for you to solve. Can you reason out the explanations by yourself? If not, perhaps you will find the answers quickly by consulting this textbook and other references.

   a. Many veins can be traced for part of their course by looking at the skin. You cannot do this with your arteries. What does this indicate about the location of veins? of arteries? Why would it be much more dangerous to have arteries located where so many of the veins are?

   b. This problem may puzzle you a bit. Shock and fainting are accompanied by a drop in blood pressure. Some persons may faint with a systolic blood pressure of 60. Yet there are extremely healthy trained athletes with a *normal* systolic blood pressure of 60 or a bit lower. Put these facts together and try to find an explanation.

2. If you have the use of a microscope, you will enjoy observing the path of blood through the blood vessels in the tail of a goldfish. Cover a small goldfish with wet absorbent cotton, leaving only the tail exposed. Inexpensive goldfish are fine for this purpose. Lay the fish on a Petri dish or a clean, thin glass plate and place a glass slide over the tail to hold it flat. Examine under the low-power objective of the microscope. Should the fish flip its tail or leap off the dish, add water to the cotton or add more wet cotton, dry off the lens of the microscope, and examine again. Can you see the blood moving rapidly in spurts? Is it moving more slowly in the opposite direction in another vessel? Try to explain what you see. Return the fish to a bowl of cool water within 15 minutes.

Probing Further /

Biological Science: An Inquiry into Life, by J. A. Moore and others, Harcourt Brace Jovanovich, 1968. Many interesting facts about the hearts and blood vessels of man and other animals are included in this textbook.

The Low Salt, Low Cholesterol Cookbook, by Myra Waldo, Putnam, 1972. Do you like to cook? Miss Waldo tells how to prepare tasty food intended to spare our hearts and arteries.

The Heart and Sport, by Ernst Jokl, Thomas, 1964. Read how exercise and athletics affect and are affected by the circulatory system.

Health Concepts in Action /

Does this statement help express what you have learned? Would you change or add to it?

> **The circulatory system transports the blood, with dissolved substances, throughout the body.**

Applying this concept of circulation, which health practices would you

— continue?

— change?

— begin?

Will you now, as a result of your study, change any of your health objectives?

18 / *Keepers of the Blood*

A young boy was bitten by a rattlesnake. The venom soon paralyzed his kidneys. Since the kidneys could no longer do their normal work, poisonous substances began to pile up in the boy's blood. He was rushed to a hospital, where a "kidney machine" took over the job of the boy's kidneys. It carried wastes away from his blood while his own kidneys had a chance to heal.

A PROBE INTO THE FILTERING OF THE BLOOD — What keeps the composition of your blood more or less the same? To find out, you will be probing questions like these:

1. How does your liver act as a watchdog?

2. What is bile? How is it useful?

3. Why are the kidneys so important? Why is urinalysis an important medical test? How can people survive in good health after removal of one kidney?

4. How useful is the spleen? Why is it still a bit of a puzzle?

5. How may social and environmental conditions affect the health of the liver or kidneys?

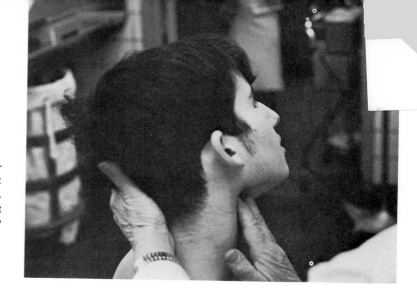

18-1 Checking for enlargement of lymph nodes is part of a physical examination. What might enlargement indicate?

HOW CAN THE BLOOD CHANGE AND YET REMAIN THE SAME?

As blood circulates through the body, it constantly loses water, salt, glucose, oxygen, and hundreds of other substances. At the same time, it gains water from the villi of the small intestine and from many cells, salt from the intestine, glucose from the intestine and the liver, oxygen from the lungs, and hundreds of other materials.

Although the blood takes in and gives up so much, there is not a great net change in its composition. In fact, we could not survive if the blood did change very much. What is it that keeps our 9 to 13 pints of blood essentially the same from hour to hour and month to month?

Every gland and every cell has an effect on the blood. The great filters and cleansers of the blood are the lymph nodes, the spleen, the liver, and the kidneys.

Our Living Bacteria Traps

If you ever suffered from "swollen glands," you know about the *lymph nodes*, or lymph glands, as they are often called. These are small swellings along the course of the lymph vessels. Most of them are in the neck, armpits, groin, and abdomen. Their work is to filter out germs and foreign matter, and to make white blood cells. Roughly 25 percent of your white blood cells are made in the lymph nodes and in other parts of the lymphatic system, such as the *tonsils* and *adenoids* (AD-in-oids).

Lymph nodes are the scene of many battles between white blood cells and bacteria. They protect you against blood poisoning by stopping germs before they get into the main bloodstream. If any of your lymph nodes become swollen or painful, you should see your doctor. Sometimes an infected lymph node forms an abscess and must be opened. Any lymph node may sometimes fall victim to the bacteria it has captured. If you should have a small abscess on the face, or a feverish tooth-socket infection, the doctor will probably examine the lymph nodes at the rear of your lower jaw. If you have an infected wound in your finger, the doctor will often examine the lymph nodes under your arm.

Tonsils – Outposts Against Infection

Your supplies of air, water, and food pass through your throat cavity. Since the nose

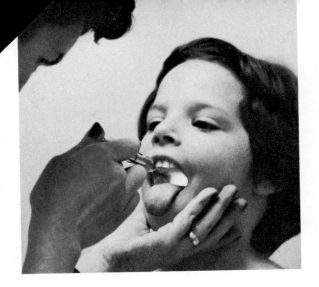

18-2 Tonsils are examined as part of a routine physical check-up. Have your tonsils been removed?

and mouth are the entrance points for most infectious diseases, vast numbers of germs also enter the throat. They ride in as hitch-hikers on dust, on food, and in water that has been contaminated. You have read about the way the air-conditioning system in your breathing passages fights against these germs. Another defense are the masses of lymphatic tissue that are placed like a ring of forts around the throat cavity. Like other lymph tissues, they make white blood cells, and they filter out and destroy bacteria.

Two of these masses—the *tonsils*—are found opposite each other, one on each side of the throat (see Figure 15-5). They become inflamed and painful when you have a sore throat. This does not necessarily mean that they are seriously diseased. It does mean that they are attempting to carry on their normal work. They are trying to hold the invading germs at bay and keep them from spreading further into the body.

Tonsil trouble, or **tonsillitis,** is most frequent in children under ten years of age. Infected tonsils are much less common in older persons, although they may be serious when they occur. The young child's body

has a problem which the older person's body has frequently solved: the child has to build up resistance to many germs. The tonsils may bear the brunt of the fight while his body makes the substances that will prevent future illness.

Sometimes the tonsils become a danger to the body, like a fort that has been captured by the enemy. They may become so large that they obstruct breathing and interfere with hearing. Sometimes they remain infected in spite of treatment. In these cases, they should be removed by a surgeon.

Doctors prefer not to remove the tonsils at the first sign of infection. They try to build up the patient's resistance and give the tonsils every chance to recover before making a decision to remove them. Tonsillitis is often cured by sulfa drugs and antibiotics.

Adenoids

The *adenoids* are a mass of lymphatic tissue in the passage between the nose and the throat (see Figure 15-5). They are similar to the tonsils and do the same kind of work. Enlarged adenoids may prevent proper breathing through the nose. Mouth breathing is undesirable since the air cannot be filtered or properly moistened or warmed. Enlarged adenoids sometimes block the Eustachian tubes that run from the throat to the middle ear, causing deafness. Enlarged or infected adenoids should be removed if they interfere with breathing or hearing.

The Spleen—
an Organ That We Can Safely Lose

You have already learned in Chapter 16 about the work of the spleen in destroying worn-out red blood cells. It is thought that the spleen makes both red and white blood cells in the developing child before birth, and also that it makes blood cells in adults after certain types of anemia. The spleen is

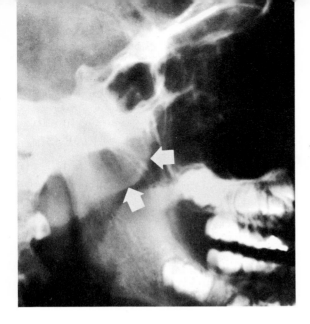

18-3 An X ray of the adenoids. What is the function of the adenoids?

part of the lymphatic system and is the largest lymphatic organ in the body.

The spleen was a puzzle to scientists two thousand years ago, and it is still a bit of a puzzle. As the blood flows through it, the spleen removes and destroys worn-out and imperfect red blood cells. It probably helps to defend the body against infection, yet at times the spleen destroys healthy red blood cells and has to be removed. It may be of some value in protecting the body against the effects of radiation. In adults, other tissues can apparently do everything useful that the spleen does for us. Hence it can be removed without danger to life.

The Liver—
Your Chemical Laboratory

Our most complicated filters and cleansing stations are the liver and kidneys.

The liver is the largest gland in your body and one of the two largest internal organs. In adults it is the heaviest organ in the body. As you grow up, your liver grows much more than your brain does. A baby's brain weighs three times as much as his liver. At twelve years of age, the brain still weighs more, but in adults, the liver weighs 10 to 20 percent more than the brain. The liver is located on the right side of the body, just below the diaphragm, and is protected by the lower ribs.

No one could live more than a few hours without his liver. Without it, he would be in serious trouble digesting food. Many of the things he ate could not be changed chemically so that his body could use them. He would soon be injured by wastes that body cells are always producing and by poisons that the body produces or takes in. The liver collects substances that would be dangerous if allowed to accumulate and changes them into harmless ones.

The Liver As Your Watchdog

The liver and all other organs in your body receive blood from arteries, but unlike other organs, the liver also receives blood from a vein. The large *portal* (POR-t'l) *vein* brings to the liver all of the blood that has passed through the walls and tissues of the organs in the digestive system (except the mouth, salivary glands, and gullet). The liver receives in this way all of the digested foods before they go to your body cells (except most of the fat, which gets into the blood by way of lymph vessels). Suppose that bacteria, viruses, or poisons are swallowed with food or water and manage to get into the blood. They must still break through the liver's defenses before they can invade other parts of the body.

The Star Cells—
Sentinels in the Liver

Lining some of the blood vessels that serve every part of the liver are peculiar cells that act much like white blood cells. Each of these cells looks something like a starfish.

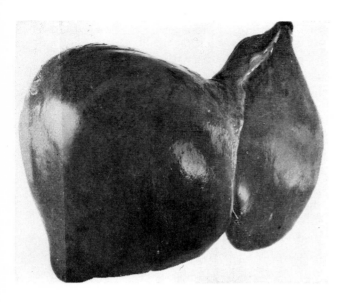

18-4 The liver is the largest gland in the body. What are some of the functions of the liver?

Most books call them the **Kupfer** (KOOP-fer) *stellate* (STEL-ate) liver cells. We shall call them the **star cells.** (*Stellate* means "star-shaped.")

The star cells destroy bacteria, fragments of dead red blood cells, and tiny floating bits of tissue. In other words, star cells remove dead or dangerous particles from the blood before it leaves your liver.

The Liver's Chemical Work

The liver takes sugar, vitamins, and other useful substances from the blood and gives them back when the body needs them. The fact that the liver stores so much food explains why animal liver is sometimes recommended as part of the diet. It is rich in iron, vitamin A, and in a number of the B vitamins. (Vitamins were discussed in Chapter 3.)

Your liver is a wonderful chemical laboratory. Here are some of its functions.

1. Since too much sugar in the blood would be harmful, the liver changes some of the sugar to a starchlike substance called *glycogen*, which it stores. Whenever your cells need fuel, the liver changes the glycogen back into sugar and gives the sugar to the blood.

2. After protein foods have been digested to form amino acids, the liver removes any excess amino acids not needed by body cells for tissue building and repair. The liver also takes out of the blood the amino acids from cells that are destroyed in the body. It makes sugar from these amino acids and forms *urea* (yoo-REE-uh) from what is left. It pours the urea into the blood a little at a time to be removed by the kidneys. The sugar made in this process is saved.

3. It removes hemoglobin from the millions of worn-out red blood cells destroyed by it or the spleen every day. It uses them and other materials to make *bile*. It sends the bile into the small intestine, where it helps digest fats.

4. It stores vitamin B_{12}. This substance is necessary for the development of red blood cells, thus preventing anemia (you read about anemia in Chapter 16).

5. It forms the fibrinogen needed to make your blood clot. It is also believed to make another blood protein, plasma albumin, and two other substances concerned with blood clotting. One of these substances is needed to cause fibrinogen to change to solid fibrin (see Chapter 16); the other acts to prevent clotting at the wrong time.

How the Liver Rebuilds Itself

A large part of the liver may be removed without lasting damage. As soon as the wound heals, liver cells start to grow and divide, provided that there is no serious disease in what is left of the liver. Soon there is enough new liver tissue to carry on all of the liver's normal work.

How the Liver Makes Bile

Twenty-four hours a day the liver uses substances it saves from broken-down red blood cells to make bile. It pours the bile into many tunnel-like tubes that run together to make the bile duct, which carries the bile to the gall bladder and the small intestine. Figure 18-5 is a diagram of the structure of the liver. In making bile, the liver uses over and over much of the material it saves from old red blood cells, as long as this material returns to the liver in nearly the same quantity as before. It removes the iron and part of the protein from the hemoglobin of dead red blood cells and saves these materials for use by the bone marrow in making new blood cells. Then it takes another part of the hemoglobin to use in making bile. This part is brightly colored, being composed of an orange-red substance and a green one. The resulting bile, although mostly water, is orange or yellow in color. (In birds and cows and certain other animals, bile is green in color.)

Chemicals called **bile salts** are found in bile. They are needed in the small intestine to break up fat into tiny drops that are easier to digest. We say that an **emulsion** (ee-MUL-shun) has been formed of fat with the watery liquid in the intestine. In addition, most of the digested fat has to combine with bile salts before it can be absorbed by your blood. As soon as the fat and bile salts have been absorbed, the bile salts are carried by veins back to the liver. Thus, the same bile salts are used over and over in making bile.

The Gall Bladder— Where Bile Is Stored

Your liver makes bile all the time, but the bile goes to the small intestine only when it

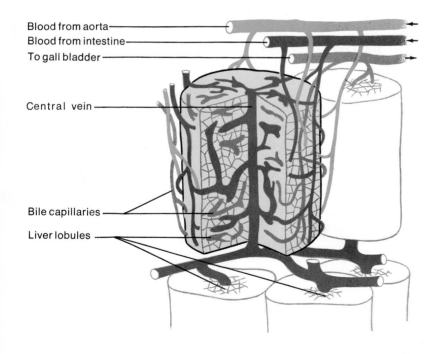

Blood from aorta
Blood from intestine
To gall bladder

Central vein

Bile capillaries
Liver lobules

18-5 A diagram of one tiny lobule in the liver, with four others shown in outline. Can you follow the detailed structure and explain the movement of blood and bile? *Hint*: Blood flows in, toward the center; bile flows out, toward the edges.

is needed, as after a meal when there is food in the intestine.

■ How does bile help break up fat? Try this. Pour some liquid fat (vegetable oil) into a container partly filled with warm water. Notice that the fat comes to the top and forms a continuous film. (See Figure 18-6.)

Now add soap powder, shake well, and look again. You see that the fat has broken up into tiny drops. Bile, like the soap you used, breaks up fat into tiny particles. These can be reached more easily by digestive enzymes.

Bile goes from the liver through the bile duct to the *gall bladder* (see Figure 14-3). As soon as fats or acid foods pass from the stomach into the intestine, the wall of the gall bladder contracts. This makes bile flow from the gall bladder to the intestine.

There is only one entrance to the gall bladder; it is on a one-track branch of the duct that goes from the liver to the small intestine. Sometimes stones form in the gall bladder. These **gallstones** may be made of cholesterol. (You read in Chapter 3 that this substance sometimes does harm in another way—by helping to cause arteriosclerosis.) Other gallstones may be formed of calcium and bile substances that harden as a result of infections or other reasons not well understood.

About one adult out of ten has gallstones, and many more women than men have them. Gallstones are more common in persons who are overweight, and in older persons. However, occasionally younger women may develop gallstones after pregnancy.

Often gallstones give no trouble but sometimes they cause pain or indigestion. *Colic* (KAH-lik) results when a stone clogs the outlet from the gall bladder. Colic is severe abdominal pain. The preferred treatment for gallstones is surgical removal.

18-6 The top photographs show what happens when oil is mixed with water. In the bottom photograph, what has happened to the oil? Why?

Jaundice

During World War II, some soldiers found that they were growing very weak. They lost their appetites and often were nauseated. Sometimes their skins itched so badly that no amount of rubbing or scratching could relieve them. Looking in a mirror, they saw that the whites of their eyes had turned yellow—as yellow as the yolk of an egg. These men suffered from **infectious jaundice** (JAWN-diss), a virus disease of the liver.

Jaundice comes from the French word *jaune* (yellow). The word jaundice by itself is not the name of a special disease, but of a condition in which bile cannot pass on to the small intestine. Consequently, it backs up into the bloodstream. Normally, bile helps in digestion, but it now acts as a poison throughout the body. Yellow color shows in the skin and the eyes, and severe itching may result.

Jaundice may be caused by:

1. Infection by a virus. This condition, called infectious jaundice or *infectious hepatitis*, is caused by drinking water or eating food contaminated by the virus. *Serum hepatitis*, which is more difficult to cure, is transmitted by blood transfusions from a donor with the virus, or by contaminated needles or syringes (see Chapter 16).
2. Certain poisons, such as mercury, phosphorus, arsenic, and carbon tetrachloride.
3. Blockage of the main bile duct by one or more gallstones.

Jaundice of any of these three types is a serious matter. Newborn infants sometimes have a harmless type of jaundice that lasts for four or five days after birth.

Other Liver Damage

Since you could live only a few hours without your liver, it is important to protect it. Fortunately, the liver has wonderful powers of recuperation. It needs them!

The liver has four important kinds of enemies:

1. *Parasites* (PAIR-uh-sytes) that cause liver disease. (Parasites live in the body and use its food or destroy tissue.) These include viruses (as described above) and bacteria. They also include larger parasites, such as the liver fluke, a kind of worm common in some tropical coun-

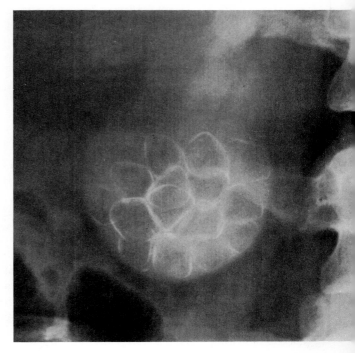

18-7 An X-ray photograph of the gall bladder, showing gallstones. How can gallstones obstruct the flow of bile? Gallstones sometimes enter the bile duct.

tries, but rarely found in the United States.
2. Poisons and alcohol.
3. Eating too little protein and vitamins.
4. Overeating.

Alcohol can be one of the liver's worst enemies. In time, heavy drinking may be followed by an incurable hardening and scarring called *cirrhosis* (sih-ROH-sis), or "hobnail" liver. This permanently disables the liver cells. You will read more about this condition in Chapter 33.

Sometimes the liver stores too much fat. We call this condition *fatty liver*. Whether cirrhosis and fatty liver are *directly* caused by alcohol is not certain. Many doctors think that these troubles are due to lack of protein or certain vitamins. Since alcoholics may not

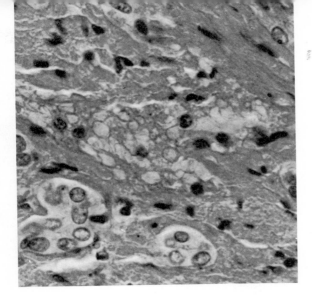

18-8 Photomicrograph of a portion of a liver that has been damaged by cirrhosis. The condition leaves the liver badly scarred. Alcoholism often contributes to it.

eat properly, they could easily develop liver trouble. At any rate, a great deal of liver trouble in the undeveloped countries is caused by too little nourishment, mostly by too little protein. Certain proteins help the liver protect itself against the effect of too much fat. Protein and some of the vitamins help the liver to recover after damage due to alcohol, poisons, or disease.

Eating too much may hurt the liver. Large amounts of fat and rich foods are especially bad. The doctor often has to advise the patient with liver trouble to avoid much fat, especially fatty dishes that are hard to digest. Many people cannot digest greasy stews, rich pastry, and dishes containing fats or oils that have been burned or scorched. Do you have any trouble digesting such foods? If so, what type of diet should you try to maintain?

Exercise and the deep breathing that results from active exercise stimulate circulation of blood through the liver. Each time you inhale, the diaphragm presses down on the liver and gives the blood in it a push forward in the circulation.

YOUR LIVING FILTERS—THE KIDNEYS

Your kidneys are two bean-shaped organs situated one on each side of the back, behind the other abdominal organs. They are just above your waist (Figure 18-9). Each kidney is about 4 1/2 inches long and weighs a little over half a pound. The kidneys do three vitally important things to the blood that passes through them:

1. They remove excess water, taking a large amount of it from the blood when the blood has much more water than it needs, and taking only a little when the supply is low.
2. They filter out wastes prepared for them by the liver. One of these, urea, you have already read about. These wastes are included in the *urine* which is passed out of your body.
3. They regulate the amount of *sodium chloride* (SOH-dee-um KLOR-yde — common salt) and many other substances in the blood. They do not remove the small amount of sugar normally present

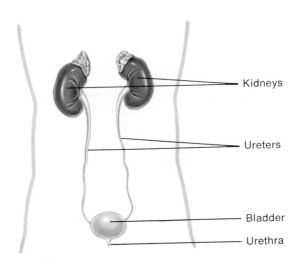

18-9 The urinary system. What are the functions of each part of this system? Why are the kidneys called "your living filters"?

in the blood; the liver normally controls the sugar level, as you have read. However, in a person with **diabetes** (dy-uh-BEE-tiss), the kidneys remove a large part of the excess sugar.

The kidneys are a part of the urinary system. In addition to the two kidneys, the urinary system includes two long tubes, called **ureters** (yoo-REE-ters), that carry the urine to a storage reservoir called the **bladder**; and a short canal, the **urethra** (yoo-REE-thruh), leading from the bladder to the exterior of the body. Figure 18-9 shows the kidneys, ureters, bladder, and urethra.

Arthur F. Jacques, Rhode Island Hospital

18-10 Photograph of a human kidney, approximately two-thirds actual length. At the left, you see the artery and vein that serve the kidney. The tube running down from the kidney is the ureter, leading to the bladder.

How the Kidneys Work

Each kidney has inside it about a million tiny tubes, each called a **nephron** (NEF-ron — from a Greek word meaning kidney). Each nephron is a long coiled tube (Figure 18-11). One end of the nephron is closed and cup-like in shape. The cavity formed by this cup contains a network of capillaries. There are also many other capillaries surrounding the tubule of the nephron. The other end of the nephron opens into a duct that collects the urine.

Blood laden with wastes, nutrients, salts, and water flows from the renal artery into the capillaries in the cavity of each nephron. This blood is under high pressure. The blood fluid containing all blood material except red blood cells, white blood cells, platelets, and blood proteins is filtered from the cells into the nephron cavity. While this is happening, cells of the cavity are reabsorbing useful substances from the fluid and passing them back to the capillaries. You can see that there is a two-way traffic through the cells of the nephron. As the fluid continues to pass through the nephron, more useful substances are returned to the blood. More waste materials are also removed from the blood. Water is reabsorbed into the bloodstream in the lower part of the nephron. By the time the fluid reaches the open end of the nephron, it is urine. Urine, then, is a fluid from which nearly all the useful substances have been removed and returned to the blood.

To test kidney function, the doctor may inject a dye into an arm muscle. The dye should appear in the urine in five to ten minutes.

About 150 quarts of liquid are filtered from the bloodstream into the nephrons every day. As 150 quarts is about twelve times as much as the entire amount of blood in the body, this may seem impossible. The explanation is simple. Only about 1 to 2 quarts

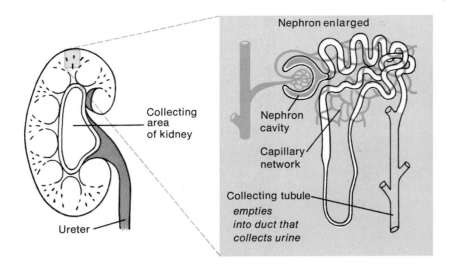

Collecting area of kidney

Ureter

Nephron enlarged

Nephron cavity

Capillary network

Collecting tubule *empties into duct that collects urine*

18-11 Kidney and enlarged nephron. How is blood filtered through the nephron? Where is water reabsorbed? Why is this so important?

of urine are excreted daily. The remaining liquid, including glucose and other substances needed by the body, passes back into the blood capillaries through the coiled tubules.

Reserve Power

A young man was dismayed when his doctor told him that his left kidney would have to be removed. Today, thirty years after the successful removal, he is working as hard as ever and enjoying life as much. That one kidney has taken him through several serious illnesses, including hepatitis, appendicitis, and peritonitis. When a diseased kidney has been removed, the patient may live in good health to a ripe old age. Is this true with any other organ of the body?

The reserve power of the kidneys depends partly on the fact that only a portion of the nephrons work during normal body activity. As there is more need, more nephrons go to work. When one kidney is removed, vast numbers of resting nephrons go into activity in the remaining kidney. As they fill up with liquid from the blood, they expand. As a result, the remaining kidney may increase greatly in size.

Kidney Disorders

There is a close connection between certain kinds of kidney trouble, heart conditions, and high blood pressure. In fact, it has been claimed that the kidneys produce a substance called *renin* (REE-nin) that may act to increase blood pressure. In any case, very high blood pressure may injure the kidneys.

The kidneys are often blamed for conditions that have nothing to do with them. Many backaches, for example, are due to muscular strains and not to kidney malfunctions. However, anything that poisons the rest of the body is likely to injure the kidneys. Mercury, other poisons, large amounts of alcohol, and bacteria may damage the kidneys. The bacteria that cause some kinds of kidney abscesses and inflammation may come from infected tonsils, gall bladder, or teeth, from boils, or from diseases like scarlet fever. Hardening of the arteries, like high blood pressure, is likely to lead to damage to the kidneys.

Nephritis (ne-FRY-tis) includes several serious diseases in which the kidneys are inflamed and damaged. Formerly these diseases were called Bright's disease, for the English doctor who first described this type of ailment. Usually, in these conditions, protein is allowed to pass out with the urine and thus is lost to the body. Some types of nephritis are due to diseases in other parts of the body; others are the result of kidney infection by various bacteria.

Kidney stones sometimes form in the kidneys. They may reach a large size without pain if they stay in one place. They may cause great pain if they slip into the ureter and remain there to block the passage of urine. The cause is not known, but it has been suggested that they are more likely to form when there is infection, blockage causing stagnant urine in the kidneys, or very concentrated urine with excess minerals. Fortunately, hard drinking water does not seem to cause stones. Hard water is water with a large amount of mineral matter.

Sometimes kidney stones pass out of the body with the urine without any treatment, and often the doctor can relieve the condition by purely medical treatment. Sometimes he must operate to remove the stone. A stone may pass down from the kidney to the bladder, remain there, and continue to grow.

Uremia (yoo-REE-mi-ah) is a condition in which the kidneys cannot get rid of many waste products. As a result, these wastes accumulate in the blood and have a poisonous effect. As the wastes accumulate in the tissues, a person becomes extremely fatigued and may suffer from lack of appetite, breathlessness, anemia, and loss of weight and strength. Uremia is not itself a specific disease, but is the result of kidney disease, such as infection or an obstruction that blocks the passage of urine.

Kidney failure, like heart failure, may occur in greater or less degree. Sometimes, during nephritis, shock, severe injury, hemorrhage, or heart failure, the kidneys suddenly "go on strike." They become unable to produce more than a very small amount of urine, so that the patient is soon suffering from the damaging effects of uremia. Com-

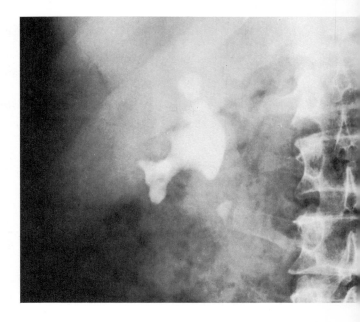

18-12 An X-ray photograph of the kidneys showing kidney stones. How are kidney stones formed?

plete lack of urine output is called *anuria* (a-NYOO-ri-ah).

Artificial Kidneys and Kidney Grafts

Kidney machines, or *artificial kidneys*, have saved many lives when kidney failure would otherwise have been fatal. Plastic tubes are connected with the patient's blood vessels, and the blood is pumped through a series of filters until the patient's own kidneys are again working efficiently.

Many persons have donated one of their own healthy kidneys to desperately ill patients so that the donor's kidney could be grafted into the body of the sick person. The difficulty here is that the human body may "reject" organs or tissues that are grafted into it. A certain measure of success has been achieved, however, and a tremendous amount of research is going on in the field of grafting organs.

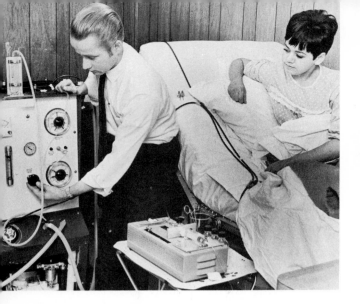

18-13 The artificial kidney has saved many lives. This man is adjusting the machine for his wife. The room was added to their home especially to house the machine. She uses it twice each week.

18-14 Kidney transplants are becoming more and more common. These ten-year-old twins have undergone kidney surgery. Joyce (*left*) is the recipient, and Janet (*right*) is the donor.

Urinalysis— and What It Tells the Physician

A most important source of information for the physician is the ***urinalysis*** (yoo-rih-NAL-ih-sis), or analysis of urine. The urine is tested for glucose, albumin, and many other substances. This analysis usually shows whether there is any likelihood or presence of kidney disease, even in the early stages. It also helps to reveal abnormal conditions in other parts of the body. This is because the liver and other glands and the spleen may cause changes in the blood and consequently in the urine. As a result, urinalysis often shows how these other organs are working.

Like all medical tests, the urinalysis needs to be studied by a physician who knows his patient. Sugar in the urine often indicates diabetes. Sometimes, however, sugar may appear because of excitement or having recently eaten a large amount of sweets. Pro-tein in the urine may mean infection or kidney disease, but sometimes it is found as a result of perfectly normal conditions. Cloudiness may be the result of infection, or it may merely show the presence of normal salts in the urine. Color may vary a good deal without indicating that anything is wrong. In any case, a urinalysis is an important part of a general physical examination.

Bladder Difficulties

As the inner lining of the bladder is very resistant to infection, most infections of the bladder are conveyed to it from the kidney or other organs. Bacterial infection of the bladder lining is called ***cystitis*** (sis-TY-tis). Urine containing pus, painful urination, and, in severe cases, pain over the bladder and fever and chills are frequent symptoms. If urine accumulates in the bladder and continually stays there, it may cause serious trouble in the kidneys. Older men frequently suffer from this condition due to enlargement of the *prostate* gland. This is an organ found only in the male; it surrounds the part of the urethra through which urine is excreted from the bladder. Ordinarily the prostate enlarges and causes difficulty only in men over fifty.

Avoiding Kidney Damage

You can help to keep the kidneys healthy by maintaining your overall health and by seeking prompt treatment for any disorder, such as infection.

In the past, much painful bladder disease was the result of the venereal disease *gonorrhea*, which is discussed in Chapter 29.

Drink plenty of water. The kidneys do not seem to be injured by the quantity of water that they have to get rid of, but they cannot do the best job unless they have sufficient water to dilute wastes. A healthy adult needs about six to eight glassfuls a day, or somewhat less when he takes sufficient quantities of other liquids. In practice, you should find your sense of thirst a good guide. Salty foods increase the need for water. You need more water when you perspire freely, or when you have a cold, fever, or other disease in which the kidneys have to get rid of an unusual amount of wastes and poisons. A doctor should be immediately informed when there is any difficulty, burning, or pain when passing urine.

Don't try to doctor yourself. You do not have the knowledge to judge whether advertised kidney remedies would help you. Only a physician can judge the value of any drug in any particular case.

ENVIRONMENTAL FACTORS AFFECTING THE HEALTH OF THE LIVER AND KIDNEYS

It is interesting to compare different countries in relation to disorders that seem to be affected by social-environmental factors. Cancer starting in the liver is rare in western countries, but comparatively common in Africa. Formerly it was thought that the principal cause of liver cancer was lack of sufficient protein. But much of the liver cancer in Africa, and perhaps in other places, has been caused by eating peanuts infested by a certain kind of mold. The poison made by this mold is called *aflatoxin* (a-flah-TOCKS-in).

To show how important social conditions can be to health or survival, consider the artificial kidneys or kidney machines that can do the job of a diseased kidney and thus save a person's life. There are so few of these machines and they are so expensive that comparatively few of the patients who need them can have the use of one. The patient shown in Figure 18-13 is particularly fortunate.

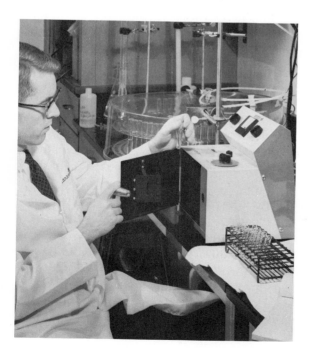

18-15 Urinalysis is an important source of medical information. What are some conditions tested by urinalysis?

Polycythemia — too many red blood cells, cause unknown sometimes due to heart or lung disease

What kind of health practices should you apply in maintaining your health? Check your understanding of the chapter. On a separate sheet of paper, number 1 through 24 and insert the answer from the vocabulary list below. Use each expression, but use each one only once.

11 aflatoxin	8 jaundice	13 portal vein
6 bile	5 kidneys	2 star cells
10 cirrhosis	1 liver	16 sugar
19 diabetes	12 liver fluke	24 tonsils
15 fibrinogen	23 lymph nodes	4 urea
7 gall bladder	21 nephritis	22 uremia
3 glycogen	18 nephrons	20 ureters
9 infectious hepatitis	17 plasma albumin	14 vitamin B_{12}

As the blood circulates over and over again through the body, it gives up useful substances, such as oxygen and digested foods, and takes in waste products that the body must get rid of. The (1) *liver* may be thought of as the "watchdog" of the blood because poisons and germs swallowed with food must break through its defenses before they can invade other parts of the body. In this organ, the (2) *star cells* devour bacteria and floating dead particles.

The liver acts like a living chemical laboratory. It changes some of the sugar it receives into (3) *glycogen* and it changes amino acids into two very different substances, sugar and (4) *urea*. This last substance is carried to the (5) *kidneys* which remove it. Although the liver does not send digestive enzymes to the intestine, it produces (6) *bile* which helps digest fats. This substance is stored in the (7) *gall bladder* until it is needed.

The condition that causes bile to back up into the bloodstream and may make the whites of the eyes turn yellow is called (8) *jaundice*. This is often the result of the virus disease (9) *infectious hepatitis*. (10) *cirrhosis* is an often incurable hardening of the liver. Cancer of the liver, rare in western countries, may be due to eating too little protein or too much (11) *aflatoxin* found in moldy peanuts. Another condition, fortunately rare in this country, is invasion by a parasitic worm, the (12) *liver fluke*.

The liver receives blood from arteries and also from the (13) *portal vein*. It stores iron and (14) *B12* needed for making normal red blood cells. It makes (15) *fibrinogen* which changes to fibrin when the blood clots. Whenever the cells need fuel, the liver changes glycogen to (16) *sugar*. Besides fibrinogen, the liver is believed to make the protein (17) *plasma albumin*.

Each kidney contains about a million tiny tubes called (18) *nephrons*. In the disease (19) *diabetes* these tubes allow part of the excess sugar to pass from the blood to the urine. The (20) *ureters* are the long tubes that carry urine from the kidneys to the bladder. The term (21) *nephritis* includes several serious diseases in which the kidneys are inflamed and damaged. As a result of these diseases or of severe injuries or other diseased conditions, the kidneys may be unable to get rid of waste products, which therefore accumulate in the blood. This condition is called (22) _uremia_

Our (23) _lymph nodes_ in the neck, armpits, and other places protect us by stopping germs before they get into the main bloodstream. Our (24) _tonsils_, one on each side of the throat, also help to protect us against invading germs.

What You Can Do

The following are health practices. Are these practices helpful or harmful? Change the poor health practices to make them into good health practices. While doing this, keep as much of the original wording as you can.

1. You do not need to be careful about eating or drinking things that may be poisonous since the liver will make them harmless.

2. Since slightly swollen or painful lymph nodes are not important, you do not need to bother to see a doctor when you have a slightly painful swelling in the armpit following a wound in your finger.

3. There is no use looking for trouble when you feel quite well; hence a urinalysis when you take your physical examination may be merely a waste of time.

4. While it is true that drinking too much alcohol may cause one to act differently, there is no evidence that alcohol is likely to do any _physical_ harm to the body.

5. Plan to drink very little water, because water only takes up space and keeps one from eating nourishing food.

6. To help keep the liver in good condition, one should eat plenty of fats and minerals, but one should not eat very much protein or vitamins.

7. Exercise and good posture may be beneficial for one's muscles, but there is no reason to think that they can benefit the liver.

8. We do not need to take medical precautions when we have an infection in another part of the body as such an infection is not likely to spread to the kidneys.

Things to Try

1. The artificial kidney and the heart-lung machine are two of the most hopeful recent advances in medical practice. Learn about machines that can do the work of the living human kidney in "Artificial Kidneys: Where We Stand," by B. T. Burton in _Today's Health_, July 1967.

2. Just as hopeful for the future welfare of mankind is the work now being done in transplanting kidneys and other organs. You can make an exciting report to your class about research and surgical efforts in this direction. Invite the members of your class to give their opinions of the work described in your report. What may be the results of the remarkable progress that physicians are making in the replacement of defective human organs?

Probing Further /

Human Physiology, by T. F. Morrison, Holt, Rinehart & Winston, 1966. This is a more advanced book for those who want to probe more deeply into the systems of the body.

The Body, by Alan E. Nourse and Editors of *Life*, Time, 1964. You will enjoy the beautiful color illustrations and the brief explanations of the work of the kidneys and the liver in this up-to-date book.

The Machinery of the Body, by A. J. Carlson, Victor Johnson, and H. M. Cavert, University of Chicago Press, 1961. An advanced but interesting book from which you can learn many facts about the organs discussed in this chapter.

Health Concepts in Action /

Does what you have learned support the following statement?

> ***Wastes and poisons are filtered from the blood and other body fluids by specialized organs.***

Applying this concept, which health practices would you

— continue?

— change?

— begin?

Will you now, as a result of your study, change any of your health objectives?

19 / Balances in the Body

Many years ago a carnival entertainer known as the "Fire King" would alarm his audience by walking into a large, hot oven. The oven was kept at a temperature of about 220°F—eight degrees above the boiling point of water. Dressed in heavy clothes, the Fire King would remain in the oven broiling slices of meat rare, medium, or well-done as the audience called out their choices. How was it possible for him to remain in this intense heat?

A PROBE INTO THE BODY'S FEEDBACK MECHANISMS—How is your internal environment kept more or less constant in spite of a changing environment? To find out, you will be probing these questions:

1. How does your body's cooling system work? How does our body temperature vary in health and in disease? Why could the "Fire King" remain in the oven?

3. What is heatstroke? heat prostration? heat cramp? How would you give first aid for each of these conditions?

2. What are some of the feedback systems in your body? Why is negative feedback important for life? Why is positive feedback dangerous?

4. How may your feelings affect breathing, heartbeat, and heat regulation?

HOW WE CONTROL OUR TEMPERATURE

Some schools have nature rooms with plants, fish, tadpoles, and perhaps a snake or two. If you took a snake outdoors on a cold day, it could not go far. It would soon be stiff with cold even though you and other **warm-blooded** animals felt fine. Suppose you took the snake to a hot desert. If the sun were very hot and the snake could not make its way to the cooler shade, it would probably die.

All animals are said to be either warm-blooded or **cold-blooded.** Man is warm-blooded, as are dogs, rabbits, and cats. Cold-blooded animals, such as snakes, fish, and frogs, actually feel cold when you touch them. Yet if these animals are exposed to great heat, their temperature may rise 20 degrees or more above ours. The important difference is that warm-blooded creatures can keep their temperature more or less the same, regardless of the temperature around them, while the cold-blooded animals cannot do this. Your body has a system of built-in controls that keeps heat production and loss in proper balance to counteract the effect of changes in the temperature around you. As a result, your temperature does not change much whether you are waiting on the corner for the school bus on a very cold day or lying on the beach in the middle of summer.

Your Heating System

Each of the billions of cells in your body oxidizes digested foods. In the process the cell releases chemical energy and stores some in readily available compounds, but it also loses a significant amount of energy as heat. You read about this in Chapter 3.

■ You can demonstrate to yourself the presence of heat in your body, as well as its loss. Put the palm of your hand near your mouth and blow against it. What do you feel? See Figure 19-1.

The temperature of the air you breathe out is close to the temperature in your lungs. Your cells can give off enough heat to keep you warm in freezing weather as long as you wear clothing sufficient to keep the heat from escaping too rapidly.

Speeding Up Heat Production

Anything that increases the rate of **oxidation**—the rate at which energy is released from food in the cells—will increase the amount of heat produced in your body. Hence, your body is warmed mostly by:

1. Exercise, which if vigorous enough may raise your temperature temporarily from 1 to 4 degrees or more.
2. All the normal work of your body cells. The liver, the largest of the glands, contributes more heat than any other gland. However, your muscles do far more than your glands to keep you warm.
3. Eating. The digestion of the meal itself results in extra heat production. The food also supplies substances that

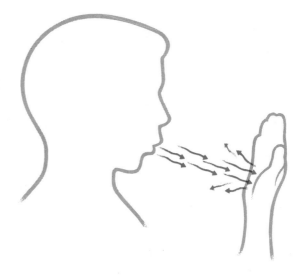

19-1 Does your breath feel warm against your hand? How is it warmed?

stimulate the oxidation of food in the cells.

4. Shivering, which is a sort of *involuntary* exercise. When you shiver, your muscles contract and relax slightly, producing a bit more heat.

The fact that exercise increases body temperature helps explain why Arctic explorers and mountain climbers caught in blizzards keep moving until they find shelter. To lie down to rest without protection from the cold would be fatal.

Your Cooling System

Though you must produce heat to live, you must also get rid of it to live. A rise of only eight to ten degrees above your normal body temperature is fatal if not corrected.

Your cooling system begins with the blood, which distributes heat more evenly through your body. The blood absorbs heat from active muscles and busy glands and carries it to the lungs and skin. This helps to protect you in three ways: (1) it cools organs that are too warm; (2) it warms parts of the body that do not produce much heat; (3) it provides a route of heat escape. As you grow too warm, capillaries near the skin widen and let more blood pass through. With more blood flowing not only to your skin but to your lungs, more heat exchange occurs as cooler air comes in contact with your warm skin.

About 75 percent of the heat you lose escapes through your skin. The air around you gains some of the body heat as long as it is cooler than your skin. This is the same way heat escapes from a steam radiator or a stove.

Another 15 percent of the heat you lose also escapes through the skin—as you perspire. See Figure 19-2. In this case you lose both heat and water. As the perspiration evaporates from your skin, it takes with it the heat that helped it change into water vapor. For a speeded-up version of how this works, try a simple test.

19-2 Perspiration is a valuable aid in keeping your body from overheating. In what other ways does your body cool itself?

Wet the back of your hand with rubbing alcohol. Let the liquid evaporate. Why does the back of your hand feel cooler?

Just as the alcohol vapor goes off into the air taking heat with it, so does perspiration, although at a slower rate. On very hot days, when the temperature of the air equals or exceeds your skin temperature, you have to rely on perspiration and breathing to keep you from overheating.

Going back to the "Fire King" mentioned in the introduction to this chapter, scientists have proved that it was possible for him to do what he claimed to do. It was the evaporation of vast amounts of perspiration in the hot, very *dry* air of the oven that saved him—this and being shielded from the oven's hot rays by his thick clothing. If the air had been moist he would have been overcome by heat and might have died.

Every time you exhale the air that you have in your lungs, you lose heat with it. About 10 percent of the heat you lose escapes in this way.

Maintaining Heat Balance

If you grow too cool, the blood capillaries in your skin contract. Less blood reaches your skin; thus less heat is lost by the skin to the air around you. When the balance shifts the other way, the capillaries widen, and more blood flows through the skin. More heat again is lost by the skin.

The water balance in your body plays a part in heat balance. When you are too hot, your tissues give up fluid to the bloodstream; this increases the volume of blood that circulates to your skin. When you are cooler again, the tissues reabsorb more fluid.

Maintaining heat balance is one of hundreds of your body's tasks of *homeostasis* that you read about in Chapter 1. In perfect health, your temperature goes up and down a little each day and there is a difference between the normal temperatures in different parts of your body. However, your body will not function properly if your temperature is too high or low.

How Body Temperatures Vary

"Normal" mouth temperature is 98.6° F. The temperature on the surface of the skin is lower. To test this, place a thermometer under your armpit. You will find that your temperature there is about one degree less than in your mouth. The temperature deeper inside your body is about one degree higher than in your mouth. Very often the hands and feet are much cooler than the rest of the body; many people suffer from cold feet. Infants, young people, and aged people have about one degree higher temperature than most adults. Most women have a slightly higher temperature than men. Even in healthy people of the same age and sex, working under the same conditions, the temperatures may be slightly different.

There is a regular daily rise and fall of about two degrees. Most people wake up in

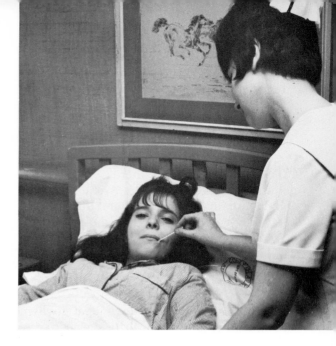

19-3 Body temperature usually rises when you have an infection. How do temperatures vary? What is *your* "normal" temperature?

the morning with a temperature of from 96° F to 98° F. Different people reach their high temperature point at different times of the day. Meals, exercise, hot and cold baths, clothing, time of year, and climate also cause slight changes.

Your feelings of warmth or cold cannot be relied upon to tell you what the temperature is inside your body. You need a thermometer for this purpose. A cold wind makes you feel cold; summer sunshine makes you feel warm. Yet a thermometer would show your temperature to be normal at both times. What you *feel* is the condition affecting the nerve endings in your skin, not the true temperature inside your body.

Your Living Thermostat

The thermostat in a building keeps the temperature indoors from going too high or too low. Inside your head, as you learned in Chapter 12, you have a wonderful thermostat that keeps your temperature from varying more than a few degrees. The principal piece of equipment of your thermostat is a portion of the **hypothalamus**, a small part of the brain that lies below the *cerebrum*. The front part of the "built-in" thermostat protects you against overheating by sending out impulses to lower the body's temperature. Behind this are the nerve cells that protect against chilling. They send impulses that cause the capillaries to contract, and they make you shiver and do the other things that cause you to produce and save heat. If this section of the hypothalamus is removed, a profound drop in temperature follows. Your thermostat is apparently influenced in two ways: (1) by the temperature of the blood flowing around it and (2) by nerve impulses brought in from the skin.

HOW FEEDBACK KEEPS US ALIVE

All thermostats, including the metal one that keeps the temperature in a building from going too high or low and the living thermostat that keeps your temperature within a normal range, work by **feedback**. When the temperature of the air around a thermostat in a building drops too low, the thermostat sends, or *feeds back*, an electric "command" to make the furnace send up more heat. If the temperature goes too high, the thermostat feeds back a signal to make the furnace send less heat. Feedback is a helpful term because the temperature of a room (largely due to the activity of the furnace) indirectly causes the output of the furnace to be adjusted to bring the temperature up or down to the desired level.

The heating-control systems both in a building and in man work by **negative feedback**. A *rise* in building or body temperature causes the furnace or the hypothalamus to act to lower the temperature. A fall in building or body temperature causes the control system to take the reverse action.

Feedbacks in the Human Body

Many other feedback systems work to keep your internal activities in balance. You have such automatic controls for breathing, rate of heartbeat, the amount of water in your tissues and blood, the amount of sugar in the blood, maintaining the proper degree of acidity and its opposite, alkalinity, in the fluids of the body, and many other purposes. These various activities must be controlled to maintain health, and sometimes to maintain life. Most of the time you are not aware of the constant readjustments that are made without your ever having to think about them.

All of the controls mentioned above work by negative feedback. Negative feedback for such functions as temperature control is necessary for life. **Positive feedback** can be disastrous. Think again of the thermostat that controls the heating of a building. If it had positive feedback, it would send a signal to make the furnace send *more* heat when the

19-4 Is this scene familiar to you? How often have you shivered while waiting for a bus? What makes you shiver?

temperature of a room rose. If positive feedback continued, the thermostat would signal for more and more heat as the building became hotter and hotter.

Our negative-feedback balance systems operate only within certain limits. If a man's body temperature rises to about 108° F, the negative feedback breaks down, and a deadly positive feedback goes to work. As chemical reactions go on faster as temperature rises, his cells carry on respiration and other chemical changes faster and faster, producing more and more heat. More heat makes the chemical reactions speed more and more. Unless this process of positive feedback can be stopped, the patient will die.

Heatstroke and Heat Prostration

Heatstroke is a breakdown of the body's negative-feedback heat-regulating system. This breakdown is followed by a positive, heat-increasing feedback that is a serious threat to life. It most often follows exercise or physical work during prolonged exposure to very high temperature or the direct rays of a hot sun along with lack of circulating air. *Sunstroke* is heatstroke resulting from exposure to the sun.

Heat prostration, or *heat exhaustion,* is alarming but much less dangerous than heatstroke. It also follows exposure to excessive heat, but the heat-regulating system does not function as poorly as in heatstroke. Few people die from heat exhaustion.

First Aid for Heatstroke and Heat Prostration

Heatstroke and heat prostration require very different treatment. Both call for immediate care by a doctor. Heatstroke victims have a high fever and a flushed face. The pupils of their eyes are usually dilated, the skin dry and hot, and the pulse rapid. Place the patient in a cool spot and apply ice packs, or repeatedly dash cold water over his body and head to reduce his temperature. Care should be observed not to make his temperature drop too *low*. If it does, he may again be in danger of collapse and now need applications of heat. Do not give stimulants.

The victim of heat prostration may be dizzy and nauseated. His face is pale, his skin clammy, and his pulse slow. Have him lie down in a cool spot. Loosen his clothing and give him nothing to drink but cool water. See Figure 19-5.

Heat cramp results from physical exertion in high temperatures (above 100° F), with heavy sweating and failure to eat enough salt to replace that lost with perspiration. Cramps are painful, involuntary contractions of muscles. In heat cramp, the patient may thrash about or lie flat with legs drawn up. If not treated, an attack may last for days. All that is needed to prevent heat cramp is to consume enough salt. To give first aid, have the patient lie down in a cool place and have him drink salted water. A doctor should be seen as soon as possible.

Fever

If you have ever been a patient in a hospital, you know how the nurse comes around at regular intervals to take your temperature. Fever is a rise in body temperature above its normal range. Usually we say that a person has fever if the temperature is above 98.6° F in a patient remaining in bed, or above 99° F in one who is allowed to walk about a bit. Fever follows when the body produces more heat than it can lose. In an active person, a temperature of about 99° F is no cause for alarm unless other symptoms are present. A temperature of around 100° F in an adult or 101° F in a child almost always indicates illness.

The unborn child has not yet developed an efficient temperature-control system. In fact, a new-born baby is still like a cold-

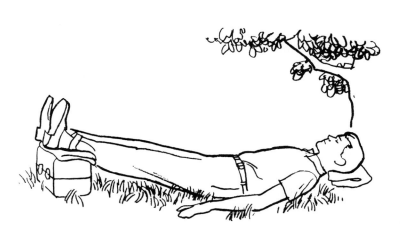

19-5 (*Top*) Treatment for heatstroke. Keep the patient as cool as possible and call a doctor immediately. (*Bottom*) Treatment for heat prostration. The patient should lie on his back with his feet slightly elevated. If the victim is conscious, give him sips of cool water.

blooded animal in this respect. This is why it is so very important to keep a new baby properly warm. The temperature of young children goes up and down more readily than that of adults. A given amount of fever is usually more serious in an adult.

Is Fever Ever Helpful?

Scientists are still investigating whether fever is part of the body's defense against germs. A high temperature may increase production of antibodies, substances the body makes to fight germs or their toxins. Fever may check the growth of the bacteria that cause many diseases. The problem sometimes is whether the fever is doing more harm to the germs or to the patient.

Generally speaking, the doctor's aim is to treat the disease that is causing the fever. Sometimes the fever rises so high, or causes such distress and discomfort, that the physician takes steps to reduce fever itself along with treatment to cure the disease. Aspirin is the best-known anti-fever drug. It acts on our thermostat in the brain. Large or continued doses should not be taken except on doctor's orders. Aside from the disease or condition

FIGURE 19-6 CONDITIONS THAT CAUSE HIGH BODY TEMPERATURES*

Condition	Causes	Symptoms	Treatment
Heatstroke or sunstroke	Breakdown of heat-regulating system following overexertion in hot weather or prolonged exposure to sun.	Collapse or weakening, with skin dry despite heat, face flushed, pupils usually dilated, pulse rapid. Perspiration rate extremely low despite high body temperature.	A serious threat to life— call a doctor at once. Move victim to shaded spot and apply ice packs or cold water liberally.
Heat prostration or heat exhaustion	Exposure to excessive heat, resulting in accumulation of body heat at a faster rate than perspiration can remove.	Fainting, or dizziness and possible nausea. Face pale, skin damp, pulse usually slow.	Move victim to shade, loosen his clothing, have him lie down, and give him cool water to drink. Patient should be advised to see doctor if recovery not prompt.
Heat cramp	Physical exertion in high temperatures, causing heavy sweating leading to excessive loss of salt from body.	Painful cramps of the muscles, infrequently lasting for several days if not treated.	Move victim to shade and give salt tablets with water. Patient should be advised to see doctor.

* Conditions listed above do not include infections.

which causes it, extremely high fever can itself be fatal.

A review of some conditions that affect the body's heat balance is given in Figure 19-6.

Chills

When you have a chill and feel coldest, it may be just an early stage of a hot fever on its way. A person with a chill feels miserably cold, shivers, sometimes violently, and usually has pale or blue lips. Frequently he has aching pains in his joints. Chills are usually followed by fever. In malaria and a few other diseases, chills and fever are repeated at regular intervals. As a general rule, the worse the chill, the hotter the fever that follows. A person with a chill may already have a high fever in his internal tissues although he feels very cold.

Good evidence indicates that there is a *center* (a group of nerve cells) in the hypothalamus that brings on a chill when stimulated. If bacteria, other germs, or substances made by bacteria enter the blood, they may cause the "chill center" to go into action. When a chill occurs, water passes from the blood through the capillary walls into the tissues. This reduces the volume of circulating blood and thus causes less blood to go to the small vessels of the skin. Receiving so little blood, the skin becomes cold and sends messages to the thermostat in the brain, telling it to act to increase body temperature. The thermostat now causes still less blood to flow to the skin and still more to flow through the internal blood vessels. This is a case of the *positive* feedback, which can be destructive unless proper care is given.

Chilling in Surgery

There is danger that tissues may die for lack of oxygen in operations in which, for a time, blood supply has to be cut off to certain organs, such as the heart or the brain. The amount of oxygen needed by a tissue goes up and down with temperature. Hence, if organs can be safely chilled well below normal temperature, some delicate operations can be performed that would not be safe at normal temperatures.

Your Feelings and Their Effect on Heat Regulation

In addition to the center of heat balance, several other important centers are also in the hypothalamus, as you have read. Some of them are intricately involved with your emotional responses—fear and anger are examples. When you become afraid or angry, nerve impulses stimulate some of your body's endocrine glands (Figure 22-1, page 403). Their secretions, called *hormones*, are released into your bloodstream. One of these

hormones, *adrenaline*, is among those secreted into the blood. It and **ACTH**, another hormone that is released by a gland very near the hypothalamus, cause energy-yielding sugar to be released into the blood, too. Adrenaline speeds up your heartbeat and brings about other changes. At the same time, sympathetic nerve impulses slow digestion to put you into an emergency state. You oxidize sugar at an increased rate. More heat is produced as you oxidize more sugar in your emotional stress. You will learn more about the endocrine glands in Chapter 22.

With your emotions and your heat regulation both affected by the hypothalamus, is it any wonder that your temperature is affected by your behavior and emotions? When something makes you blush, you may actually *feel* the change in your skin temperature as the blood capillaries dilate in your skin and a hot flush creeps up your face. Your internal temperature also may go up, briefly.

Your skin temperature may go up markedly when you lose your temper. Anger feeds anger in a way, because the nerve- and hormone-stimulated reactions, once set up, have your body adjusted for quarreling, shouting, and fighting with heart pounding rapidly, muscles contracting and relaxing (trembling), blood pressure going up, face flushing, body temperature going up, and other emergency changes occurring. Your body has thrown the switches for violence and, as a result, you grow angrier still—an example of the dangers of positive feedback from the body's emergency state.

People often say that it is best to get angry once in a while and "get it out of your system" rather than "choke it down." Is this true? If you do not get too ruffled in the first place, you will not have much anger in "your system" and will have little "to choke down." Better still, you are more likely to think clearly and do the right thing, instead of doing something you may regret. How do you react in such situations?

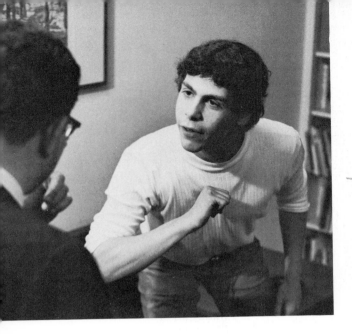

19-7 There are many day-to-day situations that result in anger. How should they be handled?

Your temperature can be affected to some degree by almost all intense emotion. Whatever effect fear may have upon your body temperature, it can make your face turn pale, your hands grow cold, and cold perspiration stream from your body.

We have not discussed all the effects of your feelings upon your temperature. Perhaps you can think of more as you consider the things that happened to you today. You might want to compare your reactions with those of your classmates.

Social and Environmental Effects upon Heat Regulation

Figure 19-6 lists some of the extreme effects of environmental conditions upon heat regulation. Shivering as you wait outdoors on a cold day or perspiring heavily on a hot day are more common examples.

Environment means more than climate. Your surroundings, whatever they may be, are an environment. After a few minutes in a crowded room you may find yourself think-

ing, "It's stuffy in here—I wish someone would open a window." If no one does, you soon feel very warm. The air temperature has gone up somewhat, but it may not be high. One thing that has happened is that the room's atmosphere has become moist with exhaled vapor from the breath of the people in the room. Humidity has gone up so much that your perspiration does not evaporate readily. Your body temperature may have changed little, but you feel "hot" because of the moisture on your skin. The atmosphere of the room is so humid that perspiration cannot evaporate.

Exercise raises the body's temperature measurably. When you play tennis with a friend, or put on a glove and join in a baseball game, your temperature soon may be up 1° F to 4° F. The actual amount depends upon how hard you work at the game, and also upon the working of your heat-regulating system. This temperature change is nothing to be alarmed about—in fact, the exercise is probably good for you. When you stop play, however, put on a light jacket, even if the outdoor temperature is moderate. Otherwise you may chill as perspiration continues to evaporate. If the day is cool, wear a heavier jacket or a coat after the game.

Day in and day out, your feelings of comfort or discomfort are closely related to heat regulation. If you feel too hot or "clammy," or too cold, you lose time and enjoyment at study and play. This is true of all of us and is one of the reasons why a great deal of planning and expense goes into temperature and humidity control for modern classrooms, offices, auditoriums, restaurants, and other indoor places where people meet, work together, eat, and enjoy entertainment. Not everyone is comfortable at the same temperature and humidity; there are individual differences. But *most* people can be made comfortable, or at least less uncomfortable than they otherwise would be.

Some scientists foresee a day when an

19-8 A crowded, stuffy room can ruin your enjoyment of a party or other social gathering.

entire city may be placed under a dome in which weather conditions are controlled (Figure 19-9). Indoors and "outside," the conditions would be those most suitable for the comfort and efficiency of most of the population.

FEEDBACK IN BREATHING AND HEARTBEAT

Normally your breathing, like your temperature, is regulated by *negative feedback*. You make constant adjustments without having to think about it, as you read in Chapter 15. But, unlike most other functions kept in balance by your body, your breathing may be switched to your conscious control any time you please. It also is affected by your emotions, so that you have several systems of feedback for how frequently and how deeply you breathe.

Heartbeat is closely related to breathing. It and your breathing rate are controlled by the medulla of your brain. They work together in maintaining the oxygen-carbon dioxide balance in your body. Heartbeat is associated with other body balances, too. Unlike your breathing, it cannot usually be consciously controlled.

Feedback to the Medulla— and Its Responses

What kinds of feedback due to changes in the oxygen–carbon dioxide balance go to the medulla to cause it to regulate your heartbeat and breathing? Since all your body cells require oxygen, you might guess that too little oxygen in blood circulating to the medulla is the feedback stimulus. Actually, too much carbon dioxide in the blood initiates the feedback. As blood with an excess of carbon dioxide passes through the medulla, the medulla sends more nerve impulses to your diaphragm and your rib muscles. You begin to breathe more deeply, *lowering* the carbon dioxide content of the blood (and increasing the oxygen content). Usually the heartbeat is not measurably affected unless the imbalance is considerable, as during exercise.

Do you see how, once again, *negative feedback* works to maintain a balance? Too much carbon dioxide is a stimulus causing its concentration to be *lowered*.

Another feedback system is triggered by oxygen concentration, but our understanding of it is not complete. You read in Chapter 15 that there are nerve-cell endings in the main arteries in your neck. There are also other

19-9 *(Left)* An artist's conception of a temperature-controlled city under a dome. *(Right)* Temperature control may also be possible in this artist's conception of an underwater city.

nerve-cell endings in the arch of the aorta, just above this great artery's point of departure from the heart. Blood is under great pressure as it passes these points. If the oxygen level in the blood falls only moderately low, these nerve endings appear not to be stimulated. If the oxygen level falls extremely low, they are stimulated. They send impulses to the medulla; connections are made, and other impulses are started on their way to your diaphragm, rib muscles, and your heart. You begin to breathe very rapidly, and your heartbeat suddenly increases.

Your Feelings and Your Oxygen–Carbon Dioxide Balance

Both your feelings and your habits may affect your breathing. Some boys and girls (and some adults) hold their breath when they try very hard to concentrate on a particular thought or problem.

Fear produces a change in breathing. Just when the fear begins, breathing may subside, almost as if the person who is afraid wants to escape notice and feels that his breathing may draw attention to him. Controlling your breathing in this way only accelerates the effect of fear upon the heart, which pounds away at a much more increased pace.

Often when you feel sleepy "without reason" (assuming that you know you are getting enough sleep), your position may be partly the cause. Blood circulation to parts of your body may be sluggish because you have remained in one position too long. You may find it difficult to keep your attention focused on what you are doing. The air in the room may help to make you sleepy. The air may be stagnant or too cool or too warm. Stand up and move around for four or five minutes before you return to what you were doing. Take a few deep breaths. Try to plan a similar break in activity each hour.

Your school schedule is planned with frequent breaks to help keep you from becoming fatigued, drowsy, or sluggish. You have a short recess between classes, and you move to another room in the school for your next class. Some teachers plan their class periods for a change in activity midway in the period. All these things help maintain good balances in the body—including your oxygen–carbon dioxide balance.

Social and Environmental Influences on Oxygen–Carbon Dioxide Balance

We already have discussed some environmental influences. Your environment may have a great deal to do with your feelings, not only in your school but wherever you are. Social and environmental influences extend much further—beyond their influence upon your feelings and emotions.

One of the severest environmental problems today is smog. Contributing to it—in and near every large city—are smoke from chimneys, automobile exhaust fumes, and

19-11 How does a mountain altitude affect your oxygen-carbon dioxide balance? Do people who live in such an environment ever adjust to it?

industrial exhaust products. It isn't easy to feel refreshed as you walk along a street inhaling the exhaust fumes from thousands of automobiles.

At moderate-to-high altitudes in the mountains of the western United States you begin to breathe more heavily, and your heart beats more quickly. There is less oxygen than you are accustomed to in the air around you; hence moderate exercise may make you short of breath. In time you adjust, as an increased supply of red blood cells is made by your body. How will this help?

The greatest natural effect of your environment upon your oxygen–carbon dioxide balance is the one that makes your life possible—your relationship to green plants. Can you explain it?

BALANCE IN THE BLOOD AND OTHER TISSUES

Twice you have learned that the blood is one bearer of feedback. You will see this more as you read of other body balances. Blood is not only a "messenger service" for

19-10 An awkward position may contribute to your feeling sleepy. Can you explain why?

homeostasis—it is a means of making supplies available to cells everywhere in the body, and also a means of collecting their wastes. The remarkable thing is that the supplies and wastes also serve as feedback to the organs that keep their quantities in the right balance. Intake and output of oxygen and carbon dioxide are examples, with the medulla of the brain the regulator. Heat balance is another example, as you know, with the hypothalamus the regulator. There are scores of other feedback mechanisms in the blood and in the cells of your body. In each case, the composition of the blood affects the balances in the cells of the body, and vice versa.

Salt and Water Balance

The table in Figure 19-6, page 356, includes a condition caused by excessive loss of salt in perspiration. Salt balance is a very important part of your overall body balance. Normally your tissue fluids and blood are about 0.9 percent solutions of various salts, over half of which is common table salt. If you eat more salt than you need, your kidneys remove it. If you eat less than you need, you are in trouble. If there is too much salt in the tissue fluid, the extra salt is absorbed by the blood. As the blood circulates through the kidneys, the kidneys remove the surplus salt and excrete it in the urine. The remedy for not eating enough salt is simple—eat more. However, far more people eat too much salt than too little.

Sugar Balance

Sugar, too, must be present in your blood. When you eat a meal rich in carbohydrates, your blood sugar level goes up. To deal with the increase in sugar, certain cells in the pancreas secrete the hormone *insulin* (IN-suh-lin). Insulin from these cells enters the blood and circulates throughout the body.

Some insulin molecules pass through the walls of the capillaries and attach themselves to cell membranes throughout your body. There they cause your body cells to take in and use sugar until the blood sugar level is lowered. The liver also helps lower the blood sugar level by changing glucose to glycogen and then storing the glycogen, as you read in Chapter 18.

What happens when your blood sugar level falls too low? Now there is too little glucose in the blood circulating through the hypothalamus of the brain. This results in a complicated negative feedback. First, nerves from the hypothalamus carry "messages" to the *pituitary* (pih-TOO-ih-tare-ee) *gland* near the hypothalamus and the *adrenal* (a-DREEN-al) *glands* atop your kidneys to make the pituitary release ACTH and the adrenals release adrenaline. You can see these glands in Figure 22-1, page 403, and you will read more about the ACTH and adrenaline they release in Chapter 22. These hormones enter the bloodstream and cause the liver to go to work breaking down glycogen and releasing glucose into the blood. Thus, the blood sugar level is raised again.

Check and countercheck keep the blood sugar level between certain limits. Here, as in the other feedback systems you have read about, negative feedback keeps you in the vital state of homeostasis.

Red Blood Cells

You read in Chapter 16 that we usually lose about 2,000,000 red blood cells each second and get the same number of new ones during the same time. Suppose that as a result of an accident someone has lost a considerable quantity of blood. A spoonful of blood holds two *billion* red blood cells. The victim of the accident would probably lose many spoonfuls of blood containing many billions of red blood cells. But what would the laboratory technician observe if

19-12 There may be great blood loss in a serious automobile accident. How does the body make up this loss?

the doctor ordered a blood count a few weeks later? If the accident victim did not lose a *very great* amount, his laboratory tests would probably show a normal number of blood cells. In some way that we do not yet understand, loss of red blood cells results in the blood-making cells of the bone marrow working a little faster. This is another example of negative feedback. The feedback may result from the fact that a smaller number of red cells carry less oxygen. But once the number of red blood cells rises to normal, the bone marrow slows down its manufacture of red cells to the normal rate.

In your day-to-day activities, any time that you need more fluid or more red blood cells in circulation, the spleen, liver, and other internal organs allow stored blood with billions of red cells to go out through their veins. This may increase the number of red cells in circulation by 10 or even 15 percent in a few minutes. Note that this does not increase the total number in the body. It is, however, another example of the operation of feedback, as during heat regulation or during a visit to unaccustomed altitudes.

Even a bit of hard physical exercise causes your muscles to have a temporary need for much more oxygen. The liver and spleen come promptly to your aid, allowing a sufficient number of red cells to circulate. After you have rested awhile and no longer need the extra oxygen, some of the red cells are again put in storage in the spleen.

Acid-Alkaline Balance

Most of the fluids in the body are either *slightly* acid or *slightly* alkaline. Gastric juice is the only fluid that is *strongly* acidic, as you read in Chapter 14.

The blood is normally slightly alkaline. When it becomes less alkaline, *acidosis* (a-sih-DOH-sis) results. When it becomes more alkaline, *alkalosis* (al-ka-LOH-sis) results. In acidosis, the blood is not actually acidic; it is merely a little less alkaline than it should be. In alkalosis, the blood is a little *more* alkaline than it should be. "A little more" or "a little less" acidity or alkalinity can be very important in the make-up of blood and tissue fluids, for the chemical reactions in your cells proceed best in specific acid or alkaline surroundings. Severe acidosis may cause weakness, nausea, dizziness, drowsiness, unconsciousness, and shock. Severe alkalosis may result in irritability, lightheadedness, fainting, and convulsions.

Feedback to prevent the blood and body tissues from going too far in either direction comes from substances always present in the blood—examples are sodium bicarbonate and carbonic acid. Carbonic acid is formed by reaction of carbon dioxide with water. Prolonged deep breathing (*hyperventilation*) can cause alkalosis, while breathing too long in a confined space could cause acidosis (you are not getting rid of enough carbon dioxide, which forms more carbonic acid in your tissue fluids and your blood).

The breathing rate is readily affected by the emotions. Nervousness or excitement often causes unnecessarily deep breathing in some people. As a result, there may be a temporary alkalosis.

Acidosis and alkalosis are caused by a number of different chemical changes. Faulty breathing is but one example.

Feedback in Thirst and Hunger

You drink water when you are thirsty and stop when you have quenched your thirst. You become hungry, eat, and no longer feel hungry. The sensations of thirst and hunger are part of feedback systems that run from body cells to the hypothalamus, then back to other body cells and also to the cerebral cortex. When men fast for a long time, the hunger feedback may break down, so that a starving man may no longer feel hungry. You can see how useful these feedbacks normally are—they drive us to seek water and food, to consume enough to satisfy thirst and hunger, and then to stop. "Appetite" is not the same as hunger; in fact, appetite can lure us to eat more of certain foods than is good for us—which brings us again to the role of your feelings.

Your Feelings and the Balances in Blood and Body Tissues

Are you unhappy at times? Unhappiness is an imbalance that some people have trouble correcting. When they cannot (or do not) attack its source directly, they sometimes make it a kind of feedback that stimulates appetite! Eating brings feelings of physical-emotional contentment that help mask the mental-emotional unhappiness. It is a peculiar kind of negative feedback system: depression stimulates eating, which promotes physical pleasure and comfort—a substitute for happiness.

Your feelings can affect an otherwise normal balance in the blood and cause an imbalance that further affects your feelings!

19-13 The sensation of thirst is another part of our feedback system. How does it work? Is it positive or negative feedback?

Nervousness and excitement can lead to hyperventilation and alkalosis in the blood. The physical reaction then may affect the state of your feelings.

Blood, Hormones, and Nervous System— the Network of Feedback

The blood, hormones, brain, and nerves can be linked together because they are the chief parts of the feedback systems that work to maintain your homeostasis. This has become evident in just the few examples that you read about in this chapter. Another thing that has become evident is that homeostasis involves your feelings.

Somewhere at the center of it all are your brain and endocrine glands. Both affect your intelligence and your behavior, and their regulation. Nerves can stimulate the secretion by endocrine glands of regulatory hormones; hormones can stimulate sensory nerve endings. Nerve endings even give off their own chemical substances not unlike hormones! The tissue that forms the hypothalamus as a specialized part of the brain also forms part of the pituitary gland, early in life. The pituitary is something of a "master" gland that affects other hormone-producing glands. It secretes not only the ACTH you have read about, but many other vital hormones that flow through the blood and stimulate other endocrine glands to release their hormones. All these hormones, too, circulate in the blood and affect organs and tissues, nerves, and the pituitary itself, which, as a result, may stop secreting some of its hormones.

What starts the pituitary secreting its hormones? Nerve impulses from the hypothalamus affect it, as do insufficient quantities of hormones from other glands. You will explore this endless feedback more fully in Chapter 22 when you consider all the things that hormones help determine — growth, sexual maturity, emotional adjustments, body build and appearance, and many more.

The nervous system has its own lines of communication — the nerves. The endocrine system has the blood. And the blood itself carries chemical feedback of hundreds of kinds — to the liver, kidneys, medulla of the brain, and hypothalamus.

Do not be surprised if you read in a newspaper in future years that a hormone that helps trigger one or more emotions also has another, homeostatic function — keeping some requirement in balance in your body cells. And do not be surprised that a hormone we have thought helps only to balance a chemical requirement in the blood and in body cells may be found also to affect intelligence. We already know of such instances, and more are predictable from *the interaction among blood, hormones, brain, and nerves in everything you do.*

What You Have Learned

What kind of health practices should you apply in maintaining your health? Check your understanding of the chapter. On a separate sheet of paper, number 1 through 24 and insert the answer from the vocabulary list below. Use each expression, but use each one only once.

17 adrenaline
21 alkalosis
18 carbon dioxide
2 cold-blooded
13 fever
16 glucose
11 heat cramp
9 heatstroke

7 hypothalamus
15 insulin
14 malaria
19 medulla
muscles
10 negative feedback
8 nerve endings
12 98.6° F

3 oxidation
6 perspiration
23 pituitary gland
positive feedback
20 prolonged deep breathing
4 red blood cells
5 shivering
1 warm-blooded

Man and the animals that can maintain their body temperature regardless of the temperature of the air around them are said to be (1) _warm_ while animals that cannot do this are called (2) _cold_. Heat is produced in the body by (3) _oxidation_, in which energy is released in our cells. Our (4) _red blood cells_ do more to keep us warm than any other structures in the body. (5) _Shivering_, a sort of involuntary exercise, may help to warm the body. When the surrounding air is warmer than our internal temperature, we protect ourselves by losing heat by means of (6) _perspiration_.

Our temperature is controlled by our internal thermostat in the (7) _hypothalamus_. Like the metal thermostat in a building, your living thermostat—and the other control systems that keep your breathing rate, heartbeat, and other vital activities in proper balance—all work by (8) _nerve endings_.

At least three different serious conditions may follow exposure to intense heat. You would use different first aid methods if called upon to help victims of these conditions. Ice packs may be used in treating a person suffering from (9) _heat stroke_. In this condition, a person's heat-regulating system may break down and be followed by a (10) _negative feedback_, in which a high fever brings on a still higher fever that may be fatal. A person suffering from (11) _heat cramps_ should lie down in a cool place and drink salty water. (12) _98.6°_ is considered a normal temperature, while a temperature of 100° F is referred to as (13) _fever_. (14) _malaria_ is a disease in which fever and chills are repeated at regular intervals.

The hormone (15) _adrenalin_ helps to cause the liver to release sugar into the blood. To do this, the liver changes glycogen to (16) _glucose_. Another hormone, (17) _insulin_, is needed to deal with the sugar released into the blood. An excess of (18) _carbon dioxide_ in the blood passing through the (19) _medulla_ stimulates deeper breathing. Hyperventilation due to (20) _altitude_ could cause (21) _alkalosis_. As persons living at very high altitudes breathe air with less oxygen, they secure a better balance of oxygen and carbon dioxide by producing more (22) _____.

The (23) _pituitary_, a "master" gland, helps to maintain balances in the body by stimulating other endocrine glands. Nerves resemble glands in that (24) _____ give off substances resembling hormones.

What You Can Do

All of the following statements are false. Explain why each is false and give your authority for your statement, whether it be this book, another book or magazine, or your teacher. Give the title and date of any book that you quote and mention the page on which you found your reference.

1. It is impossible for a person to remain for five minutes in a room where the temperature is more than 30° F above body temperature.
2. The fact that snakes are found in hot deserts shows that snakes can stand higher temperatures than men can.

3. Exercise lowers the temperature of the body.
4. Our glands contribute no heat to the body.
5. Your temperature should be 98.6° F day and night.
6. Your internal thermostat is in your cerebellum.
7. Feedback is of little importance in the body because the body can regulate itself.
8. Positive feedback is more beneficial than negative feedback.
9. A temperature of 100° F is more serious in a small child than in an adult.
10. Adrenaline slows heartbeat and speeds digestion.
11. Perspiration exerts its greatest cooling effect when it remains on the skin instead of evaporating.
12. The air in mountain regions contains less smoke and exhaust fumes and therefore is richer in oxygen.
13. The spleen stores glycogen and changes it to glucose when the rest of the body needs sugar.
14. Too much carbon dioxide in the blood may cause alkalosis.
15. Since the pituitary gland is a "master" gland, it is not influenced by the activity of other glands.

Things to Try

1. If your library is fortunate enough to have space for storing old magazines, try to locate *Natural History* Magazine for December, 1955, and *Today's Health*, August, 1955. The article "How Hot Can You Stand It?" in *Natural History* (one of whose authors is the famous explorer Vilhjalmur Stefansson) tells how men have remained exposed to temperatures above the boiling point. The article by Ruth and Edward Brecher in *Today's Health* tells "How Your Body Beats the Heat."

2. You or some other member of your class might make an interesting report on the article "Physiology of Fear and Anger" in *Scientific American*, May, 1955. You could then explain to the other members of your class how these emotions may affect the body's many chemical balances.

3. With the consent of your teacher, try to arrange for a physician to address your class on the subject of "Homeostasis," how the body continuously makes the adjustments that allow you to remain in good condition.

4. If your class can obtain a sound projector, try to arrange to see the film *Stress* (McGraw-Hill). This film illustrates the theory that stress (whether due to disease, injury, or mental pressure) sends a general alarm reaction throughout the body, reinforcing or upsetting our many chemical balances. This theory was originated by Dr. Hans Selye of Montreal.

Probing Further

Controls in Your Body, by Navin Sullivan, Lippincott, 1971. Compares the internal controls of your body to the thermostat of a furnace. Includes helpful illustrations of the regulating organs.

Biology: Its Principles and Implications, by Garret Hardin, W. H. Freeman, 1966. This first-year college text is interestingly written and gives a clear account of homeostasis, with explanations of examples of negative and positive feedback.

Penguin Science Survey 1966 B, edited by Anthony Allison, Penguin Books, Baltimore, 1966. This accurate and interesting paperback book contains brief, well-written explanations of human temperature regulation. It also gives up-to-date accounts of chilling the body for surgery and the use of cold for preserving corneas of the eye.

Health Concepts in Action

Does this statement bring together the ideas you have gained from this chapter?

> **The body reacts to keep its internal environment relatively constant despite wide fluctuations in the external environment.**

Applying this concept, which health practices would you

—continue?

—change?

—begin?

Will you now, as a result of your study, change any of your health objectives?

UNIT FIVE
Your Changing Self:
Growth and
Development

20 / *Your Biological Heritage*

369-414

The birth of a baby—an important time. We were all the center of attention when we were born! The first question is—will it be a boy or a girl? Mother, father, grandparents, aunts, uncles—all wonder what he, or she, will be like. Whom will the child look like, the mother or the father? Whose temperament will it have? Will the child inherit the uncle's talent for music, or the aunt's talent for painting?

A PROBE INTO YOUR HEREDITY—Why is even a single cell from your body uniquely you—and not anyone else on earth? To help you decide, you will be probing these questions:

1. What great discovery was made by Mendel? How does a *dominant* trait differ from a *recessive* one?

2. How are genes transferred from one generation to the next?

3. In what sense do we "inherit directions"? How is it possible for DNA to carry so many different hereditary directions, or *genetic codes*?

4. How can the harmful effects of some genes be controlled by proper environment? Give examples.

5. Why is it difficult to make predictions about what sort of people children will grow up to be?

inherit directions

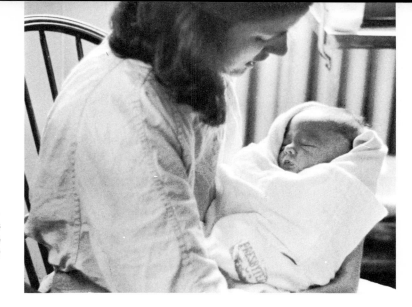

20-1 A newborn baby. What are some of his inherited traits? What are some of his "possibilities"?

WHAT DO WE INHERIT?

Do we inherit intelligence, sense of humor, industry, strength (or weakness), blue eyes, or a good appetite? Take yourself, for example. Make a table like Figure 20-2 showing similar traits for yourself, your parents, brothers, and sisters.

You can make this more interesting by including grandparents, aunts, uncles, and cousins. If you do this, indicate whether an uncle, for example, is your father's or your mother's brother. Also, list the parents of each cousin. How many other characteristics can you think of to compare? Perhaps you would want to make a second table and fill it out.

Now compare yourself with your parents, brothers, sisters, and other relatives. Does this table seem to indicate that any of the traits are inherited—which ones? As you read this chapter, you will learn many more interesting facts that scientists have discovered about human heredity.

You Inherit Possibilities

If you and your parents show the same traits, does this mean that you inherited the traits from your parents? Were your eye color, hair color, ability, and disposition passed along in the microscopic fertilized egg (about 1/200 inch in diameter)? It doesn't seem likely, does it?

Blue or brown eyes, blond or black hair, a long nose or a short one, could not be passed along directly with the egg. What you and all of us inherit are *directions*. Given the right conditions, the human fertilized egg develops into a boy or girl. The egg has tiny structures within it that direct it to develop into a particular human being, already different from any of the other billions of persons on our earth. Most living things, including birds, elephants, mice, grasshoppers, and redwood trees develop from eggs. The fertilized egg of a redwood tree can only become a redwood, not a pine or an oak. Some human eggs cannot become persons with blue, gray, hazel, black, or green eyes—only brown.

From $\frac{1}{200}$ Inch to Six Feet Tall

You read in Chapter 2 that a sperm from the father and an egg from the mother must fuse to produce the fertilized egg. The human egg is very small, but it is enormously

FIGURE 20-2

Traits	Self	Mother	Father	Sister	Brother
Left- or right-handed	right-handed	right-handed	right-handed	right-handed	right-handed
Eye color	brown	blue	brown	blue	blue
Hair color	light brown	dark brown	light brown	light brown	dark brown
Height	6 ft. 2 in.	5 ft. 7 in.	6 ft. 4 in.	5 ft. 7 in.	6 ft.
Body build slender, stout, or average	slender	average	slender	stout	slender
Color blind?					
Can roll tongue?					
School marks high, average, low					
Bashful or not bashful					

20-2 A table like the one above will enable you to see some of the similarities and differences among members of your family. Perhaps your table could include additional traits.

larger than the sperm. If it contained nothing else, the egg membrane would have room for about 90,000 sperms. Yet the sperm contributes as much to the traits of a new baby as the egg does.

In human beings, an egg is released from an *ovary* about every 28th day, roughly once a month. (You will learn more about this cycle on pages 412–413.) The sperms, however, are produced in hundreds of millions. When fertilization takes place, there are usually about 200 million sperms present. This may seem wasteful, considering that only one sperm can unite with an egg. The other 199,999,999 sperms are by no means wasted. It has been discovered that no one sperm can fertilize the egg unless millions of other sperms are present. During her life, a woman may produce 400 eggs, any of which can be fertilized. During the same time a man may produce 250,000,000,000 sperms. Therefore, the vast majority of sperms and eggs soon die without taking part in producing the next generation.

BLUEPRINTS FOR LIFE AND GROWTH

A robin's egg can only develop into a robin. The human egg can only develop into a human being. Furthermore, a certain human egg, if all goes well, can only develop into a person with brown eyes, curly hair, and a tendency to freckle. What in the fertilized egg determines that this egg can become, first, a human being, and, second, a human being with his or her individual possibilities? Besides physical possibilities, such as eye color and hair color and type, there are mental possibilities, such as ability to learn.

A little more than a hundred years ago a monk named Gregor Mendel discovered that the pea plants in his garden often seemed to inherit traits that their parent plants did not have. For instance, some of the offspring of very tall plants were dwarfs, even when planted in rich, well-cultivated soil. Their heredity made them dwarfs, and they lacked the ability to grow tall. Perhaps you have known boys or girls with blue eyes, both of whose parents had brown eyes. Often you may find that these blue-eyed boys or girls had a grandparent with blue eyes. If you search back far enough in their "family trees," you are almost certain to find blue-eyed ancestors.

Mendel knew, as you do, that any physical trait inherited from grandparents or other ancestors must be passed on by one or both of the parents. To be more exact, something that *causes* the trait must be passed on. As he did not know what this something could be, he called it a *factor* (from a Latin word meaning something that makes something). He thought that some tall plants carried a factor for being dwarf without themselves being affected by the dwarf factor.

All scientists agree with Mendel today, only they call his factors *genes*. Every cell, except sperms and eggs, in every human being contains *two* genes for each inherited trait. We can speak of these as *pairs* of genes. If both genes are the same, say two genes for tallness in the pea plant or two genes for brown eyes in a person, we say that the plant or the person is **pure** for this trait. If a person has one gene for brown eyes and one for blue, we say that he is **hybrid** for the trait of eye color. It has been noticed that persons with dark-brown eyes sometimes have blue-eyed children. But a married couple who both have clear, light-blue eyes never have brown-eyed children. The explanation is that some brown-eyed persons are hybrid for eye color, having one gene for brown eye color and one for blue. If two such persons marry, each parent might pass on a gene for brown eyes. The child then would be pure for brown eyes. One parent might pass on a gene for brown, and one a gene for blue. In this case, the child would have brown eyes, but he would be hybrid for brown. Finally, each parent might pass on a gene for blue eyes. The child would then be pure for blue eyes and could not pass on any genes for brown because he would not have any.

Mendel used the word **dominant** (from a word meaning master) for the trait that appeared in a hybrid and the word **recessive** for the trait that did not appear in a hybrid.

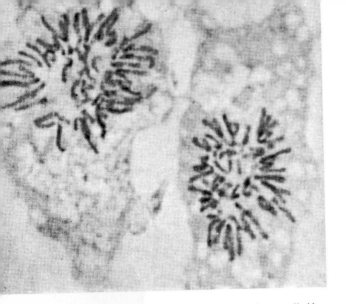

20-3 Chromosomes of a human spleen cell. How many pairs of chromosomes are found in human cells? Do *all* human cells have the same number of chromosomes?

We sometimes speak of a trait "skipping a generation" when we refer to traits such as blue eyes in grandchildren and grandparents but not in the middle generation.

We have thousands of different genes. They are not scattered about in our cells, but are in the nucleus of each cell. We have evidence that genes are particular parts of the *chromosomes*.

Like genes, chromosomes are in pairs. One of the genes for a trait is on one chromosome; the other gene is on the other chromosome of the pair. Humans have 23 pairs of chromosomes in body cells.

Genes are made up of *deoxyribonucleic* (dee-OKS-ih-ry-boh-nyoo-KLEE-ic) *acid.* We call this substance **DNA**. As the model shows (Figure 20-4), a DNA molecule can be thought of as a twisted ladder. The "sides of the ladder" are made up of repeated units of phosphates and sugars; the steps are made of four other molecular units, which are nitrogen compounds. These units are arranged in millions of different ways, making different kinds of DNA.

How Genes Are Carried from One Generation to Another

Before a new individual is born, sperms and eggs have to be formed, and one sperm and egg have to unite to become the fertilized egg. The fertilized egg can then develop into the new person. The cells that make up the body of a human being each have 46 chromosomes (23 pairs). Red blood cells are an exception as they have lost their nuclei and, hence, have no chromosomes. As a result, they cannot grow, and they do not live long.

As we mentioned before, sperms are produced in the *testes,* the male sex glands. Each sperm has a head containing the nucleus and a long, whiplike tail that enables it to swim. See Figure 13-5, page 232.

Eggs are produced in the female sex glands, the *ovaries.* When we say that sperms and eggs are produced, we refer to the fact that they are produced in the only way that cells *can* be produced—by *cell division.* When certain cells in the testes divide, each of the new cells becomes a sperm. When certain cells in the ovaries divide, some of the new cells grow in size and become eggs.

If each human sperm had 46 chromosomes (like the trillions of cells that make up our bodies), and if each human egg had 46 chromosomes, the fertilized egg resulting from the fusion of egg and sperm would have 92 chromosomes. If mature men and women developed from fertilized eggs with 92 chromosomes and themselves produced sperms and eggs with 92 chromosomes, the generation following them would have 184 chromosomes in each cell—provided that human beings could live and develop with so many chromosomes.

What keeps the number of chromosomes from doubling in each generation? Certain cells in the testes and ovaries go through what we call **reduction division** just before

20-4 A model of a portion of a DNA molecule. What submolecules make up DNA?

the sperms and eggs are formed. Instead of each egg and sperm receiving a pair of chromosomes, each sperm or egg receives only *one* chromosome of each pair. Thus, each sperm has only 23 chromosomes, and each egg also has only 23 chromosomes. Therefore, a fertilized egg receives 23 *pairs* of chromosomes, or 46 chromosomes. As you will recall from Chapter 13, cell division that produces the sex cells is called *meiosis.* See Figure 20-5.

What Is "The Genetic Code"?

Every time new *body* cells are formed, the new cells get the full number of 46 chromosomes, or 23 pairs. The type of cell division in which this occurs is called *mitosis.*

To compare mitosis with *meiosis,* the kind of cell division that produces the sex cells, compare Figures 20-5 and 20-6.

As we have said, genes are thought to be segments of the chromosomes. Different genes have different arrangements of the four kinds of nitrogen compounds that are part of DNA. These nitrogen compounds are *adenine* (AD-uh-neen), *thymine* (THY-meen), *guanine* (GWA-neen), and *cytosine* (SYE-toh-seen). They may be abbreviated as *A, T, G,* and *C.*

Sometimes we speak of all the genes in our chromosomes as being the hereditary *blueprint* that directs the way our bodies form from the time the egg is fertilized. You may have heard of another expression—the *genetic* (juh-NET-ihk) *code.* The word genetic refers to heredity, and your particular genetic code depends on the arrangement of the A, T, G, and C compounds in your DNA.

In recent years, scientists have developed evidence of how the genetic code probably works. Remember that the genes are sections of the long DNA molecule that stretches lengthwise along the chromosomes. Remember, too, that each gene has its own arrangement of the nitrogen compounds, which we refer to as A, T, G, and C If we think of these compounds as letters, we can then think of the genetic code as an alphabet with only four letters.

Each group of three nitrogen compounds can be said to form a word in the genetic code, for example: AGC. We can then think of a gene as a sentence giving instructions.

An entire chromosome would resemble a book of instructions, and all the chromosomes together would be like a set of books giving instructions for building all the proteins and other substances that make up our cells.

During the time that cells are not dividing the chromosomes seem to lie quietly in the cell's nucleus. Quiet as the chromosomes seem, they are doing work that brings about growth and development and maintains the life of the cell. The "three-letter words" in DNA cause another kind of nucleic acid, ribonucleic (RY-boh-noo-klee-ik) acid, or *RNA,* to form.

These RNA molecules are called *messenger*

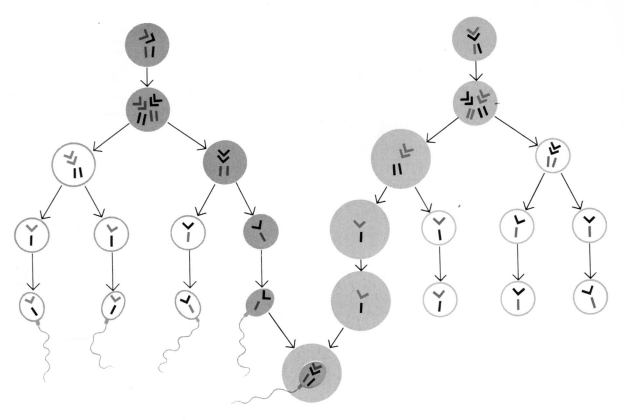

20-5 Cell division of the sex cells is called meiosis. What is happening in each part of this drawing? How does meiosis differ from mitosis? Why is meiosis necessary?

20-6 Mitosis includes all cell division except that of the sex cells. What is happening in each part of this drawing? Compare this drawing with Figure 20-7.

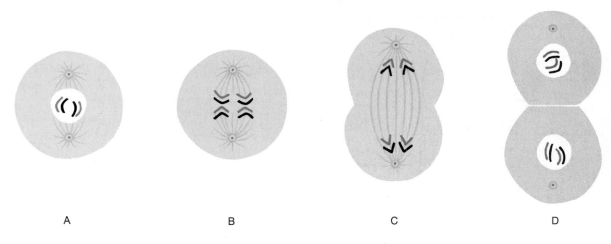

A   B   C   D

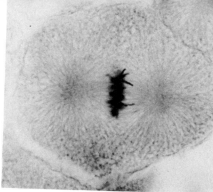

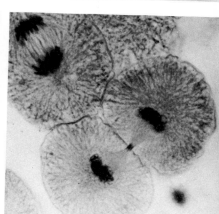

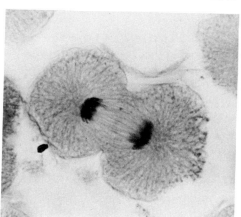

20-7 The four stages of mitosis. Can you describe what is happening in each of the stages shown?

RNA because they break away from the DNA and carry "instructions" they have picked up from the DNA. The molecules of messenger RNA move out of the nucleus to a microscopic assembly line in the cell's cytoplasm. Here the messenger RNA's attach themselves to the *ribosomes*, centers of protein production. You will recall reading about ribosomes in Chapter 13.

Other smaller RNA molecules move about in the cytoplasm. They pick up amino acid molecules and take them to the messenger molecules. These smaller RNA molecules are called *transfer RNA* because they pull, or transfer, amino acids from their previous location in the cytoplasm and line them up against molecules of messenger RNA. The result of all this activity is the joining to-

gether of the proper number and kind of amino acids to build a particular protein, usually an enzyme.

The whole amazing operation works efficiently because the sequence of A's, T's, C's, and G's in each gene dictates the building of a protein (usually an enzyme) by the RNA in the cytoplasm. As enzymes control all the living activities of each cell, the DNA of the genes thus directs how each cell will grow. Through the individual cells, DNA directs how the baby will develop from the fertilized egg and what hereditary traits he will receive. Will he have blue eyes or brown eyes? Will he have a thick head of hair in old age or begin to show a bald spot in his twenties? These traits are determined by the "three-letter words" of DNA.

How Is Sex Determined?

Long before there were any scientists to study the subject, people noticed that there were just about as many boys around as girls—just about one boy for each girl. Why is this true? Also, what causes some fertilized eggs to develop into boys and others into girls? To answer these questions, think about facts that you already know. There are 23 pairs of chromosomes in human body cells. One chromosome of each of the 23 pairs came from the father through the sperm, while the other chromosome of each pair came from the mother through the egg. Figure 20-8 shows chromosomes from a human cell arranged in pairs. You will note that twenty-two pairs consist of two chromosomes similar in size and appearance. The last pair consists of *chromosome X* and *chromosome Y*, which are very different in size. The X chromosome is much larger. We know that these chromosomes are from a man or boy because male human beings have one X and one Y chromosome. If the cell had been taken from a woman or girl, there would have been two large X chromosomes.

The sex of a child is determined the moment a sperm cell fertilizes an egg cell. If the sperm carries the Y chromosome, the child will be male (XY). If the sperm carries the X chromosome, the child will be female (XX).

What Are Sex-Linked Traits?

Certain traits are called *sex-linked* because their genes are carried on the X chromosome but not on the Y chromosome. More than thirty human sex-linked traits have been reported, with the male suffering much more often from the defective trait in each case. Examples include double eyelashes, a juvenile form of glaucoma, and degeneration of the optic nerve.

The X and Y chromosomes help to explain why there are more color-blind boys than color-blind girls. As the X chromosome is so much larger, it contains a number of genes not present in the Y chromosome. The size

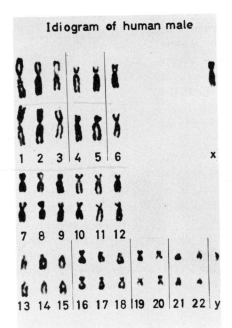

20-8 Paired chromosomes from a human male (*left*) and a human female (*right*) arranged in accordance with the internationally accepted classification system.

Tjio, J. H. and Puck, T. T., *Proc. Nat. Acad. Sci. 44,* 1229 (1958).

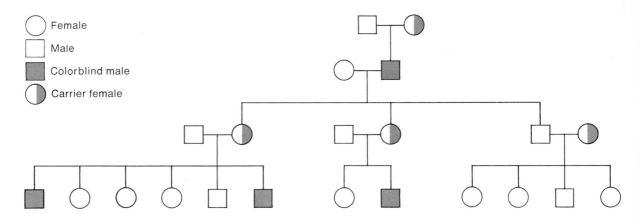

20-9 A pedigree chart showing sex-linked inheritance. What are some of the inherited conditions that are sex-linked?

difference is apparent in Figure 20-8. A girl may have two dominant genes for normal color vision on her two X chromosomes; she may have one normal gene and one for red-green color blindness, or she may very rarely have two recessive genes for color blindness. If a boy gets the dominant gene for normal color vision on his only X chromosome, he should see colors perfectly well. However, if he should get the gene for color blindness on his X chromosome, there is no gene on his Y chromosome that affects color vision. You have already read about color blindness in Chapter 11.

More than 2,000 years ago, the ancient Greeks had noted that some human traits might appear in a father but not in any of his children. Then the trait might reappear among his grandchildren—among his grandsons, the children of his *daughters*. Figure 20-9 shows how this sort of inheritance is carried on.

Almost all of those known to suffer from hemophilia are males, as you read in Chapter 16. A male bleeder can never pass the gene for hemophilia on to his sons because his sons can receive only duplicates of his Y chromosome, not of the X. Furthermore, his daughters, all of whom will receive a recessive hemophilia gene from him on the X chromosome, cannot have the disease unless the mother is that rare person, a female hemophiliac, or at least a hybrid, having a normal gene on one X chromosome and a recessive hemophilia gene on the other X chromosome.

WHY YOU ARE DIFFERENT FROM EVERYBODY ELSE

When human eggs and sperms are formed, there can be many different arrangements of the chromosomes in each sex cell, as indicated in Figure 20-5. Whenever an egg and a sperm unite (that is, whenever an egg is fertilized), the number of possible combinations between the 23 chromosomes of the male and of the female is 8,388,608. But the chance of the *same* combination of chromosomes taking place another time is only about one in 70,000,000,000,000. This figure is about 23,000 times the present population of the earth. This is a good reason why you can expect each human being to be different in various ways from all the millions of others.

Dwarfs with Tall Children

A few years ago, *Life* magazine printed pictures of a smiling, sturdy husband and wife, both dwarfs, and their normal-sized children. The male dwarf was of the type that may serve as the strong men in a dwarf stage or circus act. This type of dwarfism is caused by a dominant gene, which explains why such a dwarf couple may have normal children. Another type of dwarf, often called a midget, is of normal proportions and usually delicately built. The famous Tom Thumb was a midget. He grew slowly and finally reached his full height of about three feet. He married another midget, but their only child died in infancy. Another famous midget was only 18 inches tall when full grown. This type of dwarfism is due to a recessive gene. Dwarfs of both these types are usually of normal intelligence, unlike *cretins* (KREE-tins) who are subnormal in intelligence unless treated in time with *thyroxin* (thy-ROKS-in), a hormone secreted by the *thyroid* (THY-royd) *gland.* You will read more about this in Chapter 22.

Many disorders are known to be inherited. Among these are some kinds of deafness, some kinds of blindness, and muscular dystrophy—a disease in which voluntary muscles waste away.

How About Identical Twins?

You see two sets of twins in Figure 20-10. One boy, John, differs in eye color, size, and shape of face from his brother, Bill. The other twins, Carol and Ellen, look so much alike that visitors never know which is which. These two girls have exactly similar chromosomes and identical genes.

John and Bill are *fraternal* (fra-TER-nal) *twins.* In their case, two sperms fertilized two eggs. Hence their genes are by no means identical. Carol and Ellen, however, are *identical twins.* Only one sperm fertilized

20-10 Two sets of twins. John and Bill are fraternal twins, and Carol and Ellen are identical twins. How does each type develop?

one egg. Either the two cells resulting from the first cell division of the fertilized egg separated or the early embryo split apart with each part continuing to develop.

Identical twins may be called *one-egg twins* because both arise from one fertilized egg. Fraternal twins are *two-egg twins.* How many twins of each kind do you know? About one birth out of 87 results in twins. About one third of the twins born are identical and two thirds fraternal.

Triplets occur in about one out of 7,570 births and quadruplets (four babies at one birth) about one out of 658,000. Triplets and quadruplets are very rarely identical. You will probably never meet any quintuplets. They occur at the rate of one about every 57,290,000 births. Have you read newspaper accounts that suggest these figures for multiple births may be changing with the use of various modern drugs?

Even though identical twins have the same kinds of genes, they are never *exactly* alike. It is true that hair color and texture, eye color, and most other physical features are the same. Fingerprints, which are used by detectives to help trace the person guilty of a crime, are very similar. Sometimes the fingerprints are what we call the mirror image of each other. In this case, you would have to hold one twin's prints up to a mirror to have them match those of the other.

Identical twins show similar resistance or susceptibility to disease. Their intelligence and even their dispositions tend to be similar.

How Social and Environmental Influences Affect Identical Twins

As you have read, identical twins are never exactly the same. One twin may be smaller than the other. A drug taken by the mother or a disease that she suffered from might affect one twin more than the other. After the twins are born, it is impossible to keep all the conditions that affect them exactly the same. Without anyone intending it, one twin may receive better attention at times than the other. One may be dropped, frightened, or injured without this happening to its brother or sister. If the twins are separated, they will be exposed to varying influences and, consequently, tend to differ in various ways. Identical twins raised together are usually strikingly similar in intelligence as well as in appearance. However, such twins sepa-

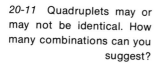

20-11 Quadruplets may or may not be identical. How many combinations can you suggest?

rated at birth or soon afterward may show different traits of personality or a definite difference in *intelligence quotient* (QWO-shunt) or *IQ*. Intelligence quotient is often used to measure learning ability. You will read more about this in Chapters 21 and 25.

Gladys and Helen, identical twins, were adopted by different foster parents and never saw each other from the ages of eighteen months to thirty-five years. Gladys was raised in comparative poverty and received little education. Helen's foster parents were more prosperous, and they saw to it that Helen received a college education. At thirty-five, the two women were strikingly similar physically. Their difference in weight was only 1½ pounds, and each had just six filled tooth cavities. However, there were marked differences in manner, personality, and the impression they made on others. Gladys was ill at ease, Helen graceful and socially confident. Helen's IQ test score was 24 points above that of Gladys.

Other identical twins separated from infancy until adulthood may be as similar in personality and ability as they are physically. Fred and Edwin had been separated as babies, and neither knew that the other existed. One was raised in the East and one in Iowa, but at the age of twenty-five they were living in the same city. They learned that they were brothers only after they had been frequently mistaken for each other. Each had about the same amount of education; each had become an expert telephone repairman; each married a very similar girl in the same year; each had a baby son; and each owned a fox terrier named Trixie.

How Heredity and Environment Affect Intellectual Development

Is intelligence controlled by heredity or by environment? Heredity and environment are both important in the development of our intelligence, as they are in our physi-

cal development. One child may be born with a combination of genes that gives him average abilities, which he develops to the fullest because of a favorable environment. Another baby may be born with a very different combination of genes that would permit him to become a genius. However, abuse, starvation, disease, or lack of education or encouragement may prevent him from ever developing the abilities that could have made him famous.

WHAT CAN WE DO ABOUT OUR HEREDITY?

Before the various blood groups were discovered, there was little that medical science could do for victims of hemophilia. When a victim of the disease seemed in danger of hemorrhage, the usual means to stop bleeding were used—pressure and application of bandages. Recently, scientists found that a person with hemophilia lacks a certain antibleeding (or antihemophilic) protein in his blood. Ever since it became safe to give blood transfusions, the most effective way to cope with bleeding emergencies has been to give blood transfusions or infusions of plasma. The blood of a hemophiliac may now be made to clot much faster by injecting small amounts of *serum globulin* (one of the important proteins of the plasma). One type of globulin is the protein that is missing in hemophiliacs. While this treatment gives relief, it does not cure the condition and has no effect on the genes responsible for the defect. Recently, many universities and other organizations have sponsored genetic counseling clinics for married couples. These clinics can help couples with Rh incompatibility (see Chapter 16) or other genetic problems to plan their families.

The Problem of Mental Retardation

There are children who never learn to speak, to dress themselves, or to find their way home after being led a few blocks away.

There are others who learn foreign languages correctly, master volumes of advanced research findings, and become expert mathematicians before they reach their teens. No doubt about it—some persons possess far more ability than others.

In a number of cases, these differences may be due to heredity—to differences in genes. However, mental retardation is also caused by brain damage occurring before, during, or after birth, or by other environmental factors.

Whatever the cause of the retardation, it is becoming increasingly clear that with adequate training even very dull persons can learn to do useful work and to live reasonably satisfactory lives. Even in our industrialized society, there are many simple jobs. Mentally retarded persons can be happy doing repetitive work that might be painfully boring to persons of average intelligence. Efforts are being made to persuade employers to hire mentally retarded persons for such jobs.

Diets that Prevent Retardation

Among the most important of all social and environmental influences are those resulting from medical progress. Today we are learning how to remedy or alleviate the effects of some of the rare, recessive genes that cause physical disorders and mental retardation.

As you read on page 380, feeding thyroid extract to infant cretins has saved many from a short life of physical and mental weakness.

We have also learned how to alter babies' diets to prevent the disastrous effects of a hereditary condition known as *phenylketonuria* (fee-nil-kee-toh-NOO-rih-ah). This condition used to cause more than half of its victims to become severely retarded—with IQ's of less than 20 (compared to a normal of 100). The condition is due to the absence of a dominant gene needed for the formation

20-12 These mentally retarded youngsters are being taught to work with their hands. What conditions can cause mental retardation?

of a certain enzyme. This enzyme is necessary for the harmless use of the amino acid *phenylalanine* (fee-nil-AH-lan-in) in the body. When a person receives two recessive genes for this condition, phenylalanine and an acid derived from it accumulate and cause a rapid lessening of mental power.

At birth, children with phenylketonuria seem normal. For this reason, in many states all newborn infants are routinely tested for the condition before they leave the hospital. A sample of blood is taken from the heel and sent to a laboratory for testing. If the test indicates that the infant has phenylketonuria, more extensive testing is done and treatment is started immediately.

Treatment is simple but not always easy to carry out. All human beings must have a certain small amount of phenylalanine to live. Therefore, the amount of phenylalanine eaten by a child with phenylketonuria is reduced to only a little more than what is necessary. Protein foods are treated with

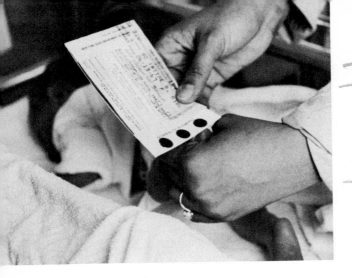

20-13 Newborn infants are routinely tested for phenylketonuria in many hospitals. What causes this disease? How can it be treated?

enzymes that break them down into the amino acids the proteins consist of. The baby is then fed other needed amino acids and only a small, essential amount of phenylalanine. If this treatment is started early enough, the child's mentality is likely to be in the normal range.

Controlling Other Hereditary Conditions

The likelihood of your developing certain diseases or harmful conditions is influenced by your heredity. Also influenced by your heredity is your susceptibility to many infections.

However, whether you actually become ill with such a disease may depend upon many environmental factors. For example, a hereditary factor is probably important in many cases of diabetes; however, diet and stress have much to do with whether the diabetes actually develops in a given person.

Some infants carry recessive genes that make it impossible for their bodies to handle milk. It seems strange that milk could be fatal to babies, but many of these infants have died from drinking milk, even their mother's milk. The difficulty arises because their par-

ticular genes make it impossible for them to deal with *galactose* (gah-LAK-tohs). Galactose is a simple sugar derived from the digestion of milk sugar or **lactose** (LAK-tohs).

These children lack the enzyme needed for changing galactose so that it can be used properly by the body. The condition is called *galactosemia* (ga-lak-toh-SEE-mee-uh). Careful control of such children's diet now prevents the harmful effects of the genes. Such children are forbidden to drink milk or to eat cheese or other milk products. They are fed special protein preparations made from other foods that do not contain lactose. They can eat certain fruits and vegetables, and sugars other than lactose.

Mutations

In past ages, such genes as those for hemophilia, galactosemia, or other hereditary conditions had a far more drastic effect upon the lives of those who carried them. Many were weakened by the ailments, died as infants, or if they grew to adulthood were too weak to marry and have children. It would seem, therefore, that the proportion of faulty genes would decrease over the centuries and the proportion of normal genes would increase.

However, the proportion of babies born with hereditary defects has tended to remain much the same from generation to generation. Thus, new supplies of defective genes must be coming from somewhere.

Defective genes continue to arise from *mutations* (myoo-TAY-shuns). A mutation is some change that takes place suddenly in the chemical makeup of a gene. The gene will now cause at least one different enzyme to be formed than before; in other words, it will be giving different instructions to the cell. Beneficial mutations do occur, but most are harmful.

Mutations are inherited. However, most harmful mutations are recessive; therefore, the offspring would have to receive two of

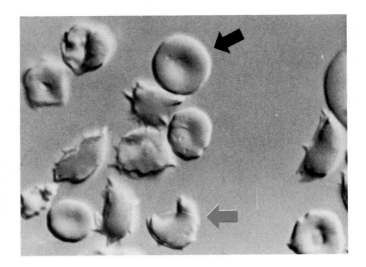

20-14 Red blood cells showing the sickle-cell trait. The black arrow points to a red blood cell of normal shape; the blue arrow points to a typical sickle-shaped cell. Under what conditions do red blood cells take on the sickle shape?

these genes to show the new trait.

At present we know of no way to stop mutations, and therefore no way to stop the reappearance of hereditary defects. However, researchers are making progress. They have discovered some of the environmental conditions, such as X rays during certain periods of a pregnancy, that may cause mutations in the unborn child.

The Sickle-Cell Trait

Many people in tropical Africa—as well as some people in India, the middle East, and the Mediterranean areas—have blood whose red cells take on a crescent or sickle shape when the blood's oxygen content is low. This condition has been named *sickle-cell trait* because of the characteristic shape of the cells. See Figure 20-14. A large number of Americans, including about 10 percent of those with African ancestry, are likely to carry the sickle-cell trait.

The sickle-cell trait appears in persons who carry one gene for an abnormal structure of hemoglobin. This gene will cause sickling of the red blood cells at certain times. No sickling occurs unless the person is in a situation in which his or her oxygen supply is limited. This may occur during heavy exercise, travel in high altitudes, infection, or anesthesia given for surgery. Then many of the cells change from the normal round shape to the sickle shape and cannot pass properly through the blood vessels.

Carrying one gene for the sickle-cell trait is not as severe a medical problem as carrying two genes for the trait. If a person inherits two sickle-cell genes rather than just one, he will have *sickle-cell anemia.* This is a much more serious ailment causing recurring symptoms such as pain and weakness. Children with the disease are very susceptible to infection, and show poor growth.

The sickle-cell gene is so common in much of Africa and in parts of India and Greece that some researchers have suggested that there must have been a survival advantage for people carrying one sickle-cell gene. The researchers speculate that these people had more protection against malaria than persons who carried genes for only normal hemoglobin. Something about the sickle-cell hemoglobin gave greater resistance to the germ that causes malaria.

At present, many researchers are working on the problem of sickle-cell anemia. Drugs for treatment and prevention of the episodes of pain are being studied. Work is also underway on pre-natal diagnosis.

What You Have Learned

What kind of health practices should you apply in maintaining your health? Check your understanding of the chapter. On a separate sheet of paper, number 1 through 24 and insert the answer from the vocabulary list below. Use each expression, but use each one only once.

cell division	genes	phenylketonuria
chromosomes	genetic code	proteins
directions	hemophilia	recessive
DNA	identical twins	RNA
dominant	Mendel	sex-linked
fraternal twins	1/200 inch	sickle cells
G	ovaries	testes
galactosemia	pea plants	Y chromosome

We really do not inherit blue eyes or curly hair. What we inherit are the (1) _____ for developing these traits. About one hundred years ago, a scientist named (2) _____ made important discoveries concerning heredity. He experimented with (3) _____, and he used the word (4) _____ for a trait that appeared in a hybrid and the word (5) _____ for a trait that did not appear. We know now that heredity is controlled by (6) _____ which are arranged on long threads called (7) _____. Genes are made of a substance called (8) _____. DNA is built up of six kinds of sub-molecules. Four of these are often referred to by their abbreviations, A, T, C, and (9) _____. The arrangement of these four sub-molecules along the chromosomes is now often called the (10) _____. Instructions are carried from the DNA to an "assembly line" in the cytoplasm by (11) _____. Molecules of this substance carry directions for making (12) _____.

Human eggs, which are about (13) _____ in diameter, are made in the (14) _____; sperms are made in the (15) _____. Like all other cells, sperms and eggs are made by the process of (16) _____. All fertilized eggs which have received a (17) _____ from the sperm develop into male babies. Twins that develop from one fertilized egg are called (18) _____, while twins developing from two eggs are (19) _____. Color blindness is an example of a (20) _____ trait. (21) _____ is a more serious sex-linked condition.

Eating only the minimum required amount of a certain amino acid can prevent mental retardation due to the hereditary defect, (22) _____. In (23) _____, milk can be fatal to babies. The gene that causes (24) _____ is more harmful when a person inherits two such genes.

What You Can Do

1. You can find many interesting articles on our biological heritage in such newspapers and magazines as *Life, Time, Scientific American,*

and *Science Digest.* Consult *Readers' Guide* in your school or public library for articles in other magazines. You will find the three following articles in *Senior Science,* a magazine for high school students published by Scholastic Magazines:

"Induced Galactosemia in Rats," by Gladys Watrob, May 5, 1967.
"Using Plants to Identify Blood Groups," by Ruth Garms, February 10, 1967.

Both of these articles describe original experiments done by these students. Remember that doctors do not use plants for identifying blood groups.

"Abraham Lincoln and the Marfan Syndrome," February 10, 1967.

Lincoln's unusual build resembled that of men with the Marfan syndrome. What is the Marfan syndrome? Does the article convince you that President Lincoln did have the gene for this condition?

2. What is Lesch-Nyhan disease? As you read newspapers and magazines, be on the lookout for mention of this disorder, in which the victims strike out at other people and mutilate themselves. Mothers pass the genes on to their sons. The illness was first identified in 1964.

3. Copy the following list of personal characteristics and discuss it with a few of your classmates. Note that the characteristics appear in the left column, the influences which might have caused them in the right column. Discuss each characteristic and what influences you think may have caused them. (Hint: You may find interesting facts and ideas in a biology textbook such as *Biological Science: An Inquiry into Life,* Harcourt Brace Jovanovich, or in the "Probing Further" section at the end of this chapter.)

1. aggressiveness	a. Entirely due to heredity.
2. cheerfulness	b. Due more to heredity than to environment.
3. eye color	
4. attractiveness	c. Due about equally to heredity and environment.
5. height	
6. musical talent	d. Due more to environment than to heredity.
7. hair color	
8. muscular strength	
9. shyness	e. Entirely due to environment.
10. talent for drawing	

Things to Try

Do you know of traits inherited in your family? For example, can you or any of your relatives roll your tongue the way the girl in the picture on the next page is doing?

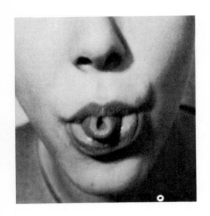

Make a chart to show the history of the tongue-rolling trait (or of some other trait) in your family.

For each man or boy, draw a square: ☐ For each woman or girl,

draw a circle: ◯

Write *yes* or *no* in each square or circle to indicate tongue-rolling ability. Your chart should look something like this, depending on the tongue-rolling situation in your family.

Parents   [No]——(Yes)

Children   (Yes)   (No)   [Yes]

Make similar charts for eye color, hair color, or any other characteristic that interests you.

Probing Further

Heredity in Humans, by Amram Scheinfeld, Lippincott, 1971. Human inheritance of a variety of traits is clearly explained in this well-organized book.

Genetics Is Easy, by Philip Goldstein, Viking (Compass, paperback), 1970. A clear, simple account of important facts about heredity.

Heredity and Your Life, by A. M. Winchester, Dover Publications, 1960. An excellent explanation of human heredity.

Health Concepts in Action

Does this statement help express what you have learned?

An individual's growth and development depend upon the interaction of his heredity and environment.

Applying this concept, which health practices would you

—continue?

—change?

—begin?

Will you now, as a result of your study, change any of your health objectives?

21 / *Your Cultural Heritage*

Why are high school boys and girls so much taller today than their grand-parents were at the same age? Are their genes changing? Are mutations for greater height spreading throughout the United States? There is no evidence of a great change in heredity. Instead, an improved environment, with better nutrition and medical care, allows genes that we inherited from our grandparents to "express themselves" more completely.

A PROBE INTO CULTURAL ENVIRONMENT—What are the different cultural environments that affect a teen-ager's development? To help you decide, you will be probing questions like these:

1. When does a child begin to learn? From whom do we acquire our early beliefs? What role does tradition play in our learning?

4. What are some of the advances made by American Indians before the Europeans arrived here? Why do some Indians living on reservations make low test scores?

2. What are some of the realities that adolescents must face? What are some problems of the later years?

3. How different are city and country education today? How different were they in former years? How do these differences affect us?

5. What kinds of difficulties were faced and overcome by famous men such as Lincoln, Steinmetz, Clarence Day, and George Washington Carver?

SOCIAL AND ENVIRONMENTAL INFLUENCES THAT AFFECT YOUR LIFE

A child begins to learn the day he is born. To some extent learning continues as long as we live. Much of what we learn is from our parents who learned it from their parents who learned it from theirs, and so on back in time. Whether we eat with a knife and fork or with chopsticks, whether we eat any meat or fish that we wish, or whether we abstain from beef, or pork, or all meat, is usually taught to us by our parents who may have carried on a tradition that goes back for thousands of years. We may also develop a dislike for a certain food just because our parents do not like it.

More important than these customs are our beliefs, our principles, our notions of right and wrong. These come to us largely from what our parents indicate they should be, just as our parents learned their customs and many of their beliefs from their fathers and mothers. Prejudiced people often acquire their prejudices unconsciously from parents and companions who acquired their beliefs without being aware that they were becoming prejudiced.

Seven Stages of Life

To better understand what came before and what will come after your present stage of life, we can divide our lives into these seven stages:

Prenatal (before birth)
Neonatal (during birth and just after)
Infancy (usually taken to mean the baby's first year)
Childhood
Adolescence (usually means the "teen years")
Middle years
Older years

Prenatal

In the nine months between *conception* (con-CEP-shun) or fertilization and birth, the embryo grows fast. At birth most babies weigh between five and one half and ten pounds, with the average about seven pounds. This is about two billion times as much as the fertilized egg. After two months' growth, the embryo is called a *fetus* (FEE-tuss). It is then about one inch long, and its limbs are fairly well developed. Later it grows a coat of fine hairs that it loses before birth. The fetus lies inside a living bag, called the *amnion* (AM-nih-on) that is filled with liquid. This liquid cushion helps to protect it from blows and shocks.

Neonatal

At birth the newborn emerges from the darkness and safety of the mother's uterus to the outside world. For the first time, he must do a few things for himself. He must breathe, and he must cry when he is hungry, annoyed, or in pain.

Infancy

The baby continues to grow and change rapidly, but not nearly as rapidly as he did in the months before birth. He usually doubles his weight by the fifth month and triples it by his first birthday. An infant has a few in-born reflexes that he loses later on. For instance, he has a grasping reflex. Place your finger in his palm and he will automatically grasp it so firmly that you can pull him upright. He cannot, of course, yet support himself in a standing or even a crawling position. Yet if you hold him upright with his feet on a hard surface he will show "stepping movements."

At four months an infant reacts to bright objects. At six or seven months he will reach for objects with one arm. Soon he will be exploring with his eyes, hands, and mouth.

Around one year of age, he usually begins to say things like "ma-ma," "da-da," and "bye-bye."

His muscular control proceeds in a head-to-foot direction—first, head control, then, some arm and hand control, and last, control of legs and feet.

Childhood

Don't worry if your little brother or sister fails to follow the average developmental schedule exactly. The following is what usually happens.

Two-year-olds: say a two or three word sentence; go up and down stairs alone; run without falling; can identify parts of body, such as arms, feet, and hands.

Three-year-olds: know their own full name; can ride a tricycle; can feed themselves; play by themselves.

Four-year-olds: can partly dress themselves; start to play in groups; can carry out simple directions.

Five-year-olds: know names of days and which events of the day come before others; print first name, large and irregular; like to print, draw, and cut out things; normal for boys to play with dolls.

Six-year-olds: have better sense of time; can print own full name; learn to tell their right hand from left hand.

Between six and twelve years: baby teeth and the baby look are lost. Weight doubles. Muscular strength increases, especially in boys. There is great improvement in running, jumping, and all sports. As the child grows, he tends to be taller and heavier than his ancestors were—because of his improved environment.

Adolescence

This is a period of rapid physical and psychological change. A boy or girl enters adolescence as a child and leaves it as an adult. As adolescence begins, the sex glands

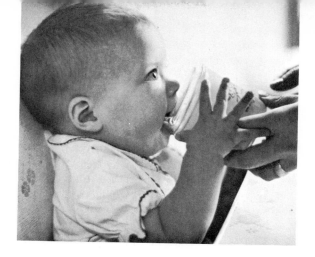

21-1 Infancy is a time of rapid growth and change. If you have the opportunity, study a young infant for a few hours. How many kinds of activities can you observe?

21-2 Young children are constantly learning. Your younger brothers and sisters would make interesting case studies.

begin to produce larger amounts of their hormones. These hormones help to cause the changes that result in the little boy developing into a man and the little girl into a woman. There is a period of rapid growth in which some "shorties" find themselves becoming much taller than they ever thought

21-3 Adolescence is perhaps the stage of life you know the most about. What do you think are the major problems of the teen years?

they would be. The voice boxes begin to grow so that both sexes lose their childish voices.

Adolescence is a time when both school work and the friends and acquaintances we make in school are of great importance. Now one has to prepare for further education or a job and for heavier future responsibilities. Whether we realize it or not, most of us are also preparing for marriage. We need to learn the give and take that makes life with other people possible. Adolescence is a time of emotional problems, of successes and disappointments that may seem small to adults, but are very important to teen-agers.

One of the most important things that we all have to do in adolescence is simultaneously to learn the duty of accomplishing what we can, to respect the rights and feelings of others, and also to accept and respect ourselves. We must accept our physical build, tall or short, thin or stout, strong or weak. In the same manner, we can do no good to ourselves or others if we blame ourselves because we cannot learn mathematics as easily as Charlie, get as high grades as

Marlene, or make witty remarks like Alice. Continued self-blame can lead to unhappiness and to doing poorer rather than better work.

Boys and girls of your age often undergo a conflict between a desire to be free and independent and assume adult responsibility and the opposite wish to remain childish and avoid responsibility.

Young Adulthood

By eighteen in girls and by twenty or twenty-one in boys, physical growth is usually complete. From this time you will no longer increase in height, because the bones in your arms and legs can no longer lengthen. Before you leave high school, you must decide whether you plan to go to college, continue in further vocational training, or seek a job. Sooner or later most young people face the problem of making a suitable marriage. By the time you are thirty, you will probably have children and will be concerned about how *they* are going to get through the stages of their lives.

21-4 The middle years are a time of great responsibility for most people. Marriage, job advancement, and rearing a family are all important parts of these years.

21-5 The older years are perhaps the most difficult. Keeping occupied is very important. How do your grandparents spend their time?

Middle and Older Years

The greatest accomplishments come at different periods of life in different kinds of activity. The young adult period—from 20 to 25—is the peak time for most athletes, although many of our great ice-skaters and swimmers win their championships while still in their teens. Many scientists and poets do their best work before thirty. On the other hand, a great many scientists, writers, teachers, professors, business men, public officials, and doctors, continue to improve in their knowledge, skill, and understanding past the age of fifty. In fact, political leaders of fifty are often referred to as "young."

Health problems such as heart disease and arthritis, become more common from the middle forties on. Women reach the upper limit of child-bearing in the middle or late forties. Both men and women may be regretful that they are no longer young.

After sixty, diseases related to aging grow more common and old people often feel lonely and unwanted. On the other hand, many old people find that they finally have enough leisure time for their friends and hobbies.

HOW MANY CULTURAL HERITAGES ARE THERE?

There is a world-wide cultural heritage— all that has been passed on to us in art, science, medicine, law, social customs, and all other human activities. No one can absorb more than a small amount of this total heritage. Each nation, each region, each social class, and each profession has its own fraction of the entire heritage. The heritage is not exactly the same for every family, and two brothers may absorb different fractions of the heritage available to them.

An Iowa boy would know little of the cultural heritage of the Congo Republic, and a boy raised on a farm in China would not acquire the language or customs of a native of Paris. How much difference is there in the cultural background of an American farm boy and a boy raised in a large American city?

In one city high school class fifty years ago, the only boy who could at a glance identify kinds of birds and trees from a distance was a boy who had been raised on a farm. His grades and *intelligence quotient* or IQ were not very high. Intelligence quotient is a measure of your capacity to learn. You will read more about IQ in Chapter 25. (The IQ test, of course, had been prepared for use with students with a typical, complete elementary school education which this boy had not had.) Other students with higher grades and IQ scores could only identify the trees after closely examining the bark and leaves. They could not recognize many of the birds.

Although the farm region in which the first boy spent his early years was only fifty miles from the city, a good part of the actual cultural heritage of the young people in the two regions was quite different. This boy was two years older than most city pupils when he first attended school. For several years he started school late in the term in

21-6   Do you live in the city or in the country? Years ago the educational opportunities for city and country residents differed greatly. Today they are very similar. What are some of the factors responsible for closing the gap in educational opportunities? What are some of the advantages and disadvantages of going to an urban school? a rural school?

order to help gather the crops. His school had only a tiny library and his teacher had to teach several grades.

At present there is far less difference in the educational opportunities offered to the city and country student. The school year was once shorter in rural districts. Today city and country children are more likely to attend school for about the same number of days. Elementary school and high school education are both much more similar in city and country than they were. Public libraries, radio, and television help to offer enlightenment as well as amusement to the entire nation.

Taking Tests Written for Someone Else

Foreign-born students and members of underprivileged groups often fail to show their true ability in school grades and IQ scores. A teacher entering a very high grade for a girl who had arrived from Europe the year before was surprised to find her IQ score listed as 95. He had the girl retested. This time her score was 125. During a year and a half in this country her knowledge of English had improved and she now understood the questions much better than when she had taken the test.

Many persons belonging to underprivileged groups may fail to reveal their true ability in tests and regular classroom work. Often IQ tests are geared to the middle-class population and many items on such tests are unknown to the underprivileged groups. Partly on account of the handicap imposed upon children from underprivileged homes, many educators believe that *group* IQ tests should be abolished. Group tests are tests given to an entire class or school at the same time.

IQ and Environment

The first settlers in New England and Virginia learned much from Indian friends. Indians taught the Pilgrims how to "plant" a fish as fertilizer in each hill of corn. In Canada, Indians showed the French how to chew spruce needles to prevent scurvy. Before the Spaniards arrived in Yucatan, the natives had worked out a calendar at least as good as that of the Europeans. Yet Indians living on reservations in the United States in this century made lower scores on intelligence tests than most of the rest of the population. What was wrong? The trouble was not that the Indians lacked inherited potentiality, but that their education and their life on the reservations did not stimulate them to perfect themselves in reading and the other skills measured in IQ tests. When Indian children were placed in white foster homes, they were later found to average about 102 in their IQ, a little above the national average.

21-7 These children of migrant workers are being taught to speak English. What are some of the factors that might contribute to lower intelligence scores among these children?

What Answer Would You Have Given?

There are valleys among the mountains of Kentucky where the local people have been comparatively isolated for generations.

In some valleys the natives earned a meager living by hunting and farming. In others they depended on coal mining, and when the mines closed many families became desperate. During the Great Depression of forty years ago, an intelligence tester was questioning a boy. He asked: "If you went to the store and bought six cents worth of candy and gave the clerk ten cents, how much change would you receive?" "I never had ten cents," said the boy, "and if I had, I wouldn't spend it for candy. Anyway candy is what your mother makes." The answer tells a great deal about conditions at that time and place—and also indicates that this was probably a rather bright boy.

When Environment Fights Against You

Some boys and girls are born into environments that help them to develop whatever favorable tendencies they may have inherited. Others run into discrimination, neglect, poverty, or disease that make it difficult to survive at all. Think about men like Lincoln, who rose from poverty in the "backwoods" to become a great president, or Steinmetz, physically disabled from birth, who became a great scientist, or Clarence Day, who wrote *Life with Father* while lying paralyzed flat on his back. We wonder how much an individual's success is due to his genes or biological inheritance, and how much to his environment.

Think also of men and women who rose from the most unfavorable of all environments, slavery. Among the black Americans who escaped from slavery to become famous was Frederick Douglass who fled to freedom disguised as a sailor and was later acclaimed as an antislavery leader in England and France as well as in the United States. One

21-8 The environment we are brought up in is very important to our future life. The life of this old Navajo woman, who lives on an Indian reservation, is similar in many ways to that of her ancestors. How can we help the American Indian to improve his place in American life?

21-9 Jackie Robinson had a long way to go to overcome his environment. The youngest son of a poor sharecropper, he became the first black man to play in major league baseball. After retiring from baseball, Robinson had successful careers in both business and public life.

of our best-known American scientists was George Washington Carver, the son of slave parents, who never saw his mother after she was kidnapped by raiders. As a boy he was too frail to work in the fields. From the age of ten, when he first went to school, he worked to support himself. He always had a struggle with poverty. It was not until he was about twenty-six that he was able to enroll as a student at Iowa State College. Later, he became famous for his work on the chemistry of peanut products and in the education of farmers.

Jackie Robinson, who became the first black player in major league baseball, was the youngest of five children of a poor sharecropper. His father died when Jackie was a baby, leaving his mother to do her best to support the children as a servant and a laundress. Often there was not quite enough to eat. Even during the depression of the 1930's, Mrs. Robinson managed to keep the children in school. From the first, Jackie was a success in school—as a good student, as a well-liked person, and as an outstanding athlete for his age. He became famous after Branch Rickey, manager of the old Brooklyn Dodgers, signed him up for that team. After his baseball success he went on to other successful careers in business and government.

Abraham Lincoln, Clarence Day, George Washington Carver, and Jackie Robinson can be inspirations for all of us. They profited from good use of the cultural heritage and their own talents, even though their immediate environment was unfavorable.

What You Have Learned

What kind of health practices should you apply in maintaining your health? Check your understanding of the chapter. On a separate sheet of paper, number 1 through 24 and insert the answer from the vocabulary list below. Use each expression, but use each one only once.

Abraham Lincoln	George W. Carver	neonatal
adolescence	grasping reflex	nutrition
American Indians	group test	physical growth
amnion	heart disease	prenatal
beliefs	IQ	seven pounds
Charles Steinmetz	Jackie Robinson	stepping movements
Clarence Day	later years	tradition
cultural heritage	liquid cushion	uterus

Our principles and our (1) _____ come to us largely from our parents. People who abstain from eating certain kinds of food because they have been taught that it is wrong for them to eat such foods are often carrying on a (2) _____ that may be thousands of years old. All that has been passed on in social customs, knowledge, skills, and manners forms part of our worldwide (3) _____.

Before birth, the embryo develops in the mother's (4) _____. For a better understanding, we can divide our lives into seven stages. The first of these is the (5) _____ stage. This is followed by the (6) _____ stage. At the beginning of this stage, at birth, babies average about (7) _____ in weight. Before birth the fetus is contained in a baglike structure called the (8) _____, and is protected from shocks and blows by a (9) _____. Place your finger in the palm of a very young infant and he will use his (10) _____. Hold him upright with his feet on a hard surface and he will show another reflex, (11) _____.

Boys and girls lose their childish voices during (12) _____. Due to better medical care and (13) _____, teen-agers are taller than they used to be. Tall or short, (14) _____ usually ceases at about the age of 21. Conditions such as arthritis become more common in the (15) _____, and (16) _____ is also more frequent at that time.

Foreign-born students have often failed to show their true ability in (17) _____ scores. A test given to an entire class or school at the same time is known as a (18) _____. So-called primitive peoples have often made important discoveries. An example of this is the discovery by (19) _____ that spruce needles prevent scurvy.

Many men have made their way to achievement in spite of unfavorable environment. (20) _____ rose from "backwoods" poverty to become one of America's greatest leaders. (21) _____ who had to support himself from the age of ten, became a famous chemist. (22) _____, whose poor sharecropper father died when he was a baby, became a famous athlete. Although disabled, (23) _____ became a great scientist. *Life with Father*,

a popular book and a great success as a play, was written by (24) _Clarence Day,_
while he lay paralyzed on his back.

What You Can Do

Which interesting and important men and women would you like to know more about? Think about those mentioned in this book, or persons you have read about in your history, English, and science classes. Consult other books or magazines.

Write a report on the cultural heritage of a person who interests you and on how he reacted to this heritage. You will probably do best with someone you think you would have liked. However, you might also write a valuable and possibly amusing report about someone you disapprove of and think you would have disliked. Here are some things you may want to include:

1. When and where did this person live?
2. What was his physical appearance?
3. What were his parents and other relatives like?
4. How much education did he receive?
5. Did he receive any special advantages?
6. What difficulties did he face, and how did he manage to deal with them?
7. What is interesting about his friends (and about his enemies, if he had any)?
8. How did he come to accomplish whatever important things he did?
9. Was his life happy according to what you know about him?
10. For what reasons do you consider him important, or very interesting?

Things to Try

1. You can learn more about how social and environmental influences help to make us what we are by inviting a group of foreign students to talk to your class. If you have no foreign students attending your school, perhaps there are some attending the local college or university who would be willing to visit your school. You should familiarize yourself with the countries that your speakers are going to talk about before your guests come to class. By reading ahead, you will be able to ask interesting and intelligent questions during the discussion period. Talking with other students and teachers who have visited those countries may also help to prepare you for talking with your foreign guests.

2. Beautiful and interesting bulletin-board displays can be prepared to illustrate the cultural heritage of any country. You can find valuable articles and fascinating pictures in *The National Geographic, Life, Look,* and many other magazines.

3. There are several good films dealing with growing up and with how different people have coped with their environments. To learn how one scientist triumphed over heartbreaking difficulties, try to obtain a sound projector and show *George Washington Carver* (Bailey Films, Hollywood, Calif.). There are six films in the *Ages and Stages Series* (McGraw-Hill), showing a child's development from babyhood on through the teens. Two films on family life that you and your classmates may find interesting are *Your Family* (Coronet) and *The Family* (Universal Education and Visual Arts).

Probing Further /

Getting It Together, by John Seder and Berkelee G. Currell, Harcourt Brace Jovanovich, 1971. This book tells the success stories of sixteen black Americans, often in their own words. They overcame powerful environmental handicaps to pursue a professional or business career.

A Guide to African History, by Basil Davidson, Doubleday, 1971. You can learn about the history of Africa from the origins of man to the independent countries of today.

Baseball Has Done It, edited by Charles Dexter, Lippincott, 1964. In this book you can learn how Jackie Robinson was accepted into big league baseball and was eventually elected to the Baseball Hall of Fame.

Edward Jenner and Smallpox Vaccination, by Irmengarde Eberle, Franklin Watts, 1962. This book tells how Edward Jenner battled against prejudice, ill fortune, and ridicule to provide defense against a great killer.

George Washington Carver, by Rackham Holt, Doubleday, 1963. You may be inspired by this true story of a man who overcame obstacles that made even getting started in his education seem an almost impossible feat.

Indians of the Plains, edited by American Heritage, Harper, 1961. This beautiful book tells you about the cultural heritage of the last independent Indians in the United States. It explains their history, customs, warfare, and ceremonies.

Martin Luther King: The Peaceful Warrior, by Edward T. Clayton, Prentice-Hall, 1968. The inspiring story of the man who became the nonviolent leader in the fight for civil rights and who won a Nobel prize in Peace.

Story of My Life, by Helen Keller, Doubleday, 1954. Helen Keller, who died in 1968 just before her eighty-eighth birthday, was one of the outstanding women of the twentieth century, despite what would seem to have been overwhelming handicaps. You may enjoy reading her autobiography to find out how she overcame deafness and blindness, learned how to speak, earned a college degree, and became a successful author and lecturer.

The Life of Abraham Lincoln, by Stefan Lorant, New American Library. You will enjoy the hundreds of pictures as you learn about the cultural heritage and the difficult environment of one of the best-loved presidents who ever lived.

Health Concepts in Action

Does this statement agree with your own ideas?

> *Cultural heritage influences an individual's physical, mental, and social development.*

Applying this concept, which health practices would you

—continue?

—change?

—begin?

Will you now, as a result of your study, change any of your health objectives?

22 / Regulators of Growth and Development

Whenever fourteen-year-old Lois went to the teen department to shop for clothes, the saleswoman would send her to the children's shop. Lois was most unhappy about the fact that she had a childish figure, particularly when she recalled that her older sister had already developed a shapely figure at that age.

When her mother took her to the family doctor, Lois pleaded with him to give her "hormones." After examining her, the doctor assured her that nothing was wrong. He explained that individuals, even in the same family, mature at different rates. Sure enough, at fifteen, Lois began developing the more rounded figure that marked her approach toward womanhood.

A PROBE INTO THE BODY'S CHEMICAL CONTROLS—How do hormones affect a teen-ager's development? To find out, you will be probing questions like these:

1. How do endocrine glands differ from other glands? What is a hormone?

2. Which gland is called the "master" gland? Why was it given this name?

3. Which hormone causes giantism? Which two hormones may be involved in preventing dwarfism?

4. How is the thyroid gland related to goiter? to cretinism? to myxedema?

5. What are our "glands of combat" and where are they located?

6. Which glands influence the development of male and female body characteristics?

THE ENDOCRINE GLANDS

As you read in Chapter 2 and Chapter 19, there are several *endocrine glands* in our body. They are called *ductless glands* because their secretions pass directly into the bloodstream. Other glands, such as the salivary glands, produce secretions that are carried to another organ or tissue by a duct, or tube. They are called *exocrine* (EX-oh-krin) *glands*.

What Is a Hormone?

The secretions of the endocrine glands have widespread influence, and they are effective in very small amounts. These secretions are called *hormones*. The word hormone, derived from the Greek, means *to excite* or *set in motion*. As scientists learned more about the endocrine system, they found that hormones may have an inhibiting effect on some distant tissue or organ. That is, a hormone may interrupt or lessen a particular reaction in the body, rather than speed it up. In either case the hormone *regulates* the reaction.

The hormones are chemicals that are secreted by the ductless glands and transported by the bloodstream to other tissues in the body where they exert their effects. The general effect of the hormones is to help in the regulation of chemical reactions in our bodies. The mechanisms by which the hormones act are very complex, and in many instances we do not know exactly how they do their work.

What Do the Endocrine Glands Do?

Scientists use many methods to find out what the various endocrine glands do. For example, surgical removal of the *thyroid* gland during the growth period results in retardation of growth. Growth is resumed when thyroid hormone is administered. Absence of thyroid hormone in infancy results in mental retardation, but this may be corrected by treatment with the hormone. An excess of the thyroid hormone increases the irritability of nerves, and the reverse is also true. In studying one gland scientists discover effects which that gland has on other glands in the endocrine system. Thyroid removal results in cellular changes in the *pituitary* (pih-TYOO-ih-ter-ee) gland; and the removal of the pituitary gland results in changes in the thyroid gland.

Many of the endocrine glands have important relationships to each other. That is, they work together to maintain a delicate balance in the body's metabolism.

The endocrine glands include the pituitary, the thyroid, the *parathyroids* (pair-uh-THY-roids), the *adrenals* (ad-REE-n'ls), the *pancreas* (PAN-kree-us), the *gonads,* or sex glands (*testes* in the male and *ovaries* in the female), and two mysterious glands called the *thymus* (THY-mus) and the *pineal* (PIN-ee-ul). See Figure 22-1.

The Pituitary Gland

The pituitary gland is located in a bony cavity on the floor of the brain. See Figure 22-2. It is about the size of an acorn. The part of the pituitary that is situated in front (anterior lobe) is sometimes called the *master gland* because its hormones regulate other glands in the endocrine system.

It secretes hormones that stimulate:

1. Growth of the skeleton
2. The gonads (testes and ovaries)
3. The thyroid gland
4. The adrenal gland
5. The mammary glands

The anterior lobe of the pituitary regulates the rate of secretion, metabolism, and size of the adrenal cortex (which will be described later), the gonads, and the thyroid gland. These hormones are called *trophic*

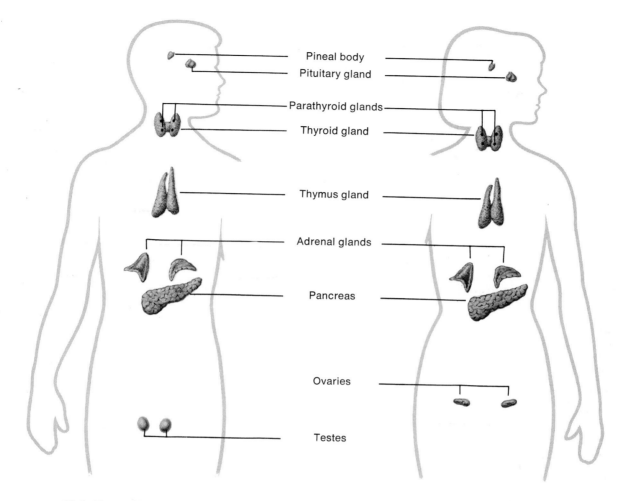

22-1 The endocrine glands. How many endocrine glands are there? How do the endocrine glands differ from the exocrine glands? What is a hormone? How are hormones distributed? How do hormones regulate the many chemical processes in the body?

(TRO-fik) hormones. ***Adrenocorticotrophic hormone*** (shortened to ACTH) does its work by stimulating the adrenal cortex to produce cortisone and other related substances. ***Gonadotrophic hormones*** act on the ovaries in the female and the testes in the male. The effects are to (1) regulate the production of eggs and sperm, and (2) to stimulate the production of sex hormones. ***Thyrotrophic*** or thyroid-stimulating hormone (called TSH) acts directly on the thyroid gland.

Growth hormone (sometimes called ***somatotrophic***) is an important pituitary hormone. It had been thought that the pituitary influenced growth, but the human growth hormone was not isolated chemically until the mid-1950's. It stimulates bone growth and is believed to act upon body cells of all kinds, speeding the formation of

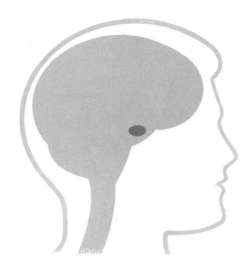

22-2 The pituitary gland is located in a bony cavity on the floor of the brain. Why is the pituitary sometimes called the *master gland*?

Extracts of the posterior lobe reveal two hormones—one of these hormones is a substance called **vasopressin** which is responsible for controlling the water balance in our bodies. It does this by acting on the small tubules of the kidneys, thus regulating the amount of water that is lost through the excretory system.

The other hormone is called **oxytocin.** Its main action is on the pregnant uterus. Near the time of delivery the uterine muscles become very sensitive to this hormone (sometimes called **pitocin**) which causes these muscles to contract. Under certain conditions physicians use this hormone to cause labor to start.

Oxytocin also has an effect on the milk ducts of the mother. It does not stimulate the actual production of milk, but does promote its flow.

proteins from amino acids. The total effect of the growth hormone results from its action with other hormones such as thyroxin, **insulin** (in-SUH-lin), and the gonadotrophic hormones. This is an example of the "working together" of the different glands of the endocrine system.

The pituitary hormone which stimulates the mammary glands to produce milk is called **prolactin.** Apparently this hormone, together with the female sex hormones, is responsible for breast development and for the production of milk after the birth of an infant.

The posterior lobe of the pituitary gland has important functions too. This part of the pituitary has many nerve connections with the *hypothalamus* (a part of the brain just above the pituitary). Some scientists believe that the hormones of this part of the pituitary are manufactured in the brain cells of the hypothalamus and migrate down the tiny nerve endings and are stored in the posterior pituitary. From here the hormones pass into the bloodstream to produce their action.

Disorders of the Pituitary

From this discussion of the many influences of the pituitary you can see how disorders of this small gland could result in a number of abnormal conditions. Tumors arising in the pituitary or near it can cause alterations in function, resulting in certain **syndromes** (SIN-droms). Syndrome is a term meaning the changes in the body that characterize an abnormal condition. In any event, if the glandular secretions of the pituitary are increased it results in **hyperpituitarism;** and if the secretions are decreased **hypopituitarism** results.

Too much pituitary hormone may cause **giantism.** This condition can occur in childhood and early adolescence, resulting in abnormal growth of the long bones of the body. The rate of growth is unusually fast and extreme heights are reached (See Figure 22-3).

The pituitary may also affect water balance. The anterior lobe may enlarge so much that it exerts pressure on the posterior lobe and thus prevents the secretion of enough vasopressin. Not getting enough vasopressin, the kidneys excrete far too much water. This condition is called *diabetes insipidus* (in-SIP-ih-dus). This disease should not be confused with the more common *diabetes mellitus,* (me-LI-tus), a true diabetes (see page 408).

When excess secretion of growth hormone occurs in adulthood, after the growth centers of the long bones are no longer active, the condition is called *acromegaly* (ak-ro-MEG-uh-lee). The bones cannot increase in length, but they increase in bulk. The bones of the face enlarge and produce a distorted appearance. Hands and feet may enlarge greatly. As in giantism, there may be other associated glandular effects, such as hyperthyroidism and diabetes.

Cushing's syndrome also may result from a too active pituitary gland. This condition is

22-4 Pituitary dwarfism may result when there is a deficiency of the pituitary growth hormone during the growing period.

22-3 Too much of one pituitary hormone can result in giantism. The man on the right is over eight feet tall. The bellhop is five feet tall.

rare in children and males. It is most common in females between fifteen and thirty-five years of age. It is characterized by a rounding of the face, called "mooning," an increase of fatty tissue around the face, neck, and trunk, but not of the arms and legs. Blood pressure is elevated. Protein and carbohydrate metabolism are interfered with. There may be an increased growth of hair on the trunk, upper arms, and face. The exact cause of this syndrome is unclear, but it is believed to result from increased secretion by the adrenal cortex, resulting from excess production of ACTH by the pituitary.

Deficiency of the anterior lobe hormones can also have widespread influence. Body metabolism is interfered with, and in the absence of the stimulation of pituitary hormones, other endocrine glands fail to produce enough of their hormones. When the growth hormone is deficient, a condition called *pituitary dwarfism* results. It is thought that some of these deficiency conditions may be inherited disorders, though there may be other causes such as the destructive action of tumors.

Pituitary dwarfism becomes apparent during childhood, and there may be an arrest of growth or growth at a very slow rate. The body is well proportioned, and there is no mental defect. See Figure 22-4.

The Thyroid Gland

The thyroid gland is located in the neck. It has two irregularly shaped lobes, lying on either side of the larynx, or voice box (Figure 22-5).

Thyroxin, the thyroid hormone, regulates the rate at which your body oxidizes food (uses oxygen). The gland manufactures and stores the hormone, releasing it as the body requires it. This gland secretes other related hormones, but thyroxin is considered the main one.

Iodine is necessary in the formation of thyroxin. In fact, this is the main use of iodine by our bodies. If not enough iodine is available, too little thyroxin is produced and the thyroid enlarges. This enlargement of the gland is called a goiter. An enlarged thyroid that produces *too much* thyroxin is also called a goiter.

The iodine necessary for formation of thyroxin is available in our diets from such foods as salt-water fish and vegetables grown in soil that contains iodine. Some sections of the world yield foods that do not contain adequate amounts of iodine for human requirements. One such section in the United States is the region around the Great Lakes. At one time, there were so many cases of thyroid enlargement in this area it was called the *Goiter Belt*. This situation was remedied

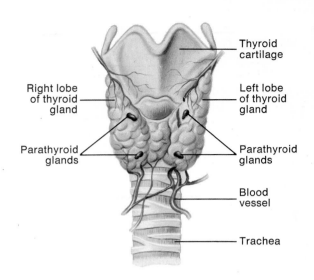

22-5 The thyroid and parathyroid glands. What hormones do these glands secrete? What are some of the main functions of these hormones?

when it was discovered that iodine could be added to table salt. Look at the box of salt in your kitchen. The chances are that it is labeled *iodized*, meaning that iodine has been added to it. Iodine can be added to other foods as well, but when the diet naturally includes enough iodine-containing food, it is not necessary to eat iodized foods.

Disorders of the Thyroid Gland

The chief disorders of the thyroid gland are *hypothyroidism* and *hyperthyroidism.* Too little thyroxin is produced in the first condition; too much in the second. Both conditions range from mild to very severe.

A form of hypothyroidism present from birth is called *cretinism*. It is caused by an absence of thyroid hormone. This absence of hormone may be related to: (1) absence of the thyroid gland at birth; (2) deficiency of iodine; (3) some defect in the thyroid that interferes with its use of iodine; and (4) possibly absence or deficiency of TSH from the pituitary.

If unchecked, cretinism results in retarded physical and mental development. The onset is gradual and must be diagnosed early so that thyroid hormone can be given to the child. Fortunately, with modern methods of diagnosis it is fairly easy to detect cretinism at an early stage of life and this disorder is becoming increasingly rare.

Hypothyroidism can have its onset during adolescence, but the outlook is much better than in cretinism since physical and mental development have been normal up to this time.

When hypothyroidism develops in adolescents and adults to a marked degree, it is called *myxedema* (mik-suh-DEE-ma). The basal metabolic rate of the body is lowered and bodily activity is slowed down. Facial features become coarse, the skin is dry, hair becomes coarse, speech is slow, pulse rate slows, intellectual alertness is hindered, and emotional responses are blunted. The condition is treated by thyroid hormone.

Hyperthyroidism is a complex disease and even though all its causes are not clear, it can be treated successfully.

Symptoms of this disease include an increased metabolic rate, nervous excitability, rapid speech, anxiety, instability, weight loss, even though the appetite is increased, increased heart rate, tremor of the hands, and excessive sweating.

Treatment may be in the form of medicine that blocks the production of thyroid hormone. Sometimes surgery is necessary, and in some cases radiation therapy is used.

How Is Thyroid Function Tested?

As part of a physical examination, the physician may use some special tests to help him find out how a person's thyroid gland is working. One of the tests commonly given today is called the *Protein Bound Iodine (PBI)* test. In this test the amount of iodine in the blood serum is measured. This measurement gives a direct indication of the amount of thyroxin that is being secreted by the thyroid gland.

Another useful test that is sometimes used is the *Iodine-Uptake Test.* A small amount of radioactive iodine is administered to the patient, and the amount taken up and retained by the thyroid gland is measured by placing a Geiger counter over the neck. The rate of clicking of the Geiger counter depends on the amount of radioactive material taken up by the thyroid gland. The figures are then compared with the uptake of a normal thyroid.

The Parathyroids

The parathyroid glands derive their name from their location beside (para) the thyroid gland. Usually there are four parathyroid glands, lying on the back surface of the thyroid gland. They are small and often irregular in shape.

At one time these glands were thought to be a part of the thyroid gland. But experimental work with animals, involving the removal of the thyroid and parathyroid glands, together and then separately, showed that the two glands had different functions. When the parathyroids were removed, the animals almost always died in *tetany* (a state of extreme muscular contraction). The blood of these animals contained less calcium and more phosphorus than normal. The deficiency of calcium is thought to cause the increased irritability of muscles.

The main hormone of the parathyroids is called *parathormone.* This hormone appears to have as its primary function the maintaining of an optimum balance of calcium in the body.

Too much parathormone results from a

parathyroid tumor or increased growth of the glands. It leads to the loss of calcium and phosphorus from the bones. This weakens the bones and may result in unusual fractures. The excretion of excessive calcium and phosphorus by the kidneys may result in the formation of kidney stones. Disease of the parathyroid glands is quite rare in children and adolescents.

Pancreas

The pancreas lies in the abdomen near the stomach. It is a compound gland, part exocrine and part endocrine. As you read in Chapter 14, the exocrine part of the pancreas produces the pancreatic juice needed in digestion.

The endocrine parts of the pancreas are called the *islets of Langerhans* (LAHNG-er-hahnz), named for the German anatomist who first described them. These are small masses of cells scattered throughout the gland. It is estimated that there are from 250,000 to 2.5 million of these islets in the human pancreas. The main hormone secreted by these islets is called *insulin*. It was first isolated in the 1920's by Banting and Best, two physiologists at the University of Toronto, Canada. Insulin is necessary for the release of energy from carbohydrates, although other endocrine glands also have some influence on carbohydrate metabolism. Although we do not know exactly how insulin works, we know that it (and the more recently discovered *glucagon*) help regulate sugar metabolism in our bodies.

Disorders of the Pancreas

Glucose is the main form in which carbohydrates are used in the cells. Glucose is stored in the liver after being changed to *glycogen*. Insulin is necessary for storing glycogen and changing glycogen back to glucose. If the amount of insulin is inadequate, the body is unable to utilize the glucose properly and some of it will pass out of the body in the urine. This condition is known as *diabetes mellitus* or true diabetes and is a major health problem in the United States today.

The cause of inadequate production of insulin by the islets of Langerhans is unknown. Several factors have been implicated, however. There is a history of diabetes in families in as many as 50 percent of cases studied. This suggests an inherited condition. In identical twins, the incidence of diabetes in both twins is about 65 percent; but in fraternal twins it is about 22 percent. Diabetes occurs in childhood, but is not common in this age group. It is most common in people in their fifties or sixties. This disease occurs about equally among men and women, and it is estimated that between 1 percent and 2 percent of the population in the United States has diabetes. Fortunately, since 1922 when insulin became available for treatment, diabetes can usually be controlled.

The principal symptoms of diabetes are excessive thirst, increased flow of urine, weakness, excessive appetite, and weight loss. Healing of injuries may be more difficult in people with diabetes; hence special care should be given to cuts and bruises.

Physicians are alert to the symptoms of diabetes, and as a part of routine physical examinations the urine is checked for sugar. If this test is positive, the physician will then test the level of sugar in the blood. Also, a *glucose tolerance test* may be necessary before the physician can be sure that the patient has diabetes. In this test the physician gives the person a specific amount of glucose by mouth and measures the blood sugar level at intervals to test the body's ability to handle sugar. The body of a diabetic person has less ability to handle this extra sugar than the normal body has.

22-6 These children are diabetics enjoying a month of camping at Camp Nyda, a training camp where diabetics learn to care for themselves properly.

Treatment of Diabetes

Although there is no cure for diabetes, most diabetics can lead normal lives if they are given proper treatment. The person who has diabetes will have to follow the diet prescribed by his physician. A diet must be planned for each individual, depending on age and nutritional state, with attention to protein, carbohydrate, and fat requirements. Also, he may have to take insulin to help in his use of carbohydrates. There are fast-acting, slow-acting, and mixtures of fast- and slow-acting insulin, that are given by injection. These different forms of insulin enable the physician to adjust the dosage to the needs of the individual patient. Oral medicine can be used in some cases. Best treatment results from understanding and cooperation on the part of the patient. Therefore, he is taught, whenever possible, to check his own urine for sugar and to give himself injections of insulin. He must learn to take proper care of himself to avoid the complications that can occur with diabetes.

Hypoglycemia

Hypoglycemia (HY-poh-gly-SEE-me-ah), or a blood sugar level below normal, may result from many different causes. It can occur from fasting, from disorders of the anterior pituitary lobe, and in destructive disease of the *cortex* or outer part of the adrenal gland. It can occur, also, from an overdosage of insulin; hence it is extremely important that insulin dosage be individually adjusted. Hypoglycemia produces a feeling of dizziness, intense hunger, weakness, and even loss of consciousness. Diabetics are advised to carry a piece of candy at all times in the event that symptoms of a low blood sugar level develop. Further, as a safeguard, diabetics should carry a card stating that they have the disorder and should receive emergency medical attention if any of these symptoms occur.

The Adrenal Glands

What brings about a state of readiness for emergency action? It is brought about

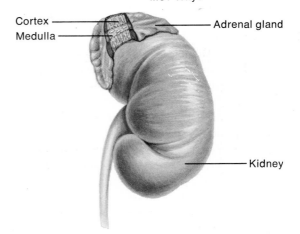

22-7 Adrenaline may be secreted when you are very excited. In what other situations may adrenaline be secreted?

22-8 The adrenals are compound glands. What hormones are produced by each part? Which hormone is necessary for life? Why?

Cortex

Medulla

Adrenal gland

Kidney

through the complex actions of your nervous and endocrine systems. Your adrenal glands pour *adrenaline* into your bloodstream, with lightning quick response to an emergency situation. In fact, the adrenal glands have been called "the glands of combat."

The two adrenal glands, each lying near the upper end of a kidney are relatively small and irrgeularly shaped glands. They are very important members of the endocrine group. Each adrenal is a compound gland (see Figure 22-8). The inner part of the gland is called the **medulla** (me-DUHL-uh), while the outer part is called the *cortex*. The cellular structure of the two parts of the gland are quite different.

Epinephrine (ep-ih-NEF-rin) or *adrenaline*, as it is also called, is the main hormone secreted by the medulla or inner part. A second hormone secreted by this part is called *norepinephrine*. Both have their major effects on the heart and circulatory system and aid the body in responding to emergency situations.

Although a person can survive under ordinary circumstances without adrenaline, the hormone is valuable in emergencies. Here are the chief reactions that it produces:

1. Blood vessels—vessels of skin and kidneys become constricted; muscle and coronary arteries are dilated.
2. Heart rate and cardiac output of blood increase. Blood pressure rises.
3. The blood clots much more quickly.
4. The basal metabolic rate is increased,

meaning an increase in oxygen use and heat production.

5. Stores of sugar in the body are made available.

Adrenaline is used in a number of instances in medical practice: in some operations to prevent excessive bleeding, to stop a nosebleed, and to prolong the effect of a local anesthetic by slowing its absorption through the constricted blood vessels. Adrenaline may relieve a severe attack of asthma by relaxing the muscles of the respiratory tract.

The adrenal medulla is the only endocrine gland, with the possible exception of the pineal body, known to have a direct nerve connection with the sympathetic division of the autonomic nervous system (refer to Chapter 12). This connection makes it possible for the brain to signal the adrenal medulla instantly to secrete adrenaline preparing the person for emergency reactions in the face of danger.

Unlike the medulla, the *cortex* is necessary for life. The cortex produces a large number of chemically related hormones known as *steroids.* The cortex's production of the life-sustaining steroid hormones is stimulated by the pituitary hormone ACTH. Some steroids influence salt and water metabolism. Others have an effect on carbohydrate, nitrogen, and fat metabolism. Some have an anti-inflammatory or antiallergic action. Still others influence the development of secondary sexual characteristics in both men and women.

One of the most important steroids is *cortisone,* a very potent hormone used in the treatment of a number of diseases, such as arthritis and certain kidney disorders. It is a life-saving medicine in **Addison's disease,** a condition in which the adrenal cortex produces insufficient amounts of hormones. Cortisone may produce undesirable side effects, and it must be used with extreme care under close medical supervision.

The Thymus and Pineal Glands

There are two glands that long have puzzled scientists and have only begun to reveal their secrets.

One of these glands is the *thymus,* located behind the upper end of the breast bone. The gland is quite large in infants and children, but begins to shrink by adolescence and is quite small in adults.

For some time the thymus was thought to be related to many diseases, but nothing definite was proved. Experimental work in the past few years now indicates that the thymus may have an important role in the body's immune reactions. There are indications that during infancy the thymus produces those cells that are vital in setting up the antibody-manufacturing machinery in the spleen and lymph nodes. This work gives rise to some exciting possibilities. One possible outgrowth may be that foreign-tissue proteins needed by the body could be injected in infancy, *before* the body would recognize them as not being its own and reject them.

The other mysterious gland is the *pineal,* a small gland about the size of a pea located deep inside the brain. Its functions remain obscure. But the most recent studies suggest that it may have an inhibitory influence on sexual development during childhood. This inhibitory influence is thought to result from an endocrine secretion from the gland. We know that removal of the pineal in certain laboratory animals has resulted in early sexual development. Tumors of the pineal gland result in early sexual development in male children. It is believed that the early sexual development occurs because the tumor injures the pineal, thus preventing the effect of its hormone.

Some observations suggest that the pineal may serve as a kind of "biological clock" regulating the rhythmic or cyclical effects of some of the endocrine glands.

THE GONADS AND SEXUAL DEVELOPMENT

There are four important phases of human reproduction.

1. Mature eggs and sperms must be produced. (See pages 372–376.)
2. The egg is fertilized while inside the mother's body.
3. The fertilized egg has a long period of development inside the mother's body. This period of development is known as pregnancy.
4. After birth, the child is fed for some time.

As you know, the testes and ovaries (Figure 22-1) have major roles in reproduction. They produce the sperms and eggs. However, they do not start producing mature sperms and eggs, capable of reproduction, until the time in late childhood known as **puberty** (PYU-ber-tee). Puberty commonly occurs somewhere around the age of twelve in girls and fourteen in boys. However, the age varies from individual to individual.

At puberty, the testes also start to secrete large amounts of the male hormones, and the ovaries large amounts of the female hormones. Sexual drives arise in response to these hormonal changes. These hormones are also responsible for the development of the other differences between the sexes, called **secondary sexual characteristics.** Small amounts of these hormones are secreted by the testes and ovaries in infancy and childhood, but much larger amounts are secreted during adolescence. (Hormones from the pituitary gland stimulate this increased secretion.)

Each sex produces both male and female hormones. But men produce a greater amount of male than female hormones; women produce a greater amount of female than male hormones. As a result, a boy or girl develops the secondary sexual characteristics of his or her sex.

The Testes

The chief male hormone produced by the testes is **testosterone** (tes-TOS-ter-ohn). The male hormones are responsible for such male secondary sex characteristics as enlargement of the muscles, the development of body and facial hair, the enlargement of the larynx, and the deepening of the voice.

The Ovaries

The chief female hormones produced by the ovaries are **estrogen** (ES-troh-jen) and **progesterone** (proh-JES-ter-ohn). Estrogen, in particular, is responsible for the development of female characteristics such as growth of the breasts, widening of the pelvic bones, and the development of a more rounded figure in general.

The female hormones are also involved in the monthly cycle that begins in girls at puberty. The ovaries release a mature egg about once a month. This is known as **ovulation** (ov-yoo-LAY-shun). (Usually only one egg is released each month. If two are released and each is fertilized, fraternal twins can result. See page 380.) With ovulation, the inner lining of the uterus thickens and holds a good supply of blood. This prepares the uterus to receive the fertilized egg.

If the egg is not fertilized, the thickened part of the lining of the uterus is shed by the body, about two weeks after ovulation. Some blood is lost in this process, which is known as **menstruation** (men-stroo-AY-shun). Menstruation lasts, on the average, about five days.

The time from one menstruation to the next is roughly about twenty-eight days. Somewhere around the middle of that time, an egg is released by the ovary and is ready for fertilization. However, the actual time of ovulation in relation to menstruation may be quite variable.

If the egg released by the ovary is fertilized, it attaches itself to the lining of the uterus and pregnancy begins. Now the thickened lining of the uterus will not be shed; therefore, the next menstruation does not take place. Also, no more eggs are released by the ovaries. The whole monthly cycle of ovulation and menstruation stops as long as pregnancy continues.

The Placenta

During pregnancy, a spongy tissue gradually forms where the fertilized egg is attached to the uterus. This tissue is the *placenta* (pluh-SEHN-tuh). A tubular **umbilical cord** connects the fetus with the placenta. See Figure 22-9.

Through the placenta, the developing fetus gets food and oxygen from the mother and gives off wastes. The blood of the mother does not pass through the placenta to the child. However, some harmful substances in her blood may pass through—for example, antibodies from an RH-negative mother (See page 301) and some drugs. This is why a pregnant women should be under a doctor's care and never take any drugs—even headache remedies—without her doctor's approval.

Although the placenta is not a gonad, it takes over some of the hormone-producing work of the gonads. It produces most of the estrogen and progesterone needed during the second part of pregnancy.

Hormones from the placenta also seem to check milk production in the developing milk glands of the mother. When the child is born, the umbilical cord attached to the child's navel is cut and tied. Later the placenta (which is known as the "afterbirth") is discharged from the mother's body. Once the placenta is discharged, milk production begins.

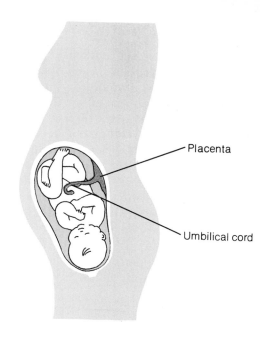

22-9 The uterus is stretched to many times its normal size to hold the developing fetus.

Medical Use of Sex Hormones

Sex hormones have many uses in medical practice. For example, the female hormone estrogen has been used to relieve some types of pain.

The male hormone testosterone has been reported to be of some value in treating men who are unable to become fathers because of low sperm count.

Treatment with female hormones is helpful in some forms of menstrual disorders. Female hormones have also helped some women to become pregnant and to carry the fetus the full term of the pregnancy. You may have read, on the other hand, about pills taken to prevent pregnancy. The active agents in these pills are synthetic female hormones. They are given in dosages that temporarily prevent an egg from being released by the ovary, or prevent the egg from imbedding itself in the uterus lining.

A MASTER CONTROL SYSTEM

Taken together, all the endocrine glands discussed weigh less than the contents of a soda bottle. Yet the hormones from these glands have major influences on the body. Some of the hormones exert their influence on our growth and development according to an orderly timetable. For example, the growth hormone from the pituitary has its peak effects in early childhood and again at puberty. At puberty, the sex hormones join them to modify physical appearance, producing the secondary sexual characteristics.

Normally, a remarkable state of balance exists among the endocrine glands and their secretions. For example, if the thyroid pro-duces too much thyroxin, the pituitary re-duces its output of thyroid-stimulating hormone, TSH. If the thyroid produces too little thyroxin, the pituitary pours out more TSH. The level of circulating thyroxin "tells" the pituitary gland how much stimulation the thyroid gland needs. This is an illustration of the important "feedback" mechanisms of the body which you learned about in Chapter 19.

Studies indicate that other tissues, like brain tissue, may produce substances that act as hormones. Scientists tell us that they have no more than scratched the surface in understanding the work of the endocrines.

What You Have Learned

What kind of health practices should you apply in maintaining your health? Check your understanding of the chapter. On a separate sheet of paper, number 1 through 24 and insert the answer from the vocabulary list below. Use each expression, but use each one only once.

acromegaly	gonads	myxedema
ACTH	growth	PBI
cortex	hormones	puberty
cretinism	hypothalamus	secondary sexual characteristics
dwarfism	insulin	thyroxin
endocrine	iodine	trophic
"glands of combat"	"master"	TSH
goiter	menstruation	uterus

Growth, sexual development, and even intelligence are affected by the secretions of different glands located in various parts of the body and called the (1)_____ glands. The powerful secretions of these glands are called (2)_____. The pituitary gland is closely connected with a part of the brain called the (3)_____, and is itself often called the (4)_____ gland. (5)_____ hormones made by the pituitary stimulate other endocrine glands. (6)_____ stimulates the adrenal gland and (7)_____ stimulates the thyroid gland. Too much (8)_____ hormone may result in giantism and too little of this hormone in (9)_____. An excess of one pituitary hormone in adults may cause (10)_____, in which the bones of the face enlarge and the long bones grow more bulky, but not longer.

A (11)____ is an enlargement of the thyroid gland. To make its hormone, (12)____, the thyroid must have a sufficient supply of (13)____. Lack of thyroid hormone from birth results in the serious condition called (14)____. In adolescents and adults, hypothyroidism may cause (15)____. One test doctors give patients to find out how the thyroid gland is working is called the (16)____ test.

The adrenal glands have been called the (17)____. One part of the adrenal glands, the (18)____, is necessary for life. Another gland, the pancreas, produces both a digestive juice and the hormone (19)____.

The hormones of the (20)____ bring about many of the physical differences between men and women known as (21)____. These physical changes start to take place at (22)____. At this time, the testes and ovaries begin to produce sperms and eggs that are ready for reproduction. When an egg is released by an ovary, the lining of the (23)____ thickens. (24)____ is the monthly discharge of blood as the thickened lining is shed.

What You Can Do

How much do you now know about the endocrine glands and their effect on growth and sexual development? The following statements are all made false by an italicized word or words. Copy the statements in your notebook, replacing each incorrect term with the correct one. Do not write in this book.

1. Testosterone is the major hormone secreted by the *ovaries*.
2. An egg must combine with a *fetus* to start a new life.
3. A fertilized egg becomes attached to the lining of the *pancreas*.
4. Weakness, excessive thirst, and sugar in the urine are symptoms of *acromegaly*.
5. In hypoglycemia, the level of *estrogen* in the blood is below normal.
6. Too much thyroxin makes a person *sluggish*.
7. The islets of Langerhans are important endocrine tissues in the *parathyroids*.
8. An endocrine gland releases its hormones into *ducts*.
9. Diabetes may be controlled by proper diet and injections of *adrenalin*.

Things to Try

You may find it very interesting to do some research on the discovery of hormones and the benefits that have followed the medical use of hormones. One topic you might like to investigate is "What's Being Done by Doctors with Hormones Today?" Consult some of the books listed in the "More You Can Learn" section. Then go to the library and use the *Readers' Guide* to find recent articles on hormones and their use. You may find advanced books on health helpful.

Other interesting subjects would be the story of individual hormones, including the effect of insufficient amounts of each hormone and remedies attempted before the particular hormones were discovered.

Probing Further

Human Growth, New School Edition, by Lester F. Beck, Harcourt Brace Jovanovich, 1969. This book may answer some of your more detailed questions about human reproduction. It discusses sexual development, the female and male reproductive systems, becoming parents, the development of the fetus and the birth of the baby.

The Body, by Alan E. Nourse and the editors of *Life,* Time, Inc., 1964. Clear explanations (rather brief) and beautiful colored illustrations make this book a pleasure to read.

The Communication System of the Body, by David F. Horrobin, Basic Books, New York, 1964. If you like to read and have even a slight interest in either hormones or the nervous system, you should find this book fascinating. It clearly explains how our glands, nerves, and brain work together to make us what we are and to help us to remain the same or to change, whichever is best at the time.

Health Concepts in Action

Would you agree with the following statement? Would you change or add to it?

The individual's physical, mental, and social development is regulated by endocrine secretions.

Applying this concept of development, which health practices would you

    —continue?

    —change?

    —begin?

Will you now, as a result of your study, change any of your health objectives?

UNIT SIX
Your Changing Self: Social Development

23 / Your Personality

You are learning new ways of being with people. Perhaps you are still struggling within yourself to overcome some of your earlier, "less mature" ways. You are also spending a great deal of time thinking about yourself and your problems.

You are forming new friends, and your feelings for friends of longer standing may be changing. You are moving toward independence. Is it any wonder that you may feel insecure and awkward at times, when so many important, new things are happening to you?

A PROBE INTO PERSONALITY—What are some of the major influences on personality development? To find out, you will be probing these questions:

1. What do we usually mean by personality?

2. How may personality development be influenced by inherited characteristics? By parents and family, or by other environment factors?

3. Give an example from your own experience of each of these emotional needs: recognition, love, independence, responsibility.

4. Can you change your personality now? As you grow older? If so, how? yes

yes

23-1 Do you form opinions about teachers before you even meet them? What are these opinions based on? How does personality enter into the picture?

No

MANY DIFFERENT FACTORS AFFECT YOUR PERSONALITY

It's the beginning of the term at Madison High. Walking through the halls, you might hear the following comments: "Did you get stuck with Mr. Peterson again for English?" or "I'll never get through chemistry with Miss White teaching the class." These are very familiar conversations. But, what is it about Mr. Peterson and Miss White that provoke these comments? Are they too strict, hard to understand, or just uninteresting? If there were one word that would describe all of these characteristics and many more characteristics it would be *personality*. The comments that you are overhearing are reactions to Mr. Peterson's and Miss White's personalities.

What is meant by personality? If you continue your walk into the cafeteria of Madison High, you might overhear the following bits of conversation: "Was I ever lucky to get Miss White for chemistry," or "I can't wait for English—Mr. Peterson is the greatest!" How is this possible? Are there two Miss Whites and two Mr. Petersons? No, but the four people discussing their teachers have

personalities of their own, and the way they see other people is partly a reflection of their own personalities.

We still haven't answered the question "What is personality?" *Personality* includes many things: the way a person looks, walks, talks, smiles, and thinks are all parts of his personality. You notice some of these things at once—his gestures, his appearance, the things he talks about and is interested in, whether he seems confident or ill at ease. Other things may be more or less hidden, including the way he feels about people. *Personality is the expression of all the traits or qualities of one individual that set him apart as unique and give him an identity of his own.* Personality grows and changes, to an extent, much as the person does. It changes to reflect how he treats the world, and how the world treats him. It even changes to reflect how he *thinks* the world and he affect one another, whether this is true or not.

Our reactions to another person are influenced by both conscious and unconscious factors. Sometimes we may not be well aware, or even *remotely* aware, of the reasons for our reactions. For example, one student may be afraid of chemistry with Miss White

23-2 Many of your feelings about yourself and other persons are based on what you hear in your immediate environment. Your parents, brothers and sisters, and friends play an important role in your personality development.

because an older brother or sister took the course and constantly complained about Miss White as a teacher. The girl or boy may not be consciously aware that this is the reason for disliking Miss White, but thinks it is because she seemed strict when she took over in a study-hall period last year.

In this chapter, and in the following chapters of the unit, you will learn more about personality development and some of the reasons you react in certain ways. Your heredity has a great deal to do with personality development. You will recall reading about genes and chromosomes in Chapter 20. This might be a good time to go back and review this chapter.

What are some of your inherited characteristics that have affected your personality development? Your intelligence, appearance, and physical health are some of the qualities that will be discussed in the next few pages. Of course, you must keep in mind that heredity never operates alone, but always in combination with environment.

Intelligence and Personality Development

Do the students who achieve high marks in school have better personalities than those who don't? Certainly you can find cases where the poorest students are well liked and vice versa. The fact that a student is doing poorly is not always an accurate measure of his ability to learn. You will learn more about this in Chapter 25.

Inherited intelligence is greatly modified by environment. This was shown in *Operation Headstart* when preschool children from low-income homes were taught with the intent of broadening their experiences. Exposure to interesting learning experiences proved to be very important, and remarkable improvements were found in the children's attitudes and attention spans.

What effect does a high intelligence have on personality? It may give one a more assured feeling, a greater sense of security. But, intelligence alone will not do this—it must be accompanied by a healthy emotional outlook.

Appearance and Personality Development

Attractiveness is a prime concern of teenagers, as shown by the amount of money they spend on creams, make-up, clothing, and various other items. Notice in newspapers, magazines, and radio and television advertising how great an appeal is made to the teen-age market. Attractiveness is very closely related to good grooming. Very few people have perfect facial features or perfect figures, but good health habits and neatness in appearance make us all look and feel better.

Many teen-agers go through an "awkward" stage, especially in the early teens. Complexions tend to "break out," and figures are changing but are not yet completely matured. Generally, by the early twenties, complexions tend to clear, and facial features and figures are much more mature.

Personality may be deeply affected by a growing person's attitude toward his changing appearance. One teen-ager may find that his legs and feet have quickly grown out of proportion to the rest of his body. This boy needs to know that this is a phase of normal growth, that his body proportions will continue to change, and that many other boys also experience such uneven development. On the other hand, a boy who is not growing as rapidly as others may begin to worry that he is not developing as *he* should! But the chances are that, in a few years, both boys will come closer to each other in relative development.

More often, it is not one's actual appearance but rather a lack of self-confidence that makes one feel unattractive. It is this lack of self-confidence that makes you exaggerate the effect on your appearance of a "crop of pimples" or other such feature, and ignore all your attractive features.

23-3 Operation Headstart has benefited many preschool children from low-income areas.

Physical Health and Personality Development

Physical health—or lack of it—has a great effect on personality. If you have always been healthy, you may take good health for granted and not realize how it influences your behavior and other aspects of your personality.

A girl or boy with a physical irregularity knows much more about the effect of physical health upon personality than you may ever need to know. A lovely young woman who recently passed through adolescence—and at the same time encountered a physical problem—is Madeleine, now of marriageable age and finished with her education. Dated constantly by young men, proposed to by two of them, she is unmarried because of a complex physical and emotional problem. Madeleine's parents and a number of aunts and uncles suffered from cancer. Madeleine herself has had a malignant growth successfully removed. But Madeleine is concerned

23-4 Good grooming is important to an attractive appearance. Are you as well groomed as you might be? How might you improve your grooming?

23-5 Good health is something teen-agers rarely think about, but poor health can have a lasting influence on your personality development.

about the possibility of another such growth appearing. The doctors try to encourage her to marry and to live a normal life, but she is unable to accept this and is in despair much of the time. Her worries about poor physical health, whether or not these worries are realistic, are affecting Madeleine's personality very greatly.

General good health is a great asset. If you have been physically strong since birth and have had reasonably good care through childhood and adolescence, you are in a good position to meet and master each milestone in life.

SOCIAL AND ENVIRONMENTAL INFLUENCES ON PERSONALITY DEVELOPMENT

The environmental factors that influence personality development are often subtle and do not readily stand out. In some cases, however, they do. Life situations such as Madeleine's, just mentioned, have a major impact. So do home environments that spoil or that deprive a growing person. Environmental factors may promote a positive, or

healthy, life approach, or they may result in fearful attitudes that inhibit one's encounters with life.

Environment and Personality Development

An important study today is whether malnutrition affects the mental development of infants. What a powerful effect upon a child this would be, if true. Fortunately malnutrition is probably at an all-time low in the United States, with protein and vitamin supplements added to many foods, so that families not able to afford meat regularly can use many of these foods at less expense. But malnutrition is not altogether absent, and the care and feeding of infants will be studied closely to determine whether our nation's concern for deprived children should begin with their diet.

Data accumulated over the years strongly indicates that malnutrition in infancy can permanently impair the mental capacity of a child. If proven conclusively, this means that valuable human resources are being lost because of malnutrition.

Almost anything about the environment can affect personality. The age of exposure to certain experiences determines to an extent the effect they produce. Much has been written about the importance of good mothering of infants as preparation for the development of healthy youngsters and teen-agers. No one is going to deliberately experiment with infants, giving one group little nurture and affection, while another group is showered with attention. This would be a scientific approach, but not one that law or conscience would permit. However, there have been certain "natural" experiments from which much has been learned. For example, foundling homes that care for abandoned infants have at times had more to do than a limited staff could accomplish well. At first they cried and were restless, but soon this gave way to calm, then apathy and refusal to eat. Observers noted that some of these babies died, and a number of those who lived did not grow and develop like other babies.

What is the meaning of this? Such observations have been made often enough to support the belief that infants must have a definite amount of affection in order to develop normally. The term used to describe this lack of interaction with a mothering person is *emotional deprivation*. As illustrated by the foundling-home experiences, emotional deprivation during infancy has a profound effect on growth and personality.

Socio-Economic Position

A special case of environmental influence upon personality is the socio-economic position of one's family. By this is meant:

1. Educational backgrounds of the parents
2. Type of work done by the father or by both parents
3. Family income
4. Type of home and the neighborhood environment
5. Religous and racial backgrounds of the family in relation to other families in the neighborhood

You can easily see what extreme cases of socio-economic position could do *for* or *to* the personalities of parents and adolescents. Parents who are educated often "appear" to have more intelligent children than parents who have little formal education. In many instances, the heredity factor is difficult to measure, but the actual difference in these children, even before their first day of school, may be great. One child speaks correctly and fluently and has been exposed to many ideas. Another may have derived little stimulus to want to learn from contact with his parents and with the children in his immediate neighborhood. Continuation of such different home environments may lead to the

23-6 What advantages and disadvantages do *each* of these neighborhoods offer to children growing up in them?

growth of the educational difference between the children all the way to adulthood.

Often parents with little formal education encourage their children to do well at school. The family environment may be as much directed toward education for the children as in any other home.

In all of these home environments other factors affect personality development—

especially in teen-agers. The attitudes involved are not necessarily a direct reflection of the parental attitudes. Instead, they are the attitudes of the girls and boys themselves, reflecting emotions, from pride to shame, about the kind of work the father does, how much he earns, the kind of house or apartment the family lives in, the religious or racial background of the family, and the part of town where their home is located. Sometimes real family problems are indicated, but often only the attitude of the girl or boy is at fault. In time this attitude is often corrected.

Your Personality and Where You Live

Growing up in a large city has both advantages and disadvantages in terms of your personality. The advantages of the city are numerous but not equally available to all. Sometimes you can meet and come to know interesting people from many states and countries. Libraries and museums are excellent and are either free or inexpensive. Plays, operas, concerts, world's fairs, and some but not all exhibits by industries and other agencies are more expensive. Many economically deprived teen-agers are unable to avail themselves of the city's opportunities, where even transportation becomes an expense. The city may be so large that one can get "lost" in it and have trouble meeting people outside his neighborhood.

On the other hand, growing up in a small town enables you to feel part of the town. You know most of the people, and they tend to take a genuine interest in you and your family. You also have the benefits of less-crowded conditions and a healthy environment to grow up in.

You may have some special concerns about living in a large city or a small town. Can you think of reasons for a teen-ager to feel lost in a large city? In another way, can he feel lost in a small town? What are some of the factors that make the city a more or less desirable place than a small town to grow up in? What are some factors that make a smaller city or town a better place to raise children? What are some of the drawbacks to growing up in a small town?

23-7 Lincoln Center is one of the focal points for the many cultural activities that take place in New York City and represents one of the advantages of city living. What are some of the disadvantages?

THE EFFECT OF PARENTS AND FAMILY ON PERSONALITY DEVELOPMENT

During your childhood your most important relationships are with your parents. In the family's daily activities, parents become the basic models from whom children learn many important attitudes. In some cases, an aunt, grandparents, or other adults take over the role of parents.

Setting Goals

Parents usually have certain wishes and goals for their children—whether stated or unstated, conscious or unconscious. These goals may concern education, social position, or acquiring money or a certain kind of job. They may concern the child's going to what the parents consider the right school, or his having the right friends, or his belonging to the right church.

Of course, within reason it is the responsibility of parents to guide their children and to help them establish goals. However, as a teen-ager you also take part in setting up the goals toward which you will strive. Most parents recognize the increasing ability of their children, as they grow and mature, to help set their own goals.

Sometimes parents cannot help their children as much as they would like to because of unavoidable circumstances. A greater responsibility then falls on the children to be more self-sufficient at an earlier age than other children are.

To give just one example, James and Paul are twin brothers whose father died when the boys were very young. The mother works. Her small income does not permit her to hire a housekeeper for her sons. Neighbors try to "keep an eye on" the two boys, but this is not effective. James becomes truant. He stays out of school so much that his mother is notified to appear with him in

23-8 Parents help their children to set future goals. These parents are helping their son to fill out college applications.

juvenile court. Paul, the twin brother, is a good student who has set goals for himself that keep him well-adjusted both at work and at play. He is almost never "at loose ends." The mother has taken her problem with James to a social agency. It is too soon to tell if the agency's help will be effective.

At the opposite extreme from parents who are unable to do enough are those who try to do *too* much in setting goals for their children. Consider the following example.

Ned's father attended an excellent university. It played an important part in preparing him for a successful career. His sons are growing up and he wants them to go to the same university. The first son follows in his father's footsteps, doing what the father expects of him. Ned comes along and is not nearly as good a student as his older brother and father were, but the expectation is that he will do as well as they have done. Directly and indirectly there are pressures that mold his life in such a way as to head him straight for that school. He is vaguely aware that this is not the right choice for him, but he loves his father and wants to please him. It would not occur to Ned to openly oppose the plan that has been laid out for him. He goes to the university and finds that his father's name and his older brother's name are "magic" words at the school. He knows of their brilliant academic records and realizes that he is expected to carry on the tradition. But he is not the student that they were, and he is not capable of achieving at their level. When it is apparent that he is not measuring up, he tries all the harder but to no avail. Finally, he must withdraw from school because he is not making passing grades. The boy, his brother, his father, and the university faculty are all disappointed. Many problems could have been avoided if Ned's father had been wiser in helping his second son be the individual he is.

Though your parents' responsibility has not ended, yours has already begun. How well do you work with your parents?

Relationships with Your Brothers and Sisters

In spite of their day-to-day disagreements, teen-agers in a family learn much from each other. Generally there is a strong affection between teen-agers that is taken for granted and perhaps unexpressed openly until a time when one of them faces some disappointment or threat. Then the other teen-ager usually comes to the rescue with action or sympathetic encouragement.

Even so, rivalry among children in a family is a normal thing, and it exists in every family where there is more than one child. In *young* children the rivalry may be quite direct and open. When a new baby comes along, the next-older child expresses his feelings at having to share parents with the newborn by such open expressions as "I hate him." Or, there may be attempts to physically harm the newborn, and the parents at first may have to protect the baby from the older child. In one family, Chris, the older child, was much more clever in his rivalry. "I love you, Mommy. I love her, too." He pointed to the baby, then bent to kiss her. A few minutes later, when the mother looked out from the kitchen, Chris was spanking the baby soundly with one of his toys, while still insisting, "I love her, I love her."

Chris was then not quite two years old. Soon it occurred to him that he *did* love the baby, although he still sometimes pushes her over from her sitting position to announce his annoyance with her presence.

By the time you are a teen-ager, rivalry may have lessened considerably, but often it may still be present. Fights are possible, but the rivalry more often is expressed in a much different manner than it would be by younger children. A girl in her mid-teens may view a younger sister who has just entered her teens as "a mere child." The newly developing interests of the younger sister may, in some instance, pose a real threat to the older girl who will attempt to downgrade the interests and activities of this "child" in the family. The rivalry may also express itself in competition for grades or for social prestige.

Have you brothers or sisters, and is there rivalry among you? If so, what can be done?

Are You an Only Child or a Middle Child?

An only child is often in the position of receiving special care, not only materially but also emotionally. This can be both an advantage and a disadvantage. You may have heard the expression "Susie is an only child and that means she is spoiled." This is not necessarily true, but being an only child can have its hazards in terms of personality development. An only child usually reflects the attitudes of the adults around him. If the only child has limited association with other children, he may feel a sense of defeat in trying to compete with the adult world. Or, he may feel at ease with adults and experience difficulty in relating to others his own age.

23-9 These sisters enjoy shopping together. Do you have a sister or brother close in age? How well do you get along with each other?

The middle child or in-between child is in a special position and may require some special thought by parents. He has an older brother or sister who is more capable of doing things because of age and who has more privileges than the middle child. He also has a younger sister or brother who receives a lot of attention. There may be a tendency for the middle child sometimes to be "left out."

Being the "middle child" also may have its advantages. The teen-ager who is a middle child may feel that he is in a favorable position. He is neither the oldest, of whom much may be expected, nor is he the youngest, who may still be regarded as "the baby" by his parents. The family situation permits the teen-ager more freedom than the younger child and less responsibility than the older brother or sister has.

If you are a middle child, how do you feel about your position in the family?

Divorce and Remarriage

If your family, like the majority of American families, is unaffected by divorce, you may have thought little about it. When a teen-ager's parents are divorced, the impact on his personality may not be as great as it would have been during his earlier years. Nevertheless, divorce in a family can be extremely difficult for the teen-ager, and he may even be embarrassed about what the community or his friends think about the divorce. Anguish may also occur when a girl or boy must take sides with one parent and reject the other. This is not easy to do, and many parents who obtain divorces recognize this and make it possible for teen-agers to see the parent who moves away.

However much at fault either of the parents may be, it is generally true that both contribute something to the conflict or conflicts that make the marriage unworkable. It is also true that however disappointed one may be in a particular parent, somewhere within him exist good feelings for that parent. Therefore, as a general rule, when divorce occurs,

23-10 Divorce is a very difficult problem for the family to adjust to. What positive ways can you suggest that will help this adjustment?

some relationship between the children and the absent parent should be continued.

Remarriage is quite common in American families. Some parents remarry each other, but the majority of remarriages involve another partner. The remarriage may be a time of particular stress for a teen-ager, who may harbor resentment for either or both of the parents. If this resentment is excessive, he may view the remarriage as personal rejection, and he may express his feelings in rebellion and lack of cooperation. On the other hand, many remarriages are welcomed by teen-agers. A remarriage can establish family life more fully.

ADOLESCENT PERSONALITY NEEDS

Everyone has basic needs—physical and emotional. Physical needs are fairly constant, but emotional needs change in kind and degree. The kind of love that an infant needs is very different from the kind of love that a teen-ager needs. What are some of our emotional needs? How strong are these needs?

Recognition

Recognition is an important emotional need. One teen-age boy stated it this way: "Everybody needs to be recognized, but teen-agers have to learn that everybody cannot be recognized in the same way. For me it may be making good grades in school, and for another boy it may be his athletic ability." There are hundreds of ways to be recognized.

It is a stress for teen-agers if they have the feeling that in order to be recognized they must always be outstanding. Everybody cannot be outstanding, and you need recognition for trying and for just being a part of something.

While recognition by parents, teachers, coaches, and acquaintances is important to you, so is recognition by other teen-agers. You may find this recognition through your talents and abilities and by belonging to a group. Belonging is extremely important because it helps you find points of common interest with others your age. Think of yourself in relation to the need for recognition. How are you recognized? What are the things that you do as an individual and as a member of a group that give you a sense of recognition? How does this strengthen your personality? What are some ways in which boys and girls you know seek a kind of recognition that could have a harmful effect on personality development? a good effect on personality development?

Love

Love, while difficult to define, describes qualities about our feelings for each other. There are many kinds of love, and these will be discussed in Chapter 26.

An adolescent needs love from his parents, but this love has a different quality from parents' love for an infant or a small child. Parental love is seen in respect for the teen-ager as an individual, and in confidence in his ability to make increasingly more difficult decisions. It is the support they give in the face of some disappointment. Parental love is expressed by setting a limit for behavior, and by not permitting one to flounder in such a way as to encounter repeated failure. A part of love is learning that children and parents can disagree, and even have angry feelings about some matter, and still have good feelings for each other. As a teen-ager's world expands, love comes to include friendships, romantic love, and eventually a more mature and realistic love resulting in choice of a marriage partner.

Independence

Much has been written about the "struggle for independence" that teen-agers experience. The word "struggle" implies an uphill journey, yet this is not necessarily a journey without benefits. Parents like to be assured that a teen-ager can use his growing independence wisely, before they can accept such independence. In our complex society, there has to be a much longer time of preparation for adult responsibilities than in simpler societies.

Imagine for a moment how you might have felt if, when you became a teen-ager, your parents and society had put you entirely on your own. You would be faced with many obstacles if you were entirely independent. It would be difficult to get an education, make a living, get married, and perhaps have children of your own, and to rely completely on yourself for all your decisions. It is for these reasons that your independence is limited—but growing.

Vocational or Educational Goals

From the time that you were quite small you have been imagining yourself as being many things when you become an adult. During the teen years you begin to consider more about what you want to do. These are the years when you must come to some understanding of your special interests and abilities and begin to make plans for the future. At this time it is important for you to learn about what is needed in the way of ability and preparation, and about the realistic possibilities of your pursuing a particular occupation. You may make your career decisions yourself, but you may need assistance. Parents, teachers, and school advisers will be of great help.

You may have no idea of what you want to do. You may want to have the benefit of aptitude testing to help you understand your interests and capacities. But even if such testing indicates that you have the capacity to become an engineer there is no guarantee that you will be a successful engineer. Along with the capacity there must be *motivation*—

23-11 A part-time job or volunteer work may be of valuable experience in your future career and will help you along the road to maturity.

enough drive and interest to carry you through years of training. Here again your increasing independence and responsibility will help you. So will your family, friends, and teachers.

Codes and Ideals

Your codes of behavior and ideals have their origin early in life. They depend on your parents' standards, as well as the standards of the community and the culture in which you live. Teachers and religious leaders may have played an important part. Some of your ideals and codes of conduct have also come from your friends. All these people and social influences are affecting your personality.

The inconsistencies and contradictions that you see around you may make the teen years seem very trying. What do people really stand for, and what do they believe in? Sometimes people say one thing and do another. This can be confusing, but it seems to be the way life is. You are not likely to discover neatly-wrapped, signed, sealed, and delivered sets of codes or ideals that cannot be questioned. Indeed, this is a time when you must question, weigh, and evaluate that which you see around you and hopefully develop a workable code of conduct and set of ideals that will enable you to live your own life with more satisfaction.

PERSONALITY TESTING

Everyone would like to know more about himself if it could help him live a happier life. Psychologists and testing specialists have worked for many years to try to make this possible.

Can Our Personalities Be Tested?

There are certain tests that have come to be known as *personality tests*. They can be very helpful, but they cannot assure a complete and accurate picture of your personality. Some of these tests are *projective* tests. Such tests provide visual stimuli to which you react. It has been found that people with certain personality traits react in definite ways to the stimuli. Thus the tests suggest certain aspects of your personality and of

23-12 This card is one used in the Rorschach Test. What do you see in this "inkblot"?

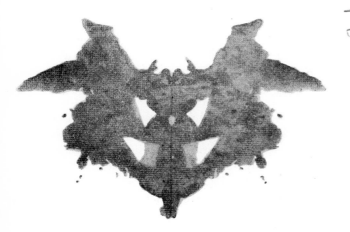

your relationships to the world and to people around you.

One of the tests in common use is the **Rorschach Test** (ROR-shok), originally devised by a Swiss psychiatrist in the 1920's. It has had widespread use by psychologists all over the world. This test is commonly called the "inkblot test" and consists of a series of ten cards on which there are inkblots of symmetrical design. These cards are presented, one at a time, to the person being tested, and he is asked to describe what he sees in the inkblot. Some of the inkblots are black, and some are in color. There are many shapes so that the stimuli presented are quite varied. In evaluating the responses to such a "personality test," the examiner will record whether the person describes human beings, landscapes, animals, animate or inanimate objects, and whether there is attention to whole scenes or attention to minute details. The reaction time is important, and the kinds of responses, whether usual or unusual, will also be noted. All of these responses are analyzed, and the person's responses are compared with responses most commonly given. Of course, responses are interpreted only by thoroughly trained persons. An example of a card used in the Rorschach Test is shown in Figure 23-12.

Other tests are the Minnesota Multiphasic Personality Inventory, the Thematic Apperception Test, and the Children's Apperception Test. These and other tests are designed to learn more about the feelings, ideas, and attitudes of the person being tested.

Personality Changes

A natural question to ask is "When is a personality fully formed?" For different people it occurs at different ages *after the ages of greatest change—infancy, childhood, and the teen-age years.* No single answer to the question is possible, since *some* changes may occur all your life. They will be fewer than the changes that can occur now, when you are younger.

There are many things that you do in a conscious way to modify your personality so that it approximates more closely an ideal that you have in mind. You observe others and the qualities that they have which contribute to their popularity, and you borrow some of these qualities and try them out for yourself. Ultimately, borrowing is not enough if you wish to develop new qualities securely. The *skills* related to the qualities should be your goal—learning to swim, to dance well, to do the other things that affect the qualities you have in mind. Most of these qualities have to do with how well you like and are liked by other people who influence your life. The more things you learn to do well and to enjoy, the more you may associate with others who like these things, too. Personality changes grow constructively out of experience.

23-13 The teen-agers above are gaining vocational skills through a Mobilization for Youth program. Because this training may influence their future goals, it could bring about some personality changes.

What You Have Learned

What kind of health practices should you apply in maintaining your health? Check your understanding of the chapter. On a separate sheet of paper, number 1 through 18 and insert the answer from the vocabulary list below. Use each expression, but use each one only once.

adolescence
age
appearance
attitudes
constant
degree

future goals
independence
infancy
intelligence
kind
love

parents
personality
physical
projective
recognition
Rorschach

The traits or qualities of a person that set him apart as unique and that give him an identity are the characteristics of his (1)_____. Heredity has a great deal to do with your personality development. Your inherited traits include (2)_____, (3)_____, and (4)_____ health. Your environment also influences personality development, and the (5)_____ at which you are exposed to certain experiences will, to some extent, determine the effect of the experience.

During childhood your most important interpersonal relationships are with your (6) _parents,_ who provide the model from whom you learn (7) _attitudes_ and who lay basic patterns of reactions. Everyone has certain basic personality needs. The physical need for air, water, food, and protection is (8) _constant,_ but the emotional needs change both in (9) _kind_ and (10) _degree._ As you grow toward maturity, your emotional needs vary somewhat in harmony with your heredity and environment, but for everyone there is the need for (11) _love,_ (12) _recognition;_ (13) _independence,_ and (14) _future goals._

You have heard of people taking personality tests in order to learn more about themselves. Some of the common personality tests are (15) _projective_ tests. Such tests contain certain visual stimuli to which the person reacts and thus reveals information about his personality and his relationship to the world and to other people. One such test now in common use is the (16) _Rorschach_ test. Your personality may change to some extent, but the greatest period of change comes between the ages of (17) _birth_ and (18) _adolescence._

What You Can Do

1. Select several members of your class to act as roving reporters. Have the reporters approach students, teachers, and other adults. Try to obtain an answer to such questions as "What is personality?" and "Can you change your personality?" Later, read the answers to the class, discuss and evaluate them in terms of what you have learned in this chapter.

2. What kind of personality traits are important for meeting the responsibilities of marriage and making a happy marriage? In what types of dating activities do boys and girls reveal more of their personalities to each other? Compare your opinions on these questions with the opinions of classmates of the same sex, and then of the opposite sex. How do you account for differences?

Things to Try

1. Try a general class discussion on a topic such as "Our Emotional Needs — How to Recognize and Handle Them." Divide the class into four discussion groups and assign each group one of the basic emotional needs — recognition, love, independence, or responsibility. In each discussion group everyone will discuss his topic, raise questions, agree, and disagree. Finally one member of the group, the secretary, will make a list of the agreed ways to recognize and handle the topic. Later on, the lists from all four groups will be presented and discussed by the entire class. When the class has agreed on a final list, put the list on the chalkboard for everyone to copy.

2. Try this little experiment in observation. Select a friend whom you see very often and are well acquainted with. Invite your friend to join you in the experiment. Over a period of perhaps a week you will observe each other as you go about your regular activities. Jot down all of the personality traits that you observe. At the end of the experiment, go over your lists together. Are you agreed on the traits listed? Have any observable traits been omitted? Can you explain where the traits on your list came from? How many items on your list are inherited traits? Where do the others come from?

Remember to include in your observations such things as manner of speech and walking, ability to get along with other people, ability to concentrate. Also note whether your friend worries a lot, is happy and contented most of the time, has an easily aroused temper, likes his family and neighborhood, and many other traits that may come to mind.

Probing Further

Psychology: Its Principles and Applications, by T. L. Engle and L. Snellgrove, Harcourt Brace Jovanovich, 1969. The chapter on personality explains the principal theories of personality and how psychologists attempt to measure personality.

How to Be a Successful Teen-ager, by W. Menninger, Sterling, 1966. This book discusses how to get along with others.

How to Improve Your Personality, by Roy Newton and H. H. Green, McGraw-Hill, 1963. The authors of this book give advice on how to adjust successfully to other people.

Health Concepts in Action

Does this statement seem to bring together the ideas in this chapter?

Personality—expressed by the sum total of behavior—is the product of heredity and environment.

Applying this concept of personality, which health practices would you

—continue?

—change?

—begin?

Will you now, as a result of your study, change any of your health objectives?

24 / Your Behavior

"Why don't you snap out of it?" Henry's sister said when she found him sulking in his room after he had lost the tennis match. "I was going great," Henry replied, "until the referee called that hit out. I know the ball hit right on the line and it made me mad to lose that point. After that, my game was all off."

What did Henry's sister mean by "snap out of it"? What kind of behavior had Henry demonstrated during the tennis match? What kind of behavior is he demonstrating by sulking? How can his sister be of help to Henry?

A PROBE INTO BEHAVIOR—Why do you think human behavior has been called "personality in action"? To explain, you will be probing questions like these:

1. How would you define behavior in its simplest sense? in its broadest sense?

2. What contributions to the knowledge of human behavior are made by anthropologists? sociologists? psychoanalysts?

3. Do emotions play a part in intelligent behavior? Give an example to explain your answer.

4. Give some instances of constructive group behavior and destructive group behavior.

5. What is meant by conscience? How does it develop?

6. What are some of the mechanisms by which we respond to conflicts?

24-1 A young monkey and two "substitute mothers" used by Dr. Harlow and his associates in their studies of behavior.

PRINCIPLES OF BEHAVIOR

In its simplest sense, behavior is a response to a stimulus. It may involve only a cell, or cells of a few tissues. For example, clouds move away from the sun, and bright sunlight strikes your eyes. Nerve cells pass the information to the brain, and other nerve cells carry a message to the muscles of the irises of your eyes. The pupils of your eyes contract.

More often, however, behavior involves much more of you than a few cells or tissues. In its broadest sense, behavior is everything you do and why you do it. "Tomorrow you will have a quiz on Chapters 21 and 22," announces your teacher. What a stimulus! You may respond all over. Does your heart beat more rapidly, and your face feel warm? Perhaps you feel butterflies in the pit of your stomach. Thoughts flash past: *which* chapters are Chapters 21 and 22? *What* will she ask? *Not* essay questions, I hope! How much do I remember? You may feel certain that you cannot relax until after the test. Yet by lunchtime you are chatting gaily with your friends, almost as if nothing had happened.

How Do We Study Behavior?

Many studies of behavior begin with child-rearing practices. Many observations and speculations have been made about the effect of the infant-mother interaction on later behavior. Scientists have attempted to learn more about these interactions by studying mammals and their young. One example is the work of Dr. Harry Harlow and his associates at the University of Wisconsin. They have conducted fascinating experiments with newborn monkeys and substitute mothers. They devised plain wire mothers and terry-cloth–covered wire mothers. Given a choice of these two artificial mothers, the babies preferred the one with terry-cloth covering. When these baby monkeys were frightened, they would run to the terry-cloth mother rather than to the plain, wire-mesh mother. From these experiments Dr. Harlow's group concluded that something about the texture of the terry-cloth mother was more satisfying to the infant monkeys. This scientific work supports more casual observations that infants need to be provided with pleasurable touch stimuli by the mother. The monkeys that were "reared" by the plain wire mothers did not get along well with other monkeys. They demonstrated many behavior problems, such as being aggressive and antisocial, and they later had difficulty in finding mates. The females that mated and had young were poorer mothers themselves. This kind of work with animals is one way of studying behavior, and it lends strong support to the theory that infancy and early childhood are critical times of development.

There are many other ways to study behavior. For example, *neurophysiologists* (people who study the nervous system) have conducted elaborate experiments on the brains of animals to learn more about the effect of different parts of the brain on behavior. They have learned that when the cerebrum of a dog is removed, many changes occur. He will not come when called, nor will he look for food or attempt to learn new tricks. He does not recognize old friends. Even so, the dog is still alive. He breathes, and his heart beats. When food is placed in his mouth, he will eat it, and digestion will follow. If a human cerebrum is damaged by accident or some disease process, similar responses occur. What does this tell us about the function of the cerebrum?

24-2 Understanding of the brain's relationship to behavior is gained from animal studies.

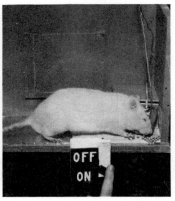

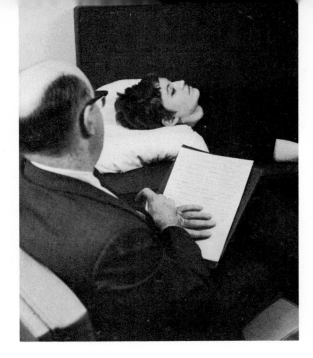

24-3 Psychoanalysis helps many people and is also one of the methods used to learn about human behavior. Do you know someone who has been psychoanalyzed?

Psychoanalysis (SY-co-uh-NAL-uh-sis), one method of studying human behavior and its motivation, has contributed much to our understanding of behavior. It has been used as a treatment method, as well as an investigative tool. The analyst and patient explore together the patient's random thoughts and wishes as he expresses them. They use these "free associations" as clues to the unconscious needs that contribute to the patient's behavior.

Anthropologists have lived for extended periods of time with other cultural groups in many parts of the world. They have noted the habits and customs of such people. By comparisons with our own way of life, anthropologists have attempted to draw conclusions about the development of behavior. *Sociologists,* in a similar way, are concerned about the forces in society that shape group behavior. You will read more about this kind of behavior later in this chapter.

Behavior Is Motivated

Much of your behavior seems to be motivated by needs, wishes, goals, and problems. Stated another way, human behavior is basically concerned with moving from a state of unpleasantness, tension, or pain toward a state that is more pleasurable. Let's think about an example that is not unusual. Mary is walking from geometry to modern literature class when one of her friends greets her in the hall with "Hi, chubby." Over the next few weeks, several others make similar comments about her weight. At home she studies herself in the mirror and notices that her dresses *are* getting tight. Seams have begun to bulge, and zippers are more stubborn than usual. She is putting on weight. She admits to herself, "I'm not fat, but very close to it." Concern begins to develop. "I'll need new clothes. The spring dance is coming up. Will I have a date? Milk shakes are *so* good though —and potato chips, too. What will I do?"

Mary decides to go on a diet. For a few days she sticks to her resolution and eats sensibly. But it is hard to give up the milk shakes after school, and she misses seeing friends at the drugstore. The diet is a failure.

Mary is in a state of discomfort—disappointed with herself. She confides in a friend who happens to be putting on too much weight, too. They talk it over. Then planning starts, and together they work out their calorie requirements. They enlist their mothers' help in not making so many of their favorite desserts. At first too much food is as hard to resist as ever, but after a week they are not so hungry, and the bathroom scale at Mary's house reports that they have lost a few pounds. The uncomfortable feeling begins to lessen, and after several weeks both Mary and her friend hear what they have been waiting to hear from a classmate, "Say, you've lost some weight, haven't you?" It was all worthwhile. Mary has become close friends with another person with the same problem;

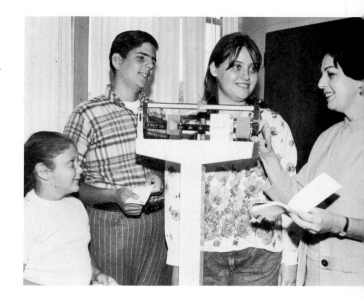

24-4 How many different motives can you think of for a teen-ager to try to lose weight?

they have helped each other and are pleased that they had the willpower. The motivation for this sequence of events was to move from a less comfortable state of mind to a more comfortable one. What are some of the things that motivate your behavior?

Instinctive and Learned Behavior

Many scientists attempt to define the motivation for our behavior under two very broad categories: (1) drive for *self-preservation* and (2) drive for *species-preservation*. There are, of course, many variations on these two basic themes. *Drive* is a term often used to describe inborn forces that motivate us toward certain kinds of behavior. Probably little if any of this behavior is purely *instinctive behavior* that involves no learning and is not modified by learning. A wasp that lays eggs on an insect it has stung and paralyzed is providing food for the larvae that will hatch from the eggs, but it will lay the eggs anyway if an observer removes the paralyzed insect. The wasp does not learn to provide another

24-5 What kind of behavior are these boys showing? Is there a better way for them to handle their problem?

insect, indicating that its "intelligent" way of providing for its offspring involves no intelligence at all, but is instinctive behavior, inborn and unvarying, directed toward preservation of the species.

Humans have inborn responses, too, but we are not sure that any of these are unvarying, although some are modified less than others by learning. A baby's sucking movements and crying are inborn, but both are either inhibited or modified later in development. Some of our *learned behavior* even affects such things as the sizes of the pupils of our eyes, which we normally think of as affected only by bright or dim light in an inborn pattern. Psychologists have discovered that most people show changes in pupil size in response to strong likes or dislikes, or even the difficulty of a homework assignment! You read about this in Chapter 11.

Whatever the relation of instinctive behavior to learned behavior in man, it is the learned behavior that has the more important role in your life and your associations with others.

Intelligent Behavior

When learned behavior begins to involve reasoning and related processes, it becomes *intelligent behavior*. A chimpanzee piles boxes on top of one another to reach a banana hung at the top of his cage. This is intelligent behavior. When Mary and her friend (page 437) plan and carry out a dieting campaign, they are working beyond the abilities of a chimpanzee. In humans, reasoning permits anticipation and planning, ability to generalize from experience, capacity to delay gratification and to think in terms of consequences, ability to conceive of and act according to abstract concepts, and use of symbolic language. These abilities go far beyond Mary's use of them in undertaking her diet. These abilities have made possible our civilized society.

The Role of Emotions

Emotions contribute regularly to intelligent behavior. They either interfere with it or are the important parts of a situation that calls more for *feeling* than for *thinking*.

In some cases, emotions will help solve a problem. In other cases, emotions will stand in the way of finding a solution. It depends on the problem. Suppose that a girl has decided to talk with her mother about being permitted to stay out as late as her friends. Let's see what will happen if we know the following facts about the case:

1. This girl is the only member of her group who has to be home at 9:30.
2. Her mother has her own reasons, though, and is not going to agree to a change.

Here no solution is in sight, and we can guess that emotional behavior will win in a situation in which both the girl and her mother will be the losers. If either would try to understand better the other's point of view, some change might be possible. At least a more intelligent appreciation of their differences might exist.

The situation between the girl and her mother illustrates a class of encounters that range from actual fights to heated exchanges to "the cold shoulder" (in which no one speaks). These encounters are responsible for a great deal of emotional behavior that we afterward would like to forget (between two politicians, or a soldier and a sailor, or two boys fond of the same girl, or a student and a teacher about which answer to a test question is correct—how many more can you name?). Many of these encounters develop accidentally, and you must learn by experience how to sort out your thoughts and feelings to avoid unreasonable anger and frustration.

But if emotions can be our enemies at times, they also add purpose to intelligent behavior. Love in its many roles, from personal to humanitarian, is chief among constructive emotional feelings that lead to family and civilized society. What other emotions are positive and constructive?

Group Behavior

People in groups often exhibit behavior that is quite different from what they would do as individuals. It is a kind of mass reaction. The behavior may be humanitarian and constructive, as in the aftermath of a disaster such as a flood or a fire. Or, group behavior may be violent and destructive, as in the case of a riot touched off by some relatively minor incident.

Group behavior, especially that of protest groups, has almost become a national pastime. A great deal of time and effort is required to organize an effective protest group, and often the goals are worthy. Sometimes, for example, group protests are directed toward causes such as civil rights or peace. Here the goal is not the problem, but rather how to attain it in a lasting way. Protest groups of university students seeking more control of their universities are effective as mass demonstrations, but are often less clear in their purpose. How the university would be improved if the protesting students had more control over its policies may be partly obscured by the youthful emotions of many of the demonstrators.

Often, especially among teen-agers, group behavior is directed toward approval rather than protest, and centers around performing musical groups or individual celebrities. Group behavior of this type is highly emotional. Very often the group may get into a frenzy and do things they would never think of doing individually or even in a small group. Have you ever acted in this way? See Figure 24-6.

Group behavior is not new. Look at photographs of our political party conventions over the years and you will see examples of highly emotional group behavior. The causes and motivations may change from year to year, and from decade to decade, but people have always reacted in groups, and much social change has been brought about through group action.

24-6 Group behavior is often highly emotional: (*above*) fans at a rock festival; (*below*) a recent national political convention. Why do you think that groups create such strong emotional feeling? What are some good and bad aspects of group behavior?

Behavior Is Conscious and Subconscious

Behavior may occur as a result of a ***conscious*** (KON-shus) process or as a result of a ***subconscious*** process of the mind. To be conscious implies a state of alertness and a state of knowing. You may have a homework assignment and suddenly discover that you have no paper on which to do the assignment. You say to yourself "I have no paper, therefore I must buy some in order to do my homework." This is a state of awareness. You know that you have homework to do, you know that you need paper to write on, and you know the steps that you must take to obtain the paper. We will call this *conscious behavior.*

What do we mean by *subconscious behavior?* From time to time we meet persons that we are immediately attracted to, and we also meet people whom we immediately dislike. Sometimes we can identify qualities in the other person that may explain our reactions. But often we do not know why we feel a particular way. It may be that we perceive qualities in the personality of the other person at a subconscious level. We may not be aware of it, but memories of other people may cause us to react to an individual in a certain way. Thus, our behavior is influenced by subconscious memories.

All of the experiences and information that we have that are not in the conscious mind are conceived of as being in the subconscious mind. These experiences are buried in the mind and are not readily available to us. With some effort at concentration we can reach this information and put it into words. The process of psychoanalysis, referred to earlier, is aimed at making unconscious memories and information available to the conscious mind, so that its effect on personality and behavior can be understood more clearly.

Dreams may tell us much about the subconscious part of a person's mind. Dreams that are repeated often are most likely related to something in the subconscious. Such dreams may reveal something that the person has forgotten or does not want to admit to himself because it was unpleasant. By studying dreams, psychiatrists are often able to learn more about the fears, wishes, hopes, and aspirations that a person may have somewhere deep in his subconscious mind. Some of these thoughts may go back as far as early childhood. It is frequently found that these subconscious conflicts influence later behavior.

Behavior Is Directed Toward Goals

All behavior appears to be directed toward some goal. Every day is filled with many goals. The goal for classwork may be learning, a passing grade, or an *A*. That may be the *immediate goal*, and the *long-range goal* may be acquiring adequate grades to gain admission to college or to prepare you for a job. Still a longer-range goal is acquiring a better understanding of yourself, other people, and the world.

Most goals are learned. As we grow and mature, we add new wishes and desires to our old ones. We establish goals for ourselves that will help us meet our immediate and long-range plans.

Behavior Is Developmental

The first "friendship" an infant has is with his mother. Then his father and brothers and sisters come into the relationship. In his second and third years a child may be with other children his age; but though they are a group, he will be playing pretty much by himself. The next step is moving toward children his age in cooperative play, and here "give and take" friendships begin to form in earnest. In the preteen years there are very intense friendships among members of the same sex. Gradually in the teen years the

24-7 Goals, and behavior related to achieving them, change many times as we mature.

friendship interests fan out to include members of the opposite sex, again in groups. From this stage the movement is to intense friendship with the opposite sex, and finally to marriage. By this time the person is both secure and mature enough to enter into and sustain friendships with adult members of both sexes. But look back at the many steps through which he learned how to relate to others and how to form friendships. The overall goal was relating to other people, but methods of reaching that goal were modified at the different age levels.

You can think of many other examples. For example, a small child's behavior in trying to acquire a shining glass bead will be quite different from the behavior that she uses when she becomes a young woman and wants to acquire a very special dress. The goal in each case is to get an object that will bring pleasure. But, instead of grasping for the object, the young woman has learned to plan a series of behaviors over a period of time—such as working overtime and saving money—that will result in her getting the dress.

24-8 Behavior is developmental. (*Top left*) Small children advance from playing by themselves to sharing friendships. (*Bottom left*) During the preteen years, interest in the opposite sex begins to develop, but boys and girls of this age often have difficulty mingling at parties. (*Right*) In the middle and late teens, boys and girls enjoy dating and being with each other alone or in groups.

Conscience

Conscience (KON-shintz) is that aspect of personality that tells one what behavior is acceptable and what is unacceptable. How does this aspect of personality develop?

Actually it has its origins very early in life and is derived largely out of our relationship with our parents. Every society has a wide range of behavior that it will tolerate, and one that it will not tolerate. Behavior has a value on it, and certain behavior is accept-

able for an adolescent. For example, the very small child may take a treasured object or plaything from a small friend. Because he is a child, his act carries with it no idea of stealing. Although this behavior is unacceptable, no great concern is felt. On the other hand, if an adolescent takes a treasured object or possession, such as a watch or a piece of jewelry, from a friend, this act is regarded by society in an altogether different light.

The conscience develops gradually as a result of the day-by-day activities for which the child receives parental approval or disapproval. When first told that he cannot do something, a child may refrain from the act only because the parents are present and he fears some kind of punishment. But, as time goes on, he gradually comes to build into his personality a quality that tells him what he can and cannot do, even in the absence of the authority of parents.

This process of accepting the value systems of our parents and society is known as *internalization.* That is, through our daily experiences over a long period of time the attitudes of others about right and wrong are adopted and become a part of our personalities. Parents begin the process. Later on, other persons become important in transmitting society's expectations. School teachers, scout leaders, religious leaders, and friends influence and modify the conscience.

Conscience is both necessary *socially* and a source of conflict *personally.* Many times you may be torn between what you want to do and what you feel is right to do. At times even something you have done with good intentions may be judged otherwise by someone else, and there are consequences that you had not expected.

Conflicts can be even more complicated. Sometimes we may not wish to face certain aspects of ourselves—certain traits or motives or wishes that are in conflict with the traits and motives we would like to have. We all have certain common ways of dealing with this kind of conflict. These adaptations are normal, as described in the following sections. In Chapter 28 you will see that, when carried to extremes, they can lead to abnormal behavior.

METHODS OF ADAPTATION

The mental or emotional adaptations we commonly use to avoid facing conflicts or frustrations are often called *defense mecha-*

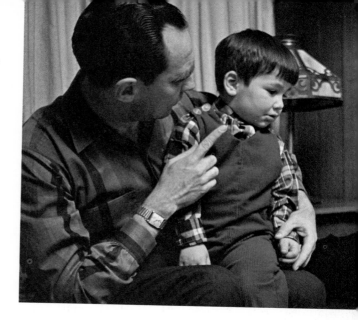

24-9 Conscience develops gradually with the aid of parents who show approval or disapproval of a child's behavior.

nisms, which implies that we use them protectively.

Repression

Repression (re-PRESH-un) is a mechanism which we use to avoid anxiety about feelings that we do not want to face. It is a way of putting these motives and feelings out of our mind. The feelings are pushed down into our subconscious mind.

Thoughts that we repress may be those that would endanger our *self-concept.* Self-concept means the view or opinion that an individual has of himself. If a thought makes a person feel too unworthy, too guilty, or too foolish, he may deal with it by repressing it.

Often we speak of *repressed hostility.* A boy may want to drive his father's car to a neighboring town to attend a ball game. The father may love his boy very much, and the boy may know this, but at the same time the father may be very strict in his attitude about letting his son drive the car on long trips. He might refuse to let him do this. Meanwhile the boy may have promised a couple of friends that he would get the car and take them to the game. When he cannot get the car, he experiences a feeling of frustration and has angry thoughts and wishes about his father. He knows that his father loves him and that his father is trying to do the best thing for him, even though he may not agree with his father's methods. He thinks of all of the fine things that his father has done for him. If he permits these angry feelings toward his father to become conscious thoughts, he will feel a sense of guilt that is painful to him. Therefore, he represses the angry thoughts. He must find some other way of reaching his goal, or else change his goal.

Regression

As a child, Jim was subject to temper tantrums when he was faced with a frustration. He might have an outburst of temper and stamp his feet, throw his arms in the air, and finally fall on the floor kicking. We would think this a rather ineffectual way for a teen-ager to deal with a frustration, and indeed it would be. Most young children have temper tantrums but usually get through this stage fairly promptly. However, if parents always come around and reverse their decision when a child has a tantrum, it is not uncommon for the child to hang on to such a mechanism for reaching his goal. This process of returning to an earlier method of reacting to frustration is called *regression* (re-GRESH-un).

Displaced Aggression

Paul has just had a disagreement with his father. He goes angrily to his room. Soon his younger brother knocks on the door and asks to borrow a necktie to wear to a party.

In great anger, Paul refuses and yells at his brother for even asking. Paul has reacted out of proportion to what might ordinarily be viewed as a reasonable request. He has *displaced* his *aggression* toward his father onto his younger brother. This is the same as the story of the employee who is chastized by the boss; he cannot hit the boss so he comes home and kicks his dog. Has a similar situation ever happened to you?

Projection

Suppose that you are at fault and do not want to face the truth. To do so would hurt too much. To escape from facing up to yourself, you simply put the blame on someone else.

Suppose that on a recent test you did poorly. This makes you unhappy, and you know that your parents will be displeased because they urged you to study ahead of time. But you cannot accept the blame; it makes you too anxious and uncomfortable. So you try to deal with it by putting the blame on the teacher. "She didn't ask questions about the material that was discussed in class. She never does. She always asks the wrong kind of questions." This mechanism is called *projection*—you have projected the blame onto someone else. There is also another type of projection. Suppose that, for some reason you do not understand, you dislike a classmate, Joan. She has not done anything to you, so there is no good reason for you to react with hostility. You do not like this feeling in yourself and feel guilty about it. In this form of projection you turn the tables and attribute the hostility to your classmate, saying "Joan doesn't like me."

Rationalization

Everybody uses *rationalization* (rash-un-uh-luh-ZA-shun) to some degree. We try to avoid an inner conflict by explaining it

24-10 When is the last time you "kicked the cat"? Why did it happen?

away. This is the same as finding a "good" excuse for something.

Often we use rationalization to "explain away" our failures to measure up to our self-concept. Bill fancied himself a good athlete, and in fact he measured up quite well in his school. But when he ran in a race against a team from another school, he finished last. The other school had some very outstanding runners. But Bill's finish was a real blow to his self-esteem, and he began making excuses for his failure. He said the other team had more practice and came from a larger school with more boys to choose from.

You have probably rationalized a few times today. Can you think of one instance?

Compensation

Compensation is a way we have of replacing one goal, which we are having difficulty obtaining, with another goal. Carolyn was a high school junior whose father and mother had divorced about three years earlier. She was quite upset by this and embarrassed that her classmates might not like her when they found out about the divorce. She had been an average student, but in her preoccupation with family problems her school work began to suffer. Carolyn blamed her mother for the events leading up to the divorce, and there was continual discord between them. Her mother criticized Carolyn for not doing well in school, and Carolyn used this as a weapon against her mother.

Earlier, Carolyn had been active in drama, and this had brought her considerable attention; so she turned more actively to the area of drama. She dropped out of the high school drama club and became involved in a local community theater group, spending practically every evening at the theater working backstage and occasionally taking part in the productions. This was an older group, and she received considerable recognition and praise for her hard work and dedication to community theater. Meanwhile her school grades continued to suffer, and she finally was asked to withdraw. Carolyn had compensated for her problems at school and at home by becoming interested in the theater group. But this compensation still left her with many problems. What were some of these problems?

Sublimation

Jeff was a young high school boy who was extremely aggressive and who seemed to go around with a "chip" on his shoulder, daring anyone to knock it off. At the slightest provocation he would try to pick a fight. His aggressive behavior made him very unpopular, and he used the resentment of his classmates as an excuse for being more hostile. It was a vicious cycle.

24-11 What are some of the ways in which you can "sublimate" a desire for adventure and for travel to distant places?

The wrestling coach in Jeff's high school became interested in him. He convinced Jeff to direct his energies into wrestling, where he could be aggressive but where he had to conform to established rules. With the counseling that the coach gave Jeff, and the redirection of Jeff's energy into an acceptable channel, the boy developed into an outstanding athlete. This reflected favorably on Jeff and on the school and brought him attention from faculty and classmates. Consciously Jeff knows nothing about **sublimation**, but he is pleased that he is recognized as a wrestler and doesn't need to "throw his weight around" any more.

Possibly you have sublimated some characteristic of your own, but it is unlikely that you would be fully aware of it.

Reaction Formation

Sometimes a person will react in a way that is completely opposite to the impulse that he feels like expressing. Occasionally almost anyone can have strong feelings of anger and hostility, but not many react with the opposite kind of behavior by being extremely polite and kind. This can be a useful mechanism in getting one through a difficult situation, but if carried to the extreme of becoming a "way of life" it may not be the best mechanism of adaptation. For example, Julie was a high school student whose mother had been ill for many years. This made it necessary for Julie to spend all of her spare time caring for her mother and doing the housework. In fact, she had to dash home from school at noon to prepare lunch for her mother and then rush back to school. Julie was known to her friends and to all of the people in the neighborhood as a very sweet, kind, gentle girl who was dedicated to taking care of her mother. This was what showed on the surface, but underneath there was intense resentment at having all of her time and energy consumed in caring for her mother. Yet, when these feelings tried to break through into consciousness, she became very anxious and felt extremely guilty for having such feelings. Would it have been better for Julie to have sought professional advice? yes

Who Uses Mechanisms of Adaptation?

At some time or other all of us use these various mechanisms of adaptation, and within reason they are quite normal. At any one time we may use a combination of mechanisms. Such mechanisms are, for the most part, on a subconscious level, and we are not aware that we are using this particular way of adapting. However, we do become aware of whether or not we are being reasonably successful, and in thinking about our behavior, we often develop an awareness of how we have been functioning. At such times we may have a keen insight into our personalities that can result in healthier and more effective adaptation.

What You Have Learned

What kind of health practices should you apply in maintaining your health? Check your understanding of the chapter. On a separate sheet of paper, number 1 through 18 and insert the answer from the vocabulary list below. Use each expression, but use each one only once.

- 13 conscience
- 9 conscious
- 7 emotional
- 8 group
- 5 instincts
- 6 intelligent
- 12 investigating
- 2 neurophysiologists
- 3 pain
- 14 parents
- 4 pleasurable
- 16 projection
- 11 psychoanalysis
- 17 rationalization
- 15 regression
- 18 repression
- 1 stimulus
- 10 subconscious

In its simplest sense, behavior is response to a (1) _____. Among the specialists concerned with behavior are the (2) _____ who study the nervous system. Human behavior generally moves from a state of unpleasantness, tension and (3) _____ toward a more (4) _____ state. Behavior is motivated by many forces, some of which are inborn ones called (5) _____. Behavior is also motivated by learned ideas that may produce a different type of behavior called (6) _____ behavior. Then there is behavior that may occur when strong feelings are aroused. This is (7) _____ behavior. In addition to individual behavior there is also (8) _____ behavior.

Behavior is partly (9) _____, that is, you are aware of what you are doing. But there is also (10) _____ behavior that may be provoked by memories, thoughts, and feelings of which you are not aware. The procedure used to make unconscious memories and information available to the conscious mind is called (11) _____. This procedure is helpful not only for treatment but also for (12) _____ human behavior.

That aspect of your personality which tells you what behavior is acceptable and what is not acceptable is your (13)_____. It has its beginning early in life and develops gradually as the child receives approval or disapproval from his (14)_____. Conflicts in your personality are frequently resolved by using methods of adaptation. There are many types of these defense mechanisms. For example, when you are frustrated over some difficulty and revert to childish behavior, it is called (15)_____. Or, when you have failed a test and put the blame on the teacher, you are using the mechanism of (16)_____. When you failed to win in a sports contest and made an excuse by saying the judges were partial to the other school, you were using the mechanism of (17)_____. We use the mechanism of (18)_____ as a way of putting thoughts out of our mind.

What You Can Do

1. A committee from your class might be appointed to prepare a shelf of interesting reference material on the subject of behavior. The material could include books, magazines, photographs, cartoons, and films. The material could cover the behavior of animals and various primitive tribes as well as adolescents. See if you can find anything in common between the animal and human types of behavior. What differences do you observe? What accounts for the differences?

2. You might select one person whom you know quite well for observation. Observe the behavior of this person when he is eating lunch following a tough mathematics test, at a football game, or while attending a school dance. What types of behavior have you observed? Can you find reason for such behavior? How does this behavior correspond with your behavior?

Things to Try

1. Arrange for a class debate on such topics as "Does behavior express your personality?" or, "Who should decide on what is acceptable behavior for teen-agers?"

2. Observe your favorite television drama. Jot down on a piece of paper the various reactions of the star in different situations that he faces. Try to determine what type of behavior he is using—instinctive, intelligent, or emotional. Would you be inclined to behave in the same way?

3. Often you are asked to join a group to protest some school rule or to gain a privilege you think you deserve. Based on the section on "group behavior" in this chapter, make a list of the types of behavior

you would probably display if you were to agree to join such a group. Check your list to see if these are the types of behavior you would normally want to display.

Probing Further

Building Your Life, by J. T. & M. G. Landis, Prentice-Hall, 1964. Two valuable books written especially for teen-agers by outstanding authorities in the field of guidance.

How to Be a Successful Teen-ager, by W. Menninger, Sterling, 1966. You will find excellent advice on how to act in a group, how to get along with others, and how to be efficient in your school work.

Ways to Improve Your Personality, by V. Bailard and R. M. Strange, McGraw-Hill, 1965.

Health Concepts in Action

Does this statement help express what you have learned? Would you change or add to it?

An *individual develops patterns of behavior* by which he interacts with his environment.

Applying this concept of behavior, which health practices would you

—continue?

—change?

—begin?

Will you now, as a result of your study, change any of your health objectives?

25 / How You Learn

"Come on Paul," said his older brother Ken, "put the banjo away and get with your history for tomorrow's test." "OK," replied Paul, "but it's no use, I can't make an A no matter how much I study." "Who said you had to make an A?" Ken asked. "Well," said Paul, "every time Mr. Hall returns my tests he says Ken would have made an A."

Do you think brothers and sisters should be expected to be alike in their ability to learn? Think of the suggestions you could make to Paul as you continue with this chapter.

A PROBE INTO LEARNING—Have your learning goals changed in recent years? To what do you attribute any changes? You might begin by probing these questions:

1. How do hereditary and environmental factors affect our capacity to learn?

2. How is the intelligence quotient, or IQ, derived?

3. How may learning be affected by anxiety? by low motivation? by competition?

4. What techniques can you develop to help you learn more effectively?

5. Why are skills for test-taking important?

25-1　What are some of the reasons that your attention may wander during class? What can you do to improve your concentration?

FACTORS THAT AFFECT LEARNING

Do you ever take a moment to look at your classmates while the teacher is talking? Some are listening attentively, but you might see John staring out the window, Nancy fixing her hair, Anne whispering to Paul, and Jane aimlessly turning the pages of her book. Are all of your classmates learning? Can they concentrate on what the teacher is saying while doing other things? Why is it difficult for some of them to concentrate? Is the work boring, or too difficult, or can one or more of your classmates have an emotional problem that is occupying his mind? In this chapter we will *learn* about *learning*—what it is, how we learn, and problems that interfere with learning.

Suppose John is walking to school on an April morning. The sun is shining and the birds are singing. He is swinging along, thinking alternately of the class picnic that is coming up next Saturday and of a topic for a term paper due soon. Almost before he notices, a few scattered clouds have scurried together and others have hurried from over the horizon to form a slow-moving layer that blankets the sky. There is a

moment of stillness, a few raindrops fall, the air is chilled, and then the downpour comes. John dashes under an awning and in a few minutes the dark clouds pick up speed and move on; the sun comes through again. John had sense enough to come in out of the rain. His behavior was *intelligent*. He was able to make associations in his mind with past experiences and realize the uncomfortable consequences if he had not behaved appropriately. John's behavior was *learned*, as is most behavior.

Let's imagine that the experience on that April morning sparked his imagination. He began to think about rain and sun, about the seasons of the year, and about weather in general. He wanted to know more. Indeed, this might be a good subject for his term paper! How did he go about learning more about weather? First he recalled what he knew from his own experience and from his reading. He studied sections on weather in the encyclopedia and in his science books. He talked with a neighbor who was an airline pilot and he listened to weather forecasts on television. He learned how weather affects agriculture, shipping, and other kinds of business. Over a few weeks John compiled a lot of information and ideas and many un-answered questions. And after some hard work he had a term paper that pleased him. John had done a great deal of learning. What are some of the characteristics of this learning?

The Complex Nature of Learning

Human learning is a complex process that is still being investigated. Much remains to be understood. Here we can take just a brief look at some of the things that had to happen for John to learn to "come out of the rain."

First of all, we need to recognize that John did not simply "see" the changes in the weather. He *perceived* them. **Perception,** the process by which we become aware of our environment, is not a passive process involving only the sense organs. On the contrary, it is an active process in which the brain interprets the evidence gained through the sense organs.

John had already had many such experiences with changes in the weather. He had watched the changes that preceded rain and then the rain that followed. He was able to *associate* the first events with the second. After many such associations, he was able to *form a concept* about when it is likely to rain.

Through **memory,** John was able to store these earlier learnings and to recall them at the appropriate time.

It was all of this (and more) that enabled him to *interpret* what was presently happening, to *predict* that rain would come shortly, and to *decide on an appropriate behavior*— taking shelter in time.

John also had the capacity to form more involved concepts about the weather. He prepared a report for his class about the effects of weather on man's activities, such as farming and famous battles. In preparing his paper, John expressed his concepts in symbols—letters arranged in a manner that had meaning for him and his readers. John

25-2 A number of factors are involved in effective learning. When you are learning something new, do you take all of these factors into consideration?

used **symbolic processes** not only throughout his reading and writing but also throughout his thinking. That is, he used ideas, mental images, words, and so on, to represent things.

These are just a few of the complex functions carried out by the brain in learning. You may want to look into some of the theories of how different kinds of learning take place, of different kinds of memory, of how we attain concepts, and of other aspects of learning.

Capacities for Learning

People have different capacities for learning, based on heredity and environment. How much of each is involved is impossible to say. Anyone who has worked with students who come from emotionally and materially deprived backgrounds can cite examples of some who were very able. The reverse is also true. Many boys and girls of these backgrounds initially appear to have lowered capacities for learning—but their abilities seem to increase when their life experiences are enriched. Still other students from widely differing backgrounds remain more closely identified with the level of learning they first demonstrate upon entering school. Thus, although both hereditary and environmental factors affect the capacity for learning, these factors must be evaluated for each individual. It is not wise to generalize. We can, however, try to distinguish what some of the learning factors are.

Purpose of IQ Tests

From the beginning, children vary in ability to learn, and a recognition of this is important for parents and teachers. Although a trained observer, such as a child psychologist, can determine some of a child's abilities in the preschool years, it is usually in relation to schoolwork that abilities and inabilities become most evident. This is because the school is usually the first organized experience in which a child is expected to participate with a group of children his own age. Marked learning inabilities as well as lesser handicaps become apparent as more difficult material is presented in school.

Any attempt to help a child who is having difficulty learning should include a study of his physical and emotional problems as well as an estimate of his intelligence. He should be helped as early as possible so that he can avoid frustration and increased difficulty. Otherwise, he may develop behavior problems. More and more, the schools are taking into account the differences among children. They are providing special programs for children of varied abilities, interests, and backgrounds.

In the beginning of this section we pointed out the difficulty in accurately pin-pointing how much of the capacity to learn depends on heredity and how much on environment. In this connection, it is important that you understand something about **intelligence quotient** (QUO-shunt) or IQ. This term has become an everyday word, often misused. IQ refers to the measurement of the rate of growth of intelligence. One way in which it is determined is by dividing the mental age

25-3 This boy is a prize-winner in a Westinghouse Science fair. His project took many hours of investigation and research.

(MA) of a person, as demonstrated in testing, by the chronological age (CA), which is simply one's age in years and months. The result is multiplied by 100 in order to avoid decimals. The procedure is expressed by this formula:

$$\frac{MA}{CA} \times 100 = IQ$$

What is MA or mental age? It is the level of intellectual performance that you have reached. This figure is arrived at by comparing your performance on a particular test with that of many others, some the same age as you, but others younger and older. Let's assume that you are fifteen years old and that on a test you accomplish the usual tasks that most other fifteen-year-olds can do. Then your mental age or MA is 15. The formula would be expressed:

$$\frac{15}{15} \times 100 = 100$$

Your IQ would be recorded as 100. About 100 is taken as the average IQ; MA and CA are the same. An MA higher than the CA shows that you are performing higher than the average person your age; an MA lower than the CA places you in a lower-than-average group. What if there were two children, one aged ten and another aged six, and both had the same MA? This means that the intelligence of the six-year-old had developed at a faster rate than the intelligence of the ten-year-old.

IQ tests, or intelligence tests, today are undergoing much study and revision. Concern has been expressed that some tests formerly administered do not measure a true MA because they are based on language and experience—in and out of school—that is not typical of all schools and all neighborhoods. Suppose, for example, that you cannot do certain tasks on a test because you have not been taught how. You might be *intelligent* enough, but not *informed* enough.

It is true that no test can be perfect, and group tests (administered to entire classes at once) are not as reliable as individual tests. But if the MA on such tests is not completely reliable, it does indicate whether your learning compares favorably with that of other students your age.

Motivation

Motivation to learn is closely related to motivation for all your behavior. Just as Mary (Chapter 24) became uncomfortable when called "Chubby," so, too, you may become uncomfortable if you don't do as well as others do on class quizzes. You don't enjoy facing the criticism of classmates, teachers, or parents. Moreover, you even face criticism from yourself, partly because of your conscience and *internalization* (also Chapter 24). You recall that *internalization* is the process of adopting as your own the value systems of your parents and of society. From then on, your conscience motivates you.

25-4 These teen-agers are partaking in a program conducted at Mount Holyoke College to help able, motivated, but poorly educated students achieve their goal of admission to college. Several similar programs are being tried throughout the country.

Adopting the values of others around you may work both ways. In your school and in your neighborhood, you may feel much better and happier when you do tasks well and earn the encouragement and approval of others. However, some groups of young people place little value on school achievement. They may be in a hurry to get out of school and start working for the many material things they want, such as a car and expensive clothes. They may see no connection between doing well in school and getting good jobs later.

Family illness and economic problems may also make it hard for some teen-agers to concentrate on school work. Their frustrations at trying again and again and *not* succeeding may cause some of them to "give up." Many of these boys and girls will need the encouragement of adults with a strong belief in their ability to succeed. See Figure 25-4.

Fortunately, you are far more than a passive product of your environment. Your heredity gives you a unique combination of traits, a different combination than that of either of your parents. You have affected your environment and have set many of your own goals. Increasingly you want to learn *for your own reasons* as well as those you have adopted from your parents and from society. You have your likes and dislikes, and your favored and less-favored school subjects, and other interests. You have begun to learn *selectively* for a better understanding of the things *you* want to know. This is *self-motivation*, which includes many factors your parents and society have not instilled in you.

In school, "favorite" teachers often have much to do with the development of your interests, and with your motivation to learn. Favorite friends and their interests also may affect your motivation—and you affect theirs.

25-6 Trying out for the cheerleading squad is a highly competitive experience. Do you enjoy competition of this kind?

25-5 Young children are usually eager to learn reading and writing. Could motivation explain their interest?

Are You Competitive?

Do you compete with your friends? Wherever you turn there is competition, and it can be a healthy kind of interaction when kept within limits.

For example, you compete for grades, for a place on the team, for good scores on exams, and for a job. Competition may serve to stimulate you to learn more effectively. You can model yourself after someone who competes successfully and learn from him. Your efforts at competing may also inspire someone else. Competitive achievements may help improve self-esteem.

For some people competition is an end in itself; winning can become so important that the means used to win may get out of hand. If you find yourself in this position, you may need to examine your sense of values. Some teen-agers still carry with them

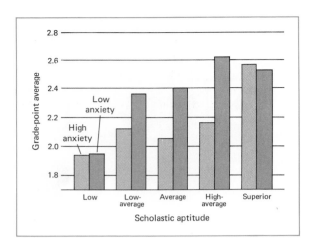

25-7 The bars show the College Board scores of students of different ability levels. For each level of ability, the scores of "high-anxiety" and "low-anxiety" students are compared. In which ability levels is high anxiety connected with lower scores?

the sense of frustration they felt as children in relation to their struggles with parents, or their competition with a brother or sister for parental attention. Some people carry this "sibling rivalry" over into their daily lives and constantly compete with everyone for attention. This is an unhealthy form of competition that seldom leads to personal happiness.

What are your own attitudes toward competition? Remember that as you become more mature you are more in competition with yourself. You need to be concerned with acquiring a realistic view of your capacities and abilities, and with developing your potential in an effective manner.

Anxiety

Anxiety can be caused by competition, conscience, or reasons we don't always know. We define anxiety as an unpleasant state of apprehension, often without an awareness of what stimulates the feeling. Are anxiety and

fear the same? Fear usually relates to a specific threat, but the two concepts are similar enough that we shall consider them closely related.

How does anxiety affect learning? It can have a positive or negative effect. Mild anxiety, according to many people, is an aid to learning. For example, you may want to go out for a school sport. Your motivation may be high. For several reasons it may be quite important to you to belong to the squad. You may approach tryouts with considerable anxiety. It is quite possible that the anxiety increases your level of alertness, improves your coordination and the tone of your muscles, and quickens your reflexes to the extent that you perform more effectively than you thought possible.

But what about being too anxious? Perhaps you can recall some occasion when you were so tense that you could not do your best. Maybe you were so tense you could not

25-8 Learning to drive can be an anxiety-producing experience. Does anxiety help or hinder such learning?

coordinate your muscles as well as usual. Maybe you were so "worked up" over an exam that your performance suffered. What caused the anxiety? If you are continually so anxious that you do not do your best, ask yourself why. Many times, with some honest thinking about your anxiety, you can find and evaluate the causes. Only then can you find ways of decreasing the tension caused by anxiety. Being anxious about an examination is normal, but extreme anxiety may interfere with your attention and concentration.

Health

Problems that hinder learning are not "all in the head." When a student is not learning properly, a complete physical examination should be made. Several kinds of anemia affect physical health, motivation, and concentration. Hormones, especially, affect learning. A marked hypothyroid condition, for example, could result in laziness and apathy. Or, though the symptoms would be quite different, a hyperthyroid condition also could interfere with learning. Very often glasses or a hearing aid may be the answer to a learning problem. A physician's attention is usually most helpful in unravelling a learning problem.

DEVELOPING EFFECTIVE STUDY HABITS

A learning factor that you can do a great deal about is your study habits. *Skills of learning* are as important as *skills of accomplishment.* In fact, skills of learning *are* skills of accomplishment—of a special kind.

Many a boy spends a lot of time training his muscles to throw a baseball with speed and control. Many a girl spends a lot of time learning to sew or knit. How many boys and girls know that by practice they can train their brains to do more work in less time? Suppose that you can now learn a certain assignment in one hour. If you practice better methods of learning, you might be able to learn the same assignment in half the time— and remember it longer! Would you like to learn more quickly and remember better what you learn? Try the following suggestions.

Some Useful Techniques

1. *Pay attention.* Keep your mind on what you are trying to learn. Try to become interested. Give the subject a chance! Then your mind will be more alert and ready for action. If some part of the work interests you very much, think of that from time to time. This will help you to go on to the less interesting parts.

2. *Get the central thought first.* To do this, skim the lesson first. Then, as you study the details, you will find that the parts fit together. Outline the main points and use this outline for review. You will find this procedure one of the best ways to understand and remember how ideas are related. You will also find that understanding an idea makes remembering it almost automatic.

3. *Associate the new facts and concepts with each other and with what you already know.* Do you remember John and the associations he made between a rain shower and a school project? Or the later associations he made between weather and man's activities? Say to yourself from time to time, "What does this have to do with our lives and with what we have already studied?" Think, "What is this connected with?" And don't skip lessons. You can't expect to understand the work if you leave out the connecting links.

4. *Get your ideas in as many ways as you can.* Learning cannot be poured into

25-9 Study habits are a major factor in learning. How might the girl on the left study more effectively? If your study habits are poor, how can you improve them? Do you give your studying a chance, as the girl on the right does? Check your study habits tonight.

you, like milk into a glass. You learn only when you think, feel, or do something. If you learn by reading, you use one sense (sight). Yet reading involves understanding and memory of what you have learned through all of your senses. Use such aids to learning as the shop or laboratory, diagrams, pictures, films, and records. A slightly different approach between your book and another source of information may help you *conceptualize*, just as such different sources of information helped John form *his* own ideas and concepts in a project about the weather.

5. *Practice the material to be learned.* Review it. Do you know the saying, "Practice makes perfect"? Don't expect to learn most lessons by reading

them once. Think a lesson through again, and again and again if you need to. As you do this, pay most attention to the main points. Use your own outlines or those in the book. Try to think of examples to illustrate or make clear each of the main points.

6. *Get satisfaction from what you learn.* If you know that you have done a lesson well, it will help you to remember it. You have reached the age when your own feeling of pride in good work should be enough. You should not have to depend upon praise or rewards.

7. *Budget your study time.* Plan how much time you will give to each subject. Do the hardest thing first. Then your mind is more relaxed for the rest of the work. Try to follow your time-schedule closely.

Improving Your Memory

Certain aids have helped many others build good memories. They will probably help you.

1. *Don't try to remember everything.* Don't make your mind carry details that are not important. That is a waste of energy. Write down appointments, plans for the day, and shopping lists. Be sure to remember where you put your notes!

2. *Make it a habit to review properly.* Let many small ideas grow into a big one. Then fix this large, general idea in your mind. In books, the italics, summaries, and conclusions all help you to pick out the important ideas and make reviewing easier.

3. *Concentrate.* Do one thing at a time. Keep away from radio and television while studying. Don't interrupt your studying with phone calls. Your date for the school prom is important and so is your choice of dress for the picnic! However, put these matters out of your mind during the time you have allotted for studying.

4. *Connect your ideas.* The idea of association cannot be overemphasized. Learn to relate facts and ideas, not only for study, but for learning names, places, dates, and instructions. Connect a name with something about the person. Connect a date with a birthday, or something that happened on that day in history.

5. *Try to relax.* Your brain works best if you are not overanxious. Have you ever tried hard to recall a name and found that you could not think of it? The name often comes quickly to your mind after you pass on to another point. You know what happens if you try to run, skate, dance, or write with your muscles too tense. The same principle operates when you learn.

25-10 Taking tests is one way of finding out what you know—and what you need to learn.

Taking Tests

We live in a culture that gives great importance to testing. There is a test for just about everything: intelligence tests, personality tests, school tests. You would not make any special preparation if you were to take either of the first two tests. But if you have observed the suggestions about study and memory, your chances of being successful with school tests will be greatly increased. Before the test, attend to what has been discussed in class and you can anticipate many of the questions. Quickly assess the entire test. If there are questions that you know will take more time or that you don't know, answer the others first. If you do not know an answer to a question, don't let this damage your efforts on questions that you do know. No test can determine everything you know. It can test you on some things you know and can tell you what you need to learn. When you get the test back, review the results and learn what you did not know.

What You Have Learned

What kind of health practices should you apply in maintaining your health? Check your understanding of the chapter. On a separate sheet of paper, number 1 through 18 and insert the answer from the vocabulary list below. Use each expression, but use each one only once.

anxiety	health	100
brain	intelligence	perception
competition	internalization	practice
concentration	IQ	selectively
concept	language	self
experience	memory	values

A basic part of learning is (1) _____, the ability to interpret the evidence of our senses. The capacity to store impressions of previous experiences and to be able to recall them is known as (2) _____. When you are able to relate many experiences and form a general idea from them, you have attained a new (3) _____.

Since people vary in their capacity to learn, certain tests are used to estimate learning capacity. One of these is a test devised to show how well one performs the usual intellectual activities for a person his age. This test is called an (4) _____ test. Intelligence tests are not completely reliable for all situations because they are based on (5) _____ and (6) _____. When your mental age has been established and you already know your chronological age, it is possible to determine your (7) _____. You use the formula of dividing your mental age by your chronological age and multiplying the result by (8) _____.

As you grow and develop from childhood onward, there are many factors that affect your learning. Among these factors are the (9) _____ of those around you, and then (10) _____. Later you begin to learn (11) _____ that is, to learn things you want to understand rather than just those things that your parents and society want you to learn. You have become (12) _____-motivated, to a greater or lesser extent.

Learning can be handicapped when you experience an unpleasant state of apprehension without an awareness of what stimulates the feeling. This state is called (13) _____. Sometimes this apprehensive state is brought about by too strong a sense of (14) _____, which can be an effective stimulus for learning and achieving if kept within healthy limits. Another hindrance to learning is poor physical (15) _____.

Study habits are another learning factor. Developing effective study habits, like learning a skill, requires persistent (16) _____. You can train your (17) _____ to do more work in less time. Everyone admires a person who has a good memory. You can build a good memory, and the key to this skill is (18) _____.

What You Can Do

1. Invite the school psychologist to give your class a talk on tests of various types. Perhaps he could give some sample questions that might be used to test for verbal ability and for performance ability. Ask the psychologist to lead a class discussion at the close of his talk. What questions would you ask? Would you like to know what your own IQ is? What would you have to do to find out? Can you be tested for aptitude before choosing a career? Where could you go for such a test?

2. You have learned that anxiety is an unpleasant feeling of misgiving or uncertainty but you don't know what causes this feeling. Put another way, you have "butterflies in your stomach" and you don't know where they came from. Let's suppose that the principal has called you to his office. Naturally, you will feel some anxiety, just as a workman might feel if his boss called him to the office. Using this call to the principal's office as an example, write down the feeling you might first experience. What causes these feelings? Why were you sent for? Is your principal friendly and understanding?

Things to Try

1. Copy the seven suggestions for effective study from your text into your notebook. Read them carefully before you start studying your next assignment. Practice each one faithfully. Talk about the lesson with other people and get their ideas, look up the topic you are studying in the encyclopedia and get more ideas. After practicing using the suggestions for some time, how do you feel about learning in this way? Do you feel more "at home" with the subject? Are you ready to ask questions? Are you better able to answer questions?

2. Draw a large circle on a sheet of paper and put a small circle in the center. Divide the circle into 24 even segments to represent 24 hours of time. Using different colors, block in the number of hours as you now spend them and name the activity. For example, your list of activities might include:

8 *to* 9 *hours sleeping*
6 *to* 7 *hours attending school*
2 *to* 3 *hours studying out of school*
1 *to* $1\frac{1}{2}$ *hours eating meals*
1 *to* $1\frac{1}{2}$ *hours bathing, dressing, etc.*
$1\frac{1}{2}$ *to* 2 *hours play or work after school*
$19\frac{1}{2}$ *to* 24 *hours*

How does your circle work out? Have you allowed enough time for study out of school? Since learning is at this time your primary responsibility, it becomes an important item in your list. Suppose a test is announced and you temporarily need even more time to study. From which of the other items could you safely borrow some extra time for study? Do you need to modify your schedule? What are some of the factors which make you realize that you should do so?

Probing Further /

Introduction to Psychology, by E. R. Hilgard and R. C. Atkinson, Harcourt Brace Jovanovich, 1971. Read the chapters on how we learn, and how and why we remember and forget.

Psychology, by W. J. McKeachie and C. L. Doyle, Addison-Wesley, 1970. Learning is emphasized throughout this advanced book. If you like to read and are a good reader, you should find some of the accounts of human and animal learning very interesting.

You and the Next Decade, by Adrian A. Paradis, McKay, 1965. Written for high school students, this book discusses how you can best learn to be a successful high school graduate. It discusses your progress through college or on the job to adult life.

Health Concepts in Action /

Would you now agree with this statement? Would you change or add to it?

> *An individual's capacity to learn is influenced by heredity and environment.*

Applying this concept of learning, which health practices would you

— continue?

— change?

— begin?

Will you now, as a result of your study, change any of your health objectives?

26 / *Your Emotions*

Sally got the part she wanted in the school play. One scene in the play called for her to be kissed. She asked her boy friend whether he would mind her taking the part. Although he did mind, he hid his feelings and told Sally to go ahead.

Sally took the part. The actor who played opposite her was handsome and popular. For weeks after, Sally's boy friend was kidded about his "competition." Sally discovered that her dates with her boy friend were now always ending in some petty argument. At one point, she and her boy friend almost broke up. It took months before they became close again.

Could this situation have been prevented? If so, how?

A PROBE INTO YOUR EMOTIONS — What influences the way we express our emotions? You can begin your probe with questions like these:

1. What body systems play a major role in emotional states?

2. What physical changes accompany the emotion of fear?

3. Give some examples of emotional behavior that would be acceptable at age six but not at age fifteen.

4. What are three principal influences on individual emotional development?

5. What are four kinds of love? How do they differ?

6. In what ways can anger and fear help? Is anxiety ever helpful?

26-1 Have you recently had an embarrassing thing happen to you? How did you handle it?

WHAT DO WE MEAN BY EMOTION?

You may not be able to define *emotion*—but you certainly know when you experience it! When someone you are strongly attracted to comes unexpectedly into the room, you feel elation that actually sends a physical sensation surging through your whole body. If, perhaps, you would rather not let your feelings be known, you wonder uncomfortably whether your flushed face, quickened breathing, alert posture, and the tone of your voice are showing all too clearly how you feel about that person.

Recall some less pleasant experiences. A small incident of no real importance causes you embarrassment; you feel you have "made a fool of yourself." Oddly enough, the physical signs accompanying these feelings are much like those of elation: face flushes, breathing speeds up, heart pounds, and mouth feels dry. Yet the first experience was distinctly pleasant, and the latter was quite the opposite!

Your emotions are always present. You're about to start an important examination and feel you are not well prepared. You just sit quietly, waiting for the papers to be given out, but the tell-tale physical signs of "nervousness" appear. Your face may become pale instead of flushed, breathing steps up, mouth becomes dry, palms sweat, and, perhaps, your hands tremble.

"You seemed pretty emotional about it," a friend may recall later. Yet perhaps you did as well as you had hoped you might. The friend may have been very confident about the examination beforehand, without doing nearly as well. How can you explain the different emotions different people feel in the same situation?

You could name varying emotional states—anger, resentment, fear, joy, anticipation, surprise, guilt, sympathy, and many more. Yet certain physical reactions are very similar regardless of the type of emotion, especially when the emotion is very intense. No wonder we find the emotions so confusing and difficult to define.

Theories About Emotions

Scientists who study human behavior also have trouble defining emotion. Some say it is a stirred-up state of the whole physical organism. It arises from conflict or tension, and the physiological changes serve to reduce the tension and reestablish balance. Others say this stirred-up state has a purpose in preparing the organism to meet emergencies—enabling it to react to threat through either aggression or escape.

Both general physiological disturbances and emergency reactions can vary in degree from mild to severe. Again the experts differ, some regarding only extreme physiological upsets or crisis reactions as emotions. By this definition, emotional states are relatively rare. Others claim that *every* experience has an emotional side and that *all* behavior expresses something of what you are feeling.

It is enough for us to recognize that any form of *feeling*, mild or severe, is a special kind of experience that includes both mental and physical activity. The emotion that we feel is our *interpretation* of the bodily changes that take place. In different situations, we may interpret the same bodily changes differently, and therefore feel different emotions.

Scientists differ in the number of distinct emotions they recognize. Most consider that there are only three basic emotions: *love, fear,* and *anger.* They feel that the others are all derived from them. Some reduce the three to two: *pleasure* and *displeasure.* But all agree on one important thing: the infant starts life with very limited emotional equipment, and the rich variety of feelings experienced by the teen-ager and adult result from a long, gradual learning process.

26-2 Teen-agers are capable of a rich variety of emotions. What emotions do you think this boy and girl might be experiencing? How much of a variety of emotions do you experience daily?

Your Whole Body Participates

Carla came dancing into the room, twirled about three times, and flung herself into a big chair. Her heart was pounding, her cheeks flushed, her pulse very fast. She had felt light as a feather, then pleasantly relaxed as she fell into the chair. The reason for her behavior? Several pieces of paper in her hand—a letter from a boy named George.

Several miles away, in the sprawling building of a large factory, Mike ground his teeth. He, too, had a piece of paper. As he shoved the dismissal notice into his pocket, his face went red, his big biceps and forearm muscles contracted, and he took short, quick breaths. He could almost feel the plant manager's jaw against his fist as he gave him an imaginary punch.

When people experience emotions, the most important physiological changes are related to the autonomic nervous system and the endocrine, or ductless, glands. You may want to refer to Chapters 12 and 22 for a complete review of these systems. You remember that the autonomic system lies outside the brain and spinal cord, and its operation is partly independent of all our other nerve activities. It regulates basic life functions such as heart action and digestion, *over which we have no voluntary control.* The sympathetic division of the autonomic system is dominant during emotional states. It speeds up heart action, slows down or stops digestion, quickens breathing, causes the pupils of the eyes to dilate, and sends an increased blood supply to the skeletal muscles.

At the same time the adrenal glands become active. They release a hormone (adrenaline) into the blood stream and facilitate the release of blood sugar from the liver. These changes make more energy available for the voluntary muscles, which enables people under stress to perform incredible acts of strength and endurance. This accounts for the theory that emotion prepares the organism for *fight or flight.* But if the threatening situation occurs in the classroom or office, where vigorous physical feats are not called for, the adrenaline may cause muscles to quiver from sheer tenseness, thus adding to the general disturbance.

What is the involvement of the brain? This is the part we know least about at the present time. Many researchers are trying to find out what parts of the brain are affected and what takes place to initiate emotional reactions.

The intricate details of these physical changes do not concern the nonprofessional. But it is important for us to learn from laboratory studies that the process is very complicated. As you have seen in earlier chapters, the parts of the nervous system and the several glands are interdependent and react upon each other. This makes the total reaction in an emotional state highly variable between one individual and another, and often quite variable for a single individual from one situation to the next. Sometimes the physical reaction is so sudden and so far ahead of awareness that one does not even realize what the stimulus was that triggered the emotional response.

You Started with So Little!

Observation of infants and young children has shown that their emotions are few and uncomplicated. For the newborn it is correct to describe *all* emotion as just a stirred-up state, or, as it is more commonly called, a **generalized excitement,** of which the external evidence is only crying and thrashing about. However, a baby's emotional growth is rapid. Soon we see the difference between excitement that is tinged with delight, happiness, or displeasure, and distressed excitement. The delight reaction usually turns into affection for specific persons, while the distress signals express anger, fear, or physical discomfort. By the age of two, jealousy, love, and hate appear.

Learning to experience these varied feelings develops along with the baby's social

26-3 Infancy is a period of rapid emotional growth. This baby shows a delight reaction.

learning. As he experiences day-by-day care by various adults, he associates certain occurrences with particular people. He gradually begins to distinguish relationships that have meaning for him. This overlapping, or interdependence, of social and emotional learning continues through infancy, childhood, adolescence, and on to adulthood.

Although the *kinds of reactions* of which all newborns are capable are the same, the *degree of intensity* with which responses are exhibited is widely variable — right from the moment of birth. Some babies react to a puff of air or sharp noise by showing a strong *startle* pattern or by crying. Others remain quiet and relaxed. Their heart beat, blood pressure, and other physiological measurements also differ over quite a range even at this just-born stage.

Here we may have a partial answer to the question, are some people *overemotional* and others *unemotional?* The evidence suggests there are indeed biological differences. The infant who overreacts to a puff of air may be more inclined, when he grows up, toward a quick and vigorous reaction to any form of exciting stimulus, pleasant or unpleasant. The quieter baby may be less susceptible to stimulation in his adult behavior patterns.

YOUR "EMOTIONAL AGE" OR MATURITY

Have you ever heard someone ask "Is he *emotionally mature?*" This question is based on the concept that we change as we gain experience. Certain behavior that is appropriate and acceptable at one age is not suitable at a later age. But such change in emotional behavior is not automatic. If a person's "emotional age" lags behind his chronological age, we say he has not attained emotional maturity—no matter how grown up he may appear to be physically.

As the baby learns to experience different kinds of feelings, he expresses them in direct physical terms: a smile and happy gurgling for pleasure, and frowns, tears, or screams of rage for displeasure. A few years later, the young child still shows his feelings openly and actively. He jumps and skips about and laughs with happiness over a new toy that he likes. He hits and kicks, to the accompaniment of loud protests, when a strong desire is frustrated.

A teen-ager or adult often will substitute talk for direct physical action. This in itself is a big step toward emotional maturity. But other changes also occur. A teen-ager has acquired a wider "vocabulary" of feelings to express, and he distinguishes many different shades of meaning among stimuli to which he once would have reacted on an all-or-none basis—*all good* or *all bad.* Some stimuli that call forth strong reactions from a youngster do not even exist as emotional stimuli for the teen-ager.

You may be disappointed if you have to miss a movie in order to get homework done. But you are not as emotionally upset as a baby appears to be when his toy is taken away. When disappointment is really devastating, you do not express it as the baby would by anguished crying, at least not in public! Both in your emotional *reactions* and in your emotionally expressive *behavior*, you have come a long way from infancy.

Some Adults Never Grow Up

There are instances when infantile behavior persists—not only into the teen years, but through adulthood. The grown man who is cranky when his evening is spoiled, and the woman who cries whenever she wants her own way—both are using behavior techniques that are suitable only for the small child who has smashed his spaceman's helmet. Can you think of other examples of emotional behavior that are acceptable at six but unacceptable at twenty-six?

Some examples of emotional immaturity are not clear-cut. A boy makes a lame excuse for refusing to participate in a group activity

26-4 What do we mean by "emotional immaturity"? How emotionally mature are you?

because he is afraid of the social competition of a popular classmate. Figuratively speaking, he is not crying over a smashed space helmet. He is avoiding the possibility of damage to his toy—or his ego—by taking his space helmet and going off by himself!

A girl is jealous of a classmate who gets the prize part in the school play. A four-year-old would push a playmate away and step into the spotlight herself. But the high school girl may pretend friendship for her rival while finding some way to make her look ridiculous in the part. This is the four-year-old's behavior pattern in disguise!

FACTORS INFLUENCING EMOTIONAL DEVELOPMENT

Many factors account for individual differences in the way people develop emotionally. We can't touch on all the influences here, but by and large they fall into three categories—factors related *to environment*, to *health*, and to *intelligence*. You can see that these factors are similar to the factors that influence the development of personality (Chapter 23). Of course, the emotions that you are in the habit of feeling and expressing make up a major part of your personality.

Environment

Different environments set different patterns for the handling of emotions. Your manner of expressing your emotions may be influenced chiefly by the patterns set by your community, or by your ethnic group or your family. Moreover, the patterns set by these three may be in conflict.

Some environments call for more direct expressions of emotions; other environments call for more restraint. In some homes, parents may expect one pattern of behavior from their children, and yet not follow that pattern themselves.

All these different standards may make it difficult for you to develop a consistent, satisfying pattern of handling and expressing your emotions.

There is, for instance, the case of the child who grows up in a family where shoving and striking and "fighting back" is taken for granted. When he gets to school, he is bewildered to find that such actions are not allowed. The hardest part of his problem is that he goes on living in the pushing-and-shoving atmosphere at home all through the years when he is trying to learn a more controlled kind of behavior at school. It is not surprising, then, that his adjustment is difficult, perhaps even as far along as in high school.

Health

Health has an important effect upon emotions. Many life-maintaining functions are regulated by the autonomic nervous system and the endocrine glands. But the autonomic nervous system and endocrine glands also have a major part in producing our emotional states. Fatigue, poor diet, illness, convalescence, and other adverse health conditions may upset the body chemistry controlled by the autonomic nervous system and endocrine glands. In such cases, bodily changes may arise that produce negative, painful emotions, even though the actual situation which the person finds himself in does not normally cause each emotions.

Many experiments with inadequate diets, lack of sleep, or other interference with body functions have shown that subjects experience both physical and emotional effects, including a tendency to overreact to stimuli invoking anger or panic. During these times the capacity for sympathy, loyalty, and other feelings natural to love and friendship may diminish.

Frequent or prolonged emotional upheavals often have an adverse effect upon physical health. The result may be *psychosomatic illness*. You will read more about this in Chapter 27.

Intelligence

Intelligence is related to emotions in that our capacity to reason and think *can* affect our emotional behavior. Although intelligence can have an important influence on emotional behavior, there is no guarantee that it will!

We know that the physiological aspect of emotion is beyond our conscious control. But there are three stages in a complete emotional experience. First, there is the *stimulus*, or external condition, that arouses a certain emotion. The second stage is the *emotion* itself. Finally, there is the *conscious behavior response* through which the emotional reaction is expressed. It is in the first and third stages that emotional maturity develops. In these two stages reasoning power exerts its influence — if we let it.

Unfortunately, there is a tendency to ignore or deny the relationship between intelligence and emotion. When people behave rationally, we tend to say they act unemotionally — implying that if intelligence is present, emotions must be absent. This is not so.

A trifling, everyday situation will illustrate the relationship between intelligence and emotion. Two drivers are waiting in a long line of traffic. When the cars finally begin to move, the car ahead is slow in starting. Pete reacts as if the driver ahead were purposely and deliberately interfering with his right to go ahead. A sense of outrage comes over him, and he "lets him have it" in the form of a blast of the horn. Jim, in the same spot, brushes the whole thing off as unimportant. He probably reacts with an impatient frown or gesture, but not as loudly as Pete. He realizes two things: the other driver was not intentionally inconsiderate, and, more important, the gap in the slow-moving line will immediately close anyway.

26-5 How would you react if you were to meet this driver on the highway?

By making little outward display of the slight annoyance he felt, Jim actually *ceased to feel the annoyance* more quickly than did Pete. This seems to contradict what we are so often told — that the built-up emotion must have an outlet if we are to get relief. But, notice that Jim did not let himself get angry and *then* try to control his actions. He *avoided* a big emotional build-up by interpreting the stimulus sensibly in the first place. He actually *felt* less strongly about the situation; then, by not prolonging the incident through tense verbal and muscular behavior, the slight feeling that he did have quickly drained away.

The difference in the two boys' responses did not lie in control of pulse or heart beat—which we know is impossible. The whole difference was in the way each one saw the situation and the kind of behavior response he considered appropriate. Pete's was an infantile reaction—Jim's was emotionally mature. Or to put it another way, Pete reacted in a purely emotional way while Jim used his head.

SOME BASIC EMOTIONS

The ability to interpret stimuli in various ways in order to make a reasonable choice among possible behavior responses is the result, largely unconscious, of a long learning process. This applies not just to "emotion" in general, but to various specific emotions: to love, hate, anxiety, fear, and anger.

Four Kinds of Love

The infant's only love capacity is for *self-love*. Until he experiences social relationships, he himself is the center of his world. An infant's love is soon directed toward his mother or another adult who cares for him. A little later it is extended to other *relatives and friends*, and, a few years later, to favorite playmates. This is *give-and-take love*, or *sharing love*. The physical changes of puberty bring about the most marked development, leading to *romantic love* (unromantically described as love for the opposite sex). But puberty is not the only factor; learning still goes on. We are not born with social know-how or with knowledge of mature sexual behavior—these arts must be acquired. More important even than this—we have to learn to give and accept love on an adult, instead of a childish, basis. When this is achieved, we call it *mature love*—and a tragic number of adults never achieve it. But fortunately an even larger number do.

Actually we have to build each of the four basic kinds of love (except self-love, of course) on the foundation of the preceding stage, for the earlier stages are not discarded. The infant's self-love persists, forming for the adolescent and adult the basis of such very acceptable and important emotions as self-respect, self-reliance, and the fundamental security one must have before love can be extended to someone else. Of course, the infantile ways of expressing self-love are outgrown and replaced by others. It is appropriate for the baby to play with his toes and take frank delight in his body. When a grown-up is too absorbed in his or her own physical attractiveness, we call it *narcissism* (NAR-si-sizm)—and again label him emotionally immature.

In the same way, ties to family and friends are lasting, but the focus shifts. When romantic and mature love develop, both parents and friends quite properly move out of the spotlight. The ties are still there, but the affection is of a different kind and is differently expressed. These different love relationships can be experienced at the same time, because they are not really competitive and not of the same degree of intensity.

Hate, Anger, and Fear

Hate is different from love in that there are no clearly marked stages through which we progress. Children, teen-agers, and adults all may feel hate as a mixture of anger, resentment, jealousy, and even fear. Perhaps most confusing of all is the contradiction between hate and love when both are felt for the same person. But this will be discussed further in Chapter 27, which is concerned with emotional conflicts.

Anger and fear are negative emotions when the anger leads to aggression and the fear to unreasoned withdrawal. A child reacts to physical things—anger over loss of a plaything, or fear of being physically hurt. In

26-6 Four kinds of love are illustrated in the photographs above. (*Top left*) self-love; (*top right*) give-and-take or sharing love; (*bottom left*) romantic love; (*bottom right*) mature love. As we develop the capacity to experience each kind of love, do we completely abandon the stage that preceded it? Do you have different kinds of love for different people in your life?

teen-agers, the reaction is more often to frustrations and threats of social life. Late adolescents and adults are capable of being stimulated by more remote or abstract situations, such as problems of government and war.

Both anger and fear can be useful when reactions are not too violent, and when they are not irrational and destructive. They keep us alert to dangers—"keyed up," so to speak, to notice clues and make necessary adjustments before provocation or disaster occurs. *Anxiety* differs in this respect. Where fear is specific and puts us on guard against a recognized threat, anxiety is vague and unfocused—a generalized sense of helplessness and uncertainty. It is the apprehension we feel when a fundamental value seems to be threatened and we don't know the exact source of the danger, just when it will strike, or what—if anything—we can do about it.

26-7 New experiences are often accompanied by some anxiety. Is this an abnormal or a normal reaction to stress?

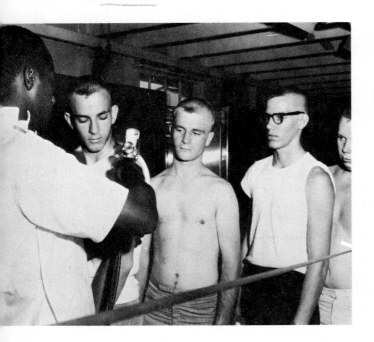

Anxious? You Are Not Alone

Anxiety is not always abnormal—everybody experiences it—but too much, or too intense, anxiety can give rise to serious neurotic problems (as may too much, or too intense, emotion of other kinds). We will have more to say about this in Chapter 27. Among teen-agers, however, anxiety that is quite normal—but nevertheless responsible for much misery and unhappiness—is all too common. New experiences and relationships may produce insecurity, and appropriate behavior patterns have to be sought by the uncertain method of trial and error. The great majority of boys and girls have some understandable fears at this time: fear of disapproval by their age-mates; of being different in appearance, speech, or manners; of revealing inexperience in something that "everyone" else has done. Often the actual cause of these worries is not clear. Then a nagging, hopeless, continuing anxiety takes the place of a more wholesome fear that would characterize specific situations.

The teen-ager often has a heavy emotional burden, but he need not fall apart under it. There are many sources of help, and it is some comfort just to know that practically all other teen-agers have the same problems.

Emotional Control Does Not Mean the Elimination of Emotions

Of course we have to control emotions—for if we do not, they will control us. But it is too bad that talk of controlling emotions so often sounds as if it would be even more desirable to eliminate them. Without a fully developed emotional life, existence would be dull and drab. If no one ever felt anger, few wrongs would ever be righted. If no one felt fear, no changes would bring about greater security and peace for the future. You need a richly developed emotional experience for a full and happy life.

26-8 Without emotions your life would be dull and uninteresting. Experiencing the full spectrum of emotions is part of living a rich and happy life.

What You Have Learned

What kind of health practices should you apply in maintaining your health? Check your understanding of the chapter. On a separate sheet of paper, number 1 through 24 and insert the answer from the vocabulary list below. Use each expression, but use each one only once.

adrenal	environment	maturity
adulthood	fear	neurotic
anger	health	progress
autonomic	intelligence	romantic
destructive	irrational	self-love
development	learning	sex
emotion	love	sharing
endocrine	mature	useful

Any form of feeling, mild or severe, that differs from purely mental or purely physical activity is called an (1) _____. Most scientists consider that there are three basic emotions, (2) _____, (3) _____ and (4) _____. When you experience an emotion, the most important physiological changes are related to the (5) _____ nervous system and to the (6) _____ glands. The (7) _____ glands, for example, pour their secretions into the bloodstream and also facilitate release of blood sugar from the kidneys.

When a person's "emotional age" lags behind his chronological age, he has not attained emotional (8) _____. There are instances where infantile behavior persists through (9) _adulthood_. Many factors account for individual differences in emotional development. The three basic factors are those related to (10) _nerve_, (11) _health_, and (12) _intelligence_. The ability to interpret stimuli in order to make reasonable choices among possible behavior responses is the result of a long (13) _learning_ process. For example, the infant's love capacity is for (14) _self_. Later this extends to love of family and playmates and becomes (15) _other_ love. Soon the physical changes of puberty produce marked development, leading to (16) _romantic_ love. This means love for the opposite (17) _sex_. Finally there emerges an understanding and sensitivity to another person's needs, as well as to personal needs. This is called (18) _mature_ love.

Hate is different from love in that there are no clearly marked stages through which we (19) _progress_. Both anger and fear can be (20) _useful_ when reactions are not too violent and when they are not (21) _prolonged_ and (22) _destructive_.

Anxiety is not always abnormal, but an intense feeling of anxiety can lead to (23) _mental_ problems. Along with emotional control you need emotional (24) _balance_ so that your emotions will serve you and not destroy you.

What You Can Do

1. Recall a recent situation at school or at home where you observed someone who was involved in an emotional situation. Describe the event. What emotional reaction did you notice in this person's behavior? Do you think he handled the situation adequately? How would you have behaved?

2. During the next week test your own emotional reactions. Check such things as how you felt when you made a mistake and the class laughed. Can you laugh at your own mistakes? Suppose that a person you dislike is out of school with an illness. Do you feel sympathetic toward him? Do you feel a little pleased? Do you feel both of these things? Which reaction should you try to cultivate?

3. What does the word _anxiety_ mean to you? How do you cope with it? Compare your ways of coping with anxiety with those of your classmates.

Things to Try

1. Collect three newspaper articles that report on what individuals did in an emotional crisis. Can you determine, in general terms, what emotional need each person was trying to satisfy by his actions? Can you agree with his behavior? How else might his emotional need have been met?

2. Try making a list of your emotional strengths and weaknesses. Do

you believe your strengths can be further developed? How would you go about developing them? How can you correct your weaknesses?

3. Try to spend some time with young children. How does an infant show self-love? Study him carefully and make a list of the things he does that reveal self-love. At what age does a child extend his love to other members of the family? Provide some actual examples of give-and-take love that you observe in a young child.

Probing Further /

Dear Teen-Ager, by Abigail Van Buren, Pocket Books, 1971. The author has received hundreds of letters from teen-agers. She gives you the benefit of what she has learned in this pocket-sized paperback.

One Hundred Ways to Popularity, by Joan O'Sullivan, Macmillan, 1963. How many of these ways to popularity have you already mastered? Like all of the other books listed on this page, this one is easy to read and interesting.

Health Concepts in Action /

Does this statement help express what you have learned?

An individual's emotional development is interrelated with his physical, mental, and social development.

Applying this concept of emotional development, which health practices would you

—continue?

—change?

—begin?

Will you now, as a result of your study, change any of your health objectives?

27 / Handling Your Emotions

Jack and Ted were good friends and often went on double dates together. Usually this worked out well. But, on one occasion, Jack found himself very attracted to the girl that Ted had brought. Jack felt that the girl returned his interest.

During the weeks that followed, Jack could not get the girl out of his thoughts. He decided to phone her. And then he decided not to, for he knew that Ted would resent this. Jack's mood remained low for weeks as he struggled with this conflict. What might Jack have done about his conflicting wishes?

A PROBE INTO EMOTIONAL CONFLICTS — What needs and goals are likely to create conflicting feelings in teen-agers? To help you decide, you will be probing these questions:

1. What is meant by emotional conflict? Why are there usually more emotional conflicts during the teen-age years than other years?

2. What are your standards for dating behavior? What rules of behavior do your parents insist on? How can you resolve any conflicts between their standards and yours?

3. What are the advantages of going steady? the disadvantages?

4. What should you consider before you decide on college, vocational school, or job?

5. Why is it important for you to distinguish between short- and long-range goals?

27-1 Teen-agers on a senior class trip. Suppose your parents said they could not afford to send you on such a trip. How would you react?

THERE ARE MANY KINDS OF CONFLICT

Spring vacation is just a week away. Four of Ellen's friends have saved their allowances for a train trip to a nearby city, where an aunt of one of them has planned an enjoyable weekend. Ellen is invited, and a sixth friend, too, but their allowances are no match for the cost of the trip. Ellen knows her father cannot afford to give her the money, but she thinks it is "unfair" not to be able to go. What will Ellen do? Will she manage to be good-natured and plan things to do locally with the sixth friend, who also cannot afford to go? Or will she have a fight with her parents over the money?

What Is Conflict?

Emotional conflict is universal and occurs wherever there are tendencies in two different directions. That is often, because human beings can make choices, and when more than one possibility confronts us the stage is set for conflict. The conflict may be within ourselves or between us and others (or the environment). Ellen's conflict, for in-stance, is within herself if she does not blame her father for not having the money to let her go away with her friends. But if she "has it out" with her parents, then the conflict is between her and them.

Confusion or uncertainty is very much a part of many conflicts. Suppose Ellen also is waiting for Mike to ask her to the junior prom. The prom date is nearing and Mike has not called. While she is at home over the weekend her friends are away, the phone rings and it is Arthur asking her to the prom. What should she do? Should she accept the date and risk losing a date with Mike, or refuse and risk not going?

Consider the same problem from Mike's point of view. He likes Ellen and *wants* to ask her to the prom, but he knows her friends, too! When he and Ellen double-date with them, some of the other girls often ask to do things he can't afford. If he asks Ellen to the prom and she wants to double-date again, he may be embarrassed by a request to eat afterward at a place that is too expensive.

Mike has a conflict, too. He can resolve it by asking Helen to the prom. She is nice and likes just to be with him. Actually Ellen, too, would rather be with him than with her friends, and if he will only call her and explain the problem, they can happily go to the prom on Mike's budget.

Unfortunately, we don't know how it will all turn out. All we know is that Ellen and Mike both have *conflicts*, and that they will either resolve them or be frustrated.

How Is Frustration Related to Conflict?

Frustration results from interference in reaching our goals. It arouses many unpleasant emotions. Something must be done about the conflict to restore a state of balance. What we do about the conflict is important, for character develops out of our ways of dealing with a conflict, and character has much to do with what we are and who we are. When conflicts arise we can change our methods of reaching a goal or we can change our goal, or a combination of both. This mental flexibility is a remarkable and frustration-saving quality in all of us.

During adolescence one is concerned more with emotions than at any later time. This is so because a teen-ager still feels some of his childhood emotions and at the same time is learning to cope with many new emotions that are a part of being an adult. This provides an inevitable source of conflict and frustration.

Do You and Your Parents Disagree?

Many conflicts with parents may concern *dependence* versus *independence*. If you think about the conflicts you have had with your parents over past weeks, you will probably be able to recall some examples. You and your parents may disagree over use of the car, the time to be home, the kind of clothes to wear, friends, or numerous other problems. The conflict may occur in any area of daily life, and often the very thing, idea, or

event around which the conflict develops may not be as important as the fight for independence. Being home at 11:00 o'clock instead of a half hour later is not so terribly critical. But the principle involved of independence vs. dependence is important both to parents and teen-agers.

In a way your growing independence is really a struggle for **identity.** By refusing at times to accept your parents' ideas you are really trying to assert your own individuality. In most parent–teen-ager conflicts each is well motivated from his point of view. It is reasonable that each parent wants to guide and direct his children in the best way. Parents sometimes have cause to recognize in a teen-ager a certain lack of maturity or lack of responsibility. This may cause them to curb some of his wishes and actions. Parents especially will discourage their son or daughter from a headlong rush into a situation that is dangerous or carries a high possibility of injury, either physical or emotional. How do they know the risk involved? *They often*

27-2 How frequently do you and your parents disagree? What is the best way to discuss a problem that arises?

know first-hand from their own youthful experience. They also have lived longer than you and understand more about individual and group emotions and resulting actions. On the other hand, they may have great trust in you but may not wish you to be placed in too many situations, all at once, that are going to involve conflicts for which a person needs time to adjust.

Do Teen-agers Get Upset Too Easily?

Possibly you get upset easily—some of you more than others, and some of you show it more than others. But adolescence is a time of rapid change, learning, and adjustment. A teen-ager has been likened to a young colt galloping in a pasture. He needs room to move around in, but he also needs fences.

There are many factors that contribute to your feeling things so intensely and sometimes getting upset too easily. There are the hormonal changes going on in your body, directing your growth from a child to an adult. Your body is rapidly changing and you are faced with accepting these new dimensions. There are new feelings that go along with the body changes, and there are new social relationships that are encouraged and others that are premature, or dangerous to your future, or both. You are forming new relationships with your own sex and the opposite sex. New feelings inevitably accompany these relationships.

How to Discuss a Problem

How can you sensibly discuss a conflict with your parents? If you take the time to sit down and discuss the problem, you may find that the point of disagreement may not warrant a battle. You may also discover that there are actually many points of agreement. What you might hopefully discover is that you and your parents are of two generations, who will never agree completely,

27-3 When a problem involves the entire family, it is best to sit down quietly and discuss all the aspects of the problem.

but who can hold a meaningful conversation. Recognition of this may be enough, and out of the recognition many helpful things can develop. Hopefully you will gain a mutual respect for each other, with the conscious awareness that each has certain rights and privileges and that each can permit the other to function in his own right. Often such discovery means a compromise on the part of each. But rather than a compromise on *principles* it is more often a compromise on a *plan of action*. It may mean you're putting off something you want to do. Or sometimes it means that your parents can help you achieve your goal. After all, your parents have lived longer, and hopefully that is worth something, even if they *aren't* perfect.

27-4 "Do I like myself?" How often do you ask your-self this question?

Do You Like Yourself?

What do you think of yourself? How do you add up your assets and liabilities, and what can you do to change liabilities into assets? During the teen years you are developing a composite picture of your total self, and this picture is continually changing. Questions you may often think of are "Who am I *to myself?*" and "Who am I *to others?*" or "How do I fit in with the world?"

Every other teen-ager must tackle these same questions. The answers that you eventually find help make up your "self" and contribute to your self-concept. As a sense of mastery develops, self-confidence is increased. Mastery does not mean perfection, but it means a willingness to try and an ability to solve problems to some degree of satisfaction. A sense of being able "to do" is the basis of developing self-confidence.

At some time or other most boys and girls are concerned about their feelings about themselves in regard to **sexual identity.** Am I *feminine* enough? Am I *masculine* enough? These private thoughts are seldom expressed in words, yet this is a universal concern among young people. As your confidence in yourself increases there comes an increasing self-esteem and acceptance of yourself. These self-doubts tend to diminish with time.

Are You Really So Different?

Teen-agers often feel lonely. It is a feeling that is fairly universal, though some experience it far more than others. Loneliness can occur in childhood, middle age or old age, but perhaps it is more prevalent during the teen years.

Loneliness is increased when you feel you are different from the boys and girls you know. You are not sure what you are doing, yet everyone else appears more certain. You seem to be the only one having difficulty. You are on a journey and cannot turn back, but the way seems uncertain and baffling and sometimes downright confusing. You may feel lost, but you try to forge ahead and not show how you feel.

You are not asked to a party. "What's wrong with me?" Or you go to a party, but you never can find the right thing to say. You want someone of the opposite sex to like you and yet you are afraid of them liking you. Perhaps you have your own party, and your father comes in to meet your guests wearing his old Bermuda shorts. Would you be embarrassed if your mother and father joined the party and "acted young"? Does anyone else have parents who act that way or dress like that? Relax! You've just been initiated into full adolescence.

27-5 Have you often found yourself in this situation? How did you feel about it?

You *are* different, and it is your responsibility to recognize your uniqueness and to develop your skills and talents. But you are not *that* different. Other people are unsure, too. Human emotions are common to mankind throughout recorded history. You find this in the literature of all peoples, in their folklore, and in their art. Though the settings are quite different, the young boy growing up in an isolated fishing village in Japan has the same basic emotions and feelings as the young boy growing up in a large city in the United States.

Is There Enough Time in the Day?

A junior in high school was reciting a list of her activities and engagements. She was trying to fit another activity into her already busy schedule. She was complaining about the lack of time. The guidance counselor said, "Well, you do have a busy schedule. Why must you add another activity? You know that will take time too!" The girl said, "I just have to do this. You see, I might miss something and I wouldn't want that to happen."

This conversation is typical of the attitudes of many teen-agers. It is a time of learning, of storing up experiences. There are often

27-6 How many activities can you successfully engage in? Try to schedule your time carefully to allow for school and social activities. Try to work in a little free time, too!

so many activities in which they can engage. Often the external pressures, as well as their own internal pressures, urge them on. There is a sense of urgency that time is passing and something might be missed. Before they know it they can be loaded down with so many activities and commitments that school work begins to suffer. Then a real conflict exists. "What can I give up?" "What will others think if I don't continue participating?" No one can fit everything into a twenty-four-hour day. This kind of conflict requires some weighing of values by the teen-ager, and often some support and guidance by parents and teachers. The candle can sometimes be burned at both ends, but it is not wise to do so continuously.

YOU AND DATING

Few experiences will give you more problems or cause more conflicts than dating. You may be unsure of yourself and be shy on dates, have problems with dating and your parents, or even have too many dates. Regardless of the problems, most of you will date, fall in love, and eventually marry.

Teen-agers in Other Societies

Perhaps in some ways it might be easier if you lived in a primitive society where the rules are clear and definite. Then you would know exactly what was expected of you. If on one given day you were told, "Now you are an adult," it might be reassuring. This does happen in some societies that are not as complex as the one in which you live. Generally in the more primitive societies, there are puberty rites that move a youth from childhood to adulthood in a short time. The very nature of the primitive society determines what the youth's future will be and what his pattern of living will be. In most cases, he will be a hunter or a farmer.

He will take a mate at a certain age, often in the very early teen years. He will do what everyone else in the group does. In primitive groups, the concern of the society is for basic survival and a simple style of life is necessary. But for many reasons this simplified existence is not possible in our society. What are some of the conflicts that arise concerning dating and marriage in our complex society?

When Should You Start Dating?

Parents in some communities encourage dating before the young teen-ager is ready for it. Dating may serve as a **status symbol** for the parents. Parents should encourage their youngsters to participate in group social life until they are mature enough to date individually. This is a matter that usually takes care of itself. Parents and teen-agers together can work out a common-sense approach to dating that will provide suitable social participation for teen-agers.

Some communities have established worthwhile projects, such as a "teen canteen" in a church or community center. This is especially popular during the summer months when many teen-agers have prolonged time on their hands and activities are not as scheduled as they are during the school year. The projects that are most successful usually involve the teen-agers in the planning, during which codes of conduct and other regulations are worked out jointly by them and their parents. Such groups may meet two or three times a week and focus around dances and other social activities.

Some Problems in Dating

It is important for you to get to know many other young people of your age. All the group activities in the community and school provide an excellent opportunity for you to do this.

27-7 Preteen-agers and many early teen-agers are not yet ready for dating. What would be some more suitable and enjoyable activities for youths in this age group?

Group activities in your early teens give you practice in social relationships with other boys and girls. Do not underestimate the advantage of *practice.* You would not expect to be an accomplished musician without practice. The same is true in social interactions. Practice makes you feel more at ease, teaches you to understand the opposite sex better: how they think, how they feel, their interests and their behavior. Young teen-agers are often easily embarrassed. Group social activities can help to overcome these feelings.

In asking for a date, it is usually suitable to say "Mary, there is a movie at the State Theater that is supposed to be great. Would you like to go with me Friday night?" This is declaring your intent; it is being definite. The girl may have to ask her parents, but do not be offended at that. If the girl cannot accept, she should have a good reason.

A girl may ask boys and girls to a small party at her home or several girls may plan a party together at one of their homes and invite boys. A girl may ask a boy to a movie or some other event if she knows him well enough and happens to have tickets. This is considered in good taste in many communities.

Mistakenly you may have felt that you have to say something profound or speak in a sophisticated way when talking with the opposite sex. This *never* has been so. Instead, discuss things you know about—school, activities, mutual friends, sports, current events —the commonplace things. Planning an activity such as playing or watching games or listening to records will make conversation easier. If you talk about topics you know about and in which the other person is interested, the conversation problem will not be as difficult as you might imagine.

Going Steady

Patterns of dating vary in different communities. In the majority of American communities the teen-ager who is fifteen or sixteen will begin occasional dating, again most often in a group or on double dates. If this is the pattern in your community your parents are likely to approve of your doing likewise. But most parents will want to know whom you are dating, where and how you are going, and what time you will return. They have a right to know this, even though you might feel otherwise at times.

By the last year of high school some teenagers are dating fairly regularly. Then the question of "going steady" arises. Often the question arises earlier than this. "Going steady" usually means dating one person exclusively. Sometimes "going steady" provides a false kind of assurance to the boy and girl that they will not be left out of things. In most cases there is plenty of time for "going steady" and it is far more important for a teen-ager to have a variety of dating experiences. Only by getting to know more boys (or girls) can you eventually make the wisest choice of a marriage partner. "Going steady" can easily lead to an emotional involvement that you may not be mature enough to handle.

Teen-age Marriages

What about teen-age marriages? The pre-adolescent has hardly given this possibility a passing thought. The early teen-ager may have thought briefly about himself in relation to marriage. Many late teen-agers see marriage as a definite event not too far in the future.

Howard, an eighteen-year-old, complained with bitterness, "Why shouldn't I get married. I love Linda and she loves me. We've known each other since we were twelve. It's just not fair!" Howard acted

27-8 What are some of the advantages and disadvantages of "going steady"?

accordingly and married his seventeen-year-old schoolmate. Everything went well for a while, with the newlyweds living with Howard's parents, who were supporting the couple. Soon Howard's feelings about parental support contributed to his dropping out of school and finding employment at a garage while Linda continued in school. Later he was inducted into the Army and was sent overseas. Linda finished the school year, but friction developed between her and Howard's parents. The focus of the friction was her acceptance of a classmate's invitation to a party. Howard's parents objected, but she went anyway. This happened several times, and someone wrote Howard about it. Angry, hurt letters were exchanged. Linda left in an angry state to live with her parents. Howard hinted in a letter that he was dating a girl in Germany. Things were in a state of turmoil with a divorce being planned. Linda left home to go with a girl friend to another city to work to "get away from it all" and did not return to school that fall.

This is not a typical teen-age marriage. Many teen-age marriages do work out. But this account does demonstrate some of the problems that are more likely to arise in teen-age marriages:

1. The boy and girl may have been mature enough physically, but not psychologically.
2. Educational-vocational opportunities were limited when the boy left school.
3. The married couple could not support themselves.
4. Complications arose because of their having to live with parents where, though married, they were "treated like children."
5. Social life was restricted because of marriage vows, and neither was mature enough to accept or adjust to this situation.

27-9 What are some of the problems that are likely to arise in a teen-age marriage?

In Howard and Linda's marriage there were no children, but you can see how children could complicate matters further for everyone involved.

The incidence of teen-age marriages has increased in recent years, as has the incidence of teen-age divorces. Many of these divorced young people are disillusioned, frustrated, and hurt. The same obstacles are present in any marriage, you might argue. But the chances of any marriage succeeding are increased if there is a greater psychological maturity and a readiness to accept the responsibilities of marriage.

VOCATIONAL AND EDUCATIONAL PROBLEMS AND CONFLICTS

Once in a while a person may know early in life what vocation he wants to follow. But more often he will change his ideas many times between then and the time that

27-10 A teen-age married couple who must live with their parents have many additional problems.

he really begins to pursue a particular line of work. Yet this wide-ranging interest in elementary and high school years is of value; it affords the student an opportunity to learn something about many kinds of work before he makes a final choice.

What Will You Do After High School?

In this half of our century, school has taken on increased importance, particularly in view of the increasing technological and scientific innovations. Children and teen-agers are under greater pressure to achieve academically in order to be able to enter the college of their choice. In fact, many persons believe that too much stress is laid on the competitive aspects of getting good marks in school. Competition is necessary, but the human mind and body also needs time to relax.

Is College Always the Answer?

Our country and the world need creative thinking, but people differ in their capacities for achievement, and when the only accepted value system is high academic achievement, someone is bound to be disappointed. Not everyone should go to college and graduate school; not everyone can become a scientist; not everyone can go to the most prestigious colleges and universities. There are many other kinds of work not requiring a college education, and some (although not most) of these have as good an earning potential.

Before going to college or vocational school or taking a job, there are certain considerations that should be taken into account:

1. *Am I interested in this work?* Many times a boy or girl will go to a particular school or take a job because of pressures from his family. It may be that his father or mother had the same occupation. Once in it he may find that he is not interested in the job. You should find out all you can about a job by reading, talking with someone in this line of work, or taking a part-time or summer job that will give you a closer look at the particular work you have in mind.

27-11 Is going to college the right choice for you? What are the reasons for your decision?

2. *Do I have the ability (physical, mental, and emotional) to pursue my choice successfully?* Teachers and guidance counselors should be of help in making this decision. Aptitude testing may help also.

3. *Will I be able to finance any necessary training?* There is much more financial assistance available now for students who need it than there was a few years ago. Such help is available on the basis of merit scholarships, work scholarships, athletic scholarships, state and federal scholarships, long-term low interest loans, and many other sources. A guidance counselor will know about such help.

4. *Will the work enable me to make a living that will offer reasonable security and will it enable me to contribute to the society in which I live?* Both are important. One of man's basic needs is gaining satisfaction from his relationships with other human beings. He also must have something to offer to those around him.

Do My Short- and Long-range Goals Conflict?

It is absolutely necessary for teen-agers to develop an awareness of the differences between long-range and short-range goals in life. The two may conflict, and it is sometimes a real struggle to clarify the most sensible course of action.

A fisherman may be out at sea in his small boat; the afternoon is growing late, and the catch is good. But he reads the signs of nature—the gathering clouds, the color of the sky, the stillness of the water—and all tell him that a storm will break within the hour. The fisherman's conflict is whether to stay another half-hour and fill his boat (short-range goal) or whether to head for home with what he has and know that his boat and he will be safe to return tomorrow or the next day (long-term goal). He weighs anchor and starts for the shore; there will always be other days and more fish.

Think of the conflict between a boy's wish to be married and his educational-vocational goals. He can choose marriage, and it can be successful if circumstances are right;

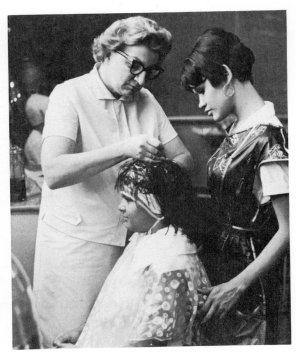

27-12   There are many good jobs available that do not require a college education. These boys and girls are learning valuable trades. How are you preparing for your future?

but there are many potential conflicts. His educational goal may be thwarted by his quickly acquired responsibilities. He may be able to continue his education if his wife can work to support him. This is done many times, but there is an additional potential conflict here. His young wife may feel very frustrated at her own inability to continue her education. Resentments may develop. Further, with the widening gap between their educational preparation, they may grow apart. Their social worlds may also grow apart. The rift may widen until they feel cheated and bitter and can no longer continue the marriage.

Too often the teen-agers who rush into marriage are the very ones without strong motivation for further education or vocational preparation. A long-range direction may be awakened in such teen-agers by discussion with adults who can offer guidance, such as parents, school counselors, a minister, or family physician. Aptitude tests may also provide valuable guidance.

What You Have Learned

What kind of health practices should you apply in maintaining your health? Check your understanding of the chapters. On a separate sheet of paper, number 1 through 21 and insert the answer from the vocabulary list below. Use each expression, but use each one only once.

adult	guidance	school counselor
character	identity	short-range
childhood	independence	social
composite	long-range	status symbol
emotional conflict	parents	support
frustration	psychological	vocational
going steady	relationships	yourself

When you have a choice to make and you are pulled in two different directions, you experience (1)_____. This experience may be within (2)_____ or between you and your (3)_____ or environment. When you set a goal for yourself, such as making the tennis team, and something interferes with your plans, you experience (4)_____. The ways in which you handle these experiences is important in the development of your (5)_____.

During adolescence emotions are a major problem because you still feel some (6)_____ emotions while learning to handle emotions that are part of being an (7)_____. Many conflicts arise with parents from your natural desire for (8)_____ and your search for your own (9)_____. You strive to develop a (10)_____ picture of yourself that involves you and your relationship to the world.

The early teen-age years are a time of group interests, and you are wise to seek group (11)_____ life where you get to know others of your own age. Group activities provide you opportunity to practice social (12)_____ that are essential to growing up. The age at which teen-agers begin dating varies with individuals and with communities. Some parents encourage early dating. To them, dating may be thought of as a (13)_____. (14)_____ is the exclusive dating of one person. This practice has some advantages, but generally it is preferable for teen-agers to broaden their experience by dating a variety of people. The incidence of teen-age marriages has increased in recent years, as has the incidence of teen-age divorces. Teen-age marriage partners may encounter such problems as a lack of (15)_____ maturity, limited educational and (16)_____ opportunities, and an inability to (17)_____ themselves.

It is vital for you to develop an awareness of the goals you seek. There are the immediate ones or (18)_____ goals. There are also future or (19)_____ goals. Sometimes these two types of goals are in conflict with each other. When this happens, it is well to discuss your ideas with your parents, (20)_____, and others who may be able to give you (21)_____.

What You Can Do

1. Suppose you have decided to seek employment after high school and are uncertain about your abilities. You can get an idea of your aptitude for various types of work by taking an aptitude test. Consult your school vocational counselor about where you can be tested. After learning the results of your tests, consider the areas you did best in and consult your counselor as to what kinds of jobs are available and what the requirements are. Try to arrange a visit with someone working at a job that you are considering. If the job appeals to you, try to find a summer or after-school job of a similar type and try it out. You will want to know what the chances for advancement are and whether it requires additional training. Will the company provide the advanced training or will you be expected to pay for it? Why is it important to find out these things before you take a job?

2. Suppose you have decided to go to college and already know what your major subject area will be. See if you can answer these questions: Why did you select this major? How did you become interested in this subject? Is a close friend also interested in this area? How much do you know about the college requirements for that major? Do you believe you have the abilities needed for success in that major? Will the successful completion of courses in that major enable you to find satisfactory employment? Have these questions helped you to understand your feelings about your choice of a major subject area?

Things to Try

1. Try writing out a list of the rules your parents have made about your social activities. Include such things as places you may and may not go, the time you must be home at night, spending a night with a friend, going camping with a mixed group, dating, and other activities that will come to mind. Some of the items may trouble you. Beside each of these, write out your idea of what the rule should be and give your reasons. Check to see how often your reason is that "all the other kids do it." Why isn't this a good reason for accepting your idea? What other reasons can you think of?

2. Try checking your similarities and differences with a friend. Together make a list of the ways in which you are most alike. Make another list of ways in which you are most different. Include such things as your emotional reactions to parental and school rules, to winning and to defeat, and to facing difficult situations. Do you find that you and your friend are quite different? If your differences are worthy ones, should you discard them and try to be more like your friend? Can people who are quite different remain good friends?

Probing Further

Your Personality and You, by Sara Splaver, Messner, 1965. An experienced psychologist discusses many of the problems you face as a teen-ager, including problems of dating, popularity, communicating with parents and teachers.

The Personal World: An Introduction to the Study of Personality, by Harold G. McCurdy, Harcourt Brace Jovanovich, 1967.

Psychology, by R. J. McKeachie and C. L. Doyle, Addison-Wesley, 1970.

Specific Analysis of Personality, by Raymond B. Cattell, Penguin Books, 1966. You can learn much about emotions and emotional conflicts from the last three, rather advanced, books.

This Is Mental Illness, by Vernon W. Grand, Beacon Press, 1963. While mainly concerned with mental illness, this work also discusses emotional conflict in mentally healthy persons.

Health Concepts in Action

Does this statement help bring together the ideas in this chapter?

Emotional conflict may result from contradictory expectations, goals, and needs.

Applying this concept of emotional conflict, which health practices would you

—continue?

—change?

—begin?

Will you now, as a result of your study, change any of your health objectives?

28 / The Troubled Personality

Suppose a member of your class has been mentally ill, has recovered, and will soon return to your class. What will your attitude be toward this student? Will it be the same as it would be if the student had been away from school for an appendectomy? What action can you take to help this student feel at home in your class? What support can you give him as he renews his school and community activities?

A PROBE INTO EMOTIONAL DISORDERS—When and where should a person seek help for his emotional problems? To find out, you will be probing questions like these:

1. Give examples of different kinds of troubled feelings and behaviors. Which seem the most serious? Why do you think so?

4. In general, what are some of the differences between neurotic and psychotic reactions?

2. What are some social and environmental influences that contribute to troubled personalities?

3. To whom can you turn for help in dealing with troubled feelings?

5. How can the mentally ill be helped?

28-1 Everyone benefits by spending some time alone, reading, studying, or thinking. If carried to an extreme, solitary habits may be a sign of a troubled personality.

WHO HAS A TROUBLED PERSONALITY?

Almost anyone has a troubled personality at times. Among the ingredients are difficult choices that we must make, important events that we cannot control, repeated failure to achieve our goals (or those that others expect of us), or even excessive self-criticism when we believe we are doing much worse than we actually are. At times we may react to situations like these unrealistically or try to ignore them. So long as our unrealistic reactions are temporary and are replaced by more realistic attitudes and behavior there is usually no serious problem.

The approaching end of the school year is an event that a boy or girl cannot control. Do you worry about all the tests? The chances are that you do, to an extent. Probably you are able to step back and look at the situation, put your emotions into their proper perspective, and find effective ways of dealing with the approaching time of stress. You may even look forward to the tests as a way of getting your school affairs in order. Whatever your feelings, you take a long-range point of view. That is a healthy approach.

Jim, faced with the same events, acted differently. He rebelled at the idea of disciplining himself ahead of time. Instead of studying he spent all of his spare time playing baseball and fixing up an old car. In the end, he failed two of his final tests and was very bitter about it.

Eloise also retreated from the threat of tests. She always feared failure and withdrew into her own fantasy world. This world did not include tests or examinations. She daydreamed about a childhood that was free of problems. She did not even go to school on the days the tests were given.

Would you say that Jim's and Eloise's reactions were normal? No: both had troubles that reached beyond the normal. Jim, although experiencing partial failure, carried on his school work. His baseball and car-tinkering activities may have had some constructive value for him. And, even by his expression of bitterness, you would guess that he had some awareness of the reasons for his failing the exams. Eloise, however, was far more troubled and denied reality by creating her own fantasy world into which she escaped.

28-2 Although not yet ready for dating, these teenagers are enjoying each other's company through a common interest. Do you think there is a "normal age" for everyone to start dating? What are your reasons?

What Is Normal?

The difference between the "normal personality" and the "troubled personality" is often one of quantity rather than quality. The same human feelings are common to all of us, but when certain feelings are exaggerated, distorted, or denied, it may indicate a troubled personality. For instance, no one is happy all of the time. It is normal to be afraid, sad, or depressed. Normal persons feel strong anger and even hate on some occasions. Everyone at some time has "bad" thoughts that would result in trouble if translated into action. But having "bad" thoughts is quite different from acting on them in an uncontrolled and uninhibited manner.

Where Is the Dividing Line?

How is one to know the difference between normal and abnormal behavior? Sadness or anger in and of themselves are not sufficient for us to say that someone is mentally ill, emotionally disturbed, or socially maladjusted. On many occasions these emotions are appropriate.

Note these descriptive terms—*mentally ill, emotionally disturbed, socially maladjusted.* These are terms used to describe "the troubled personality," and many people use them interchangeably. Here are some examples that will help you to understand them.

1. *Mentally ill.* Bob, a sixteen-year-old, had not attended school for several years. His behavior was peculiar, being characterized by apathy, inability to relate to people, strange mannerisms, hearing voices, seeing things, and often not recognizing familiar faces.

2. *Emotionally disturbed.* Lucy did not like herself. She was extremely critical of her own efforts and thought she was unattractive. Her prevailing mood was one of sadness and loneliness. She preferred not to try because, "I can never do anything right."

3. *Socially maladjusted.* Henry had friends who belonged to a gang, and he was very loyal to them. But outside of the gang his relationship to society was different. He was filled with hate for people in the next block or across town. They were his perpetual enemies, and he stole their belongings and destroyed their property.

Right now we are concerned with a working definition of the troubled personality. Personality has been discussed in Chapter 23 *as being all of those qualities or characteristics that set a person apart as an individual.* Each person must live with himself, with

28-3 All teen-agers have frequent and often rapid changes in moods. A feeling of depression or anxiety may quickly be replaced by one of happiness and confidence.

other individuals, and with society in general. He is expected to do this in such a way as to bring satisfaction to himself and to others. He is also expected to live in a manner that is neither destructive to himself nor to others.

In each of the examples cited we could speculate about the causes of the behavior. But the important point is that in each case we would have to say that the behavior was *excessive,* that it was troubled behavior. The individuals were having an unusual amount of difficulty in living effectively and with reasonable harmony with themselves, with others close to them, and with society.

Social and Environmental Influences on the Troubled Personality

With the physical changes taking place in the teen years along with rapidly changing roles, any teen-ager is going to have some troubled feelings. These troubled feelings may range from mild anxiety to intense turmoil. Fortunately, most of these troubles are self-limited; that is, within a reasonable length of time they solve themselves. A problem that looms large in your life today may be gone tomorrow or in a few days. You need to recognize this aspect of adolescence, as it will help you through some troublesome periods. Through the tensions and stresses that arise and the successful mastery of them, your capacities for coping with life are increased.

What are some of the common social and environmental influences that contribute to the troubled personality?

1. *Early childhood experiences.* Hardest to pinpoint are the influences that many psychologists and psychiatrists recognize are derived from early childhood, at least in part. Generally a person is no longer aware of his earliest experiences, but some of their effects persist. If these include troublesome symptoms, professional help may be needed.

28-4 Teen-agers need and are grateful for guidance from their parents, despite their increasing desire for independence.

2. *Conflict with parents.* This is a primary source of trouble and one which has been discussed in Chapter 27; but it is so important that it requires reemphasis. Your thirst for greater independence is an absolute requirement for growing up. So is continued guidance from your parents on all matters you are not yet prepared to handle completely on your own. Real trouble develops if the parents or the teen-agers take extreme attitudes. An unwillingness of teen-agers to assume some responsibility, or the unwillingness of parents to let them do so, is one extreme. A demand that parents refrain from *any* interfering, or the complete surrender of responsibility by the parents, is the other extreme. Neither extreme is satisfactory. If both parents and teen-agers recognize a "middle-

ground" approach, trouble is less likely to follow.

3. *Acceptance of self.* A teen-age boy may worry about his long legs or his big feet. A girl may worry about her figure or her hair. "I am not as pretty as other girls" is a frequent complaint. "I am not as good an athlete as the other boys" is heard often. All of this may be true, but it does little good to think continually about your differences. You are not like any other teen-ager, but you have your own unique qualities. You will, of course, compare yourself with others; but at the same time it is important to recognize your own assets and to overcome liabilities in a healthy manner. You cannot be another person, but you can accept yourself.

4. *Conflict over current practices in adolescent behavior.* There are certain ways of dress and grooming that are common to teen-agers in a particular area. With modern communication these fashions tend to be more alike throughout the country. Being a part of the current scene means belonging to something, and nothing is more important to the teen-ager than belonging. It lessens isolation and loneliness. Fashion changes need to be seen for what they are—a way of belonging to one's own social group. Long hair and "mod" trousers in and of themselves do not make delinquents of boys, although they make acceptance by mature standards difficult. Trouble may develop when a family imposes its own strict standards on its teen-agers and isolates them from the current scene. But still worse trouble may follow if parents give up all influence and control.

5. *Other stresses cause tension and worry.* Teen-age concerns include popularity, acceptance by peers, school failure, family discord, economic status, condi·

28-5 Are you a slave to fashion? Your mode of dress can make you feel a part of the group but may bring about conflict with adults.

tions of skin (acne), physical development, social skills, femininity, masculinity, and many other matters. Even though at a given moment a problem may appear insurmountable, it will usually be solved in the course of daily living. When problems remain unsolved a troubled personality may result.

Seeking Help in Solving Problems

You may be troubled by one or a combination of the stresses discussed above. Who are some of the people that you can turn to for help in dealing with your troubled feelings?

1. *Parents.* Parents are listed first because they are usually the best people to turn to with your problems. But, certain problems like those you meet in school should also be discussed with teachers and counselors. Still other "teen-age" problems might best be discussed with friends.

2. *Other teen-agers.* You have each other, and this is probably the greatest source you have for comparing ideas, information, and feelings. Together teen-agers have a wealth of practical knowledge, since each has in some way a different background of experience. Concern about school, dating, dress, and conduct can be examined from many points of view. Such sharing among teen-agers leads to clarification, fosters a sense of belonging, and lessens feelings of isolation and of being different. Through

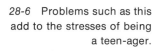

28-6 Problems such as this add to the stresses of being a teen-ager.

28-7 Talking with a favorite teacher can help resolve a conflict. Are you overlooking this resource?

discussions with friends you gain a greater sense of being an individual and of knowing who you are. To know that you are not alone is a great source of assurance and comfort.

3. *Teachers and counselors.* A favorite teacher or counselor at school can be of great help in solving many of your problems. Sharing your concerns about current course work or future vocational or educational plans with school personnel is vital. These are professional persons who can listen objectively and help you evaluate a situation. Many teachers do far more than teach the content of a particular course, and you miss an important resource if you do not consult them about your problems.

4. *Religious leaders.* Today most of the ministers, priests, and rabbis have extensive training in human relationships, psychology, and sociology. They can provide direction for you by individual and group counseling. Such counseling will be valuable in helping you to develop an ethical code of conduct by which you can live a more satisfactory and effective life.

5. *Family doctor.* In your routine visits to a family doctor, a health clinic, or other medical facility, you may want to ask many questions about growing up. Such questions may concern your body functions. Doctors can provide you with valuable information and guidance. Many teen-agers want to ask questions but hesitate for fear of exposing their ignorance. You are not expected to know everything! Professionals will not laugh at your questions, and your privacy will be respected.

We have been discussing normal concerns and worries of teen-agers and sources of help and guidance. At times more help is needed for problems. The help of a **mental health professional** is often desirable. But, it is important to know that seeking and obtaining such help does not brand one as "some kind of nut."

There are severely troubled personalities for which more extensive and specialized treatment is required. Now we shall direct our attention to these disorders and the kinds of treatment available.

MENTAL ILLNESS

Some people become so troubled that their effective functioning is markedly impaired. Many of these persons require admission to a hospital for treatment. However, the trend has shifted from prolonged hospitalization to shorter periods, with an attempt to return the person to his home and community as promptly as possible. In fact, many patients with serious mental illness are being treated on an out-patient basis today, meaning that the person lives at home and goes periodically to a hospital for treatment. Physicians now recognize that prolonged isolation of a mentally ill person from family and society may make his reentry into normal life very difficult. Change in social attitudes toward the mentally ill has made a more normal family life possible for them.

A Brief History of the Mental Health Movement

A few historical notes will help you to appreciate the change in attitude toward persons with mental illness. In the mid-eighteenth century, the Pennsylvania Hospital in Philadelphia was the first hospital in the United States to have a section for the confinement of the mentally ill. In the latter part of that century the first public mental hospital was established in Williamsburg, Virginia. Most mental hospitals of this kind, even into the early part of the twentieth century, were constructed in rural areas, away from population centers. One reason for this was that it was thought that quiet surroundings would be beneficial for mentally ill patients, but another reason was to isolate such "deranged" people from society.

Many persons became interested in the welfare of the mentally ill and crusaded for better facilities and care. Dorothea Lynde Dix, a New England school teacher in the nineteenth century, was one of the most vocal, and her crusading resulted in many improvements in the care of the mentally ill. By 1913, sufficient interest had been generated to result in the formation of a national mental health association.

Recognition of the need for a more comprehensive approach to the problems of the mentally ill resulted in establishment of the National Institute of Mental Health in the 1940's as one of the Institutes of the Public Health Service. This Institute and its support by the Congress of the United States has brought a national focus on the problems of mental health, and many worthwhile developments have resulted from the increased interest in this area of health.

One of the most important developments has been the forming of treatment centers within the community, rather than isolated from it as the earlier hospitals were. Some persons can now receive treatment as out-patients; this means that they can remain with their families and continue working at their jobs.

Scope of the Problem

The overall statistics on mental illness are complex and often confusing. This is understandable when you realize that reporting methods leave much to be desired, and that many of the causes of these illnesses are not specific and easily recognizable. However, a few figures will illustrate why mental illness is a major problem.

You may be surprised to learn that there are approximately 800,000 beds in hospitals in the United States for the care and treatment of the mentally ill. This is a large figure when compared with a total number of somewhat less than two million hospital beds in this country for the care and treatment of all illnesses.

In a recent year, there were about 5,800 children under fifteen in our public mental hospitals, and more than 26,000 patients between the ages of fifteen and twenty-four. In this same year, there were more than 4,000 first admissions below the age of fifteen, and more than 24,000 first admissions from fifteen to twenty-four years of age. These figures tell us nothing about readmissions, nor do they include admissions to private mental hospitals.

Kinds of Mental Illness

Professional workers continually try to classify mental illnesses more accurately as they learn more about these disorders. They usually classify mental illnesses into two groups—*neuroses* (nyoo-ROH-sees) and *psychoses* (sy-KOH-sees).

Most of the illnesses falling in both groups are presently considered *functional*. This means that they relate to a person's ability to adjust to the tensions of his environment. In other words, most of these diseases are not *organic* (or-GAN-ik); they are not believed to be caused by physical factors.

NEUROSES

The symptoms of a *neurotic* (nyoo-ROT-ik) disorder may occur during childhood, adolescence, or later. However, the conflicts that underly the neurosis seem to have had their beginning in early childhood.

You have learned that we deal with our conflicts by using a variety of defense mechanisms. But under environmental or physical stresses, certain conflicts may become stronger; then we may not be able to use the usual mechanisms to resolve the conflicts satisfactorily.

The stresses might include hormonal changes and social drives in adolescence, competition in college, marriage adjustments, work responsibilities, economic troubles, and acute or chronic illness. At such times of stress, the personality structure may be threatened as old conflicts start to break through into awareness.

The formation of neurotic symptoms occurs as a kind of protection. The symptoms can be thought of as extreme forms of defense mechanisms. They keep a person from becoming aware of his conflicts.

The pages that follow give brief descriptions of some of the more well-known neurotic symptons.

Anxiety Reactions

An *anxiety reaction* may be a general, all-pervading feeling of anxiety, or it may be an acute anxiety attack.

Suppose that in early childhood a boy had a great fear of his demanding father but managed to repress this fear. Later in a new job with an exacting supervisor his old conflict might be revived. He would not be aware of the origin of the problem, but he might become extremely anxious. His hands might perspire, his heart beat fast, and his mouth get dry. This reaction might continue out of all proportion to the threat, and as a result, his effectiveness on the job might be seriously impaired.

Dissociative Reactions

This condition is a type of personality disorganization that is usually short-lived. You may have read in the newspapers of persons who have wandered from home, forgetting their names and not knowing where they are. During wartime, such reactions occasionally are seen among young soldiers who, in the face of battle, convert an enormous amount of anxiety into specific symptoms, such as amnesia, stupor, or sleep-walking. These are all neurotic reactions though they resemble certain psychotic reactions that we will discuss later in this chapter. They are temporary neuroses but may be serious.

Dissociative reactions may occur under less obviously stressful circumstances than battle. Jim, a fourteen-year-old boy, had been warned by his father not to play with his pistol. One day the father returned unexpectedly and caught Jim shooting the gun in the yard. The father was angry and Jim dropped the gun and ran. When found wandering hours later, he could not remember his name or the gun incident. His dissociative reactions were gone in a short time, but the underlying anxiety was not. It would continue to express itself in other ways.

Conversion Reactions

In a *conversion reaction,* great fear and anxiety are converted into a more localized physical symptom. An example of an extreme form of conversion reaction is a soldier so overwhelmed with fear and anxiety in the face of battle that he experiences a temporary paralysis of his arms or legs. Such extreme forms of conversion reactions are rare, but less severe forms occur with greater frequency.

An example of the more common, less severe form is Jo Anne, a bright sophomore whose parents had great expectations for her. She was somewhat of a perfectionist and became upset when she made a grade less than an "A" in any of her school work. She was having a difficult time with Latin and was quite apprehensive that she might not measure up to the expectation of her parents and herself. Over a period of two or three weeks prior to her final exam in Latin, she became sick and was unable to attend school because of abdominal pain and nausea. These symptoms were worse in the morning and would subside somewhat during the day.

The doctor was unable to find any physical disorder, but recognized the anxiety that Jo Anne had about her school work and the possible disapproval that she would face. With the help of the doctor, Jo Anne and her parents were able to understand the origins of the anxiety that had been expressed in physical discomfort. With the assurance that her parents would still love her even if she did not make an "A," she was able to revise her expectations of herself. Her symptoms rather promptly subsided and she was able to return to school and work satisfactorily toward taking her final exam in Latin.

Phobic Reactions

In a *phobic reaction* the anxiety resulting from conflict is directed toward a specific object or situation in daily life. This is done by use of the mechanism of displacement. Refer to Chapter 24 for a review of displacement reactions.

A person may, for example, be fearful of riding in elevators or of being confined in other enclosed places. Or he may be afraid of some harmless, common item such as a toy. In such cases, he remains unaware of the unconscious conflicts that are actually causing him anxiety. He tries to avoid his anxiety by avoiding the object on which he has displaced his fears.

Neurotic Depression

Neurotic depression is not unusual in teenagers, whose feelings are likely to shift more rapidly than those of adults. The reaction is set in motion by a current situation, most often by some loss sustained by the person. The loss may be the friendship of a boy or girl friend, or loss of self-esteem because of failure in some endeavor. The current loss may be associated with feelings of guilt over past losses or failures.

If the person harbors a great amount of guilt the reaction may be severe. The anxiety underlying the situation is relieved to some extent by the person's depression and self-blame.

Hypochondria

The word *hypochondriac* (HY-poh-KON-dre-ack), like "neurotic," is often used freely without real understanding. You have probably called your friends "neurotics" many times; yet they do not really suffer from the conditions we are discussing here.

Hypochondria is a neurosis that is based on anxiety. The hypochondriac is abnormally concerned with physical illness. He may imagine symptoms that do not exist and may be constantly alert for new remedies for his illnesses.

John was always complaining about being sick. He would go from one doctor to another with various symptoms, but none of them could find anything physically wrong with him. John's visits to the doctors, the attention he exacted from his family, the symptoms he suffered—all served some inner needs of which he remained unaware.

PSYCHOSOMATIC DISORDERS

This term has also come into popular use in recent years. It refers to physical disorders that we believe to be at least partially caused by emotional stress.

The organs involved in psychosomatic disorders are supplied by the nerves of the autonomic system, the same system that produces body changes during emotional states. If a chronic and exaggerated emotional state affects a particular organ over a long period of time, structural changes in the tissues of that organ may result. Some of the more common disorders that may be influenced by emotional factors are certain forms of asthma, allergies, high blood pressure, and ulcers and certain other stomach and intestinal problems.

PSYCHOSES

The person with a psychosis has a mental illness that is more severe than a neurosis. Whereas the neurotic has not lost effective contact with the real world around him, the psychotic has a more profound personality impairment and often is out of touch with reality. He may not know time, place, or actual events, but may live in his own fantasy world. Therefore, the psychotic person is more likely to need hospitalization than the neurotic person.

Manic-Depressive Reactions

Psychotic (sy-KOT-ik) reactions for which no underlying organic cause exists (or has been discovered) are called *functional psychoses.* One such disorder is ***manic-depressive reactions.***

In this disorder, there is usually a rapid alternation between depression and elation. These marked alternations of mood are accompanied by disturbances of thought and behavior. There may be ***delusions*** (false ideas and beliefs) and ***hallucinations*** (imaginary sensations, of people and voices that are not there). In some persons, the manic-depressive reactions tend to clear up for a while but then recur.

Psychotic Depression

A ***psychotic depression*** may occur independently of manic-depressive reactions and have no connection with that illness. There is no history of repeated depressions or marked mood changes. In addition, specific environmental factors can usually be traced as precipitating the depression. This type of depression can often be cleared up without too prolonged a treatment.

The psychotic depression is much more severe than the neurotic depression. There may be a misinterpretation of reality with delusions and hallucinations. Most frequently it occurs in middle or old age, but it can occur in adolescence.

Involutional Psychosis

Involutional psychosis is another disorder that first appears in middle age. It is more frequent in women than in men, and it often occurs around the time of the menopause in women. It is characterized by feelings of depression and unworthiness. In some cases it is considered a neurotic rather than a psychotic depression.

This disorder seems to occur at a time that the person loses his (or her) major role in family life or business life. He feels that his vigorous, productive years are over, and that he is unimportant to those he loves.

Schizophrenia

The term *schizophrenia* (skiz-oh-FREH-nee-uh) applies to a variety of psychotic reactions that some experts believe should be grouped as separate disorders. *Schizophrenia* means *split mind,* and suggests the splitting away of the mind from reality and from its own emotions.

The shift from reality, or back again, can take place unpredictably and is evidenced by behavioral, emotional, and intellectual disturbances in varying degrees and combinations. There may be inappropriate behavior, such as unpredictable giggling. In one form, motor activity may be greatly inhibited, and the person may stay in one position for hours. In another form there may be delusions of persecution. Sometimes, instead, there may be delusions of grandeur—the person may imagine that he is some figure from history. In severe cases a complete withdrawal from human relationships may take place.

28-8 Psychiatric treatment is beneficial to many mentally ill people and often helps them to make an adjustment to life.

A person with schizophrenia may be severely impaired in his functioning, although many such persons make a partial adjustment to life. Schizophrenia sends more persons to mental hospitals than any other category of mental illness. Many patients must return to the hospital at intervals throughout life. There are childhood forms of this illness, but in the majority of cases symptoms appear in the late adolescent and early adult years.

What Causes Psychoses?

The cause of schizophrenia is unknown. At various times different possible causes have been implicated, such as social and environmental stress, genetic factors, and metabolic disorders. In each instance highly suggestive evidence has been found to support a particular hypothesis. For instance, if one parent is schizophrenic, the incidence of the disorder in the children in the family is higher than in the general population. If one identical twin has schizophrenia, the other twin will be far more likely to develop the same disorder than someone in the general population. These findings suggest a genetic factor. Those favoring an environmental cause refute this theory, saying that both twins were reared in the same environment. However, studies of identical twins reared apart—one twin with the disorder—still showed the other twin more likely to have the disorder than someone else in the general population.

Current investigation is focusing more on metabolism, with scientists searching for abnormal metabolism in schizophrenic patients. Some encouraging findings have been reported, but as with other theories the results are not conclusive. Many psychiatrists suspect that there are multiple causes for the kind of disorder that we call schizophrenia.

In addition to the functional psychoses, there are many psychoses caused by physical, or organic, factors. These causes include encephalitis (brain infection), syphilis, brain changes of old age, vitamin deficiencies, brain tumors, and drug intoxication. Since so many causative agents can produce a psychosis, a patient with suggestive symptoms must have an exhaustive medical examination.

WHAT IS BEING DONE TO HELP THE MENTALLY ILL?

From what you have read you can understand that mental illness is a complex problem, with contributing factors ranging from environmental stress to a specific physical cause. Efforts to help the mentally ill may be divided into three major areas: prevention, treatment, and rehabilitation.

28-9 Prevention of mental illness begins with giving infants the care, love, and attention they need for a good start in life.

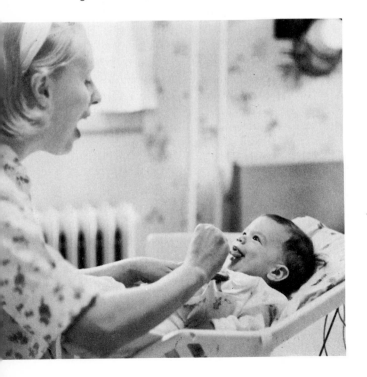

Prevention

Prevention of mental illness includes directing all efforts toward good infant care with the goal of giving each person a good start in life so that he will be less vulnerable to physical and emotional stress. It also includes an attempt to identify the various stresses that are most prevalent at the different stages of life.

For you, as a teen-ager, prevention includes helping to make you aware of your total health needs. It includes helping you to be aware of the particular stresses during the teen years—your search for an identity, your need for growing independence, and your changing self-concept. It means helping you to evaluate yourself in relation to other teen-agers, your family, and society, and helping you to think about long-range goals and decisions in your life.

Prevention also includes scientific research. Such research has led to the theory that schizophrenia may be caused by changes in brain chemistry. If so, can these changes be corrected or prevented? Research is constantly going on to search for answers to the problems of mental illness.

Prevention also includes the efforts directed at improving the lot of those whose lives are materially and culturally deprived. It aims to break the despair so often associated with mental illness—to help people to belong, to lessen their feelings of isolation, and to give them purpose in life.

Treatment

Early treatment provides the best opportunity for recovery. Thus, early detection of those who are emotionally disturbed or mentally ill is very important. Treatment of such diverse problems requires many approaches. There is no one form of treatment; it depends on the nature and degree of the disturbance. Some of the more widely used methods follow.

28-10 Helping elderly people find companionship and interests is an important part of preventing mental illness. These people are learning to garden at a summer camp for older people.

1. **Psychotherapy** (SY-co-THER-a-pee). This is the basic form of treatment of the mentally ill; it is supported by other methods. Psychotherapy has as its goal the relief of symptoms and the development of insight or understanding in the patient. The process relies on verbal communication between therapist and patient, which is aided by the interpersonal relationship between the two. Psychotherapy requires special training and the **psychotherapist** must have a thorough understanding of his own personality. Many persons other than psychiatrists are trained to do certain forms of psychotherapy. These people include physicians, psychologists, social workers, ministers, and nurses. Such treatment, especially with the more severe disorders, always should be under the direction of a psychiatrist, who is also trained as a physician.
2. **Group therapy.** This is a form of psychotherapy in which a small group, usually six to twelve, meet regularly to discuss their problems. They not only learn insights from the group leader, but also from interactions with others in the group.
3. **Occupational therapy.** This is a form of treatment often used with patients in a hospital. The patients learn special skills in arts and crafts which give them a sense of accomplishment. Their projects are selected on the basis of personality needs. For instance, an aggressive, hostile person might be directed to a project requiring hammering or pounding for the release of feelings in constructive ways.
4. **Recreation therapy.** Patients are directed in games and social activities that foster release of tension as well as an improvement of their relationships with others.
5. **Play therapy.** This is a special form of psychotherapy that is used mainly with younger children who have not

28-11 Many forms and combinations of treatment are used to help mentally ill people. Some of the commonly used treatments are group therapy (left) and occupational therapy (below left). (Below right) Playing musical instruments is beneficial to many patients.

developed good verbal skills. The children reveal their conflicts through their choice and use of different play materials.

6. *Chemotherapy.* One of the newest methods of treating the mentally ill is the use of chemical agents, or *chemotherapy* (KEM-oh-THER-a-pee). Many medicines have proved valuable in the treatment of the mentally ill. Some of the drugs have a tranquilizing effect, while others elevate the mood of depressed persons. None of the drugs is a cure, but all are aids to the success of other forms of therapy. The drugs must be taken under close supervision of a physician.

7. *Electro-shock therapy.* This form of treatment became widely used during the 1940's and early 1950's. It consists of passing a current briefly through the brain, resulting in a temporary confusion of the thought processes. This treatment has been of benefit to certain kinds of depressed patients.

   Recent research suggests that electro-shock therapy may work by increasing brain activity, much the way the drugs do that relieve depression.

8. *Insulin therapy.* This form of treatment is seldom used now. Before the advent of modern drugs, insulin was in common use in severe forms of mental illness. Again, as in electro-therapy, a temporary confusion of thought processes was induced by the administration of insulin, which lowered the blood sugar and caused the patient to go into insulin shock.

Rehabilitation

Many persons who have been mentally disturbed are left with lowered self-confidence and self-esteem. They feel that there is no real place for them and that others will view them as different. Rehabilitation involves identifying the strengths and skills of a person recovering from a mental illness and aiding and encouraging him in useful work. Sometimes this means that the person must be trained in a new skill. If there are certain emotional or mental handicaps, he will be guided into some work in which he has the optimum chance of success. The vocational rehabilitation programs around the country are doing an outstanding job of getting former mentally ill patients back into the mainstream of life and living highly successful lives.

There is scarcely a family that, sometime or other, has not had a member who has been disturbed enough to require special treatment. When we think of mental illness in this way we realize that it is prevalent enough to require the effort and concern of all citizens to work for better preventive measures, care, and treatment facilities. What can we do as individuals and as groups of individuals? We can support efforts to obtain more money for research, clinics, hospitals, and the training of workers in the field of mental health. We can read about the problem and learn other ways in which we can help. With a concerted effort at all levels, we undoubtedly will make great progress against mental illness in the last half of the twentieth century. Great strides have already been made in just the past decade.

The Best Prevention — You

Fortunately people have an enormous capacity to adjust. How we use that capacity is an important measure of mental health. Nearly all of our activities have more helpful than harmful features. Activities that have not met this test tend to be eliminated by law or social pressure. *How you respond* is partly a habit that you acquire as you gain experience. Keeping the balance in your favor is an important function of family, school, church, country, and you.

What You Have Learned

What kind of health practices should you apply in maintaining your health? Check your understanding of the chapter. On a separate sheet of paper, number 1 through 27 and insert the answer from the vocabulary list below. Use each expression, but use each one only once.

acceptance
anxiety
behavior
conflicts
despair
emotionally disturbed
family doctor
hypochondriac
isolation

mentally ill
neuroses
organic
parents
prevention
psychoses
psychosomatic
quality
quantity

reality
rehabilitation
religious
schizophrenia
socially maladjusted
stresses
teachers
teen-agers
treatment

The difference between the normal and the troubled personality is one of (1) ____, not (2) ____. The complex nature of troubled feelings makes them difficult to describe but, in general, these descriptive terms can be useful: (3) ____, (4) ____, and (5) ____. Some of the common social and environmental influences that may contribute to a troubled personality are (6) ____ with parents, (7) ____ of self, and conflict over current practices in adolescent (8) ____. Among the people who can help you with troubled feelings are (9) ____, (10) ____, other (11) ____, (12) ____ leaders, and your (13) ____.

Mental illnesses that are discussed in this chapter may be grouped as (14) ____ and (15) ____. Scientists are still investigating to what extent these illnesses are caused by (16) ____ changes as well as psychological problems.

An (17) ____ neurosis is characterized by a general feeling of anxiety or uneasiness. The (18) ____ is abnormally concerned with physical illness. (19) ____ disorders refer to physical disorders believed to be at least partially caused by emotional stress.

The psychotic has a more profound personality impairment and often is out of touch with (20) ____. (21) ____, which means "split mind," applies to a group of psychotic reactions characterized by disturbances in reality relationships.

Mental illness, as you have learned, affects a large proportion of our total population, including a high percentage of teen-agers. National, state, and local mental health organizations conduct continuing programs in an effort to help the mentally ill. These programs are divided into three major areas: (22) ____, (23) ____, and (24) ____. To prevent mental illness, we must know the particular (25) ____ of each age group. Prevention also includes research into causes of mental illness and attempts to lessen feelings of (26) ____ and (27) ____.

What You Can Do

1. What can you do as an individual to improve mental health? You can start by learning all you can about mental health and how it can be maintained. Then apply what you have learned to your daily living. Beyond this you should try to take an intelligent attitude toward the mentally ill. Do what you can to help others realize that mental illness is a real illness that requires medical treatment. It is an illness from which many persons recover and return to their homes and occupations. Many old fears and superstitions still haunt mental illness; try to help dispel these misconceptions. Visit your local Mental Health Society, obtain their bulletins, and offer the society your help.

2. There are many interesting career opportunities for mental health personnel. Perhaps some of your classmates are interested in the requirements for a career as a psychiatric nurse, clinical psychologist, or psychiatric social worker. For detailed information write for the U.S. Public Health Service pamphlets on careers in mental health, Superintendent of Documents, Government Printing Office, Washington, D.C. 20201.

3. Invite a psychiatrist or a mental health officer from the Public Health Service to talk to your class about the appropriate attitudes of the class and of people in the community toward those who are mentally ill.

Things to Try

1. What do you know about the mental health facilities in your community? Perhaps you could make it a project to try and find out. Often there are both official and voluntary agencies engaged in the prevention, treatment, and rehabilitation of the mentally ill. What types of organizations would you look for? Here are some suggestions: Is there a public mental health clinic? Is there a psychiatric ward in your local hospital? How many private psychiatrists are listed in your telephone directory? How many mental hospitals are in your state? What is the nearest one to you? Are there any hospital-supported mental health clinics? Are there any children's psychiatric clinics? Are there state, county, or local mental health societies that function in your community? Are there any rehabilitation centers, workshops, or halfway houses in your area? This is information every citizen should know and share with those who may have need for such facilities.

2. Select a committee from your class to collect a display of pamphlets, books, and periodicals on mental health subjects. Divide the

materials among the class for reading. Have a class session where each
member reports on his readings. Discuss the reports and summarize
what you have learned. Here are some topic suggestions: How can
you deal with the tensions of everyday life? How can a person with
emotional problems help himself? When must he seek help from
others? Are dogs and other animals ever neurotic?

Probing Further /

Psychology: Its Principles and Applications, by T. L. Engle and L. Snellgrove, Harcourt Brace Jovanovich, 1969. You will find in this textbook
an interesting account of mental illness and modern methods of
treatment.

Toward Mental Health, Pamphlet No. 120A; New Medicines for the Mind,
Pamphlet No. 228; Schizophrenia, Pamphlet No. 460. All are published
by the Public Affairs Press, Washington, D.C. In these pamphlets you
will learn about mental health and the treatment of mental illness.

Health Concepts in Action /

Does this statement help express what you have learned?

**Mental health depends upon successful adaptations to emo-
tional conflicts.** yes

Applying this concept of mental health, which health practices would you

—continue?

—change?

—begin?

Will you now, as a result of your study, change any of your health
objectives?

UNIT SEVEN
*Protecting
Your Health*

29 / The Nature and Causes of Diseases

512 - 614
test #7

Long before men began to be civilized, they wondered about the nature of disease. What could it be that gave them headaches, toothaches, stomach aches, sore joints, paralysis, and other ills? Most of their early ideas were wrong. One of the many early notions was that too much blood caused certain diseases. When George Washington fell ill with a serious throat infection, his doctors bled him four times in six hours. We now suspect that this hastened his death.

A PROBE INTO COMMUNICABLE DISEASES—What can you do to avoid infections? To help you decide, you will be probing these questions:

1. What are some of the causes of disease? What are some tests for detecting unsuspected disease?

2. What do we mean by infection?

3. What are the major ways in which communicable diseases are spread? How may environment affect the spread of disease?

4. How do disease germs enter the body?

5. What are some characteristics of virus diseases? bacterial diseases? fungus diseases? Give some examples of each kind.

6. Why must treatment for venereal diseases be sought even if symptoms are mild and go away?

29-1 Most people enjoy good health throughout their lives. Many elderly people live full, active lives.

WHAT IS DISEASE?

Disease is any departure from the state of good health or any condition in which normal structure or function in the body is impaired. It may be mild or severe, brief or long-lasting. It may affect only a small area of the body, or it may involve the entire body.

Disease may cause great suffering or produce no noticeable symptoms at all. Tapeworm may remain in the intestine for years but cause few symptoms. Other diseases, such as *syphilis* (page 525), may not be noticed for years but gradually progress and eventually cause symptoms years later. Still others, such as tuberculosis, may be held in check by the body's defenses for many years, but may break out if the defenses weaken.

Some diseases, such as the common cold, may subside or disappear without any treatment. Other diseases may be severe and even fatal if not treated, but may be completely controlled with proper treatment. For example, pneumonia usually responds to antibiotics, and acute appendicitis is cured by surgery.

What Causes Disease

Most people enjoy good health throughout most of their lives. When we consider all of the many ways in which we might become sick, it is really surprising that we are free of illness so much of the time. We owe much of our good health to a large variety of defenses that protect us from disease. Sometimes these defenses break down or the forces of disease become too great; then we become ill. Certain types of disease may occur when organs or tissues begin to function poorly, chemical reactions in the body go awry, or tissues grow in an abnormal or uncontrolled fashion. Sometimes disease is caused by outside forces in the form of bacteria or other living organisms that break through the body's defenses.

Age and Disease

How long a person would live if disease had never occurred is not known. Many diseases develop with advancing years and are common in elderly people. But whether or not these diseases are associated with deteriorating processes that occur as a result of the wear and tear of a long life is not entirely clear. Most of what we know about these diseases of aging seems to indicate that they are due to chemical alterations within the body. What might be expected if every disease were conquered? Will we some day reach the point when people can live their life span free of disease? Some medical scientists have speculated that people could live two hundred or more years if it were not for disease.

Types of Disease

Diseases that come on suddenly and run a brief course are *acute diseases.* The common cold and tonsillitis are acute conditions. Other diseases start slowly and run a long course. These are *chronic diseases.* Most forms of heart disease, for example, and most cancers are considered chronic. Other diseases flare up at times and then quiet down only to flare up again at one or more intervals over days, weeks, months or even years. These are said to be *relapsing diseases.* Malaria is an example of a relapsing disease.

Symptoms of Disease

When disease occurs it may cause no symptoms at all and may only be discovered by accident when the doctor is examining a patient and finds something he thinks abnormal, such as a lump or swelling. Unsuspected disease may be discovered in a routine chest X ray, a blood test, a urinalysis, or an electrocardiogram. Many cases of diabetes, tuberculosis, kidney infection, and cancer are detected in routine examinations of patients who have not suspected that anything was the matter. This is one reason it is wise to get a medical examination from your doctor regularly.

Most diseases produce symptoms that are troublesome enough to make the patient seek medical attention. Certain symptoms are frequently encountered. Pain is the most common symptom; many types occur. A doctor often gets a clue about the nature and severity of the disease from the location and character of the pain. Other important symptoms for diagnosing disease include fever, *malaise* (ma-LAYS—a vague feeling of illness with generalized aching or discomfort), loss of appetite, loss of weight, lumps or swellings, abnormal bleeding, and abnormal body functions.

INFECTIOUS DISEASES

Infectious (in-FEK-shus) diseases are the commonest forms of disease among older children, teen-agers, and young adults. These diseases are characterized by *infection,* the invasion of the body tissues by germs that are capable of producing injury. Disease-causing organisms are termed *pathogenic* (path-oh-GEN-ik) organisms. Most of them are bacteria and viruses, although certain other small organisms also may invade the body and cause disease.

Because infectious diseases can be transmitted from one person to another either directly or indirectly, these diseases are called *communicable* (kom-MUN-ik-a-bul). Figure 29-2 lists some important infectious diseases, their symptoms, and their mode of transmission.

The Course of Infectious Diseases

Most infectious diseases follow a more-or-less definite course, usually with three distinct stages:

1. The period between the entrance of the germs into the body and the first symptoms of the disease is the *incubation period.* During the incubation period, the germs are growing and multiplying

in the body. In some diseases, the incubation period may only be a day. In other diseases, it may be several weeks or even months.

2. The period of *active illness* is a short period for most infectious diseases and is usually accompanied by fever and symptoms of the disease. Some infectious diseases such as tuberculosis or malaria may remain active for years. Today many of the infectious diseases are treated with potent antibiotics or other medications that shorten the period of active illness and terminate the disease more quickly.

3. The period of *convalescence* (kon-vuh-LES-ense) lasts from the time the symptoms disappear until the patient feels completely well. In general, the more severe the disease, the longer the convalescence. Virus diseases often leave people feeling tired, easily fatigued, and weak for periods of weeks or months after the active disease has terminated.

In many diseases you often hear of the danger of *complications*. There are several kinds.

1. The disease may begin to attack other organs or parts of the body. Thus, a patient with pneumonia may develop a bloodstream or heart-valve infection as a complication.

2. Other types of germs may invade the body after the original disease has left the patient weakened. Influenza or pneumonia, for example, may follow a bad cold or pneumonia may follow influenza. Often bacterial infections develop as complications of virus infections, particularly in the respiratory system.

3. The stress of the infection may cause malfunction of certain body organs and systems. Thus, a patient who has a weakened heart after a severe case of pneumonia may develop heart trouble. A patient who has suffered severe diarrhea or vomiting may have complications involving a disturbance in the salt content of the blood or the acid-base balance which you read about in Chapter 19.

How Communicable Diseases Are Spread

Communicable diseases are spread chiefly by the following means:

1. *Direct bodily contact* with sores in the skin or mucous membranes of an infected person or animal. Some examples are syphilis and gonorrhea, the two most frequent diseases involving sexual contact (you will read more about these diseases on pages 525-26), and skin diseases such as impetigo. Possibly *infectious mononucleosis* (mon-oh-NU-klee-oh-sis) is transferred by direct contact. You will read more about it, too, on page 521.

2. *Indirect contact* with articles contaminated by a diseased person. Colds, influenza, pneumonia, tuberculosis, and similar diseases are often spread in this manner. Common sources are food, dishes, silverware, handkerchiefs, toilet articles, bedclothes, or anything else that is used or touched by a diseased person.

3. *Droplet infection* from the spray of coughing or sneezing, or the saliva and discharges from the nose and throat of a person with disease in the respiratory tract or lungs. Such diseases include many that you studied in Chapter 15— colds, sore throats, influenza, whooping cough, bronchitis, and pneumonia. Saliva and discharges from the nose and throat can also transmit measles, mumps, chicken pox, smallpox, diphtheria, scarlet fever, strep throat, polio,

Disease	Organism Responsible	Mode of Transmission	Symptoms
Chickenpox	virus	nasal discharge, droplets	mild fever, weakness, skin erupts
Common cold	virus	contact, droplet infection	headaches, cough, nasal discharge
Conjunctivitis	virus	contact	red, itchy conjunctiva; pus
Diphtheria	irregular, rod-shaped bacteria	carrier, direct contact	sore throat, fever, vomiting, difficult breathing
Dysentery	short, rod-shaped bacteria	flies, food, feces, water, carriers	fever, vomiting, diarrhea, abdominal pain
Encephalitis	virus	mosquitoes, ticks, or mites	headache, vomiting, drowsiness, convulsions
Gonorrhea	diplococcus bacteria	sexual intercourse	redness, swelling, pus, frequent and burning urination
Infectious hepatitis	virus	direct contact, food, water	fever, vomiting, weakness, jaundice
Influenza	virus	contact, droplet infection	fever, muscular pain, chills
Measles "regular" (rubeola)	measles virus	contact, droplets	fever, rash, conjunctivitis, cold symptoms
"German" (rubella)	German measles virus	contact, droplets	milder symptoms, but more dangerous to the unborn of pregnant women
Mumps	virus	direct contact, droplets, contaminated articles	swollen salivary glands, may involve sex glands in adults

Disease	Cause	How Spread	Symptoms
Pneumonia	diplococcus bacteria (a milder form of pneumonia is caused by a virus)	droplet infection	chills, chest pain, rapid breathing, jaundice
Polio	virus	contact, houseflies, food, water	fever, headache, neck stiffness, paralysis
Q fever	rickettsia	contact, raw milk, ticks	high fever, chills, muscular pains
Rabies	virus	bite of a rabid animal	muscle spasms, convulsions, paralysis; always fatal if virus reaches brain
Rocky Mountain spotted fever	rickettsia	ticks	sudden chills, high fever, headache, rash
Scarlet fever	streptococcus bacteria	droplets, direct contact	sore throat, fever, cough
Smallpox	virus	direct contact, droplets	high fever, skin eruptions, headache, backache
Strep throat	streptococcus bacteria	droplet infection, infected milk	severe sore throat, high fever, aching
Syphilis	spiral-shaped bacteria	sexual intercourse	hard, painless sore; skin rash
Tetanus	spore-forming, rod-shaped bacteria	bacteria in soil entering through wound	spasms of muscles, convulsions, lockjaw
Typhoid	short, rod-shaped bacteria	flies, food, water, feces, carriers	nausea, fever, vomiting, severe abdominal pain, diarrhea
Typhus	rickettsia	body louse	chills and fever, general aching, skin eruptions
Tuberculosis	irregular, rod-shaped bacteria	direct contact, droplet infection, food, milk	cough, fever, loss of weight, fatigue
Undulant fever (brucellosis)	bacteria	direct contact with cattle, infected milk	fever, pain in joints
Whooping cough	small, short, rod-shaped bacteria	droplets projected during cough	coldlike symptoms, cough

29-3 Some diseases can be spread by contact with cooking utensils and silverware that have been handled by a diseased person.

29-4 Droplet infection is the most common way of acquiring communicable diseases. What kind of infections are spread this way?

and tuberculosis. Since the germs are spread through the air, these infections are called *air-borne infections.* More communicable diseases are spread by air-borne infection than in any other way, and sneezing and coughing represent the commonest forms of disease transmission. We acquire more diseases by breathing in germs in air or on droplets than by any other way.

4. *Water,* especially from open wells and streams, is a common way in which communicable disease germs are spread. There is an old saying in some European countries, "He died from drinking water." In many parts of the world it is dangerous to drink from the local water supply, which may be polluted by the intestinal discharges of men and animals and may contain the germs of such diseases as typhoid fever, *cholera* (KOL-er-uh), and *dysentery* (DIS-en-ter-e). Present methods of sewage disposal and water purification have made these diseases rare in the United States and in many parts of western Europe.

5. *Milk and other foods.* One of the most important reasons for the much lower death rate today is the precautions taken to keep germs out of our water, milk, and other foods. In many parts of the world where human wastes are still used as fertilizers it is dangerous to eat raw fruits and vegetables, and it is

29-5 A new pump, installed by UNICEF (see page 557) and a clean water supply help keep this Chilean boy healthy.

best to wash any raw foods before eating them. Many varieties of bacteria are able to live and multiply in milk. If cows are not healthy, if unsterilized milking utensils are used, or if the hands of an infected person come into contact with the milk, the milk may be infected and can transmit such diseases as tuberculosis and typhoid. The problem of making milk safe for use has been solved by *pasteurization* (pas-tur-ih-ZAY-shun), a process developed by Louis Pasteur whereby milk is disinfected by maintaining it at a temperature of about 142° F for thirty minutes and then cooling it rapidly. Pasteurization destroys all common disease germs. Another process called the Flash method sterilizes milk at a temperature of 160° F for fifteen seconds.

6. *Bites of insects and ticks.* Certain mosquitoes transmit germs of malaria and yellow fever. The rat flea carries germs of bubonic plague. Tick bites transmit the organisms that cause Rocky Mountain spotted fever. Typhus germs are carried by lice. A number of other diseases can be transmitted from one person to another through the contamination of food or water by germ-carrying insects such as flies. In this case, the germ is passively carried on the insect's feet from one area to another. In the case of disease spread by insect bites, the germ actually enters the body of the insect and spends part of its life inside the insect.

7. *Carriers.* A few people may continue to carry the germs of a disease for weeks, months, or even years after they have recovered from it. Other people may carry the germs of a disease which they never contract themselves. During an epidemic of a disease such as meningitis, many people can be found carrying the germs who are not themselves sick,

and in the winter many people harbor the streptococci in their throats which can cause severe strep throat in others. Typhoid Mary was a famous carrier who harbored live typhoid germs in her gall bladder. She was a cook and infected twenty-eight people over a six-year-period before she was finally discovered. Other diseases in which people may be carriers include polio, dysentery, diphtheria, and hepatitis.

8. *Other ways in which germs may reach us.* Rabies is transmitted by the bite of a warm-blooded animal, such as a dog or a bat, that has the disease. If a person with rabies were to bite another person, he could also transmit the disease that way. *Tetanus* (TET-uh-nus) is usually transmitted when the germs get into the body through a puncture wound or cut, particularly when the instrument that caused the wound is dirty.

You see that communicable diseases can be transmitted through other organisms or through person-to-person contact (or contact with articles handled by diseased persons). If other organisms (such as mosquitoes, insects, and ticks) are not necessary to transmission of the disease germs, we say that the disease is not only communicable but *contagious* (kon-TAY-jus).

How Disease Germs Enter the Body

There are five avenues of entry into the body for disease germs. These include:
1. The nose and respiratory tract.
2. The mouth and digestive tract.
3. The delicate membranes surrounding the eyes.
4. The skin when it is broken by cuts or bites of insects or animals. Some diseases are caused by the agent entering the skin directly.
5. The urinary tract and the reproductive organs.

29-6 What are some of the dangers involved in walking barefoot?

Fortunately, in most cases, infected persons can only transmit germs to others during certain stages of the disease. This period of communicability is known for most diseases. Most disease germs can only live a short time if they are exposed to light, dryness, and atmospheric temperature. However, some disease germs are very resistant and survive a long time in spore form. They retain their capacity to infect and do so when environmental surroundings are right.

Environment and the Spread of Disease

Environment affects disease in many ways. Obviously, certain diseases are more common in certain areas. Respiratory illnesses are more common in areas where the air is contaminated with pollutants than in other areas where the air is clean. Nutritional illnesses are more common in underprivileged and underdeveloped countries than in our country. However, in disadvantaged areas of the United States, nutritional diseases still occur. Some diseases, such as hypertension

and ulcers, occur more commonly in areas where people are subject to greater environmental stresses.

Environment also affects how widely a disease spreads. Respiratory illnesses, carried by air-borne germs, will spread more readily in large cities where populations are dense and people come in close contact with each other. Epidemics are much more likely to occur where people are in close contact, and the rates of certain diseases are also much higher in large cities where there is overcrowding, poor heating and ventilation, and inadequate sanitation. Diseases that are spread by rats and flies may occur with much higher incidence in such areas than in areas which are less crowded and have better living conditions. On the other hand, some diseases have a higher incidence in rural areas. Examples are *trichinosis* (tri-ki-NOH-sis), caused by a worm that infests pork and

29-7 Air-borne infections spread rapidly in crowded places such as beaches, and epidemics can result. How can you protect yourself and others under these conditions?

that may survive in improperly cured or cooked pork; tetanus, which may be acquired from a puncture wound caused by a contaminated instrument or object; **undulant fever,** acquired by contact with cattle infected with **brucellosis;** and Rocky Mountain spotted fever, carried by ticks.

Virus Diseases

Viruses are far too small to be seen with an ordinary microscope. It is not known for certain whether they are living organisms or merely chemical entities. Viruses are composed of complex chemical substances known as nucleic acids, wrapped within an envelope of proteins. They have characteristic sizes, shapes, and appearances and can be seen only through very powerful **electron microscopes.**

When virus particles cause disease, they actually invade the individual cells of the body and live within these cells. They cannot live outside of cells and are dependent upon the cells in which they live for their nourishment and development. They cannot multiply outside of cells. Unlike bacteria, they cannot be grown on culture media, such as broths or jellies. It was not until the development of tissue cultures composed of living cells that viruses could be grown outside living organisms.

Virus diseases are usually unaffected by sulfa drugs or antibiotics. The only exceptions to this are a few of the larger viruses such as the one that causes parrot fever, a form of pneumonia that people can get from parrots or parakeets.

Most of the common childhood diseases such as measles, mumps, chicken pox, and whooping cough are virus diseases. Other well-known virus diseases are polio, encephalitis, common colds, and influenza.

Infectious mononucleosis is believed to be due to a virus but this has not been definitely proven. This disease, also known as

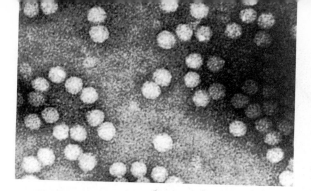

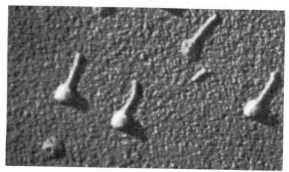

29-8 Viruses cause disease in many types of organisms. The viruses shown here infect cucumbers (top) and bacteria (bottom).

glandular fever, is common in adolescents and young adults and has been thought to be spread by kissing. While it seems that many people have acquired the disease after close contact with others who have had it, the mode of transmission, like the cause, has not been definitely proven. Refer to Figure 29-2 for some common infectious diseases caused by viruses.

Rickettsial Diseases

Rickettsias are microorganisms that are somewhat larger than viruses but smaller than bacteria. These organisms are large enough to be seen under an ordinary microscope but, like viruses, can only live and multiply inside the cells of susceptible animals. Rickettsias live in insects such as lice and fleas, and also in ticks and mites, but while they live in these small animals, they

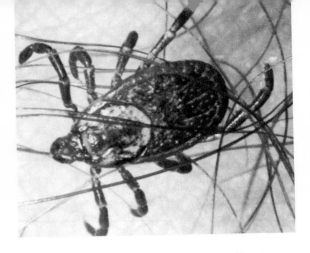

29-9 Ticks, such as this one sucking blood from a man's arm, spread diseases caused by rickettsias. How do rickettsias differ from viruses?

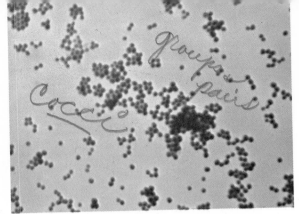

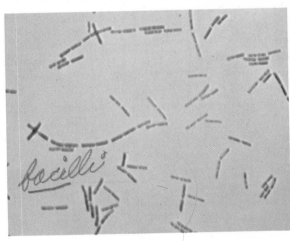

do not cause disease in them. The rickettsial organisms are transmitted to people by the bites of the insects or ticks and mites, and when inside people, are capable of causing disease. Most of the diseases caused by rickettsia are illnesses with a rather sudden onset and high fever, and many of them are accompanied by a skin rash. The most common forms of rickettsial disease include typhus, Rocky Mountain spotted fever, and Q fever.

Bacterial Diseases

Bacteria cause a tremendous variety of infectious diseases, probably more than any other kind of microorganism. Bacteria are larger than rickettsias, and they vary considerably in size and shape. All bacteria are too small to be seen by the naked eye. In fact, bacteria are so small that it would take about four hundred million of them (twice the number of people in the United States) to fill a space the size of a grain of sugar.

There are three different types of bacteria according to shape. The *cocci* (KOK-sigh) or spherical bacteria are often grouped in long chains, short chains, pairs, or clusters. Some bacteria are rod-shaped or elongated.

29-10 Three kinds of bacteria: (*top*) cocci; (*middle*) spirilla; (*bottom*) bacilli. Describe the different shapes of these bacteria. How do bacteria differ from viruses and rickettsias? Where do these three types of organisms live?

elongated in shape

These are the *bacilli* (buh-SIL-eye). They form chains of rods. The *spirilla* (spy-RIL-uh) are spiral-shaped and resemble twisted rods. See Figure 29-10.

Many bacteria are harmless to man and many others are useful. All of us have billions of bacteria on our skin, in our noses, mouths, and throats, and inside our intestinal tract. Bacteria can cause such diseases as dysentery, pneumonia, and meningitis as well as tuberculosis, syphilis, and osteomyelitis (a chronic infection of bone). They can infect nearly all parts of the body. Some bacteria can cause different diseases by infecting different parts of the body. *Staphylococci* are common bacteria that often cause skin infections but can attack the heart, the bloodstream, the lungs, the bones, and even the central nervous system. *Pneumococci* most often cause pneumonia but can also affect the heart, the abdominal cavity, or the central nervous system. When *meningococci* (mening-oh-KOK-sigh) infect the membrane enclosing the spinal cord and brain, they cause meningitis, but they can also invade the bloodstream and attack many other parts of the body.

Unlike viruses and rickettsias, bacteria can live and grow outside body cells. They can be grown on culture media such as various types of broth, or a jellylike substance called *agar.* This makes it possible for doctors to isolate them from an infected area in the body and grow them so that they can be identified and studied. Thus, when a person with pneumonia coughs up sputum, the material can be put on an agar plate or in a broth and kept in an incubator at body temperature. In a matter of hours or days, the bacteria causing the pneumonia will have multiplied in the culture media and can be identified. Since a number of different types of bacteria can cause pneumonia, it is helpful to doctors to know which bacteria are causing the infection in a particular case.

Bacteria also can be grown from urine in patients with kidney or bladder infections, or from a throat smear taken from someone suffering from a bad sore throat. Refer to Figure 29-2 for some diseases caused by bacteria.

Mycoplasma

Mycoplasma (MY-ko-plaz-muh) are a special group of bacteria. They are characterized by a thin and flexible cell wall. Because of this, they can squeeze through much smaller holes than most bacteria. In the days when viruses were first being studied, the viruses were separated from bacteria by being passed through filters with holes so small that the bacteria were trapped. It was for this reason that viruses were first called *filterable agents.* The mycoplasma were once thought to be viruses because they passed through these filters. However, they proved to be bacteria smaller than most others, and with cell walls so pliable that they could squeeze through the tiny holes in the filter. Mycoplasma cause a group of diseases affecting the lungs and bronchial tubes. The best known disease caused by mycoplasma is a form of pneumonia that for many years was

29-11 Mycoplasma are a type of bacteria that cause certain respiratory diseases. How do these bacteria differ from other bacteria?

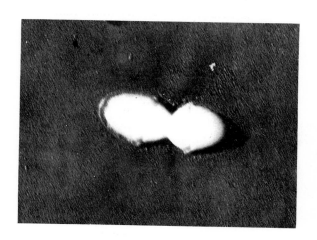

confused with *virus pneumonia.* Because the mycoplasma organisms resemble another group of bacteria that cause *pleuropneumonia* in cattle, they have also been called the pleuropneumonia-like organisms, abbreviated as PPLO.

Fungus Diseases

Fungi (FUN-jye) are plants that have no roots, stems, or leaves and no chlorophyll (the substance that gives most plants their green color). Because they lack chlorophyll, fungi are unable to synthesize carbohydrates in sunlight. This process is known as *photosynthesis* (FOH-toh-SIN-the-sus). Fungi therefore are *parasites* or *saprophytes* (SAP-roh-phyts). *Parasites* are organisms that live off other living organisms. *Saprophytes* feed upon dead or decaying organisms.

Some fungi form masses of tiny hairlike filaments. Others, such as the yeasts, form colonies of cells.

The vast majority of fungi are harmless or helpful. A few fungi, however, are capable of causing disease. Fungus diseases are often very mild and frequently involve superficial parts of the body, such as the skin. Many people have had fungus infections of toenails or of the feet. Athlete's foot and ringworm are both fungus infections (page 155). More serious forms of fungus infection involve the lungs. Occasionally fungus infections can spread throughout the entire body and threaten life. Fortunately these infections occur only rarely.

Protozoan Diseases

Protozoa (PROH-toh-ZOH-uh) are one-celled organisms. Protozoa are considerably larger than bacteria or yeasts. They can easily be seen under a microscope. The most common forms of protozoan disease are malaria and amebic dysentery. Another protozoan disease is African sleeping sickness.

Diseases Caused by Parasitic Worms

Trichinosis (page 520) is not the only disease that is caused by worms. Until a few generations ago, in the United States and Western Europe a large number of people had *tapeworms* or *roundworms* living inside their intestines. Worm infestations are still common in many parts of the world. Certain types of worms are still fairly common in this country. One kind of tapeworm is acquired by eating infected beef and another by eating infected pork. Tapeworms may grow to be as long as twenty feet but cause few, if any, symptoms. Live tapeworms may remain for years or even a lifetime inside a person. However, with government inspection of meat, education on how to cook meat properly, and with better safeguards in the preparation of commercially available meats and sausages, tapeworm is disappearing from this country.

Hookworms are roundworms that can be acquired only when the baby worm, passed in the feces of an infected person, directly enters the body, usually through the skin of the feet. Once inside the body, hookworms suck blood from the walls of the intestines and produce anemia. Today, with the increase of adequate plumbing facilities and with most people wearing shoes, hookworm disease is becoming less prevalent. However, it remains a health problem in very economically deprived areas where plumbing is absent and people go barefoot.

Trichina (tri-KIN-uh) *worms* cause the disease trichinosis. The disorder is acquired by eating infected, insufficiently cooked pork. Through government supervision of commercially available pork and pork products and a better understanding of the necessity of adequately cooking pork, trichinosis is gradually disappearing in the United States. Nevertheless, the best protection against trichinosis and other diseases spread by infected meat is to cook all meat thoroughly before eating it.

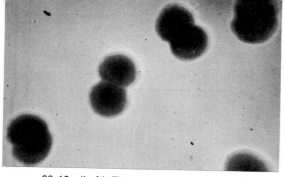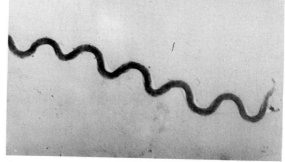

29-12 (Left) The gonococcus, which appears in pairs, is the bacterium that causes gonorrhea. (Right) The spirochete is the corkscrew-shaped bacterium that causes spyhilis. Both gonorrhea and syphilis have increased in recent years. What are some of the reasons?

VENEREAL DISEASES

Venereal diseases are infectious diseases that are spread from person to person chiefly through sexual intercourse, and also through other intimate body contacts involving infected mucous membranes. The two most common venereal diseases, *syphilis* and *gonorrhea*, are caused by bacteria that do not survive outside the body, and are readily destroyed by soap and water. Therefore, these diseases cannot ordinarily be spread through contact with clothing or other objects.

Syphilis and gonorrhea are serious health problems. They are the nation's leading communicable diseases after the common cold. It is estimated that in the United States each year there are over 70,000 new cases of syphilis and over a million and a half new cases of gonorrhea. Many of these new cases occur among young people. According to some estimates, venereal disease strikes one teenager every 11 minutes.

Environment and Venereal Diseases

Venereal diseases are found among people in all economic groups and in all areas — suburbs, rural areas, and cities. However, venereal diseases are much more common in overcrowded urban areas. One infected person may have contact with many others. In large cities it is harder for public health officials to trace all of these contacts and make certain that treatment is provided before the disease is spread to others.

Gonorrhea

Gonorrhea is the most common venereal disease. It is caused by a **gonococcus,** a form of bacteria appearing in pairs (Figure 29–12). The organism multiplies readily on mucous membranes.

Gonorrhea starts as a local infection. In about two to nine days after contact with an infected person, a male may have painful urination or a puslike discharge. The female, however, may show no symptoms of the infection at all. Any symptoms that are noticed soon disappear without treatment, *but the infection does not disappear.* Therefore it is essential to go for medical help whenever exposure to the disease is suspected.

Most cases of gonorrhea respond very well to treatment with penicillin or other antibiotics. However, if gonorrhea is untreated or inadequately treated, it can cause serious diseases of the urinary or reproductive systems, with sterility as a common result.

Gonorrhea is not inherited. However, the disease may be spread from an infected mother to a baby during its birth. If the baby's eyes are infected, blindness may result. For this reason, special medication is placed in the eyes of newborn babies at birth to prevent any possibility of infection.

Syphilis

Syphilis is caused by a *spirochete* (SPY-roh-keet), a slender bacterium that is shaped like a corkscrew (Figure 29-12). This bacterium, too, thrives only in the body.

Like gonorrhea, syphilis begins as a local infection. However, the first symptoms may appear as late as ninety days after contact with an infected person. A painless pimple or open sore may be noticed where the bacteria have entered the body; in the female, the sore may be internal and go unnoticed altogether. In both sexes, these early sores disappear even without treatment, but unfortunately the syphilis infection does not. Left untreated, the disease soon spreads throughout the body.

Weeks later, the second stage begins. Common symptoms in this stage are a skin rash, sore throat, headache, or fever. These symptoms resemble the symptoms of so many other diseases that syphilis may not be suspected. Again, the symptoms will disappear without treatment—but again, the disease remains. During these first two stages of syphilis, the infected person can spread the disease readily to others.

If syphilis remains untreated, the symptoms gradually clear up, and then the patient may go along for many years with no symptoms at all. This is the third, latent stage of syphilis. During this stage the disease germs are slowly growing in various parts of the body. Years later, symptoms appear again. By then vital parts of the body such as the heart, blood vessels, and nervous system may be affected. This may lead to heart trouble, insanity, crippling, or blindness.

Syphilis is not inherited. However, an untreated, infected mother can pass on the disease to her unborn child through the placenta. The infection can result in the death of the unborn child. If the child is born, serious defects resulting from the infection, such as deafness, may show up later.

Where to Seek Help

There is no "quick cure" at the local drugstore for syphilis or gonorrhea. However, people who believe that they may have been infected can get help from several sources. Their private doctors can arrange to test whether they have the disease and give them treatment if needed. Most communities also have clinics supervised by the local Boards of Health, where venereal diseases are diagnosed and treated without charge.

Treatment and recovery from a venereal disease does not give immunity to the disease. A person may be infected by the same venereal disease—and by the same sexual partner—more than once; he will need treatment each time. Moreover, he can have both syphilis and gonorrhea at the same time.

Controlling the Spread of Venereal Diseases

When penicillin was first used to treat gonorrhea and syphilis, these diseases became less common. People soon became careless about avoiding venereal diseases and about seeking complete treatment for the diseases when they acquired them.

Then penicillin-resistant bacteria appeared. Because of this, many patients are now not cured as readily as before.

Moreover, since venereal diseases are transmitted chiefly through sexual intercourse, any increase in casual sexual contacts increases the chances of becoming infected.

These are just some of the reasons given for the rise in venereal disease cases in recent years. Public health officials are presently trying to educate people about the dangers of venereal diseases, how to avoid them, and what to do about them if infection occurs.

To help control the spread of syphilis, a majority of the states now require blood tests for syphilis before marriage.

What You Have Learned

What kind of health practices should you apply in maintaining your health? Check your understanding of the chapter. On a separate sheet of paper, number 1 through 24 and insert the answer from the vocabulary list below. Use each expression, but use each one only once.

acute	droplet	mycoplasma
bacilli	filterable	protozoa
bacteria	fungus	relapsing
carrier	hookworms	rickettsia
chronic	incubation	tapeworms
cocci	infectious	ticks
contagious	malaise	trichina
convalescence	mosquitoes	viruses

Communicable diseases are also called (1)_____ diseases. Diseases which may pass from one person to another merely by touch or breath or by means of clothing or bedding are called (2)_____. Some diseases are spread by water or food, some by biting insects, and some by (3)_____ infection from the spray of coughing or sneezing. Typhus germs are carried by lice, and the (4)_____ that cause Rocky Mountain fever are carried by (5)_____. The germs that cause malaria invade our bodies by means of the bites of (6)_____. Measles, mumps, whooping cough, and polio are caused by (7)_____.

Although too small to be seen by the naked eye, (8)_____ are larger than viruses or rickettsias. Among this group of organisms, those that are spherical are called (9)_____, while the (10)_____, on the other hand, are rod-shaped or elongated. (11)_____ are a special group of bacteria that were once thought to be viruses. Viruses were first called (12)_____ agents.

Athlete's foot and some serious infections are (13)_____ infections. Malaria and amebic dysentery are caused by (14)_____. Although the inhabitants of the United States and western Europe suffer far less from parasitic worms than do those of many other parts of the world, there are at least three kinds of intestinal worms that we should know about. (15)_____ may be acquired by eating infected fish, beef, or pork. (16)_____, which suck blood from the wall of the intestine, usually get into the body through the bare feet. (17)_____worms, which are much less common than they used to be, are swallowed along with insufficiently cooked pork.

Diseases that come on suddenly and run a brief course are called (18)_____ diseases. (19)_____ diseases start slowly and run a long course. Diseases that flare up at times, then quiet down and later flare up again, are said to be (20)_____ diseases.

Among the important symptoms of disease are pain, fever, loss of appetite, and (21)_____, a vague feeling of illness. In infectious diseases, the time between the entrance of the germs into the body and the first symptoms is the (22)*incubation* period. As the patient's condition improves, (23)*convalescence* lasts from the time symptoms disappear until the patient feels completely well. A (24)*carrier* is a person who carries the germs of a disease after he has recovered or without ever having had the disease.

What You Can Do

1. Test yourself on what you have learned about the nature of disease. In your notebook, briefly explain the difference between each of the following pairs of terms.
   a. acute diseases—chronic diseases
   b. incubation period—convalescence
   c. infectious—contagious
   d. viruses—bacteria
   e. rickettsia—protozoa
   f. pathogenic organisms—nonpathogenic organisms
   g. bacilli—cocci
   h. parasite—saprophyte
   i. hookworm—trichina
   j. relapsing diseases—chronic diseases

2. If your health teacher approves, you might try to secure a speaker to address your class (or perhaps the school assembly) on "The Nature of Disease" or "The History of Medical Discovery." Perhaps your own teacher, another health teacher, a biology teacher, or a history teacher may be especially interested in one or both of these subjects. Your classmates would no doubt enjoy being addressed on these subjects by a physician. If none of you knows a doctor that you would like to invite, you could get in touch with the local medical society or the local hospital.

3. You could prepare a very interesting bulletin board exhibit based on these four themes: (a) "Medicine Long Ago," (b) "Medicine Yesterday," (c) "Medicine Today," (d) "Medicine Tomorrow."

   In each case, you could show pictures, clippings from newspapers or magazines, typed quotations from books, original essays or reports, and even cartoons clipped from publications or made by students. For "Medicine Long Ago," try to find reports about our cavemen ancestors and about medical practices in ancient and medieval times. For "Medicine Yesterday," tell about vaccination and the great discoveries of Pasteur, Lister, Koch, and other pioneers of the germ theory of disease. For "Medicine Today," tell about the revolution in medicine due to antibiotics and about the pioneer work going on now in kidney and heart machines and in transplanting organs. For "Medicine Tomorrow," look through daily and Sunday newspapers, magazines like *Life, Look, Medical Digest, Today's Health, Science Digest*, and *Science News*. If your library has it, always consult the *Reader's Guide* when seeking interesting magazine articles.

Things to Try /

1. You will most likely never see a virus, but in this respect you are not more deprived than most doctors and scientists, because only a very few of the largest viruses can be *seen*, even with the highest power of the light microscope. There are, however, many pictures of viruses, such as the one on page 521, made by means of the electron microscope.

   However, you can see bacteria if your doctor or the biology department of your school can let you examine some stained, prepared slides under the *oil immersion* microscope. This is a special microscope, magnifying 1,000 times. Many schools may not have this type of microscope.

2. Here is another problem that you may want to carry out with the aid of a biology teacher. Perhaps a teacher can let you borrow some sterile Petri dishes which have been prepared for growing bacteria.

   The jellylike film in the bottom of each dish is the result of boiling flakes of *agar* (made from seaweed) with a nutrient broth. Each dish has been heated until it is sterile — that is, all living things in it, such as bacteria, have been killed.

   Hold one dish at arm's length and expose it to the air in a still room which has not been swept recently. Breathe gently and slowly through your nose into another dish. Drop some dust from the floor of a busy hall into the third. Sneeze or cough into the fourth. Close each dish immediately after exposing it to the particular condition.

   Place the dishes in an incubator or keep them in a warm place for a few days. In how many of the dishes do you find circles of white, red, yellow, gray, or other colors? If the circles are smooth and waxy, they are colonies of bacteria. If they look furry or woolly, they are probably molds. Try to account for any differences that you observe in the number of colonies present. Each mold growth contains thousands of threads of mold, and each bacterial colony has millions of bacteria.

Probing Further

What You Should Know About Venereal Disease, by K. L. Buxbaum and C. S. Lindenmeyer, Harcourt Brace Jovanovich, 1973. Dr. Buxbaum and his co-author share with you important information about this critical health problem: the history, symptoms, spread, effects, and prevention of the various venereal diseases.

Man, Nature, and Disease, by Richard Fiennes, New American Library, 1965. An extremely interesting paperback discussing the nature of disease, with several important diseases described in detail. Many interesting true stories from the author's own experience.

Microbiology, by M. J. Pelczar and R. D. Reid, McGraw-Hill, 1972. You can learn a great deal merely from studying the drawings, photographs, and colored plates of this authoritative and very complete textbook. It explains the life of microbes, from viruses to protozoa.

The Wonderful World of Medicine, by Ritchie Calder, Doubleday, 1969. Illustrated in full color, this accurate history of medicine from the time of the witch doctors to modern laboratories is still one of the best books on the subject.

Health Concepts in Action

Would you agree with the following statement? Would you change or add to it?

Disease can be caused by a variety of organisms.

Applying this concept of infectious disease, which health practices would you

— continue?

— change?

— begin?

Will you now, as a result of your study, change any of your health objectives?

30 / Defenses Against Disease

It happened just a little over one hundred years ago. "We are going to try something very new," said the famous English surgeon, as he prepared to amputate the hopelessly infected leg of his patient. Ether for anesthesia had been first used in Boston shortly before. The patient breathed the ether fumes, and twenty-eight seconds later the leg had been removed.

Today we marvel at this operation not because of the ether used to deaden pain, but because the operation was carried out without any method of controlling infection. Indeed, the operation had to be done in the first place because no one knew how to prevent infection of wounds—just a brief century ago.

A PROBE INTO CONTROL OF COMMUNICABLE DISEASES—How can your resistance to infections be strengthened? To find out, you will be probing these questions:

1. What are the body's first defenses against invading microorganisms?

2. Once microorganisms have entered the body, what are some cellular defenses against them?

3. How do antibodies combat infection?

4. How does passive immunity differ from active immunity?

5. What are some of the diseases controlled by vaccination? by antibiotics and other chemical agents?

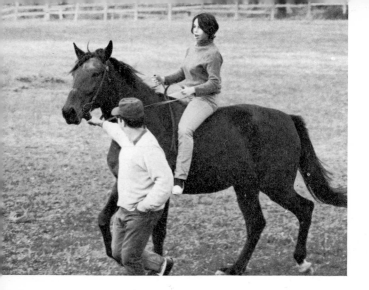

30-1 Do you enjoy good health most of the time? A properly cared for body is better able to resist disease and injury.

DEFENSES OF THE BODY

Most people enjoy good health most of the time. They stay well because they are defended in many ways against the forces that could so easily destroy them.

The processes of evolution and natural selection that have been going on ever since life began on earth have provided most of us with a sound, healthy body that functions well, resists disease and injury, and has a great capacity to repair and heal. These *natural defenses* are the best that any men down through the ages have possessed. Other, different characteristics that occurred in the past as gene mutations (Chapter 20) have not survived. We picture the reason for this as a natural result of the people with these characteristics having been more susceptible to diseases—they died, often before they had a chance to reproduce. The genes they carried were not passed on to succeeding generations. Natural selection favored other people, who survived to become your ancestors and passed along to you the genes that gave them better defenses against disease.

A number of your most basic defenses against disease have always been built-in features of the whole human species. Some of these are listed below.

Built-in Defenses

You have many built-in defenses. The first of these is the skin, which provides your body with a protective covering. It not only protects you from physical injury but also from invasion by viruses, bacteria, and larger organisms.

The eyes are protected by eyelashes, by the blinking reflex, and by tear secretion. Tears contain an enzyme called *lysozyme* (LY-so-zime) that destroys many bacteria that are carried in the air. In addition, tears wash out small particles of foreign material, including bacteria.

The *cilia* of the nose present a physical barrier that traps material that is breathed in. The cells lining the breathing passages in the windpipe and its major branches also have cilia that are constantly in motion. The cilia tend to sweep in an upward direction, carrying bacteria, dust, and other minute particles and foreign material in the direction of the throat, away from the lungs.

The *mucous membranes* that line the inside of the nose, throat, and windpipe, secrete mucus, which covers the surfaces of the air passageways. This mucous blanket, like the tears that protect the eyes, contains lysozyme, which destroys many bacteria. The mucus is sticky, and dust, germs, and many other small particles adhere to it. Thus, the nose, throat, and windpipe prevent the entrance of much foreign material and most germs into the lungs.

Foreign material is either swallowed or coughed up when it reaches the throat. Our cough mechanism also is stimulated when foreign material gets into the windpipe or the lungs themselves. The cough is a sudden, explosive breathing out of air, which tends to expel foreign material.

In the stomach there are several built-in defenses against disease. The very acidic stomach juice kills most of the bacteria that are swallowed in food. In addition, the entire intestinal tract tends to respond to irritation from toxic substances by expelling them. When the stomach is irritated, the person becomes nauseated and vomits. When the intestines or colon are irritated, diarrhea may develop. These mechanisms are useful in ridding the body of substances that might be dangerous or harmful. In addition, many poisonous substances that are absorbed into the bloodstream are carried directly to the liver where they are chemically changed and rendered harmless.

Cellular Defenses

When germs and foreign materials invade the body, a variety of protective mechanisms are called into play. First, there are cells called *phagocytes* (FAYG-oh-sites) that can engulf and destroy invading organisms. This process is called *phagocytosis* (FAYG-oh-sy-TOH-sis). Some phagocytes are located in special organs such as the liver, the spleen, and the lymph nodes. They remain in these

30-2 Many Indians died from diseases brought to the New World by European settlers. Can you explain why?

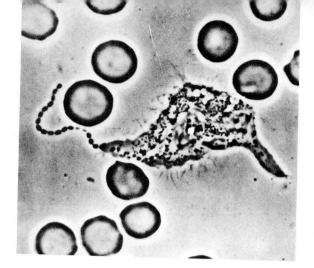

30-3 A white blood cell engulfing a chain of bacteria. What are phagocytes? Where are they located?

Cells that can engulf & destroy invading organisms

organs, removing germs and impurities delivered by the blood, lymph, or tissue fluids.

In addition, many of the white blood cells are phagocytes. They circulate through the bloodstream and destroy foreign particles and bacteria at the point at which they invade the body. See Figure 30-3. When an infection occurs, bone marrow is stimulated to produce great numbers of these white blood cells which tend to migrate to the site of the infection. The number of these white blood cells increases so greatly when an infection is present that a white cell count is a useful diagnostic test. For example, when a doctor suspects appendicitis, he may order a blood count and if the white cell count is high, it may help confirm his diagnosis of an infected appendix.

When infection occurs, the body temperature rises. Some scientists believe that a function of fever is to create an environment that is harmful to the bacteria, tending to inactivate or destroy them. The body also produces *fibrin* in infected areas. Fibrin is composed of minute strands of hairlike structures that form a net around the area of infection. This net may wall off and prevent the spread of the infection to other parts of the body. As time goes on, fibrous tissue, or scar tissue, even more effectively walls off the infection. An abscess is an example of this walling-off process.

Clotting of the blood is another protective mechanism. A clot serves to stop bleeding by closing a tear in a blood vessel through which blood is flowing. The clot may also cover an open wound and prevent bacteria from entering. You read about blood clotting in Chapter 16. It, too, involves fibrin.

The body also protects itself through its capacity for repair and regeneration. Cuts heal and damaged tissue regenerates. Old and worn-out tissue is constantly replaced by healthy new tissue.

Natural Immunity

You have some degree of **natural immunity** to infectious disease, acquired through natural selection among people in the past. Some of this immunity is very broad, indicating that the natural selection occurred over a very long time and involved many diseases. Some of the immunity is specific to certain diseases, and still varies among people today. Your defenses against tuberculosis, for example, may be high or low depending upon where your ancestors lived. Tuberculosis has been known in Europe for as long as man's medical history has been recorded. Starting long ago, the most susceptible Europeans in each generation died out. The survivors and their descendants tended to have greater natural immunity to the bacteria that cause the disease. In North America, however, tuberculosis was unknown until introduced by European settlers. The toll among American Indians was staggering, and even today the descendants of native Americans are far more susceptible to tuberculosis than others are.

Measles is another disease for which natural immunity varies. Smallpox is another, but vaccination has made it no longer a major problem.

Acquired Immunity

Immunity—a state in which the body is resistant to disease—may be natural or acquired. We have already discussed the *natural immunity* that one person may have against a germ that may cause disease in another person. **Acquired immunity** is immunity that an individual obtains or develops as a result of having suffered an attack of illness, through contact with a diseased person or from a poison that the disease germ produces. From these exposures, he acquires a capacity to resist that illness on any future exposure to it.

Immunology, the study of immunity, took its first steps forward when Lady Mary Wortley Montagu brought *variolation* (var-e-oh-LAY-shun) to eighteenth century England from Constantinople. Variolation consisted of inoculating the skin of children with material taken from the pustule of a person with a mild case of smallpox. The children generally developed smallpox, with mild symptoms and a few scattered pox, and subsequently were immune to the disease. Shortly thereafter, Jenner wondered about the tales of dairy maids being immune to smallpox. His subsequent experiments introducing cowpox material (it was not known in those days that this material contained viruses) into the skin of children created an immunity to smallpox, and laid the basis for the whole modern concept of immunology and *vaccination* (vak-sih-NAY-shun).

Subsequently, the work of Pasteur and others helped put the concepts on firm footing. Pasteur discovered, for example, that if chickens were inoculated with very old cultures of the bacteria that caused chicken cholera, the animals developed only mild symptoms and recovered. Afterwards, the chickens were immune to the disease. This

The Bettmann Archive, Cartoon by James Gillray

30-4 This eighteenth-century cartoon shows Edward Jenner vaccinating people against smallpox. You can see that the cartoonist, and many people who lived during that time, did not have faith in this method of preventing disease. What kind of immunity does vaccination confer?

observation led Pasteur to conceive the notion that microorganisms could be altered in such a way as to make them less dangerous without impairing their ability to create immunity to disease.

Antibodies

We have learned much since the days of Jenner and Pasteur. We now know that the body is capable of developing immunity after exposure to bacteria or viruses by developing *antibodies*. You first read about antibodies in Chapter 16. Antibodies are proteins found primarily in the fraction of the blood protein called the gamma globulin. Antibodies are produced by certain cells in the body, such as the *lymphocytes* (LIM-fo-sites), which are a type of white blood cell. Some antibodies circulate in the bloodstream. Other lymphocytes remain fixed in various local tissues.

Antibodies are produced when a foreign substance, known as an *antigen* (ANT-ih-jen), enters the body. Invading organisms are capable of being antigens. When a foreign material, or antigen, enters the body, the body reacts by creating antibodies to it. These antibodies have the capacity to react with the antigens and inactivate them. Unfortunately, the antibody reaction is not fast enough to protect us against our first exposure to the organism. But once the antibodies have been developed, we are protected as long as they remain within the body.

Fortunately, many of the diseases that afflict us do so in such mild form that we are never aware that we have been infected at all. Thus, in the days before immunization against poliomyelitis, a large number of people who never knew that they had had polio could be demonstrated to possess antibodies against polio virus. In the same way, many people who never knew that they had tuberculosis or mumps could be shown to have had previous contact with the disease organisms and to have antibodies against them.

The presence of particular antibodies can be demonstrated by skin tests. In these tests, material from a disease-causing organism is injected into the skin. If the person has previously had a mild attack of the disease and has built up antibodies to it, he will react by forming a firm red spot at the site of the injection. This reaction indicates an *antigen-antibody response*, which would occur only in an individual who possesses an immunity to that disease.

Immunity against bacteria can take two forms. It can involve the bacteria directly. In this case, antibodies against the bacteria are produced and react with chemical substances that coat the bacteria. This causes the bacteria to clump and to be more easily destroyed or inactivated. Antibodies to the toxic products, or poisons, that bacteria produce can also be built up in the body. These antibodies are called *antitoxins.* Thus, a person infected with diphtheria will build up antitoxin that will destroy or inactivate the toxin produced by the bacteria.

We have already discussed the use of skin tests to determine the presence of antibodies. Such tests can also be used to determine the presence of antitoxins. For example,

if a person has had diphtheria, he has built up antitoxin against the diphtheria toxin. A test called the **Schick test** can demonstrate the presence of diphtheria antitoxin. Another test called the **Dick test** is used to determine whether an individual has had scarlet fever.

The amount and duration of immunity that an individual gains after exposure to an antigen varies considerably from person to person and from antigen to antigen. Thus, most people who have had measles will develop a lifelong immunity to it, though some weak-antibody formers may get a second infection. Antibodies to viruses that cause the common cold are relatively short-lived, and so it is possible for people to get frequent colds.

Passive Immunity

Suppose that you suffer a puncture wound and become infected with tetanus germs. Your chances of surviving the disease and producing your own antitoxin to the tetanus toxin are not very great. *You need antitoxin right now.* The doctor can give it to you, in blood serum taken from a horse previously exposed to tetanus organisms. In this case you will not make your own antitoxin, because the antitoxin from the horse will prevent the occurrence of the disease. Inoculation of a person with serum containing antitoxin or antibodies produced in another animal or person confers *passive immunity.* It is passive because the individual who is immunized is not making antibodies himself. Such immunity is short-lived because the antibodies themselves do not last for more than a few weeks or months. For some people, the passive immunity introduces another risk. Horse serum, for example, is itself a potent antigen, and many people who have been given horse serum containing antibodies to a particular disease may develop *antibodies against the horse serum.* They may then have serious reactions

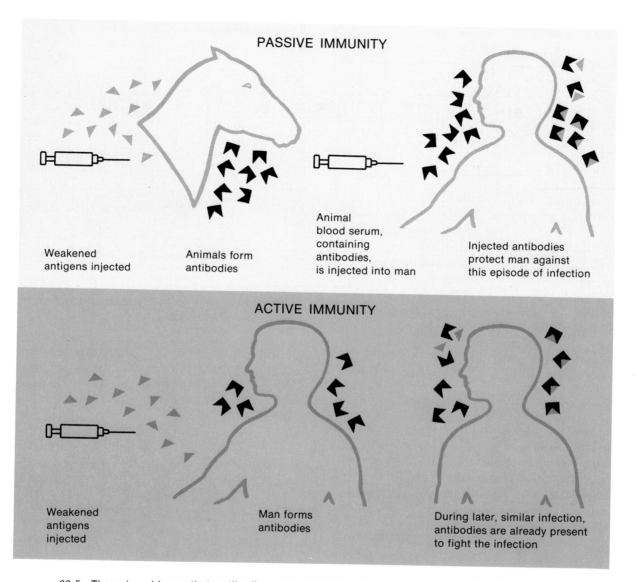

PASSIVE IMMUNITY

Weakened
antigens injected

Animals form
antibodies

Animal
blood serum,
containing
antibodies,
is injected into man

Injected antibodies
protect man against
this episode of infection

ACTIVE IMMUNITY

Weakened
antigens
injected

Man forms
antibodies

During later, similar infection,
antibodies are already present
to fight the infection

30-5 There is evidence that antibodies may combine with antigens (such as bacteria and their toxins) to make them harmless. Where do the antibodies come from that produce passive immunity in people? That produce active immunity in people?

horse

to any further injection of horse serum.

Newborn babies often possess passive immunity to certain infections as a result of acquiring antibodies from their mother. This form of immunity is also short-lived and a baby still has to develop antibodies.

We have already mentioned that the anti-bodies that a person produces are carried in the blood in the gamma globulin. Doctors often use gamma globulin to impart passive immunity for certain diseases. If gamma globulin is taken from the blood of many people and pooled, it will contain many antibodies.

Active Immunity

Active immunity is more desirable than passive immunity. Active immunity develops when a person builds up his own antibodies. It occurs naturally when a person recovers from a disease. Doctors also have been able to stimulate the development of active immunity by injecting vaccines. This is essentially what Pasteur and Jenner did. Vaccines contain either dead organisms or weakened, living organisms that still maintain their antigenic properties. Their introduction into the body stimulates the body to produce antibodies against them.

Today, we have vaccines against a host of diseases such as whooping cough, smallpox, typhoid, tetanus, and polio. The widespread use of the vaccines in this country has caused these diseases to become rare or to vanish entirely from the medical scene. Doctors look forward to the day when other vaccines will make still other diseases rare or extinct.

Your Responsibility and Immunity

. The job of maintaining immunity is the responsibility of each person. Apart from maintaining a good state of nutrition and hygiene, it is important to be immunized against those diseases which are common and for which immunization is available. Commonly today, all children are immunized against smallpox, whooping cough, diphtheria, tetanus, and polio. The use of vaccines for both regular measles and German measles (rubella) may soon become routine procedures.

Many people are immunized against such diseases as typhoid, typhus, cholera, plague, and yellow fever, particularly when they travel to foreign countries. Immunization requirements depend on the area of the world to which a person is traveling. In order to help your doctor, it is important to keep track of just what shots you have had and when you had them. It is also very important to

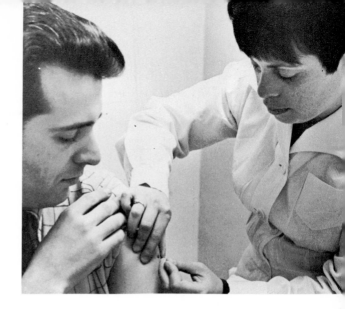

30-6 When you are inoculated with a vaccine, you develop active immunity. How does active immunity differ from passive immunity? *doesn't last*

periodically get booster shots. It is particularly important to have a booster shot if a disease for which there is immunization breaks out in your community. Many people, for example, do not keep their smallpox vaccinations up to date and only get revaccinated when they travel abroad. Occasionally cases of smallpox break out in this country and all the people living in that area are urged to be vaccinated.

Allergies

In general, we develop antibodies primarily to injurious substances. Some people, however, develop them to such harmless substances as dust, pollen, dander, feathers, hair, or certain foodstuffs. In the course of antigen-antibody reactions in your body, one of the chemical substances that may be secreted is the chemical called *histamine* (HIS-tuh-meen). In certain people who develop antibodies against commonly encountered harmless materials, a reaction which they may get to the release of histamine and other substances causes symptoms that can be annoying and severe. When this occurs, a state of *allergy* is said to be present. Some allergies cause relatively minor symptoms. For example, sufferers from hay fever are likely to develop sneezing; a running, itching nose; tearing, burning eyes; and a dry, itching mouth. This occurs in the spring, summer, or autumn, when certain pollens are prevalent in the air. The symptoms of allergies such as hay fever are caused by the release of histamine. Often these symptoms can be controlled by drugs that block the release of histamine. These drugs are called *antihistamines*.

An allergy that may be much more severe is **asthma** (AZ-muh), in which the bronchi go into spasms as allergic reactions occur within their walls. This makes it very difficult for asthmatic people to breathe; they wheeze, gasp, and cough.

Other allergies may take the form of hives, in which an itchy skin rash or larger skin swellings develop. These reactions often follow eating such foods as chocolate, strawberries, or seafood, and taking sulfa or penicillin.

Your Feelings and Allergies

Allergies are basically not psychosomatic diseases. In order to have an allergic reaction, there has to be a combination of antigen and antibody that is built up within a sensitive individual. Lacking antigens and antibodies, there cannot be allergic reactions. However, psychological factors are very important in the development of allergic reactions. Allergic reactions appear to occur much more frequently in people who have emotional problems. They are also more likely to be quite difficult to control in people who are emotionally upset or disturbed. However, lacking the underlying sensitivity and the presence of both antigens and antibodies, there can be no allergic reactions, no matter how emotionally disturbed an indi-

30-7 How many possible allergy-producing items can you identify here?

vidual may be. Many allergic reactions occur in the absence of emotional disturbance. In general, emotional factors seem to be more important in the asthma type of allergy than they are in some other allergic reactions such as allergic reactions to penicillin, sulfa, or other drugs.

Anaphylactic Shock

Occasionally an allergic reaction is so severe that it takes the form of shock. This may lead to death if not attended to immediately by a doctor. The shock usually occurs very rapidly after an antigen is injected into the body. This kind of reaction may occur when a person who is allergic to bee stings is stung by a large number of bees. In these reactions, the blood pressure suddenly drops, the pulse becomes rapid, or the heart may stop altogether. **Anaphylactic** (an-uh-fuh-LAK-tik) reactions to drugs can also occur.

Autoimmune Diseases

Sometimes the body loses its capacity to distinguish between its own and foreign material and builds up antibodies against its own tissues. This may occur when the tissues are altered or disturbed by previous infection with a microorganism. A possible example of this type of disorder is rheumatic fever. Affected people are first infected with *streptococci* bacteria. A number of weeks later, they develop rheumatic fever. This disease does not represent an allergic reaction to the streptococcus organism, but perhaps an allergic reaction to the tissues of the body. In the case of rheumatic fever it is the joint tissues and often the heart that are involved. It has been suggested that these tissues act as antigens, and the body builds up antibodies against them, leading to an immune reaction that causes the disease. Any disease of this nature is called an *autoimmune disease.*

Transplant Rejection

In recent years, doctors have become increasingly interested in transplanting healthy organs to replace diseased ones.

The first transplants commonly done were skin transplants. It was found that when skin from one person was transplanted or grafted to an area where skin had been destroyed on another person, the new skin would not survive the transplant. It would gradually be destroyed in what was found to be an allergic or immune reaction. The body of the person who received the transplant rejected the new skin because it was foreign. It was later found that the only skin transplant that would hold was skin transplanted from one area of the body to another in the same individual. Thus, it became apparent that allergic reactions were going to pose a problem in organ transplants since the body of one person would reject, as foreign, tissue transplanted from another person.

With subsequent experiments in organ transplantation, doctors found that if they used donor tissue from an identical twin, in most cases it would not be rejected by the recipient. It was also found that certain types of tissue did not seem to evoke this allergic, rejecting response. Thus, the cornea of the eye can be transplanted from one person to another without being rejected. Organ transplants are not as easily performed. Today doctors are experimenting widely with kidney and heart transplants, using drugs that suppress the immune reaction and prevent the recipient from developing antibodies to the donated kidney or heart. You will read more about heart transplants in Chapter 32.

DRUGS AND THEIR USES

The most widely used method of treating diseases is the use of chemical agents, or drugs. Drugs may be **nonspecific** or **specific.** Nonspecific drugs merely treat symptoms. For example, aspirin will reduce pain and fever, and cough medicines will control a cough. Specific drugs affect the basic causes of a particular disease. These include such medicines as antibiotics and sulfa drugs that are effective against bacteria and certain viruses. Other specific drugs include various hormones, such as insulin which is effective in the treatment of diabetes.

Antimicrobial Drugs

Antimicrobial drugs are drugs that are effective against germs, or microbes. These include *chemotherapeutic agents* and *antibiotics.* Chemotherapeutic agents are derived from chemicals; antibiotics from living organisms, particularly molds.

The first use of chemical agents to combat infections occurred long before anyone knew about the existence of germs. Certain herbs and roots were known to be good remedies against certain illnesses long before the causes of these illnesses were ever recognized. For example, cinchona bark was used as a treatment for malaria in the seventeenth century. It was many years later before the organism that caused malaria was recognized, and before the quinine in the bark was isolated and found effective against the malaria parasite. Another example is digitalis, a plant that has been used for certain heart diseases for centuries.

Modern chemotherapy began in the early 1900's when the German scientist, Paul Ehrlich, developed a drug that he called 606. This drug was effective against syphilis and was used until the development of penicillin.

In 1932, Dr. Gerhard Domagk (DOH-mag), another German scientist, showed that a dye called protonsil was effective in the treatment of certain bacterial infections. In 1940 it was found that a part of the protonsil molecule, which could be separated from the rest, was the active substance *sulfanilamide* (sul-fah-NIL-a-myd). This was the first of the sulfa drugs, and in the years since many new and better ones have been developed. Sulfa drugs, or sulfonamides, as they are also called, are still widely used by doctors today.

The era of antibiotics began with the development of penicillin. Penicillin was discovered by Alexander Fleming almost by accident. In 1929, Dr. Fleming was working with certain bacteria that he had been growing on culture plates. One of his culture plates was contaminated by a mold. He was struck by the fact that no bacteria grew in the ring around the mold. It occurred to him that perhaps the mold was secreting a substance that destroyed bacteria. He subsequently isolated this substance and named it penicillin after the mold, penicillium, that produced it. It was first used by doctors in 1940. This began a new era in antibacterial treatment.

In rapid succession in the years that fol-

30-8 Penicillin mold. Does it look familiar? It is the mold you often see on citrus fruit.

lowed, a number of very effective drugs were obtained from molds and fungi. One of the most important was *streptomycin*, discovered in 1944 by the American scientist, Dr. Selman Waksman. It was of particular importance because it was the first drug to be effective against the germs that cause tuberculosis. Many other antibiotics have been discovered in recent years. Some are only active against a limited number of germs. Others, known as **broad spectrum antibiotics,** are effective against many different germs.

Some of these drugs cause serious toxic or allergic reactions in certain individuals. These reactions can range from minor skin rashes to serious or even fatal reactions. Therefore, doctors advise that these drugs be used only when necessary.

Another reason for doctors avoiding the unnecessary use of these antibiotics is that many bacteria are capable of developing resistance to them. Thus, strains of resistant bacteria have increased in recent years and have become a serious medical problem. *Staphylococci,* a type of bacteria that often cause boils and skin infections, at first were

streptomycin
Penicillin

30-9 Dr. Selman Waksman (*left*) and Dr. Alexander Fleming (*right*) have made great contributions to our knowledge of antibiotics. Name an antibiotic drug credited to each of them.

very sensitive to most antibiotics. Over years of exposure to antibiotics, sensitive strains of staphylococci began to disappear, but resistant strains remained and flourished. The problem of resistant staph infections has now become a serious one.

When penicillin was first used in the treatment of gonorrhea, it was uniformly effective. Today however, about 20 percent of patients with gonorrhea are infected with resistant strains that do not respond to penicillin treatment.

Drug Safety

No drug is completely safe. Most drugs cause some undesired reactions. Sometimes these reactions are allergic or toxic. For example, some drugs may damage the liver, kidneys, or bone marrow if used for a long period of time or in large quantities. Certain individuals will develop bad reactions to drugs that do not cause these reactions in most people. These phenomena are called *drug idiosyncracies* (id-e-oh-SIN-kruh-seez). Do you have any drug idiosyncracies?

Every time a drug is used, the doctor must be sure that the advantage to be gained by the use of the drug outweighs the risk that is involved in giving it. He considers carefully what dose of the drug he is going to give in order to achieve the desired effect. The amount of a drug needed to cause a desired effect in a sick person is called the *therapeutic dose*. The amount of drug that will cause unpleasant or serious reactions is called a *toxic dose*.

Drug Testing

Before a drug can be safely dispensed to people, it must be carefully tested to determine that it is both safe and effective. The process of drug testing is lengthy, time-consuming, and expensive, but it is absolutely necessary to be sure that people will not be given harmful drugs. When scientists are working to develop new drugs, they first test them on diseased animals. Once they are satisfied that the drug appears to have promise in the treatment of a particular condition, the drug must be tested for safety. These tests or experiments are first performed on animals. Two types of

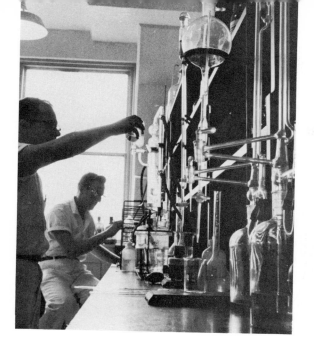

30-10 To ensure safety, drugs are analyzed for purity at all stages of preparation and are tested extensively in animals before they can be used in humans.

experiments are performed. First, *acute experiments* are carried out to determine how much of the drug can be given at once or over a short period of time without seriously injuring the animal that is receiving it. This gives the scientist an idea of how safe the drug is when given over a short-term period and what quantities can be safely administered. After acute experiments have been completed, the drug is tested in *chronic experiments.* Here, small safe doses of the drug are given to animals over extended periods of months or even years to be sure that long-term use of the drug is not going to be dangerous or harmful.

After the drugs have been extensively tested in the laboratory with a variety of animals, they are subjected to tests on sick humans. This is *clinical testing.* The first of these tests are usually conducted on small numbers of patients under carefully controlled circumstances. After clinical tests

have demonstrated that the drug is effective and safe, it is then released for broader clinical testing. Often many different doctors working together will conduct tests and studies with the drug to determine more about its effectiveness. It is only after the drug has been extensively tested in the laboratory and on humans under carefully controlled conditions that its effectiveness and safety can be assured. Then it is released on the market to be sold to people on doctors' prescriptions.

A federal agency known as the Food and Drug Administration (FDA) is responsible for approving all new drugs to be released on the market. An application for a new drug is made to the FDA which reviews all of the testing that has been conducted on the drug. The drug is not approved until the FDA is satisfied that it has been adequately tested, and that it is effective and safe.

Problems in Drug Testing

Some years ago the drug *Thalidomide* was marketed in certain countries. It was found later that a very sizeable percentage of pregnant women who took this drug gave birth to deformed infants. Many of these infants lacked arms or legs. The catastrophe of Thalidomide taught a very important lesson about drug safety. It emphasized again the importance of testing thoroughly for safety before any drug is made available for general use.

No matter how thoroughly a drug has been tested in the laboratory with animals, it cannot be safely used until it has been adequately tested on people. However, testing in humans raises problems. Recently, there have been claims that some patients have been tested without their permission or consent. When this has been done, the drug tested was usually harmless and the patients were carefully watched for possible bad reactions to the drug. If a patient is told that he is being tested it may detract from the value of the test. The patient may expect an effect and feel better because he is getting a

30-11　This child was born with deformed arms because her mother took Thalidomide when she was pregnant. What can be done to prevent tragedies like this from happening again?

drug that he thinks is going to help him. The important thing is that drug testing must be done under proper supervision and under conditions that assure safety to the patient.

What You Have Learned

What kind of health practices should you apply in maintaining your health? Check your understanding of the chapter. On a separate sheet of paper, number 1 through 24 and insert the answer from the vocabulary list below. Use each expression, but use each one only once.

- acquired immunity
- anaphylactic
- antibodies
- antigens
- antitoxins
- bone marrow
- cholera
- cilia
- cough
- fibrin
- gamma globulin
- gastric juice
- hay fever
- histamine
- Jenner
- mucous membrane
- mucus
- penicillin
- phagocytes
- polio
- Schick test
- skin
- streptomycin
- tears

Your body has the capacity to resist disease and injury and to repair and heal itself. The eyes are protected by eyelashes, by the blinking reflex, and by (1) *tears*. The (2) *cilia* that lines our air passages secretes a (3) *mucus* blanket. The (4) *cilia* keep bacteria and dust moving away from the lungs. The explosive breathing out called a (5) *cough* helps us to get foreign matter out of the windpipe. Many bacteria that reach the stomach are killed by (6) *gastric juice*.

Many germs that invade the body are engulfed and killed by cells called (7) *phagocytes*. (8) *____* comes to your aid in infection by producing many white blood cells. Strands of hairlike (9) *fibrin* often wall off infecting germs. (10) *____* often develops as a result of having suffered an attack of a disease. (11) *Jenner* used cowpox virus to immunize people against smallpox. Pasteur made chickens immune to chicken (12) *cholera*.

After exposure to germs, we often produce (13) *antibodies*, which then give us protection. These substances inactivate (14) *antigens* which enter the body. Before we had immunization for (15) *polio*, many persons had antibodies for this disease, although they were never aware of having suffered from it. Presence of antibodies against tuberculosis can be shown by a (16) *skin* test. (17) *antitoxins* are antibodies to poisons produced by bacteria. A positive (18) *test* indicates that a person has had diphtheria or has been exposed to the germs. Antibodies that a person makes are carried in his blood in the (19) *bone marrow*.

In persons subject to allergies, release of (20) *histamine* often results in a dry mouth, burning eyes, sneezing, and an itching, running nose in sufferers from (21) *hay fever*. (22) *anaphylactic* shock is an allergic reaction which may lead to death.

Fleming began a new era in medicine when he discovered (23) *penicillin*. Waksman discovered (24) *streptomycin*, the first antibiotic effective against tuberculosis.

What You Can Do

1. Test yourself on your knowledge of disease and defenses against disease. Select the word or words that best complete each statement. Then copy each complete statement into your notebook.

   a. Streptomycin is used in treating (1) diphtheria, (2) tuberculosis, (3) typhoid fever, (4) typhus.

   b. Cells that engulf and destroy germs and foreign matter are (1) erythrocytes, (2) platelets, (3) phagocytes, (4) antigens.

   c. Injection of antitoxin is intended to give (1) active immunity, (2) passive immunity, (3) no immunity, (4) permanent immunity.

   d. Preparations containing dead organisms or altered living organisms are called (1) antitoxins, (2) toxins, (3) toxoids, (4) vaccines.

e. A puncture wound is most likely to be followed by (1) tetanus, (2) tuberculosis, (3) typhoid fever, (4) typhus.

f. Hives are usually an indication of (1) allergy, (2) bacterial infection, (3) virus infection, (4) malnutrition.

g. A disease that may be the result of autoimmunity is (1) cholera, (2) Q fever, (3) rheumatic fever, (4) typhoid fever.

h. One of the structures least likely to be rejected when transplanted from one person to another is the (1) cornea, (2) heart, (3) kidney, (4) liver.

2. Do you make it a habit to follow good health practices for protecting yourself and others from infectious diseases? Copy the following list in your notebook, then rate yourself "yes," "no," or "sometimes" on each item. In class, discuss the reasons for each practice and its value. Determine to improve your own health practices if they are not as good as they should be. *Do not write in this book.*

Do you:

a. Keep your fingers away from your eyes, nose, and mouth?

b. Drink from your own glass?

c. Cough or sneeze into a disposable tissue—and always carry a supply of tissues when you have a cold?

d. Try to stay away from others when you have a cold?

e. Keep your distance (as far as you can politely) from people who have colds or show other signs of infection?

f. Carry a clean handkerchief?

g. Avoid touching a drinking fountain with your lips?

h. Refrain from kissing pet dogs, cats, or other animals, and always wash your hands with soap after petting them?

i. Wash raw vegetables and fruits before eating them?

j. Get enough sleep and rest?

k. Use your own washcloth and towel?

Things to Try

You can find excellent articles on which to base class reports in quite a few magazines, such as *Harper's, Atlantic Monthly, Senior Science,* and *Scientific American.* Both current and old issues of *Scientific American* often contain articles on disease and the fight against it. You might find some of the following interesting: "Infectious Drug Resistance" (December, 1967); "Kinship of Animal and Human Diseases" (January, 1967); "German Measles" (July, 1966); "Rheumatic Fever" (December, 1966); "Viruses of the Common Cold" (December, 1960); "How Cells Make Antibodies" (December, 1964); "How Cells Attack Antigens" (February, 1964); "Malaria" (May, 1962); and "The Germ of Tuberculosis" (June, 1955).

Probing Further

The Medical Garden, by Geoffrey Marks and William K. Beatty, Scribner's, 1971. Describes the origin of, use of, and folklore surrounding seven important drugs: aspirin, cocaine, colchisine, digitalis, penicillin, opium, quinine. Describes the role of both amateur and professional scientists in developing these drugs.

Man Against Disease, by Geoffrey Lapage, Abelard, 1964. This accurate book is very interesting and easy to understand.

Health Concepts in Action

Does this statement bring together the ideas you have gained from this chapter?

The body has structural, cellular, and chemical defenses against disease organisms.

Applying this concept of body defenses, which health practices would you

—continue?

—change?

—begin?

Will you now, as a result of your study, change any of your health objectives?

31 / Guarding Community Health

"I ought to know something about raising children," said the old woman. "I've buried six." So she had, and of her three surviving children, one was pale with tuberculosis, one had narrowly escaped death from poisoning from germ-laden food, and the third had recently recovered from typhoid fever caught by drinking polluted water.

That was in the "good old days," when little was known about guarding community health, and public health services were much less widespread than they are today.

A PROBE INTO COMMUNITY HEALTH—How does your community help to protect your health? To determine the many different ways, you will be probing questions like these:

1. What are some of the public health services of your federal, state, and local government?

2. Describe some of the voluntary health agencies and their activities.

3. What are some programs for cutting the cost of medical care to the average citizen? to the aged?

4. What steps are being taken to improve health services in the developing countries?

5. What are some of the health careers for which you might prepare? Which career appeals most to you?

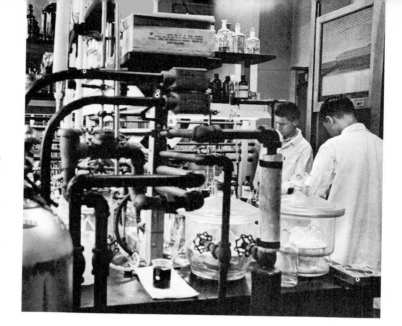

31-1 The Public Health Service conducts its own medical and biological research programs and also supports research carried out at universities and other institutions throughout the country.

PUBLIC HEALTH SERVICES

Your health is protected by many government health agencies. You have already learned, for example, of government measures to safeguard your water, food and air (Chapter 5) and to prevent communicable diseases from spreading (Chapters 29 and 30).

Many other aspects of your physical and mental well-being are promoted by federal, state, and local health agencies.

Federal Health Services

On the federal level, there are a number of agencies concerned with your health and the health of all of us. Many of these agencies are in the Department of Health, Education, and Welfare. One of the most important is the *Public Health Service.*

The Public Health Service had its beginnings in 1789, when Congress passed a law to provide hospitals for the care of merchant seamen. Through the years, new laws reorganized the original agency. Its health services were extended to many other parts of the population and began to include preventive medicine as well as healing medicine.

Today, the Public Health Service is one of the major health services of the country. Some of its general functions are to:

1. Conduct and promote programs of medical research and health education.
2. Help communities expand their physical and mental health services by giving financial or other assistance for health centers and for training of personnel.
3. Provide certain kinds of direct health care, as in quarantine centers.
4. Identify and take steps to control hazards in certain consumer products and services.
5. Collaborate with foreign governments and international organizations in world health activities.

The Public Health Service now consists of three major agencies headed by the Surgeon General. See Figure 31-2 on the next page for some of the duties of these agencies.

NATIONAL INSTITUTES OF HEALTH

Carries out research for the prevention, diagnosis, and treatment of serious diseases through many research institutes, including:

National Cancer Institute
National Heart and Lung Institute
National Institute of Neurological Diseases and Stroke
National Eye Institute

Maintains the world's largest collection of medical literature in the National Library of Medicine.

Cooperates with other health organizations to collect and spread information on medical advances.

HEALTH SERVICES AND MENTAL HEALTH ADMINISTRATION

The National Institute of Mental Health conducts and supports programs for the prevention and treatment of mental illness, drug dependence, alcoholism, and other problems related to mental health.

The Center for Disease Control enforces quarantine regulations and takes other measures to eradicate or control communicable diseases.

The National Center for Health Statistics collects and publishes statistics on health needs and resources.

Provides direct medical care in the Indian Health Service and in health programs for federal employees.

FOOD AND DRUG ADMINISTRATION

Enforces the federal Food, Drug, and Cosmetic Act and its amendments.

Sets standards for food labeling to show clearly nutritional content, food additives, exact amount packaged. Conducts research, inspections, and food recalls to control food-borne illnesses.

Sets standards for many drug industry practices, such as the testing, advertising, and labeling of prescription drugs. Reviews prescription-drug manufacturers' safety tests and claims for new drugs before these are put on the market. Inspects and recalls contaminated or mislabeled drugs.

Maintains district offices to respond to consumer inquiries about product safety.

Radiation Control

The discovery of radioactivity has proved to be both beneficial and dangerous to man. For example, X rays have made possible both the early diagnosis of cancer and the treatment of certain forms of cancer. Yet careless exposure to radiation can result in serious damage. Thus, all uses of radiation require close supervision.

The federal **Atomic Energy Commission** has established procedures for the safe use of radioactive materials in hospitals and research laboratories throughout the country, and for the disposal of radioactive wastes. The Commission also investigates accidents involving radioactive materials.

State governments have also become concerned, along with the Atomic Energy Commission, in the inspection of facilities that use radioactive materials.

Through the work of several agencies, the federal government tries to carefully monitor the amount of radiation in our water and food and in the rest of our environment. It has set standards for the maximum levels of radiation exposure that are considered safe. At present, the federal agency that is responsible for setting and enforcing environmental radiation standards is the Environmental Protection Agency. You have read about other responsibilities of the EPA in Chapter 5.

At this time, the amount of radiation to which we are exposed in our daily lives is not considered to be near a dangerous amount. Nevertheless, it is important that we all do what we can to limit our exposure to unnecessary radiation and to know the dangers that are involved in the use of any nuclear weapons.

In addition, the peacetime uses of nuclear energy will be increasing. This will present the problem of safe disposal of radioactive wastes (see page 82). This problem will be concerning all of us in our efforts to control environmental pollution.

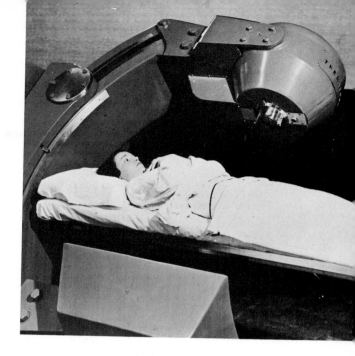

31-3 Radioactive materials are used in the treatment of such diseases as cancer. What measures are taken to use them safely?

The Federal Trade Commission

This commission supervises the advertisement of drugs bought over the counter without prescription. It makes certain that advertising claims for drugs are not exaggerated or misleading. It acts to assure us that labeling of drugs is clear, meaningful, and understandable to the potential user and that any dangers involved in their use are clearly spelled out.

It is important that drug manufacture, distribution, sale, and labeling be supervised in order to prevent *medical quackery*. Many people, and particularly those who are faced with desperate health problems, are likely victims of salesmen who are dishonest, or honest but unwitting. Medical quacks with claims for cancer cures or false remedies for serious incurable disorders prey on thousands of people each year. Federal regulation tends to minimize the activities of medical quacks. See Figure 31-4.

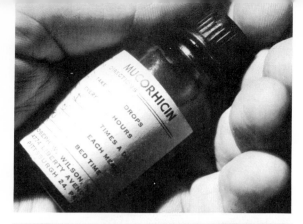

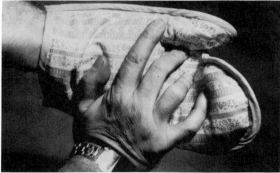

31-4 The Federal Trade Commission helps guard against the sale of quack "cures," such as (*top*) medication claimed to cure cancer and (*bottom*) a glove claimed to cure arthritis. What should you do to avoid purchasing such worthless and possibly dangerous "cures"?

Department of Agriculture

The Department of Agriculture is another division of the federal government that is concerned with public health. This department studies diseases that affect livestock and poultry. It requires that all meats sold in interstate commerce be inspected. Inspectors working in packing houses examine animals. If approved, they stamp them as inspected and passed by the Department of Agriculture. In addition, this department grades meats for quality and labels them as prime, choice, good, commercial, or utility. In the Department of Agriculture, the *Veterinary Service* conducts inspections of domestic livestock.

The *Agricultural Research Service* conducts research on livestock and products related to livestock to prevent, control, and eliminate animal diseases and parasites.

State Health Services

Many health problems are not national, but regional. For this reason, in addition to the federal health agencies, there are state and local agencies. State health departments work in cooperation with federal and local health agencies. Each state establishes its own disease control laws and its own sanitary codes. It operates laboratories where physicians may have tests made, particularly tests related to diseases of public concern, such as infectious illnesses. State health departments operate many of the state hospitals, particularly those designed to deal with mental health problems, tuberculosis, and care of the aged. They establish ordinances relating to health, such as those requiring blood tests for syphilis prior to the issuance of a marriage license.

31-5 State and local health workers run regular checks on food that could spread disease.

The bulk of the responsibility for the maintenance of public health lies with the local health departments, which are operated on a municipal or, in rural areas, on a county level. The functions of local health departments are many and they cover a scope of activities that affect all of our lives.

Through laws, codes, statutes, and regulations, health authorities make certain that the food we get is clean, free of contamination, and safe for us to eat. They check to see that food is properly packaged and labeled. Food stores and restaurants are inspected to assure cleanliness and sanitation. People that handle food are examined to make certain that they do not have a communicable disease and are not disease carriers. Insect and rodent control helps prevent food contamination. Local health departments are also concerned with purification of the water that we use.

Local health departments are concerned with the production and distribution of milk. Dairies are inspected to be sure that sanitary conditions prevail. Controls are maintained over the pasteurization, processing, and the distribution of milk so that we may be sure that our milk supply is clean and free of disease. Before milk was pasteurized and distribution was so stringently controlled, many diseases, including tuberculosis, were spread through milk.

Local health departments have many other responsibilities. They concern themselves with preventing illegal use of narcotics, barbiturates, and tranquilizers, with treatment of alcoholics, and in some cities, of chronic smokers. They are concerned with family planning and may operate agencies that disseminate birth control information. They maintain or supervise agencies for adoption of children. Through bureaus of child guidance, they deal with the problems of juvenile delinquency and are concerned

also with the inspection of hotels, trailer camps, public buildings, parks, beaches, and local recreational areas in order to be sure that these are clean and sanitary and that health codes are maintained. They maintain city morgues and medical examiners' offices where autopsies are performed when a question arises involving public health, safety, or infraction of law.

The local health departments collect statistics and record births and deaths. Health codes require physicians to report communicable diseases to local health authorities, who then compile information and statistics on the frequency and severity of communicable diseases. Accidental deaths and suicides are recorded. Information relative to the effects of extreme weather conditions on the health of the community is also collected. With these statistics, the health departments are better able to understand, predict, and deal with the spread of communicable diseases in communities and with the various causes of mortality that may occur.

OTHER HEALTH SERVICES

In addition to the various governmental organizations concerned with public health, there are many private organizations and public and private hospitals that serve important health functions, and another governmental agency that today is concerned with medical insurance.

Major Health Associations

The **American Medical Association** or AMA was organized in Philadelphia in 1847 to raise the standards of medical education and practice in the United States, to combat medical quackery, and to promote public health. It comprises over 1,900 county and district medical societies and 53 state and territorial societies. The AMA, which is an organization of practicing doctors, is concerned with many aspects of national health. It studies and makes recommendations to the government concerning issues related to public and individual health problems. It sets standards for hospitals and medical schools that it supports and aids. It stimulates and aids research activities throughout the country. It supervises the training of interns and residents and helps set standards for certification of medical specialists. It provides an information service for physicians and publishes a variety of medical journals, thus playing a major role in disseminating medical information.

There are many other voluntary health organizations. The *American Cancer Society* supports cancer research and provides services and aid to cancer victims. The *National Heart Association* conducts the same type of activities in the field of heart disease, and a host of other organizations are concerned with specific diseases such

31-6 Refugees from flooding brought about by a hurricane are evacuated to safe ground by American National Red Cross workers.

as arthritis, kidney disease, and tuberculosis.

The *American National Red Cross* is another important health service. This organization provides assistance and money to individuals in time of such disasters as floods, fires, and hurricanes. It supervises a blood procurement program and operates donor centers where people can give blood. It also operates laboratories where blood is fractionated, producing such by-products as plasma and gamma globulin. It assists servicemen in time of personal emergencies or family tragedies and, through the International Red Cross, helps in such matters as exchange of prisoners in time of war. It also provides educational programs in first aid, water safety, home nursing and other fields.

Our Hospitals and Clinics

An important line of defense in guarding the health of the community is the network of hospitals and clinics spanning our country. Hospitals basically are of three kinds. First there are *government hospitals,* including federal hospitals. Some are under the auspices of the United States Public Health Service, such as the Clinical Center in Bethesda, Maryland, and the hospitals for treating drug addiction in Lexington, Kentucky, and Fort Worth, Texas. Others are operated by the Veterans Administration. Still others are maintained by the Armed Forces, such as the Army's Walter Reed General Hospital and the Naval Hospital in Bethesda, Maryland.

Many other governmental hospitals are operated by states. Most states have a number of mental hospitals. Many have large university hospitals as part of medical centers associated with state universities. Finally, on a local level, there are county and municipal hospitals, including such famous institutions as Cook County Hospital in Chicago and Bellevue in New York City.

The second major type of hospital is the *voluntary hospital.* Many of the large and well-known hospitals in our country are voluntary hospitals. These hospitals are nonprofit organizations, financed by private contribution and by the monies taken in as fees for services given in the hospital. These hospitals are tax-exempt institutions and are designed and operated to serve the welfare of the community. Many of them are associated with medical schools and include the more famous teaching hospitals throughout the country. The majority of the voluntary hospitals are fairly large, having from 150 to 1,000 beds.

The third type of hospital is the *private hospital.* Private hospitals are usually small and are operated as a business, designed to make money for their owners, as well as to care for the sick. In general, private hospitals do not concern themselves as much with community health functions as do the voluntary or government hospitals but they do provide valuable health care.

Voluntary and government hospitals serve several functions. They maintain beds for sick patients in need of hospital care. They also have out-patient clinics which primarily serve persons in a low economic bracket. Often the clinics are separated into specialty clinics so that patients can have health problems attended to by doctors who specialize in those particular types of diseases. Such clinics include surgical clinics, medical clinics, pediatric clinics, and obstetrical clinics. In addition, many hospitals operate emergency rooms. Some hospitals have home-care programs, in which the members of the hospital staff visit the patients in their homes when they are too sick to come to the clinic. Most hospitals have laboratory services that are used not only by the hospital, but by the doctors in the community. Patients may be referred to the hospital for X-ray, blood, or bacteriological studies.

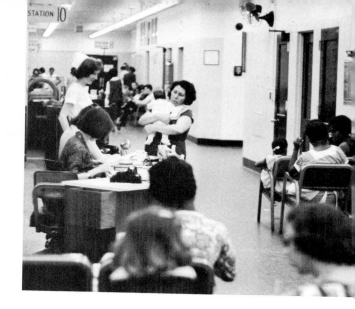

31-7 Excellent medical care is provided through hospital out-patient clinics.

In recent years, clinic functions have been assumed by other organizations. Many large industries have their own health centers operated by management. Unions have also set up health clinics in many major cities throughout the country. In addition, a number of voluntary health agencies operate specialized clinics and services. For example, there are many mental hospitals throughout our country that are operated by mental health associations and are organized and financed on a local level. Various tuberculosis health associations operate clinics where patients can obtain chest X rays or skin tests for tuberculosis, and where patients with tuberculosis can be treated.

Varied Research Facilities

If we are to look to a brighter and healthier tomorrow, we must explore means of maintaining better health and combating illness. The constant fight to extend the horizons of knowledge and understanding of disease and its treatment is conducted in research institutions and laboratories throughout the country. Some of these are operated as pure medical research institutions, such as the National Institutes of Health. Others are part of the sphere of activity of university medical centers where much research is conducted. Some is carried out in private laboratories operated by industries, such as the pharmaceutical industry. Although most of this research is supported by the Federal Government, much is supported by industry, private agencies, organizations, and foundations.

Health Insurance

The cost of medical care is a problem of ever increasing magnitude. Because of the tremendous complexities of a hospital, services today are extremely expensive. A relatively brief stay in a hospital may cost many hundreds of dollars and a prolonged illness may cost thousands of dollars. For many families a major illness can be an economic catastrophe. Because of this increase in the cost of medical care, there has been a steady growth in medical insurance plans. In return for regular payments to the insurance organization, an individual may recover all or part of his medical costs if he becomes ill and requires hospitalization or other treatment. Many different plans for prepaid medical care, covering both hospital costs and physicians' fees, have been developed.

Most insurance plans are sponsored by private insurance companies and are regulated by the states in which they operate. Their widespread acceptance has been promoted by business, industry, unions, and fraternal organizations. Government has sponsored other insurance programs for its employees. Because of the promotion of medical insurance on so broad a scale, a substantial percentage of the population has medical coverage of one sort or another.

However, there still remains a large part of the population for whom private insurance plans are too expensive. These include the underprivileged segment of the population and the aged, who are often retired on limited incomes. Since these people present greater risks for illness, insurance premiums for them tend to be quite expensive. To cover the cost of medical care for these people, new, more imaginative plans have been developed on a state and national basis.

Medicare and Medicaid

The **Medicare** program went into effect in 1966. It provides medical insurance through Social Security to almost all citizens over sixty-five. In addition, the federal government will assist states in developing insurance programs for the needy. Many state legislatures are adopting medical care plans of their own to provide insurance for low-income families regardless of age. These programs have been named **Medicaid.**

These new medical insurance plans have provided the aged and the needy an opportunity to receive medical care without concern about expense, and with the assurance that they will have available to them the same facilities as anyone else. However, these programs have also introduced new problems into our society. The medical profession does not have the facilities to handle the increase of patient load that will accompany the widespread adoption of plans for prepaid medical care. There is a critical shortage of hospital beds, doctors, nurses, and technicians. There is no quick or easy solution to the problems raised by this increased availability of medical care.

WORLD HEALTH

So far we have discussed the health needs of our American community. Our problems

31-8 The ship *HOPE* brings medical care and education to remote, underdeveloped areas. Would you be interested in participating in such a project? How could you help?

are small indeed, when compared to those in other parts of the world. Many of the underdeveloped areas and emerging nations have virtually no medical facilities at all. Infectious diseases that have practically been eliminated in the United States continue to be major killers in other parts of the world. Malaria, smallpox, cholera, tuberculosis, typhoid, yellow fever, typhus, and sleeping sickness are all diseases that still claim an enormous toll of lives throughout the world. Worms and parasitic infections are common, as are starvation and deficiency diseases which claim millions of lives. In parts of the world, people live their entire lives without ever seeing a doctor. Sanitation is primitive. The water supply is impure. Milk and other foods are contaminated. Broken bones go unset and cuts unsutured. There are no surgeons to operate on a child with acute appendicitis; no specialists to treat trachoma, a virus disease of the eyes which is very common in many parts of the world and which leads to blindness if untreated. Many women die in childbirth because they are attended by untrained persons. Many infants die in their first years of life because of lack of medical care and poor nutrition.

International Health Agencies

To meet these challenges, a number of international health agencies have been established. Organizations such as *CARE* and *MEDICO* have sent doctors, nurses, and supplies to remote areas of the globe. Religious organizations have established mission hospitals in many needy areas.

The American people, by voluntary contributions, have outfitted and supported a ship known as project *HOPE* to bring medical care and education into remote areas. This ship visits various parts of the globe where health facilities are inadequate. The ship's personnel help train local health workers and educate the population in health matters, hygiene, and nutrition.

Government agencies are sponsoring technical assistance programs to send personnel and supplies to help emerging nations cope with the problems relating to health, sanitation, agriculture, and food technology. The *Peace Corps* has also supplied needed personnel in many of the health services. *UNICEF* has been established under the auspices of the United Nations to help children thoughout the world.

World Health Organization

The **World Health Organization** (**WHO**) was established by the United Nations to function as a public health service for the world community. It is one of the most important international health services. Its objective is to attain the highest possible level of health for the world population.

The functions of WHO include directing and coordinating international health work, assisting governments upon request in strengthening health services, and providing technical assistance and necessary aid in emergencies. WHO also operates to stimulate and advance work in eradicating disease and to improve nutrition, nursing, and sanitation. WHO promotes cooperation among scientific and professional groups that contribute to all phases of the advancement of health. Fostering activities in the field of mental health, promoting and conducting health research, and promoting improved standards in teaching and training in health, medical, and related professions are additional responsibilities of WHO.

WHO has attempted to deal with major problems in a broad way rather than attending to the medical needs of individuals. It has been concerned with the eradication of malaria, broad-scale vaccination programs against smallpox, control of cholera, development of programs of sanitation and purification of water, and adequate disposal of sewage. WHO is gradually making progress in the eradication of diseases that are taking a large toll of lives in so many underdeveloped areas.

Much remains to be done. Illness is still one of the world's major problems. Millions of people die unnecessarily each year from injury, disease, or malnutrition. But major strides are being made every year by an army of dedicated people working as individuals or in teams, attempting to bring modern medicine into remote communities.

CAREERS IN HEALTH

The health services provide promising careers for young people today. There are more than 200 different health occupations now available to you. Still more are being added as medical science takes over some of the discoveries of the space age.

Trained people for these occupations are greatly in demand. Many recruitment programs, aimed at bringing young people into the health fields, are being sponsored by local, state, and national organizations. In a number of cases, financial aid is provided to help people train for the work. You may know of such a recruitment program going on in your school or community. If you are interested, or think you might become interested in a health career, you can obtain information from a local health-careers association or project or from your public health department.

Many Types of Specialties

A career in one of the health fields offers opportunity for just about every type of personality, aptitude, or degree of schooling.

Figure 31-9, on the next page, merely begins to suggest how varied the health occupations are. See, also, the photo essay, *Careers in Health,* on pages 565-72, for examples of occupations related to hospital services.

If you are trained in a health occupation, you can choose to work in many other facilities besides hospitals. You might work in some public health service, such as a federal health agency, school health program, or community health center. Or you might choose to work in a private medical office or laboratory, or in an industry producing some health product. If you are interested in sales, you might consider selling medicines or health equipment. You might even plan toward a business of your own providing some health product or service.

Do you like desk or laboratory work?

Air pollution meteorologist
Dietician
Health information specialist
Laboratory, medical, blood bank, or X-ray technician
Pathologist
Pharmacist
Medical illustrator
Medical librarian
Medical secretary
Medical photographer
Sanitarian
Science writer or editor
Nuclear medicine technologist

Do you prefer to work with people?

Aides to the mentally or physically handicapped
Dental hygienist
Health instructor
Hearing, occupational, physical, recreational, or speech therapist
Hospital administrator
Nursing aide
Practical nurse
Psychiatric or medical social worker
Psychiatrist
Physician in general practice
Public health educator
Receptionist
Registered nurse
Vocational rehabilitation counselor

Do you enjoy working with figures, graphs, and statistics?

Medical statistician
Morbidity and mortality recorder
Population data analyst
Research specialist
Vital record registrar

31-9 Health careers are so varied that there is a place for persons with almost any interest, aptitude, or level of training. The chart suggests just a few of the many possibilities.

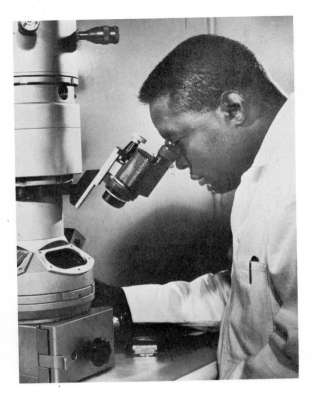

31-10 Today, many health careers involve training in the use of new equipment. This cancer researcher is using an electron microscope to study the mouse leukemia virus, which cannot be seen under an ordinary light microscope.

Some of the Advantages in a Health Service Career

As the American public expects higher standards of living and as our population continues to increase, the demand for trained, qualified personnel in the field of health will continue to exceed the supply. A health career may well appeal to you as a lifetime vocational opportunity. These specialties provide satisfactory financial return for the expenses involved in your preparation. You may expect about the same salary range as in other fields of service requiring a similar background of education, skill, and experience.

Since the health professions and specialties are so varied you will find opportunity to use them almost anywhere you may live. If you want to travel you will find many of these specialties in demand in the armed forces, the World Health Organization, the U.S. Public Health Service, and in many U.S. governmental agencies. Here at home, job opportunities are available in industry, hospitals, clinics, public health departments, voluntary health agencies, professional health organizations, medical schools, and dental schools.

In addition to learning the skills and techniques of a health specialty, there are other factors you may well consider. A career in health is likely to be one of service, in which you will contribute to the welfare of other people. At times you will be a member of a team, which calls for an ability to cooperate with others. You may find it necessary, at times, to lay aside your personal desires in the service of the team. Then again, you may be entirely on your own, fully responsible for an entire project.

What Kind of Training Will You Need?

Both men and women find work in health careers. The amount and kind of education and skills you will need depends on the particular specialty you choose. Some skills may be learned on the job while others require many years of study and preparation. For some of the professions requiring long periods of preparation, the expense may seem high but the rewards will be comparable.

Your school counselor can provide you with more detailed information regarding any particular health career that you may find appealing. The references at the end of this chapter will also give you useful information.

What You Have Learned

What kind of health practices should you apply in maintaining your health? Check your understanding of the chapter. On a separate sheet of paper, number 1 through 24 and insert the answer from the vocabulary list below. Use each expression, but use each one only once.

advertisement
appendicitis
biomedical
CARE
code
communicable
fractionated
gamma globulin
health associations
Health, Education, and Welfare
local health
pasteurized
pathologist
physical therapist
Public Health Service
radioactive materials
safety
sanitation
Social Security
trachoma
UNICEF
voluntary
WHO
yellow fever

Most federal agencies concerned with public health are in the Department of (1)_____. One of our oldest government agencies, the U.S. (2)_____, was organized soon after this nation became independent. It includes the National Institutes of Health, the government's primary agency for (3)_____ research. The Food and Drug Administration tests drugs for (4)_____. The Atomic Energy Commission has established procedures for the use of (5)_____. The Federal Trade Commission, which has many other duties, supervises the (6)_____ of over-the-counter drugs.

Each state establishes a sanitary (7)_____. Local health services inspect food stores to make sure of (8)_____. Milk, fortunately, is (9)_____ at present; before this custom was adopted, many diseases were spread by milk. Doctors are required to report cases of (10)_____ diseases to (11)_____ authorities. The American National Red Cross operates laboratories where blood is (12)_____ to produce plasma and (13)_____.

Varied diagnostic and educational health services are provided by (14)_____. Most of the more famous teaching hospitals are (15)_____ hospitals. Medicare provides medical insurance through (16)_____ for almost all citizens 65 or older.

In many of the underdeveloped countries, diseases that have practically been eliminated in the United States continue to kill many people. Among these are malaria, smallpox, and (17)_____. Often there is no one to operate in case of (18)_____, and persons with the eye disease (19)_____ go untreated. The organization called (20)_____ sends doctors and supplies to remote regions. Two important agencies established under the auspices of the United Nations are (21)_____, intended to function as an international public health service, and (22)_____, designed to help children in all countries.

You might do well to prepare yourself to enter one of the more than 200 different health professions. If you prefer working with people, you might like to become a (23) _____. If your greatest interest is in the medical sciences, you might be happiest as a (24) _____.

What You Can Do

When you protect yourself against infection, you are making a contribution to community health because every time a person becomes ill with a communicable disease, the germs multiply enormously. Without meaning to, the sick person makes it more likely that others will become ill. Copy the following health practices in your notebook and look up the reasons for each. In most cases you will find an explanation for each practice. In one case, you may need to look up a word in the dictionary. Now put all of these good practices into operation as often as you can.

1. Look for the inspection stamp when you buy meat.
2. Place garbage in a watertight can with a close-fitting top, or wrap securely.
3. Wash your hands with soap before preparing food and before each meal.
4. Keep your fingers out of your eyes, and don't put on anyone else's eyeglasses.
5. If you wear contact lenses, don't touch them with unwashed fingers and don't place them on your desk or on any other germ-laden object.
6. Place milk, meat, and fish in the refrigerator as soon as they are received, and keep them there except when they are being used.
7. Don't leave food around where insects, mice, or rats can obtain a free meal.
8. Carry a supply of tissues, use them, and promptly dispose of them in a sanitary manner.
9. Scald eating and cooking utensils after washing them.
10. Cook pork until well-done.

Things to Try

1. You and your class should find it worthwhile to see how some of the agencies that guard the health of your own community work. Below is a partial list of agencies and offices guarding health in Manhattan Borough, New York City:
   As part of the Department of Health: Birth and Death Records, Health

Centers, Child Health, Contagious Diseases, District Health Services, Food Complaints, Food Poisoning, Health Education, Research Laboratories, Public Health Nursing, Poison Control, Preventable Disease, Radiation Control, Sanitary Engineering, Sanitary Inspection, School Health, Social Hygiene, Tuberculosis, Vaccinations, and Veterinary Medicine.

Other large departments concerned with community health: Department of Sanitation, Health and Hospitals Corporation, and Department of Water Resources.

Then there are comparatively new departments: Department of Air Resources, Office of Emergency Control Board-Civil Defense, and Mental Health and Mental Retardation Services.

If you and some of your classmates would like to do some research on community health, you might first make up a list for your own community like that given above. A smaller community would probably not require such a large number of offices. With your teacher's approval, you could then visit some of the agencies (after making sure that your presence would be welcome). Try to arrange an interview with an official, and, if possible, arrange for a class trip to observe the community water department or the garbage or sewage disposal plants.

Caution: Not more than one student should telephone or write to any one official. It is unfair to take up the time of busy men.

2. The booklet *Health Manpower Source Book,* Public Health Service Publication No. 263, Section 21, obtainable from the U. S. Government Printing Office, Washington, D. C. It shows the range of health fields and the variety of occupations in each field. Which occupations have you never heard of before? Choose two or three of the occupations that you know *least* about. Do library research or interview someone in these occupations to find out the training for and functions of the job. Report to your class what you have found out.

Probing Further

Careers and Opportunities in the Medical Sciences, by Arthur S. Freese, Dutton, 1971. This is an informative book that gives much insight into the lesser known medical professions. It gives accurate descriptions of the work of, for example, a medical computer programmer, a physicist working in the field of medicine, and a physical therapist. It will open your eyes as to the vast number and variety of medical specialists other than doctors and nurses.

Black Pioneers of Science and Invention, by Louis Haber, Harcourt Brace Jovanovich, 1970. This book tells of fourteen black scientists who have played important roles in this country's medical and industrial progress.

Health Careers Guidebook, National Health Council, Washington, D. C., 1965. An interesting book that includes many well-known and not so well-known careers in health.

Wanted: Medical Technologists, Public Affairs Pamphlet 442.

Mental Health Jobs Today and Tomorrow, Public Affairs Pamphlet 384.

A Career in Social Work, Public Affairs Pamphlet 458.

Do you have a future in one of these health careers? These pamphlets may help you decide. They are available at low cost from the Public Affairs Committee, 381 Park Avenue South, New York, 10016.

Routes of Contagion, by Andre Siegfried, Harcourt Brace Jovanovich, 1965. An interesting study of the paths by which diseases travel throughout the world.

Health Concepts in Action

Does this statement help express what you have learned?

> **The community organizes to promote the physical and mental health of its members.**

Applying this concept of community health, which health practices would you

— continue?

— change?

— begin?

Will you now, as a result of your study, change any of your health objectives?

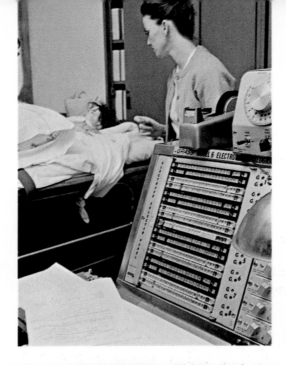

Each year, many young men and women become qualified to join the health force of the nation. Some become doctors and nurses. Many more choose to serve our health needs in other ways, for the opportunities in the field of health are many and varied. In the following photographic tour through a large, modern hospital, you will see some of the many functions that must be fulfilled to provide vital health services.

One of the important people in a smoothly functioning hospital is the **admissions interviewer,** who records personal data of patients. These records, like medical records, are kept on file by **medical record clerks.** Determining a course of treatment requires extensive examination by **doctors** (*right, bottom*) and, sometimes, testing by other specially trained people, such as the **electroencephalograph technician** who records brain-wave activity (*right, top* and *center*).

Another person who helps doctors to reach a diagnosis is the **X-ray technician,** who takes X-ray photographs of troublesome areas (*right, top*). The doctor interprets the photographs, sometimes with the help of a **radiologist,** a doctor with special training in this work. Problems that show externally may be photographed by the **medical photographer** (*below*). These visual records are kept on file as part of the patient's medical record and for teaching purposes.

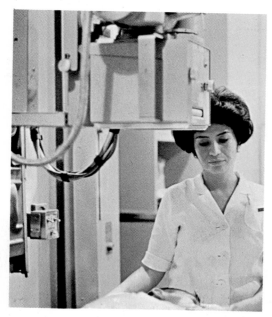

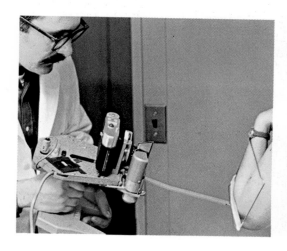

Learning is a never-ending process within a hospital. In the emergency room, where quick decisions save lives, young **interns** and **nurses** work with more experienced colleagues. Here, and in recovery rooms and intensive care units, there are often **inhalation-therapy technicians** who observe seriously ill patients and administer oxygen or mechanical breathing aids when necessary, freeing doctors and nurses to concentrate on other problems.

/ **567**

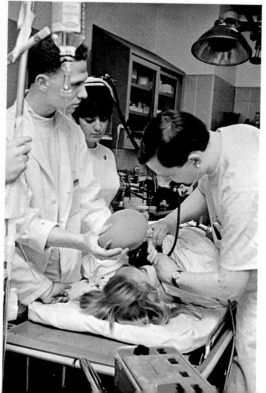

Many people who perform valuable health services in a hospital are never seen by the patients who benefit from their help. These **certified laboratory assistants** make tests on blood specimens taken from patients. They count the white blood cells, check the hemoglobin content and clotting ability, and look for abnormal blood cells.

In the blood bank, reserves of blood are always on hand to replace blood lost because of accidents, operations, or disease. The blood may be obtained from a large blood-collecting center or from people who donate blood at the hospital. Before it is stored, **blood banking technologists** carefully determine the blood type (*right*). **Laboratory aides** in the blood bank keep the storage facilities at the proper temperature and keep track of dates on the containers, since blood cannot be stored indefinitely.

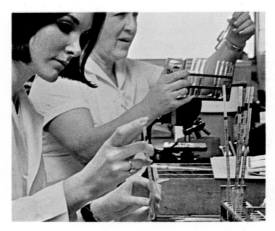

Medical technicians in the bacteriology laboratory aid doctors in identifying the exact cause of patients' infections so that proper treatment can be instituted. Samples from infected areas are streaked on dishes containing a sterile nutritive medium. The dishes are then stored under conditions that encourage the growth of bacteria. If bacteria are present, they will grow into a colony and can be identified. The doctor then prescribes the antibiotic that is most effective against the bacteria.

In many large hospitals, research into the causes and possible cures of diseases is carried on. A variety of specialists such as **microbiologists, pathologists,** and even **electronic-computer operators** may be involved in a research project.

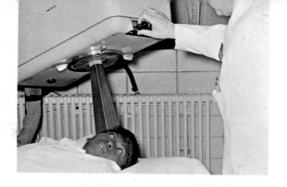

In the histology laboratory (*below*), a **histologic technician** slices tissues into very thin sections, each of which is then mounted on a slide and stained to bring out its characteristics. A doctor who is a **pathologist** examines the stained slides under a microscope to determine if the tissue is diseased and the nature of the disease.

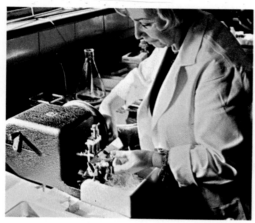

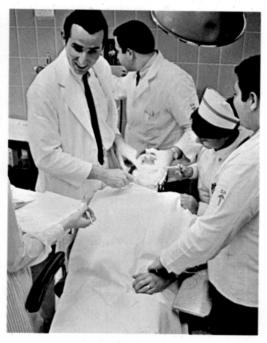

Doctors who work in a hospital often complete many additional years of schooling and training after earning their medical degrees in order to become specialists. This means that they are highly qualified to practice medicine in a particular field. The doctor in the top photograph at the right, for example, is a **radiologist**, who uses X rays and other forms of radiation to treat cancer and certain other diseases. Another type of specialist is the **surgeon** (*right, bottom*). Many large hospitals have at least one **dentist** and **dental assistant** (*right, center*) on the staff to care for dental problems associated with disease and to perform oral surgery.

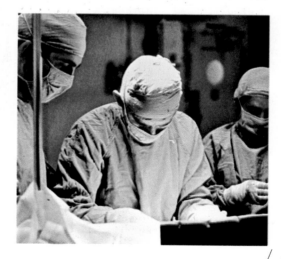

Through rehabilitation, patients are helped to return to a normal life after their illness has been cured. The **audiologist** below is testing a patient's hearing, while the **physical therapist** (*bottom, left*) and the **occupational therapist** (*bottom, center*) direct patients in activities that will help them to regain muscular strength. The **pediatric nurse** (*bottom, right*) has had special training in dealing with the problems of hospitalized children.

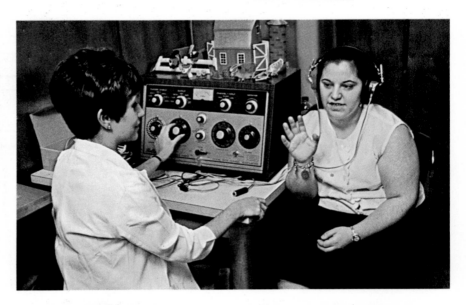

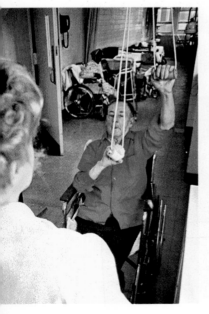

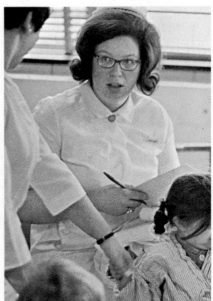

Directing the kitchen staff, planning meals for patients and staff, and providing special diets are among the responsibilities of the **dietitian** (*top, left*). The **hospital administrator** (*bottom, left*) makes sure that all facets of the hospital function smoothly, including the **payroll and accounting departments** (*bottom, right*). Amidst all the activities of the hospital, training of medical students, the future members of the health team, goes on (*top, right*).

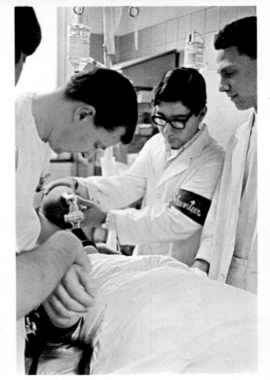

One good way to investigate career opportunities in the health field is to work as a **hospital volunteer,** as the teen-agers shown on this page do. Volunteer work enables you to help others while you determine your reactions to a possible future career.

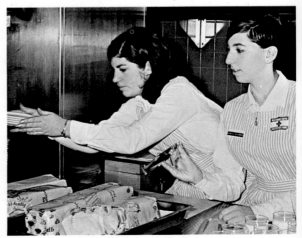

You have not met all the people who help to run the hospital on this photographic tour. There are the **heating and maintenance staffs,** the **groundskeepers,** the **orderlies,** the **medical librarians,** **ambulance attendants,** and many others who perform essential work. Remember, too, that many opportunities for health careers exist outside the confines of a hospital. **Public health service, teaching, medical editing or writing,** and **social work** are only a few of the other careers you may wish to explore.

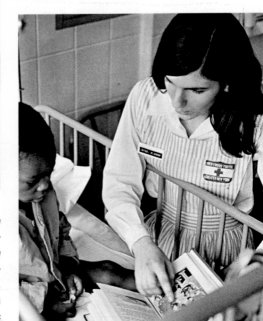

32 / The Big Killers — Heart Disease and Cancer

With the advance of science, our disease problems have changed. Infectious diseases that were once deadly have become just pages in medical history books. For example, the development of good sanitation has made typhoid a rare disease, and the establishment of tight quarantine ended yellow fever in the United States.

But as old, dreaded diseases have been conquered, certain chronic diseases and diseases connected with aging have taken their place as major health problems.

A PROBE INTO CHRONIC DISEASES — How can you reduce the risk of developing heart disease or cancer? To help you find out, you will be probing these questions:

1. What are the leading causes of death in the United States?

2. What can be done to prevent rheumatic heart disease?

3. Which is the commonest form of heart disease? What factors may contribute to the development of diseases of the heart and blood vessels?

4. What are some causes of stroke?

5. How do malignant and benign tumors differ?

6. What are the "seven danger signals?" Why should medical advice be sought as soon as one of these symptoms appears?

7. How does the microscope help in diagnosing cancer?

HEART DISEASE—THE MAJOR KILLER

Today, the major killers are diseases of the heart and blood vessels—including stroke—and cancer. The many advances in medicine have enabled people to live longer today than ever before, and more people are surviving to an age when these diseases tend to occur. Hence, the incidence of these diseases is increasing. Presently, heart diseases, stroke, and cancer account for about seven out of every ten deaths in the United States.

Congenital Heart Defects

A *congenital* (con-JEN-ih-tol) heart defect is one that a person is born with and is due to abnormal development of the heart before birth. In this country between 30,000 and 40,000 children are born with congenital heart defects each year. There are many kinds of congenital abnormalities of the

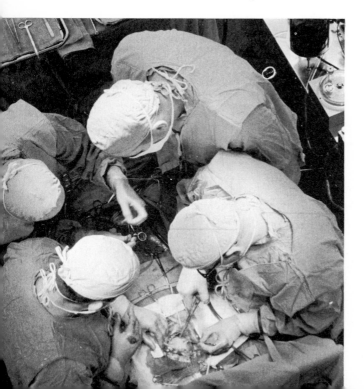

32-1 Open-heart surgery can correct many congenital heart defects. How do congenital defects differ from other heart defects?

heart. The most common defect is holes in the *septa,* or sheets of muscle, that divide the left side of the heart from the right side. Other kinds of congenital abnormalities include abnormal positioning of the major blood vessels around the heart and the failure of a small connection between the aorta and the pulmonary artery to close after birth. Sometimes babies are born with only one ventricle, a condition known as a three-chambered heart. The septum that normally divides the two ventricles does not develop. The congenital defects we have listed allow the mixing of arterial and venous blood, resulting in a "blue baby." A blue or pale purple discoloration of the baby's skin is a symptom of the insufficient oxygen distribution. The more proper name for the condition is *cyanosis* (sy-uh-NO-sis); it must be corrected by surgery. Often, two or more congenital defects occur in the same heart.

Many of the heart defects can be corrected by heart surgery. The development of *heart-lung machines* permits surgeons to open the heart while the flow of blood is by-passed around the heart through the machine. It allows surgeons to perform time-consuming, complicated open-heart surgery with much less danger to the patient.

Rheumatic Heart Disease

A type of heart disease that appears in children and young adults is rheumatic heart disease. This kind of heart disease may be the aftermath of repeated *streptococcal* infections in some susceptible persons; therefore such infections should be carefully followed by the physician.

Weeks after the streptococcal infection, some children or teen-agers may develop rheumatic fever. In some cases, not only do the joints become inflamed and painful but the heart may be affected as well. During the time that the heart is affected, it functions poorly. Far more frequently, however, the

32-2 This is a heart-lung machine. Until this complicated piece of equipment was developed, it was impossible to perform life-saving open-heart surgery.

A key feature of the machine is its ability to handle blood gently, thus conserving the natural properties of the blood. The machine includes a pump, heat exchanger, blood filter, and bubble trap.

case of rheumatic fever is mild and does not cause severe problems.

However, the valves of the heart may be affected, and as healing occurs, they become scarred. Repeated attacks of rheumatic fever may cause further scarring. Scarring may damage the heart valves and thus cause a strain on the heart muscle. If the damage is mild, particularly if it is limited to only one valve, there may be no symptoms at all because the strain on the heart is slight. If, however, the damage is more severe, then a greater stress is placed on the heart, and over the years the strain may begin to tell.

At first, the heart muscle responds to the strain by becoming thicker. Later, the muscle begins to weaken and stretch, and the heart enlarges. The enlarged heart is not as efficient. It cannot pump out blood in quantities sufficient to meet the needs of the body. Thus, more blood flows into it than can be pumped out with each heartbeat.

When a patient has rheumatic heart disease

with damaged valves it is often possible to operate on the valves. Narrowed valves are widened and leaky ones are repaired or replaced.

To avoid the possibility of rheumatic fever, streptococcal sore throats should not be neglected. Anyone who has a sore throat should consult his doctor to make certain that the condition is not caused by streptococci. This is particularly true of people who have had rheumatic fever in the past, since it is repeated inflammation that damages the heart.

The best way to avoid rheumatic heart disease is to prevent the recurrence of rheumatic fever. This is now widely accomplished by giving children who have had rheumatic fever sulfa drugs or penicillin or another antibiotic all year round in order to prevent the development of a streptococcal infection. If a child never gets a streptococcal infection, he cannot get rheumatic fever or develop rheumatic heart disease.

Other Valvular Diseases

A valve in the heart known as the aortic valve, which leads from the left ventricle to the aorta, may become damaged and leaky from infection or other causes. This creates the condition known as *aortic insufficiency.* Or the wall of the aorta itself may become weakened and balloon out, causing a condition known as *aortic aneurysm.*

Aortic aneurysm and insufficiency can sometimes be treated by surgery, but often this is a difficult technical problem.

In the past, syphilitic heart disease was an important cause of aortic disease. Syphilis, if untreated in its early stages, goes into a long latent period when a patient shows no symptoms of disease at all. But during this time, heart damage can occur. The best way to avoid syphilitic heart disease is to prevent syphilis. With widespread testing for syphilis and treatment with penicillin and other antibiotics, syphilitic heart disease is gradually vanishing. However, with the recent increase in venereal disease among teen-agers, the threat of new cases of syphilitic heart disease concerns many public health officials.

Heart Failure

Heart failure refers to the failure of the heart to carry on its work properly because it has been weakened by some disease.

With heart failure, the tissues of the body become congested. When the left side of the heart fails, the lungs become congested, the patient develops difficulty in breathing, and often he cannot breathe comfortably lying down. When he tries to walk or run, he finds himself quickly getting out of breath. When the right side of the heart fails, fluid collects in the tissues, usually first in the legs about the ankles, causing swelling. Later, this fluid accumulates in the many organs in the abdominal cavity, and later it accumulates in the chest.

Hypertensive Heart Disease

A common form of heart disease among middle-aged and older people is *hypertensive heart disease.* It occurs in some people who have long-standing high blood pressure, or *hypertension.* When the blood pressure is high, the heart muscle pumps harder, and this may eventually strain the heart and blood vessels and even other organs, such as the kidneys.

High blood pressure arises from different causes. Drugs, restricted diet, and other treatments are now available to control most cases of high blood pressure.

Cardiac Arrhythmias

Another group of heart diseases includes disorders of the rhythm of the heartbeat. These are known as the *cardiac arrhythmias* (ar-RITH-me-uhs). There are many kinds of arrhythmias. In some, the heartbeat is abnormally slow, and there is a long pause between one beat and the next, during which time the blood pressure tends to fall. Thus, not enough blood flows to the tissues, particularly to the brain. When this occurs, people may have fainting spells. In other forms of arrhythmia, the heartbeat is abnormally fast, sometimes regular and sometimes irregular. This condition is called *fibrillation* (fib-ril-LAY-shun). When the heart beats very rapidly, it becomes inefficient. One beat follows the next so quickly that the heart does not have time to fill with blood between beats. Each heartbeat, therefore, pumps out a very small amount of blood. The effect is a reduction in the total output of blood from the heart.

Arrhythmia may occur in the presence of other forms of heart disease, such as acute rheumatic fever or heart failure. It may also occur as an accompaniment of other diseases, as a result of drugs that are used to treat heart disease when the heart muscle is damaged, injured, or inflamed, or as a result of heavy smoking or excessive nervous tension and stress.

The treatment of arrhythmias depends on their cause and type. They can be corrected by the use of a variety of drugs and with a device that shocks the heart with a brief jolt of direct electric current. Drugs have also proven useful in preventing certain arrhythmias in situations where they are likely to develop.

Coronary Artery Disease

The commonest form of heart disease is coronary artery disease. The heart muscle, like all other tissues of the body, has to be supplied with blood. It gets its blood supply from the coronary arteries that arise just outside the heart. As people get older, these arteries tend to become hardened and narrowed. This condition is known as *arteriosclerosis*. If the arteries become hardened as a result of cholesterol deposits in the blood-vessel walls, the condition is called *atherosclerosis*. You read about this in Chapter 3. Genetics may also play a role. The incidence of atherosclerosis in some families is striking. But in whatever manner genetic factors may be involved, an abnormally high level of certain fats and cholesterol in the blood may be the significant observable cause in many patients — or so many doctors believe. When coronary arteries are narrowed, the heart muscle does not receive as much blood as it needs, particularly at times when the demands on it are greatest, such as during exercise or stress. When this happens, the patient may suffer a tightness or squeezing pain called *angina pectoris* (an-JY-na PEK-tor-is). It is relieved fairly quickly by rest. Angina pectoris is a warning sign to the patient that he is doing too much, and that he should rest because his heart muscle is working too hard. The treatment of angina pectoris usually involves giving drugs

that widen or dilate the narrowed coronary arteries, thus improving the flow of blood and relieving the pain.

Sometimes a small blood clot blocks one of the coronary arteries, particularly at a site where it is narrowed by arteriosclerosis or atherosclerosis. When this happens, the patient suffers a heart attack, or *coronary thrombosis*. Blood cannot flow through the blood vessel, and the heart muscle beyond is deprived of its blood supply and dies.

Doctors do not know why blood clots form inside blood vessels. The roughening of the lining of the blood vessels from cholesterol deposits may be a factor. Other things that seem to be related are stress and tension, heavy cigarette smoking, obesity, overeating, and possibly sudden excessive physical stress.

When a person suffers a heart attack, he usually is stricken with pains in his chest, similar to, but generally far more severe than, the pain of angina pectoris. Instead of going away quickly with rest, the pain tends

32-3 Making an electrocardiogram is one of the important steps in diagnosing heart disease. Are the results always conclusive?

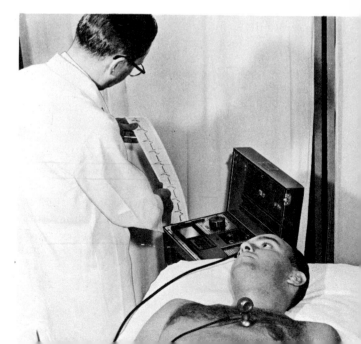

to persist. Sometimes patients have heart attacks with very little pain and occasionally without any symptoms at all. Doctors find *electrocardiograms* useful in diagnosing heart attacks. An electrocardiogram is a magnified line record of the electrical impulses formed in the heart. The electrical impulses travel from the patient through wires to the *electrocardiograph* where they are magnified a thousand times and are recorded. Usually afflicted patients show certain characteristic changes in the cardiograms. However, it may take several days or more before these changes become evident. A number of blood tests, in addition to the cardiogram, may help the doctor make the diagnosis. Often he has to keep a patient under observation for several days, repeating the cardiograms and blood tests every day, before he can be sure whether or not the patient suffered a heart attack.

When a heart attack occurs, the patient is put to bed. Often medicines are given to thin the blood and prevent further clotting. The patient is usually kept at rest for a period of several weeks until the heart has mended and scar tissue has formed. Then the patient is gradually allowed to resume activities but generally is kept under observation, and often very extreme activities are not permitted. Many patients, after recovering from a heart attack, lead long, productive, and active lives, scarcely limited at all by their healed heart injury.

Your Feelings and Your Heart

Your feelings may affect your heart in a number of ways. Stress, anxiety, and emotional tension can raise blood pressure and accelerate the pulse. Whether or not stress has a direct relationship to heart attacks is not entirely clear. Certainly factors other than stress play a role in coronary heart disease, coronary thrombosis, and high blood pressure. People with heart disease are more likely to worry about themselves and, thus, a vicious cycle may be established, with anxiety and stress aggravating heart disease and the heart disease aggravating the anxiety and stress.

Social and Environmental Effects upon the Heart

While all of the causes of hardening of the arteries are not known, it is evident to doctors that social and environmental factors play a role. There seems to be little doubt that eating habits are related to atherosclerosis. In populations whose diet is rich in fat, particularly meat and dairy products, the incidence of atherosclerosis tends to be higher than in populations that eat less well. Nevertheless, many people who eat rich foods never develop atherosclerosis, and others on a very deprived dietary intake may develop the disease.

Evidence that smoking plays a role in heart disease and is a contributory factor in death from coronary heart disease, in particular, is rapidly accumulating. The incidence of hardening of the arteries is higher at any given age in heavy smokers than in nonsmokers, and life expectancy for smokers is much lower than for nonsmokers. It appears that cigarette smoking increases the heart's need for oxygen but also decreases the amount of oxygen available for use by the heart.

Drinking does not appear to affect the heart except in severe alcoholics who may develop a kind of heart disease thought to be associated with nutritional disturbances.

Another environmental factor that may have an important relationship to heart disease and the development of heart attacks is the increased tensions that our environment and society place upon us. Most medical scientists feel that good physical fitness, adequate exercise, avoidance of overeating, and restriction of smoking are the best things for protecting the heart.

Recent Contributions to the Health of the Heart

In the last decade, many advances have been made in the treatment of heart disease. Methods for surgical correction of various kinds of heart defects have been of great importance, particularly to people afflicted with disease of the valves or with various forms of congenital heart defects. The development of heart-lung machines has permitted surgeons to do open-heart surgery. The development of plastic material to replace damaged valves, or close holes, or replace damaged parts of blood vessels has also been a great advance. Another development is *electronic pacemakers*, which make the heart beat at a proper rate in certain disorders of the heartbeat. In addition, there is a variety of electronic equipment that permits doctors and nurses to monitor the heart action of patients who have had heart attacks, and to treat sudden disturbances in rate, rhythm, or even the sudden cessation of the heartbeat. This care is often administered in **intensive care units** of the hospital.

Many new drugs have also been developed to treat heart disease and to deal with various types of emergencies that may affect the heart. One of the newest of these drugs brings down the cholesterol level and, hopefully, may slow down or prevent the development of atherosclerosis. It may even cause regression of the disease. But it will be many years before the effects of this drug have been adequately evaluated.

Heart Transplants

Millions of persons who have died of heart disease might still be alive and in good health if a successful substitute for their own failing hearts could have been transplanted into their chests. Victims of fatal accidents frequently have healthy hearts that possibly could replace the incurably weak-

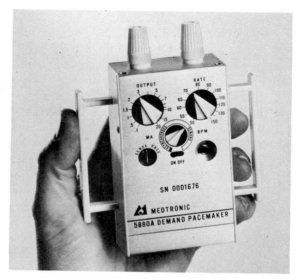

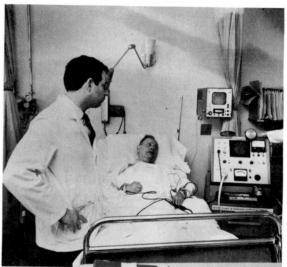

32-4 *(Top)* An electronic pacemaker that is worn strapped to the chest. *(Bottom)* A patient in an intensive care unit. Notice the machines that monitor his heart and breathing.

ened hearts of others. In 1967 and 1968, many heart transplants were performed. Heart patients received living hearts, and their own diseased hearts were removed, *immediately* after the death of other people

32-5 Some current directions in heart surgery. (*Left*) Damaged parts are being replaced by artificial parts, such as this heart valve. It is made of highly polished metal, silicon rubber, and Teflon—materials that can be safely implanted in the body. (*Right*) A nuclear-powered artificial heart is being developed as an alternative to heart transplants.

whose healthy hearts were made available. The first heart transplant was performed in Capetown, South Africa. Dr. Christian Barnard performed this surgery. Unfortunately the increasing number of subsequent heart transplants did not prove encouraging. We must look into the body's natural defenses against germs and other "foreign" materials to understand the kinds of problems that arose in heart transplants.

You have read about the body's defenses against bacteria and other invaders. If germs manage to invade the tissues and escape being destroyed by white blood cells or digested by enzymes, they still may have to face antibodies which may destroy them or make the germs and their products harmless. As you read on page 535, our bodies tend to make antibodies and to "reject" not only disease germs, but also any other living thing or substance that invades our tissues. This is the main reason why almost all of the

early attempts at transplanting hearts and other organs were failures. The body's methods of defending itself against germs, transplanted organs, and other "foreign bodies" are called *immune reactions.*

When a heart is transplanted, the medical team attempts to suppress the immune reactions enough to prevent the rejection of the organ by the patient's body. This raises a serious problem: to find drugs that will check both the small lymphocytes that make antibodies and the larger white blood cells that destroy bacteria, dead tissue cells, and eventually the transplanted organ. X-ray treatment, and certain drugs, can suppress the immune reaction, but doctors must maintain a fine balance between too much of these treatments—which would leave the patient open to fatal attack by many different disease germs—and too little—which would allow the body's blood cells and antibodies to act upon and destroy the transplanted organ.

How these difficult problems can be solved successfully will make fascinating reading for you as you follow events in heart (and other organ) transplants in the nation's newspapers and magazines. Many doctors believe that success is relatively near and that organ transplants may soon add years of life to many cases now considered hopeless.

STROKE

Stroke is caused by a stoppage of blood supply to part of the brain, or by hemorrhage in the brain. The most common form of stroke is **cerebral thrombosis,** a condition that affects the brain in the same way that a heart attack affects the heart muscle. A clot forms in a blood vessel leading to the brain, usually a vessel narrowed by arteriosclerosis. When such a clot forms, the area of the brain normally fed by that vessel is damaged.

The symptoms of a stroke depend on what part of the brain is affected. The most common symptom is paralysis of the side of the body opposite the side of the brain affected by the blood clot. In mild cases there may be only a slight weakness involving the arm or leg. In severe cases the entire side of the body, including the face, becomes paralyzed. The patient often has difficulty with speech or swallowing.

Recovery after a stroke may be limited or almost complete, and may be fast or may take as long as a year or two. Physical and speech therapy may aid a patient to recover some of the functions he has lost and teach him to use other muscles to do the work of paralyzed ones.

Sometimes a stroke results from a blood clot in an artery leading into the brain at a point in the neck. Some of these strokes can be treated by surgery. With the removal of the clot, the flow of blood through the vessel is reestablished.

In a stroke caused by hemorrhage, blood leaks from a small tear, or rupture, in a weakened segment of the wall of a blood vessel supplying part of the brain. Severe, long-term hypertension might be a contributing cause. If the blood vessel involved is small and the bleeding is not too great, the symptoms may be indistinguishable from those of most strokes caused by a blood clot. More often, however, the bleeding is of a considerable degree, and the effects are more severe. Usually a patient so affected will quickly lose consciousness. We say that he has suffered a **cerebral hemorrhage.**

Occasionally, brain hemorrhage occurs when a blood vessel has a congenital defect with an area of weakness in its wall that balloons out. This is called an *aneurysm.* You will recall our discussion of aortic aneurysms on page 576. These aneurysms occasionally burst, leading to severe headache and often loss of consciousness and death. When patients survive bleeding from ruptured aneurysms, they are sometimes operated upon, either to remove the aneurysm, if it is accessible, or to tie off the blood vessel involved. This will stop the bleeding and prevent its recurrence.

Another type of stroke, which occurs only rarely, is known as **cerebral embolism** (EM-buh-liz'm). A blood clot that is formed elsewhere in the body, usually within the heart, breaks from its lodging and is carried through the bloodstream into the blood vessels leading to the brain and eventually lodges in an artery where the size of the vessel is too small to permit it to go any further. This plugs the artery.

Measures being taken to reduce diseases of the blood vessels should also reduce the incidence of strokes.

CANCER

Cancer is one of the most dreaded of all diseases because most people believe that cancer always progresses to death. This, of course, is not at all true. Some types of cancer grow so slowly that they cause no trouble for many years. Some seem hardly to grow at all. Many others make their presence known early enough that, when properly treated with drugs, surgery, or radiation, cures can be obtained in a large percentage of cases. One of the most important reasons for death from cancer is delay between the time the first symptoms appear and the time the patient seeks treatment. A good example of this involves breast cancer. If all patients were treated when cancer was first detected, the rate of cure would probably be well over two thirds. Unfortunately, on the average, almost a year passes between the time the first symptom of cancer is noticed and the time treatment is begun.

What Is Meant by Benign and Malignant Tumors?

Tumors are a type of abnormal growth of tissue. Some tumors have certain characteristics that doctors call **malignant** (muh-LIG-nant). These tumors are cancers. Other tumors do not have the characteristics of a malignant or cancerous tumor and are called **benign** (be-NINE). Examples of some benign tumors are warts and fatty tumors. Cysts are also benign tumors. Benign tumors are characterized by the fact that they are contained inside a capsule, do not invade surrounding tissue, and never spread to distant parts of the body.

When the cells of a benign tumor are viewed under the microscope, they look like the tissue from which they arose, and they are growing in an orderly fashion. Benign tumors often cause no ill effects at all. When they do, the effects are created by simple pressure of the tumor on surrounding structures.

At times, benign tumors arise in glands that produce hormones, and then the patient

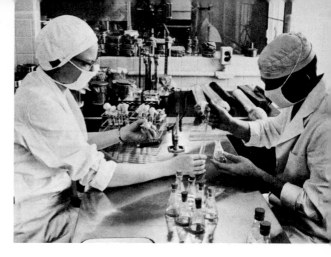

32-6 These research workers are investigating a virus that causes leukemia in chickens.

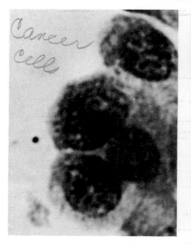

32-7 Early cancer of the neck of the uterus (cervix) may be detected by the Papanicolaou test, or "Pap smear." Scraped-off cells are examined under the microscope. Pre-cancerous or cancer cells (*left*) appear quite different from normal cells (*right*).

may develop symptoms of too much of that hormone in the body. For example, if a benign tumor arises on the thyroid gland, a person may develop symptoms of excessive thyroid function, or *hyperthyroidism*.

Treatment of benign tumors is usually effective. If treatment is required, it is accomplished in most cases by surgical removal of the tumor. Benign tumors rarely recur, and, therefore, pose no serious threat.

Cancers, or malignant tumors, generally grow much more rapidly than benign tumors and are not contained inside a capsule. Some types of cancer tend to spread into the surrounding tissues, often destroying them. As a cancer spreads into surrounding tissues, it invades small blood vessels and lymphatic channels, and cancer cells are often carried away from the original cancer by the blood and lymph. The vast majority of the cells carried away in this fashion do not survive. But some may begin to grow and multiply elsewhere in the body. This spread of cancerous growth is called *metastasis* (meh-TAS-tuh-sis). Metastasis can take place in almost any part of the body, but it occurs most often in the lymph nodes, the liver, the lungs, the bones, and the brain.

Under the microscope, cancer cells usually do not look like normal cells, but appear to be poorly organized. Many cells are dividing, indicating that they are being produced at an uncontrolled rate.

Types of Cancer

Cancers are of several types. One type, called *carcinomas* (kar-sin-OH-muhs), arises from epithelial tissue, such as the lining of the air tubes of the lungs, or the lining of the stomach, or the outer layers of the skin. Another type, called *sarcomas* (sar-KOM-uhs), arises from supporting structures, such as bones, cartilage, and other fibrous and connective tissue. A group of cancers related to sarcomas includes those arising from blood-forming organs and lymph glands. This group includes the *leukemias* and the *lymphomas* (lim-FOM-uhs). Leukemias behave as though they were cancers of the blood. Although some experts believe they are not true cancers, they are usually classified as such and behave generally in the same manner that cancers do.

Do We Know What Causes Cancer?

Although many theories have been proposed, the causes of cancer remain unknown. It is possible that certain underlying factors make a person a potential cancer victim but that cancer only occurs in the presence of certain other factors. Some scientists in the field of cancer research have suggested that we are all born with cells that have the capacity to become cancerous but that we all possess a variety of defenses, or containing mechanisms, that hold these cells in check and prevent them from becoming cancerous. It is possible that the disease that we recognize as cancer represents some impairment of the resistance that normally prevents such cells from growing. The same *immune reactions* (page 580) that have caused patients to reject heart transplants may be useful in protecting persons against cancer cells.

While we do not know what the underlying factors are, there is some suggestion, at least in some types of cancer, that heredity may play a role. In some animals, such as mice, strains can be developed that have a high incidence of cancer.

Much is known about some of the factors that may stimulate certain kinds of cancer. For example, we know that cancer of the skin may develop in an area that is subject to continued irritation. Cancer of the skin of the face is much more common in people who are exposed to sunlight and wind than in people who spend much of their life indoors. Cancer of the lip may occur in pipe-smokers. Lung cancer occurs much more commonly in people who smoke a great deal than it does in nonsmokers. Cancers in other tissues or organs are also more common in individuals subject to chronic forms of irritation.

Cancers may develop after repeated exposure to radiation. Years ago, it was common practice to give X-ray treatment for certain types of arthritis of the spine and for inflamed tonsils. Many years later, it became evident that a certain percentage of those people who had been treated with X rays developed leukemia, and some patients who had their tonsils frequently X-rayed developed cancers of the thyroid.

Another theory is that some cancers are related to virus infections. Animal studies have suggested that some leukemias and certain other types of cancers may be caused by viruses or in some way may be stimulated by the presence of certain types of virus infections. The theory that virus infection of some sort is related to cancer is the subject of intensive study in many research institutions throughout the world.

Whatever the cause, cancer represents a form of uncontrolled growth. The normal mechanisms that allow growth to proceed in an orderly and controlled fashion appear to have been lost. Many cells of our body are reproducing at very rapid rates all of the time. We are constantly making new red blood cells at a fantastic rate, and yet cancer does not usually develop in the bone marrow. The cells lining our intestinal tract are constantly being replaced and yet this, too, is growth that proceeds in an orderly fashion. When cancerous tumors occur, the order and the control are missing. When scientists know more about normal tissue growth, they will have a better understanding of the growth of cancers.

Helping to Detect Cancer

It is important to remember that early cancers seldom reveal themselves by causing pain. But there are seven danger signals of which you should be aware. Keep in mind that these signs may be symptoms of other diseases, but the appearance of any one of the symptoms that are listed should be immediately investigated by your doctor.

1. Any sore that fails to heal properly.
2. Any lump or thickening in the breast or elsewhere in the body.
3. Any unusual bleeding or discharge.
4. Any change in the appearance of a wart or mole, and any new growth on the skin.
5. Persistent indigestion or difficulty in swallowing.
6. Persistent hoarseness or cough.
7. Any change in normal bowel habits.

To these danger signs should be added any unexplained loss of weight or chronic feeling of fatigue. Occasionally, a cancer that causes no symptoms may be detected in the course of a routine physical examination.

Where and How Often Does Cancer Occur?

Cancer kills almost a third of a million people annually. While more common in older people, it does occur among young adults and even infants and children. The frequency and type of cancer differ according to the part of the world one lives in and one's age group and sex. Thus, certain types of bone cancers are most common in children. Lung cancer is much more common in men than in women. Liver cancer, rare in this country, is one of the most common forms of cancer in the Orient. Frequency patterns also change with time. Thirty years ago cancer was more frequent in females; now it is more frequent in males. Stomach cancer was the most common type of cancer in males thirty years ago, and lung cancer was rare; now lung cancer is common, and stomach cancer occurs much less frequently.

Skin cancer and lung cancer are the most frequent forms of cancer in men today. Other common cancer sites in males are the prostate gland, colon and rectum, stomach, and pancreas. Among women, the common sites are the skin, breast, colon and rectum, uterus, ovary, and stomach.

The Treatment of Cancer

The treatment of cancer in many cases is surgical—the cancerous tissue is removed by an operation.

Some types of cancer, however, are best treated by radiation, which is given either through X-ray treatment or through the use of cobalt or other radioactive materials known as *radioisotopes.* Often surgery is used in combination with radiation of one form or another.

In recent years, a number of chemical substances have been developed that are effective in treating certain forms of cancer, particularly the lymphomas and leukemias. The first of these was nitrogen mustard, a substance derived from poisonous mustard gas. Nitrogen mustards were developed in the early days of World War II when army chemists were studying derivatives of mustard gas for their potential use in gas warfare. Since then, many other chemicals that suppress certain cancerous growths have been developed. They have been effective in relieving symptoms and prolonging life for extended periods of time.

Sex hormones have proven helpful in certain types of cancers, particularly those arising from the sex organs. For example, symptoms of prostate cancers may respond well to treatment with female sex hormones, and breast cancers may respond to treatment with male hormones.

Research in the treatment of cancer continues. More effective chemical agents, methods of radiation, and surgical techniques are being developed each year.

What You Have Learned

What kind of health practices should you apply in maintaining your health? Check your understanding of the chapter. On a separate sheet of paper, number 1 through 24 and insert the answer from the vocabulary list below. Use each expression, but use each one only once.

aneurysm	electrocardiograms	malignant
angina pectoris	faint	metastasis
atherosclerosis	fibrillation	rheumatic fever
benign	heart failure	70 percent
blue baby	heart-lung machine	stroke
congenital	hemorrhage	syphilitic
coronary artery	hypertension	valves
coronary thrombosis	liver	warts

Heart disease, stroke, and cancer now account for about (1) _____ of all deaths in the United States. The commonest form of heart disease is (2) _____ disease. This condition is often preceded by pain called (3) _____. (4) _____ follows when a clot blocks an artery in the heart. Some babies are born with abnormally developed hearts. Such defects are called (5) _____ defects. A (6) _____ is born when such a defect allows arterial and venous blood to mix. Surgeons can now perform difficult heart operations in which they open the heart while the blood is by-passed through a (7) _____

(8) _____ follows some streptococcal infections. This disease often results in injury to the (9) _____ of the heart. A form of heart disease that is rapidly disappearing is (10) _____ heart disease. An (11) _____ is the ballooning out of the wall of a blood vessel. Swelling of the legs about the ankles may be a symptom of (12) _____. Strain on the heart due to overwork may result from high blood pressure, also called (13) _____ When there is a long pause between one heartbeat and the next, blood pressure tends to fall and a person may (14) _____. In (15) _____ on the other hand, the heart beats abnormally rapidly. Older people tend to suffer from (16) _____, in which cholesterol is deposited in blood vessel walls. In these patients, as in others, (17) _____ are useful in diagnosing heart attacks.

When the blood supply to a part of the brain is cut off, the result is likely to be a (18) _____. Sometimes this condition can be caused by (19) _____ in the brain.

(20) _____ growths are called cancers. (21) _____ growths, on the other hand, are contained within a capsule and never spread to distant parts of the body. Among growths of this kind are (22) _____ and cysts. Invasion of distant tissues by cells from a tumor elsewhere in the body is called (23) _____ Organs likely to be invaded in this way include the brain, the bones, and the (24) _____

What You Can Do

1. In each of the following sentences, the italicized word or words make the statement false. Replace the italicized words with those that will make the statement true. Then copy the corrected list of statements in your notebook.

   a. *Cerebral* arteries supply blood to heart muscle.
   b. *Warts* are malignant growths.
   c. Rheumatic fever may develop after a *virus* infection.
   d. The major cause of death in the United States is *stroke*.
   e. Metastasis is a very serious development in cases of *stroke*.
   f. Any defect with which a person is born is said to be *hereditary*.
   g. A blue or purple discoloration of the skin may be called *apoplexy*.
   h. In atherosclerosis the artery walls are thickened by deposits of *carbohydrate*.
   i. A ballooning out of the wall of a blood vessel is called an *embolism*.
   j. Certain cancers may be caused by *protozoan* infections.

2. Good health practices, by individuals as well as by the community, are of the greatest importance in preserving life and health. Also vitally important, of course, are proper medical treatment and adequate cooperation by the sick person with the physician. For each of the conditions listed below, tell (a) what good personal health

practices would help to prevent the development of the condition, (b) what good community health practices could help to protect people from the condition, and (c) what medical treatment is likely to be most helpful for victims of the condition. If you cannot find that any personal or community health practices could prevent the condition, say so, and try to give an explanation as to why not.

a. congenital heart defects

b. rheumatic heart disease *Sore throat*

c. heart failure

d. high blood pressure

e. coronary artery disease

f. atherosclerosis

g. stroke

h. cancer - *Checkups*

Things to Try

1. You and your class can learn much about the nature of cancer and about modern developments in cancer treatment by following current articles in newspapers and magazines. The following magazine articles may be helpful in developing a report for your class: "The War on Cancer: Progress Report," *Newsweek,* February 22, 1971; "Perspectives on Cancer: Viral Link Elusive," *Science News,* February 19, 1972; "How Safe are X-rays?" *Today's Health,* June, 1968.

   The National Cancer Institute at Bethesda, Maryland, and your local chapter of the American Cancer Society will also supply helpful pamphlets.

2. You can write a valuable report on one of the topics related to the health of the heart. The subject could be: Transplanting Hearts; Your Heart and Sports; How to Protect Your Heart; What Can Be Done About Stroke?; Artificial Hearts or Heart Transplants—Which Goal for the Future?; How Smoking Affects the Heart.

   You can obtain free pamphlets from the American Heart Association and the Metropolitan Life Insurance Company on the prevention of heart disease. In addition, articles like the following offer useful information: "Heart Attack: Curbing the Killer," *Newsweek,* May 1, 1972; "Mending Hearts at Home," *Today's Health,* November, 1967; "What You Should Know About Strokes," *Today's Health,* August, 1968, "Fighting the Masked Crippler: Rheumatic Fever," *Today's Health,* March, 1968.

Probing Further

Cancer Explained, by Maurice Sutton, Hart, 1967. This readable book describes the current status of cancer treatment and some of the danger signals that should be investigated by a doctor to rule out cancer.

Cancer Facts and Figures, American Cancer Society. Your local division of the American Cancer Society will provide this up-to-date pamphlet as well as other valuable pamphlets on cancer.

Hypertension: High Blood Pressure, National Institute of Health, No. 1714.

A Handbook of Heart Terms, Public Health Service Publication No. 1073.

Rheumatic Fever Can Be Prevented, Public Health Service Publication No. 144.

Varicose Veins, Public Health Service Publication No. 154.

You can obtain the above pamphlets at low cost from the Superintendent of Documents, U. S. Government Printing Office, Washington, D. C. 20402.

Handbook of Heart Diseases, Blood Pressure, and Strokes, by C. Anthony D'Alonzo, Collier, 1962. A paperback that is interesting and easy to read.

Strokes, How They Occur, and What Can Be Done About Them, by Irving H. Page and others, Collier, 1963. This paperback gives helpful information about strokes.

Health Concepts in Action

Does this statement bring together ideas you have gained from this chapter?

> **Disease can be caused by impaired body structures that interfere with normal functioning.**

Applying this concept of chronic disease, which health practices would you

—continue?

—change?

—begin?

Will you now, as a result of your study, change any of your health objectives?

33 / *The Problem of Alcohol and Tobacco*

About forty boys and girls are waiting for the doors to open in front of a large city high school. Some are in groups, talking or laughing. Others stand alone. A few are trying to study. A dozen or more are puffing cigarettes, some with satisfaction, some really hating the taste of the tobacco.

One boy is embarrassed when he refuses a cigarette someone offers. He doesn't care for smoking, and his common sense tells him that it is a dangerous habit. Yet he feels miserable at the thought that the others in the group will look down on him.

A PROBE INTO CHOICES YOU MUST MAKE—Do the risks in smoking or drinking outweigh any possible advantages—for you? To help you decide, you will be probing these questions:

1. What is alcohol? Why does alcohol work so fast when one drinks it? How does it affect the drinker?

2. What are some of the social and psychological influences that encourage occasional drinking? heavy drinking?

3. What kinds of help are available for dealing with alcoholism?

4. What are some of the reasons for the widespread habit of smoking?

5. How does smoking affect organs of the respiratory system? circulatory system? digestive system?

6. Smoking is a contributing factor in certain diseases that affect the life span of smokers. What are some of these diseases?

C₂H₅OH   *ethyl alcohol*

THE USE AND ABUSE OF ALCOHOL

Alcohol is a drug. **Alcoholism** is a disease. These are about the only simple statements that can be made about the problem of alcohol. Alcoholism is one of the most complex health problems facing our nation.

The number of people in the United States who drink alcoholic beverages is estimated as high as 100 million. More than 6 million of these drinkers are believed to be "problem drinkers." That is, they have developed unhealthy drinking habits that interfere to varying degrees with their job performance, family responsibilities, and life in general.

What is Alcohol?

The alcohol we drink is **ethyl** (EHTH-il) **alcohol,** a simple compound (C_2H_5OH). It is produced by the fermentation of grain or fruit sugars by yeasts.

Scientific studies show that the effects of alcohol upon the body are that of a **depressant.** It acts upon the nervous system to slow down body functions. When a person drinks, his mental processes become dulled and he becomes less efficient at his tasks.

Yet many people take a drink "as a stimulant." They claim that they can work better, think more imaginatively, be stronger, funnier, and more clever when they have a few drinks. This is a false impression which they get from the way that alcohol affects the nervous system. Alcohol acts first upon the higher centers of the brain—those involved with judgment, worry, and inhibitions. When these centers are dulled, the drinker tends to feel a sense of elation and release. For someone who is tense and worried, the immediate effect of a small amount of alcohol may therefore be relaxing. It is for this kind of **sedative** purpose that a doctor occasionally prescribes a drink before dinner for some patients.

However, drinking alcohol is also an **intoxicant,** which is another way of saying that it has a harmful, toxic effect on body functions if taken in excess. In large amounts it is also a **hypnotic,** putting the drinker to sleep. It can also act as an **analgesic,** dulling pain without causing loss of consciousness.

There are many forms of alcohol used in medicine and industry. In medicine, alcohol is a component of important drugs. It is also used as a **disinfectant** in strong concentrations, to kill bacteria on the outside of the body.

Denatured alcohol, used for industrial purposes, is ethyl alcohol mixed with substances that make it poisonous if taken internally. Another kind of alcohol, **methyl** (METH-il) **alcohol,** is made from wood. Methyl alcohol is highly poisonous and has no medical uses.

Kinds of Alcoholic Beverages

There are basically three kinds of alcoholic beverages:

1. Beer and ale, which are produced by the action of yeast on a mash containing grain and malt. Beer contains about 4½ percent alcohol. Ale is slightly stronger, containing possibly 6 to 8 percent alcohol.

2. Wines, which are produced by the fermentation of fruit juices by yeast. They contain somewhat more alcohol than beer and ale, generally from 10 to 14 percent.

3. Whiskey, gin, rum, brandy, vodka, and other liquors, which are distilled beverages. These usually have an alcoholic content of between 40 and 50 percent, although some liquors may contain up to 60 or even 65 percent alcohol.

The term **proof** indicates the alcoholic content by a number which is twice the actual percentage of alcohol. Thus a drink that is 45 percent alcohol is called 90 proof. Pure or absolute alcohol is 200 proof.

methyl alcohol—made from wood poisonous

33-1 Is he really the "life of the party"? Or does he just *think* he is because alcohol has dulled his judgment?

Why Alcohol "Works So Fast"

The effects of alcohol are felt quickly because it begins to be absorbed as soon as the drink is taken. Absorption begins even before swallowing, because some alcohol is absorbed through the mucous membranes of mouth and throat.

When the alcohol reaches the stomach, it is rapidly absorbed into the bloodstream, passing directly through the walls of the stomach without being changed by any digestive process. Within a few minutes after taking a drink, detectable amounts of alcohol appear in the blood and shortly thereafter can be detected on the breath. About twenty percent of the total amount of alcohol that is consumed is absorbed from the stomach. The rest passes into the small intestine where it is absorbed about as quickly as it is received.

Absorption of alcohol is affected by a number of factors, the most important being the amount of food with which it is taken. Alcohol consumed on an empty stomach is absorbed much more rapidly than alcohol taken after a meal. The concentration of alcohol in the drink also affects the rate of absorption. Psychological factors that influence the emptying time of the stomach will affect absorption. The presence of certain other drugs in the body also affect absorption time.

The Body Rids Itself of Alcohol Slowly

Once absorbed from the digestive organs, alcohol is carried to the liver. The liver can oxidize only a small part of the alcohol at a time. The rest is carried in the blood throughout the body. The alcohol tends to concentrate in tissues that have the highest water content. The greatest concentration is in the nerves and brain.

The alcohol remains in the blood and tissues of the body until all of it is oxidized at the rather slow rate of about half an ounce an hour. Thus, it may take many hours to get rid of only a few drinks. A small percentage of alcohol that is not removed by oxidation is excreted through the lungs, the skin, and the kidneys.

33-2 Mixing drinking with driving is a major cause of tragic automobile accidents.

Effects of Alcohol on Behavior

Alcohol affects first the *cerebral cortex*, the part of the brain that controls the highest intellectual functions, such as judgment and the ability to reason. Therefore normal control of emotions may be lost, and behavior tends to become uncontrolled. An individual may grow silly or aggressive, depressed or irritable, and may be inclined to do things that he would not do under normal circumstances.

As the concentration of alcohol increases, the cerebellum and the rest of the nervous system are affected. Muscular coordination is impaired. Reaction time is slowed. Speech becomes thickened and slurred, and there is loss of ability to perceive things accurately.

If the concentration of alcohol rises still higher, consciousness is affected. A person may become sleepy and may actually pass into a coma. His blood pressure drops and his pulse is slowed. The rate of breathing is decreased and body temperature may drop. If the concentration of alcohol in the blood is as high as 0.50 percent, life is endangered.

When discussing smaller quantities, it is difficult to predict how much alcohol will produce a given effect in any given person. One person will act drunk after he has a single sip of champagne, while another can have five or six drinks and *appear* to be in control of himself. Even the same individual may react differently from time to time, depending on such factors as fatigue, physical condition, and food eaten recently.

Drinking and Driving

Thousands of Americans die each year as a result of automobile accidents that involve alcohol. There is actually no dividing line beyond which one can say a man is drunk. Nevertheless, safety experts point out that a person with only 0.04 percent alcohol in his blood is already influenced by the alcohol, and is not as safe a driver as he would normally be. This blood level of alcohol can appear in a 155-pound man who drinks rapidly just 3 ounces of 90-proof whiskey on an empty stomach.

Blood concentration of alcohol has given us a legal definition of drunkenness. According to the laws of some states, a driver is definitely intoxicated if the concentration is over 0.08 or 0.10 percent. Other states set a legal limit of 0.15 percent alcohol in the blood as a sign of intoxication. If the average person drinks two martinis before dinner, he will probably have a concentration close to 0.15 percent in his blood by the time he sits down to eat.

Social and Environmental Influences on Drinking

Why do so many people drink? Perhaps one of the greatest influences is advertising. Just turn on the television or open a magazine and you will see that drinking alcoholic beverages is linked with popularity and success. But there are other influences, too.

Socially, drinking is considered acceptable. In fact, many people who don't really like to drink find themselves drinking at business luncheons and cocktail parties. People tend to conform to what the society around them is doing. Of course, there are many people who do enjoy a drink or two. They may like the taste or find it relaxing at the end of a tense day. Certainly, the complexity of today's society with its fast pace of living has increased the number of drinkers. These people are not *alcoholics* or problem drinkers as long as they can control their drinking habits. Only if they develop a need for alcohol and find that it is a continuing and daily necessity are they problem drinkers.

Psychological Reasons for Drinking

Social and environmental reasons for drinking only tell part of the story. Many people drink for a number of psychological reasons. These people usually drink in excess and are called problem drinkers. Some people drink because they want to feel accepted. By drinking they may be able to "let themselves go" and become part of a group. Because of certain psychological or emotional problems they could not feel comfortable in a group situation unless they were drinking. When they drink, they feel more secure, competent, and in command of themselves and others. They like this feeling and continue to drink. Others drink because problems may have left their life with little meaning and they feel they have nothing better to do than to drink. Some drink as an escape from their problems. But, it is only a very temporary escape. When they wake up the next morning with an alcoholic hangover, the problems may loom larger than ever. Some drinkers cannot get along without alcohol. They are completely addicted and their lives revolve around drinking. These people are alcoholics—people who drink excessively and without control.

33-3 Many people drink for social reasons. Bars are popular meeting places, and cocktail parties are a common way of entertaining at home. Do you think it is necessary to drink to be sociable? *No*

33-4 The "morning after" often brings much physical and mental discomfort. This man is suffering from a hangover.

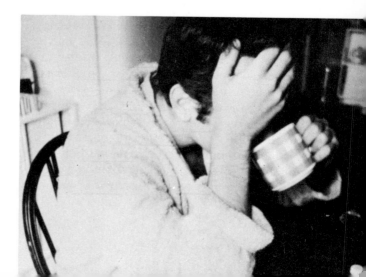

What Is Alcoholism?

The causes of alcoholism have been studied by many, but we still have few answers. However, alcoholism is now recognized as not only a disorder involving human behavior, but also an illness to be treated medically.

The problems of alcoholism involve not only medicine and psychology, but other fields such as law, criminology, religion, ethics, sociology, and economics. When people are for or against alcohol, many emotional attitudes are involved, and it becomes even more difficult to look at the problem of alcoholism objectively.

The alcoholic has been defined by the National Council on Alcoholism as "a person who is powerless to stop drinking and whose drinking seriously alters his normal living pattern." Sooner or later, alcoholism affects every phase of a person's life. It undermines the stability of the family and leads to dissension and often separation and divorce. Children in the family of an alcoholic are often neglected, both emotionally and financially. So for every alcoholic there are innocent victims of the disease.

Alcoholism also affects the productivity of the patient. It is difficult for an alcoholic to keep a job because he often stays home from work—and when at work, he produces much less than the nonalcoholic. Subsequent jobs become harder to find. The result is financial problems for the family.

As drinking continues, the alcoholic's health may be affected. Persons who drink heavily usually lose their appetite and eat poorly. Because of this, they often suffer vitamin deficiencies and other forms of malnutrition. These disorders lead to physical wasting, and often to intellectual impairment and disturbed behavior. Sometimes an alcoholic suffers from severe mental illness.

Many patients who drink heavily develop inflammation of the stomach. Drinking causes additional problems for ulcer patients. Liver disease is also very common among alcoholics. First, fat accumulates in the liver. Some people, if they continue to drink, develop *cirrhosis* of the liver, in which liver cells are replaced by scar tissue. Alcoholics are also likely to become involved in accidents of one sort or another, particularly automobile accidents if they drink when they drive. For all these reasons, the average life span of alcoholics is definitely shortened.

How Does Alcoholism Affect the Nation?

The public health problems created by drinking are great. The number of automobile accidents, injuries, and deaths in which alcohol plays a role are incalculable. It has been estimated that one third of all serious automobile accidents involve alcohol.

In addition, alcoholism contributes to crime. People under the influence of alcohol are more likely to commit violent actions, sexual crimes, and even murder. Furthermore, because of the difficulty in holding a job, and the cost of buying liquor, alcoholics often resort to crime to pay their bills.

The cost to society is very great. To combat the crimes associated with alcohol, there must be added police protection and increased legal and penal facilities. Looking at another aspect of the problem, alcoholism costs industry huge sums of money in absenteeism, poor productivity, and inferior work.

What Is Being Done for the Alcoholic?

Treatment of the alcoholic is a complicated problem. The many steps in one recovery program are shown in Figure 33-6. It is simple to say that the solution to the alcoholic's problem is to stop drinking. Unfortunately, it is not that easy. If the alcoholic suddenly stops drinking, his body suffers uncomfortable, often serious, and occasionally fatal effects because it has become

IF *you know someone who—*

✓ attempts to solve problems with a drink . . . .

✓ has blackouts . . . .

✓ often drinks more than he really means to . . . .

✓ needs a drink the morning after . . . .

THEN *you know someone who has a treatable disease—ALCOHOLISM*

33-5 A check list of some of the symptoms of alcoholism. What is being done in your community to help the alcoholic?

accustomed to alcohol. The patient may become jittery, nervous, and irritable. He may develop a condition known as *delirium tremens* (TREE-menz), or d.t.'s, in which he has hallucinations that are often terrifying for him. He may develop a high fever, a dangerous drop in blood pressure, or an increase in his pulse rate. Occasionally patients suddenly withdrawn from alcohol develop a form of mental illness known as *alcoholic psychosis.* These conditions may also occur when an alcoholic continues to drink.

The treatment of alcoholism cannot be a simple, abrupt withdrawal of alcohol. It must be a gradual decrease in the daily consumption until alcohol is completely withdrawn. In addition, many patients who are alcoholics need intensive psychotherapy, dietary treatment, and often rehabilitation. The psychotherapy is the most difficult part because these patients generally have very deep-rooted problems that cannot be easily solved.

Many clinics have been established to help alcoholics. Physicians are beginning to treat alcoholism as they do other chronic medical conditions with a tendency toward relapse. There is hope for the alcoholic if he will only accept the fact that he has a problem and realize the necessity of doing something about it before it is too late. The sooner that society in general recognizes that alcoholism is a disease that responds to treatment, the easier it will become for the alcoholic to seek help.

Alcoholics Anonymous, Al-Anon, and Alateen

Perhaps the greatest boon to the alcoholic is *Alcoholics Anonymous (AA)*, an organization founded in 1935 by alcoholics to help each other. While only about one fifth of all alcoholics ever join and stay with an Alcoholics Anonymous group, about three quarters of those who do are significantly benefited. Members of Alcoholics Anonymous never refer to themselves as cured. They recognize that, if they start to drink again at any time, all of the old problems will return. In Alcoholics Anonymous, patients meet with other alcoholics, and discuss and begin to understand their problems. Many people who have been alcoholics have, through AA, built productive and rewarding lives for themselves.

Another important organization is *Al-Anon* which organizes Al-Anon family groups. These groups are for spouses, relatives, and friends of alcoholics who band together to

33-6 PHASES OF ALCOHOLISM AND RECOVERY

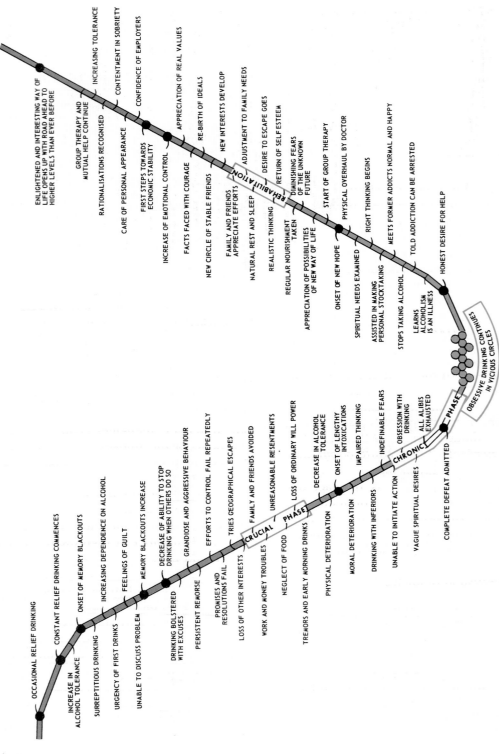

OCCASIONAL RELIEF DRINKING

INCREASE IN ALCOHOL TOLERANCE

CONSTANT RELIEF DRINKING COMMENCES

ONSET OF MEMORY BLACKOUTS

SURREPTITIOUS DRINKING

INCREASING DEPENDENCE ON ALCOHOL

URGENCY OF FIRST DRINKS

FEELINGS OF GUILT

UNABLE TO DISCUSS PROBLEM

MEMORY BLACKOUTS INCREASE

DRINKING BOLSTERED WITH EXCUSES

DECREASE OF ABILITY TO STOP DRINKING WHEN OTHERS DO SO

GRANDIOSE AND AGGRESSIVE BEHAVIOUR

PERSISTENT REMORSE

EFFORTS TO CONTROL FAIL REPEATEDLY

PROMISES AND RESOLUTIONS FAIL

TRIES GEOGRAPHICAL ESCAPES

LOSS OF OTHER INTERESTS

FAMILY AND FRIENDS AVOIDED

WORK AND MONEY TROUBLES

UNREASONABLE RESENTMENTS

NEGLECT OF FOOD

LOSS OF ORDINARY WILL POWER

CRUCIAL PHASE

TREMORS AND EARLY MORNING DRINKS

DECREASE IN ALCOHOL TOLERANCE

PHYSICAL DETERIORATION

ONSET OF LENGTHY INTOXICATIONS

MORAL DETERIORATION

IMPAIRED THINKING

DRINKING WITH INFERIORS

INDEFINABLE FEARS

UNABLE TO INITIATE ACTION

OBSESSION WITH DRINKING

VAGUE SPIRITUAL DESIRES

ALL ALIBIS EXHAUSTED

CHRONIC PHASE

COMPLETE DEFEAT ADMITTED

OBSESSIVE DRINKING CONTINUES IN VICIOUS CIRCLES

LEARNS ALCOHOLISM IS AN ILLNESS

STOPS TAKING ALCOHOL

ASSISTED IN MAKING PERSONAL STOCKTAKING

SPIRITUAL NEEDS EXAMINED

MEETS FORMER ADDICTS NORMAL AND HAPPY

TOLD ADDICTION CAN BE ARRESTED

HONEST DESIRE FOR HELP

RIGHT THINKING BEGINS

PHYSICAL OVERHAUL BY DOCTOR

ONSET OF NEW HOPE

START OF GROUP THERAPY

APPRECIATION OF POSSIBILITIES OF NEW WAY OF LIFE

REGULAR NOURISHMENT TAKEN

DIMINISHING FEARS OF THE UNKNOWN FUTURE

RETURN OF SELF-ESTEEM

REALISTIC THINKING

DESIRE TO ESCAPE GOES

NATURAL REST AND SLEEP

ADJUSTMENT TO FAMILY NEEDS

FAMILY AND FRIENDS APPRECIATE EFFORTS

REHABILITATION

NEW CIRCLE OF STABLE FRIENDS

NEW INTERESTS DEVELOP

FACTS FACED WITH COURAGE

RE-BIRTH OF IDEALS

INCREASE OF EMOTIONAL CONTROL

APPRECIATION OF REAL VALUES

FIRST STEPS TOWARDS ECONOMIC STABILITY

CARE OF PERSONAL APPEARANCE

CONFIDENCE OF EMPLOYERS

RATIONALISATIONS RECOGNISED

CONTENTMENT IN SOBRIETY

GROUP THERAPY AND MUTUAL HELP CONTINUE

INCREASING TOLERANCE

ENLIGHTENED AND INTERESTING WAY OF LIFE OPENS UP WITH ROAD AHEAD TO HIGHER LEVELS THAN EVER BEFORE

From "GROUP THERAPY IN ALCOHOLISM" M. M. Glatt, M.D., D.P.M. Warlingham Park Hospital offer friendship, hope, and solutions to common problems resulting from living with an alcoholic. In these groups are people from all walks of life who have a loved one who is an alcoholic.

Alateen groups serve the same purposes as Al-Anon and accomplish much for teen-agers who have an alcoholic parent. These boys and girls have problems which are unique to their age and they find much comfort in talking with other teen-agers who have lived under the same or similar circumstances. Many find a great deal of hope and help from attending Alateen meetings. These groups have no dues or fees; personal anonymity is protected and no one is under obligation in any way. The doors are open and all are made to feel welcome.

33-7 This "smoking machine" helps us investigate the effects of cigarette tars. The machine puffs away on cigarettes and traps the tars in the cigarette smoke. The tars are then painted on the backs of mice to determine their ill effects.

THE SMOKING HABIT

Smoking is a serious and increasing public health problem. In the United States, about 45 million persons over the age of 17 are cigarette smokers, and it is cigarette smoking that appears to be the most hazardous form of smoking. About 4 million of these smokers (or three percent of the adult population) smoke two packs a day or more.

Of particular importance is the fact that each year an estimated 1 million teen-agers start smoking. However, in a recent study, more than half the teen-age smokers looked forward to *not* smoking in the future.

How Dangerous Is Smoking?

We are constantly reminded by newspapers, magazines, and doctors that smoking is harmful. A notice of the danger of smoking is printed on every cigarette package sold in this country. See Figure 33-8.

We are warned that cigarette smoking shortens life. The more cigarettes a person smokes and the earlier he starts to smoke, the more likely he is to die at an earlier age than if he had never smoked.

Unfortunately, while these warnings prompt many to try to stop smoking, relatively few heavy smokers succeed in doing so. Moreover, teen-agers continue to swell the ranks of the smokers. It appears that the barrage of cigarette advertising, along with social pressures, is sufficient to overcome the advice of physicians and scientists.

Just what it is in tobacco that is harmful is the subject of much study. Tobacco smoke contains a number of ingredients. The most active and best understood is *nicotine* (NIK-uh-teen). In its pure form, it is an oily, poisonous liquid that can be very harmful even in small amounts. It speeds up the heart rate, causes blood pressure to rise, and causes small blood vessels to contract. In addition, cigarette smoke contains a number of tars, resins, and other residues that are irritating and, in all likelihood, poisonous.

Some of these products are filtered out by the unsmoked tobacco, but the more of a cigarette one smokes, the less of a filtering

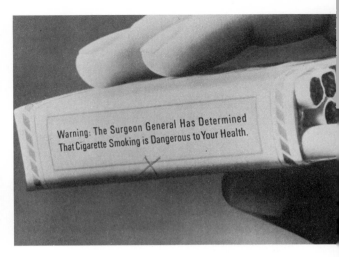

33-8 In October, 1970, an earlier warning label on cigarette packages was changed. Which label do you think is the later one? Why do you think it was changed?

action the remaining tobacco provides. The widespread use of filters on cigarettes may decrease to some degree the presence of these harmful products. But there is no method known today of completely eliminating these substances.

■ Ask a smoker to make this test with his brand of filter cigarettes. Have him breathe out through a folded handkerchief after having inhaled a puff. Do the smoke residues discolor the handkerchief? These tarry substances lodge in the lungs.

Some Effects of Smoking

There are many harmful effects of smoking.

Smoking stimulates the stomach to secrete abnormal amounts of acid. Smoking may therefore prevent the healing of stomach ulcers.

Cigarette smoke causes constriction of small blood vessels. This is particularly dangerous in people who have a circulatory disorder. They may develop gangrene of the fingers or toes; eventually one or more amputations may be required.

Smoking also affects the heart and promotes hardening of the arteries. Just exactly how smoking causes its adverse effects on the heart and blood vessels is not entirely clear. However, death rates from coronary heart disease are at least double among smokers as among nonsmokers.

The products of smoking are also irritants that cause inflammation in the back of the mouth and the throat. In many chronic smokers the larynx is irritated, which results in chronic hoarseness. Smoke also irritates the bronchial tubes and causes many smokers to cough. Any brand of cigarettes will produce this irritation. The degree of irritation will vary from person to person and be dependent to a large extent on the amount that he smokes. Inhaling definitely increases the irritating effects of smoking on the throat, the air passages including the sinuses, and the lungs.

Thus, smoking seems to be a factor in many diseases that shorten the average life span of smokers as compared with nonsmokers. The diseases include not only peptic ulcer and heart and blood vessel diseases, but also emphysema (page 281), and cancer of the larynx, esophagus, and lungs.

Smoking and Lung Cancer

Fifty years ago lung cancer was a rare disease. Today, it is quite common and causes over 25,000 deaths a year. It is one of the most common cancers among men. It is also one of the most lethal, and must be caught very early to be cured.

The incidence of lung cancer has increased almost directly as the incidence of smoking has risen. Correlations between smoking and lung cancer have been noticed since the 1930's, and a relationship is now well established. Lung cancer in nonsmokers is rare: about eight in a hundred cases. The remaining cases occur in smokers.

The frequency with which lung cancer appears in smokers is almost directly related to the amount they smoke. Thus, lung cancer is about twice as common in one-pack-a-day smokers as in half-pack-a-day smokers and twice that common in the two-packs-a-day smokers. Most victims of lung cancer could have been spared the disease had they never smoked.

Some people have stated that it is not cigarette smoking, but air pollution, gasoline fumes, and the highly pressured lives of some heavy smokers that tend to cause lung cancer. It is certainly true that lung cancer occurs more commonly among people who live in large cities than among people who live in rural areas. The possibility that exhaust fumes, smog, and other air pollutants play a role cannot be dismissed. But most scientists who have studied the question consider cigarette smoking to be the most significant factor.

Social and Environmental Influences and Smoking

Among high school pupils, who smokes? And why do students smoke? A study of 22,000 high school students in Portland, Oregon, and nearby areas showed that pupils were most likely to smoke if:

1. Their parents smoked.
2. Their grades were lower than average.
3. They were above average age for their class.
4. They were not preparing for college.
5. They did not take part in extracurricular activities.

Most people would never start to smoke unless their friends were smoking. In any large high school, you can see many boys and girls smoking cigarettes even though they get no pleasure from smoking—simply

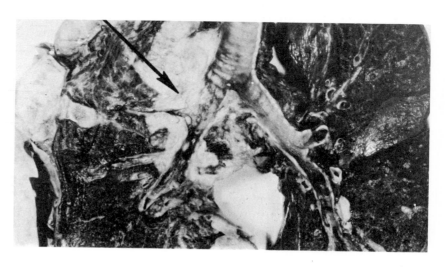

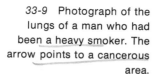

33-9 Photograph of the lungs of a man who had been a heavy smoker. The arrow points to a cancerous area.

33-10 Clinics of various kinds have been formed to try to help smokers give up the habit. This photograph shows the meeting of participants in a smoking clinic for teen-agers.

because everyone else is smoking and they want to be part of the group. Some of the reasons why young people smoke are

1. *To be accepted.* Many boys and girls feel like outsiders. They fear that their fellow students or the boys and girls that they associate with don't really accept them as full and equal companions. A boy may want to show that he is a "man," and a girl that she is one of the group.

2. *To be sociable.* This is not the same thing as feeling that one is accepted. Smoking with a group, or even with one other person, is doing something together. No doubt it can do something to build a feeling of friendship. Most of us like to go along with a friend or with the crowd. What boy or girl wants to be a wet blanket? We may fear that saying *no* all the time separates us too much.

3. *To cover up bashfulness.* Are you sometimes upset because you think that people notice all of the awkward things that you may say or do? Many boys and girls suffer severely in this way. They worry before they arrive at a party because they fear they will be unable to think of anything to say that is worth hearing. They feel awkward and fear that they will look ill-at-ease. A cigarette often helps them feel poised.

4. *To give needed satisfaction once one has the habit.* Heavy smokers may feel that they get satisfaction or a "lift" and may be uneasy, nervous, and dissatisfied if they do not smoke. A heavy smoker's body seems to "need" tobacco. Some smokers become nervous and irritable when they quit or try to smoke less. Some heavy smokers think that they can't quit. Yet many people do quit smoking, and once they have succeeded they feel much better. The main thing is to *want* to stop and to be *determined* to stop.

How Can the Smoking Habit Be Broken?

Once a person has started to smoke, it becomes increasingly difficult to do without cigarettes. Smoking becomes a habit that one has difficulty in breaking. Heavy smokers actually crave tobacco and may feel physically uncomfortable and even sick without it. This has led many scientists to think that one can actually become addicted to tobacco.

Mark Twain once said, "Breaking the smoking habit is the easiest thing in the world. I have done it a hundred times myself." Smokers like to feel that if they exert enough will power, they can stop by sheer force of self-discipline. But for many smokers it is not as easy as that. While heavy smokers often manage to abstain for periods of days, weeks, or even months, many take up smoking again, and within a year of withdrawal are smoking as much as they ever did previously. Some people have been able to stop either by slowly cutting down or discontinuing abruptly.

There are a variety of programs to help the smoker who wants to stop smoking. A number of medications are available and are helpful to some smokers. Some people try chewing gum or change from cigarettes to cigars or pipes, which seem to be less injurious to health. Some people undergo hypnosis or take courses designed to instruct them on how to stop smoking. Others attend smoking clinics or go to psychiatrists.

Some persons find that they can cut down on their smoking gradually. Other persons find that the only way that works for them is to stop entirely, all at once. The day may come when some medicine or treatment will be the answer for the heavy smoker. But until that day, a doctor can only advise his patient to try to stop smoking in whatever way may seem best to him.

In view of the very serious effects of cigarette smoking on health and considering how difficult it is to break the habit, doesn't it seem wiser never to start smoking, regardless of social or other pressures?

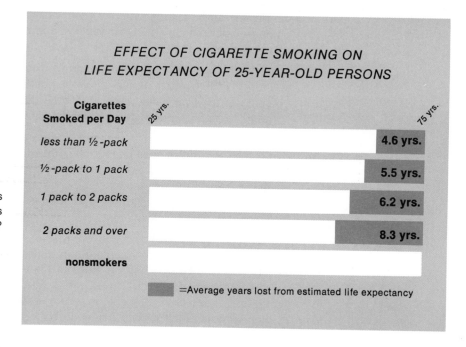

33-11 Do these statistics convince you that smoking is a dangerous habit?

EFFECT OF CIGARETTE SMOKING ON LIFE EXPECTANCY OF 25-YEAR-OLD PERSONS

Cigarettes Smoked per Day	25 yrs. — 75 yrs.
less than ½-pack	4.6 yrs.
½-pack to 1 pack	5.5 yrs.
1 pack to 2 packs	6.2 yrs.
2 packs and over	8.3 yrs.
nonsmokers	

=Average years lost from estimated life expectancy

What You Have Learned

What kind of health practices should you apply in maintaining your health? Check your understanding of the chapter. On a separate sheet of paper, number 1 through 24 and insert the answer from the vocabulary list below. Use each expression, but use each one only once.

18 Al-Anon	*12* coma	*24* lung cancer
19 Alateen	*15* delirium tremens	*8* methyl
17 Alcoholics Anonymous	*2* disease	*10* oxidized
13 business	*5* disinfectant	*4* problem drinkers
11 cerebral cortex	*3* divorce	*16* psychotherapy
21 cigarettes	*1* drug	*9* store
23 cigarette smoking	*6* ethyl	*20* tobacco
14 cirrhosis	*22* lower	*7* yeast

Alcohol is a (1) _____ and alcoholism is a (2) _____ which often leads to joblessness, dissension, and (3) _____. There are thought to be between five and six million (4) _____ in the United States. When a doctor wipes your arm with alcohol before giving you an injection, the alcohol acts as a (5) _____. (6) _____ alcohol, the kind of alcohol that people drink, is made by the action of (7) _____ on sugar. (8) _____ alcohol, which is made from wood, is a dangerous poison.

The body cannot (9) _____ alcohol, and about 98 percent of the alcohol that a person drinks is (10) _____. The first part of the brain to be affected is the (11) _____. Persons who drink too much may first show impaired judgment, poor reasoning, and giddiness, and may eventually become sleepy or pass into a (12) _____.

Men who really don't like to drink may find themselves drinking at (13) _____ luncheons. Some alcoholics suffer from a scarring and hardening of the liver called (14) _____. Other alcoholics may have attacks of (15) _____ with its terrifying hallucinations. Most alcoholics need both a proper diet and (16) _____.

Many alcoholics have been rehabilitated through the work of (17) _____, an organization of alcoholics and former alcoholics whose members never refer to themselves as cured. (18) _____ organizes groups including wives or husbands, relatives, and friends of alcoholics for help to the alcoholics and to each other. (19) _____ organizes groups of teen-agers who have an alcoholic parent.

More than 45 million people in the United States use (20) _____. Most of these smoke (21) _____. A study of high school students showed that cigarette smokers made (22) _____ grades than the average. The practice of (23) _____ has increased greatly in recent years, and along with this increase has come a much higher incidence of (24) _____. Cigarette smoking also has adverse effects on the heart and blood vessels.

What You Can Do

1. Would you and your classmates enjoy producing and acting in a short play written by one or more of you? Use your imagination. You and others in your health class could write interesting, brief plays based on the important problem "Why Do Boys and Girls Smoke?" Each of the four reasons why young people smoke (as explained in the section "Social and Environmental Influences and Smoking" in this chapter) can serve as the basis for a number of different short plays.

2. Test yourself on what you have learned about alcohol and tobacco. Copy the following statements in your notebook. If the statement is correct as it stands, simply underline the word that is italicized in this book. If the italicized word or words make the statement incorrect, replace the incorrect term with one that makes the statement true. *Do not write in this book*.

   a. A drug that speeds up cell activity is called a *depressant*.
   b. Alcohol *should* be considered as a food.
   c. Alcohol in the bloodstream *slows* one's vital reactions.
   d. *Al-Anon* groups are composed of the wives or husbands, relatives, and friends of alcoholics.
   e. Alcohol is correctly considered a *stimulant*.
   f. *Nicotine* is an oily, poisonous liquid.
   g. Nicotine *slows* the heartbeat and *decreases* blood pressure.
   h. Lung cancer is about *twice* as common among those who smoke two packs of cigarettes a day as among those who smoke half a pack a day.
   i. Smoking stimulates the stomach to produce *acid*.
   j. A pint of whiskey contains about *ten* times as much alcohol as a pint of beer.

Things to Try

An address by a doctor on "Smoking" or "Drinking" or on both topics could be a profitable experience for your health class. If such a talk can be arranged, ask the doctor if he is willing to answer questions from the class. If he says yes, make sure that you and other members of the class are prepared to ask sensible questions. If your teacher and the principal of the school think it a good idea, it might be worthwhile to have the doctor speak at an assembly meeting.

Probing Further

Al-Anon Faces Alcoholism, by Al-Anon Family Group, published by Al-Anon, 1968. Tells how the alcoholic's family can meet the problems of his or her alcoholism.

How to Stop Smoking, by Herbert Brean, Pocket Books, 1970. A most helpful book for a difficult problem.

Facts About Smoking and Health, by Eva J. Salber, M.D., D.P.H., Science Research Associates, 1968. Contains many interesting facts about why people smoke, why some people never start, and what you can do if you want to stop smoking.

Facts About Alcohol, by Raymond G. McCarthy, Science Research Associates, 1967. Gives the reasons why people drink and tells you the effects of drinking.

Tobacco and Your Health: The Smoking Controversy, by Harold S. Diehl, McGraw-Hill, 1969. Summarizes the evidence that smoking is an important health hazard and gives advice on how to stop smoking.

Health Concepts in Action

Does this statement help express what you have learned? Would you change or add to it?

> **Mood-altering substances in established use affect mental and physical functions and, in excess, can impair health.**

Applying this concept of alcohol and tobacco, which health practices would you

- continue?

- change?

- begin?

Will you now, as a result of your study, change any of your health objectives?

34 / The Problem of Heroin and Other Drugs

Thousands of football fans packed the stadium. Millions more waited at home, near their radios, to hear the famous sports announcer, Bill Stern, report the game. But he never even got to announce the starting lineup. While the eager public waited, he "came apart at the seams" and could not continue.

His collapse was due to a drug habit that had victimized him all through the days of his great success. He had first started using narcotics for pain following an automobile accident in which he lost his leg. Then he began to use narcotics for every real and imaginery pain. His habit now threatened not only his job, wealth, and fame, but his family life as well. In his autobiography *The Taste of Ashes,* Bill Stern tells how he became cured of his habit and successful again in his profession.

A PROBE INTO DANGEROUS HABITS—What problems does drug-taking create? To find out, you will be probing questions like these:

1. What is drug abuse? drug dependence? Why is the taking of narcotic drugs, other than as prescribed by a doctor, unlawful?

2. Why do some people become drug-dependent? What measures have been used to treat drug-dependent people?

3. What are typical effects of each of the following: narcotics, barbiturates, tranquilizers, amphetamines, hallucinogens?

4. What is marijuana? How is it related to hashish?

5. How serious is the problem of barbiturate abuse?

DRUG ABUSE

Among the most tragic problems today are *drug abuse* and *drug dependence.* Drug abuse is the excessive use of drugs by people for nonmedical reasons. A major danger in drug abuse is that it may lead to drug dependence, and with it serious injury or even death.

Drug dependence is a complex problem, partly medical, partly psychological, and partly sociological. It is a particularly tragic problem because, unlike other diseases, drug dependence is self-inflicted.

You may wonder, "Why should I be concerned with a problem that does not affect my daily life?" Drug abuse and drug dependence are problems that are not far removed from any of us. Drug abusers include not only those we usually refer to as "addicts," who are dependent on illegal drugs, but also many who misuse legal drugs. Among some groups of young people, drug abuse spreads like a dangerous disease, and the number of drug-dependent young people has been increasing rapidly.

What Is Drug Dependence?

In drug dependence, there is an overwhelming desire for the drug, an overpowering need to continue taking it, a tendency to increase the amount taken, and either a psychological or physical dependence upon the drug, or both.

In psychological dependence, the drug abuser cannot meet the stresses of daily life without the help of drugs.

In physical dependence (commonly called "addiction"), the body chemistry changes. Drug *tolerance* develops. That is, larger and larger doses of the drug are needed to get the same effects that were obtained originally from small doses. Eventually the body cannot function without the drug. If the drug is suddenly withdrawn, extremely unpleasant physical symptoms result. These symptoms

may include nausea, headaches, muscular spasms, and even more dangerous effects. These symptoms are part of *withdrawal sickness.* Withdrawal sickness is serious and can be fatal. Medical supervision is therefore always advisable in trying to overcome a drug habit.

NARCOTICS

A number of different types of drugs are frequently abused. First and foremost are the *narcotics* (nar-KOT-iks). In small doses, narcotics relieve pain and produce drowsiness. In very large doses, they may produce stupor or even death. All narcotics can produce physical, as well as psychological, dependence if used repeatedly.

Heroin and Other Opium Products

Narcotic drugs in common use in this country today are products of *opium* (OH-pee-um), which comes from the opium poppy. *Morphine* (MOR-feen) is a powerful narcotic extracted from opium. It is used medically to relieve severe pain. A less powerful narcotic made from opium is *codeine* (KOH-deen), which is weak enough to be used in some cough medicines.

There are other products of opium considered too dangerous to use medically. The one creating the most serious problem today is *heroin* (HEHR-oh-in). In the United States it is illegal even for doctors to prescribe heroin, because it is so strongly addicting. Heroin is widely used by narcotics addicts, who obtain it through illegal sources. It is smuggled into this country by highly efficient, well-organized narcotics rings.

Methadone

Chemists are constantly trying to develop narcotics that are less dangerous than the opium products in present use. One of these,

34-1 Is drug abuse in your community the major problem suggested by these headlines? If so, what measures are being taken?

City Asks U.S. to Curb Barbiturates

Methadone Program Is Praised And Attacked by Drug Experts

Drugs Are a Bad Scene Ex-Addicts Tell Students

NARCOTICS DEATHS ON INCREASE HERE

450 Fatalities to June 30, Most in 15-35 Age Group

Drug Use Rises in City's High Schools

---

methadone (METH-uh-dohn), is used to treat some heroin addicts. (See page 609.) Methadone is also addicting, but does not seem to have the disabling effects of heroin. As part of a hospital program, the addicts are given methadone free as a substitute for heroin. Eventually they will not crave heroin, although they will need a daily supply of methadone instead.

Cocaine

Cocaine (koh-KANE) is classified by law among the narcotics although its action on the body is that of a stimulant. The narcotics classification means that the federal laws on illegal narcotics can help control its sale.

Cocaine is derived from the leaves of the coca plant. (This is not the same plant as the cacao tree, from which we get chocolate and cocoa.) Cocaine has been occasionally used medically as a local anesthetic.

Abusers of cocaine tend to develop extremely strong psychological dependence on the drug. Repeated use of the drug may cause violent and criminal behavior.

DEPENDENCE ON NARCOTICS — A SOCIAL AND PSYCHOLOGICAL PROBLEM

The number of narcotics addicts in the United States is estimated at well over 250,000. Most live in poor economic circumstances, and four out of five are young men.

The hopelessness of the life of the addict is difficult to imagine. All his energies are devoted to getting drugs. He hates his dependence on drugs and despises his world of fellow addicts; yet he is unable to escape his way of life.

Since the narcotics addict has to obtain drugs illegally, he finds the cost of narcotics staggeringly high. He may need $20–$100 a day to support his habit. To get the money, he almost always has to resort to theft or other crimes. Since he gets only a small percent of the value of his stolen goods when he sells it, he often has to steal many hundreds of dollars worth a day in order to get enough money to buy drugs. Of course, any family or social life is disrupted. Thus, society, as well as the individual, pays an enormous price for narcotics addiction. It has been estimated that the cost of each addict to New York City, for example, is at least $25,000 a year.

Why Do People Turn to Narcotics?

What causes people to use narcotics (or other drugs) in the first place? A small number of people use narcotics prescribed by their doctors for a time to relieve pain from disease. Many of these patients become physically dependent on the narcotics; however, few of them have any serious problem getting off the drug when they no longer need it—unless psychological dependence complicates their problem.

A greater number of people use narcotics because of the hopelessness of their lives and their inability to cope with difficult living conditions. While using narcotics, they feel good. Life seems rosier; worries vanish; time seems to stand still.

Many persons are prodded into trying narcotics and other drugs by friends who are addicts. They feel that they must use drugs, too, to be part of the group. They fear that if they don't, they will be rejected and isolated from the group.

Younger people may start taking drugs because of a desire for "kicks," or a need to rebel against parental authority. These young addicts may begin first with a milder drug like marijuana, which itself is not physically addicting, but may lead to trying heroin.

Once a person starts taking heroin, whether by mouth or by sniffing it, he easily becomes addicted. Eventually he may have to inject the drug directly into the veins (a practice known as "mainlining") to obtain the desired effects. Many confirmed addicts need to take a shot every few hours.

Once addiction occurs, the search for drugs rules the person's life. Accidental death from overdose eventually claims the lives of many addicts. Some die from an infection acquired because of a nonsterile needle, or from a disease acquired because of lowered resistance.

Can Narcotics Addicts Be Cured?

Most narcotics addicts had emotional problems before they ever started using drugs. Psychological dependence is the main factor in their addiction problem. It is this which makes their treatment so difficult and the cure so very hard to achieve.

Most narcotics addicts, under medical supervision, can be withdrawn from addicting drugs in a matter of a few weeks. But once withdrawn from drugs, they usually return to narcotics—unless emotional or environmental stresses are eased. Psychological help, occupational help, and drug withdrawal must go hand in hand for the addict to break the habit permanently.

Treatment Programs

Hospital therapy is one form of help addicts may seek. Addicts may, for example, commit themselves voluntarily in hospitals like those run by the U. S. Public Health Service in Lexington, Kentucky, and Fort Worth, Texas. In the hospital, physical withdrawal from the drug is carried out with medical help in a short time. But getting rid of psychological dependence on the drug usually takes months of treatment which may tax crowded hospital facilities. Moreover, many patients do not remain for the length of time needed.

Another form of help has come from laws passed by several states including California and New York, and by large cities with major drug problems, like New York City. The laws focus more on helping the addict than on punishing him, and provide that addicts may be committed to **treatment centers** rather than prisons.

The treatment centers are showing a higher cure rate than hospital confinement. However, in both kinds of treatment, there is still a high rate of relapse. For when the addict leaves, he returns to the way of life and the environment where his addiction began.

Another effort to help the addict depends upon *methadone maintenance,* mentioned earlier. A patient taking methadone as a substitute for heroin finds that he can live a normal life outside the hospital. He can take methadone by mouth just once a day, while heroin would have to be injected every few hours. When taken by mouth, methadone does not give the "high" that heroin does. At the same time, methadone blocks the craving for heroin. It also blocks the exhilarating effects of heroin if heroin should be taken again.

Methadone programs have mushroomed around the country because of their low cost and high success rate. Supporters of the program point out that many of those on methadone maintenance have been able to complete their schooling, become self-supporting, and lead useful lives. Others object, however, that the program switches addicts from one addicting drug to another addicting drug, which they will have to take for the rest of their lives.

Self-help residential groups like *Synanon* use a relatively new form of treatment. These groups operate much like Alcoholics Anonymous, except that during treatment addicts must live in the residence provided by the group. People who were once addicts themselves provide psychological support for those trying to conquer their addiction. Addicts must give up drugs completely; substitute drugs are not allowed. Instead, with the aid of the group, addicts face the reasons for their dependence on narcotics and learn to cope with the problems of living without dependence on drugs.

Narcotics Controls

Efforts are constantly being made to restrict the traffic in narcotics on an interna-

34-2 Narcotics are kept under lock and key in doctors' offices, and dispensary records are examined regularly by federal agents.

tional as well as national basis. Federal officers constantly hunt down shipments of narcotics being smuggled into the United States. Local officers also crack down on distributors and pushers. But thus far the efforts have not kept pace with the traffic, which continues to grow because of the powerful underworld forces behind the traffic.

There is considerable disagreement as to whether there should be a tougher crackdown on the addicts themselves, or whether the addict should be regarded as a sick person and committed for treatment under civil, rather than criminal, law.

In some countries, such as Great Britain, addicts are being supplied their daily drug requirements legally, through clinics. The purpose is to remove the profit in illegal drug traffic and thus reduce the underworld's interest. However, some authorities claim that a good part of these legally distributed drugs are reaching illegal markets elsewhere and still making profits for the underworld.

On the other hand, the opposite extreme of stepping up legal penalties for drug traffic and use has also failed. If the narcotic problem is ever to be controlled, it must be attacked on a number of fronts—not only as a law-enforcement problem, but also as a medical problem, a psychological problem, and a social problem.

OTHER ABUSED DRUGS

Besides the narcotics there are a number of other groups of abused drugs. The groups include not only illegal drugs, but also drugs prescribed by doctors for medical purposes. It seems that almost any drug that can change mood or behavior tends to be abused. See Figure 34-3.

The "Pep Pills"—Amphetamines

Doctors prescribe *amphetamines* (am-FET-uh-meens) to check fatigue and create a feeling of well-being, or to curb appetite at the start of a reducing diet. Amphetamines commonly used are *Benzedrine, Dexadrine,* and *Methedrine* (often called "speed"). Many people in all walks of life abuse amphetamines.

The amphetamines are stimulants. (See page 221.) They speed up body processes, including heart action and breathing rate. Even in small doses, the amphetamines may cause irritability in some people, and a very uncomfortable letdown after the effects wear off. Moreover, stimulants may make a person who is tired and uncoordinated mistakenly feel that he is operating on an efficient level. For example, a driver of a truck who took amphetamines to keep himself awake was responsible for a 36-car accident.

The body quickly develops a tolerance to amphetamines, and larger and larger doses are needed to produce the same effect. Here is where the trouble begins. The huge doses, obtained legally or illegally, have been known to cause serious emotional breakdowns, and dangerous mental confusion. Methedrine abusers, who take massive, illegal doses, have shown such deranged behavior that they have come to be known as "speed freaks."

The "Sleeping Pills"—Barbiturates

Sedative drugs such as the *barbiturates* (bar-BICH-yur-its) are prescribed by doctors to make people drowsy and encourage sleep. Prescription sleeping pills, such as *Seconal* and *Nembutal,* are barbiturates.

Unfortunately, these useful drugs have been increasingly abused. It is estimated that about 20 million people in this country take barbiturates, and that half the barbiturates produced are sold illegally.

The barbiturates depress the nervous system. Therefore, even small doses of barbiturates combined with alcohol (another depressant) can slow the breathing rate to a deadly standstill. Over 3,000 people die each year from overdoses of barbiturates, often accidental.

Barbiturates cause strong physical dependence, as narcotics do. During early stages of addiction, the user will need more and more barbiturates. Once hooked, the average barbiturate addict takes from 20 to 40 pills a day. Abrupt withdrawal is even more dangerous than withdrawal from narcotics, and may be fatal. Safe withdrawal requires a slowly decreasing dose each day. This often takes from four to six weeks or longer to accomplish, and should be carried out under close medical supervision.

Tranquilizers

In carefully selected cases, the more potent tranquilizers have helped many people overcome emotional breakdowns and return to normal living.

Amphetamines	Classification	stimulant
	Medical use	dieting, relieve depression of narcolepsy (brief attacks of deep sleep)
	Common types	amphetamine, diphetamine, methamphetamine (examples: Benzedrine, Dexadrine, Methedrine)
	Nicknames	A's, bennies, speed, pep pills, ups
	How taken	orally, injection
	Effects	talkativeness, excitability, mood uplifting, hallucinations
	Dependence	psychological
	Tolerance	yes
	Physical complications	fatigue, malnutrition, diseases related to needle contamination (hepatitis)
	Comments	When used to stay awake for long periods, the severe drain of the body's energy may result in severe fatigue as the drug wears off—a possible cause of automobile accidents.
Barbiturates	Classification	depressant
	Medical use	sedation, treatment of epilepsy, high blood pressure, and insomnia
	Common types	phenobarbital, pentobarbital, secobarbital, amobarbital (examples: Nembutal, Seconal, Amytal)
	Nicknames	barbs, goofballs, yellow jackets, redbirds, downs
	How taken	orally, occasionally by injection
	Effects	staggering, slurred speech, quick temper, drunkenness
	Dependence	physical and psychological
	Tolerance	yes
	Physical complications	coma, respiratory failure, shock, death
	Comments	When combined with alcoholic beverages, death may result. Withdrawal from barbiturates is more dangerous than withdrawal from narcotics.
Deliriants	Classification	volatile chemical
	Medical use	none
	Common types	airplane glue, paint thinner, cleaning fluid, lighter fluid, gasoline
	How taken	inhalation
	Effects	intoxication, exhilaration, blurred vision, slurred speech, stupor, vomiting
	Dependence	psychological
	Tolerance	possible
	Physical complications	some types may damage the liver, blood, central nervous system, and the kidneys
	Comments	Psychotic behavior has resulted in some cases.
Hallucinating Agents		hallucinogen
	Medical use	research
	Common types	marijuana, LSD, STP, mescaline, psilocybin, peyote, hashish
	Nicknames	pot, grass, acid, cubes, trips, psychedelics, sacraments
	How taken	smoking, orally, inhalation, injection
	Effects	distortion of perception, hallucinations, rambling speech, giddiness
	Dependence	psychological
	Tolerance	yes
	Physical complications	LSD may break chromosomes
	Comments	Long-term psychotic effects have resulted from the abuse of hallucinating agents. Spontaneous recurrences of the experience ("flashbacks") may occur weeks or months after the last dose of LSD.
Opiates	Classification	depressant
	Medical use	pain relief after surgery, burns; in final stages of terminal diseases
	Common types	heroin, morphine, codeine, methadone
	Nicknames	horse, H, junk, dope, hard stuff
	How taken	injection, sniffing, orally
	Effects	stupor, drowsiness, possible nausea and slow breathing
	Dependence	physical and psychological
	Tolerance	yes
	Physical complications	addiction may come quickly and is not known until withdrawal syndrome appears; overdose may result in shock and death; sharing of injecting equipment may spread hepatitis and venereal diseases.
	Comments	Heroin is the most addicting of the group and is the drug of choice for most addicts. It is not used medically in this country.

Adapted from *Drugs: A Pocket Primer* and reprinted by permission of the New York State Narcotic Addiction Control Commission.

34-4 Young mothers and hard-working executives must contend with stress-producing situations every day. Will taking drugs help them to meet the demands of their work? How might they better cope with their problems?

Unfortunately, the milder tranquilizers are often requested by patients to calm them and relieve them of daily tensions which should probably be dealt with more realistically. Many of these people become psychologically dependent upon the tranquilizers.

Overdoses of tranquilizers cause people to become sluggish and sleepy, have slurred speech, and walk with a stagger. Extremely large doses can cause convulsions and death.

Marijuana

Marijuana, often called "pot" or "grass," is prepared from the dried leaves and flowers of the hemp plant. The hemp plant grows wild in many parts of the United States and Mexico. The illegal cigarettes made from marijuana are referred to as "joints" or "reefers."

The effects of marijuana vary from user to user. Some users become giddy and uninhibited. Others have mild hallucinations, confused vision, hearing, and speech. Still others become withdrawn and sluggish.

There are different strengths of marijuana, depending upon the variety, so that the user never knows what he is getting. This may help explain some of the conflicting results obtained by researchers testing the harmful effects of marijuana. *Hashish* (HAHSH-eesh), produced in the Middle East and India, is made from a stronger concentration of the hemp resin. It is from five to ten times as strong as the marijuana commonly used in America.

Although people do not become physically dependent on marijuana, they often become psychologically dependent. Researchers are continuing to test the possible harm of long-term, repeated use.

LSD—A Powerful Hallucinogen

The **hallucinogens** (ha-LOO-sin-uh-jinz) are the so-called "consciousness expanding" or "psychedelic" drugs. They have become a dangerous, illegal plaything for people seeking "thrills."

Marijuana is a mild hallucinogen, while **lysergic acid diethylamide** (DY-eth-ul-AM-ide), or **LSD,** is the most powerful known. LSD, commonly called "acid" is colorless, odorless, and tasteless, and has been taken by people unwittingly. It is so powerful that one ounce yields 300,000 doses.

Under the influence of LSD, a person sees, hears, smells, or tastes things that are not real. For example, sounds may seem to have color. Such distorted sensations may be exciting to some, but terrifying to others.

The effects of LSD on the users are dangerously unpredictable. As the result of a "bad trip" with LSD, some have committed violent acts, suffered mental breakdown, and been hospitalized. Moreover, there is some evidence that LSD may kill or disrupt brain cells permanently. No protection exists, therefore, for one who takes the tragic risk of using LSD, for doctors neither understand the nature of the drug's action on the body as yet, nor know of an antidote for it.

Volatile Chemicals

Airplane glue, paint thinners, dry cleaning fluids, and many other chemicals in ordinary use are **volatile chemicals.** That is, they contain solvents that change rapidly from a liquid to a gas. If inhaled in a room that has no free movement of air, such substances can be poisonous. They have been known to cause delirium, severe kidney and liver damage, and irregular heart action and brain damage leading to death.

DRUG USE VERSUS DRUG ABUSE

Although the word *drug* has become a synonym for "dope," or the abused drugs, a drug is actually a chemical product used to treat some undesirable physical or mental condition. Drugs are helping to rid mankind

34-5 Drug-taking becomes a vicious cycle for some people who take sedatives to fall asleep, stimulants to stay awake on the job, and tranquilizers to calm them down. How can such a pattern be changed?

not only of minor ailments but also of polio, tuberculosis, and other major diseases that have caused much suffering in the past. (See pages 540-44.) It is therefore most unfortunate that the abuse of some drugs is destroying lives today.

To avoid drug abuse, one bit of advice is safe: take a drug only if prescribed by your doctor for you, and only in the dosage prescribed. At all other times depend upon your body to maintain its state of health with your help—through a good diet, proper exercise and rest, and a useful balance between work and play.

What You Have Learned

What kind of health practices should you apply in maintaining your health? Check your understanding of the chapter. On a separate sheet of paper, number 1 through 13 and insert the answer from the vocabulary

abuse	LSD	psychological
amphetamines	methadone	tranquilizers
barbiturates	narcotics	volatile chemicals
Benzedrine	opium	withdrawal sickness
heroin	prescribed	

Drug (1)_____ is the excessive use of drugs for nonmedical reasons. Drug dependence may be physical or (2)_____. The unpleasant symptoms suffered by a drug-dependent person when he is suddenly deprived of the drug are called (3)_____.

(4)_____ relieve pain and, in large doses, may produce stupor. Codeine and morphine are both made from (5)_____. Another drug derived from the same source, (6)_____ is so dangerous that it is not used medically. Substitution of the drug (7)_____ is being used as a treatment for heroin addiction.

Sedative drugs that may cause dangerous physical dependence are the (8)_____. Increasingly abused are the (9)_____, sedative-type drugs used to reduce tensions. Also commonly abused are the group of stimulant drugs, the (10)_____. (11)_____ is one of these drugs. Marijuana is a mild hallucinogen, while (12)_____ is a powerful one. The liver and other organs may be severely damaged if (13)_____ are inhaled. To use drugs safely, use only (14)_____ drugs, in the dosage ordered by the doctor.

What You Can Do

1. Form a committee of students from your health class to find out and report how prescription drugs, over-the-counter drugs, and illegal drugs differ. How is the sale of each kind of drug controlled? What

are the general hazards in the use of each kind? Can these hazards be prevented? If so, how? What are common examples of each kind of drug?

2. How much do you remember of what you have studied? If a statement is false, correct it by replacing the italicized words. Write all the statements, in correct form, in your notebook. Do not write in this book.

   a. When a person develops drug tolerance, *smaller* doses produce the same effect that was produced by the original dose.

   b. *Morphine* is a drug often used in cough syrups.

   c. A person who cannot stop taking a drug is *drug-dependent.*

   d. Cocaine is a product of the *cacao* tree.

   e. One of the most dangerous hallucinogens, which should never be used is *Synanon.*

   f. Marijuana affects all users *alike.*

   g. There are *no* treatment programs for people who become dependent on illegal drugs.

Things to Try /

Join with your classmates to prepare a list of questions that you would like answered about drugs. With your teacher's approval, invite a doctor, health department official, nurse, or teacher who has worked with drug problems to review the questions in advance and discuss them with your class.

Probing Further /

What You Should Know About Drugs, by Charles W. Gorodetzky, M.D. and Samuel T. Christian, M.D., Harcourt Brace Jovanovich, 1970. This very readable book on drugs gives the origins and effects of the commonly abused drugs. The book includes teenagers' own accounts of their experiences with drugs, including alcohol.

Drugs—Facts on Their Use and Abuse, by Norman W. Houser in consultation with Julius B. Richmond, M.D., Lothrop, Lee & Shepard, 1969. A clearcut account, clarifying terms like physical and psychological dependence.

Drug Abuse—What Can Be Done?, by Jules Saltman, Public Affairs Pamphlet No. 390A, 381 Park Avenue South, New York 10016, 1971. Up-to-date information on abused drugs, drug traffic controls, and the variety of methods used to help the narcotics addict.

The Taste of Ashes, by Bill Stern with Oscar Fraley, Holt, Rinehart & Winston, 1959. The facts about Bill Stern at the beginning of this chapter were taken from this life story.

Health Concepts in Action

Does this statement bring together ideas you have gained from this chapter?

> *Dependence upon mood-altering substances impairs mental, physical, and social health.*

Applying this concept of drug dependence, which health practices would you

— continue?

— change?

— begin?

Will you now, as a result of your study, change any of your health objectives?

UNIT EIGHT
You Can Make Safety a Habit

35 / *Preventing Accidents*

617-654

"If we hurry," said Paul to his five friends in his car, "we'll get to camp before Bob and his gang do." Just at that moment, Bob's car whizzed by and the race was on.

Car racing can offer fine competition when it is properly supervised and conducted in controlled areas. But highways are public places built for the convenience of everyone; they cannot be supervised or controlled for racing. The thoughtless use of highways for racing endangers the lives of many innocent people, as well as the driver's life.

A PROBE INTO LIVING SAFELY—What habits of work and play can help you to avoid accidents? To help you find out, you will be probing questions like these:

1. What are some of the human factors— physical and emotional—that contribute to accidents? What are some environmental causes of accidents?

2. What are the four most frequent causes of highway fatalities? Why does the trained driver have fewer accidents? How can highway hazards be reduced?

3. What are some precautions for preventing fires? firearm accidents? poisoning? school accidents?

4. What safety habits should bicycle riders develop? What additional safety habits are needed by motorcycle riders?

5. List some job-safety techniques that we can apply in our daily activities.

35-1 Highway accidents claim an astonishingly high number of lives each year. What safety habits can help to lower the toll taken?

ACCIDENTS DON'T JUST HAPPEN

Accidents are undesirable, unplanned events that often result in injury and sometimes in death. Injuries can deprive you of pleasure in sports and social activities. They can be both physically and mentally painful. An injury could, for instance, seriously affect your schoolwork. If you are ever out of school for a long period of time due to injury, you may find yourself far behind in your classwork.

You will, of course, find hazards that may cause accidents in all types of activities. But most of these can be overcome by observing certain precautions. In this chapter you will find suggestions that can help you become alert to such hazards, and some precautions to take to protect yourself against accidental injury.

Actually, forming habits of safe living is a lifelong task. With the constant flow of new equipment and gadgets on the market, there are always new directions and rules to learn. A good understanding of accident causes and how to deal with them will be of use to you as long as you live.

Accidents Are a Leading Cause of Death

Did you know that the fourth leading cause of death in this country is accidents? Only heart disease, cancer, and stroke outrank accidents as a cause of death. But these are degenerative diseases, mainly of older people. Among persons between the ages of one and twenty-five, accidents lead all other causes of death.

About 1 million Americans died in wars fought by the United States from the American Revolution to 1970. But during the much shorter period from 1900 through 1970, almost 2 million Americans died in motor-vehicle deaths.

In a recent year, not only were over 54,000 people killed on our highways, but about 2 million people received disabling injuries. To these figures must be added the accidents that happened during that year in other public places and at work and in the home: another 60,000 fatal accidents and almost 9 million disabling injuries!

Accidents do not happen only to the so-called "accident-repeaters." In fact, most of the drivers in fatal accidents were considered

35-2 ACCIDENTAL DEATHS
BY TYPE OF ACCIDENT

Type of Accident	Ages 15 to 24 Total	All Ages Total	All Ages	
			Male	Female
Motor vehicle	16,543	54,862	39,788	15,074
Falls	409	18,651	9,314	9,337
Fires, burns	332	7,335	4,296	3,039
Drowning	2,030	7,372	6,265	1,107
Firearms	764	2,394	2,049	345
Ingestion of food and objects	185	3,100	1,821	1,279
Poison (solid, liquid)	481	2,583	1,616	967
Poison by gas	339	1,526	1,128	398
All other types	1,929	17,041	13,147	3,894
Total	23,012	114,864	79,424	35,440

Adapted from *Accident Facts, 1971 Edition*, published by the National Safety Council.

35-2 This chart shows the many kinds of fatal accidents among people of all ages and in your own age group in a single year. Automobile accidents account for well over two-thirds of these deaths. Note how many more men are affected than women. Can you say why?

"good" drivers according to one study. Eight out of ten of them had no record of previous accidents.

Notice, in Figure 35-2, that motor vehicle deaths lead all other categories of fatal accidents. Motor-vehicle deaths accounted for almost half of the accidental deaths in the population at large and over half of the deaths in the 15 to 24 age group.

Falls and fires are usually the next causes of accidental deaths among people of all ages. However, among those from 15 to 24 years old, drownings are the second leading cause of death followed by injuries from firearms (over 700 deaths).

From Figure 35-2 you can also see that many more accidental deaths occurred among males than among females. What percent of the total number of accidents occurred among males? among females?

Perhaps this striking difference may be attributed to the fact that boys and men engage in more hazardous types of work and are, in general, permitted to be more venturesome in their activities than are girls and women.

The statistics in this table reveal another striking difference. At all age levels, accidental deaths from motor vehicles are more than twice as frequent for men (39,788 deaths) as for women (15,074 deaths). However, we know that men drive more miles than do women and this may account, in part at least, for their greater number of fatal accidents.

The Number One Killer of Teen-agers

Let's face it, accidents are the number one killer in your age group. You often hear accidents spoken of as just "bad luck." They are bad luck, but we know that *accidents do not just happen; they are always caused*, and often there is more than one cause. Usually a chain of careless behaviors leads to injury or death. For example, a man waits in a closed garage while the motor of his automobile warms up. He is overcome by carbon monoxide gas and dies. Or someone walking backward while chatting with friends injures his head on a low-hanging sign.

Factors That Cause Accidents

One of the important factors associated with accidents is the way you feel physically and emotionally. When you are fatigued, for instance, your reaction time is slower and you are likely to make mistakes in time, distance, and space. When you are worried over some problem, it is difficult to concentrate on what you are doing. Suppose that you forget to turn off the switch of the iron when you finish pressing your jacket. While you are thinking of something else, the iron may burn a hole in the ironing board—or an even more serious fire may occur.

Another factor that is involved in accidents is the way you think—your attitude. Do you, for example, wear the protective gear that is provided for some sports or do you neglect this and say, "I got away with it before, didn't I?" Your attitude about rules of any kind will go far toward determining how free you will be from accidents.

Then there are the environmental or external factors that can contribute to injury or death. Some common dangers are firearms, knives, electric and gas appliances, glass doors, scatter rugs, cleaning fluids, and cluttered stairways. Also, there are the outdoor hazards, such as poisonous spiders and

35-3 An accident is about to happen. What chain of events is leading up to it?

reptiles, insect sprays, and power lawn mowers and hedge clippers. There are also water hazards near a lake or river.

Many of the potential environmental hazards can be eliminated by proper protective devices. For instance, you can put eye-level markings on glass doors, skid-proof mats under scatter rugs, and handrails and lights on stairways. And you can join efforts to keep our air, water, and food safe—as described in Chapter 5. However, you also need to learn to protect yourself against certain elements of nature, such as fog, blizzards, lightning, and tornadoes. In Chapter 36, you will find suggestions for protecting yourself against the destructive force of some of these natural hazards.

As you see, it is possible to modify and eliminate many of the environmental hazards. But the human factor, your general physical and emotional health and your attitudes, are not so readily altered. This takes time. First you must want to change and then be willing to practice until safe living becomes a habit.

Highway Fatalities Lead the Teen-age Accident List

Since highway accidents are associated with three fifths (Figure 35-2) of all fatal accidents among teen-agers, we will consider them first. Insurance agencies have already taken into account one of the statistics shown in Figure 35-2—the fact that boys and young men have almost four times as many fatal highway accidents as do girls and young women. As a result, boys and young men must now pay higher premium rates for automobile insurance.

Accident-causing Drivers

Extensive research findings gathered from all parts of the country have pinpointed some of the factors contributing most frequently to highway fatalities.

1. Driving too fast is a cause in one out of three fatal accidents.
2. Violating traffic laws is a factor in three out of four fatalities.
3. The use of alchohol is involved in about one half of driver and about one third of adult pedestrian fatalities.
4. Unsafe cars are high contributors to fatal accidents.

From these frequent causes of fatalities you see that human factors, mentioned earlier, are significant. We can add to these causes those potentially dangerous drivers who are socially maladjusted, selfish, careless, discourteous, and who show poor judgment. When any one of these dangerous traits occurs in combination with speed, intoxication, or a defective car, there is almost certain to be serious trouble.

Importance of Driver-Training

Statistics show that people who have been taught how to drive by a professional teacher have fewer accidents. This should recommend to you the importance of taking and passing a driver education course before you attempt to drive an automobile.

In many states, driver-training courses are required of all high school students, and in others they are offered on a voluntary basis. If your school does not offer this course, you may find one given by a nearby motor club or some civic organization. There are also driver-training courses offered by private agencies, usually for a fee.

The final test of driver-training is, of course, your ability to pass the state driver licensing test. But obtaining a state license to drive does not make you an "expert" driver. It takes many hours of driving in all types of traffic and weather and on roadways that require you to make different types of judgments before you can qualify as a sure, safe driver.

35-4 Driver-education in classes such as this has proved effective in reducing the number of accidents involving teen-age drivers.

Defensive Driving

In addition to courses in driver-training, **defensive driving** courses are now offered in many areas for the general public. This is sometimes referred to as "driving for yourself and the other fellow too." Here are a few of the principles emphasized in defensive driving:

1. Never "tailgate." The practice of following too closely the car ahead is the most common cause of rear-end collisions. Stay back one car length for each ten miles of speed you are traveling. When another driver "tailgates" you, slow down and encourage him to pass.
2. Expect the driver ahead of you to put on his brakes without warning. Be alert to situations in which he might slow down or stop.
3. Stop smoothly and gradually and signal your intentions of stopping, slowing down, or turning.
4. Look to the left and right when approaching an intersection. Never assume the other driver will yield the right-of-way.

35-5 This young man is a defensive driver. When you drive, do you drive for yourself and for the other fellow, too?

5. When in doubt never pass. Use your turn signal when passing. Make sure someone behind you is not trying to pass you at the same time. When passing, sound your horn or flick your lights to alert the driver ahead. Accelerate and pass quickly, getting back into your lane after you can clearly see the car you passed in your rear-view mirror.

Accident-causing Automobiles

Motor vehicles fall into the class of environmental accident-causing factors. This includes the entire vehicle, inside and outside. Unlike many environmental factors, the automobile moves and changes. It sustains stresses and pressures at the will of the driver and in conformity to the surface of the road. Sometimes, this is referred to as "the deadly triangle" — the car, the driver, and the highway. From the statistics in Figure 35-2, it is obvious that drastic action to reduce injury and death on our highways calls for action on all three of these fronts.

Present Provisions for Car Safety Challenged

In the past few years many articles and books have been published on the topic of highway safety. Some authors put the primary blame for highway fatalities on human factors while other authors emphasize the need to improve the safety features of the car. Almost everyone agrees that roadway improvement is essential to the reduction of automobile fatalities.

Unsafe at Any Speed by Ralph Nader (Grossman Publishers, N. Y., 1965) is among the many publications that deal largely with the need to improve the safety features of the car. *Unsafe at Any Speed* presents facts — it is well documented — in the hope that a better informed public will demand safer cars. It suggests that a crashproof car is a possibility.

Mr. Nader challenges a theory that for a long time has had the support of national, state, and voluntary agencies. This theory is that the driver is the primary cause of vehicular accidents. He points out that among accidents involving all modes of transportation — trains, ships, planes, and motor vehicles — the motor vehicle was responsible, in a recent year, for 92 percent of the deaths and 98 percent of the injuries. Further, while there now are safety standards established for all other modes of transportation, there are no such uniform safety standards for motor vehicles.

At about this same time, 1965–1966, the findings of extensive research into national automobile safety were also published. These findings, along with those of Mr. Nader, stimulated national concern and debate. As a result of this concern, congressional committees conducted hearings and called

35-6 Ralph Nader testifies before a congressional committee investigating automobile safety. Nader's persistent attack helped to bring about new automobile safety standards.

Miles per Hour	Reaction Distance, ft	Braking Distance, ft	Total Stopping Distance, ft
5	5.5	4	9.5
10	11.0	8	19.0
15	16.5	13	29.5
20	22.0	20	42.0
25	27.5	28	55.5
30	33.0	40	73.0
35	38.5	52	90.5
40	44.0	72	116.0
45	49.5	92	141.5
50	55.0	118	173.0
55	60.5	148	208.5
60	66.0	182	248.0
65	71.5	220	291.5
70	77.0	266	343.0

These distances are based on tests made by the Bureau of Public Roads. The chart shows how greatly braking distances and danger zones increase when you increase your speed.

35-7 In a driver-education course, you will learn important safety facts like these:

If you see a danger and want to come to a full stop, it will take about ¾ second before you press the brake pedal (average reaction time). During this time, your car will have moved a certain distance, depending upon its speed. This is known as *reaction distance.*

Even after you apply the brakes, your car will travel a certain distance before stopping. This is the *braking distance,* also dependent on speed.

Under the best road conditions, how far will you travel after you decide to stop your car? To find out, add the reaction distance and braking distance for a particular speed.

Why is "brake early" an important driving caution?

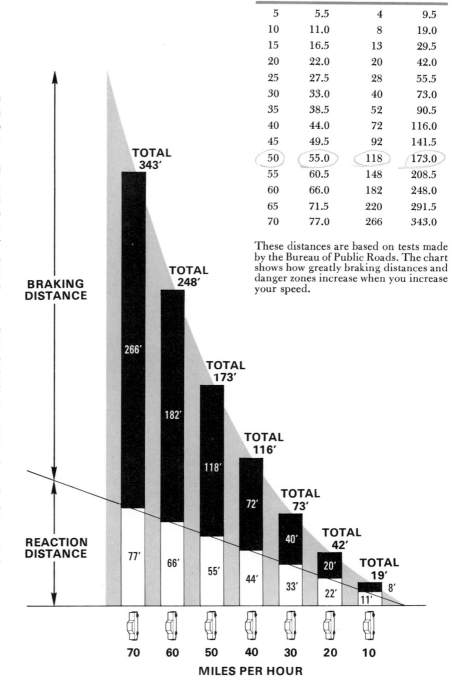

BRAKING DISTANCE

REACTION DISTANCE

TOTAL 343'
TOTAL 248'
TOTAL 173'
TOTAL 116'
TOTAL 73'
TOTAL 42'
TOTAL 19'

266'
182'
118'
72'
40'
20'
8'

77'
66'
55'
44'
33'
22'
11'

70 60 50 40 30 20 10

MILES PER HOUR

35-8 Lap and shoulder safety belts are now required by law in all new automobiles in the United States. It is estimated that the belts will save at lease 10,000 lives each year. The automobile shown has another important safety feature—a collapsible steering wheel.

Nader to testify along with research experts of national prominence and officials of the automotive industry.

Because of such conferences, federal laws have been passed establishing minimum safety features for new motor vehicles. These safety standards are constantly being improved. They include the design of such car features as door latches, mirrors, brakes, and dashboards, as well as safety belts. See Figure 35-8.

In addition, many states are attempting to improve their motor vehicle inspection programs. These inspection programs will help to make certain that cars already on the road are being maintained in safe operating condition.

Accident-causing Roadways

Nearly two thirds of our 3.6 million miles of streets and roads were originally laid out and in use before we had automobiles. While vast improvements in roadways have been made, they have not kept pace with the increasing numbers of motor vehicles. There are now said to be about 90 million motor vehicles and 100 million drivers who drive more than 870 billion miles per year on our roadways.

Automobile crashes have become a critical national problem, not only in lives lost and disabling injuries, but in cost. The cost per year was recently estimated at 9.8 billion dollars.

Highway Improvement Programs

Along with concern about safer vehicles and better driver training has come concern about highway safety design.

Studies of highway accidents suggest many changes that can make present roads less hazardous. Such changes include clearer signs, better guardrails and pedestrian walkways, safety areas for vehicles that have to leave the road, and so on.

Senseless road "booby traps" are found the country over. Most of these hazardous conditions can be eliminated or remedied. Installing a stop light at a dangerous intersection, trimming a hedge that obscures the view, eliminating left turns into oncoming traffic, improving entrances into fast-moving superhighway traffic, and similar "spot improvements" can greatly decrease traffic crashes and casualties.

Citizens are urged to report hazardous spots to local or state highway officials or to the American Automobile Association (AAA). They may also be reported to the United States Bureau of Public Roads, Matomic Building, 1717 H Street, N.W. Washington, D.C. 20235. Here is a worthy activity for teen-agers. You can help locate and report these danger spots.

Safe Cycling

Bicycling is becoming more popular every year for recreation and transportation. A trend in this direction has developed among high school and college students and among adults seeking exercise to offset sedentary occupations. Cycle tours, already popular in Europe, are attracting people of all ages in America. To provide more pleasant and safer conditions for these tours, bicycle paths are being constructed along the highways in many parts of the country. Regular traffic signs along the pathways warn cyclists of highway and railroad crossings and other hazards.

The growing number of cyclists creates a problem in roadway safety. The National Safety Council reports that in a recent year there were 34,000 cyclists injured and 600 killed in highway accidents. Shocked and alarmed by these figures, the 11 million members of the General Federation of Women's Clubs are crusading for bicycle safety with the same zeal that they campaigned for seat belts.

Bicycle manufacturers now have an array of safety devices, most of them designed to make the bicycle more visible at night. A pedal that lights up when in action creates a circular light that should help motorists see the outline of the bicycle.

Other devices recommended and available include reflector tape, bells, horns, headlights, and the "wiggler." The "wiggler" can be seen in the dark and is similar in size to an automobile antenna. As the bicycle moves along it causes the device to vibrate or wiggle.

Cyclists in most states are required to obey the same traffic regulations as motorists. You will find these regulations in your state driver's manual. The Bicycle Institute of

35-9 A bicycle club sets off for new and interesting territory to explore.

America has compiled the following list of characteristics of good cyclists in their publication "Rules for Bicycle Riders":

1. He obeys all traffic laws.
2. He gives pedestrians the right-of-way.
3. He never rides against traffic.
4. He looks for cars pulling out of driveways and parking areas.
5. He does not "hitch on" to cars or weave in and out of traffic.
6. He does not carry another person on his bicycle.
7. He always dismounts and walks his bicycle across heavily traveled intersections.
8. He keeps his bicycle in good condition.
9. He rides single file on busy or narrow streets and never rides more than two abreast.
10. He always rides with consideration of others.

Motor bikes and motorcycles, like bicycles, have become a popular means of transportation, especially in congested city areas. They are inexpensive to buy and operate, in comparison to automobiles, and they are easier to park. The operator of a motor bike or motorcycle must obey the same traffic laws as automobile drivers. Accident records show a high rate of crashes, particularly among motorcyclists. This has caused a number of states to require motorcyclists to wear a helmet when riding. Some of the dangers inherent in the use of these small, easily manipulated power cycles are the tendency to weave in an out of traffic, "jump" lights, pass on hills and curves, and drive too fast on uneven surfaces. Unfortunately, motorcycles and motor bikes upset easily, especially on uneven ground or when the road surface unexpectedly becomes slick.

Pedestrian Safety—Everyone's Concern

There are reasons why motorists should be protective and courteous to pedestrians. The nondriver pedestrian does not know how difficult it is to stop a car quickly or to spot a pedestrian on a busy street. The experienced driver knows that among pedestrians there will be small children whose actions are unpredictable and elderly persons with slow reactions. There may be persons who are ill, crippled, deaf, or distracted by some problem. Although the blind can be distinguished by their white canes, there is no such warning device for persons with other handicaps.

The pedestrian and the motorist are both expected to observe safety precautions but their accidents seem uniformly to be due to either not knowing what the precautions are or disregarding them. Based on years of observation, the AAA has compiled the following list of pedestrian safety precautions:

35-10 Motor scooters have become a common sight—and so have the protective helmets that all drivers should wear.

1. Look in both directions before crossing any street or roadway.
2. Never step into the street from between parked cars.
3. Cross streets only at intersections and on a green light or walk signal.
4. Watch for cars that are turning, especially cars making left turns.
5. If you are waiting for a bus in an unprotected zone, face the oncoming traffic.
6. Never cross behind or in front of a vehicle from which you have just stepped.
7. On rural roads, use side paths if provided. Otherwise, walk on the left side of the road facing oncoming traffic.
8. Step off the road when nearby cars are about to pass.

9. At night, wear something white or carry a flashlight. Remember that you can see the headlights of an approaching vehicle long before the driver can see you.

SAFETY AT HOME, SCHOOL, AND ON THE JOB

The number of accidents that occur in and around your home are second only to those that happen on our highways. In a recent two-year period there were 20 million accidental home injuries. About one half of these were serious enough to require bed rest while two million of the more seriously injured were hospitalized.

Fatal Home Accidents

Among the fatal home accidents, *falls* account for about one half of the total number. Many of these falls could have been prevented. For example, the top and bottom steps of stairways should be painted with luminous or white paint. Elsewhere in the home, such preventive measures should be taken as putting nonskid pads in bathtubs, hand grips on showers, and side rails on beds for children and elderly persons.

Every home should have a stepladder. Its use prevents falls from chairs, table tops, and other unreliable means of getting up to hang curtains, change light bulbs, and perform similar household tasks. Notice the high incidence of falls listed in Figure 35-2.

After falls, next in frequency among fatal accidents are those associated with *burns*, *fires*, and *firearms*. Many of these can be prevented by keeping electric cords in repair and out from under rugs; using safety matches and keeping all matches out of the reach of children; screening open fireplaces; learning the discipline of never smoking in bed; and keeping firearms safely put away.

Knowing the protective measures to use in case of fire can help save lives and property. If you awake at night, for example, and smell smoke, first get everyone out of the house. Then call the fire department and next post someone out front to direct the firemen to your house. If you discover a grease fire in the oven while meat is being roasted, turn off the range. Then open the oven door and throw a handful of salt or baking soda into the oven. Close the oven door and the fire will be smothered.

The common remark heard in cases of firearm fatalities seems to be, "I was sure he unloaded his gun before he put it away." For protection against the human tendency to forget to take precautions, all firearms should be unloaded in the presence of another person, then stored under lock and key.

Poisoning by mouth or inhalation ranks high in fatal home accidents, especially among young children. Calling drugs "candy" as a means of bribing children frequently leads to the child's taking an overdose. According to figures from the poison control centers, aspirin is the great offender in fatal accidents among small children. When using insect sprays or spraying paint on walls and furniture you should maintain good circulation of air in the room. A more difficult problem is that of fumes from gas or sewer lines. No time should be lost in locating the source of the fumes and obtaining immediate repairs.

Precautions must be taken against other potentially fatal hazards in your home. A discarded refrigerator should have its door removed as a safety precaution; an abandoned cistern should be filled in and boarded over.

At the end of this chapter under "What You Can Do," you will find a home safety checklist. If you can answer YES to all 26 questions, then you are safe in your home. If you answer 23 or less as YES, you need to do some "homework" to eliminate the hazards and improve your safety habits.

35-11 Accidents in the home, as elsewhere, do not just happen—they are caused. How many bad practices that are likely to lead to an accident can you spot here?

35-12 Medicines and cleaning supplies should be totally inaccessible to young children. Is this safety practice observed in your home?

Accidents at School

Accident statistics are especially alarming during the school years, since accidents are responsible for more deaths among those in the age group of 5 to 17 than the next several leading causes of death combined. As you have seen, boys in that age group are involved in more accidents than are girls.

School administrators have a legal and moral obligation to provide buildings, grounds, equipment, and supplies that meet the highest standards of safe and healthful living. You have learned in your many safety lessons that students also have a personal obligation for their own safety and a social obligation for the safety of others. Many states have laws that apply to the supervision of school activities. These laws are designed to insure that school activities are conducted under conditions that are safe for the students and for school property.

In school, the greatest number of accidents occur in physical education classes, sports programs, and recreational activities.

It is recognized that there are certain inherent hazards in these school activities, just as there are inherent hazards in such a common daily activity as walking across a busy street. But many hazards can be reduced to a minimum so that you can participate in activities at an optimum level of safety. You can do this by observing the four points listed later in this chapter on page 632.

Other areas in school in which accidents are frequent are the shop and the science laboratories.

In the shop, you need space to use your tools and to avoid harming students working near you. Using the correct tool for the job at hand makes a job easier as well as safer. A sharp tool is safer to use than a dull one. Your clothing can also be a hazard. Avoid loose sleeves, flowing ties, and flying shirttails that can get caught in machinery and pull you in with them. Before using a new tool or piece of machinery, always read the instructions. If the instructions are not clear, consult your teacher.

In the laboratory, it is vital to your safety to follow directions in mixing chemicals or in performing experiments. Never perform an experiment when your teacher is absent. Handle test tubes and beakers with care to avoid cuts from breakage. Never use beakers for drinking glasses; there may be a chemical residue in them. Spilled chemicals should be cleaned up immediately.

If a chemical splashes on your skin, wash the area immediately with clear water and continue the treatment for at least five minutes. Chemicals splashed into the eye are painful and dangerous. The eye should be washed or irrigated in running water for at least ten minutes. Following this, immediately see your ophthalmologist. Wash your hands thoroughly at the end of each laboratory period.

There are many other school hazards; those mentioned are the more frequent and dangerous ones. The safety rules posted in

35-13 What kinds of shop activities require more eye protection than these goggles give? Why?

Welding

your school are there for your protection. Learn them thoroughly and make them a habit.

At the end of this chapter there is a sample accident record that you may find interesting to keep in your classroom.

Safety on the Farm

It is often said that somewhere on a farm there is "an accident waiting to happen." In a recent year approximately 11,300 farm residents lost their lives both on and off the farm and about one million were injured.

Prevention and preparedness are the watchwords for farm hazards. Every effort should be made to remove as many hazards as possible. When injuries do occur, the farmer must be prepared to give first aid. Most farms are far away from doctors and hospitals, so the farmer, his family, and his workers need a good knowledge of emergency care; and they should have plenty of first aid supplies at hand.

Hazards abound on farms—machinery, power tools, tractors, insect sprays, wells, pits, and animals. Bulls and boars are dangerous animals and everyone must learn that they should not be treated as pets. Then there are the dangers of lifting loads that are too heavy, with resulting muscle-straining injuries, and of driving heavy tractors over uneven ground, with the ever-present danger of the tractors overturning and crushing their drivers. These are just a few examples of possible farm accidents.

Occupational Safety

The importance of safety on the job lies not only in saving lives and preventing crippling injuries but also in the enormous effect such accidents have on our economy. The man-days lost at work due to injury, in a recent year, were 230 million. This work loss is estimated at a cost of one billion dollars to industry and to the workers. And these figures do not include the cost in human suffering, or medical and hospital expenses.

In the face of such figures it is difficult to believe that occupational accidents have been declining steadily for some years. This decline is believed to be due to new safety devices that have been added to machines and power tools for worker protection. Also, supervisors are now required to enforce the rule that workers use such safety equipment as goggles, helmets, insulated gloves, and metal-reinforced shoes. The decline in occupational accidents encourages us to believe that eventually similar declines may be expected in other activities.

SAFETY SHOULD BE A HABIT

Safe living does not come "just naturally"; it has to be learned. You learn how to concentrate on what you are doing and to obey safety rules. You learn, too, how to deal with danger in the environment. There are many ways to go about this and all of them require something of you. You must form habits of safe behavior in everything you do.

Learning habits of safe behavior is much like learning to swim. You recall that it took a great deal of practice, concentration, and determination before you got anywhere in the water. So it is with learning safety habits. Here are some simple skills or principles of safe behavior.

How to Make Safety a Habit

1. Look for hazards in whatever you may be doing. Once you recognize a hazard you will become alert to it. Suppose, for example, that you are asked to mow the lawn, just as you are about to go play ball. Because you are in a hurry to get the mowing done, you may fail to look for such hazards as pebbles in the grass. If a pebble glances off the blades of your mower and strikes you above the eye, you won't have to finish the mowing, but you won't be able to play ball either.

2. Remove any hazard that you can. Perhaps you see a skateboard on the lawn or roller skates in the driveway. You can step over them; or you can pick them up, store them in a safe place, and prevent an accident from happening to someone else.

3. There are hazards that you cannot remove, such as wet streets. But you can compensate for them if you are driving by allowing more time to get where you are going, by driving more slowly, staying well behind the car in front of you, and avoiding putting on your brakes suddenly.

4. Avoid creating new hazards by such acts as running down the "up" stairs at school, leaving dresser drawers standing open at home, leaving the iron on, or failing to completely drown-out your campfire.

It is possible, by taking sensible precautions, to live safely in almost any environment. The above easy-to-remember principles are a guide to use for your own safety and the safety of society.

What kind of health practices should you apply in maintaining your health? Check your understanding of the chapter. On a separate sheet of paper, number 1 through 21 and insert the answer from the vocabulary list below. Use each expression, but use each one only once.

accidents	fewer	motor vehicles
cancer	fires	"naturally"
concentrate	flashlight	precautions
death	heart disease	slower
defensive	highways	speed
falls	injury	stroke
feel	motorists	white

Accidents are unplanned events that often result in (1)_____, and sometimes in (2)_____. Statistics show that accidents cause more deaths than (3)_____, (4)_____, or (5)_____. The number one killer in your age group is (6)_____. Accidents do not just happen, they are always caused. An important element in accidents is how you (7)_____, physically and emotionally. When fatigued, your reaction time is (8)_____, and when you are concerned over some problem, it is difficult to (9)_____ on what you are doing.

Accidents that occur on (10)_____ lead the teen-age list, and one frequent cause of these fatalities is (11)_____. Statistics show that people who have been taught how to drive have (12)_____ accidents. "Driving for yourself and the other fellow too," called (13)_____ driving, is now offered as a course in addition to driver training. The records show that among accidents involving all modes of transportation, (14)_____ have the highest percentage of deaths and injuries.

When you ride a bicycle, motorbike, or motorcycle, you are required to obey the same traffic rules as do (15)_____. Pedestrians are also expected to obey safety (16)_____, one of which is to wear something (17)_____ or to carry a (18)_____ at night. Among fatal home accidents, (19)_____ are the cause of about one half the total number. Next in frequency are fatal accidents associated with (20)_____. Safe living does not come (21)_____; it has to be learned.

What You Can Do

Accidents that occur in and around the home are second only in frequency to those that occur on highways. Copy the list on the next pages; then make a tour of your home and check the various items on the list.

If you can answer "yes" to all 26 items, you are probably safe in your home. If you answer "yes" to 23 or less, you need to eliminate the existing hazards and improve your safety habits. How can you obtain help in removing hazards? What must you and your family do to make your home safer?

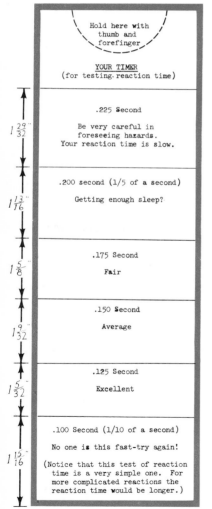

35-14 "Timer" shown here has been reduced in length. Use the marked measurements when you make your own.

yes   no   In The Kitchen:

____ ____ 1. Do you keep floors dry and clean at all times?

____ ____ 2. Do you keep matches in metal containers out of reach of small children?

____ ____ 3. Is a sturdy step stool available for use in reaching high cabinets and shelves?

____ ____ 4. Are all household poisons like lye, bleaches, cleaning materials, and rat and bug killers stored where small children cannot get them?

____ ____ 5. Do you keep handles of cooking utensils turned inward on the stove?

____ ____ 6. Do you keep knives and scissors sheathed and out of reach of children?

In The Bathroom:

____ ____ 7. Are aspirin and other medicines locked up and out of reach of children?

____ ____ 8. Do you have nonskid mats on the floor and in the tub or shower?

____ ____ 9. Do you stay in the bathroom with small children to prevent their being drowned or scalded?

____ ____ 10. Are the electric pull-chains properly insulated?

In The Bedroom:

____ ____ 11. Are screens fastened to protect children from falling through open windows?

____ ____ 12. Is there a light near the bed so that you need not walk and stumble in the dark?

____ ____ 13. Do you make it a rule *never* to smoke in bed?

____ ____ 14. If you have a gas or oil heater in your bedroom, is the room well ventilated?

In The Living Room:

____ ____ 15. Do you have a metal screen for your fireplace?

____ ____ 16. Do you keep passageways clear of electric cords?

____ ____ 17. Are rugs anchored with nonskid materials?

____ ____ 18. Is the furniture arranged so that low tables and footstools will not be tripped over?

____ ____ 19. Do you make sure all matches, cigars, and cigarettes are out before going out or to bed?

On The Stairs:

___ ___ 20. Do you keep all toys, brooms, mops, and other articles off the steps to prevent falls?
___ ___ 21. Are all stairways well lighted and equipped with suitable handrails?
___ ___ 22. Are there gates at the bottom and top of stairs to keep the baby from falling?

In The Basement:

___ ___ 23. Do you keep the floor dry to prevent electrical shock when handling a light fixture or electrical appliance?
___ ___ 24. Are trash, newspapers, and discarded furniture thrown out regularly to eliminate a fire hazard?

In The Yard:

___ ___ 25. Are the yard and driveway kept free of trash and clutter to eliminate fire and tripping hazards?
___ ___ 26. Are garden tools and outdoor playthings stored in proper places promptly after use?

(Prepared by the Accident Prevention Section—North Carolina State Board of Health.)

Things to Try

1. Using a chart similar to the one below, keep a record posted on your tackboard of all the accidents that happen to members of your homeroom. Every so often have a class discussion of each accident.

Kind of accident	Where it happened	Why it happened	What to do to prevent it from happening again
skinned knee	tennis court	tripped on shoelace	stop and tie lace when undone
fractured ankle	cellar stairway	stairway dark no handrail	install light and handrail

2. Make a careful survey of the area adjacent to your school to find out if there are any traffic "booby traps" that should be reported. Look for such things as shrubs, trees, and walls that obscure the driver's view. Is there a dangerous intersection that needs a stoplight? Is the area properly marked as a school zone?

3. Cut a stiff piece of cardboard 11½ by 3 inches and measure off the distances as shown in Figure 35-14. The cardboard is now your

"timer." To test a friend, hold the timer at the top, with its lower portion slightly above his hand. Have him hold his thumb and forefinger apart, so the timer can slip between them. Instruct him to grasp the timer as quickly as he can when you drop it. The point at which he grasps the timer gives his approximate simple reaction time in thousandths of a second. Keep in mind that this test of reaction time is a very simple one. For a more complicated reaction like that on page 625, reaction time would be longer.

4. Look through the rest of this book to develop a manual containing safety hints that are especially important to you in *your* activities. Check, for instance: safety in sports, pages 173-79; avoiding poison gases, pages 283-4; how to stop bleeding, pages 297-99; avoiding ear damage, page 197.

Probing Further

Sportsmanlike Driving, Sixth Edition, by the American Automobile Association, Washington, D. C., Webster Division, McGraw-Hill, 1969. This book is useful for the experienced driver as well as the beginner. It has an especially interesting chapter on the effects of alcohol on driving.

"Taking the Hazards Out of Bicycling," *Today's Health,* July 1965. This article describes the many ways that a bicycle can be made safer.

Unsafe at Any Speed, by Ralph Nader, Grossman, 1965. This is the well-known book whose author aroused public debate over the lack of safety features in automobiles.

Health Concepts in Action

Does this statement help express what you have learned?

> **Health depends upon personal and community practices that prevent accidental injuries.**

Applying this concept of safety, which health practices would you

— continue?

— change?

— begin?

Will you now, as a result of your study, change any of your health objectives?

36 / Coping with Disaster

Some dangers in our environment build up slowly—such as the pollution of our air and water. You have read about these accumulative dangers in Chapter 5. Other environmental dangers face us suddenly. In spite of their suddenness, there are ways you can prepare to maintain health during such emergencies. Because doctors and nurses are generally scarce at such times, everyone has an essential role to play during a disaster.

A PROBE INTO EMERGENCY LIVING—How can you maintain health during prolonged periods of emergency? To find out, you will be probing questions like these:

1. What are some natural hazards in the environment? How can you protect yourself and others against each hazard?

2. What measures can you take in advance of disaster to reduce the possibility of fire? disease? and contaminated water?

3. What do the different public warning signals mean? What procedure should you follow upon hearing each warning? Where is your nearest Civil Defense shelter?

4. What organizations are concerned with helping us prepare for environmental emergencies?

5. What courses can you take to learn how to assist yourself and others during emergencies?

CONTROLLING THE EFFECTS OF DISASTER

When an unforeseen mishap occurs, bringing with it widespread destruction of life and property, it is called a disaster. When disaster strikes, many (and sometimes all) of the conveniences of living that we depend upon may suddenly not be available. Water, heat, refrigeration, lights, telephones, elevators, and many other services may be cut off.

Almost everyone has experienced a power failure in the neighborhood and felt concern for the food that was stored in the refrigerator. Perhaps an ice storm has broken the telephone lines in your part of town and you have experienced the inconvenience of being without a telephone. These are relatively minor mishaps but they serve as reminders of the problems that are to be faced under disaster conditions.

36-2 A first aid class learns a rather difficult procedure—how to apply a head bandage. Have you this and other first aid skills?

Origins of Disaster

Disaster may originate from such uncontrollable forces of nature as earthquakes, blizzards, floods, hurricanes, lightning, and tornadoes. It may be caused by man-made explosives and devices, including thermonuclear attack. When confronted by a disaster each person must be able to assume certain responsibilities. One of these is to be able to take care of yourself, to be self-sustaining during the emergency. There is also a civic responsibility—your obligation to be of assistance in your neighborhood and community. In order to discharge these responsibilities well, you will need preparation and training. It is no small task to learn how to live and survive without protective equipment.

Preparation for Disaster

There are many ways to go about preparing and training for self-preservation and for assistance to other people during emergencies. Some of these methods relate to you, some to your home, and some to the area in

36-1 A carbon-dioxide extinguisher is being used to put out a gasoline fire. This extinguisher is also useful for electrical fires, since carbon dioxide does not conduct electricity. Find out about other types of extinguishers and their purposes.

which you live. You can qualify yourself to deal with illness and injury by taking the American National Red Cross course in First Aid or in Home Care of the Sick, or both. You can take the Medical Self-Help Training course offered by your local civil defense agency. This course also qualifies you to deal with sickness and injury in a fallout shelter and in the community. All these courses are available to you in your town or in your county; all are offered free of charge.

The home should be examined in advance to determine where the safest place will be in the event of various types of disaster. In case of nuclear attack, for example, the basement probably would give the best protection. But in case of flood, the basement would be an impractical refuge. The sump pump in the basement could not be relied on to keep the basement dry and free from flooding since the pump operates on electricity and the current would probably be cut off.

Fire—an Aftermath of Disaster

One of the common aftermaths of disaster is the old enemy, fire. Homes and community buildings should be regularly inspected for fire hazards. Castaway articles stored in closets, attics, and basements and the rubbish in the backyard are all fire hazards. In addition to good housekeeping measures, there are other inspections to be made and safety measures to be taken. The electric wiring system should be checked for frayed and worn-out cords, loose sprockets on plugs, and overloading of circuits. The heating system needs at least an annual inspection for soot deposits in chimneys and pipes, rusted or cracked pipes, and fittings. These are real dangers to everyday living and require immediate attention.

Another potential fire hazard exists in the use and storage of such liquids as gasoline, benzene, naphtha, and similar fluids. None of these belong in the house, either for use or storage. When being used, their vapor can be ignited by such simple means as the spark of a light switch or the tiny flame of a gas stove pilot light. They should be used only outdoors and should be stored outside the house in closed, airtight, metal containers.

Quick action can put out fires while they are still small. To do so, you must know how and have the right tools. Perhaps if we consider what makes a fire, you can learn more easily how to prevent one from starting and how to put one out.

What Makes a Fire

Three things are needed to start a fire: fuel to burn, heat to make it burn, and air to keep it burning. The kitchen match is a good example. When you strike it the head flares hotly for a moment, setting fire to the matchstick which is the fuel. The oxygen in the air then keeps the match burning. If you drop the match into a small bottle and put a cover over the opening, the flame will smother for lack of oxygen. An even quicker way to extinguish the match is to dip it into a glass of water. The water will immediately cool the fuel so that the flame can no longer make the match burn. Most small fires can be put out by cooling or by smothering.

As a general rule, burning liquids, such as gasoline or grease, are smothered. The smothering process occurs when you throw a handful of salt or baking soda into a blazing skillet or oven or when chemical foam is used to blanket an oil tank fire. Both fires go out for lack of oxygen; they are smothered. Burning solids, such as wood, cloth, or paper, are best put out by water. When you turn your garden hose on a trash fire it has the same effect as pouring great streams of water into a blazing building. The fire goes out because the water both cools the fuel and smothers the flame.

The tools required for fire fighting in the

home need not be expensive. If you act promptly, the simplest tools will often do the job. You can use a wet mop or broom, a wet burlap bag or small rug, or any similar articles that are close at hand. However, the most useful tools are a garden hose (with an adapter so it will fit onto the faucets in kitchen and bathroom), a water pump, buckets of water and sand, and a ladder. A chemical-type fire extinguisher for the home is fine if it is in good repair and if you know how to use it. These extinguishers, however, are not easily refilled and may run dry before the fire is under control.

Fire-fighting Tips

The following measures have been suggested by civil defense groups:

1. Give your house and yard a good cleaning.
2. Keep plenty of water on hand.
3. Keep your fire-fighting equipment in good order and ready for use. Know how to use it.
4. Make your family a fire-fighting team.
5. Don't lose your head. Fires can be fought.
6. Never stop fighting a fire except to save your life.
7. Do not search a burning building alone.

Disease—an Aftermath of Disaster

A dreaded aftermath of disaster is disease. The normal protective measures used against the spread of disease are sanitation, isolation, and immunization. You can protect yourself in advance of a disaster by being immunized against disease and then remembering to regularly take the prescribed booster doses. The other two protective measures—sanitation and isolation—cannot so readily be provided for in advance of a disaster.

Sanitation becomes a problem whenever the water supply is disrupted or contaminated and whenever the means of disposing of waste, especially human waste, is interrupted or overflows. There are also the disease carriers—rats and other rodents, flies, roaches, and mosquitoes—that form a threat during disaster conditions. It has been observed that during hurricanes and floods there is the problem of a backwash of water. When the water recedes it often leaves small pools of water in low areas that form breeding places for mosquitoes.

There are several disaster problems associated with sanitation. The plumbing system may be blocked or broken, or there may not be enough water available for use in flushing. If it is safe to go outdoors, sewage can be burned or buried. If, however, you are in a fallout shelter or otherwise confined indoors, all sewage should be disposed of in waxed or plastic bags, tightly closed, and placed in covered metal containers. Powdered chlorinated lime may be sprinkled over the sewage to deodorize it and help keep insects away.

Isolation is another problem to be dealt with. In disaster conditions, when many people are sharing a relatively small space, it is difficult to effectively separate the sick from the healthy people. As a result there is the danger of spreading communicable disease through the entire group unless the members of the group have been immunized.

The Importance of Water During Disaster

The most critical need for water during a disaster is for drinking purposes. If the water mains are cracked or broken there is danger of contamination as well as shortage. Though some water may still be available in the main water system, it may not be fit to drink. Many gallons of water, however, that are still in pipes of homes or buildings will be safe to drink if the main valve is shut off before the emergency to seal the water in the pipes. A faucet in the upper part of the house should be left open to allow air to enter the pipes, and the water should be drawn off from the lowest faucet or pipe.

Water may also be found in the hot-water heater tanks and flush tanks. Although this water may be murky or filled with some sediment, it can be strained through paper towels or pieces of cloth, and it is safe to drink.

Fluids can also be found in canned fruits and vegetables, canned vegetable juices, and bottled soft drinks.

How to Purify Water

There are a number of simple methods that are recommended for purifying water.

Water purification tablets should be included in your emergency supplies in case it is necessary to use cloudy water from sources that may not be clean.

If heat is available, the water could be boiled vigorously for at least a full minute and then cooled. Another method is *chlorination* (KLO-rin-ay-shun). Ordinary household bleach can be used to purify water *if* chlorine is the only active material in the bleach. Two to four drops of chlorine bleach should be added for each quart of water an hour or so before using it. There should be a faint odor of chlorine noticeable when the water has been properly chlorinated.

Ordinary two-percent tincture of iodine can also be used as a water purifier. Add four drops to each quart of water and let it stand for at least a half hour before using it.

It is to be remembered, however, that boiling water or treating it with chemicals will not remove radioactive contamination. This is a complicated procedure for which you need advice from your local civil defense office. The best procedure of all is to store water for emergency use in plastic, airtight containers.

36-3 Broken water mains and disrupted sewage disposal systems account for widespread disease after disasters unless precautions are taken.

The Importance of Home Utilities During Disaster

During disaster of any kind, the utilities of the home become a source of concern. Everyone in the family, including children, should know how to shut off the gas valves in case a main gas line has been ruptured. Everyone should be cautioned against using any type of flame—candles, matches—when searching out a gas failure. All members of the family should know where and how to turn off the main house electric switch. Flashlights, in good repair, should be available for any such emergency. If the home happens to have a standby generator, everyone should know how to turn it on.

Although the civil defense programs were devised primarily to protect the population in the event of a nuclear attack, their provisions are of equal value in most other types of disaster situations. A home or community that is well provided with fallout shelters, stocked for a two-week survival period, will find them useful.

Coping with Disaster / **641**

36-4 Under direction of the Army Corps of Engineers, these young people are helping to strengthen earthen flood walls by piling up miles of pliofilm across them.

NATIONAL PROGRAMS
FOR DISASTER PREPAREDNESS

For many years, our nation has recognized that the defense of the civilian population in case of nuclear attack is a vital part of the total defense of the nation. The Office of Civil Defense, within the Department of Defense, has been responsible for administering the *National Civil Defense Plan* to prepare individuals, families, and communities for their roles in minimizing the effects of nuclear attack.

Increasingly, our nation is also concerned with reducing the impact of natural disasters, such as hurricanes, floods, and tornadoes. Some of the know-how already developed by the Office of Civil Defense to help the civilian population meet nuclear disasters will now be put to use to help it meet natural disasters. To this end, the Office of Civil Defense has been reorganized and

renamed *Defense Civil Preparedness Agency.*

The Agency will work with the *Office of Emergency Preparedness* when necessary. For example, it will provide OEP with "vulnerability studies" to indicate the type of disaster to which a community is vulnerable, and will give assistance in organizing the community to prepare to meet it. The emphasis will be not simply on disaster relief but on disaster preparedness.

The National Civil Defense Plan and Fallout Shelters

In the National Civil Defense Plan, each person should be ready to live under disaster conditions for a two-week period after a nuclear attack, to avoid harm from radioactive fallout. During this time, you would have to substitute for all the conveniences of daily living—normal water supply, sewage disposal, power services, telephone, fuel, drug and grocery stores, and probably even medical services.

36-5 These people are learning to use radiation detection instruments as part of a civil defense preparedness program.

Fallout shelters for these weeks of emergency living are considered the core of the civil defense program. Proper shielding in a fallout shelter is necessary to avoid harm from the radioactive fallout following a nuclear attack.

Shelter space has now been located for more than 200 million people. Surveys of buildings continue in order to locate appropriate shelter space for the entire population. Buildings that qualify are licensed as public shelters and marked with black and yellow signs. Such shelters are eligible to be stocked with food, medicine, and other emergency supplies. At present there are marked and stocked shelters for well over 100 million people.

Civil defense measures depend for their success on the cooperation of every American. Everyone is asked to carry out the following steps:

1. Learn the public warning signals and what they mean.

   The **alert signal,** used by some local governments, is a three-to-five-minute *steady* blast. It is used to get your attention in case of a natural disaster or other peacetime emergency. It may mean that the local government wants to broadcast important information on radio or television, so "tune in."

   The **take-cover** signal is a series of three-to-five-minute *wavering* sounds on sirens, or short blasts on horns or other devices. It means that an actual enemy attack has been detected and protective action should be taken. Go immediately to the nearest marked shelter.

   These signals may be modified to meet local conditions. Some communities, for example, use only the take-cover signal.

2. Learn your community plans and emergency communications. You should know the location of the marked shelter area closest to your home and to your school or your place of work. In the event of an *alert signal* or a *take cover signal,* all regularly scheduled broadcasting will cease. Selected radio stations will go on the air in the **Emergency Broadcasting System.** Official instructions to guide you will be broadcast by local civil defense officials. Do not use the telephone; it must be free for official use.

3. Learn about protection from radioactive fallout. It has been scientifically determined that adequate shielding is the only effective means of preventing radiation casualties. Approved shelters offer shielding from radioactivity. The following pamphlets on this subject may be obtained from your county civil defense office:

   In Time of Emergency
   Home Fallout Shelter (H-12 Series)
   Family Food Stockpile for Survival

4. Learn about the courses in First Aid, Medical Self-Help, and Home Emergency Preparedness which are available at your local civil defense office.

"Take-Cover" Precautions

If you are in a building when you hear the three minute warbling signal, close windows, draw the shades, and close doors. Go immediately to the closest shelter.

If you are outdoors and see a flash of light or hear a loud blast, drop to the ground and bury your head in your arms. When flash or blast has stopped, go immediately to the nearest shelter.

If you are riding in an auto and see a bright flash or hear a loud blast, park your car, close windows and ventilators, drop to the floor, and bury your head in your arms. When flash or blast has stopped, go immediately to the nearest shelter.

Speed is essential. After the detonation of a weapon, the debris forced up off the ground begins to scatter and fall to earth in the form of radioactive dust. The radiation is most intense during the first 24 hours and weakens as time goes by. However, it will be many days or even weeks before any time can be spent outside the shelter.

There are three ways to reduce your exposure to the intensity of the radiation:

1. time
2. distance
3. shielding

Therefore, protect yourself immediately by getting as far from the radiation as possible as quickly as possible, and by shielding yourself from it.

Shielding means as thick and strong a shelter as possible. The more dense and heavy the materials surrounding you—such as dirt, stone, or concrete—the better you are shielded.

The American National Red Cross Disaster Relief Program

In addition to providing for civil defense, the federal government also authorizes the relief of disaster victims during peacetime. By Act of Congress in January 1905, and subsequent amendments, the American National Red Cross is chartered to perform this function. Its mandate is "to continue and carry on a system of national and international relief in time of peace and apply the same in mitigating the sufferings caused by pestilence, famine, floods, fires, and other great national calamities, and to devise and carry on measures for preventing the same. Disaster is defined as a situation catastrophic in nature in which a number of persons are plunged into helplessness and suffering and

36-6 Telephone linemen arrive with a railroad crew to begin restoring vital communications after a disastrous storm in North Dakota.

as a result are in need of food, clothing, shelter, medical and nursing or hospital care, and other basic necessities of life." (*Disaster Relief Handbook*, American National Red Cross.) In addition, its congressional charter imposes on the Red Cross the duties of acting as the medium of voluntary relief and communications between the American people and their armed forces.

PRECAUTIONS AGAINST NATURAL HAZARDS

Warnings by means of the press, radio, and television are given in areas where flooding is threatened. People are advised to move away from swollen rivers and seek higher ground. When hurricanes threaten an area, the population is advised to board up windows, remove objects that are not fastened to floors or to the ground in outdoor areas, and sometimes to move inland.

When an area is threatened by blizzard, warnings are broadcast along highway routes to motorists, farmers, and ranchers. This gives people a chance to prepare to save life, both human and animal. Motorists stuck in the snow suffer from hunger and cold, and when they let their motor run for warmth, they run the risk of poisoning from carbon monoxide gas.

In regions where earthquakes occur, building codes require a more substantial structure and less height than in other areas. Earthquakes take their toll in injuries caused by falls into freshly opened cracks in the earth, from being struck by falling objects, and from spontaneous fires. Disease spreads as a result of ruptured water mains and sewage disposal pipes. Panic often follows due to shock, fear at being separated from members of the family, and confusion.

Precautions to Take in Case of Threat of Tornadoes

Some precautions can be taken to protect yourself from the harmful effects of tornadoes. It is estimated that two hundred or more tornadoes occur throughout the country each year and that these often have the power to wipe out whole towns. In general, it seems that tornadoes strike early in the year around the Eastern Gulf states; then they advance in a northwest direction toward Iowa and Kansas in the spring. Here they hover about until fall. This by no means implies that these are the only places which tornadoes strike. They may be more common in these areas, but can and do strike in other parts of the country.

In those areas where tornadoes are most frequent, people are advised to build tornado cellars in their homes. When a tornado is sighted and recognized by its funnel-shaped cloud, several actions for increasing chances of escaping injury or death should be taken immediately.

36-7 A tornado in action. What precautions should you take if you ever see a funnel-shaped cloud heading in your direction?

1. When time permits—go immediately to a tornado cellar, a cave, or an underground area that has an air outlet to help equalize the air pressure.
2. When outdoors—move at a right angle to the tornado's path. It usually moves ahead at 25 to 40 miles per hour. If there is not time to escape from its path, lie flat in the nearest depression, such as a ditch or ravine.
3. When in town—seek indoor shelter in a strong building and move along to the inside walls. Stay away from doors and windows.
4. When at home—remember that the corner of the basement toward the tornado offers greatest safety, particularly in frame houses. If there is no basement in the home, move heavy furniture against inside walls and get under or behind the furniture. If time

permits, cut off electric or gas main switches and heating systems. Doors and windows of the house on the side away from the tornado path should be opened to help reduce air-draft damage.

5. When in school—move to a lower floor, the basement if possible. Stay near the inside walls and away from doors and windows. Avoid such large rooms as gymnasiums and auditoriums as there is danger of roof collapse.

Tornadoes strike swiftly and follow an unpredictable but rather narrow path, often many miles in length. This funnel-shaped whirlwind may "touch down" causing violent destruction, then rise, and "touch down" again before its whirling violence is spent. Whatever you know how to do to avoid this destructive force must be done quickly.

36-8 Lightning can, and does, strike twice. The Empire State Building is a prime target. It is protected by a lightning rod.

"The Comeback of an Old-Fashioned Killer—Lightning"

This is the title of a report published by the National Safety Council. For centuries lightning had provoked fear and superstition, but after Benjamin Franklin discovered that lightning was "a giant electric spark," fear largely subsided. Superstitions still prevail, however, and the common one is that "lightning never strikes twice in the same place." To offset this, scientists point out that the Empire State Building has been hit as many as 48 times in one year. Today, most people do not regard lightning as a serious danger. Experts in the field seem to believe that one of the reasons for lightning casualties is that too few people possess a good healthy fear of this killer.

About 600 Americans are killed each year by lightning, including those who die from fires started by lightning. It is estimated that another 1,500 are injured, and that the property damage amounts to around 120 million dollars. It is thought that about

two thirds of these accidents occurred in the open. These are some people who were killed by lightning in one summer: a golf caddie in New Jersey when he was caught in a thundershower; a 29-year-old golf-playing mother in South Dakota; an 11-year-old Wisconsin boy on a playground; a 16-year-old boy in Illinois as he was walking home from school. All of these victims were in the open.

The *Lightning Protection Institute* predicts that the rising toll of lightning victims will continue. One reason for this is that people no longer bother to go indoors when a storm approaches. Another is that new homes in suburban areas provide prime targets because they are often scattered and are the highest object in the area. In cities the large, tall buildings furnish protection to smaller buildings as well as to pedestrians on the streets. In addition, the surburban home-owner, unlike the farmer, seems unaware of the need for lightning-rod protection. It is thought that about 40 percent of suburban fires are caused by lightning.

The prime breeder of thunderstorms is a climate in which the surface air is both hot and moist. The southern portion of the United States spawns more electric storms than the north and there is more lightning east of the Rocky Mountains than west of them. The Far West seldom has surface air that is both hot and moist. Its moist air is usually cool and its hot air is usually dry. California, for example, averages about ten electric storm days a year in contrast to central Florida, which averages one hundred, the highest in the nation.

According to medical authorities, many victims of lightning could be saved if someone were at hand who knew how to give mouth-to-mouth respiration (see Chapter 10). There is no danger of shock to the rescuer in touching the victim since the electric charge travels instantly through the body into the ground. Other types of injuries observed in lightning victims include electric burns, broken bones, tingling and numbing sensations, temporary loss of hearing, impaired vision, and paralysis.

Scientists long ago provided a means of protection against lightning by installing lightning rods on buildings. The rods do not repel lightning but conduct it safely over the outside of the building deep into the ground. The rods help prevent lightning from coming through the roof and down the chimneys. But there is no protective gear as yet devised for use by people.

Precautions Against Lightning

When you are in the open and sense that a storm is coming, immediately seek proper shelter. Do not wait for the storm to break. The most dangerous time for lightning damage is just before the storm when dark clouds appear and the air is charged with electricity. The most dangerous shelter to take is under a lone tree. If no other shelter is available, just lie flat on the ground at a distance exceeding the height of the tree. Golfers, farmers, hikers, and fishermen are the most frequent victims of the dangerous practice of taking shelter from a thunderstorm under a lone tree.

Avoid being the highest object wherever you are. It is easy to become the prime target of lightning when swimming, in a boat, on a horse or bicycle, on a golf course, on a beach, plowing a field, hanging clothes on a metal clothesline, hiking on a hilltop, playing on an athletic field or playground, standing near wire fences, metal posts, and overhead wires. If you are far from shelter and your automobile is nearby, it is a safe place to take refuge in because of its metal shell and rubber tires. Only if you are in direct contact with the car metal are you likely to get even a slight burn should lightning strike the car.

When indoors it is well to stay away from exterior walls, doors, and windows. Other places to keep clear of are chimneys, furnaces, fireplaces, stoves, and electric appliances. Avoid touching all plumbing fixtures. Outside radio and television antennae should have lightning arresters attached as protection against lightning entering the building. Television antennae may not be regarded as protective lightning rods. If anything, the height of an antenna above the roof may attract lightning and carry it into the building. An example of an antenna acting as an attractor of lightning occurred recently in Indianapolis when lightning hit the antenna on the roof of a house and tore a three-foot hole in a bedroom wall. Perhaps you have heard of similar cases.

Lightning Code

The National Safety Council advises that the best source of information for personal protection against lightning is the Lightning Code. The statements on the next page are taken from the Lightning Code.

1. Do not go outdoors or remain outdoors during thunderstorms, unless necessary.
2. Seek shelter in the following places:
   Large metal or metal-frame buildings.
   Dwellings or buildings that are protected against lightning.
   Large buildings of any kind.
   Motor vehicles with metal tops and bodies.
   Trains and trailers with metal bodies.
   Enclosed metal boats or ships.
   City streets, shielded by buildings.
3. Certain locations are extremely hazardous during thunderstorms. The following should be avoided, if at all possible:
   Open fields such as farms.
   Golf courses and athletic fields.
   Swimming pools, lakes, and seashores.
   Wire fences, clotheslines, overhead wires, and railroad tracks.
   Isolated trees and hilltops.
   In the above locations it is especially hazardous to be in or on the following:
   Tractors and other farm machinery.
   Golf carts, scooters, motorcycles, and bicycles.
   Open boats without masts.

A Calm Attitude Toward Disaster

In our effort to cope with disaster there are many factors—physical and environmental—to be taken into account. Consideration must be given to the physical ability of the people involved. Their mental and social development and the range of their experience will also have an effect on their attitudes. The interrelations of these physical factors in the emergency environment will determine, to some extent, how people will react in a disaster situation.

No two people seem to react in the same manner when faced with a disaster. One person might give way to complete panic; another might not only remain calm but be able to act as a leader and organizer of other people caught in the disaster. The most desirable reaction, of course, is to remain calm. Learning in advance the steps that should be taken in an emergency and having accessible the equipment necessary for protection and survival fosters a sense of security and readiness that helps one to attain a calm attitude toward disaster.

What You Have Learned

What kind of health practices should you apply in maintaining your health? Check your understanding of the chapter. On a separate sheet of paper, number 1 through 21 and insert the answer from the vocabulary list below. Use each expression, but use each one only once.

civilians	fires	radioactive
disaster	hot	shelter
disease	hurricanes	store
drinking	lightning rods	survive
earth	moist	tornadoes
earthquakes	North	war
east	nuclear	west

When an unforeseen mishap occurs, bringing destruction to life and property, it is called a (1) _____. Such mishaps may originate from uncontrolled forces of nature, such as (2) _____, (3) _____, or (4) _____. They may be caused by manmade devices used in waging (5) _____. Two common aftermaths of a disaster are (6) _____ and (7) _____. The most critical need of water during a disaster is for (8) _____ purposes, and the best safeguard is to (9) _____ water in airtight, plastic containers.

The National Civil Defense Program is basically a plan to protect civilians against (10) _____ attack. It has been demonstrated, in recent wars, that there is increasing danger to (11) _____ during armed conflict. Civil Defense authorities emphasize that it is possible, when properly shielded in a fallout (12) _____, to (13) _____ a nuclear attack. Speed is essential since (14) _____ fallout begins to reach (15) _____ level shortly after detonation of a weapon.

In recent years, attention is called to lightning, another destructive force of nature. The prime breeder of electric storms is climate that is both (16) _____ and (17) _____. The southern portion of the United States spawns more electric storms than the (18) _____, and there is more lightning (19) _____ of the Rocky Mountains than there is (20) _____ of them. Homes and other buildings should be protected from lightning by (21) _____.

What You Can Do

1. Make a list of the articles you would take to the fallout shelter in case of an imminent attack.

2. Invite the Director of Civil Defense in your county to tell your class about the plans for the protection of your area.

3. Visit an established Civil Defense fallout shelter.

4. Talk with someone who has experienced a tornado, hurricane, earthquake, flood, or great fire. Report what you learn to your class.

Things to Try

1. Suppose you are driving in open country when some distance ahead you see a funnel-shaped cloud moving close to the ground. What force of nature are you seeing? What are the immediate actions you should take? Make a list of these actions in proper order.

2. Some Civil Defense shelters have been stocked for a two-week survival period by the federal or local government. Find out what articles are contained in these shelters. Who is qualified to dispense these stores? Could you become one of those qualified?

3. Experiment with purifying water by boiling, by using tincture of iodine, and by chlorination. Use the procedures that are described on page 641 in this chapter.

4. Make a list of the disease carriers, such as rats, that form a great threat to health during disaster conditions. What diseases are most likely to be spread? What precautions can you take against contracting such diseases?

Probing Further /

Community Involvement in Civil Defense; Fallout Protection; and *Firefighting for Householders;* U.S. Department of Defense, Defense Civil Preparedness Agency, Washington, D.C.

These free pamphlets provide important information regarding survival under disaster conditions.

First Aid Text Book and *Home Care of the Sick*, American National Red Cross, Doubleday, 1957. These two texts are important in the preparation of people for survival during disaster.

The Killer Storms: Hurricanes, Typhoons, and Tornadoes, by Gary Jennings, Lippincott, 1970. This readable book describes many unusual occurrences connected with the more violent forms of weather. It also describes the forecasting work of the Environmental Sciences Services Administration and the U.S. Air Force.

The Forest Rangers: Adventures of the Forest Service, by Montgomery M. Atwater, Macrae Smith, 1969. An easily read book on the many duties of the forest service, including avalanche work and fire prevention.

Health Concepts in Action /

Is this statement supported by what you have learned?

Both the individual and community can prepare for the safest response to environmental hazards.

Applying this concept of safety, which health practices would you

—continue?

—change?

—begin?

Will you now, as a result of your study, change any of your health objectives?

Appendix / Common First-Aid Emergencies — Condensed

This appendix reviews some of the first-aid measures that will help you meet common emergencies until medical care is obtained. More extensive first-aid procedures are discussed with related subject matter throughout the book. For such first-aid measures as, for example, giving artificial respiration or applying a tourniquet, refer to the Index.

General First-Aid Directions Worth Remembering

Give urgently needed care first—for severe bleeding, stoppage of breathing, or poisoning.

Keep the victim lying down—or at least sitting and quiet. Do not treat a victim while he is standing.

Locate all of the possible injuries and treat the more serious ones first.

Keep a cool head and plan what you do. Instruct helpers as to their duties.

Be reluctant to make statements to the victim or to bystanders. Do not diagnose, evaluate, or make predictions about the injuries.

Obtain the victim's name and address and that of his next of kin.

Give your exact location when calling a physician or ambulance. Ask the physician for first-aid instructions.

If the victim is unconscious, do not give fluids. If there is no possibility of fracture, you can turn the victim on his side with knees flexed. Put a pillow or rolled-up sweaters under his head. Turn his head to one side so that any secretions may leave his mouth and nose.

Do not leave a victim until you have turned him over to a physician or to the ambulance attendants.

Be prepared, by having first-aid supplies in your car and in your home.

Some Common Emergencies

Animal bites—Wash wounds freely with soapy water. Hold under running tap for several minutes if possible. Apply sterile gauze compress, and always see your doctor immediately. (Obtain name and address of the owner of animal, so it may be held in quarantine.)

Bruises—Apply ice bag or cold cloths for 25 minutes. If skin is broken, treat in the same manner as minor cuts.

Eyes—Chemicals—Wash eyes with clean tap water and consult physician at once, if any chemical spatters into the eyes.

Foreign bodies—Remove by gently touching with limp point of clean handkerchief. If failure results after one or two attempts, consult a physician. Never rub the eye.

Fainting—Keep the victim lying down, with head slightly lowered. Loosen any tight clothing. Pass smelling salts or aromatic spirits of ammonia gently a few inches beneath nose (not too close to nose). Sprinkle face lightly with cold water. If person does not respond within short time, summon physician at once and keep person warm with blankets until physician arrives.

Frostbite—*Symptoms*: Pain followed by appearance of grayish-white color in exposed part. *Treatment*: Gently cover frozen part with the hand, or place in water warmed to body temperature so that thawing will occur gradually. Do not rub; do not expose to stove or fire; do not put in hot water. Such procedures may cause serious, permanent damage.

Fractures—Deformity of injured part usually means a fracture. If fracture is suspected, do not attempt to move injured person; summon a doctor at once.

Heart attack—*Symptoms*: Chest pain, bluish color of the lips and finger-nails, shortness of breath, swelling of the ankles. *Treatment*: Administer prescribed medication, if the victim is under a physician's care. Call a physician. Do not move victim. Raise the head and chest, if the victim is short of breath; place in a lying-down position with legs raised, if he is faint.

Heat prostration—Caused by exposure to heat—either sun or indoors. *Symptoms*: Face pale, skin wet and clammy, pulse weak, temperature subnormal, usually conscious. *Treatment*: Keep the victim lying down with head low. Loosen clothing. Give salt water to drink (teaspoonful of salt to cup of water) in small amounts at frequent intervals (about every fifteen minutes). Call physician immediately.

Insect bites—Remove "stinger" If present. Apply paste of baking soda and water. If swelling is pronounced, apply ice bag or cold cloths over the paste.

Minor burns and scalds—Apply cold water or ice water to burned area to relieve pain. Never use grease or antiseptic on burns. If burn is deep or extensive, always consult a physician.

Minor cuts—Wash hands thoroughly. Cleanse the injured area, using plain soap and tap water. Apply soap and water with sterile gauze. Apply dry sterile gauze and bandage into place.

Minor scrapes—Sponge off gently with wet gauze, blot dry, and cover scraped area with a simple bandage. If scrape is deep and dirty, see your doctor.

Poison ivy—Wash exposed part immediately with brown soap five or six times; but do not use brush or other rough material. If area involved is extensive or seems to be spreading, consult a physician.

Puncture wounds—The danger of tetanus should be considered in all puncture wounds. Always consult a doctor. Serious infection can arise unless such wounds are properly treated.

Severe bleeding—Stop bleeding at once. Put pressure directly over the wound with a sterile cloth; in a real emergency, apply the bare hand. Use finger tips to press the supplying blood vessel against the underlying bone, if bleeding must be slowed down before an assistant can apply direct pressure over the wound. Tourniquets should rarely be used.

Shock—Caused by burns, wounds, or fractures associated with loss of large quantities of blood. *Symptoms*: Weakness, coupled with pale, moist, cool skin; beads of perspiration about the lips, forehead, palms, and armpits; nausea; restlessness; fast, weak pulse. *Treatment*: Keep the victim lying down unless breathing is difficult. Elevate the lower part of the body unless there is a head injury, difficult breathing, or pain in the lower part of the body. Prevent a loss of body heat. Administer water only with great care.

Slivers—Apply skin antiseptic, such as mild tincture of iodine, to injured part. Sterilize needle point by passing it through a flame and use it to "tease out" sliver. Again apply antiseptic; let dry and cover with suitable bandage.

Sprains—Elevate injured part and apply ice bag or cold cloths for 25 minutes immediately after injury. If swelling is pronounced, do not attempt to use injured part until seen by physician. Always have sprains X-rayed.

Sunstroke—Caused by exposure to the heat of the sun's rays. **Heatstroke** is the same condition caused by exposure to some other source of heat. *Symptoms*: Headache, skin hot and dry, red face, high fever, strong pulse, usually unconscious. *Treatment*: Keep in lying position with head elevated. Apply cold cloths to body to cool. Call physician immediately.

Toothache—If cavity is present, moisten a small piece of cotton with oil of cloves and apply to cavity. If no cavity is present, apply ice bag or hot water bottle to cheek for comfort. Consult your dentist.

Unconsciousness—Never give anything by mouth to an unconscious person. Move him only if there is no possibility of fracture. Put in flat, lying position; turn head slightly to one side; loosen any tight clothing. Always summon a physician in every case unless you are sure it is a simple fainting spell.

This summary of emergency-type accident cases and of the more common accidents you may encounter can best be supplemented by taking a course in first aid given by the American Red Cross. Such a course is often given in your school or in the community where you live.

Glossary

A glossary gives the meanings of words as they are used in the subject that is being studied. Some of the following words have other meanings listed in the dictionary, but you will find here the meaning that is important in learning about your health and safety. For a more complete understanding of the terms you are interested in, look them up in the index and then read what is said about them on the listed pages.

A

abdomen (AB duh m'n): belly; the cavity containing the stomach, intestines, liver, pancreas, and spleen; between the diaphragm and pelvis.

abdominal (ab DOM uh n'l): pertaining to the abdomen.

abscess (AB sess): a localized collection of pus.

accommodation (uh kom uh DAY sh'n): the ability of the eye to focus either on nearby or distant objects.

acidosis (a sid OH sis): a condition in which the blood is less alkaline than it should be.

acne (AK nee): a skin condition marked by pimples, especially on the face.

acromegaly (ak roh MEG al ih): the enlargement of the head, hands, and feet, caused by too much pituitary hormone.

ACTH: see *adrenocorticotrophic hormone.*

actinomycosis (AK tin oh my KOH sis): a fungus disease that often causes sores about the jaws.

active transport: the process by which a cell forces molecules to pass in or out through its cell membrane *against* the force of diffusion.

addict: a person who cannot stop taking alcohol, narcotics, or other drugs.

Addison's disease: a condition caused by insufficient production of hormones by the adrenal cortex.

adenine (AD e neen): one of the four nitrogen compounds used to build DNA.

adenoids (AD in oids): a mass of tonsil-like tissue in the upper part of the throat at the end of the nasal cavity.

adolescence (ad uh LES 'ns): the teen-age period; the stage of growth between childhood and adulthood.

adrenal (ad REE n'l) **glands:** two endocrine glands, one of which is located just above each kidney.

adrenaline (ad REN uh lin): a hormone made in the medulla of the adrenal glands; a stimulant.

adrenocorticotrophic hormone (a DREEN oh cor tih koh TROH fik HOR mohn): a hormone from the pituitary gland that stimulates the adrenal cortex to secrete its hormones; ACTH.

aerobics (air OH biks): an exercise program that increases the oxygen-delivering capacity of heart and lungs.

air sac: one of millions of microscopic air-filled cavities in the lungs. The blood takes oxygen from and gives up carbon dioxide to the air sacs.

albumin (al BYOO min): a type of protein. One kind of albumin is present in blood plasma; another kind is in the white of an egg.

alcoholism: a condition of chronic or relapsing dependence on alcohol.

alimentary (al ih MEN tuh ree) **canal:** the tube from mouth to rectum into which food is taken and digested, and from which food wastes are eliminated. It includes the mouth, esophagus, stomach, small and large intestines, and anus.

alkali (AL kuh ly): a bitter substance that acts to offset the effect of an acid.

alkalosis (al kah LOH sis): a condition in which the blood is more alkaline than it should be.

allergy (AL er jee): an abnormal sensitivity to certain substances, such as pollen, food, dust, serum, etc.

alveolus (al VEE oh luss); pl., **alveoli** (al VEE oh lye): one of the lungs' microscopic air sacs.

ameboid (uh ME boyd) **motion:** some cells (including white blood cells) move about by pushing out part of their cytoplasm with the rest of the cell flowing into the projection. This is *ameboid motion,* named for the tiny one-celled animal, the *Amoeba.*

amino (uh MEE noh) **acids:** the end products into which proteins are separated during digestion.

amnion (AM nih on): a living bag, filled with liquid, which protects the unborn child.

amoeba (a MEE bah): a microscopic one-celled animal.

amphetamines (am FET ah meenz): these drugs act as stimulants. They can be dangerous.

analgesic (an al JEE sick): a substance that relieves pain.

anaphylactic (an uh fih LACK tic) shock: a severe allergic reaction that may cause death.

anemia (uh NEE mee uh): a condition in which a person has too few red blood cells or too little hemoglobin.

anesthetic (an us THET ik): a drug that causes partial or complete loss of the ability to feel pain.

aneurysm (AN yoo rizm): a permanent bulging out of the wall of an artery.

angina pectoris (an JY nuh PEK toh ris): a painful heart condition caused by narrowing of the coronary arteries.

Anopheles (uh NOF eh leez) mosquito: the mosquito that carries the germ of malaria.

anthrax (AN thraks): a bacterial disease of cattle, other hoofed animals, and, sometimes, man.

anthropologist (an throh POL oh jist): a scientist who studies anthropology, the study of human racial groups, cultures, and social relationships.

antibiotics (an tee by OT iks): germ-killing substances produced by certain living things, chiefly molds. A few antibiotics are now made synthetically.

antibodies (AN tih bod eez): substances in the blood that act against disease germs or their poisons.

antidote (AN tih doht): a substance used to counteract a poison.

antigens (AN tih jenz): substance that may stimulate the formation of antibodies.

antihistamine (an tee HISS tuh meen): a drug used to treat allergies or to relieve the symptoms of a cold.

antiseptic (an tih SEP tik): a substance that prevents the reproduction of germs.

antiserum (an tih SEE rum): a serum containing antibodies.

antitoxin (an tih TOK sin): an antibody that neutralizes the poison, or toxin, produced by a bacterium.

antivenin (an tih VEH nin): an antibody to snake poison, or poison from some other animal.

anuria (an YOO rih ah): the failure of the kidneys to secrete urine.

anus (AY nus): the outside opening of the rectum, through which undigested food wastes are eliminated from the body.

anvil (AN vihl): one of the three small bones in the middle ear.

aorta (ay OR tuh): the largest artery in the body; it carries blood from the left ventricle to all parts of the body except the lungs.

apoplexy (AP uh pleks ee): a stroke; the condition resulting from the breaking, or stoppage by a clot, of a blood vessel in the brain.

appendix (uh PEN diks): a small blind tube projecting from the caecum of the large intestine (near where the small intestine joins the large intestine). Infection and inflammation of the appendix is appendicitis (uh pen dih SY tis).

aptitude (AP tih tood): the ability to learn or do something.

aqueous (AY kwee us) humor: the watery fluid that fills the space between the cornea and the lens of the eye.

arteriosclerosis (ahr teer ee oh skler OH sis): hardening of the arteries.

artery (ART er ee): a blood vessel that carries blood away from the heart.

arthritis (ar THRY tis): a condition causing swollen and painful joints.

ascorbic (uh SKOR bik) acid: vitamin C.

asphyxiation (ass fik see AY sh'n): the effect of a lack of oxygen; the result may range from unconsciousness to death.

association areas: parts of the cerebrum of the brain having to do with interpretation of nerve impulses, or messages.

associative neuron: a neuron (nerve cell) that carries impulses between other neurons, often from a sensory neuron to a motor neuron.

asthma (AZ muh): a condition in which the breathing passages become constricted, probably as a result of an allergy.

astigmatism (uh STIG muh tizm): a defect of vision due to an irregular curvature of the lens or cornea.

Atabrine (AT uh breen): a drug used to treat malaria.

atherosclerosis (ATH er oh skleh ROH sis): a type of hardening of the arteries in which fatty substances and cholesterol are deposited in the inner walls of arteries.

athlete's foot: a foot infection caused by a fungus.

atonic (a TON ick): weak; weak tone in speaking.

atrium (AY trih um): the same as an auricle of the heart.

audiogram (AW dih oh GRAM): a graph showing the hearing power of an individual.

audiometer (aw dih OM uh ter): an instrument for testing the power of hearing.

auditory (AW dih tor ee): pertaining to the sense of hearing. The *auditory nerve* connects the ear with the brain.

auricle (AW rih k'l): one of the two upper chambers of the heart, which receive blood from the veins.

autonomic (aw tuh NOM ik) **nervous system:** the nerves that carry impulses to smooth (involuntary) muscle and glands not under conscious control.

axon (AK son): a nerve fiber that carries impulses away from the cell body.

B

bacillus (ba SIHL lus); pl., **bacilli** (ba SIHL ly): rod-shaped bacterium.

bacteria (bak TIHR ee uh); sing., **bacterium** (bak TIHR ee um): microscopic one-celled organisms, some of which cause disease.

barbiturate (bahr BICH yur it): a type of drug used to make a person sleep.

barium sulfate (BEHR ee um SUL fayt): a white substance used to make organs of the body show up clearly in X rays.

basal metabolic (meh ta BOL ick) **rate:** the basal rate of cell activity, measured by the amount of oxygen used while awake but resting. Often referred to as *basal metabolism.*

benign (bih NYNE) **tumor:** a noncancerous tumor; one that does not invade and destroy the surrounding tissue.

Benzedrine (BEN zuh dreen): a drug that acts as a powerful stimulant. One of the amphetamines.

beriberi (BEHR ee BEHR ee): a disease of the nervous system, caused by a lack of vitamin B_1.

biceps (BY seps): the large muscle on the front of the upper arm.

bicuspids (by CUS pihdz): the fourth and fifth teeth from center front in each jaw. Each has two raised parts, or *cusps.*

bile: a juice made by the liver, stored by the gall bladder, and used in the small intestine to help digest fats.

binocular (bihn OC yoo lar): relating to both eyes.

biopsy (BY op see): the removal and microscopic examination of a small bit of tissue from the living body.

biotin (BY oh tin): one of the B complex vitamins.

blackhead: a collection of dried oil clogging a skin pore.

bladder: a hollow, muscular organ that receives urine from the kidneys and stores it until it is excreted.

blastomycosis (blas toh my COH sis): a disease caused by a fungus; usually causing open sores in the lungs.

blind spot: the center of the back of the eyeball where the optic nerve enters.

blood clot: a mass of blood cells held together by fibrin.

blood count: a count of the number of red or white blood cells in a measured area under the microscope. Blood counts are used to determine whether a person has the normal number of cells in his blood.

blood pressure: the pressure of the blood against the walls of the arteries.

booster: a small amount of vaccine or toxoid given to reinforce the immune effect in a person who has already had injections of the same vaccine or toxoid.

brain stem: a lower part of the brain that connects the cerebrum, cerebellum, and other parts of the brain with each other and with the spinal cord. The medulla is part of the brain stem.

Bright's disease: nephritis; an inflammation of the kidneys.

broad spectrum antibiotics: those which stop the growth of a large number of different kinds of germs.

bronchial (BRONK ee ul) **tubes:** tiny tubes that branch off from the bronchi and carry air to the air sacs of the lungs.

bronchitis (bron KY tis): inflammation of the bronchial tubes.

bronchus (BRONK us); pl., **bronchi** (BRONK eye): one of two large branches of the windpipe. One bronchus leads into each lung.

C

caecum (SEE k'm): a pouch at the beginning of the large intestine. The appendix is attached to the caecum.

calcaneus (cal KAY nee us): heel bone.

callus (KAL us): a hard, thickened cuticle that forms to protect the skin underneath. The word *callus* is also used for the first solid deposit formed around a broken place in a bone.

calorie (KAL er ee): the unit used to measure the amount of energy (in the form of heat) released when food combines with oxygen. As used in this book, a calorie (great calorie) represents the amount of heat needed to raise the temperature of one kilogram of water 1° Centigrade.

calorimeter (kal er IM uh ter): a device used to measure the energy content of food in terms of heat given off when the food burns.

cancer: a growth of cells that invade and destroy nearby tissues and spread to other parts of the body.

capillary (KAP 'l air ee); pl., **capillaries:** one of the smallest blood vessels, carrying blood from the smallest arteries to the smallest veins.

capsule (KAP s'l): in the body, a membrane or sheath covering a part or organ.

capsule ligament (KAP s'l LIG uh ment): a ligament that surrounds and encloses a joint.

carbohydrate (kahr boh HY drayt): a nutrient composed of carbon, hydrogen, and oxygen. Sugar and starch are carbohydrates.

carbon (KAHR b'n): one of 92 naturally occurring elements; one of the three elements basic to most foods. It is found in sugars, starches, fats, nucleic acids, oils, proteins, and vitamins.

carbon dioxide (dy OK syde): CO_2; the gas produced when sugar and most other foods are oxidized in the body.

carbon monoxide (mon OK syde): CO; a deadly poisonous gas.

carbon tetrachloride (tet ruh KLOR ide): a liquid used for professional dry-cleaning. It is poisonous, but it will not burn.

carbuncle (KAHR bunk'l): a number of boils occurring together in one place.

carcinoma (kahr sih NOH mah): a cancer that arises from epithelial tissue, such as the outer layers of the skin.

cardiac (KAHR dee ak): pertaining to the heart.

carotene (KAIR oh teen): orange or yellow pigment in plants such as carrots and green vegetables. It is changed to vitamin A after being eaten.

carpal (KAHR pal) **bones:** bones of the wrist.

carrier: an apparently healthy person who carries disease germs in his body and spreads the germs to other people.

cartilage (KAHR tih lij): firm, smooth, elastic connective tissue. It forms part of the skeleton, pads the ends of bones, and gives shape to the tip of the nose and to the ears.

cassava (kuh SAH vuh): a starchy food obtained from the roots of the tropical plant of the same name.

cataract (KAT uh rakt): cloudiness of the lens of the eye, a condition causing poor vision.

catarrh (kuh TAHR): chronic inflammation of the nose or air passages.

catatonic (cat uh TON ik) **state:** a condition of stupor in which psychotic patients may remain in statue-like positions.

cell: a small, self-enclosed mass of protoplasm consisting of nucleus, cytoplasm, and cell membrane. All living things are made up of cells.

cell membrane: the thin living layer that encloses living cells.

cementum (see MEN tum): the hard outer covering of the root of a tooth. Often referred to as cement.

centipede (SEN tih peed): an insectlike animal with many pairs of legs and sharp-pointed jaws.

central nervous system: the brain and spinal cord.

centrioles (SEN trih ohlz): rodlike structures that play a part in mitosis.

centrosome (SEN troh sohm): the structure that contains the centrioles.

cerebellum (ser uh BEL lum): a part of the brain behind and below the cerebrum; necessary for balance and for making the muscles work together properly.

cerebral (SEHR uh bral) **hemorrhage:** bleeding from an artery in the brain; a cause of stroke.

cerebral thrombosis (throm BOH sis): formation of a blood clot obstructing an artery in the brain.

cerebrum (SEH ruh brum): the largest part of the brain; the center for voluntary and conscious actions.

chemotherapy (kem oh THEH rap ih): the treatment of disease by the use of chemical substances, such as sulfa drugs.

chilblain (CHIL blayn): a swelling or sore caused by chilling or frostbite of the hands or feet.

chlorination (kloh rih NAY shun): the use of chlorine to kill germs in water.

chlorine (KLOH reen): an element; a greenish-yellow gas that is used to kill disease germs in municipal water supplies (and in swimming pools).

cholera (KOL uh ruh): an infectious disease marked by vomiting, abnormal bowel movements, and severe weakness.

cholesterol (koh LESS ter ol): a white, fatty, waxy substance necessary for life, but dangerous when deposited on the walls of the arteries.

choroid (KOH roid): the black membrane between the retina and the sclera of the eye.

chromosomes (KROH moh sohms): structures found in a cell nucleus; chromosomes contain genes.

chronic (KRON ik): lasting, as a lingering disease.

chyme (KYME): semifluid, partly digested food, ready to leave the stomach and enter the small intestine.

cilia (SIL ee uh): tiny, living, hairlike projections from a cell.

ciliary (SIL ih er ee) **muscle:** a muscle that helps the eye to focus by changing the shape of the lens.

circulation: the movement of blood and lymph through blood vessels and lymph vessels.

cirrhosis (sih ROH sis): hardening or scarring of the liver.

clavicle (KLAV ih k'l): the collarbone.

cocaine (koh KAYN): a habit-forming drug, sometimes used as a local anesthetic.

coccidioidomycosis (KOK sihd dih oh id oh my KOH sis): a disease caused by a fungus, usually affecting the lungs.

coccus (KOK us); pl., **cocci** (KOK sigh): A bacterium shaped like a sphere.

coccyx (KOK siks): the lower end of the backbone, below the sacrum.

cochlea (KOK lee uh): the organ of hearing in the inner ear.

codeine (KOH dee in): a drug derived from opium, and sometimes used in cough syrup.

colic (KOL ick): a sudden pain in the abdomen due to spasm, obstruction, or distention of the intestine, gall bladder, kidney, or other organ.

colitis (koh LY tis): a severe inflammation of the wall of the large intestine.

colon (KOH l'n): the large intestine.

coma (KOH muh): a state of profound unconsciousness.

combustion (kum BUS chun): the process of burning.

communicable disease: a disease that can be transferred from one person to another. A communi-cable disease is an infectious disease. It may be contagious, or it may be passed from person to person through the bite of an insect or other indirect means.

compensation: a mental defense "tactic" in which a goal impossible of realization is replaced by another goal.

compress (KOM press): a dressing applied to a wound.

concave (kon KAYV): hollow and curved; a *concave lens* is narrowest in the middle and spreads light rays apart.

conception (kon SEP shun): fertilization of the egg by the sperm.

concussion: injury to the brain produced by a fall or a blow.

conditioned response: any automatic or semi-automatic behavior that has been acquired or learned. Includes conditioned reflexes and habits.

cones: nerve cells in the retina of the eye that are sensitive to colors.

congenital (kon JEN ih tal): refers to a condition present at birth.

congestion: an abnormal and excessive accumulation of blood in the vessels of an organ.

conjunctiva (KON jungk TY vah): the mucous membrane that lines the inner surface of the eyelid and covers the fore part of the eyeball.

conjunctivitis (kon JUNGK tih VY tis): inflammation of the conjunctiva.

constipation: difficult or infrequent bowel movements.

contagious (kun TAY jus) **disease:** capable of being communicated from one person or animal to another by direct contact or by contact with something touched or given off by the diseased person or animal.

contamination (kun tam ih NAY sh'n): the entry of bacteria, or other agents that can cause disease, into food, water, or any other material.

convalescence (kon vuh LES ens): the period during which a patient recovers health and gathers strength after an illness.

conversion (kon VER shun) **neurosis:** in a conversion neurosis, fear and anxiety are converted into a physical symptom or symptoms.

convex (KON veks): curved, as the exterior of a spherical form; a *convex lens* is widest in the middle and brings light rays to a focus.

convolutions (kon vuh LOO sh'nz): the furrows, or ridges, in the outer surface of the brain.

corn: a hard, thickened area of epidermis, caused by pressure and usually occurring on a toe.

cornea (KOR nee uh): the transparent part of the outer coat of the eyeball, through which the light passes before entering the pupil.

coronary (KOR uh nair ee) **arteries:** arteries that supply the heart muscle with blood.

coronary thrombosis (throm BOH siss): the closing of a coronary artery by a clot, which deprives part of the heart muscle of oxygen and food.

corpuscle (KOR pus 'l): a blood cell.

cortex (KOR teks): the outer layer of an organ such as the cerebrum or the adrenal glands.

cortisone (KOR tih zohn): a hormone produced by the cortex of the adrenal glands.

cramp: a painful, involuntary contraction of a muscle.

cranial (KRAY nee ul) **nerves:** twelve pairs of nerves coming directly from the brain.

cranium (KRAY nee um): the part of the skull that encloses the brain.

cretin (KREE tin): a person lacking normal intelligence and stunted in growth because of the absence or poor development of the thyroid.

crown: the part of a tooth above the gum.

culture (KUL chur): 1. The civilization and customs of a society, nation, or community. 2. The cultivation of microscopic or very small organisms or of cells or tissues.

Cushing's syndrome: a condition resulting from the overproduction of adrenal cortex hormones; it causes excessive obesity.

cuspids (KUS pidz): the large, pointed teeth, one on each side of each jaw, the third from the front. Often called *canines.*

cuticle (KYOO tih k'l): the outer layer of the epidermis of the skin; also, the hardened margin of skin around a nail.

cyanosis (sy ah NOH sis): an abnormal condition in which part or all of the surface of the body becomes blue or purple due to a lack of oxygen in the blood there.

cystitis (sis TY tis): an inflammation of the bladder.

cytoplasm (SY toh plazm): all of the protoplasm of a cell except the nucleus. The cell membrane is the outer layer of the cytoplasm.

cytosine (SY toh seen): one of the nitrogen compounds used to build DNA.

D

dandruff: scales formed on the scalp from the dead outer layer of the skin.

DDT: a chemical used to kill insects.

dead-virus vaccine: a vaccine containing killed viruses; an example is the Salk vaccine for polio.

decibel (DES ih bel): the unit for measuring sound intensity.

deciduous (deh SID yoo us) **tooth:** one of the primary teeth, which are shed and replaced by the permanent teeth.

defecation (def uh KAY shun): the act of eliminating food wastes from the large intestine.

deficiency disease: a disease caused by a lack of one or more nutrients in the diet.

delirium (deh LEER ih um): a state of wild excitement and confusion.

delirium tremens (TREE menz): a violent mental disturbance caused by excessive and prolonged use of alcohol.

deltoid (DEL toyd): a curved, triangular muscle that covers the shoulder joint.

dendrites (DEN drytes): the branches (fibers) of a neuron that carry impulses to the cell body.

dental caries (KAIR eez): cavities in the teeth.

dentine (DEN teen): a hard substance that forms the greater part of a tooth, beneath the enamel.

deodorant (dee OH der ant): a substance that masks or destroys unpleasant odors.

deoxyribonucleic (dee OCKS ih ry boh nyoo KLEE ik) **acid:** a nucleic acid found in chromosomes; genes are made of this substance. Often referred to as *DNA.*

depressant (deh PRESS unt): a drug that slows the activity of the brain and body.

dermatologist (der muh TOL oh jist): a doctor who specializes in diseases of the skin.

dermis (DER mis): the layer of the skin below the epidermis, containing nerves, blood vessels, and tiny muscles associated with body hair; sometimes called the true skin.

Dexadrine (DEKS uh dreen): a stimulant; one of the amphetamine drugs.

dextran (DEKS tran): a syrupy substance made from sugar by bacteria.

dextrin (DEKS trin): a carbohydrate produced when starch is partially digested.

diabetes (dy uh BEE tiss): a disease in which sugar is not properly used in the body; caused by a lack of insulin. This condition is also called *diabetes mellitus* (meh LY tus).

diaphragm (DY uh fram): the muscular wall that separates the chest cavity from the abdomen; important in breathing.

diarrhea (dy uh REE uh): a condition in which bowel movements are very frequent and watery.

diastolic (dy as TOL ik) **blood pressure:** the arterial blood pressure when the heart rests between beats.

Dick test: a test for immunity to scarlet fever.

diffusion (dif YOO zh'n): the process by which the molecules of a substance move from where they are more concentrated to where they are less concentrated; a process by which digested foodstuffs pass from the bloodstream into body cells.

digestion (duh JES chun): the process by which food is changed so that the body can absorb and use it.

diphtheria (dif THIHR ee uh): an infectious disease marked by fever and sore throat.

disinfectant (dis in FEKT 'nt): a substance that destroys germs; usually used to disinfect instruments, cloth, or skin wounds.

dislocation: an injury in which the end of a bone is forced out of place at a joint.

displaced aggression: a mental "defense" tactic, in which a strong emotional response is made to someone (or something) other than the person who caused it. For example, a child who has just been spanked by his mother may kick his dog in angry response.

DNA: abbreviation for *deoxyribonucleic acid.*

dominant gene: a gene that causes a certain trait to appear in an individual even if an unlike gene for the trait is present.

dropsy (DROP see): abnormal accumulation of liquid in the tissues.

drug dependence: the physical and/or psychological need for a drug.

drug tolerance: adaptation of the body to a drug, so that larger and larger doses are needed to get the same effect.

duct: a tube that carries away gland secretions.

ductless gland: an endocrine gland, one that secretes a hormone directly into the blood.

duodenum (doo oh DEE num): the first part of the small intestine, leading from the stomach.

dysentery (DIS un tehr ee): an intestinal disease causing severe diarrhea.

E

eardrum: the membrane that separates the middle ear from the canal of the outer ear.

eczema (EK suh muh): the name applied to several different types of skin disorder, usually marked by redness and the appearance of a rash.

electrocardiogram (eh lek troh KAHR dih oh gram): a record of the electrical changes that take place in the heart as it beats. The *electrocardiograph* is the apparatus that makes an electrocardiogram.

electroencephalograph (eh lek troh en SEF al oh graf): apparatus that records "brain waves," the electrical activities of the cerebral cortex.

electrolysis (eh lek TROL uh sis) **of hair:** destruction of the roots of hair by electrical means.

element: a substance that cannot be broken down into simpler substances by chemical means.

embryo (EM brih oh): a developing baby in the first months of pregnancy.

emetic (eh MET ik): a substance used to make a person vomit. Emetics are given to victims of poisoning.

emphysema (em fih SEE mah): a disease in which the air sacs of the lungs become stretched by trapped air.

empyema (em pih EE mah): a severe form of pleurisy with the formation of pus.

enamel (eh NAM el): the hard outer covering of a tooth.

encephalitis (en sef uh LY tis): inflammation of the brain; sometimes called *sleeping sickness.*

endocrine (EN duh kryne): pertaining to the ductless glands.

endoplasmic reticulum (en doh PLAZ mik reh TIH kyoo lum): a complex system of membrane-surrounded channels in a cell.

enema (EN uh muh): the injection of water or other liquid into the colon to promote a bowel movement.

energy: the capacity to do work.

enriched (cereals and bread): having vitamins and minerals added, usually B complex vitamins and iron.

entomologist (en toh MOL oh jist): a scientist who studies insects.

environment (en VY ron ment): all the external conditions and influences that affect the life and development of a person.

enzyme (EN zyme): an organic substance produced inside a living thing and used to speed up chemical changes. Digestive enzymes speed up chemical reactions in digestion, and respiratory enzymes speed up cell respiration.

epidemic (ep ih DEM ik): an outbreak of an infectious disease that affects a large number of people at once.

epidermis (ep ih DER mis): the outer layer of the skin, covering the dermis.

epiglottis (ep ih GLOT is): the flap of tissue that covers the top of the windpipe when you swallow.

epilepsy (EP ih lep see): a brain disorder that may bring on loss of consciousness or convulsions. Epilepsy is *not* a form of insanity.

epinephrine (ep ih NEF rin): adrenaline.

epithelial (ep ih THEE lih al): referring to the epithelium, skin.

epithelium (ep ih THEE lih um): the tissue that covers all the surfaces and lines all the cavities of the body; skin.

esophagus (eh SOF uh gus): the gullet; the food tube that connects mouth and stomach.

estrogen (ES tro gen): a female sex hormone.

ethyl (ETH ihl) **alcohol:** grain alcohol; a kind of alcohol used as an antiseptic and as a beverage.

Eustachian (yoo STAY kee un) **tube:** the tube connecting the middle ear with the throat.

evaporation: the process by which a liquid absorbs heat and diffuses into the air as a vapor or gas.

excrete (eks KREET): to carry on excretion.

excretion (eks KREE sh'n): the removal from the bloodstream, and the elimination from the body, of the waste materials of body metabolism.

excretory (EKS krih toh ree) **system:** the organs that remove from the bloodstream and the body the wastes produced by the cells; includes kidneys and bladder.

exhale: to breathe out.

extensor (ek STEN ser): a muscle that serves to straighten or extend a part of the body.

extrovert (EKS truh vert): a person who "turns out," who tends to be more interested in dealing with people than in working alone.

F

Fahrenheit (FAIR un hyte) **scale:** a scale for measuring temperature, in which the boiling point of water is 212° above zero and the freezing point of water is 32° above zero.

fallout: radioactive dust in the atmosphere after a nuclear explosion, which is scattered by winds and falls to the ground.

farsightedness: a condition in which one can see distinctly only at distances of approximately 20 feet or more.

fatty acids: part of the end products of the digestion of fats.

feces (FEE seez): the waste matter excreted from the colon.

femur (FEE mer): the thigh bone—the long bone in the upper leg extending from the hip to the knee.

fermentation (fer men TAY shun): chemical changes brought about by yeasts and some bacteria in the absence of oxygen. Yeast fermentation of sugar produces alcohol and carbon dioxide.

fertilization (fer tih lih ZAY shun): occurs when sperm and egg unite.

fetus (FEE tus): after two months' growth, the human embryo becomes the fetus.

fever (FEE ver): body temperature above normal.

fibrillation (FY brihl LAY shun): irregular heart action.

fibrin (FY brin): the fibers that enmesh blood cells to form a blood clot.

fibrinogen (fy BRIN uh jen): a plasma protein that changes to fibrin under certain conditions.

fibula (FIB yoo luh): one of two bones of the lower leg.

flagellum (flah JEL lum); pl., **flagella** (flah JEL luh): whiplike structure in sperms and some microscopic organisms; used for swimming.

flatulence (FLAT yoo lence): gas in the stomach or intestine.

flexor (FLEKS er): a muscle that serves to flex or bend a part of the body.

fluoridation (FLOO er ih DAY shun): the addition of fluorides to water.

fluorides (FLOO er ydes): certain mineral salts that check tooth decay when added to drinking water.

folic (FOH lik) **acid:** one of the B vitamins; it helps to prevent pernicious anemia.

follicle (FOL ih k'l): the tissue surrounding the root of a hair.

fovea centralis (FOH vee uh sen TRAY lis): the small area of the retina giving the most acute vision.

fracture: a broken bone. A **partial fracture** means that a bone is cracked. A **complete fracture** means that the bone is separated into two or more pieces. Complete fractures may be **simple** or **compound**; simple if the bone does not pierce the skin, compound if it does.

fraternal (fra TER nal) **twins:** twins arising from two different fertilized eggs.

fungus (FUNG gus); pl., **fungi** (FUN jye): a simple, nongreen plant that cannot make its own food as typical green plants do.

G

galactose (gah LAK tohs): a simple sugar; combined with glucose, it forms lactose (milk sugar).

galactosemia (gah lak toh SEE mih uh): persons with this condition cannot make use of the galactose from milk sugar, hence they must avoid milk and milk products.

gall bladder: the sac in which bile is stored. *Gallstones* are sometimes formed from the bile in the gall bladder.

gamma globulin (GLOB yoo lin): a form of globulin (blood protein) that is used to prevent certain diseases.

ganglion (GANG lee un); pl., **ganglia** (GANG lee uh): a mass of nerve cell bodies.

gangrene (GANG green): the death of tissue following stoppage of circulation.

gastric (GASS trik) **juice:** the digestive juice produced by the gastric glands in the stomach.

gastritis (gass TRY tiss): inflammation of the stomach.

genes (JEENS): the carriers of hereditary traits. Genes are functional areas of DNA in the chromosomes of cell nuclei.

genetic (je NEH tik) **code:** the way that adenine, thymine, cytosine, and guanine are arranged along the chromosomes.

germ: any microscopic plant, animal, or virus that causes disease.

gland: an organ that secretes useful substances (or, in some cases, substances the body has to get rid of). The liver is the largest gland.

glandular (GLAN dyoo lar) **fever:** infectious mononucleosis.

glaucoma (glaw KOH muh): an eye disease in which fluid pressure increases in the eyeball and disturbs vision.

globulin (GLOB yoo lin): a blood protein.

glucagon (GLOO kah gon): a hormone produced in the islets of Langerhans.

glucose (GLOO kohss): a simple sugar found in the blood; an end product of the digestion of starch and other sugars.

glycerin (GLISS er in): a sweet, colorless, syrupy liquid; an end product of the digestion of fats; also called *glycerol* (GLISS er ohl).

glycogen (GLY kuh j'n): a carbohydrate found in the liver and the muscles; also called *animal starch.*

goiter (GOY ter): an enlargement of the thyroid gland.

gonadotrophic (goh nad oh TROH fic): referring to the hormone that stimulates hormone production by gonads.

gonads (GOH nadz): the sex glands.

gonococcus (gon uh KOK uhs): the bacterium that causes gonorrhea.

gonorrhea (gon er EE uh): an infectious disease of the reproductive organs. Its germs can cause blindness if they reach the eye.

granulocyte (GRAN yoo loh syte): one type of white blood cell.

gray matter: part of the brain and spinal cord, made up mostly of cell bodies and dendrites and generally found in the outside surface of the brain and on the inside of the spinal cord.

guanine (GWAH neen): one of the nitrogen compounds used to build DNA.

gullet: the part of the alimentary canal that carries food and water from the mouth to the stomach; also called the *esophagus.*

H

habit: learned behavior more complicated than a conditioned response. A habit has to be learned or acquired, but it becomes almost automatic.

halitosis (HAL ih TOH sis): bad breath.

hallucinogen (hal LOO syn uh gen): a drug that causes one to have hallucinations, that is, to see things that are not present or hear things that are imaginary.

hammer: one of the tiny bones of the middle ear.

Hansen's disease: leprosy.

hardening of the arteries: a condition in which the

walls of the arteries lose their elasticity.

hashish (HAHSH eesh): a drug made from hemp; similar to but more powerful than marijuana.

hay fever: an allergy to pollen. The symptoms resemble those of a cold.

heartburn: pain resulting from stomach acid going up into the gullet.

heart murmur: abnormal sound made by the heart, often caused by a leaking valve.

hemoglobin (HEE moh gloh bin): the red coloring matter in the red blood cells.

hemophilia (hee moh FIL ee uh): a hereditary condition in which the blood will not clot normally.

hemorrhage (HEM er ij): excessive loss of blood.

hemorrhoids (HEM oh roidz): enlarged, painful veins of the rectum.

heparin (HEP uh rin): a substance made in the liver which tends to check the clotting of blood.

hepatitis (hep uh TY tis): an inflammation of the liver. *Infectious hepatitis* is a disease caused by a virus.

heredity (hehr ED ih tee): the passing on of traits from parents to offspring.

hernia (HER nee uh): a rupture; the condition that results when the intestine or other organ pushes out through a weak spot in the muscles of the body wall.

heroin (HEHR oh in): a powerful narcotic drug made from opium. Its possession or use is against the law.

histamine (HIS tuh meen): a substance, produced by the body that may help bring about an allergic reaction.

hives: swellings or bumps just under the skin, due to an allergy.

Hodgkin's disease: a disease resembling leukemia and marked by continuous enlargement of lymph nodes.

homeostasis (HOH mih oh STAY sis): the tendency of an organism to maintain stable conditions within itself by means of negative feedback.

hookworm: a tiny worm that attaches itself to the wall of a human or animal intestine and lives there as a parasite.

hormone (HOR mohn): a secretion from an endocrine gland. Hormones pass directly from an endocrine gland into the blood.

humerus (HYOO mer us): the large bone in the upper arm.

humidity (hyoo MID uh tee): the moisture content of the atmosphere.

Huntington's chorea (koh REE uh): an extremely rare mental disease.

hydrochloric (hy druh KLOR ik) **acid:** an acid found in the gastric juice of the stomach.

hydrophobia (hy druh FOH bee uh): rabies.

hyperopia (HY per OH pih uh): farsightedness.

hypertension (HY per TEN shun): high blood pressure; higher than normal pressure of the blood against the walls of the arteries.

hyperventilation (hy per VEN tih lay shun): deep or rapid breathing, which causes the blood to have too much oxygen.

hypnotic (hihp NOT ik) **drug:** one that produces sleep or makes one sleepy.

hypochondriac (hy poh KON drih ak): a person who suffers from imaginary ailments or who worries about his health without good cause.

hypothalamus (hy poh THAL uh mus): a portion of the lower part of the brain, near the pituitary gland. It acts to make the nerves and endocrine glands work together.

hysteria (his TEER ih uh): the name formerly given to *conversion neurosis,* in which emotions become abnormally excited and in which certain motor functions are disrupted. For no apparent *physical* cause, a hysterical person may lose his sight, or speech, or the ability to move his arms or legs.

I

identical twins: twins that developed from the division of a single fertilized egg.

identification: a mental tactic whereby a person tries to pattern himself after someone else.

immune (im YOON): able to resist a certain disease. A person with this ability is said to be immune or to have *immunity* (im YOO nih tee).

impetigo (im peh TY goh): an infectious disease of the skin.

incisors (ihn SY zers): teeth adapted for cutting; in each jaw the four front teeth.

incubation (in kyoo BAY shun) **period:** the time between the entrance of disease germs into the body and the appearance of symptoms of the disease.

infantile paralysis: polio.

infection (in FEK shun): the invasion and establishment of disease germs (or of larger living things that cause disease) in the body. A *local infection*, such as a boil, is confined to one spot.

infectious (in FEK shus) **disease:** a communicable disease; one that is caused by a germ or larger living thing.

infectious mononucleosis (mo noh noo klee OH sis): a disease common in adolescents and young adults, thought to be due to a virus.

inflammation (in fluh MAY shun): a diseased condition marked by redness, swelling, heat, and pain.

INH: the abbreviation for the scientific name of a drug used to treat tuberculosis.

inhale: to breathe in. An *inhalator* (IN huh lay ter) is an apparatus that makes breathing easier. It is used in first aid to supply oxygen.

inhibit (in HIB it): to hold back or suppress, as to inhibit a sneeze.

inhibition (in hih BISH 'n): the act of suppressing a response that could be made or might be expected. Inhibitions concerning a person's personality often involve reasons of which the person himself is unaware.

inoculation (in ok yoo LAY shun): the injection of vaccine or serum into the bloodstream.

insulin (IN suh lin): a hormone made by the islets of Langerhans in the pancreas. Lack of insulin causes diabetes.

intelligence quotient: a relative measurement of one's mental abilities; often referred to as *IQ*.

intravenous (in trah VE nuhs): pertaining to injecting a substance directly into a person's bloodstream, as in intravenous feeding.

iodine (EYE uh dyne): an element needed by the thyroid gland to make thyroxin.

iris (EYE riss): the colored portion of the eye, surrounding the pupil.

islets of Langerhans (EYE lits of LANG ger hans): "islands" of distinctively different tissue in the pancreas; they make insulin.

isotopes (EYE suh tohps): two or more different forms of the same chemical element.

J

jaundice (JAWN diss): a condition caused by bile circulating in the blood. The skin and the whites of the eyes may turn yellow.

joint: a connection between bones.

K

kidneys: two bean-shaped organs, each about the size of a fist, found in the small of the back. They remove urea and other wastes from the blood to form urine.

Kupfer cells: see *star cells*.

kwashiorkor (KWOSH ee ohr kohr): a disease due to lack of enough protein; found mostly in children in some parts of the tropics.

L

labyrinth (LAB ih rihnth) **of the ear:** the fluid-filled tubes, or canals, of the inner ear, including the cochlea.

lacrimal (LAK rih mal) **glands:** the tear glands.

lacteals (LAK tee ulz): small lymph vessels in the villi of the small intestine; they collect the digested fats.

lactic (LAK tik) **acid:** a waste by-product formed by muscle cells when they contract. The same acid is found in sour milk.

lactose (LAK tohs): the sugar naturally found in milk.

lanolin (LAN uh lin): a fatty substance obtained from wool; it has a healing effect on dry skin.

laryngitis (lair ihn JY tis): an inflammation of the larynx.

larynx (LAIR inks): the voice box, containing the vocal cords; it is located at the upper end of the windpipe.

laxative (LAKS uh tiv): a substance that speeds up peristalsis in the intestines, encouraging bowel movements.

lens: an object used to change the direction of light rays. The lens of the eye focuses light rays on the retina.

leper (LEHP er): a victim of *leprosy* (LEP ruh see), now called *Hansen's disease*—a disease marked by sores and deformities.

leukemia (lyoo KEE mee uh): a name applied to a group of diseases in which the white blood cells increase greatly in number.

ligaments (LIG uh m'nts): bands of tough tissue that hold bones together. Some ligaments also hold certain other body structures in place.

liver: the largest gland in the body; it lies just below the diaphragm on the right side of the body.

liver fluke (FLOOK): a worm that lives in the liver; a parasite. It is rarely found in this country.

live-virus vaccine: vaccine made with a weakened living virus; an example is the Sabin live-virus polio vaccine.

lobe (LOHB): a large division of an organ, not entirely separated from the rest of it, as in the liver or lungs.

LSD: the commonly used abbreviation for a powerful hallucinogen, lysergic acid diethylamide.

lumbago (lum BAY goh): a word formerly used to denote severe backache.

lumbar (LUM bar): pertaining to the small of the back.

lymph (LIMF): the fluid that bathes the body cells. It is formed from blood plasma and white blood cells and returns to the bloodstream through vessels called *lymphatics.*

lymph nodes: small glandlike bodies located at numerous points along the lymphatics. They are important in fighting infection.

lymphocytes (LIM foh sytes): white blood cells made in lymphatic tissue.

lymphoma (lim FOH mah): a group of tumors arising in lymphatic tissue.

lysozyme (LY soh zyme): an antibacterial substance in tears.

M

malaise (muh LAYZ): an indefinite feeling of uneasiness or illness.

malaria (muh LAIR ee uh): a disease that is caused by the protozoan carried by the *Anopheles* mosquito.

malignant (muh LIG nunt) **tumor:** a cancerous growth.

maltose (MAWL tohs): malt sugar. As starch is digested, the starch molecules break down into maltose molecules.

manic (MAYN ik): highly excited, with disordered thinking and lack of control.

manic-depressive psychosis: a mental illness marked by periods of manic excitement and other periods of profound depression.

marijuana (mair uh WAH nuh): the dried leaves and flower of the hemp plant. The mildest of the psychedelic drugs when smoked in cigarette form.

marrow (MAIR oh): the soft material inside bones; a site of blood cell formation.

massage (muh SAHZH): a "rubdown"; treating the body by rubbing, kneading, or tapping.

mastoid (MASS toid): a bone behind the ear. It has many hollow spaces, which sometimes may become infected.

medulla (meh DUHL uh): the lowest part of the brain, just above the spinal cord; often called the *medulla oblongata.* The *medulla* of the adrenal gland is the inner part of the gland.

meiosis (my OH sis): cell division in which each new cell gets only half as many chromosomes as the original cell had.

membrane (MEM brayn): a thin layer of tissue.

meninges (meh NIN jeez): three membranes covering the brain and spinal cord.

meningitis (men in JY tiss): an inflammation of the meninges.

menstruation (men stroo AY shun): the monthly process in which the extra lining of the uterus is shed.

metabolism (muh TAB uh liz'm): a general name for all activities of the body cells in which food is oxidized or protoplasm is built up or broken down.

metastasis (meh TAS tuh sis): the spread of cancerous growth from one place in the body to another.

methadone (METH uh dohn): a narcotic drug sometimes used in treating heroin addicts.

Methedrine (METH uh dreen): a stimulant, one of the amphetamines; often called "speed."

methyl (METH ihl) **alcohol:** wood alcohol, a poison.

microbe (MY krohb), or **microorganism** (my kroh OR gun izm): any living thing so small that it can be seen only through a microscope.

migraine (MY grayn): a variety of severe headache, which often affects only one side of the head.

milk teeth: a child's first set of teeth, later replaced by the permanent teeth.

millimeter (MIL ih mee ter): a small unit of measure in the metric system, equal to approximately $1/25$ of an inch.

mite: a small creature, related to the ticks.

mitochondrion (my toh KON drih on); pl., **mitochondria** (my toh KON drih uh): mitochondria are organelles in which energy is released from sugar and other substances for the use of the cell.

mitosis (my TOH sis): cell division in which each new cell gets the same number and kind of chromosomes as the parent cell had before division.

mixed nerve: a nerve containing both sensory and motor nerve fibers.

molars (MOH larz): the twelve permanent teeth, three on each side, at the back of each jaw.

mold: a kind of fungus; bread mold, for example. Molds are the source of penicillin and most other antibiotics.

mole: a growth on the skin, almost always darker in color than the skin itself.

molecule (MOL uh kyool): the smallest particle into which a substance can be divided without changing it into something else.

morphine (MOR feen): a narcotic made from opium.

motor end plate: the tip or tips of a motor neuron that connect it with one or more muscle cells.

motor nerve: a nerve carrying impulses from the brain, the spinal cord, or a ganglion to a muscle or gland. The nerve cells that carry these impulses are called *motor neurons.*

mucous (MYOO kuss): pertaining to tissues that produce mucus. The *mucous membrane* is the membrane lining the inside of the mouth, the nose, all of the respiratory system, and the alimentary canal.

mucus (MYOO kuss): the liquid that moistens and protects the mucous membrane. It is produced by cells in the membrane.

multiple sclerosis (MUL tih p'l skleh ROH sis): a disease of the central nervous system causing various motor difficulties.

muscle tonus (TOH nus): the very slight contraction that keeps a muscle ready for action.

mutate (myoo TAYT): to undergo a mutation.

mutation (myoo TAY shun): a chemical change in a gene that may produce a new hereditary trait.

mycelium (my SEE lih um); pl., **mycelia** (my SEE lih uh): a growth of living threads produced by a mold or other fungus.

mycoplasma (my koh PLAS muh): a group of very small bacteria with flexible cell walls.

myopia (my OH pih uh): nearsightedness.

myxedema (miks eh DEE muh): a disease due to lack of sufficient thyroxin in older children and adults.

N

narcotic (nahr KOT ik): generally, a drug that relieves pain and induces sleep. Certain drugs, such as cocaine, are classified legally but not chemically as narcotic drugs.

nausea (NAW shuh): a sensation tending to cause vomiting.

nearsightedness: a condition in which one can see distinctly only at short distances.

nephritis (neh FRY tiss): an inflammation of the kidney; also called *Bright's disease.*

nephron (NEF ron): one of about a million tiny tubes in the kidney.

nerve: a cordlike cable of nerve fibers, leading from the brain, the spinal cord, or a ganglion to another part of the body.

nerve fiber: a living thread of protoplasm extending from a nerve cell body.

nervous impulse: a chemical change and electrical charge that travel along a nerve fiber; a "message" that is carried from one nerve cell to the other.

neuritis (nyoo RY tis): the inflammation of a nerve.

neuron (NYOO ron): a nerve cell.

neurophysiologist (NYOO roh fihz ih OL oh jist): a scientist who studies the nervous system.

neurosis (noor OH siss): a mental disorder, less serious than a psychosis, and not involving loss of touch with reality.

neurotic (noo ROT ik): behaving as if suffering from a neurosis; a person who behaves in such a manner.

niacin (NY uh sin): one of the B vitamins, needed to prevent pellagra.

nicotine (NIK uh teen): a poisonous drug contained in tobacco.

night blindness: the inability to see in dim light; the condition is often caused by a deficiency of vitamin A.

nitrogen (NY truh jin): an element, a gas that forms four fifths of the atmosphere.

nitrogen mustard: a chemical used to treat some forms of cancer.

norepinephrine (nor ep ih NEF reen): a hormone produced by the medulla of the adrenal glands.

normal salt solution: a mixture of one level teaspoonful of salt to one pint of water, which is injected into the veins of a person who cannot drink water or who suffers from a lack of water.

nucleus (NOO klee us): a small oval body, a principal part of a living cell; it contains the chromosomes, which carry the genetic code.

nutrients (NOO tree ents): substances needed by the body for its energy, growth, and repair. Usually, several nutrients are found in the same food.

O

obesity (oh BEE sih tih): overweight, with excessive fat stored in the body.

obsession (ob SES shun): a persistent, unwanted idea that one cannot get rid of by reasoning.

oculist (OK yoo list): another name for an ophthalmologist, a doctor who specializes in eye care.

olfactory (ol FAK tuh ree): pertaining to the sense of smell.

one-egg twins: twins that developed from the same fertilized egg.

ophthalmologist (op thuh MOL uh jist): a doctor who specializes in eye care and eye surgery.

opthalmoscope (op THAL moh skohp): an instrument used to examine the interior of the eye.

opium (OH pee um): a narcotic obtained from one type of poppy.

optic (OP tik): of or pertaining to the eye or to sight.

optician (op TIH shun): an expert who grinds lenses and fits eyeglasses.

optic nerve: a large nerve that carries impulses from the eye to the brain.

optometrist (op TOM eh trist): a specialist in the correction of defects of vision by means of glasses.

organ: a group of tissues that are arranged to form a special structure that does a particular kind of work. The brain, the heart, and the lungs are organs.

organelles (or guh NELZ): microscopic structures in a cell. Each kind of organelle does its own kind of work for a cell, somewhat as organs function for the body.

organic (or GAN ik): of or pertaining to living things.

Orinase (OHR ih nays): a sulfa drug, used to treat diabetes.

orthodontist (or thuh DON tist): a dentist who treats irregularities in the way teeth are set in the jaw or in the way they come together when biting.

orthopedic (or thoh PEE dik): related to the prevention or correction of deformities.

osmosis (os MOH sis): the diffusion of water molecules through a semipermeable membrane.

ossify (OSS ih fy): to harden and change into bone.

osteomyelitis (os tee oh my eh LY tis): a bone infection caused by certain pus-forming bacteria.

otitis (oh TY tis): inflammation of the ear. *Otitis media* (MEE dih uh): is inflammation of the middle ear.

otologist (oh TOL uh jist): a doctor who treats diseases of the ear.

ovary (OH vuh ree): one of the two organs that produce the eggs and the female sex hormones.

ovulation (oh vyoo LAY shun): the release of an egg cell from the ovary. After ovulation, the egg is ready to be fertilized.

oxidation (oks ih DAY shun): the process by which substances unite with oxygen, producing heat and sometimes light.

oxygen (OKS ih jen): an element, a gas necessary for life and for burning. Necessary for respiration.

ozone (OH zohn): a very active form of oxygen.

P

pacemaker: a group of cells where the impulse for the heartbeat starts; in the right auricle.

palpitation (pal pih TAY shun): abnormal, rapid beating of the heart.

pancreas (PAN kree us): a gland that makes *pancreatic* (pang kree AT ik) *juice,* which contains enzymes needed in digestion. Part of the pancreas also acts as a ductless gland, making the hormone insulin.

papilla (puh PIL uh); pl., **papillae** (puh PIL ee): a tiny, fingerlike projection of the skin, as the tastebuds on the tongue.

paralysis (puh RAL ih sis): loss of power to move.

parasite (PAIR uh syte): an animal or plant that lives in or on another living thing and gets food from it. Bacteria that cause disease are parasites.

parasympathetic (pair uh sim puh THET ik) **division:** one of the two divisions of the autonomic nervous system. Its nerve impulses slow down heartbeat and speed digestion.

parathyroid (pair uh THY royd) **glands:** small glands located in or on the thyroid; their hormone, called *parathormone* (pair uh THOR mohn), regulates the body's use of calcium.

paresis (puh REE sis): a medical term for paralysis. *General paresis* is a brain disease caused by syphilis.

parotid (puh ROT ihd) **glands:** the two largest salivary glands.

PAS: the abbreviation for the name of a drug used to treat tuberculosis.

pasteurization (pas ter ih ZAY sh'n): the process of heating milk to about 143°F. for 30 minutes, or to 161°F. for 15 seconds, to kill all disease germs. Rapid heating and rapid cooling are used to help preserve the taste of the milk.

patella (puh TEL luh): the kneecap.

pathogenic (path oh JEN ik): causing disease.

pellagra (peh LAY gruh): a disease caused by a lack of the vitamin niacin.

pelvis (PEL viss): the hollow, girdlelike structure formed by the hipbones and the lower vertebrae.

penicillin (pen ih SIL in): an antibiotic, the first to come into general medical use. It is extracted from a common mold.

pepsin (PEP sin): an enzyme made in the stomach. It helps to digest protein.

peptone (PEP tone): partly digested protein.

peridontal (PEH rih DON tal) **membrane:** the membrane that anchors a tooth in the jaw.

periosteum (per ee OS tee um): the living membrane that surrounds each bone.

peripheral (peh RIHF er al) **vision:** the indistinctly seen area that surrounds what the eye sees clearly.

peristalsis (pehr ih STAL sis): the wavelike contractions of the muscles of the alimentary canal.

peritoneum (pehr ih toh NEE um): the membrane that lines the abdominal cavity.

peritonitis (pehr ih tuh NY tis): a serious inflammation of the lining of the abdominal cavity; it commonly follows a ruptured appendix.

pernicious (per NISH us) **anemia:** a form of anemia in which the body cannot make a substance needed for normal red blood cells.

perspiration (per spih RAY shun): sweat; the salty fluid secreted by the sweat glands.

pesticide (PES tih syde): a poison used to kill insects or other pests.

phagocyte (FAYG oh syte): a cell that engulfs and destroys bacteria and other microscopic invading organisms. This process is called *phagocytosis* (FAYG oh sy TOH sis).

pharynx (FAIR inks): the throat cavity.

phenylalanine (fee nil AH lan in): an amino acid.

phenylketonuria (fee nil kee toh NOO rih ah): a disease due to the lack of an enzyme needed for the harmless use of phenylalanine in the body.

phobia (FOH bi uh): a persistent, unreasonable fear of an object (or kind of animal) or situation.

phosphate (FOS fayt): a chemical substance containing phosphorus, hydrogen, and oxygen.

phosphorus (FOS for us): a solid element needed by all cells and important in building bone.

physique (fihz EEK): one's body build or type of body.

pigment (PIG ment): coloring matter.

pineal (PIN ee ul) **gland:** a glandlike structure near the brain. Its function is not known, but it may act to delay sexual development.

pinkeye: an infection of the eyelid lining and the front part of the eye.

pitocin (pih TOH sin): a pituitary hormone that stimulates smooth muscle.

pituitary (pih TYOO ih ter ee) **gland:** a ductless gland located at the base of the brain; the "master gland." It secretes hormones that cause other ductless, or endocrine, glands to secrete their hormones.

placenta (pluh SEN tuh): the structure that grows on the wall of the uterus during pregnancy. Through its connection with the placenta, the unborn child receives nourishment and oxygen from the mother and discharges wastes.

plantar (PLAN ter) **wart:** a wart on the sole of the foot.

plasma (PLAZ muh): the liquid part of the blood.

platelets (PLAYT lets): one of the three basic kinds of blood cells, much smaller than red or white blood cells and without nuclei. Platelets are important in blood-clotting.

pleura (PLOOR uh): the double membrane covering the lungs and lining the chest cavity.

pleurisy (PLOOR ih see): an inflammation of the pleura, causing painful breathing.

plexus (PLEK sus): a group of ganglia, which in turn are clusters of nerve cells.

pneumonia (nyoo MOH nee uh): an infectious disease of the lungs.

poliomyelitis (poh lee oh my eh LY tiss), often called **polio:** infantile paralysis; a virus disease that may kill motor nerve cells and thus cause paralysis.

polluted (puh LOOT 'd): contaminated, or mixed with impurities or disease germs.

polycythemia (pol ee sy THEE mee uh): a condition in which there are too many red blood cells.

polyp (POL ip): a small, grapelike growth, attached to the skin or mucous membrane by a stalk.

pons (PONZ): a part of the brain lying in front of the cerebellum.

portal (POR t'l) **vein**: a large vein that carries blood from the stomach and intestines to the liver.

posture: the way in which a person holds his body.

potable (POT uh b'l): fit to drink.

presbyopia (prez bih OH pih uh): "old sight"; a condition in which an older person's eyes lose the ability to change focus.

progesterone (proh JES ter ohn): a female sex hormone.

projection: putting the blame for one's faults on someone else; also, assuming that someone else is guilty of the "undesirable" emotion that is really one's own.

pronated (PROH nayt'd): tilted inward, as in a condition of the ankles.

protein (PROH tee in): a nutrient containing nitrogen, carbon, hydrogen, and oxygen. It is important in building and repairing tissue.

proteoses (PROH tee oh sez): products of the partial digestion of proteins.

protoplasm (PROH toh plazm): a term used to mean everything in a cell that we could say was alive. The term is not used now as much as formerly because there is no *substance* that could be called protoplasm.

protozoa (proh toh ZOH uh): microscopic one-celled animals.

psychedelic (sy cuh DEL ik) **drugs**: hallucinogens.

psychiatrist (sy KY uh trist): a medical doctor who specializes in the treatment of mental disorders.

psychoanalysis (sy koh uh NAL ih sis): a form of treatment for emotional and mental difficulties in which the patient is encouraged to try to recall early painful experiences that may have affected his present condition.

psychologist (sy KOL uh jist): a scientist who studies the mind and the way people behave.

psychosis (sy KOH siss): a mental illness marked by a loss of touch with reality.

psychosomatic (sy koh soh MAT ik): pertaining to the effect of the mind upon the body and of the body upon the mind. A psychosomatic illness may show physical symptoms resulting from mental causes.

ptyalin (TY uh lin): an enzyme in saliva. It helps to digest starch.

pulmonary (PUL muh nehr ee): pertaining to the lungs, as in pulmonary arteries.

pulp of tooth: the soft, living tissue inside a tooth. The pulp contains the tooth's supply of nerves and blood vessels.

pulse: the beat felt in an artery, as in the wrist, each time the heart beats.

pupil: the opening in the iris of the eye, through which light enters the eye.

pus: the sticky, usually yellow substance found in boils and other infected places. It contains dead white blood cells, bacteria, and plasma.

pushers: persons who illegally sell narcotics.

pylorus (py LOH rus): the muscular valve between the stomach and the first part of the small intestine (the duodenum).

pyorrhea (py uh REE uh): a disease of the gums that may spread to the bones of the upper and lower jaw.

Q

quack: a person practicing medicine without proper qualifications.

quarantine (KWAHR en teen): enforced isolation because of real or suspected infection with a contagious disease. People, animals, and even plants can be quarantined.

quinine (KWY nyne): a drug used to treat malaria; it is obtained from the bark of a tropical tree.

R

rabies (RAY beez): a disease caused by a virus that attacks the central nervous system. Rabies is usually contracted through the bite of an animal with the disease. A dog with rabies is often said to be "mad."

radioactivity: the giving off of energy by radioactive decay or "splitting" of atoms.

radioisotope (ray dee oh EYE suh tohp): an unstable isotope that gives off radiation as it decomposes. Radium is an example.

radium (RAY dee um): a rare element that continually gives off destructive radiation. It is used to treat cancer.

rationalization (rash un ul ih ZAY shun): the act or result of rationalizing.

rationalize (RASH un ul yze): to give to others (or to oneself) a reason other than the true reason for an act, thought, or belief, in order to avoid facing the self-incrimination of the truth.

recessive gene: a gene that causes a particular trait to appear *only* if two identical genes for the trait are present.

rectum (REK tum): the lower part of the large intestine.

reduction division: part of the process of meiosis in which each new cell gets only half as many chromosomes as the original parent cell had.

reflex (REE fleks): an inborn, automatic act.

reflex arc: an inborn pathway through the nervous system. Nervous impulses that travel the arc cause a reflex act.

regression: a mental "defense" tactic in which one thinks or acts in a childish way.

repression: the blotting out of unpleasant or embarrassing memories or thoughts.

reproductive system: the structures in an organism that function to produce offspring.

respiration (ress per AY shun): starts with the taking in of oxygen and giving off of carbon dioxide and water vapor. Internal or *cell respiration* is the complicated process by which energy is released from sugar and other substances in a cell. Both processes are part of body respiration.

respiratory system: the nose, throat, windpipe, bronchi, lungs, and air passages and sacs within the lungs.

response: what a living creature does as the result of a stimulus.

retina (RET ih nuh): a layer of cells inside the eye, sensitive to light. Images are brought to a focus on the retina by the lens.

Rh factor: a substance in the blood of most persons; named after the Rhesus (REE sus) monkey, in which the factor first was found. People who have it are *Rh-positive*; those who do not, *Rh-negative*.

rheumatic (roo MAT ik) **fever:** a disease that causes swelling of the joints and possible heart damage.

rhinitis (ry NY tis): an inflammation of the lining of the nostrils. Formerly called nasal catarrh.

riboflavin (ry boh FLAY vin): one of the B complex vitamins; vitamin B_2.

ribonucleic (ry boh nyoo KLAY ik) **acid:** molecules of this substance carry "instructions" from the DNA in the chromosomes to the ribosomes in the cytoplasm.

ribosomes (RY boh sohms): organelles in the cytoplasm of a cell. Proteins are made at the ribosomes.

rickets (RIK ets): poor development of the bones, caused by a lack of vitamin D.

rickettsia (rih KET sih uh): rickettsias are germs somewhat larger than viruses but smaller than bacteria.

ringworm: a fungus disease of the skin, similar to athlete's foot. It has nothing to do with worms.

RNA: the abbreviation for ribonucleic acid.

rods: cells in the retina of the eye, important for night vision.

Rorschach (ROR shok) **test:** a projective test, often called the "inkblot" test.

roughage (RUF ij): that part of food that cannot be digested.

S

sac: a pouch, or baglike part.

saccule (SAK yool): part of a fluid-filled sac in the inner ear.

sacrum (SAY krum): the five vertebrae fused together at the base of the spine, just above the coccyx. The sacrum is the point of attachment of the spinal column to the hipbones.

saliva (suh LY vuh): a digestive juice secreted by the *salivary* (SAL ih vehr ee) *glands*, which open into the mouth.

saprophyte (SAP roh fyte): an organism that lives on dead organic matter.

sarcoma (sar KOH muh): a cancer arising from connective tissue, such as that of bone and other supporting structures.

scabies (SKAY beez): the "itch"; a disease caused by a mite that burrows into the skin.

scapula (SKAP yoo luh): the shoulder blade.

Schick test: a test for immunity to diphtheria.

schizophrenia (skiz uh FREE nee uh): a psychosis in which the patient withdraws from the real world and is likely to show a "split" between his feelings and his thoughts.

sclera (SKLEE ruh): the tough, white, outer layer of the eyeball. It forms the white of the eye.

scurvy (SKER vee): a disease caused by a lack of vitamin C.

sebaceous (see BAY shus) **glands:** these are tiny glands in the skin that produce *sebum* (SEE bum), a fatty substance.

secretion (see KREE shun): all substances made by glands are secretions.

sedative (SED uh tihv): a drug that reduces activity, relieves anxiety, or calms an excited person.

self-preservation: the basic drive or impulse to save one's own life.

semicircular canals: small, loop-shaped tubes in the inner ear, concerned with balance.

semipermeable (SEH mih PER mee uh b'l) **membrane:** a membrane that allows some substances to pass through and not others, or allows some to pass through more rapidly than others.

sensation: being conscious of something reacted to by the sense organs.

sense organ: an eye, ear, or other part of the body that has collections of nerve cells especially sensitive to certain kinds of stimulation.

sensory nerve: a nerve containing sensory neurons which convey impulses from parts of the body to the brain or spinal cord.

septicemia (sep tih SEE mih uh): an infection of the blood; blood poisoning.

serum (SEER 'm): blood plasma after the fibrin has been removed. Antitoxins and other disease-preventing substances are usually contained in the serum.

shock: a condition resulting in the slowing up of vital body activities following injury or loss of blood. The circulation becomes inefficient in shock. Sometimes the word *shock* is used to mean an emotional upset.

sickle cell anemia: a severe anemia occurring in persons with two sickle cell genes.

sickle cells: red blood cells that contain a peculiar form of hemoglobin that causes them to take a crescent, or sicklelike, shape.

sickle cell trait: a less serious condition occurring in persons who receive only one sickle cell gene.

sinoatrial (SY noh AY trih ul) **node:** the pacemaker of the heart.

sinus (SY nus): a cavity in a bone or other organ. The *nasal sinuses* in certain skull bones open into the nose.

skeletal (SKEH leh tal) **muscle:** striated, or striped, muscle.

smog: a term applied originally to a mixture of smoke and fog. Now applied to various types of air pollution, particularly those resulting from the action of sunlight on industrial or automobile exhausts.

sodium chloride (SOH dee um KLOR yde): common salt.

somatotrophic (soh ma toh TROF ik) **hormone:** a growth hormone produced by the pituitary.

spastic (SPAS tik) **colon:** a functional irritability of the colon.

sperms: male sex cells.

spinal canal: the hollow inside the spinal column, occupied by the spinal cord.

spinal column: the spine; made up of the vertebrae.

spinal cord: a thick cord of nerve cells, extending down through the spinal canal from the brain.

spinal nerves: thirty-one pairs of major nerves that branch off from the spinal cord and connect with skeletal muscle, bone, and skin.

spirillum (spy RIL um); pl., **spirilla** (spy RIL uh): a bacterium with a spiral, or twisted, shape.

spirochete (SPY roh keet): a spiral-shaped, one-celled germ, usually thought to be one of the bacteria, but sometimes classed as one of the protozoa. Syphilis is caused by a spirochete.

spleen: an organ relating to the circulatory system, located to the left and back of the stomach. Among other functions, it stores blood.

spore: a single plant cell, produced by many types of plants. In molds and yeasts, spores are a means of reproduction that can carry the plant through unfavorable conditions. Certain bacteria produce spores that can stand an unusual amount of heat and poison.

sprain: an injury caused when a joint is moved too far or too suddenly.

staphylococcus (staf ih loh KOK us); pl., **staphylocci** (staf ih loh KOK sy): any of certain round bacteria that often form clusters, like grapes, and live on the skin or mucous membrane. Most boils and pimples are staphylococcus infections in skin pores.

star cells, or **stellate** (STEL it) **cells:** a type of cell found in the liver. Star cells devour bacteria and foreign particles in the blood as it circulates through the liver.

status (STAY tus): a person's standing; age, sex, appearance, ability, and one's own and other people's opinions help to determine one's status.

sterile (STEHR il): free from germs or other living things.

sterilization (stehr il uh ZAY shun): the process of making anything free from germs or other living things; also, the process of making it impossible for an animal to reproduce.

sternum (STERN um): the breastbone.

steroid (STEE roid) **hormones:** hormones with a

chemical structure somewhat similar to that of cholesterol. They include the sex hormones and cortisone.

stethoscope (STETH uh skohp): an instrument used by a doctor to listen to the heart and to breathing.

stimulant (STIM yoo lunt): a drug or other substance that speeds up the activity of the body.

stimulus (STIM yoo lus): anything to which a living thing reacts.

stirrup: one of the three tiny bones in the middle ear.

strabismus (stra BIZ mus): the inability to direct both eyes to the same object. Cross-eye and wall-eye are two different types of strabismus.

streptococcus (strep tuh KOK us); pl., **streptococci** (strep tuh KOK sy): any of certain round bacteria that usually form chains, and some of which cause infections of the respiratory passages.

streptomycin (strep toh MY sin): an antibiotic used in treating tuberculosis and certain other diseases.

striated (STRY ayt'd) **muscle:** a muscle with cross stripes along the cells. Voluntary (skeletal) muscle is of this type. Cardiac (heart) muscle also has cross stripes, or striations.

strontium-90: a radioactive isotope of the element strontium.

stupor (STOO per): a condition in which consciousness and feeling are diminished or absent.

sty: an infection of the edge of the eyelid.

subconscious: memories and information that are not in the *conscious* mind are thought of as being in the *subconscious* mind.

sublimation (sub lih MAY shun): one of the ways in which a person may react to inner conflict. It involves redirecting certain selfish or primitive impulses into channels that other people approve.

suffocation (suf uh KAY shun): death as the result of stoppage of breathing.

sulfa (SUL fuh) **drugs:** a family of drugs that act against many important disease germs. The names of most of them start with *sulfa-*, as *sulfadiazine* (sul fuh DY uh zeen) and *sulfathiazole* (sul fuh THY uh zol).

sulfanilamide (sul fuh NIL uh myde): the first sulfa drug to become well known.

sunstroke: another term for heatstroke, when this is due to prolonged exposure to hot sunlight.

The body temperature may rise to 105° F or more. It can be a serious threat to life.

suture (SOO cher): a joint at which two bones have grown together; the type of joint found in the skull.

sympathetic system: one of the two divisions of the autonomic nervous system; it speeds the heartbeat and slows digestion.

Synanon (SIN uh non): a group that operates to help addicts break the drug habit.

synapse (sih NAPS): the point at which a nerve impulse passes from one neuron to another.

syndrome (SIN drohm): a group of signs and symptoms of disease that occur together.

syphilis (SIF ih liss): an infectious disease, located at first in the reproductive organs, but later in many parts of the body.

system of organs: a group of organs that do a particular kind of work, as, for example, the digestive system.

systolic (sis TOL ik) **blood pressure:** arterial blood pressure during the contraction of the heart; the highest arterial blood pressure.

T

talus (TAY lus): a bone in the ankle.

tapeworm: a parasite; a long, flat worm that sometimes lives in the intestine.

tartar (TAHR ter): a hard deposit on the teeth.

tear duct: a tiny tube through which the tears reach the eyeball.

tendon (TEN d'n): a band or cord of connective tissue that attaches a muscle to a bone.

testes (TESS teez): the male organs that produce sperms and male hormones.

testosterone (tes TOS ter ohn): a male sex hormone.

tetanus (TET uh nus): lockjaw; a disease caused by spore-forming bacteria that thrive in the absence of oxygen, as in a puncture-type wound.

tetany (TET uh nee): a condition marked by a loss of muscular control and caused by a lack of parathyroid hormone, or by insufficient calcium.

Thalidomide (thuh LID uh myde): a drug that has led to the birth of deformed infants.

therapy (THEHR uh pee): the treatment of a disease or disorder.

thiamin (THY uh min): vitamin B_1; formerly called vitamin B.

thoracic (thor ASS ik): pertaining to the chest. The

chest is sometimes called the *thorax* (THOH raks).

thrombin (THROM bin): a substance important in the clotting of blood.

thrombosis (throm BOH siss): the formation of a blood clot, or *thrombus* (THROM bus), in a blood vessel.

thymine (THY meen): one of the nitrogen compounds needed to build DNA.

thymus (THY mus): a ductless gland in the chest, which shrinks as a person becomes adult. Its exact work is still being investigated; recent research indicates that it functions to prepare the body for the production of antibodies.

thyroid (THY royd) **gland:** a ductless gland in the neck, the hormone of which is necessary for normal energy and for proper growth and development.

thyrotrophic (thy roh TROH fik) **hormone:** a hormone, produced by the pituitary gland, that stimulates the thyroid to produce thyroxin.

thyroxin (thy ROKSS in): the hormone made by the thyroid gland.

tibia (TIB ee uh): one of the bones of the lower leg.

tick: a small animal with eight legs. Ticks attach themselves to the skin and suck blood.

timbre (TIM ber): the quality of the tone of a voice (or musical instrument).

tissue (TISH oo): a group of similar cells that do the same kind of work.

tone of muscle: the very slight contraction that keeps a muscle ready for action.

tonometer (TOH noh mee ter): an instrument that measures eye tension.

tonsil (TON sil): one of two oval masses of lymphatic tissue, located one on each side of the throat.

tonsillitis (ton sil LY tis): an infection of the tonsils.

tourniquet (TOOR nih ket): a bandage or other device twisted tightly around an arm or leg above a wound to stop bleeding from the wound.

toxic (TOK sik): having a poisonous effect.

toxin (TOK sin): a poison made by a living thing (or sometimes by dead cells or tissues). Different toxins are made by certain bacteria, snakes, toadstools, and green plants.

toxoid (TOK soyd): a toxin that has been treated with heat or chemicals to make it safe to inject into a person to produce immunity to a disease.

trachea (TRAY kee uh): the windpipe.

tranquilizers (TRANG kwuh lyz erz): drugs used to reduce emotional tension and to help a patient reach a more reasonable point of view.

transfer RNA: RNA molecules that transport amino acids to be joined together to form proteins.

transfusion (trans FYOO zh'n): the injection of blood taken from one person into the veins of another person.

trench mouth: a painful inflammation of the gums; also known as *Vincent's disease.*

trial-and-error learning: learning to solve a problem by a series of attempts without having thought out a probable solution in advance.

triceps (TRY sepss): the large muscle at the back of the upper arm.

trichina (trih KY nuh): a tiny worm sometimes found in raw or undercooked pork. It is a parasite, and it causes a painful disease called *trichinosis* (trik ih NOH siss).

trunk: the main part of the body.

trypsin (TRIP sin): a protein-digesting enzyme produced by the pancreas.

tsetse (TSET see) **fly:** a blood-sucking fly that carries the germ of African sleeping sickness.

tuberculin (too BER kyoo lin): a sterile liquid containing substances made by the tuberculosis germ. It is used in the *tuberculin test,* a skin test for possible infection with tuberculosis.

tuberculosis (too ber kyoo LOH siss): a disease caused by the tuberculosis germ. The lungs are most often infected, but other tissues may also be infected.

tumor (TOO mer): an abnormal growth of a mass of cells.

two-egg twins: twins that developed from two different fertilized eggs.

tympanic (tim PAN ik) **membrane:** the membrane that separates the middle ear from the outer ear.

typhoid (TY foyd) **fever:** a disease caused by typhoid bacteria in water or food. Houseflies may carry the germs.

U

ulcer (UL ser): an open sore on the surface or lining of the skin or other organ. An ulcer sometimes forms in the intestine or stomach.

ulcerative colitis (UL ser ay tiv koh LY tis): a severe form of colitis in which ulcers form in the wall of the colon.

ulna (UL nuh): one of the two bones of the forearm. The ulna is the forearm bone that attaches to the humerus, or upper arm bone, to form the elbow joint.

umbilical (uhm BIL ih kuhl) cord: the cord-like structure that connects the unborn baby to the placenta.

urea (yoo REE uh): a waste product of protein metabolism in the body. It is excreted by the kidneys and becomes part of the urine.

uremia (yoo REE mih uh): a condition in which the kidneys are unable to get rid of waste products.

ureter (yoo REE ter): a tube leading from each kidney to the bladder.

urethra (yoo REE thruh): the tube through which urine from the bladder is removed from the body.

urinalysis (yoo rih NAL ih siss): a medical analysis of the urine, involving the use of the microscope and chemical tests.

urine (YOO rin): the liquid excreted by the kidneys.

uterus (YOO ter us): the organ within which a baby develops before birth.

utricle (YOO trih k'l): part of a fluid-filled sac in each inner ear. It helps us to determine the position of the head with respect to gravity.

V

vaccination (vak sih NAY shun): the inoculation with vaccine in order to make a person immune to a disease. A vaccination may result in permanent immunity in some cases, but only temporary immunity in others.

vaccine (VAK seen): a preparation of dead or weakened germs, used to make a person produce antibodies against a certain disease and become immune to it.

vacuole (VAK yoo ohl): a cavity in the cytoplasm of a cell, surrounded by membrane and containing fluid.

vagus (VAY guss) nerves: a pair of cranial nerves whose branches go to the heart, stomach, and other organs. Their impulses slow the heart and speed up digestive processes. The vagus carries a great many nerve fibers of the parasympathetic nervous system.

valve: a structure that can be opened or closed by fluid pressure. It allows the flow of fluids in only one direction.

varicose (VAIR ih kohss) veins: swollen, enlarged, or twisted veins occurring usually in the legs.

variolation (var ih oh LAY shun): a former method of attempting to cause immunity to smallpox. Children were inoculated with material from persons with mild cases of smallpox.

vasopressin (vas oh PRES sin): a pituitary hormone that controls the water balance of the body.

vector (VEK tor): a living creature that transmits organisms which cause disease. Various mosquitoes are vectors for various diseases.

veins (VAYNZ): blood vessels that carry blood from the body toward the heart.

venereal (ven EE rih al) diseases: diseases usually spread as a result of sex relations.

venom (VEN um): poison secreted by certain snakes, spiders, and other animals.

venous (VEE nus) blood: blood in or from the veins.

ventricle (VEN trih k'l): one of the two lower and larger chambers of the heart. The right ventricle pumps blood to the lungs; the left ventricle pumps it to the rest of the body.

vertebra (VER tuh bruh); pl., vertebrae (VER tuh bree): one bone of the series that forms the spinal column. The human spinal column contains 33 vertebrae, some of which are fused.

villus (VIL us); pl., villi (VIL eye): any of the microscopic, hairlike projections (on the inner wall of the small intestine) through which digested foodstuffs are absorbed. Capillaries and lacteals in the villi absorb digested food, which is then circulated to all parts of the body through the circulatory system.

virus (VY rus): a germ so small that it cannot be seen through the ordinary microscope. Viruses reproduce only when in living cells.

visual purple: the pigment in the rods of the retina; it is sensitive to light.

vital capacity of lungs: the largest amount of air that a person can force out after taking the deepest possible breath. A person's vital capacity is not the same as his lung capacity, since one to two quarts of air remain in the lungs despite efforts to exhale all of it.

vitamin (VY tuh min): an essential nutrient found in very small quantities in foods. Only exceedingly small amounts of the different vitamins are required, but a person must have these amounts to remain healthy.

vitreous (VIH tree us) **humor:** the clear, colorless, transparent jelly that fills the space behind the lens in the eyeball.

vocal (VOH k'l) **cords:** two membranes stretched across the top of the voice box, or larynx. They vibrate to produce sound.

volatile (VOL uh tuhl) **chemical:** a substance that turns readily to a gas.

voluntary muscles: muscles that a person can cause to contract at will. They have cross-stripes, or striations, which are visible under the microscope. They are also called *striated* or *skeletal muscles*.

W

warts: outgrowths of the skin or mucous membranes due to virus infection. Warts may be soft, firm, horny, flat, raised, or growing from a stem.

white matter: nerve tissue composed mostly of nerve fibers that have a white protective covering.

windpipe: the tough tube of cartilage and smooth muscle that carries air from the upper part of the throat to the lungs; also called the *trachea.*

wisdom teeth: the molars farthest back in the jaw; the last permanent teeth to appear.

withdrawal sickness: the unpleasant symptoms suffered by a narcotics addict when he is suddenly deprived of the drug.

X

X chromosome: one of the two sex chromosomes; a fertilized egg with two X chromosomes develops into a female.

Y

Y chromosome: one of the two sex chromosomes; a fertilized egg with one X and one Y chromosome develops into a male.

yeasts: microscopic, one-celled fungi that cause fermentation, changing sugar to alcohol and carbon dioxide. A few yeasts cause disease, attacking the central nervous system, skin, or other organs.

Index

A

AA (Alcoholics Anonymous), 595
abscess, 294; in athlete's foot, 155; of tooth, 162
accidents, 618–36; and alcohol, 592; annual deaths from different types of, 620 (*table*); automobile, 622–26; cycling, 627–28; deaths among teenagers from, 175, 620–21, 630–31; farm, 631–32; home, 629, 630; human factors causing, 621–22; pedestrian, 630–31; sports, 173–79; *see also* first aid, safety
accommodation, of the eye, 186
acid-alkaline balance, 363
acne, 153–55, **154**; treatment of, **154**–55
acquired immunity, 534
acromegaly, 405
ACTH, 357, 362, 403, 405, 411
activated charcoal, as antidote, 261
active illness, 515
active immunity, 537, 538
active transport, 234–35
"Adam's apple," 271
addiction, *see* alcoholism, drug abuse
Addison's disease, 411
additives, 79, 80; definition of, 79; nonnutritive, 79; nutritive, 79
adenoids, **270**, 333–35, **335**
adjustment mechanisms, mental, *see* defense mechanisms
adolescence, and accidents, 620–22, 630–31; dating problems in, 482–84; drug dependence in, 608; emotional needs in, 428–430, 477–78, 496–98; family influences in, 425–28, 495–97; driver safety in, 622–24; incidence of venereal disease in, 525; marriage in, 484–85; sexual development in, 391–92, 412–13; skin care in, 148, 153–54; and smoking, 599–600; and vocational goals, 429, 485–88, 558–60, 565–72

adrenal glands, 362, 402–03, 409–11, **410**
adrenaline, 319, 357, 409–11, 465
adrenocorticotrophic hormone (ACTH), 357, 362, 403, 405, 411
aerobics, 104–105
aflatoxin, 345
age, and disease, 513–14
agranulocytosis, 295
agriculture, and air pollution, 86
airborne infections, 518
air pollution, and agriculture, 86; and automobiles, 85–86, 89; causes of, 76, 85–87, 87 (*table*); control of, 76, 86, 89; disasters, 86–87; effects on lung diseases of, 282; general effects on health and safety of, 88–89; and industry, 86; smog, 86, **87**; temperature inversion as cause of, 88
air pressure, and respiration, 277
air sacs, 24, **268**, 272–73
Al-Anon, 595–96
Alateen, 597
albumin, 296, 336
alcohol, 589–98; abuse of, 590, 594–97, *see also* alcoholism; as beverage, 590; and driving, 592; effects on behavior, 592; effects on body, 590–91; kinds of, 590; reasons for drinking, 592–93
Alcoholics Anonymous (AA), 595
alcoholism, 590, 594–97; alcoholic psychosis from, 595; definition of, 594; effects on health of, 594; as medical problem, 595; phases of, and recovery, 596 (*chart*); and problem drinkers, 593; as social problem, 594; symptoms of, 594–95, **595**; treatment of, 594–97
alert signal, 643
alimentary canal, definition of, 25, **25**; structure of, 243–44
allergy, 70, 538–39; and asthma, 539; control of, 539; to drugs, 539; and eczema, 156; and feelings, 539; to food, 64, 70, 539; to insect bites, 539; symptoms of, 70, 539
American Association for Health, Physical Education, and Recreation, 104
American Automobile Association (AAA), 626, 628
American Cancer Society, 554

American Medical Association (AMA), 553–54
American National Red Cross, 267, 554, **554**, 639; Disaster Relief program of, 644
amino acids, 43, 243, 248, 336
amnion, 390
amphetamines, 610, 611 (*table*)
analgesic, 590
anaphylactic shock, 539
anemia, 292, 457
aneurysm, 576, 581
anger, 465, 470–71
angina pectoris, 577
anthropologists, 436
antibiotics, 273, 540–41
antibodies, defined, 296; and immunity, 535–37; and RH factor, 301; and transplants, 580
antidotes, 260–61
antigen-antibody reaction, 536
antigens, 535
antihistamines, 278, 539
antiperspirants, 149–50
antitoxins, 536
antivenins, 305
anxiety, effects of on learning, **456** (*chart*); 456–57; reactions, 500; in teen-agers, 472; *see also* tension
aorta, 312
aortic aneurysm, 576
aortic insufficiency, 576
appearance, care of, 145–66
appendicitis, 250–51; symptoms of, 250–51; treatment of, 251 appendix, 250–51, **250**, **251** appetite, 364; and emotions, 64
aqueous humor, 186
arches, fallen, 126
arms, muscles of, **132**, **133**, 32–33
artery, bleeding from, 297–98; blood clot in, 314; coronary, 312, 313; definition of, 24, 317; hardening of, 312, *see also* arteriosclerosis; largest, **315**, pulmonary, 312
arteriosclerosis, 67, 313, 317, 328, 578; *see also* atherosclerosis artificial kidneys, 343–344, **344**
artificial respiration, 177–78, **178**
ascorbic acid (vitamin C), 46
aspirin, 259, 278, 629, 634
associative neurons, 205, **205**
asthma, 539

astigmatism, definition of, 188; test for, 189

atherosclerosis, 42, **314**, 577, 579

athlete's foot, 155–56

Atomic Energy Commission, 551

atonic muscles, 137

audiogram, function of, 194

audiometer, function of, 194, **195**

auditory nerve, 195

auricle, 312

autoimmune disease, 540

automobiles, and air pollution, 85–86, 89; and safety, 624–26, **625**

autonomic nervous system, 207–08, **208**, 412, 465, 468; definition of, 21, 204; divisions of, 207–08, **208**; parasympathetic division of, 207–08; sympathetic division of, 207–08, **208**

auto safety laws, 626

axons, 205, **205**

B

B complex vitamins, 250–51

"baby" teeth, 161, **161**

bacilli, 522, **522**

backbone, 114

bacteremia, 294

bacteria, 522–24; acne caused by, 154; antibiotics against, 541; appendicitis caused by, 250; blood poisoning caused by, 294; body defenses against, 293–95, 532–37; boils caused by, 155; conjunctivitis caused by, 191; cystitis caused by, 344; dental caries caused by, 162; diphtheria caused by, 281; diseases caused by, 516–17, **522**, 522–23; gonorrhea caused by, 191, **525**, 525–26; impetigo caused by, 156; in large intestine, 250; and lymph nodes, 333; in food, 79, 518; and pasteurization, 519; peritonitis caused by, 251, 259; pneumococcus, 280; pneumonia caused by, 280; salmonella, 79; scarlet fever caused by, 279; staphylococci, 79, 541; sties caused by, 191; syphilis caused by, 526; tetanus caused by, 519; tonsillitis caused by, 334; tuberculosis caused by, 280–81; types of, 522–23; typhoid caused by,

518–19; venereal disease caused by, **525**, 525–26; in water, 81, 518; white blood cells protect against, 293–95, 533

bacterial diseases, *see* bacteria

bad breath, 164

balance, 198–99

balanced diet, 57–63

baldness, 158

ball-and-socket joints, 117, **117**

barbiturates, 259, 610, 611

Barnard, Dr. Christian, 580

basal metabolism, 51, testing rate of, 407

baseball, 169

basketball, 170–71

bathing, 149

Beaumont, William, 255

behavior, 434–49; adolescent, 428–30, 477–79, 480–88, 496; alcohol and, 592; as developmental, 441–42; disturbed, 494–95, 500–04; emotions and, 438–39, 464–72; environment and, 393–96; 422–24; 495–97; as expression of personality, 418–31; family influences on, 425–28; 478–79; group, 439, **440**; kinds of, 437–41; and mental adjustment mechanisms (defense mechanisms), 443–47; motivation for, 428–30, 437, 441; studies of, 435–36; *see also* adolescence, personality

benign tumors, definition of, 582; treatment of, 582–83

Benzedrine, 610, 611

beriberi, 45

biceps, 132, **132**, 134

bicuspids, 160, **160**

Bicycle Institute of America, 627

bicycle safety, 627–28

bile, 24, 248, 336–38; salts, 337

Bill of Rights of the Athlete, 174

binaural selectometer, function of, 194

biological control, 78–79

biotin, 251

blackheads, 153; treatment of, 153

black (bubonic) plague, 77, 306

bladder, **25**, 340, 341, 344–45

bleeding, stopping, 297–99, **298**

blindness, color, 190

blindness, night, 187

blind spot, 186–87

blood, 288–310; banks, 300, **300**, 302–03; and blood poisoning, 294; cells of, **14**, **19**, **289**, **290**, 290–92, 293; clotting of, 296–97, 534; as connective tissue, 19; count, **290**, 290–91; diseases of, 292, 299–300; filtering of, 332–345; functions of, 289; make-up of, 289–90; plasma, 19, 295–96; poisons in, 303–07; proteins, 296; RH factor in, 301–02; tests, **293**; transfusions, 300–02, **302**; types, 301

blood sugar level, 362, 410; disorders of, 408–09

blood pressure, definition of, 323; diastolic, 323; high, 67, 323, 576; systolic, 323; taking of, **34**, 323, **323**

blood vessels, 313–19, **315**, 325–26; and emotions, 326; number of, 317; size of, 317

"blue baby," 574

blushing, 327

body build (physique), 131–32; acceptance of, 132; types of, 132

body temperature, 352

boils, 155

bones, 96; 110–122, **112**; of arm, 111; composition of, 117–18; defects of, 111; dislocation of, 139; of foot, 116; fractures of, 119–20, **119**; growth of, 119; of hand, 115; of heel, 116; and joints, 116–17; and ligaments, 116–17; marrow of, 117; mineral matter in, 117; muscle attachment to, 134; needs for growth and repair, 120; number in body, 20, 113; of pelvis, 115; of shoulder, 115; of thigh, 111; tuberculosis of, 120; of wrist, 115

brain, 211–13, **211**, **213**; cerebellum of, 212; cerebral cortex of, 212; cerebrum of, 212, **213**; convolutions of, 212; functions of, 212–13; gray matter of, 212; hypothalamus of, 212–13; medulla oblongata of, 213; parts of, 212–13; pons of, 212–13; and sound, 195

brain and spinal cord, 212 (*table*)

bread and cereal group, 61

breakfast, 62; sample, 63 (*table*)

breathing, method of, 274; regulation of, 274–75, 359; types of, 274–75

Bright's disease, 342

bronchi, 267, **268**; and bronchial tubes, 24, **24**, 267, **268**, 272; and windpipe, 272, **273**

bronchitis, 272

brucellosis, 521

bubonic (black) plague, 77, 306

bunions, 125–26

burns, first aid for, 652

bursitis, 139

C

caecum, 250

calcium, 43, 57, 120; sources of, 44

callus, of blood, 120

calluses, 125–26

calories, allowances at different ages, 51 (*table*), 58–59 (*table*); content of foods, 50, 52–53 (*table*); definition of, 50; weight control and, 60–62, 66–69

calorimeter, 50, **51**

Camp Nyda, **409**

cancer, 581–85; causes of, 583–84; frequency of, 584; occurrence of, 584; organs affected by, 584; and radiation, 583; and smoking, 276–77, 583, 599; symptoms of, 584; treatment of, **551**, 585; types of, 583; virus infections and, 584

capillaries, 313, 314, 316–18, **318**; definition of, 24

capillary bleeding, 297

carbohydrates, digestion of, 249; and energy, 50, 52–53 (*table*); sources of, 40, 41

carbon, in the body, 12

carbon dioxide, and respiration, 267

carbon monoxide, as air pollutant, 86; prevention of poisoning by, 283

carbon tetrachloride, 283

carbuncles, 155

carcinomas, 583

cardiac arrhythmia, 576

cardiac (heart) muscle, 138, **138**

cardiac plexus, 207

CARE, 557

careers, *see* health careers, vocational goals

carotene, 45

carotid sinus, 274, **274**

carpals, 115

Carrell, Alexis, 231

carriers, 519

cartilage, 18, **18**; kinds of, 118–19, **118**; and spinal column, 115; temporary, 118; of windpipe, 272

Carver, George Washington, 396

cataracts, 190

cells, 13–20, 228–241; age of, 236–37; DNA of, 374–75, **375**, 377; division of, 237, 374, 375, **376**, **377**; egg, **26**, 371–73, 412–413; food for, 232–34, 315–316; respiration of, 229, 236, 267; secretion in, 235; size of, 12, 235–36; sperm, **26**, **232**, 371–73; structure of, 229–31, **230**; *see also specific types of cells and cell structures*

cementum, 160, **161**

central nervous system, 21, 211–14; diseases of, 213–14, 216–17 (*table*); parts of, 204–05, **205**

centrioles, 231

centrosome, 231

cereal and bread group, 61

cerebellum, **211**, 212; functions of, 212

cerebral embolism, 581

cerebral hemorrhage, 581

cerebrospinal fluid, 212

cerebrum, **211**, 212, 353; functions of, 212, **213**; cortex of, 212, 592

chapping, 153

chemical pesticides, 76

chemical pollutants, 82

chemical stimulants, 221, 612

chemotherapy, 507, 540–42

chest, bones of, 115

chewing, importance of, 246

childhood, 391, **391**

chilling, causes of, 356–57; and surgery, 357

chlorination, 641

choking, first aid for, 267–69

cholera, 518

cholesterol, definition of, 41; and heart disease, 258, 576

chromosomes, **231**, **374**, **378**; as carriers of genes, 230, 374–79; number in human cells, 374; sex, 378

chronic diseases, 573–588; alcoholism as, 594–97; allergies as, 70, 538–39; cancer as, 581–85;

definition of 514; diabetes as 408–09; drug abuse as, 605–16; effects of smoking on, 598–99; emphysema as, 281–82; of heart and blood vessels, 312, **314**, 327–28, 574–81; hemophilia as, 299–300; hypoglycemia as, 409; mental illness as, 498–507; sickle-cell anemia as, 385, **385**; of urinary tract, 342–4

chyme, 247

cilia, 18, **18**, 232, 269, 276, 532

ciliary muscle, 187

circulatory system, 24, 311–328, **315**; and emotions, 326–27; and restrictive clothing, 325; disorders of, *see* heart *and* heart diseases

cirrhosis, definition of, 339, **340**

civil defense, 642–44

Clean Air Act, the, 89

cleansing materials, and skin, 149

clotting, of blood, 296–97, 534

cocaine, 607

cocci, 522, **522**

coccyx, 114

cochlea, 195, **196**

codeine, 606

cold-blooded, 350

colds, 278–79

cold sores, 156

colic, 338

colitis, 258

college, choice of, 486–87

colon, 250

color blindness, 190, 378–79

communicable diseases, 512–530, 516–17 (*table*), 531–547; caused by bacteria, 522–24, *see also* bacteria; body defenses against, 532–38; community control of, 76, 77, 80–82, 526, 549, 550, 552–53; and contaminated food, 79, 518–19; during disaster, 640; drugs in treatment of, 540–41; caused by fungi, 524; immunity to 534–38, **537**; as infections, 514–15; caused by parasitic worms, 524; caused by protozoans, 524; caused by rickettsia, 521–22; spread of, 515–21; caused by viruses, 521; and water pollution, 81, 82, 518; venereal diseases as, 525–26

community health, services pro-

(*table*); psychosomatic, 502; respiratory, 278–82, 333–34; of skeletal system, 120; of skin, 153–56; of urinary system, 342–43, 344; venereal, 525–26

disease germs, and entrance into body, 519–20

disinfectant, 590

dislocation, of bone, 139

disorders of central nervous system, 216–17 (*table*)

displaced aggression, 444

dissociative reactions, 500

divorce, effect on personality, 427–28

DNA (deoxyribonucleic acid) 374–75, 377; model of, **375**

doctor, visit to, 29–36 (*photo essay*)

dominant trait, 373

Douglass, Frederick, 395

dreams, 222–23, 440–41

drinking, social influences on, 592–93; and heart disease, 578; psychological reasons for, 593

driving, 619, 620, 622–26; and alcohol, 592; **592**; defensive, 623–24; training for, 622, **623**, **625**

droplet infection, 515, **518**

dropsy, 296

drug abuse, 605–16; and adolescents, 608; of amphetamines, 610, 611; of barbiturates, 610, 611; and commonly abused drugs, 611 (*table*); tolerance resulting from, 606, 610, 611; as environmental problem, 608–09; legal control of, **609**, 609–610, 612, 613; methadone program for, 607, 609; of narcotics, 606–07, 611; of opium products, 606, 611; physical dependence (addiction) in, 606, 607, 608, 610, 611, 612; and problems of addicts, 607–08; of "sleeping pills", 611; social problems caused by, **607**, 607–08; psychological dependence in, 606, 607, 608, 609, 611, 612, **612**, **613**; Synanon program for, 609; of tranquilizers, 610, 611, 612; treatment for, 608–09; of volatile chemicals, 613; withdrawal sickness in, 606, 610; *see also specific drugs:* Benzedrine, cocaine, codeine,

Dexadrine, hashish, heroin, LSD, marijuana, morphine, methadone, Methedrine

drugs, medical, 540–44; antimicrobial, 540; chemotherapeutic, 507, 540; safety of, 542; testing of new, 542–44; use versus abuse of, 613–14

drunkenness, test for, 592

ductless glands, 23, 402

duodenum, 253, **253**

dysentery, 518

dwarfism (pituitary), 380, **405**, 406

E

ear, 194–98; avoiding damage to, 197; inflammation of, 197; structure of, 195, 196; wax in, 197; *see also* hearing

eczema, 156

Ederle, Gertrude, 171

educational goals, 485–86

eggs, as carriers of hereditary traits, 374–75; development of fertilized, 390, 413; fertilization of, 26, **26**, 371–73, 412–13; number produced in life of female, 373; release of (ovulation), 372, 373, 412–13

Ehrlich, Paul, 541

electrocardiogram, **577**, 578

electrocardiograph, **22**, **577**, 578

electroencephalograph (EEG), 223, **223**

electron microscope, 521

electronic pacemakers, 320, **320**, 579, **579**

electro-shock therapy, 507

electrolysis, 158

elements, in body, 12, **12**, 13

elephantiasis, 306

embryo, 390

Emergency Broadcasting System, 643

emetic, 259

emotion (s), 463–75, 476–91; and allergies, 539; and blood vessels, 326; and body balances, 357–60, 364; and heart, 326, 578; and nervous system, 215, 217–18 and respiration, 274–75; and effect on skin, 147; in infants, 466; kinds of, 470–71; theories about, 464–65; and weight, 68, 69

emotional conflicts, during adoles-

cence, 476–91, 492–98; *see also* personality

emotional deprivation, 423

emotional development, 468–70; and environment, 468; and health, 468; and intelligence, 469–70

emotionally disturbed personality, 492–510; *see also* mental illness

emotional maturity, 467–68

emphysema, 281–82; and smoking, 282; and air pollution, 282

enamel, of tooth, 160, 161

encephalitis (sleeping sickness), 77, 213, 306

endocrine glands, **23**, 401–16; *see also names of specific glands*

energy, foods, 41; how cells obtain, 14–16, 97; individual needs for, 50–51, **51**, (*table*), 58–59, (*table*); sources of, 98

entomologist, **79**

environment, effects of, 389–400; on achievement, 395–96; on blood, 302–03, 345; on body heat regulation, 358; on dating patterns, 482; on diet, 39, 65, 257–58; on drinking habits, 592–93; on drug abuse, 608–09; on emotional development, 468; on heart, 327–28, 578; on hereditary diseases, 382–85; on identical twins, 381–82; on learning, 390, 391, 393–95; on mental health, 495–97; on nervous system, 218–19; on personality development, 422–24, 425–28, 429–30; on respiratory diseases, 278, 282–83; on smoking habits, 599–600; on spread of disease, 515–519, 520–21, 525; on venereal diseases, 525

environmental health, 75–92; 548–564; 618–636; 637–650; *see also* consumer protection, pollution, public health services, safety

Environmental Protection Agency, 76–77; 551

enzymes, 245–48; 377

epidermis, of skin, 148

epiglottis, 270

epinephrine (adrenaline), 411

epithelial tissue, **16**, 17, 18

esophagus, 25, **25**, **244**

essential amino acids, 43

essential nutrients, 40–48; common sources of, 40 (*table*); vitamins as, 44–48, 47 (*table*)

estrogen, 412, 413

ethyl alcohol, 590

eustachian tube, 195–96

excretory system, 25, 26; urinary system of, 340–45

exercise, and heartbeat, 321; and heat regulation, 358; and digestion, 254; lack of and effect on heart, 328; and physical fitness, 94–108

exhaustion, in swimming, 176

exocrine glands, 402

extensors, 134

eye, 183–94, **185**; blind spot of, 186–87; crossed, 188–89, **189**; diseases of, 190–91; doctors, 183; and effect on emotions, 193, **194**; examination of, 183–84; focusing of, 186–87; infections of, 190–91; movement of, 187; muscular imbalance of, 187; muscles of, 186; problems of, 185; protection of, 191–94; protective layers of, 186; structure of, 185–86, **185, 186**; and vision disorders, 185, 187–90, **188, 189**

eyebrows, function of, 191, 193

eyelashes, function of, 191

eyelids, function of, 191, 193

eyesight, conservation of, 191–92

F

fads, food, 70, 71

fainting, 324–27; treatment for, 325

family, influences on development, 381–382, 425–29, 468, 470, 478–79, 496

family life, preparation for, *see* sex, relationships with opposite

farm safety, 631–32

fatigue, 139–41, 219–22; causes of, 220; chronic, 220; normal, 220; pathological, 221; physiological, 220–21; and posture, 122; relief from, 140, 221; and tension, 140–41

fats, 43, 251, 337; and blood cholesterol, 41; as connective tissue, 19; digestion of, 249; as energy source, 41; functions of, 41; saturated, 41; unsaturated, 41

fatty acids, 249

fear, 465; 470–71; and anxiety, 500

feces, 250

federal health services, 549–552

Federal Trade Commission, 551–52, **552**

feedback, in human body, 353–54, 359

feelings, *see* emotions

feet, 125–27; arches of, **125**, 125–26; bones of, 116; care of, 126–27; flat, 126; problems of, 125–26

fertilization, **26**, 373, 412, 413; definition of, 26

fertilized egg, 26, **26**; size of, 371

fetus, 390, 413, **413**

fever, 354–56

fibrillation, 576

fibrin, 334, 336; definition of, 296

fibrin foam, 302

fibrinogen, 296, 336

"fight or flight" theory, 465

fingerprints, 147

fire, causes of, 629, 639–40; fighting, 629, **638**, 639–40

first aid for, animal stings, **304**, 305–07; artificial respiration as, 176–178, **177**; bleeding, 297–99, **298**; burns, 652; choking, 267–269; common emergencies (condensed directions) 651–54; fainting, 325; heat collapse, 354, 356 (*table*); poison gases, 283–84 poisons (swallowed), 259–60; shock, 324; snakebite, 303–304, **304**

flagellum, 232

flatulence, 256

Fleming, Alexander, **452**, 541

flexors, 132

fluorescent light, 191

fluoridation, 163

folic acid, 46; deficiency anemia, 292

food(s), 38–55; 56–74; allergies to, 70; basic groups of, **60**, 61; calorie content of, 50–51, 52–53 (*table*); contamination of, *see* food safety; fads, 70–71; fallacies, 71–72; and meal planning, 56–63; need for, 39; nutrients in, 39, 40 (*table*), 52–53 (*table*); preparation of, **57**, 251–52; and recommended daily allowances, 58–59

(*table*); social factors in choice of, 39, 63–65; and weight control, 65–69

Food and Drug Administration (FDA), functions of, 543, 550 (*table*)

food poisoning, 79

food safety, 77–80; and additives, 79, **79**; control measures for, 80, 519, 550, 551, 552, 553; and microbes, 79, 518–19; and pesticides, 77–79; and radiation, 80

football, 169–70

footprints, used in identification, **147**

fovea centralis, 186

fractures, 119–20, **119**; complete, 120; compound, 120; greenstick, 119; healing of, 120; simple, 120

fraternal twins, 380, **380**

freckles, 153

freely movable joints, 116

frostbite, 326

fruit and vegetable group, 60

frustration, and adolescence, 478–79; and conflict, 478

functional illness, 500

functional psychoses, 502

fungus diseases, 524; of lungs, 282; of skin, 155

G

gain, weight, 69

galactosemia, 384

gall bladder, **248**, 248, 337–38

gallstones, 338, **338**

ganglia, 207

gangrene, 289

gastric glands, 246, **247**

gastric juice, 246–47

gastritis, 259

gastroenteritis, 79

General Federation of Women's Clubs, 627

genes, 373, 375; definition of, 230; number in human cells, 374

"genetic code," 375–76

genetic counseling clinics, 382

genetic factors, and disease, 382–85; and coronary artery disease, 577; and heart defects, 574; *see also* heredity

giantism (pituitary), 404, **405**

glands, endocrine, 23, **23**, 402–14, **403**; exocrine, 402; gastric, 246,

247; oil, 148; salivary, 245; sex, 402–03, 412–13; sweat, 26, 351; tear, 191

glandular fever, 521

glare, 192

glaucoma, 190, 378; test for, 184, **184**

gliding joints, 117

globulin, 296

glucagon, 408

glucose, 362

glucose tolerance test, 408

glycerin (glycerol), 249

glycogen, 136, 336, 362, 408

goals, conflict of, 485–88

goiter, 44, **44**, 406

goiter belt, 406

gonadotrophic hormone, 403

gonads, 402, **403**, 412–13

gonorrhea, 191, 345, **525**, 525–26, 542

granulocytes, 295

gray matter, 212; definition of, 205

great calorie, 50

greenstick fracture, 119

group behavior, 439

group therapy, 505, **506**

growth hormone (somatotrophic), 403

H

habits, 210–11; eating, 68, 69; of feeling, 217–18; of relaxing, 218; safety, 632; study, 457–59

hair, care of, 157–58; excess, 158; follicle, 157; removal, 158, 159; structure of, 146, 157

hallucinations, 502

halitosis, 164

hallucinogens, 611, 613

hand, bones of, 115

handicapped, sports for, 173

hangnail, 160

hardening of the arteries, *see* arteriosclerosis

Harlow, Dr. Harry, 435, **435**

hashish, 612–13

hate, 470

head lice, 156

health careers, 558–60, 565–72; bases for choice of, 486–87, 559 (*table*); training for, 560; variety of, 565–72 (*photo essay*)

health concepts, 10, 28, 55, 74, 92, 109, 129, 144, 166, 181, 202, 226, 241, 263, 287, 310, 331, 348, 368, 388, 400, 416, 433, 449, 462, 475, 491, 510, 530, 547, 564, 588, 604, 616, 636, 650

health, definition of, 2–10; and learning capacity, 457; and emotional development, 468; mental-emotional factors in, 5–6; physical factors in, 4–5; social factors in, 6–7; symbols of, 3

health insurance, 556

health services, 548–564; federal, 76–77, 549–52, 556; international, 556–558; local, 553–54; state, 82, 552; of voluntary agencies, 553–56

Health Services and Mental Health Administration, 550

hearing, 194–98; aids, 197–98, **197**; defects, 196–97; testing, 194–95

heart, 311–331; beat of, 319–21, 359; and blood circulation, 312–19, **315**, **318**; disease, reducing risk of, *see* heart disease; effects on exercise on, 104–05, 320–21, 328; functions of, 312; pacemaker of, 319–320; muscle, **19**, 21, 138, **138**; sounds, 317; structure of, 312–13; **312**, **313**, **314**; valves of, **313**, 316–17

heartburn, 254, 256

heart disease, 319–20, 323–24, 574–81; angina pectoris and, 577; arteriosclerosis and, 67, **314**, 317, 328, 578; artificial heart for, **580**; artificial valves for, **580**; congenital, 574; coronary artery, 312–13, 576–77; diagnosis of, **22**, 317, 323, **323**, 578; and effects of diet, 42–43, 67, 328; and effects of environment, 327–28, 578; and effects of smoking, 578; and effects of tension, 328, 578; electrical pacemaker for, 320, **320**, 579, **579**; hardening of the arteries, *see* arteriosclerosis; heart attack in, 577–78; hypertensive, 576; rheumatic, 574–75; and strokes, 581; surgery for, **574**, **575**, **580**; transplants for, 580–81; valvular, 317, 574–76

heart-lung machines, 574, **575**

heat balance, 350–53; and emotions, 357; and exercise, 358

heat exhaustion, 354

heat prostration, 153, 354, **355**

heatstroke, 354, **355**

height and weight reference chart for adults, 67 (*table*)

hemoglobin, 44, 290, 336, 337; in sickle-cell anemia, 385

hemophilia, 299–300, 379

hemorrhage, 296

hemorrhoids, 259

hepatitis, 302, 303, 338–39, 516

hereditary defects, treatment for, 382–85; of heart, 574

heredity, 370–388; and baldness, 158; and body build, 132; effect of environment on, 381–85

heritage, biological, 371–85; cultural, 389–400

hernia, 139

heroin, 606, 608–09; 611

high blood pressure, 66, 323, 576

highway inprovement, 626–27

hinge joints, 117

histamine, 538

histoplasmosis, 282

Hodgkin's disease, 295

home accidents, 629–30

homeostasis, 8, 352, 362

home utilities, in disaster, 641

hookworms, 524

HOPE, 557, **557**

hormones, 296, 357, 401–16, balance of, 413–14; effect of on changes in adolescence, 391, 412–13; definition of, 23, 402; female, 412–13; functions of, 402; male, 412–13

hospitals, 554–55; clinics, 555; federal, 554; government, 554; private, 555; voluntary, 555

humerus, 111

humidity, importance of, 278

hunger, 364; pangs of, 62

hybrid, 373

hydrochloric acid, 247

hydrogen, in body, 12

hyperopia, 188, **188**

hyperpituitarism, 404

hypertension, 66, 323, 576

hypertensive heart disease, 576

hyperthyroidism, 406–07, 582

hypertonic muscles, 137

hyperventilation, 276, 363

hypnotic, 590

hypochondria, 501

hypoglycemia, 410

hypopituitarism, 404
hypothalamus, 212–13, 362, 404; and heat regulation, 353
hypothyroidism, 406

I

identical twins, 380, **380**
identity, 478
immune reactions, 580
immunity, 534–38, 537; active, 538, passive, 536–37; responsibility for, 538
immunology, 534
immovable joints, 116
impetigo, 156
incisors, 160, **160**
incomplete proteins, 43
incubation period, 514
indigestion, 255–56
industry, and air pollution, 86
infancy, 390–91, **391**
infantile paralysis (polio), 137, 213–14, 536
infectious diseases, 514–26; airborne, 518; stages of, 514–15; *see also* communicable diseases
infectious jaundice (hepatitis), 338–39
influenza, 279, **279**
inhalator, 283
inherited resistance, 384, 534
inherited traits, 372 (*table*)
inner ear, 195, **196**
insects, and disease, 306, 519; treatment for stings of, 306
insomnia, 224
insulin, 362, 404, 408–09
intelligence, and emotional development, 469–70
intelligence quotient (IQ), 382, 393, 453; effect of environment on, 393–95
intensive care units, 579, **579**
internal bleeding, 299
internalization, 443, 454–55
intestine(s), **244**; absorption in small, 248, **249**; digestion in small, 247–48; functions of large, 250
intoxicant, alcohol as, 590
intravenous feeding, 243
inversion, temperature, 88
involuntary muscles, 21, **22**, 138
involutional psychosis, 502
iodine, 43, 44; and thyroid gland

function, **44**, 406–07
iodine-uptake test, 407
iris, function of, 186
iron, 43, 44
iron-deficiency anemia, 292
islets of Langerhans, 408

J

jaundice, 338–39
jellyfish, stings of, **304**, 306–07
Jenner, Edward, 534
joints, 96; definition of, 111; kinds of, 116–17, **116**

K

kidneys, 340–45, **341**; artificial, 343; disorders of, 342–43; failure, 343; function of, 340–41; function test, 341; grafts, 343; loss of, 342; machines, 345; protection of, 345; stones, 343, **343**; transplants, 343, **344**; work of, 341–42
Kupfer stellate cells, 336

L

lacrimal glands, function of, 191
lacteal, 249, **249**
lactic acid, 136
large intestine, 250
laryngitis, 272
larynx, 271
learning, 451–59; anxiety and, **456**, 456–57; capacity for, 452–54; competition in, 455–56; effect of health on, 457; internalization in, 454–55; motivation in, 451, 454–55; study habits and, 457–59
legs, bones of, 115
leukemia, 293, 583
lice, 156
life expectancy, of alcoholics, 594; of cigarette smokers, 601 (*chart*); and environment, 258
ligaments, 20, 116–17
light, and conserving sight, 191–92
lightning, 646–48, **646**; precautions against, 647–48
liver, 248, 291; and bile, 337, **337**; functions of, 335–37; disorders of, 338–40
lobar pneumonia, 280
loneliness, 480
Los Angeles, smog in, 87, **87**

love, 465; in adolescence, 428; kinds of, 470–71; mature, 428, 470; parental, 428; romantic, 428, 470; of self, 470; sharing, 470
lumbar vertebrae, 114
lungs, 24, **24**; cancer of and smoking, 599; diseases of, 280–82; model of, **275**; structure of, **268**, 272–73; vital capacity of, 275
lymph, 48, 249, 316
lymphatic system, 316, **316**; nodes of, 295, 333
lymphocytes, 535
lymphomas, 583
lysozyme, 532

M

make-up, 151–52, **152**
malaise, 514
malaria, 77, 303
malignant tumor, 582
malt sugar (maltose), 245
manic-depressive reactions, 502
marijuana, 611, 612, 613
marriage, dating as preparation for, 482–84; problems of teen-age, 484–85, 487–88; romantic and mature love in, 470, **471**
marrow, in bones, 117
"master" gland (pituitary), 402–04
mastoiditis, 197
mature love, 470
measles, 534, 538; types of, 516
meat group, 61; nutrients in, 61
Medicaid, 556
medical examination, annual, 29–36 (*photo essay*)
Medical Self-Help Training Course, 639
Medicare, 556
medicine cabinet, and safety, 259
medicines, *see* drugs, medical
Medico, 557
medulla oblongata, 213, 359; and respiration, 274
meiosis, 375, **376**; definition of, 237
memory, techniques to improve, 459
Mendel, George, 373
meningitis, 213, 523
menstruation, 412, 413
mental health, 492–510; emotional development and, 466–470, 472, 476–91; environmental stresses

and, 495–97; handling conflicts and, 477–79, 485–88, 494–95; methods of adaptation (defense mechanisms) in, 443–47; as part of total health, 5–6; self-acceptance and, 480–81

mental health movement, 499

mental health professional, 498

mental illness, 498–507; incidence of, 499; kinds of, 500; prevention of, 504, 507–08; treatment of, 504–07, **506**

mental retardation, 382–83

messenger RNA, 377

mesentery, 248

metabolism, 236; basal, 51; testing rate of basal, 407

metacarpals, 115

metastasis, 583

metatarsals, 116

methadone, 606–07, 609

Methedrine ("speed"), 610, 611

methyl alcohol, 590

microbes, and food contamination, 79; *see also* bacteria

microorganisms, and disease, 521–26

microscope, electron, 521, **560**

middle ear, 195, **196**

milk, additives in, 79; and disease, 79, 518–19; food group, 61; nutrients in, 44, 53, 61; pasteurization of, 79, 519; and radiation, 80

mineral matter, in bones, 117

minerals, 40, 43, 44; functions of, 43; as pollutants, 82

mites, 306

mitochondria, 229, **230**

mitosis, 237, 375, **376**, 377

molars, 160, **160**

molecules, 232; definition of, 14

moles, 155

mononucleosis, 515, 521

morphine, 606, 611

motion sickness, 199

motivation, 420

motorcycles, 628

motor nerves, **205**, 205–06

mouth-to-mouth resuscitation, 177–78, **178**

mouthwashes, 164

mucous colitis, 259

mucous membrane, 16, **16**, 269, 270, 532; definition of, 17

mucus, 247

multiple sclerosis, 139

muscles, 96, **97**, 131–39; abdominal, 248; of arm, 132, **133**; arrangement of, 132; attachment to bones, **133**, 134; cells of, 135–36, **135**; ciliary, **185**, 187; contraction of, 96, 136; cramp in, 139; eye, **185**, 187; fibers of, 135; heart, 19, 21, 138, **138**; injury to, 138–39; involuntary, 21, 138; kinds of, **19**, 21, 134–35; of leg, **133**; skeletal, **97**, 134, **135**; smooth, **19**, 21, 137–38, **138**; strain, 138; striated (striped), 135, **135**; tone, 131, 137, 139; voluntary, 21, 97, 134

muscular dystrophy, 139

musculoskeletal system, 96

mutations, 384

mycoplasma, 523, **523**

myopia, 187, **188**

myxedema, 407

N

Nader, Ralph, 624, **624**

nails, 159–60; care of, 159–60, **159**

narcissism, 470

narcotics addiction, 606–10; and adolescents, 608; as psychological problem, 608, 609; as social problem, 607, 608, 609, 610; treatment programs for, 608–09; *see also* drug abuse

nasal catarrh, 269

nasal sinuses, 270, **270**

nausea, 256

National Civil Defense Plan, and disaster preparedness, 642–44

National Heart Association, 554

National Institute of Mental Health, 499, 550

National Institutes of Health, 550

National Research Council, 57

National Safety Council, 627, 646

National Tuberculosis and Respiratory Disease Association, 280

natural immunity, 534

nephritis, 342–43

nephrons, 341, **342**

nervous system, 203–226; autonomic, 207–208, **208**; central, **204**, 209–13; cells of (neurons), 19, 20, **20**, 205, **205**; diseases of central, 213–14, 216–17 (*table*); effects of alcohol on, 590, 592; effects of environment on, 218–19; effects of fatigue on, 219–

221; and feelings, 215–18; and habit formation, 210–11; importance of sleep for, 221–23; peripheral, **206**; reflex arc of, 209–10; and stress, 215, 217; types of nerves in, 205, 206, 207

neurophysiologists, 436

neuroses, 500–02; anxiety reactions in, 500, 501; conversion reactions in, 501; depression in, 501; dissociative reactions in, 500; phobic reactions in, 501

New York, smog in, **88**, **89**

niacin, 45, 46

nicotine, 597

night blindness, 45, 187

noise pollution, and hearing, **22**; and nervous system, 219

nonchemical pest control, 78, 79

norepinephrine, 411

nose, 269–70, and sense of smell, 199

nuclear attack, protection from radiation following, 642–44

nuclear membrane, 230, **230**

nucleus, 17, 229–31, **230**

nutrients, definition of, 39; *see also* food

nutrition, 38–55, 56–74; *see also* food, calories, weight

O

obesity, 257

occupational safety, 632

occupational therapy, 505, **506**

oculist, 183

Office of Emergency Preparedness, 642

Office of Civil Defense, *see* Defense Civil Preparedness Agency

Ohio Valley Water Sanitation Pact, 82

olfactory cells, function of, 199

one-egg twins, 380

Operation Headstart, 420, **421**

ophthalmologist, 183

ophthalmoscope, 184, **184**

opium, 606; products of, 606, 611

optic nerves, 21, 186, 207

optician, 183

optometrist, 183

organelles, 229, **230**

organic illness, 500

organic matter, in bones, 117

organ transplants, 343, **344**, 540; 579–81

projective tests, 430
prolactin, 404
prostate gland, 345
protein-bound iodine (PBI) test, 407
proteins, 40, 43, 251; complete, 43; digestion of, 247–28; foreign, 535; incomplete, 43
protozoa, 524
protozoan diseases, 524
psychedelic drugs, 613
psychiatrists, 327
psychoanalysis, 436, 440
psychological problems in drug dependence, 606, 607, 608, 609, 611, 612, **612**, **613**
psychoses, 500, 502–04; depression in, 502; manic-depressive reactions in, 502; schizophrenic reactions in, 503
psychosis, alcoholic, 595
psychosomatic, definition of, 7–8; disorders, 502
psychotherapist, 505
psychotherapy, 505
psychotic depression, 502
puberty, definition of, 412; physical changes during, 391–92, 401, 412
public health services, 548–64; *see also* health services
pulmonary artery, 312
pullups, 100–01, **100–01**, 103, **103**
pulp, of tooth, 160, **161**; decay in, 162, **162**
pupil, of eye, **185**, 186, 193, **193**
pus, 294
pylorus, 247

Q

quackery, control of, 551, **552**; food, 70–72; medical, 551–52
quadruplets, 381
quintuplets, 381

R

rabies, 213–14, 519
radiation, as a cause of cancer, 583; fallout shelters as protection from; 642–44; federal controls of exposure to, 551; and food contamination, 80; and water pollution, 82
radioisotopes, in testing of thyroid function, 407–08; in treatment of

cancer, **551**, 585
rationalization, 444–45
reaction formation, 446
reaction time, in driving, 625; effect of alcohol on, 592
recessive traits, 373
recommended daily dietary allowances, 57–61, 58–59 (*table*)
recreation, 218
recreational therapy, 505–06
rectum, 250
red blood cells, **289**, 290–91, **290**, age of, 237; count, 290, **290**, 292; development of, 291, **291**; loss of, 362–63; numbers of, 290, **290**; replacement of, 363; size of, 290
red corpuscles, 290
reducing, weight, 69
reduction division (meiosis), 374
referred pain, 200
reflex arc, 209–10, **209**
reflexes, 209–11
regression, 444
rehabilitation, of mentally ill, 507
remedial exercises, 103
renin, 342
repressed hostility, 443–44
repression, 443
reproductive system, 26, 232, 371–73, 412–13
research facilities, 555–56
resistance, inherited, 384, 534
respiration, 264–87; and atmospheric changes, 277–78; in cells, 236; definition of, 267; and emotions, 275–76; and poisonous gases, 283–84
respiratory diseases, 278–82; and air pollution, 89, 282–84; and smoking, 276–77, 598, 599
respiratory system, 24, **24**, 267–68, **269**; X ray of, **273**
response, conditioned, 210–11
retina, 186, **186**
retinal detachment, 190
Rhesus monkey, 301
rheumatic fever, 540, 575
rheumatic heart disease, 574–75
RH factor, 301, 313
rhinitis, 269
riboflavin (vitamin B₂), 45
ribonucleic acid (RNA), 377
ribosomes, 229, 230, 377
ribs, false, 115; floating, 115; true, 115

rickets, 46, **46**, 120
rickettsias, definition of, 306; diseases caused by, 521–22
ringworm, 155
RNA (ribonucleic acid), 377; messenger, 377; transfer, 377
Robinson, Jackie, 396, **396**
Rocky Mountain spotted fever, 521
romantic love, 470
root, of tooth, 160, **161**
root canals, 160, **161**
Rorschach (inkblot) test, 430, **430**
roughage, value of, 49; sources of, 50
roundworms, 524
rubella ("German" measles), 516
rubeola ("regular" measles), 516

S

Sabin, Dr. Albert E., 214, **215**
sacrum, 114
safety, 618–36, 637–50; in automobile design, 624, **626**; boating, 177, 179; cycling, 627–28; and driver training, 622–24, **625**; during disaster, 638–643, 648; farm, 631–32; and fire prevention, 629, 639–40; home, 629, **630**, 634–35; job, 632; during lightning, 646–48; pedestrian, 628–29; from radioactive fallout, 643–44; in road design, 626; school, 630–31, **631**; as set of habits, 632; sports, 173–79; swimming, 175–79; during tornadoes, 645–46; traffic, 622–29; *see also* accidents, first aid
saliva, 24, 245–46
salivary glands, 245, **246**
Salk, Dr. Jonas, 214, **215**
salmonella, 79
salt balance, 362
saprophytes, 524
sarcomas, 583
saturated fats, 41
scabies, 156
scapula, 111, 134
scarlet fever, 279, 536
Schick test, 281, 536
schizophrenic reactions, 503
school accidents, 630–31
scorpions, stings from, 305
screening tests for physical fitness, 99–103, **100–103**
sebaceous glands, 148

sebum, functions of, 148

secondary sex characteristics, 391, 392, 412

secretion, 235

sedative, 590, 610

self-acceptance, 132, 480, 496

self-concept, 443, 478, 480–81; and appearance, 420–21; group influences on, 480–81, 496–97, **497**; and self-acceptance, 132, 480, 496; and self-confidence, 421, 480–81; and sexual identity, 401, 480, 496

semicircular canals, 195, **196**

semipermeable membrane, 229

sense(s), 182–202; of balance, 198–99; functions of, 183; of hearing, 194–198; of sight, 183–194; of smell, 199; of taste, 199; of touch, 199

sensory cells (hair cells), 195

sensory nerves, 205, 206

septa, 574

septicemia, 294

serum, definition of, 296; globulin, 382

serum hepatitis, 302–03

sewage, and water pollution, 81

sex chromosomes, 378, **378**; and linked traits, 190, 378–79

sex, relationships with opposite, 480–85; and dating, 480–83; and going steady, 484; and marriage, 484–85, 487–88; romantic and mature love in, 470; and sexual identity, 480, 496

sexual development, and body changes during puberty, 391–92, 412–13; effect of sex hormones on, 403, 412–13

sharing love, 470

shaving, correct method of, 151

shivering, 351

shock, definition of, 323; treatment of, 324, **324**

shoes, correct fit of, 127

shoulder girdle, 115

sickle-cell anemia, 385, **385**

simple fracture, 120

sinoatrial node, 319

sinuses, 270, **270**

situps, 101, **101**, 103, **103**

skeletal growth, and posture, 123

skeletal muscles, **97**; 132–37, **132**, **133**, **134**, **135**

skeletal system, 110–129; **112**; disorders of, 120, 122; functions of, 20, 111–12; parts of, 113–14

skin, 146–56; care of, 148–51; and emotions, 147; functions of, 146; problems, 153–56; structure of, **146**, 147–78; and sunburn, 152; tanning of, 151–52; and weather, 151–53

sleep, 221–24; benefits of, 222; dreams in, 222–23; importance of, 221–22; loss of, 222; need for, 140

sleeping sickness (encephalitis), 77

slightly movable joints, 116

small intestine, 25, **25**; digestion in, 247–48

smallpox, 533

smog, definition of, 86; in Los Angeles, 87, **87**; in New York, 87, **88**, **89**

smoking, 597–601; and cancer, 27, 583–84, 599; effects of, 598; and emphysema, 282; and heart disease, 578; how to stop, 601; increase of, 597; and life expectancy, 597, 601 (*chart*); and lung cancer, 599, **599**; reasons for, 599–600; and respiration, 276–77, 598; risks in, 597–99, **601**; in teen-agers, 597, 599–600

smooth muscles, 21, 137–38, **138**

snacks, 62

snakebite, 303, 305, **304**

Snellen eye chart, 184, **184**

social factors, and behavior, 439; and dating, 482–84; and drug abuse, 607–08; and health, 6–7; and expression of emotions, 468; and learning capacity, 454–55; and mental health, 476–91, 495–97; and personality development, 422–25; *see also* environment *and specific entries such as* family

socio-economic position, 423, 487

sociologists, 436

solar plexus, 207

somatotrophic hormone, 403

sore throat, 270

spastic colon, 259

"speed" (Methadrine), 610, 611

sperm cells, 26, 232, **232**, 374, 412; numbers released, 373

spiders, 305

spinal canal, 114

spinal column, 114, **114**, 115, **115**; curves of, **114**, 115; and skeletal system, **112**

spinal cord, 114, 211; and brain, 212 (*table*); functions of, 213

spinal nerves, 206

spirilla, 522–23

spirochete, 525, **525**, 526

spirometer, **276**

spleen, 291; functions of, 334–35

sports, 167–181; baseball, 169; basketball, 170–71; Bill of Rights of the Athlete, 174; football, 169–70; for exercise, 105–06, 168; safety in, 173–78; selection of, 172; and sportsmanship, 168; swimming, 171; types of, 172

sprains, 138

squat thrusts, 102, **102**, 103, **103**

staphylococci, 79, 294, 533, 541

star cells, of liver, 335

starches, 41, 251

status symbols, 482

Steinmetz, 395

steroids, 412

stethoscope, 317

stimulants, chemical, 221, 610

stimulus, 469

stings, bee, 305; wasp, 305

stingrays, **304**, 306–07

stomach, digestion in, 246–47

strabismus, 188–89

strain, muscle, 138

strep throat, 270

streptococcal infection, 540, 574, 575

streptomycin, 281, 541

striated (striped) muscle, 135, **135**

strokes, causes of, 581; symptoms of, 581

sty, 191

subconscious behavior, 440

sublimation, 446

sublingual glands, 245, **246**

submaxillary glands, 245, **246**

sugar balance, 362

sulfa drugs, 541

sulfanilamide, 541

sun-bathing, 152

sunburn, 152

sunstroke, 354

sutures, 114

sweat glands, 26, 351

swimming, 171; competitive, 171;

of English Channel, 171; precautions in, 177; rescue, **175**, 177–78; safety in, 175–78
"swollen glands," 333
sympathetic division, 207, **208**; functions of sympathetic and parasympathetic divisions of autonomic nervous system, 207 (*table*)
Synanon, 610
synapse, 209
syndromes, 404
syphilis, **525**, 525–26
syphilitic aneurysm, 576
systolic blood pressure, 323

T

tables, accidental deaths by type of accident, 620; brain and spinal cord, 212; calory needs of boys and girls, 51; choosing a health career, 559; commonly abused drugs, 611; composition of foods, 52–53; conditions that cause high body temperatures, 356; desirable weights for men and women, 67; disorders of central nervous system, 216–17; essential nutrients, 40; essential vitamins, 17; communicable diseases, 516–17; functions of the U.S. Public Health Service, 550; increase of braking distance with speed, 625; inherited traits, 372; recommended daily dietary allowances, 58–59; roughage value of foods, 49; sample breakfast, 63; sympathetic and parasympathetic divisions of the autonomic nervous system, 207
"tailgating," 623
take-cover signal, 643
tapeworms, 524
tarsals, 116
taste buds, function of, 199
tear ducts, function of, 191
tears, 24, 191
teen-agers, in other societies, 482; marriages among, 484–85; and number of accidental deaths, 620–21; venereal disease in, 525; *see also* adolescence
teeth, 160–64; broken, 164; brushing of, **164**; care of, 163–64; cavities in, 162; decay of (caries),

162–63; deciduous, or primary, 161, **161**; development of, 161; diseased, 162–63, 164; functions of, 160; kinds of, 160, **160**; missing, 164; nourishment of, 160, **161**; permanent, 161; stained, 164; structure of, 160, 161, **161**; wisdom, 161
television viewing, 192–93
temperature, of body, 352; conditions that cause high body, 356 (*table*); control of, 350–53
temporary cartilage, 118
tendons, 134; Achilles, 134; functions of, 21
tennis, **172**
tension, 140–42; in adolescents, 496–97; avoidance of, 142; causes of, 141–42; definition of, 140; effect on heart, 328; and heart disease, 578; relief from, 142
testes, 26, 374, 402, 412
testosterone, 412, 413
tests, techniques for taking, 459
tetanus, 519
tetany, 408
thalidomide, 544, **544**
therapy, drug, 507; electro-shock, 507; group, 505, **506**; insulin, 507; occupational, 505, **506**; play, 505–07, **506**; recreational, 505 **506**
thiamine (vitamin B₁), 45
thirst, 364
throat, in respiration, 270; sore, 270
thrombin, 300
thrombosis, 297
thunderstorms, 647
thymus gland, 402, **403**, 411
thyroid gland, 380, 402, 406–07, **406**; disorders of, 406–08; testing of, 407–08
thyrotrophic hormone, 403
thyroxin, 406; definition of, 380
ticks, 305; and disease, 519
time, planning, 481–82
tissue, connective, 18–20, **18**; definition of, 17; epithelial, 16, **16**, 17; kinds of, 17–20, **17**, **18**; muscle, 19, **19**; nerve, 19, **19**
tonicity, of muscles, 137
tonometer, 184, **184**
tonsillitis, 334
tonsils, **270**, 333–34

toothbrush, selection of, 163
tooth decay, 162–64, **162**
topical application, of sodium fluoride, 163
tornado precautions, 645–46
tourniquet, definition of, **298**, 299; use of, 299
toxins, 303
trachea, 232
tranquilizers, 610, 611, 612
transfer RNA, 377
transplants, 540; heart, 579–81; kidney, 343, **344**
transverse arch of foot, 125
triceps, 132
trichina worms, 524
trichinosis, 520–21, 524
triplets, 381
trophic hormones, 403
trypsin, 248
TSH (thyrotrophic hormone), 414
tuberculin test, 280
tuberculosis, 280–81, 533; of bones, 120; care of, 281; prevention of, 281; test for, 280; X ray for, 280
tumors, 213; benign, 582; malignant, 582; treatment of, 582–83
twins, fraternal, 380, **380**; identical, 380, 383; numbers born, 381; two-egg, 381
typhus, 77

U

ulcerative colitis, 258
ulcers, causes of, 253–54; definition of, 253; and emotions, 253; treatment of, 253–54
ultraviolet rays, and vitamin D, 46
umbilical cord, 413, **413**
undertow, 177
undulant fever, 521
UNICEF, 557
universal antidote, 260
universal donor, 301
universal recipient, 301
unsaturated fats, 41
urbanization, 219, 282
urea, 336
uremia, 343
ureters, **340**, 341
urethra, **340**, 341
urinalysis, 344
urinary system, 340–45; structures of, **340**, 341; disorders of, 342–43, 344–45

Picture Credits

Key: *t*—Top; *c*—Center; *b*—Bottom; *l*—Left; *r*—Right

Unit One: p. 1. William Dippel; 4, Harbrace Photos; 5, Sybil Shelton, Monkmeyer; 6, Harbrace Photos; 7, *l*—Harbrace Photo, *r*—Sybil Shelton, Monkmeyer; 8, Harbrace Photo; 13, Harbrace Photo; 16–17, Harbrace Photos; 18, *t*—N.Y. Scientific Supply, *b*—General Biological, Inc.; 19, *t* to *b*—Harbrace Photo, Harbrace Photo, Antol Herskovitz, Montefiore Hospital, Harbrace Photo; 20, Harbrace Photo; 22, *tl*—American Telephone & Telegraph, *tr*—Judith Greenberg, *b*—Brookhaven National Laboratories; 26, L. B. Shettles; 29–36, Harbrace Photos.

Unit Two: p. 37, United Fresh Fruit and Vegetables Association; 39, Harbrace Photo; 41, National Dairy Council; 42, Harbrace Photos; 44, Percy Brooks, RBP, FBPA; 45, Harbrace Photos; 46, UNICEF; 48, UPI; 49, Harbrace Photo; 50, *t*—Kathryn Abbe, *c*—Esso Research & Engineering Co., *b*—Cities Service Co.; 57, Mimi Forsyth, Monkmeyer; 59, National Dairy Council; 61–65, Harbrace Photos; 68, The Borden Co.; 71, Harbrace Photo; 76, William Dippel; 77, *t*—F. E. Meyers & Bros., *b*—Geigy Chemical Corp.; 78, Harbrace Photo; 79, Department of Agriculture; 80, U.S. Department of Interior; 82, UPI; 83, *t*—N.Y.C. Dept. of Sanitation, *b*—UPI; 84, *tr*—Harbrace Photo, *bl*—Harbrace Photo, *br*—Hella Hammid, Rapho-Guillumette; 85, Harbrace Photo; 88, *The New York Times*; 89, Litton Industries—Aero Service Division.

Unit Three: p. 93 Kathryn Abbe; 95, Rene Burri, Magnum; 96, *tl*—Vendo Photo, *br*—General Motors Corp.; 98, UPI; 104, President's Council on Physical Fitness and Sports; 105, *tl*—Wide World Photos, *br*—Harbrace Photos; 113, *bl*—Harbrace Photo, *br*—National Football League Properties; 117, *tr*—Russ Reed, Oakland Athletics, *br*—Harbrace Photo; 118, *l*—Harbrace, *br*—Percy Brooks, RBP, FBPA; 123, Harbrace Photos; 125, *l*—Harbrace Photo; 126, Harbrace Photo; 131, Sybil Shelton, Monkmeyer; 135, Harbrace Photo; 136, General Biological, Inc.; 137, UPI; 138, *tl*—Arthur W. Ham, Chief, Department of Medical Biophysics, University of Toronto, *tr*—General Biological, Inc.; 139, UPI; 141, Harbrace Photo; 142, Pan American Airways; 147, Harbrace Photos; 149, Harbrace Photo; 151, Condé Nast Publications, Inc.; 152, UPI; 153, Condé Nast Publications, Inc.; 154, Orentreich Medical Group; 157, Harbrace Photo; 159, *tl*—Lucille Bouchard Salon, *br*—Mimi Forsyth, Monkmeyer; 161, Chicago Wesley Hospital; 163, Public Health Service; 164, Weco Products, Co.; 168, Charles Harbutt, Magnum; 169, *tl*—RCA, *tr*—Little League Baseball, Inc.; 170, *tl*—Joe Bereswill, Madison Square Garden, *tr*—Harbrace Photos, *br*—UPI; 171, UPI; 173, UPI; 175, American Red Cross; 183, Harbrace Photo; 184, *l*—Harbrace Photo, *r*—American Optometric Assoc.; 186, Univ. of California, School of Optometry; 188, Harbrace Photos; 189, Univ. of California, School of Optometry; 190, Harbrace Photos; 192, Harbrace Photo; 193, J. P. Goeller; 194, Harbrace Photos; 195, Maico Hearing Instruments; 197, Beltone Electronics Corporation; 198, Harbrace Photos; 206, Clay-Adams, Inc.; 210, Girl Scouts; 214, Virus Laboratory, Univ. of California; 215, The National Foundation; 218–20, Harbrace Photos; 222–23, Harbrace Photos.

Unit Four: p. 227, The Bettmann Archive; 229, Harbrace Photos; 230, Antol Herskovitz, Montefiore Hospital; 231, *tl*—Tjio and Puck, *br*—Harbrace Photo; 232–33, Harbrace Photos; 236–37, Harbrace Photos; 243, Harbrace Photo; 244, Chicago Wesley Memorial Hosp.; 247, *t*—Percy Brooks, RBP, FBPA, *b*—Harbrace Photo; 251, Percy Brooks, RBP, FBPA; 256, Harbrace Photo; 258, Ruth Galaid, Photo Researchers; 266, artist's concept by Roy G. Scarfo, General Electric Missile & Space Division; 269, Percy Brooks, RBP, FBPA; 271, Bell Telephone Laboratories; 273, Chicago Wesley Memorial Hospital; 276, National Tuberculosis Association; 277, George Holton, Photo Researchers; 279, Antol Herskovitz, Montefiore Hospital; 280, Harbrace Photo; 283, Jim Theologos; 284, Harbrace Photo; 289, Harbrace Photo; 290, American Optical Co.; 293, American Red Cross; 294, *tl*—Harbrace Photo, *br*—Chas. Pfizer & Co., Inc.; 296, Sorvall Co.; 298, *t*—American Red Cross, *bl*—American Red Cross, *br*—Acme Photo; 300, American Red Cross; 302, American Red Cross; 303, Harbrace Photo; 304, *tl*—Alvin E. Staffen, National Audubon Society, *tr*—Bucky Reeves, National Audubon Society; *bl*—George Lower, National Audubon Society; *br*—H. W. Kitchen, National Audubon Society; 314, American Heart Association; 318, Harbrace Photo; 320, New York University Medical Center; 322, *t*—UPI; *b*—Percy Brooks, RBP, FBPA; 323, American Heart Association; 33, Harbrace Photo; 334, Elizabeth Wilcox; 335, Antol Herskovitz, Montefiore Hospital; 336, Arthur F. Jacques; 338, Mimi Forsyth, Monkmeyer; 339, Harbrace Photos; 340, National Medical Audiovisual Center; 341, Arthur F. Jacques; 343, Antol Herskovitz, Montefiore Hospital; 344, UPI; 345, National Medical Audiovisual Center; 351–53, Harbrace Photos; 358–59, Harbrace Photos; 360, General Electric Company; 361, *bl*—Harbrace Photo, *tr*—UPI; 363, UPI; 364, Harbrace Photo.

Unit Five: p. 369, William Dippel; 371, Elizabeth Wilcox; 374, Harbrace Photo; 375, Courtesy of the American Museum of Natural History; 377, Courtesy of the Upjohn Co.; 378, Tjio and Puck; 380, *t*—Hays, Monkmeyer, *b*—Strickler, Monkmeyer; 381, UPI; 383, National Association for Retarded Children; 384, Elizabeth Wilcox; 385, National Foundation, March of Dimes; 388, Harbrace Photo; 391, *t*—Elizabeth Wilcox, *b*—Harbrace Photo; 392, *t*—Shackman, Monkmeyer, *b*—Harbrace Photo; 393, Harbrace Photo; 394, *tl*—Jefferson, Monkmeyer, *tr*—New Holland Machine Co., Pa.; 395, Myron Wood, Photo Researchers; 396, *l*—Courtesy of the American Museum of Natural History, *r*—UPI; 405, *bl*—UPI; *tr*—Wide World Photos; 409, New York Diabetes Assoc.; 410, Kathryn Abbe.

Unit Six: p. 417, William Dippel; 419, Harbrace Photo; 420, Vivienne; 421, Harbrace Photos; 422, Ed Bagwell, Montefiore Hospital; 423, *t*—Harbrace Photo, *b*—Clifford Dolfinger, Photo Researchers; 424–25, Harbrace Photo; 427, Harbrace Photos; 429, Harbrace Photo; 430, Klopfer & Davidson, *The Rorschach Technique;* 431, Burton Berinsky, Mobilization for Youth; 435, Fred Sponholz, Wisconsin Primate Center; 436, *bl*—Dr. Neil Miller, Rockefeller University, *tr*—Harbrace Photo; 437, Weight Watchers International; 440, UPI; 442–43, Harbrace Photos; 446, Mimi Forsyth, Monkmeyer; 451–52. Harbrace Photos; 453, Westinghouse Electric; 454, Mount Holyoke College; 455, *bl*—Kathryn Abbe, *tr*—Harbrace Photo; 456, Spielberger, C. D. The effects of manifest anxiety on the academic achievements of college students. *Mental Hygiene*, 1962, 46, 420–26; 458–59. Harbrace Photos; 464, Harbrace Photo; 466–67, Harbrace Photo; 471, *tl*—Kathryn Abbe, *tr*—Kathryn Abbe, *bl*—Jim Theologos, *br*—Trans World Airlines Photo; 472, UPI; 473, Farrell Grehan, Photo Researchers; 477, Elliott Erwitt, Magnum; 478–81, Harbrace Photos; 483, Harbrace Photo; 484, Kathryn Abbe; 485, Guidance Associates; 486, Harbrace Photo; 487, Guidance Associates; 488, Harbrace Photos; 493, Van Bucher, Photo Researchers; 494, Mimi Forsyth, Monkmeyer; 495–96, Harbrace Photos; 497, Guidance Associates; 498, Harbrace Photo; 503, Harbrace Photo; 504, Elizabeth Wilcox; 505, Federation of Jewish Philanthropies; 506, National Association for Mental Health.

Unit Seven: p. 511, Wyeth Laboratories; 513, Luoma, Monkmeyer; 518, *tl*—Harbrace Photo, *tr*—Harbrace Photo, *b*—UPI; 520, *tl*—Harbrace Photo, *br*—UPI; 521, *t*—Antol Herskovitz Montefiore Hospital, *b*—E. R. Squibb & Sons; 522, *tl*—John H. Gerard, National Audubon Society, *r*—Harbrace Photos; 523, E. R. Squibb & Sons;525, *l*—Society of American Bacteriologists, *r*—U.S. Dept. of Health, Education, and Welfare; 532, Harbrace Photo; 533, *bl*—courtesy of Title Guarantee & Trust Company, *tr*—Harbrace Photo; 535, Bettmann Archive; 538, Harbrace Photo; 541, Chas. Pfizer & Co., Inc.; 542, F. J. Higgins, Highland Park, N.J.; 543, *l*—Chas. Pfizer & Co., Inc., *tr*—Chas. Pfizer & Co., Inc., *br*—Lederle Laboratories, a Division of American Cyanamid Company, Pearl River, N.Y.; 544, UPI; 549, American Cancer Society; 551, American Cancer Society, 552, *tl*—U.S. Dept of Health, Education, and Welfare, *bl*—U.S. Dept of Health, Education, and Welfare, *br*—Dept. of Health, City of New York; 554, American Red Cross; 555, Elizabeth Wilcox; 557, Project Hope; 560, Pfizer, Inc.; 565, Mimi Forsyth, Monkmeyer; 566–68, Harbrace Photos; 569, Project HOPE; 570–72, Harbrace Photos; 574–75, National Institutes of Health; 577, American Heart Association; 579, *t*—Medtronic, Inc.; *b*—Ken Heyman, Montefiore Hospital; 580, *tl*—American Heart Association, *tr*—National Institute of Health; 582, American Cancer Society; 592, UPI; 593, *t*—N.Y. Daily News Photo, *c*—Bob S. Smith, Rapho-Guillumette, *b*—Harbrace Photo; 597, American Cancer Society; 598, Harbrace Photos; 599–600, American Cancer Society; 609, Harbrace Photo; 612, Harbrace Photos.

Unit Eight: p. 617, Harbrace Photo; 619, UPI; 623, Aetna Life & Casualty; 624, UPI; 626, William Dippel; 627, American Youth Hostels, Inc.; 628, Wide World Photo; 630, *t*—Inge Morath, Magnum, *b*—Humble Oil & Refining Co.; 631, Harbrace Photo; 638, *bl*—Walter Kidde Co., *tr*—American Red Cross Photo; 641, Department of Water Resources Photo; 642, *tl*—American Red Cross, *bl*—Department of Defense Photo; 644, Wide World Photo; 645–46, UPI.

Artwork by Dick Morill, Inc., New York, N.Y. Cartoons by Sukon Associates, New York, N.Y. Cartoon on page 591 by Sal Murdocca, Craven/Evans Creative Graphics, New York, N.Y.

We would like to thank Coney Island Hospital, Brooklyn, N.Y., and the Irvington School System, Irvington, N.Y., for the courtesy and cooperation they gave our photographic staff.

A
B
C
D
E
F
G
H
I
J